ESSAYS ON THE AMERICAN REVOLUTION

HRW Essays in American History Series
Paul Goodman, Editor

ESSAYS ON THE AMERICAN REVOLUTION

EDITED BY

DAVID L. JACOBSON

University of California
Davis, California

HOLT, RINEHART AND WINSTON, INC.

New York · Chicago · San Francisco · Atlanta
Dallas · Montreal · Toronto

Cover: Courtesy of the Virginia State Archives.

Library of Congress Catalog Card Number: 76–105884
SBN: 03–078015–2
Printed in the United States of America
1   2   3   4   5   6   7   8   9

Preface

As this country approaches the two hundredth anniversary of its independence, the predictable flood of works commemorating the events of the American Revolution has already begun. And one can confidently foresee that the torrent of words issued by scholars and others will increase almost geometrically over the next two decades. These words will have their effects, good ones—in overturning some of the old myths about the "Founding Fathers"—and bad ones—in enshrining some new legends. Moreover, scholars and students will have their difficulties simply in avoiding being inundated in paper. Partially to counteract this danger, and partially simply to display the quality of recent investigations of the period in American history from 1763 to 1787, the following essays have been gathered into one volume. Most of the essays are recent, suggesting the depth of inquiry into the American Revolution among contemporary scholars. Most of them have been selected primarily because of their interpretive contributions to an understanding of the events of the Revolution; a few have been chosen because their narrative accounts may help to clarify the day-to-day movement of the American people toward independence and then toward successful union.

The story that this volume attempts to clarify cannot be understood by the use of anachronistic conceptions based upon later American practices or principles. Nor can it best be comprehended by describing only what happened on the western rim of the Atlantic. For these reasons, a good deal of care has been taken to include information about the European and, particularly, the English backgrounds of American political thought, and about the interrelationships between local political issues and American reactions to the growing imperial crisis. Additionally, some essays are included that outline the reasons for particular British actions, for example, the personal and political factors that contributed to British difficulties in fighting their war for America. Since the American Revolution was a world event that became part of a much greater European struggle and helped, albeit primarily indirectly, to precipitate the crisis of the old European order, essays are included that present certain aspects of the ties between European and American events—ranging from the impact of the end of French control over Canada to Jefferson's view of the French Revolution and its broad significance.

While many of the essays defy any simple system of classification, they have been grouped into six sections. Part I consists of essays presenting an overview of the

Revolution and particularly of its institutional and intellectual background. In Part II, six writers examine particular conflicts that led the colonies from resistance against individual British policies to the decision to make a complete break with the home country. Part III considers the War for Independence, the contrasting patterns of leadership in Britain and in America, the extraordinary nature of the military efforts that the British undertook, and the confusing interrelationship of military and political goals. Part IV contains three discussions of the impact of the Revolution upon American institutions—particularly upon the forms and practices of American politics. In Part V, three authors consider different aspects of the ways in which the people of this new nation resolved the problem of making their fierce loyalty to republican institutions and local autonomy compatible with the necessity for strengthening the larger union among the states. Finally, the last three selections in Part VI discuss the relationships between the Old World and the New World—the views of an American revolutionary on events in France in the late 1780's, the ties between American and European diplomatic thought, and the peculiar contribution of the American revolutionaries to the thinking of European political reformers.

David L. Jacobson

Davis, California
February 1970

Contents

ESSAYS ON THE AMERICAN REVOLUTION

Part I

THE HISTORIANS' DEBATE

1 / The American Revolution: An Interpretation

Charles M. Andrews

Charles M. Andrews is frequently thought of as the most articulate proponent of the "Imperial School" of interpreting early American history. The approach of this school may be described as an attempt to escape a limited and parochial view of the American colonies in the seventeenth and eighteenth centuries and to view the New World in the broader context of the expansion of English and European civilization. The work of this school has tended to be less partisanly favorable to American complaints and more open to consideration of the problems that led to particular British policy decisions. Most of Andrews' work deals with the founding of the colonies and the development of their constitutional institutions in a period long before the American Revolution. However, in the following address, Andrews seeks to examine the roots of the Revolution and to explain the dispute between the colonies and mother country in terms hardly flattering to English leadership in the mid-eighteenth century. Basically, he argues that English social and political institutions were for the moment stultified and inelastic, and that English attitudes toward the colonies simply did not change as did the colonies and their expectations: "On one side was the immutable, stereotyped system of the mother country—designed to keep things comfortably as they were; on the other, a vital, dynamic organism." Andrews concludes—looking beyond the confines of the old Empire and its problem—that the American Revolution did represent a wave of change against which the staid patterns of English life could not triumph.

For further reading: Charles M. Andrews, *The Colonial Background of the American Revolution* (Rev. ed., 1931); Lawrence Henry Gipson, *The Coming of the Revolution* (1954); or on the character of British imperial institutions, Leonard W. Labaree, *Royal Government in America* (1930), and *Royal Instructions to British Colonial Governors*, 1670–1776 (2 vols., 1935).

Reprinted by permission from the *American Historical Review*, XXI (1926), 219–232.

You will not, I trust, take it amiss if, on this the occasion of our annual meeting, I select as my topic the familiar subject of the American Revolution. Quite apart from the pleasure that comes from harping on an old string, there is the conviction, which I hold very strongly, that no matter how familiar a subject may be, it can always be re-examined with profit and viewed not infrequently from such points of vantage as to set the scene in quite a new light. The writing of history is always a progressive process, not merely or mainly because each age must write its own history from its own point of view, but rather because each generation of scholars is certain to contribute to historical knowledge and so to approach nearer than its predecessor to an understanding of the past. No one can accept as complete or final any rendering of history, no matter how plausible it may be, nor consider any period or phase of the past as closed against further investigation. Our knowledge of history is and always will be in the making, and it has been well said that orthodox history and an orthodox historian involve a contradiction in terms.

The explanations of history have been characterized as a rule by overmuch simplicity. So wrote Maitland of the history of England and so with equal justice might he have written of the history of America. As with natural phenomena in the pre-Copernican days of celestial mechanics, when the world believed that the sun moved and the earth was flat, so it has been at all times with historical phenomena, that what to the superficial observer has appeared to be true has been accepted far too often as containing the whole truth. Among these pre-Copernican convictions, for example, widely held in America to-day, is the belief that the American Revolution was brought about by British tyranny. Whatever explanation of that great event comes to be accepted by competent historians and their intelligent readers as a near approach to the truth, it is quite certain that it will not be anything as easy and simple as all that. There was nothing simple about the Balance of Power or the Balance of Trade, even when construed in terms of such vulgar commodities as fish, furs, and molasses, and particularly when one must give due consideration to the doctrine, as seriously held in some quarters today as it was in the eighteenth century, that colonial possessions are the natural sources for home industries. Our history before 1783 was a much more complex and cosmopolitan affair than older writers would have us believe, for they have failed to account for many deep-lying and almost invisible factors and forces which influence and often determine human action and are always elusive and difficult to comprehend.

Recent writers have approached the subject with a full recognition of the complexity of the problems involved. They have found many and varied conflicting activities making for disagreement and misunderstanding between the mother country and her offspring, giving rise to impulses and convictions, ideas and practices, that were difficult, if not impossible, of reconciliation. Such scholars have expressed their conclusions in many different forms. Some have seen a struggle between two opposing historical tendencies—one imperialistic and expansive, the other domestic and intensive; others, a clash of ideas regarding the constitution of the British empire and the place that a colony should occupy in its relations with the mother country. Some have stressed the differences that were bound to arise between an old and settled country and one that was not only dominated by the ideas and habits of the frontier, but was opposed also to the continued supremacy of a governing authority three thousand miles away. Others have explained the situation in terms of an antagonism between the law and institutions of England and those, growing constantly more divergent, of the Puritan and non-Puritan colonies in America. All of these explanations are sound, because they are based on an understanding of the deeper issues involved; and taken together, they are illuminating in that they enable the reader to broaden his point of view, and to break away from the endless controversies over immediate causes and war guilt that have hitherto tended to dominate the American mind.

But elucidating as these explanations are, no one of them seems quite sufficient to resolve so complex a subject as the causes of the American Revolution. To-day we conjure with such words as evolution and psychology, and look for explanations of acts on the part of both individuals and groups in states of mind produced by in-heritance and environment. Fielding, acknowledged expert in the study of human experience, can say that for a man "to act in direct contradiction to the dictates of his nature is, if not impossible, as improbable as anything which can well be con-ceived." The philosophers tell us that mind can be more resistant even than matter, and that it is easier to remove mountains than it is to change the ideas of a people. That the impact of convictions is one of the most frequent causes of revolution we must acknowledge; and I believe that we have not considered sufficiently the im-portance of this fact in determining the relations of England with colonial America. If I may, by way of illustrating my point, I should like to show that certain differ-ences existing between England and her colonies in mental attitudes and convictions proved in the end more difficult to overcome than the diverging historical tendencies or the bridging the three thousand miles of the Atlantic itself.

The American Revolution marks the close of one great period of our history and the beginning of another of even greater significance. It is the red line across our years, because by it was brought about a fundamental change in the status of the communities on the American seaboard—a change from dependence to independence. We sometimes hear that revolutions are not made but happen. In their immediate causes this is not true—for revolutions do not happen, they are made, in that they are the creatures of propaganda and manipulation. But, in reality, revolutions are not made. They are the detonations of explosive materials, long accumulating and often long dormant. They are the resultants of a vast complex of economic, political, social, and legal forces, which taken collectively are the masters, not the servants, of states-men and political agitators. They are never sudden in their origin, but look back to influences long in the making; and it is the business of the modern student of the subject to discover those remoter causes and to examine thoroughly and with an open mind the history, institutions, and mental past of the parties to the conflict. In pursuit of my purpose let me call to your attention certain aspects of that most important of all periods of our early history, the years from 1713 to 1775.

The middle period of the eighteenth century in England, resembling in some re-spects the mid-Victorian era of the next century, was intellectually, socially, and in-stitutionally in a state of stable equilibrium. The impulses of the Revolution of 1689 had spent their force. English thought and life was tending to become formal, con-ventional, and artificial, and the English mind was acquiring the fatal habit of closing against novelty and change. The most enlightened men of the day regarded the ex-isting order as the best that could be conceived, and in the main were content to let well enough alone. Those who held the reins of power were comfortable and irrespon-sible, steeped in their "old vulgar prejudices," and addicted to habits and modes of living that were approved by age and precedent. The miseries of the poor were ac-

cepted as due to inherent viciousness; class distinctions were sharply marked, and social relations were cast in a rigid mould; while, as far as the mass of the poor was
concerned, the vagrancy laws and the narrow policy of the corporate towns made free
movement in any direction practically impossible. Life at large was characterized by
brutality and a widespread sense of insecurity. Little thought was given to the education of the poor, the diseases of poverty and dirt, the baneful effects of overcrowd-
ing in the towns, or the corrupting influence of life in tenements and cellars. Excessive drinking and habitual resort to violence in human relations prevailed in urban
sections; and while it is probably true that in rural districts, where life was simple
and medieval, there was greater comfort and peace and less barbarity and coarseness,
nevertheless, it is equally true that the scenes of English country life in the eighteenth
century, that have come down to us in literature and painting, are more often conventional than real. Vested interests and the rights of property were deemed of greater
importance than the rights of humanity, and society clung tenaciously to the old
safeguards and defenses that checked the inrush of new ideas. There was a great
absence of interest in technical invention and improvement. Because the landed
classes were in the ascendant, agriculture was the only national interest receiving
attention—drainage, rotation of crops, and the treatment of the soil being the only
practical activities that attracted capital. The concerns and welfare of those without
the right to vote were largely ignored; and it is no mere coincidence that the waste
of human life, which was at its worst in London between 1720 and 1750, with the
population of England declining during that period, should not have been checked
until after 1780. The age was not one of progress in government, social organization,
or humanitarianism; and it is important to note that the reconstruction of English
manners and ways of living, and the movement leading to the diminution of crime,
to sanitation, the greater abundance of food, and amelioration of living conditions—
particularly in the towns and among the poorer classes—came after, and not before,
the American Revolution.

The state of mind, to which were due the conditions thus described, permeated all
phases of British life and government, and determined the attitude of the ruling
classes toward the political, as well as the social, order. These classes were composed
in a preponderant degree of landed proprietors, whose feeling of feudal superiority
and tenacious adherence to the ideas and traditions of their class were determining
factors in political life both in Parliament and the country. They believed that their
institutions provided a sufficient panacea for all constitutional ills and could not imagine wherein these institutions needed serious revision. They were convinced that
the existing system preserved men's liberties better than any that had gone before,
and they wanted no experiments or dangerous leaps in the dark. They not only
held as a tenet of faith that those who owned the land should wield political power,
but they were certain that such an arrangement had the sanction of God. They
revered the British system of government, its principles and philosophy, as the embodiment of human wisdom, grounded in righteousness and destined by nature to
serve the purpose of man. They saw it admired abroad as the most enlightened government possessed by any nation in the world, and so credited it with their unprecedented prosperity and influence as a nation. They likened its critics to Milton's
Lucifer, attacking "the sacred and immovable mount of the whole constitution," as
a contemporary phrased it, and they guarded it as the Israelites guarded the ark of
the covenant. Woe to him who would defile it!

Nor were they any less rigid in their attitude toward the colonies in America. Colonial policy had developed very slowly and did not take on systematic form until well on in the eighteenth century; but when once it became defined, the ruling classes regarded it in certain fundamental aspects—at least in official utterance—as fixed as was the constitution itself. At first England did not take her colonies seriously as assets of commercial importance, but when after 1704 naval stores were added to the tobacco and sugar of Virginia and the West Indies, and it was seen that these commodities enabled England to obtain a favorable balance of trade with European countries, the value of the plantations in British eyes increased enormously. However, it was not until after 1750, when a favorable balance of trade was reached with the colonies themselves, that the mercantilist deemed the situation entirely satisfactory; and from that time on for twenty years—epochal years in the history of England's relations with America—the mercantilist idea of the place that a colony should occupy in the British scheme of things became fixed and unalterable. Though the colonies were growing by leaps and bounds, the authorities in Great Britain retained unchanged the policy which had been adopted more than half a century before. They did not essentially alter the instructions to the Board of Trade in all the eighty-six years of its existence. They created no true colonial secretary, even in 1768, and no department of any kind at any time for the exclusive oversight of American affairs. They saw no necessity for adopting new methods of managing colonial trade, even though the colonial situation was constantly presenting new problems for solution. Manufacturing was undoubtedly more discouraged in 1770 than it had been in 1699, when the first restrictive act was passed; and the idea that the colonies by their very nature were ordained to occupy a position of commercial dependence to the advantage and profit of the mother country was never more firmly fixed in the British mind than just before our Revolution. In fact, that event altered in no essential particular the British conception of the status of a colony, for as late as 1823, Sir Charles Ellis, undoubtedly voicing the opinion of his day, could say in Parliament that the colonial system of England had not been established for the sake of the colonies, but for the encouragement of British trade and manufactures. Thus for more than a century England's idea of what a colony should be underwent no important alteration whatever.

Equally unchangeable was the British idea of how a colony should be governed. In the long list of commissions and instructions drawn up in England for the guidance of the royal governors in America, there is to be found, with one exception only, nothing that indicates any progressive advance in the spirit and method of administration from 1696 to 1782. Year after year, the same arrangements and phraseology appear, conforming to a common type, admitting, it is true, important modifications in matters of detail, but in principle undergoing at no time in eighty-six years serious revision or reconstruction. These documents were drawn up in Whitehall according to a fixed pattern; the governors and councils were allowed no discretion; the popular assemblies were confined within the narrow bounds of inelastic formulae, which repeated, time after time, the same injunctions and the same commands; while the crown reserved to itself the full right of interference in all matters that were construed as coming under its prerogative. These instructions represented the rigid eighteenth-century idea of how a colony should be retained in dependence on the mother country. And what was true of the instructions was true of other documents also that had to do with America. For instance, the lists of queries to the governors, the questionnaires to the commodore-governors of the Newfoundland fishery, and the whole routine business of the fishery itself had become a matter of form and precedent, as conventional and stereotyped as were the polite phrases of eighteenth-century social intercourse. Rarely was any attempt made to adapt these instructions to the needs of growing communities such as the colonies were showing themselves to be; and only with the Quebec instructions of 1775, issued after the passage of the Quebec Act and under the guidance of a colonial governor of unusual common-sense, was there any recognition of a new colonial situation. In this document, which appeared at the very end of our colonial period, do we find something of a break from the stiff and legalistic forms that were customary in the earlier royal instructions, some appreciation of the fact that the time was approaching when a colony should be treated with greater liberality and be allowed to have some part in saying how it should be administered.

Without going further with our analysis we can say that during the half-century preceding our Revolution English habits of thought and methods of administration and government, both at home and in the colonies, had reached a state of immobility. To all appearances the current of the national life had settled into a backwater, and as far as home affairs were concerned was seemingly becoming stagnant. At a time when Pitt was breaking France by land and sea, and men on waking were asking what new territories had been added during the night to the British dominions, occurrences at home were barren of adventure, either in society or politics. Ministers were not true statesmen; they had no policies, no future hopes, no spirit of advance, no gifts of foresight or prophecy. In all that concerned domestic interests, they were impervious to suggestions, even when phrased in the eloquence of Pitt and Burke. They wanted no change in existing conditions; their eyes were fixed on traditions and precedents rather than on the obligations and opportunities of the future. Their tenure of office was characterized by inactivity, a casual handling of situations they did not understand and could not control, and a willingness to let the ship of state drift for itself. As a modern critic has said, they were always turning in an unending circle, one out, one in, one out, marking time and never going forward.

To a considerable extent the narrow point of view and rigidity of attitude exhibited by the men who held office at Whitehall or sat in Parliament at Westminster can be explained by the fact that at this time officials and members of Parliament were also territorial magnates, lords of manors, and country squires, who were influenced in their political life by ideas that governed their relations with their tenantry and the management of their landed estates. It is not necessary to think of them as bought by king or ministers and so bound and gagged against freedom of parliamentary action. In fact, they were bound and gagged already by devotion to their feudal privileges, their family prerogatives, and their pride of landed proprietorship. They viewed the colonies somewhat in the light of tenancies of the crown, and as they themselves lived on the rents from their estates, so they believed that the king and the kingdom should profit from the revenues and returns from America. The point of view was somewhat that of a later Duke of Newcastle, who when reproached for compelling his tenants to vote as he pleased said that he had a right to do as he liked with his own. This landed aristocracy reflected the eighteenth-century spirit. It was sonorous, conventional, and self-satisfied, and shameless of sparkle or humor. It clung to the laws of inheritance and property, fearful of anything that might in any way offend the shades of past generations. In its criticism of the manners of others it was insular and arrogant, and was mentally so impenetrable as never to understand why any one, even in the colonies, should wish things to be other than they were or refuse to accept the station of life to which by Providence he had been called.

A government, representative of a privileged social and political order that took existing conditions as a matter of course, setting nature at defiance and depending wholly on art, was bound sooner or later to come into conflict with a people, whose life in America was in closest touch with nature and characterized by growth and change and constant readjustments. In that country were groups of men, women, and children, the greater portion of whom were of English ancestry, numbering at first a few hundreds and eventually more than two millions, who were scattered over many miles of continent and island and were living under various forms of government. These people, more or less unconsciously, under the influence of new surroundings and imperative needs, were establishing a new order of society and laying the foundations of a new political system. The story of how this was done—how that which was English slowly and imperceptibly merged into that which was American—has never been adequately told; but it is a fascinating phase of history, more interesting and enlightening when studied against the English background than when construed as an American problem only. It is the story of the gradual elimination of those elements, feudal and proprietary, that were foreign to the normal life of a frontier land, and of the gradual adjustment of the colonists to the restraints and restrictions that were imposed upon them by the commercial policy of the mother country. It is the story also of the growth of the colonial assemblies and of the education and experience that the colonists were receiving in the art of political self-government. It is above all—and no phase of colonial history is of greater significance—the story of the gradual transformation of these assemblies from the provincial councils that the home government intended them to be into miniature parliaments. At the end of a long struggle with the prerogative and other forms of outside interference, they emerged powerful legislative bodies, as self-conscious in their way as the House of Commons in England was becoming during the same eventful years.

Here was an *impasse,* for the British view that a colonial assembly partook of the character of a provincial or municipal council was never actually true of any assembly in British America at any time in its history. From the beginning, each of these colonial bodies, in varying ways and under varying circumstances, assumed a position of leadership in its colony, and exercised, in a manner often as bewildering to the student of to-day as to an eighteenth-century royal governor, a great variety of executive, legislative, and judicial functions. Except in Connecticut and Rhode Island, requests for parliamentary privileges were made very early and were granted year after year by the governors—privileges that were essentially those of the English and Irish Houses of Commons and were consciously modelled after them. At times, the assemblies went beyond Parliament and made claims additional to the usual speaker's requests, claims first asked for as matters of favor but soon demanded as matters of right, as belonging to representative bodies and not acquired by royal gift or favor. One gets the impression that though the assemblies rarely failed to make the formal request, they did so with the intention of taking in any case what they asked for and anything more that they could secure. Gradually, with respect to privileges, they advanced to a position of amazing independence, freeing themselves step by step from the interfering power of the executive, that is, of the royal prerogative. They began to talk of these rights as ancient and inherent and necessary to the orderly existence of any representative body, and they became increasingly self-assertive and determined as the years passed.

Nor was this the only change affecting the assemblies to which the eighteenth-century Englishman was asked to adapt himself. The attitude of the assemblies in America found expression in the exercise of powers that had their origin in other sources than that of parliamentary privilege. They adopted rules of their own, that were sometimes even more severe than those of Parliament itself. They regulated membership, conduct, and procedure; ruled against drinking, smoking, and profanity, against unseemly, unnecessary, and tedious debate, against absence, tardiness, and other forms of evasion. They punished with great severity all infringement of rules and acts of contempt, and defended their right to do so against the governor and council on one side and the courts of the colony on the other. Nor did they even pretend to be consistent in their opposition to the royal prerogative, as expressed in the instructions to the royal governors, and in their manœuvres they did not follow any uniform policy or plan. They conformed to these instructions willingly enough, whenever it was agreeable for them to do so; but if at any time they considered an instruction contrary to the best interest of a particular colony, they did not hesitate to oppose it directly or to nullify it by avoidance. In general, it may be said that they evaded or warded off or deliberately disobeyed such instructions as they did not like. Thus both consciously and unconsciously they were carving out a *lex parliamenti* of their own, which, evolving naturally from the necessity of meeting the demands of self-governing communities, carried them beyond the bounds of their own membership and made them responsible for the welfare of the colony at large.

The important point to remember is that the plan of governmental control as laid down in England was never in accord with the actual situation in America; that the Privy Council, the Secretary of State, and the Board of Trade seem not to have realized that their system of colonial administration was breaking down at every point. Their minds ran in a fixed groove and they could construe the instances of colonial disobedience and aggression, which they often noted, in no other terms than those of persistent dereliction of duty. Either they did not see or else refused to see the wide divergence that was taking place between colonial administration as they planned it and colonial administration as the colonists were working it out. Englishmen saw in the American claims an attack upon an old, established, and approved system. They interpreted the attitude of the colonists as something radical and revolutionary, menacing British prosperity, British political integrity, and the British scheme of colonial government. Opposed by tradition and conviction to new experiments, even at home, they were unable to sympathize with, or even to understand, the great experiment, one of the greatest in the world's history, on trial across the sea. There in America was evolving a new idea of sovereignty, inherent not in crown and Parliament but in the people of a state, based on the principle—self-evident it may be to us to-day but not to the Englishman of the eighteenth century—that governments derive their just powers from the consent of the governed. There was emerging a new idea of the franchise, as a natural right, under certain conditions, of every adult citizen, an idea which theoretically is not even yet accepted in Great Britain. There was being established a new order of society, without caste or privilege, free from economic restrictions and social demarcations between class and class. There was taking shape a new idea of a colony, a self-governing dominion, the members of which were competent to develop along their own lines, while working together with the mother country as part of a common state.

For us to-day with our perspective it is easy to see the conflict approaching and some of us may think perhaps that the British ministers and members of Parliament ought to have realized that their own ideas and systems were fast outgrowing their usefulness even for Great Britain herself; and that their inflexible views of the colonial relationship were fast leading to disaster. Yet we must keep in mind that it is always extraordinarily difficult for a generation reared in the environment of modern democracy to deal sympathetically with the Englishman's point of view in the eighteenth century, or to understand why the ruling classes of that day so strenuously opposed the advance of liberalism both in England and America. The fact remains, however, that the privileged and governing classes in England saw none of these things. They were too close to events and too much a part of them to judge them dispassionately or to appreciate their real significance. These classes, within which we may well include the Loyalists in America, were possessed of inherited instincts, sentiments, and prejudices which they could no more change than they could have changed the color of their eyes or the texture of their skins. That which existed in government and society was to them a part of the fixed scheme of nature, and no more called for reconsideration than did the rising of the sun or the budding of the trees in spring. If Lord North had granted the claims of the colonists he probably would have been looked on by Parliament as having betrayed the constitution and impaired its stability, just as Peel was pilloried by a similar landowning Parliament in 1845, when he advocated the repeal of the corn laws. One has only to read the later debates on the subject of enclosures and the corn laws to understand the attitude of the British landowners toward the colonies from 1763 to 1776. To them in each instance it seemed as if the foundations of the universe were breaking up and the world in which they lived was sinking beneath their feet.

Primarily, the American Revolution was a political and constitutional movement and only secondarily one that was either financial, commercial, or social. At bottom the fundamental issue was the political independence of the colonies, and in the last analysis the conflict lay between the British Parliament and the colonial assemblies, each of which was probably more sensitive, self-conscious, and self-important than was the voting population that it represented. For many years these assemblies had fought the prerogative successfully and would have continued to do so, eventually reducing it to a minimum, as the later self-governing dominions have done; but in the end it was Parliament, whose powers they disputed, that became the great antagonist. Canning saw the situation clearly when, half a century later, he spoke of the Revolution as having been a test of the equality of strength "between the legislature of this mighty kingdom . . . and the colonial assemblies," adding further that he had no intention of repeating in the case of Jamaica, the colony then under debate, the mistakes that had been made in 1776. Of the mistakes to which he referred the greatest was the employment of the deadly expedient of coercion, and he showed his greater wisdom when he determined, as he said, to keep back "within the penetralia of the constitution the transcendental powers of Parliament over a dependency of the British crown" and not "to produce it upon trifling occasions or in cases of petty refractoriness and temporary misconduct." How he would have met the revolution in America, based as it was on "the fundamental principles of political liberty," we cannot say; but we know that he had no sympathy with any attempt to force opinion back into paths that were outworn. That he would have foreseen the solution of a later date and have granted the colonies absolute and responsible self-government, recognizing the equality of the assemblies in domestic matters and giving them the same control over their home affairs as the people of Great Britain had over theirs, can be conjectured only by inference from his liberal attitude toward the South American republics. He stood half-way between the ministers of the Revolutionary period—blind, sensitive, and mentally unprogressive—and the statesmen of the middle of the nineteenth century, who were willing to follow the lead of those courageous and far-sighted Englishmen who saved the empire from a second catastrophe after 1830 and were the founders of the British colonial policy of to-day.

The revolt of the colonies from Great Britain began long before the battles of Moore's Creek Bridge and Lexington; before the time of James Otis and the writs of assistance; before the dispute over the appointment of judges in North Carolina and New York; before the eloquence of Patrick Henry was first heard in the land; and even before the quarrel in Virginia over the Dinwiddie pistole fee. These were but the outward and visible signs of an inward and factual divergence. The separation from the mother country began just as soon as the mercantile system of commercial control, the governmental system of colonial administration, and the whole doctrine of the inferior status of a colonial assembly began to give way before the pressure exerted and the disruptive power exercised by these young and growing colonial communities. New soil had produced new wants, new desires, new points of view, and the colonists were demanding the right to live their own lives in their own way. As we see it to-day the situation was a dramatic one. On one side was the immutable, stereotyped system of the mother country, based on precedent and tradition and designed to keep things comfortably as they were; on the other, a vital, dynamic organism, containing the seed of a great nation, its forces untried, still to be proved. It is inconceivable that a connection should have continued long between two such yoke-fellows, one static, the other dynamic, separated by an ocean and bound only by the ties of a legal relationship.

If my diagnosis is correct of the British state of mind in the eighteenth century, and the evidence in its favor seems overwhelming, then the colonists were as justified in their movement of revolt as were the Englishmen themselves in their movement for reform in the next century. Yet in reality no great progressive movement needs justification at our hands, for great causes justify themselves and time renders the decision. The revolt in America and the later reforms in Great Britain herself were directed against the same dominant ruling class that in their colonial relations as well as in their social and political arrangements at home preferred that the world in which they lived should remain as it was. Reform or revolt is bound to follow attempts of a privileged class to conduct affairs according to unchanging rules and formulae. The colonies had developed a constitutional organization equally complete with Britain's own and one that in principle was far in advance of the British system, and they were qualified to co-operate with the mother country on terms similar to those of a brotherhood of free nations such as the British world is becoming to-day. But England was unable to see this fact or unwilling to recognize it, and consequently America became the scene of a political unrest, which might have been controlled by compromise, but was turned to revolt by coercion. The situation is a very interesting one, for England is famous for her ability to compromise at critical moments in her history.

For once at least she failed. In 1832 and later years, when she faced other great constitutional crises at home and in her colonies, she saved herself from revolution by understanding the situation and adjusting herself to it. Progress may be stemmed for a time, but cannot be permanently stopped by force. A novelist has expressed the idea in saying: "You cannot fight and beat revolutions as you can fight and beat nations. You can kill a man, but you simply can't kill a rebel. For the proper rebel has an ideal of living, while your ideal is to kill him so that you may preserve yourself. And the reason why no revolution or religion has ever been beaten is that rebels die for something worth dying for, the future, but their enemies die only to preserve the past, and makers of history are always stronger than makers of empire." The American revolutionists had an ideal of living; it can hardly be said that in 1776 the Englishmen of the ruling classes were governed in their colonial relations by any ideals that were destined to be of service to the future of the human race.

2 / Political Experience and Enlightenment Ideas in Eighteenth-Century America

Bernard Bailyn

In many ways, Bernard Bailyn's article complements the views of Charles M. Andrews on the relatively static nature of English institutions and the dynamism of American growth. However, Bailyn's interest primarily concerns the relationship of colonial institutions and ideas, the tension between old forms and new practices and principles. He notes the familiarity of Americans with ideas drawn from the most advanced English and continental political thinkers. Moreover, colonial practices had grown away from English patterns of restriction and privilege in the direction of greater liberty and substantial legal equality among freemen. Yet there remained the anomalies of British authority, of the exercise of some political power totally independent of popular will. As the years passed, the contrast between new ideas and old forms, between practice and pretense, and the continuing conflicts over the theoretical and actual nature of political power all culminated in a gradual popular alienation from what remained of the old system. In this context, the American Revolution provided an opportunity not so much for great change in practice as it did for great change in the rationalization for practice, an opportunity to bring "legitimacy" to American institutions by thinking through and systematizing their theoretical rationale. Enlightenment ideas thus helped Americans in thinking about and justifying the ways in which they reorganized their political life.

For further reading: Bernard Bailyn, *Pamphlets of the American Revolution* I (1966), see particularly the long introduction; Caroline Robbins, *The Eighteenth-Century English Commonwealthman* (1959); David L. Jacobson (ed.), *The English Libertarian Heritage: From the Writings of John Trenchard and Thomas Gordon in The Independent Whig and Cato's Letters* (1965); H. Trevor Colbourn, *The Lamp of Experience: Whig Historians and the Intellectual Origins of the American Revolution* (1965).

Reprinted by permission of the author from the *American Historical Review*, LXVII (1962), 339–351.

The political and social ideas of the European Enlightenment have had a peculiar importance in American history. More universally accepted in eighteenth-century America than in Europe, they were more completely and more permanently embodied in the formal arrangements of state and society; and, less controverted, less subject to criticism and dispute, they have lived on more vigorously into later periods, more continuous and more intact. The peculiar force of these ideas in America resulted from many causes. But originally, and basically, it resulted from the circumstances of the prerevolutionary period and from the bearing of these ideas on the political experience of the American colonists.

What this bearing was—the nature of the relationship between Enlightenment ideas and early American political experience—is a matter of particular interest at the present time because it is centrally involved in what amounts to a fundamental revision of early American history now under way. By implication if not direct evidence and argument, a number of recent writings have undermined much of the structure of historical thought by which, for a generation or more, we have understood our eighteenth-century origins, and in particular have placed new and insupportable pressures on its central assumption concerning the political significance of Enlightenment thought. Yet the need for rather extensive rebuilding has not been felt, in part because the architecture has not commonly been seen as a whole—as a unit, that is, of mutually dependent parts related to a central premise—in part because the damage has been piecemeal and uncoordinated: here a beam destroyed, there a stone dislodged, the inner supports only slowly weakened and the balance only gradually thrown off. The edifice still stands, mainly, it seems, by habit and by the force of inertia. A brief consideration of the whole, consequently, a survey from a position far enough above the details to see the outlines of the over-all architecture, and an attempt, however tentative, to sketch a line—a principle—of reconstruction would seem to be in order.

A basic, organizing assumption of the group of ideas that dominated the earlier interpretation of eighteenth-century American history is the belief that previous to the Revolution the political experience of the colonial Americans had been roughly analogous to that of the English. Control of public authority had been firmly held by a native aristocracy—merchants and landlords in the North, planters in the South—allied, commonly, with British officialdom. By restricting representation in the provincial assemblies, limiting the franchise, and invoking the restrictive power of the English state, this aristocracy had dominated the governmental machinery of the mainland colonies. Their political control, together with legal devices such as primogeniture and entail, had allowed them to dominate the economy as well. Not only were they successful in engrossing landed estates and mercantile fortunes, but they were for the most part able also to fight off the clamor of yeoman debtors for cheap paper currency, and of depressed tenants for freehold property. But the control of this colonial counterpart of a traditional aristocracy, with its Old World ideas of privilege and hierarchy, orthodoxy in religious establishment, and economic inequality, was progressively threatened by the growing strength of a native, frontier-bred democracy that expressed itself most forcefully in the lower houses of the "rising" provincial assemblies. A conflict between the two groups and ways of life was building up, and it broke out in fury after 1765.

The outbreak of the Revolution, the argument runs, fundamentally altered the old regime. The Revolution destroyed the power of this traditional aristocracy, for the movement of opposition to parliamentary taxation, 1760–1776, originally controlled by conservative elements, had been taken over by extremists nourished on Enlightenment radicalism, and the once dominant conservative groups had gradually been alienated. The break with England over the question of home rule was part of a general struggle, as Carl Becker put it, over who shall rule at home. Independence gave control to the radicals, who, imposing their advanced doctrines on a traditional society, transformed a rebellious secession into a social revolution. They created a new regime, a reformed society, based on enlightened political and social theory.

But that is not the end of the story; the sequel is important. The success of the enlightened radicals during the early years of the Revolution was notable; but, the argument continues, it was not wholly unqualified. The remnants of the earlier aristocracy, though defeated, had not been eliminated: they were able to reassert themselves in the postwar years. In the 1780's they gradually regained power until, in what amounted to a counterrevolution, they impressed their views indelibly on history in the new federal Constitution, in the revocation of some of the more enthusiastic actions of the earlier revolutionary period, and in the Hamiltonian program for the new government. This was not, of course, merely the old regime resurrected. In a new age whose institutions and ideals had been born of revolutionary radicalism, the old conservative elements made adjustments and concessions by which to survive and periodically to flourish as a force in American life.

The importance of this formulation derived not merely from its usefulness in interpreting eighteenth-century history. It provided a key also for understanding the entire course of American politics. By its light, politics in America, from the very beginning, could be seen to have been a dialectical process in which an aristocracy of wealth and power struggled with the People, who, ordinarily ill-organized and inarticulate, rose upon provocation armed with powerful institutional and ideological weapons, to reform a periodically corrupt and oppressive polity.

In all of this the underlying assumption is the belief that Enlightenment thought —the reforming ideas of advanced thinkers in eighteenth-century England and on the Continent—had been the effective lever by which native American radicals had turned a dispute on imperial relations into a sweeping reformation of public institutions and thereby laid the basis for American democracy.

For some time now, and particularly during the last decade, this interpretation has been fundamentally weakened by the work of many scholars working from different approaches and on different problems. Almost every important point has been challenged in one way or another.[1] All arguments concerning politics during the pre-

[1] Recent revisionist writings on eighteenth-century America are voluminous. The main points of reinterpretation will be found in the following books and articles, to which specific reference is made in the paragraphs that follow: Robert E. Brown, *Middle-Class Democracy and the Revolution in Massachusetts, 1691–1780* (Ithaca, N. Y., 1955); E. James Ferguson, "Currency Finance: An Interpretation of Colonial Monetary Practices," *William and Mary Quarterly*, X (Apr. 1953), 153–80; Theodore Thayer, "The Land Bank System in the American Colonies," *Journal of Economic History*, XIII (Spring 1953), 145–59; Bray Hammond, *Banks and Politics in America from the Revolution to the Civil War* (Princeton, N. J., 1957); George A. Billias, *The Massachusetts Land Bankers of 1740* (Orono, Me., 1959); Milton M. Klein, "Democracy and Politics in Colonial New York," *New York History*, XL (July 1959), 221–46; Oscar and Mary F. Handlin, "Radicals and Conservatives in Massachusetts after Independence," *New Eng-*

revolutionary years have been affected by an exhaustive demonstration for one colony, which might well be duplicated for others, that the franchise, far from having been restricted in behalf of a borough-mongering aristocracy, was widely available for popular use. Indeed, it was more widespread than the desire to use it—a fact which in itself calls into question a whole range of traditional arguments and assumptions. Similarly, the Populist terms in which economic elements of prerevolutionary history have most often been discussed may no longer be used with the same confidence. For it has been shown that paper money, long believed to have been the inflationary instrument of a depressed and desperate debtor yeomanry, was in general a fiscally sound and successful means—whether issued directly by the governments or through land banks—not only of providing a medium of exchange but also of creating sources of credit necessary for the growth of an underdeveloped economy and a stable system of public finance for otherwise resourceless governments. Merchants and creditors commonly supported the issuance of paper, and many of the debtors who did so turn out to have been substantial property owners.

Equally, the key writings extending the interpretation into the revolutionary years have come under question. The first and still classic monograph detailing the inner social struggle of the decade before 1776—Carl Becker's *History of Political Parties in the Province of New York, 1760–1776* (1909)—has been subjected to sharp criticism on points of validation and consistency. And, because Becker's book, like other studies of the movement toward revolution, rests upon a belief in the continuity of "radical" and "conservative" groupings, it has been weakened by an analysis proving such terminology to be deceptive in that it fails to define consistently identifiable groups of people. Similarly, the "class" characteristic of the merchant group in the northern colonies, a presupposition of important studies of the merchants in the revolutionary movement, has been questioned, and along with it the belief that there was an economic or occupational basis for positions taken on the revolutionary controversy. More important, a recent survey of the writings following up J. F. Jameson's classic essay, *The American Revolution Considered as a Social Movement* (1926), has shown how little has been written in the last twenty-five years to substantiate that famous statement of the Revolution as a movement of social reform. Most dramatic of all has been the demolition of Charles Beard's *Economic Interpretation of the Constitution* (1913), which stood solidly for over forty years as the central pillar of the counterrevolution argument: the idea, that is, that the Constitution was a "conservative" document, the polar opposite of the "radical" Articles of Confederation, embodying the interests and desires of public creditors and other moneyed con-

---

land *Quarterly,* XVII (Sept. 1944), 343–55; Bernard Bailyn, "The Blount Papers: Notes on the Merchant 'Class' in the Revolutionary Period," *William and Mary Quarterly,* XI (Jan. 1954), 98–104; Frederick B. Tolles, "The American Revolution Considered as a Social Movement: A Re-Evaluation," *American Historical Review,* LX (Oct. 1954), 1–12; Robert E. Brown, *Charles Beard and the Constitution: A Critical Analysis of "An Economic Interpretation of the Constitution"* (Princeton, N. J., 1956); Forrest McDonald, *We the People: The Economic Origins of the Constitution* (Chicago, 1958); Daniel J. Boorstin, *The Genius of American Politics* (Chicago, 1953), and *The Americans: The Colonial Experience* (New York, 1958). References to other writings and other viewpoints will be found in Edmund S. Morgan, "The American Revolution: Revisions in Need of Revising," *William and Mary Quarterly,* XIV (Jan. 1957), 3–15; and Richard B. Morris, "The Confederation Period and the American Historian," *ibid.,* XIII (Apr. 1956), 139–56.

servatives, and marking the Thermidorian conclusion to the enlightened radicalism of the early revolutionary years.

Finally, there are arguments of another sort, assertions to the effect that not only did Enlightenment ideas not provoke native American radicals to undertake serious reform during the Revolution, but that ideas have never played an important role in American public life, in the eighteenth century or after, and that the political "genius" of the American people, during the Revolution as later, has lain in their brute pragmatism, their successful resistance to the "distant example and teachings of the European Enlightenment," the maunderings of "garret-spawned European illuminati."

Thus from several directions at once have come evidence and arguments that cloud if they do not totally obscure the picture of eighteenth-century American history composed by a generation of scholars. These recent critical writings are of course of unequal weight and validity; but few of them are totally unsubstantiated, almost all of them have some point and substance, and taken together they are sufficient to raise serious doubts about the organization of thought within which we have become accustomed to view the eighteenth century. A full reconsideration of the problems raised by these findings and ideas would of course be out of the question here even if sufficient facts were now available. But one might make at least an approach to the task and a first approximation to some answers to the problems by isolating the central premise concerning the relationship between Enlightenment ideas and political experience and reconsidering it in view of the evidence that is now available.

Considering the material at hand, old and new, that bears on this question, one discovers an apparent paradox. There appear to be two primary and contradictory sets of facts. The first and more obvious is the undeniable evidence of the seriousness with which colonial and revolutionary leaders took ideas, and the deliberateness of their efforts during the Revolution to reshape institutions in their pattern. The more we know about these American provincials the clearer it is that among them were remarkably well-informed students of contemporary social and political theory. There never was a dark age that destroyed the cultural contacts between Europe and America. The sources of transmission had been numerous in the seventeenth century; they increased in the eighteenth. There were not only the impersonal agencies of newspapers, books, and pamphlets, but also continuous personal contact through travel and correspondence. Above all, there were Pan-Atlantic, mainly Anglo-American, interest groups that occasioned a continuous flow of fresh information and ideas between Europe and the mainland colonies in America. Of these, the most important were the English dissenters and their numerous codenominationalists in America. Located perforce on the left of the English political spectrum, acutely alive to ideas of reform that might increase their security in England, they were, for the almost endemically nonconformist colonists, a rich source of political and social theory. It was largely through nonconformist connections, as Caroline Robbins' recent book, *The Eighteenth-Century Commonwealthman* (1959), suggests, that the commonwealth radicalism of seventeenth-century England continued to flow to the colonists, blending, ultimately, with other strains of thought to form a common body of advanced theory.

In every colony and in every legislature there were people who knew Locke and Beccaria, Montesquieu and Voltaire; but perhaps more important, there was in every village of every colony someone who knew such transmitters of English nonconformist thought as Watts, Neal, and Burgh; later Priestley and Price—lesser writers, no doubt, but staunch opponents of traditional authority, and they spoke in a familiar idiom. In the bitterly contentious pamphlet literature of mid-eighteenth-century American politics, the most frequently cited authority on matters of principle and theory was not Locke or Montesquieu but *Cato's Letters,* a series of radically libertarian essays written in London in 1720–1723 by two supporters of the dissenting interest, John Trenchard and Thomas Gordon. Through such writers, as well as through the major authors, leading colonists kept contact with a powerful tradition of enlightened thought.

This body of doctrine fell naturally into play in the controversy over the power of the imperial government. For the revolutionary leaders it supplied a common vocabulary and a common pattern of thought, and, when the time came, common principles of political reform. That reform was sought and seriously if unevenly undertaken, there can be no doubt. Institutions were remodeled, laws altered, practices questioned all in accordance with advanced doctrine on the nature of liberty and of the institutions needed to achieve it. The Americans were acutely aware of being innovators, of bringing mankind a long step forward. They believed that they had so far succeeded in their effort to reshape circumstances to conform to enlightened ideas and ideals that they had introduced a new era in human affairs. And they were supported in this by the opinion of informed thinkers in Europe. The contemporary image of the American Revolution at home and abroad was complex; but no one doubted that a revolution that threatened the existing order and portended new social and political arrangements had been made, and made in the name of reason.

Thus, throughout the eighteenth century there were prominent, politically active Americans who were well aware of the development of European thinking, took ideas seriously, and during the Revolution deliberately used them in an effort to reform the institutional basis of society. This much seems obvious. But, paradoxically, and less obviously, it is equally true that many, indeed most, of what these leaders considered to be their greatest achievements during the Revolution—reforms that made America seem to half the world like the veritable heavenly city of the eighteenth-century philosophers—had been matters of fact before they were matters of theory and revolutionary doctrine.

No reform in the entire Revolution appeared of greater importance to Jefferson than the Virginia acts abolishing primogeniture and entail. This action, he later wrote, was part of "a system by which every fibre would be eradicated of antient or future aristocracy; and a foundation laid for a government truly republican." But primogeniture and entail had never taken deep roots in America, not even in tidewater Virginia. Where land was cheap and easily available such legal restrictions proved to be encumbrances profiting few. Often they tended to threaten rather than secure the survival of the family, as Jefferson himself realized when in 1774 he petitioned the Assembly to break an entail on his wife's estate on the very practical, untheoretical, and common ground that to do so would be "greatly to their [the petitioners'] Interest and that of their Families." The legal abolition of primogeniture and entail during and after the Revolution was of little material consequence. Their demise had been effectively decreed years before by the circumstances of life in a wilderness environment.

Similarly, the disestablishment of religion—a major goal of revolutionary reform— was carried out, to the extent that it was, in circumstances so favorable to it that one wonders not how it was done but why it was not done more thoroughly. There is no more eloquent, moving testimony to revolutionary idealism than the Virginia Act for Establishing Religious Freedom: it is the essence of Enlightenment faith. But what did it, and the disestablishment legislation that had preceded it, reform? What had the establishment of religion meant in prerevolutionary Virginia? The Church of England was the state church, but dissent was tolerated well beyond the limits of the English Acts of Toleration. The law required nonconformist organizations to be licensed by the government, but dissenters were not barred from their own worship nor penalized for failure to attend the Anglican communion, and they were commonly exempted from parish taxes. Nonconformity excluded no one from voting and only the very few Catholics from enjoying public office. And when the itineracy of revivalist preachers led the establishment to contemplate more restrictive measures, the Baptists and Presbyterians advanced to the point of arguing publicly, and pragmatically, that the toleration they had so far enjoyed was an encumbrance, and that the only proper solution was total liberty: in effect, disestablishment.

Virginia was if anything more conservative than most colonies. The legal establishment of the Church of England was in fact no more rigorous in South Carolina and Georgia: it was considerably weaker in North Carolina. It hardly existed at all in the middle colonies (there was of course no vestige of it in Pennsylvania), and where it did, as in four counties of New York, it was either ignored or had become embattled by violent opposition well before the Revolution. And in Massachusetts and Connecticut, where the establishment, being nonconformist according to English law, was legally tenuous to begin with, tolerance in worship and relief from church taxation had been extended to the major dissenting groups early in the century, resulting well before the Revolution in what was, in effect if not in law, a multiple establishment. And this had been further weakened by the splintering effect of the Great Awakening. Almost everywhere the Church of England, the established church of the highest state authority, was embattled and defensive—driven to rely more and more on its missionary arm, the Society for the Propagation of the Gospel, to sustain it against the cohorts of dissent.

None of this had resulted from Enlightenment theory. It had been created by the mundane exigencies of the situation: by the distance that separated Americans from ecclesiastical centers in England and the Continent; by the never-ending need to encourage immigration to the colonies; by the variety, the mere numbers, of religious groups, each by itself a minority, forced to live together; and by the weakness of the coercive powers of the state, its inability to control the social forces within it.

Even more gradual and less contested had been the process by which government in the colonies had become government by the consent of the governed. What had been proved about the franchise in early Massachusetts—that it was open for practically the entire free adult male population—can be proved to a lesser or greater extent for all the colonies. But the extraordinary breadth of the franchise in the American colonies had not resulted from popular demands: there had been no cries for universal manhood suffrage, nor were there popular theories claiming, or even justifying, general participation in politics. Nowhere in eighteenth-century America was there "democracy"—middle-class or otherwise—as we use the term. The main reason for the wide franchise was that the traditional English laws limiting suffrage to freeholders of certain competences proved in the colonies, where freehold property was almost universal, to be not restrictive but widely permissive.

Representation would seem to be different, since before the Revolution complaints had been voiced against the inequity of its apportioning, especially in the Pennsylvania and North Carolina assemblies. But these complaints were based on an assumption that would have seemed natural and reasonable almost nowhere else in the Western world: the assumption that representation in governing assemblages was a proper and rightful attribute of people as such—of regular units of population, or of populated land—rather than the privilege of particular groups, institutions, or regions. Complaints there were, bitter ones. But they were complaints claiming injury and deprivation, not abstract ideals or unfamiliar desires. They assumed from common experience the normalcy of regular and systematic representation. And how should it have been otherwise? The Colonial assemblies had not, like ancient parliaments, grown to satisfy a monarch's need for the support of particular groups or individuals or to protect the interests of a social order, and they had not developed insensibly from precedent to precedent. They had been created at a stroke, and they were in their composition necessarily regular and systematic. Nor did the process, the character, of representation as it was known in the colonies derive from theory. For colonial Americans, representation had none of the symbolic and little of the purely deliberative qualities which, as a result of the revolutionary debates and of Burke's speeches, would become celebrated as "virtual." To the colonists it was direct and actual: it was, most often, a kind of agency, a delegation of powers, to individuals commonly required to be residents of their constituencies and, often, bound by instructions from them—with the result that eighteenth-century American legislatures frequently resembled, in spirit if not otherwise, those "ancient assemblies" of New York, composed, the contemporary historian William Smith wrote, "of plain, illiterate husbandmen, whose views seldom extended farther than to the regulation of highways, the destruction of wolves, wild cats, and foxes, and the advancement of the other little interests of the particular counties which they were chosen to represent." There was no theoretical basis for such direct and actual representation. It had been created and was continuously reinforced by the pressure of local politics in the colonies and by the political circumstances in England, to which the colonists had found it necessary to send closely instructed, paid representatives—agents, so called—from the very beginning.

But franchise and representation are mere mechanisms of government by consent. At its heart lies freedom from executive power, from the independent action of state authority, and the concentration of power in representative bodies and elected officials. The greatest achievement of the Revolution was of course the repudiation of just such state authority and the transfer of power to popular legislatures. No one will deny that this action was taken in accordance with the highest principles of Enlightenment theory. But the way had been paved by fifty years of grinding factionalism in colonial politics. In the details of prerevolutionary American politics, in the complicated maneuverings of provincial politicians seeking the benefits of government, in the patterns of local patronage and the forms of factional groupings, there lies a history of progressive alienation from the state which resulted, at least by the 1750's, in what Professor Robert Palmer has lucidly described as a revolutionary situation: a condition

> . . . in which confidence in the justice or reasonableness of existing authority is undermined; where old loyalties fade, obligations are felt as impositions, law seems arbitrary, and respect for superiors is felt as a form of humiliation; where existing sources of prestige seem undeserved . . . and government is sensed as distant, apart from the governed and not really "representing" them.

Such a situation had developed in mid-eighteenth-century America, not from theories of government or Enlightenment ideas but from the factional opposition that had grown up against a succession of legally powerful, but often cynically self-seeking, inept, and above all politically weak officers of state.

Surrounding all of these circumstances and in various ways controlling them is the fact that that great goal of the European revolutions of the late eighteenth century, equality of status before the law—the abolition of legal privilege—had been reached almost everywhere in the American colonies at least by the early years of the eighteenth century. Analogies between the upper strata of colonial society and the European aristocracies are misleading. Social stratification existed, of course; but the differences between aristocracies in eighteenth-century Europe and in America are more important than the similarities. So far was legal privilege, or even distinction, absent in the colonies that where it existed it was an open sore of festering discontent, leading not merely, as in the case of the Penn family's hereditary claims to tax exemption, to formal protests, but, as in the case of the powers enjoyed by the Hudson River land magnates, to violent opposition as well. More important, the colonial aristocracy, such as it was, had no formal, institutional role in government. No public office or function was legally a prerogative of birth. As there were no social orders in the eyes of the law, so there were no governmental bodies to represent them. The only claim that has been made to the contrary is that, in effect, the governors' Councils constituted political institutions in the service of the aristocracy. But this claim—of dubious value in any case because of the steadily declining political importance of the Councils in the eighteenth century—cannot be substantiated. It is true that certain families tended to dominate the Councils, but they had less legal claim to places in those bodies than certain royal officials who, though hardly members of an American aristocracy, sat on the Councils by virtue of their office. Councilors could be and were removed by simple political maneuver. Council seats were filled either by appointment or election: when appointive, they were vulnerable to political pressure in England; when elective, to the vagaries of public opinion at home. Thus on the one hand it took William Byrd II three years of maneuvering in London to get himself appointed to the seat on the Virginia Council vacated by his father's death in 1704, and on the other, when in 1766 the Hutchinson faction's control of the Massachusetts Council proved unpopular, it was simply removed wholesale by being voted out of office at the next election. As there were no special privileges, no peculiar group possessions, manners, or attitudes to distinguish councilors from other affluent Americans, so there were no separate political interests expressed in the Councils as such. Councilors joined as directly as others in the factional disputes of the time, associating with groups of all sorts, from minute and transient American opposition parties to massive English-centered political syndicates. A century before the Revolution and not as the result of antiaristocratic ideas, the colonial aristocracy had become a vaguely defined, fluid group whose power—in no way guaranteed, buttressed, or even recognized in law—was competitively maintained and dependent on continuous, popular support.

Other examples could be given. Were written constitutions felt to be particular guarantees of liberty in enlightened states? Americans had known them in the form of colonial charters and governors' instructions for a century before the Revolution; and after 1763, seeking a basis for their claims against the constitutionality of specific acts of Parliament, they had been driven, out of sheer logical necessity and not out of principle, to generalize that experience. But the point is perhaps clear enough. Major attributes of enlightened polities had developed naturally, spontaneously, early in the history of the American colonies, and they existed as simple matters of social and political fact on the eve of the Revolution.

But if all this is true, what did the Revolution accomplish? Of what real significance were the ideals and ideas? What was the bearing of Enlightenment thought on the political experience of eighteenth-century Americans?

Perhaps this much may be said. What had evolved spontaneously from the demands of place and time was not self-justifying, nor was it universally welcomed. New developments, however gradual, were suspect by some, resisted in part, and confined in their effects. If it was true that the establishment of religion was everywhere weak in the colonies and that in some places it was even difficult to know what was orthodoxy and what was not, it was nevertheless also true that faith in the idea of orthodoxy persisted and with it belief in the propriety of a privileged state religion. If, as a matter of fact, the spread of freehold tenure qualified large populations for voting, it did not create new reasons for using that power nor make the victims of its use content with what, in terms of the dominant ideal of balance in the state, seemed a disproportionate influence of "the democracy." If many colonists came naturally to assume that representation should be direct and actual, growing with the population and bearing some relation to its distribution, crown officials did not, and they had the weight of precedent and theory as well as of authority with them and hence justification for resistance. If state authority was seen increasingly as alien and hostile and was forced to fight for survival within an abrasive, kaleidoscopic factionalism, the traditional idea nevertheless persisted that the common good was somehow defined by the state and that political parties or factions—organized opposition to established government—were seditious. A traditional aristocracy did not in fact exist; but the assumption that superiority was indivisible, that social eminence and political influence had a natural affinity to each other, did. The colonists instinctively conceded to the claims of the well-born and rich to exercise public office, and in this sense politics remained aristocratic. Behavior had changed—had had to change—with the circumstances of everyday life; but habits of mind and the sense of rightness lagged behind. Many felt the changes to be *away from,* not *toward,* something: that the represented deviance; that they lacked, in a word, legitimacy.

This divergence between habits of mind and belief on the one hand and experience and behavior on the other was ended at the Revolution. A rebellion that destroyed the traditional sources of public authority called forth the full range of advanced ideas. Long-settled attitudes were jolted and loosened. The grounds of legitimacy suddenly shifted. What had happened was seen to have been good and proper, steps in the right direction. The glass was half full, not half empty; and to complete the work of fate and nature, further thought must be taken, theories tested, ideas applied. Precisely because so many social and institutional reforms had already taken place in America, the revolutionary movement there, more than elsewhere, was a matter of doctrine, ideas, and comprehension.

And so it remained. Social change and social conflict of course took place during the revolutionary years; but the essential developments of the period lay elsewhere, in the effort to think through and to apply under the most favorable, permissive circumstances enlightened ideas of government and society. The problems were many, often unexpected and difficult; some were only gradually perceived. Social and personal privilege, for example, could easily be eliminated—it hardly existed; but what of the impersonal privileges of corporate bodies? Legal orders and ranks within society could be outlawed without creating the slightest tremor, and executive power with equal ease subordinated to the legislative: but how was balance within a polity to be achieved? What were the elements to be balanced and how were they to be separated? It was not even necessary formally to abolish the interest of state as a symbol and determinant of the common good; it was simply dissolved: but what was left to keep clashing factions from tearing a government apart? The problems were pressing, and the efforts to solve them mark the stages of revolutionary history.

In behalf of Enlightenment liberalism the revolutionary leaders undertook to complete, formalize, systematize, and symbolize what previously had been only partially realized, confused, and disputed matters of fact. Enlightenment ideas were not instruments of a particular social group, nor did they destroy a social order. They did not create new social and political forces in America. They released those that had long existed, and vastly increased their power. This completion, this rationalization, this symbolization, this lifting into consciousness and endowing with high moral purpose inchoate, confused elements of social and political change—this was the American Revolution.

3 / The American Revolution Considered as an Intellectual Movement

Edmund S. Morgan

Professor Morgan is a highly prolific and original historian who has proved to be equally at home in the seventeenth and eighteenth centuries. His works range from a study of the Puritan family through biographies of New England leaders such as John Winthrop and Ezra Stiles to provocative studies of the American Revolution in *The Stamp Act Crisis* and *The Birth of the Republic.* In the following essay, Morgan examines the transition from the early dominant interest of the colonists in religious matters to their concern with the great issues of the Revolution, a transition symbolized by the changing of leadership from ministers and theologians to politicians and statesmen. He notes the influence of a strong Calvinist conviction of the depravity of human nature upon the views of the Revolutionary generation, upon their willingness to believe in the evil character of English leaders, and their concern with checking the innate tendencies of man toward the misuse of power in their own governments. In the quarter-century of Revolutionary ferment in America, "the best minds . . . addressed themselves to the rescue, not of souls, but of governments, from the perils of corruption." This concern of the best minds combined with the lessons of actual American practice helped to establish new principles of representative government, a new notion of the constituent power of the people (the establishment by the action of the people of constitutional forms clearly superior to the governments themselves), and new and effective ways of reconciling larger union with local autonomy and the will of the majority with the rights of minorities.

For further reading: in addition to the selections listed for the preceding article, see: Alan Heimert, *Religion and the American Mind from the Great Awakening to the Revolution* (1966); Edmund S. Morgan, "The Puritan Ethic and the American Revolution," *William and Mary Quarterly,* 3rd series, XXIV (1967), 3–43; Perry Miller, "From the Covenant to the Revival," in James Ward Smith and A. Leland Jamison, *The Shaping of American Religion* (1961), 322–368.

Reprinted by permission of the Houghton Mifflin Company from Arthur M. Schlesinger, Jr., and Morton White, *Paths of American Thought* (1963), 11–33.

In 1740 America's leading intellectuals were clergymen and thought about theology; in 1790 they were statesmen and thought about politics. A variety of forces, some of them reaching deep into the colonial past, helped to bring about the transformation, but it was so closely associated with the revolt from England that one may properly consider the American Revolution, as an intellectual movement, to mean the substitution of political for clerical leadership and of politics for religion as the most challenging area of human thought and endeavor.

The American colonies had been founded during the seventeenth century, when Englishmen were still animated by the great vision of John Calvin, the vision of human depravity and divine perfection. Every human being from Adam onward must be counted, Calvin insisted, in the ranks of "those whose feet are swift to shed blood, whose hands are polluted with rapine and murder, whose throats are like open sepulchres, whose tongues are deceitful, whose lips are envenomed, whose works are useless, iniquitous, corrupt, and deadly, whose souls are estranged from God, the inmost recesses of whose hearts are full of pravity, whose eyes are insidiously employed, whose minds are elated with insolence—in a word, all whose powers are prepared for the commission of atrocious and innumerable crimes." If a man did not actually commit such crimes, it was not for want of a desire to do so. God might furnish restraints of one sort or another to prevent "the perverseness of our nature from breaking out into external acts, but does not purify it within." [1]

The official church of England, born of a licentious monarch's divorce, had never fully shared in Calvin's vision. Though it absorbed much of his theology during the reign of Queen Elizabeth I, it retained a more flattering view than his of human capacities and priestly powers. The more thoroughgoing English Calvinists, the Puritans, were hopeful of effecting further reforms, but during the late 1620's and 1630's the Church and the king who headed it drew ever closer to old Roman Catholic doctrines. In the 1640's the Puritans resorted to arms, killed the king, purged the Church, and turned England into a republic. But in 1660 the monarchy was restored. Puritans, now called dissenters, were dismissed from office in both church and state; and the Church of England resumed its old ways, unimpeded by Calvinism.

It is no coincidence that England's American colonies were settled before 1640 or after 1660. Emigration offered a substitute for revolution to thousands of men and women who were discontented with the Church of England and with the government that fostered it. Puritans settled all the New England colonies, overran the Catholic refuge of the Calvert family in Maryland, and later furnished substantial numbers of settlers to New York, New Jersey, and the Carolinas. They came even to Virginia, where the majority of settlers, though remaining within the Church of England, did not share in its high-church movement. After the Restoration, the colonies attracted large numbers of English Quakers and Scotch-Irish Presbyterians, not to mention French Huguenots and German Protestants of various denominations. Anglicans came too, and the Anglican Church was supported by law in several colonies, but the flavor of American colonial life was overwhelmingly that of the Reformation.[2]

[1] John Calvin, *Institutes of the Christian Religion*, trans. John Allen (sixth American edition, Philadelphia, 1932), I, 263.

[2] Cf. Frederick B. Tolles, *Quakers and the Atlantic Culture* (New York, 1960), p. 11; Babette M. Levy, "Early Puritanism in the Southern and Island Colonies," American Antiquarian Society, *Proceedings,* LXX (1960), 69–348.

The intellectual center of the colonies was New England, and the intellectual leaders of New England were the clergy, who preached and wrote indefatigably of human depravity and divine perfection. These two axioms, for the Puritans as for Calvin himself, required the eternal damnation of most mankind. And since God knew all and decreed all from eternity, it followed that He had determined in advance who should be damned and who should be saved. One of the principal tasks of the ministry was to explain to men how bad they were, so bad that they all deserved damnation. That God had chosen to save any was simply through mercy, another attribute of His perfection. No man deserved salvation, no one was less guilty than another, so that God's choice rested only in Himself.

To explain these doctrines was the easiest part of the preacher's task, for most of his audience was already persuaded of them. A more difficult assignment was to assist men in discerning where they stood in the divine scheme. No man could be certain whether he was saved until the day of judgment, but there were stages in the process of redemption that took place in this life; and ministers devoted much of their preaching and writing to descriptions of them. One of the first stages was conviction, a full recognition of man's helpless and hopeless condition. A man destined for damnation could reach this stage, but not the next one, conversion. Conversion was an act of God, infusing a man's soul with the Holy Spirit, "justifying" him through the attribution of Christ's merits. Conversion, for the Puritan, was so clear and precise an experience that a man who had undergone it could often specify the time and place. After conversion came sanctification, a gradual improvement in conduct, approximating, though only outwardly, the obedience which God had demanded of Adam. Sanctification could never be complete in this world, but it might be sufficiently marked to be discernible. Guided by the clergy, Puritans and other Calvinist Protestants became familiar with the morphology of redemption and expert in searching their own souls for signs of metamorphosis.

Just as the Puritans' theology revolved around depravity and divine perfection, so did their political theory. And Puritan ministers instructed their congregations in politics as well as religion. They taught that society originates in a contract between God on the one hand and the people on the other, whereby if the people agreed to abide by His commands (though again, only outwardly, for true, inner obedience was beyond them) He would assure them outward prosperity. Having made such an agreement, the people, in another compact, voluntarily subjected themselves to a king or to other civil rulers. This was the origin of government; and the purpose of government was to restrain the sinfulness of man, to prevent and punish offenses against God. As long as a king enforced God's commands, embodying them in human laws, the people owed him obedience and assistance. If, however, moved by his own depravity he violated God's commands or failed to enforce them, he broke the compact on which his political authority rested, and it was the people's duty to remove him lest God visit the whole community with death and destructiton.[3]

These ideas had developed in England at a time when reigning monarchs exhibited (by Puritan standards) far too much depravity. Three generations of Puritans nervously scolded their kings and queens and momentarily expected God's wrath to descend on England. Finally, in 1649, they did away with both king and kingship. But even after monarchy ended, human depravity remained, and Englishmen faced

[3] Perry Miller, *The New England Mind: The Seventeenth Century* (New York, 1939), pp. 398–431; E. S. Morgan, *The Puritan Dilemma* (Boston, 1958), pp. 18–100.

the problem of controlling it in the new context of a republic. Ideas about the maintenance of purity, probity, and stability in a republic were offered by a number of men, the most influential of whom was James Harrington. In his *Oceana* (1656) Harrington associated republican government with widespread distribution—approaching equality—of property. He also advocated religious toleration, rotation in public office, and separation of governmental powers. With the restoration of the monarchy, Harrington's work continued for several generations to excite the admiration of a small group of British political thinkers, who probed the nature of government and speculated about methods of keeping it responsible to the people.[4] The best known of them, John Locke, reemphasized the idea of a compact between rulers and people in order to justify the exclusion of James II from the throne.[5]

The English republican writers were read in the colonies, and Locke's political doctrines were assimilated by American clergymen and dispensed in their sermons along with the older ideas. Every generation learned of its duty to pull down bad rulers and to uphold good ones. The colonists did not, however, develop a separate school of republican political theory. The clergy, who continued to be the principal exponents of political ideas and the most influential members of the community, devoted their creative intellectual efforts to theology, and their congregations continued to search souls. Every Sunday they attended at the meetinghouse morning and afternoon to hear the theological expositions that were always the principal ingredient in a Puritan church service. Then they went home to write in their diaries and measure their lives against what they had learned in the sermons. Daily they read their Bibles and prayed, in private and with their families. Theology was as much a part of their lives as meat and drink.

By the middle of the eighteenth century, however, a change had begun. A series of developments, culminating in the Revolution, combined to effect a weakening of popular interest in theology and a decline in clerical leadership.

The first development, and the most difficult to assess, was the growth in England and Europe, transmitted gradually to America, of a new confidence in human reason. The achievements of Sir Isaac Newton and of other seventeenth-century astronomers and mathematicians belied the low estimate hitherto entertained of man's capacity to understand, without the assistance of divine revelation, God's government of the universe. The Enlightenment, as the new attitude came to be called, promised to reveal the mysteries of creation simply through the application of human intelligence.

New England ministers at first perceived no threat to religion from the Enlightenment. Although they thought poorly of human reason, they were themselves assiduous in making the most of it. They had applied it primarily to the Bible, but they now welcomed every new piece of observational knowledge in the assurance that it would help to fill out the data derived from the Bible. With the success of Newton to spur them, they began to pay more attention to the physical world and made observations of plants and animals, of comets and stars; and they sent these observations to England to assist the progress of knowledge about God's wonderful universe.

It became apparent only gradually—first in England, then in America—that reason, instead of assisting revelation, might replace it. Though Newton himself retained a

[4] In *The Eighteenth-Century Commonwealthman* (Cambridge, Mass., 1959), Caroline Robbins has identified and discussed this political tradition.

[5] Peter Laslett, "The English Revolution and Locke's Two Treatises," *Cambridge Historical Journal*, XII (1956), 40–55.

firm belief in the Scriptures and spent his later years unraveling Biblical prophecies, many of his admirers became deists, who believed that God reveals Himself only through the operation of His universe and not through prophets, priests, or holy scriptures. In America deism claimed few adherents before the last quarter of the eighteenth century; and it seems probable that the Enlightenment appreciably lowered the prestige of the clergy only after they had already lost much of their influence through the paradoxical operation of a religious revival.

The Great Awakening of the 1740's began when a young English minister, George Whitefield, showed American preachers how to convey the full meaning of human depravity. Traveling throughout the colonies, he preached wherever he could find an audience, whether inside a church or under a tree, and everywhere his message was the same: men deserve hell. Whitefield's talent lay in depicting the torments of hell dramatically and vividly. He could weep at will, over the fate of the men and women before him; he could impersonate God delivering the awful sentence against them. When he wept they did too, and when he pronounced the sentence against them, they fell to the ground in agony.[6]

Whitefield had already earned some notoriety by these methods before crossing the ocean. In the colonies his success was overwhelming. People flocked to him as to a new messiah. Though Anglicans remained largely unmoved, most Americans had been brought up on the doctrine of the depravity of man, and they could not find any expression of it too strong. Whitefield merely brought them a new and more emotional appreciation of truths they had known all along. Other preachers quickly imitated his methods and outdid him in the extravagance of their gestures. Gilbert Tennent of Pennsylvania made a specialty of roaring with holy laughter at sinners whom he had awakened to their helpless condition. James Davenport of Long Island liked to preach at night, when smoking candles and torches gave verisimilitude to his fiery denunciations.[7] These self-appointed apostles and dozens more like them imitated Whitefield not only in their manner of preaching but in wandering from place to place to deliver their fearful message.

Terror was the object; and terror was right. If a man faces eternal, unbearable pain, deserves it, and can do nothing to avoid it he ought to be terrified. The preachers had another word for it, familiar to all Calvinists: they called it conviction, the awareness, denied to the complacent, of one's hopeless condition. The great thing about the new preaching was that it destroyed complacency and brought conviction to thousands. And the great thing about conviction was that conversion could be expected in many cases to follow it. Calvinist ministers for two centuries had described the divine process and in the Great Awakening the course of conviction and conversion ran true to form. Not everyone who trembled in terror rose to the joy of conversion, but hundreds did.

As the churches filled with them, it seemed apparent that God approved the new method of preaching and the men who practiced it. Whether He also approved the

[6] On Whitefield, see Luke Tyerman, *The Life of the Rev. George Whitefield* (New York, 1877) and John Gillies, *Memoirs of Rev. George Whitefield* (New Haven, 1834). Originally published in 1772, Gillies's work was considerably expanded in later editions. On Whitefield in New England, see Edwin L. Gaustad, *The Great Awakening in New England* (New York, 1957).

[7] Charles Chauncy, *Seasonable Thoughts on the State of Religion in New England* (Boston 1743), pp. 127, 151–168; *Boston Weekly News-Letter,* June 24–July 1, 1742; "Diary of Joshua Hempstead," New London Historical Society, *Proceedings,* I (1901), 379 ff.

old methods was questionable. Men and women who had worshiped for years without result under the guidance of an erudite but undramatic minister, found grace after a few hours at the feet of some wandering apostle. The itinerant was often a layman who had never been to college and knew no Greek, Latin, or Hebrew, but had a way with an audience. If God selected him to do so much without learning, was learning perhaps more a hindrance than a help to true religion? The thought occurred to many converts and was encouraged by the increasingly confident, not to say arrogant, posture of the itinerants. Whitefield had warned broadly against ministers who preached an unknown and unfelt Christ. His followers did not hesitate to name individual ministers as dead of heart, blind leaders of the blind.

After such a pronouncement, a congregation, or a substantial portion of it, might desert their old minister. If they were a majority, they could dismiss him; if a minority they might secede to form a church of their own, with some newly discovered prophet to lead them. Congregations had left their ministers before, especially in New England, but never before had the desertions been so many or so bitter.

At first the deserted clergymen merely looked upon the Awakening with skepticism. But as its exponents (known to the time as New Lights) became more and more extravagant, skepticism spread and grew to hostility. Ministers who had spent their lives in the study of theology and who had perhaps been touched by the Enlightenment, were appalled at the ignorance of New Light preachers and dismissed their convictions and conversions as hysteria. Many of these opposers (Old Lights), though reluctant to recognize the fact, were already several steps down the road that led to Arminianism, Universalism, Unitarianism, and deism. The most outspoken of them, Charles Chauncy, eventually became a Universalist. But most of them pulled up short of these extremes, and those who went the whole way found few followers. The majority, clinging to the old doctrines of Calvinism, mitigated in some measure by the Enlightenment, were a humane and pious group, perhaps the most likeable of New England clergymen. Some of them retained or rewon the loyalty of large congregations. But they never regained the broad influence they had enjoyed over the colonial community before the Great Awakening.

The failure of the Old Light clergy to retain intellectual leadership was due partly to the fact that they failed to win the minds of the next generation of ministers. The New Lights, in spite of their ignorance, enjoyed the blessing of Jonathan Edwards, America's foremost intellectual. It was inevitable that bright young divinity students should follow his lead. Edwards, the most brilliant theologian the country ever produced, had already generated a minor awakening of his own at Northampton, Massachusetts, six years before the Great Awakening. By comparison with Whitefield his technique was muted: he talked almost in a monotone, and never resorted to dramatic gestures, but when he spoke of eternal torments in as matter-of-fact a manner as he spoke of the weather, the effect on a New England audience could be devastating. Observing the beneficial effects of terror, Edwards applauded when Whitefield and Tennent brought the fires of hell to New England.

In ensuing years Edwards wrote a series of treatises to demonstrate the importance of the emotions or "affections" in religion and to affirm, more rigorously than ever before in New England, the dogmas of divine perfection and human depravity. By the time he died in 1758, he had gathered a tight band of followers, who continued his doctrines and developed them into a theological system known as the New Divinity.[8] The high priest of the movement was Samuel Hopkins, who preached at Great Barrington, Massachusetts, and later at Newport, Rhode Island. Other leading figures were Edward's son, Jonathan Jr., of New Haven, and Joseph Bellamy, who from the small village of Bethlehem, Connecticut, earned the title of pope of Litchfield County.

New Divinity men were often rough and domineering with their congregations, exploding in angry denunciations; and their doctrines matched their manners. It was wrong, they said, for the unregenerate to pray, since an unregenerate man, lacking real love for God, could not pray without hypocrisy and would anger God further by his futile efforts. The only way in which the unregenerate could contribute to the glory of God was to rejoice in their own damnation—an attitude which their very unregeneracy made improbable. The New Divinity also called for a restoration of the standards of church membership that had prevailed in New England before the Half-Way Covenant of 1662: a man could join the church only if he demonstrated to the satisfaction of the other members that God had predestined him to eternal salvation. Only such persons were entitled to take communion or to have their children baptized. The remainder of the community could only listen to the minister's preaching, in hopes that God would use this means to achieve a salvation already determined though as yet undisclosed.

The New Divinity had a consistency and rigor that young intellectuals found challenging. It was the fashionable, avant-garde movement of the seventeen-fifties, sixties, seventies, and to some extent the eighties. During these years many young men had already begun to find politics or the law more satisfying intellectually than religion, but insofar as religion continued to draw young minds, they gravitated to men like Bellamy and Hopkins for guidance. As a result, by 1792 the New Divinity claimed half the pulpits in Connecticut (and an increasing number in the rest of New England), together with virtually all the candidates for the ministry—this on the testimony of Ezra Stiles, president of Yale from 1778 to 1795, who despised the New Divinity and lamented its attraction for the young men he had educated.[9]

But the success of the New Divinity among the rising generation of clergy was not matched among the people at large. Its harsh doctrines could be sustained only by intellectual or religious fervor, and the religious fervor of Americans was already waning before the complexities of the system had been completely worked out. Even as Jonathan Edwards turned out his massive justifications of the Great Awakening, that movement subsided in the manner of later religious revivals. By the time Edwards had devised an intellectual foundation for emotionalism in religion, he had begun to lose his popular audience. When he announced that he would apply new standards of church membership, excluding all but the demonstrably regenerate from the sacraments, his church at Northampton dismissed him. America's greatest intellectual of his time spent most of his later years preaching, for want of a wider audience, to the Indians, who perhaps least of any group in America could understand him.

[8] On Edwards, see Ola Winslow, *Jonathan Edwards* (New York, 1940); Perry Miller, *Jonathan Edwards* (New York, 1949). On the New Divinity, see F. H. Foster, *A Genetic History of the New England Theology* (Chicago, 1907); Joseph Haroutunian, *Piety versus Moralism* (New York, 1932).

[9] *The Literary Diary of Ezra Stiles*, ed. F. B. Dexter (New York, 1901), III, 464. Cf. Conrad Wright, *The Beginnings of Unitarianism in America* (Boston, 1955), pp. 252–259.

The careers of Edwards's disciples were somewhat more fortunate but not dissimilar. Samuel Hopkins, ministering to a large congregation at Great Barrington, saw it dwindle away until he was obliged to leave. At Newport, Rhode Island, he found another large congregation and again watched it decline. The history of New Haven's Second Church, formed during the Great Awakening by a seceding New Light minority from New Haven's First Church, reveals the same development. The new church prospered under the ministry of the Reverend Samuel Bird. But after Jonathan Edwards, Jr., took charge in 1769 and the relative simplicity of New Light gave way to the complexities of New Divinity, the congregation diminished until by 1795 there were not enough left or willing to support him.[10]

Hopkins and Jonathan Edwards, Jr., enjoyed the admiration of their ministerial colleagues, as did many other fearlessly consistent theologians of the New Divinity, but few of them could retain a popular following. Even while they justified emotionalism in religion, their sermons became complex, abstruse, metaphysical, devoted to details of theology that the layman found incomprehensible. During a revival of religion, their arid doctrines might still send shudders of horror through a receptive audience, but most of the time their congregations found them simply dull.

Their fault lay in addressing themselves more to each other than to their people. Engrossed in the details of their system, they delighted in exploring new elements of consistency in it and neglected the central problems of Christianity, until they scarcely knew how to deal with the elementary questions of salvation that their people put to them. Nowhere is the paradox of the New Divinity's intellectual success and popular failure more graphically demonstrated than in a letter from a young minister to his mentor. Medad Rogers, after graduating from Yale in 1777, had studied theology with Benjamin Trumbull, the New Divinity minister of North Haven. When Rogers began to preach, he discovered for the first time that he did not know the answers to the questions that Christians have always had to wrestle with.

"Sir," he wrote to Trumbull,

> if you do not think I desire more reproof than direction, some of your kind instructions, would be most timely to me—as also some directions how we should begin, spend, and end the day—What to say to those under concern for a future existence, when they enquire how they shall come to the foot of a sovereign God. They try to, but cannot. They would bow to Christ's sceptre but are not able. How are we to blame, say they? We would be saved but can't be saved. How are such to be dealt with? As also, if God hath decreed all things, why is he not the Author of sin? How can any man do otherwise than he does? If God hath elected a particular number, what is there for the others to do? Why had we not Just as good lie still and do nothing? Where is the criminality of their conduct in not embracing the Gospel offers, when they were not elected? What Justice, say they, in punishing those who miss of Salvation, for not accepting the offer, when they were not elected to it? Is not God partial? If we are to be saved we shall, if not we shall be cast away. Then, what good do our works do? Will persons who lived morally honest lives, have any respect shown them upon that account, in the day of Judgment, if they appear on the left hand of the Judge? Sir, if you could find yourself willing and at leasure Just to touch upon some, or all of these, you would do me a very great favour, and perhaps be a greater

[10] Stiles, *Diary,* III, 344, 438, 562.

monument of glory to you, Kind sir, at last, than if you had written an hundred thousand volumes of Phylosophy, Rhetorick, Logick, and History.[11]

Trumbull's answer to Rogers is not preserved. But the very fact that a young minister should ask such questions speaks volumes about the state of religion in New England. The clergy for the first time in their history had lost contact with the people. In the seventeenth century when Roger Williams debated fine points of theology with John Cotton, or Increase Mather with Solomon Stoddard, people had not been bored. But the New Divinity ministers were unable to carry their congregations with them.

In earlier decades when a people became disgruntled with their minister, they had replaced him. But the American population had increased so rapidly that there were not enough ministers to go around; and since the New Divinity claimed such a large percentage of ministerial candidates, congregations were regularly faced with the necessity of taking a New Divinity man or leaving their pulput vacant. The resultant discontent contributed in the last quarter of the eighteenth century to the rapid growth of Anglicanism, Methodism, deism, and what people at the time called "nothingarianism," a total indifference to religion. The clergy, once the most respected members of the community, became the objects of ridicule and contempt, especially in Connecticut, the stronghold of the New Divinity. In 1778, when the ministers of the state published a rebuke to the people for their neglect of public worship, the newspapers carried some rude answers. "We have heard your animadversions," said one, "upon our absence from Sabbath meetings, and humbly conceive if you wish our attendance there, you would make it worth our while to give it. To miss a sermon of the present growth, what is it but to miss of an opiate? And can the loss of a nap expose our souls to eternal perdition?" [12]

Such indifference to religion, edged with hostility to the clergy, was the end product of the developments we have been tracing from the 1740's. But though the clergy could blame themselves for much of their loss of prestige and for much of the decline of popular interest in religion, it was Parliament's attempt to tax the colonists in the 1760's that caused Americans to transfer to politics the intellectual interest and energy that were once reserved for religion. This reorientation was directed partly by the clergy themselves. They had never stopped giving instruction in political thought; and (except for the Anglicans) throughout the 1760's and 1770's they publicly and passionately scored the actions of George III and his Parliament against the standards by which their English Puritan predecessors had judged and condemned Charles I.

Presbyterian and Congregational ministers also raised the alarm when a movement was set afoot for the establishment in the colonies of state-supported bishops. The American clergymen developed no new general ideas about government—there was no New Light in political thought, no New Politics to match the New Divinity—but the old ideas and those imported from English political theorists served well enough to impress upon their congregations the tyrannical nature of taxation without representation, and of bishops who might establish ecclesiastical courts with jurisdiction extending beyond their own denomination.

[11] Rogers to Trumbull, March 17, 1783, Benjamin Trumbull Correspondence, Yale University Library.
[12] *New Haven Gazette and Connecticut Magazine,* July 31, October 9, 1788.

Although the clergy were a powerful influence in molding American political opinion during the Revolutionary period, they did not recover through politics the intellectual leadership they had already begun to lose. Their own principles barred them from an active role in politics. While they had always given political advice freely and exercised their influence in elections, most of them would have considered it wrong to sit in a representative assembly, on a governor's council, or on the bench. To them as to their Puritan ancestors the clerical exercise of temporal powers spelled Rome. A minister's business was, after all, the saving of souls. By the same token, however outraged he might be by the actions of the English government, however excited by the achievement of American independence, a minister could not devote his principal intellectual effort to the expounding of political ideas and political principles. As the quarrel with England developed and turned into a struggle for independence and nationhood, though the ministers continued to speak up on the American side, other voices commanding greater attention were raised by men who were free to make a career of politics and prepared to act as well as talk.

There had always, of course, been political leaders in the colonies, but hitherto politics had been a local affair, requiring at most the kind of talents needed for collecting votes or pulling wires. A colonial legislative assembly might occasionally engage in debates about paper money, defense, or modes of taxation; but the issues did not reach beyond the borders of the colony involved and were seldom of a kind to challenge a superior mind. No American debated imperial policy in the British Parliament, the Privy Council, or the Board of Trade. The highest political post to which a man could aspire in the colonies was that of governor, and everywhere except in Connecticut and Rhode Island, this was obtained not through political success but through having friends in England. Few native Americans ever achieved it or even tried to.

But the advent of Parliamentary taxation inaugurated a quarter-century of political discussion in America that has never since been matched in intensity. With the passage of the Stamp Act in 1765, every colonial legislature took up the task of defining the structure of the British empire; and as colonial definitions met with resistance from England, as the colonies banded together for defense and declared their independence, politics posed continental, even global, problems that called forth the best efforts of the best American minds. In no other period of our history would it be possible to find in politics five men of such intellectual stature as Benjamin Franklin, John Adams, Alexander Hamilton, James Madison, and Thomas Jefferson; and there were others only slightly less distinguished.

Whether they hailed from Pennsylvania or Virginia, New England or New York, the men who steered Americans through the Revolution, the establishment of a new nation, and the framing of the Constitution did not for the most part repudiate the political ideas inherited from the period of clerical dominance. Like the clergy, they started from a conviction of human depravity; like the clergy, they saw government originating in compact, and measured governmental performance against an absolute standard ordained by God. Like the clergy too, they found inspiration in the example of seventeenth-century Englishmen. Sometimes they signed their own attacks on George III or his ministers with the names of John Hampden, William Pym, or other Parliamentary heroes in the struggle against Charles I. They read the works of Harrington and of Harrington's later admirers; and after the Declaration of Independence, when they found themselves in a position similar to that of England in the 1650's, they drew heavily on the arsenal of political ideas furnished by these latter-day republicans.

Indeed, most of the ideas about government which American intellectuals employed first in their resistance to Parliament, and then in constructing their own governments, had been articulated earlier in England and were still in limited circulation there. The social compact, fundamental law, the separation of powers, human equality, religious freedom, and the superiority of republican government were continuing ideals for a small but ardent group of Englishmen who, like the Americans, believed that the British constitution was basically republican and drew inspiration from it while attacking the ministers and monarch who seemed to be betraying it.[13] It is perhaps no accident that the work in which Americans first repudiated monarchy, *Common Sense,* was written by an Englishman, Thomas Paine, who had come to America only two years before.

But if Englishmen supplied the intellectual foundations both for the overthrow of English rule and for the construction of republican government, Americans put the ideas into practice and drew on American experience and tradition to devise refinements and applications of the greatest importance. That republican ideas, which existed in a state of obscurity in England, should be congenial in the colonies, was due in the first place to the strong continuing Calvinist tradition which had been nourished over the years by the American clergy. But fully as important was the fact that during a hundred and fifty years of living in the freedom of a relatively isolated and empty continent, the colonists had developed a way of life in which republican ideas played a visible part. When Parliamentary taxation set Americans to analyzing their relationship to the mother country, they could not escape seeing that the social, economic, and political configuration of America had diverged from that of England in ways that made Americans better off than Englishmen. And the things that made them better off could be labeled republican.

England's practical experience with republicanism had lasted only eleven years. With the return of Charles II in 1660, Englishmen repudiated their republic and the Puritans who had sponsored it. Though a small minority continued to write and talk about republicanism and responsible government, they wielded no authority. The House of Commons grew more powerful but less common, and the main current of English national life flowed in the channels of monarchy, aristocracy, and special privilege. Americans, by contrast, though formally subjects of the king, had lived long under conditions that approximated the ideals of the English republican theorists. Harrington thought he had found in the England of his day the widespread ownership of property that seemed to him a necessary condition for republican government; but throughout the colonies ownership of property had always been more widespread than in England. Furthermore no member of the nobility had settled in America, so that people were accustomed to a greater degree of social as well as economic equality than existed anywhere in England.

During the 1640's and 1650's England had seen a rapid multiplication of religious sects, which produced a wide belief in religious freedom, but after the Anglican Church had reimposed its controls in the 1660's, the most that other denominations could hope for was toleration. In America, religious diversity had steadily increased, and with it came a religious freedom which, if still imperfect, surpassed anything England had ever known.

---

[13] See again Robbins, *Eighteenth-Century Commonwealthman.*

Though the English people had twice removed an unsatisfactory king, in 1649 and in 1688, the English government remained far less responsible and far less responsive to the people than any colonial government. While the members of Parliament disclaimed any obligation to their immediate constituents, the members of American representative assemblies knew that they were expected to look after the interests of the people who elected them. Nor were the voters in America only a small minority of the population as in England. In most colonies probably the great majority of adult males owned enough property to meet the qualification (which varied from colony to colony) for voting. In England, the government paid hundreds of office-holders whose offices, carrying no duties, existed solely for the enrichment of those who held them. In the colonies such sinecures were few. Americans thought that government existed to do a job, and they created no offices except for useful purposes.

Thus when the quarrel with Parliament began, the colonists already had what English reformers wanted. And the colonists were inclined to credit their good fortune not to the accident of geography but to their own superior virtue and political sophistication. The interpretation was not without foundation: since Calvinist traditions were still strong among them and since they had often learned of British republican ideas through the sermons of Calvinist clergymen, Americans retained what the Enlightenment had dimmed in England and Europe, a keen sense of human depravity and of the dangers it posed for government. Although their own governments had hitherto given little evidence of depravity, by comparison with those of Europe, they were expert at detecting it in any degree. They had always been horrified by the open corruption of British politics and feared it would lead to tyranny. When Parliament attempted to tax them and sent swarms of customs collectors, sailors, and soldiers to support the attempt, their fears were confirmed. In resisting the British and in forming their own governments, they saw the central problem as one of devising means to check the inevitable operation of depravity in men who wielded power. English statesmen had succumbed to it. How could Americans avoid their mistakes?

In the era of the American Revolution, from 1764 to 1789, this was the great intellectual challenge. Although human depravity continued to pose as difficult theological problems as ever, the best minds of the period addressed themselves to the rescue, not of souls, but of governments, from the perils of corruption. Of course the problem was not new, nor any more susceptible of final solution than it had been in an earlier time, but Americans in the Revolutionary period contributed three notable principles to men's efforts to deal with it.

The first principle, which evolved from the struggle with Parliament, was that the people of one region ought not to exercise dominion over those of another, even though the two may be joined together. It was an idea that overlapped and greatly facilitated the slower but parallel development of the more general belief in human equality. In objecting to British taxation in 1764 the colonists had begun by asserting their right to equal treatment with the king's subjects in Great Britain: Englishmen could not be taxed except by their representatives; neither therefore could Americans. Within a year or two the idea was extended to a denial that Parliament, representing the electors of Great Britain, could exercise any authority over the colonies. The empire, according to one American writer, was "a confederacy of states, independent of each other, yet united under one head," namely the king. "I cannot find," said another, "that the inhabitants of the colonies are dependent on the people of

Britain, or the people of Britain on them, any more than Kent is on Sussex, or Sussex on Kent." [14]

It took varying lengths of time for other Americans to reach the position thus anonymously expressed in the press in 1765 and 1766. Franklin stated it later in 1766;[15] Jefferson, James Wilson, and John Adams had all expressed it by the beginning of 1775.[16] It was frequently buttressed by the citation of precedents from English constitutional history, but it rested on a principle capable of universal application, the principle stated in the preamble of the Declaration of Independence, that every people is entitled, by the laws of nature and of nature's God, to a separate and equal station.

Before Independence this principle offered a means of reorganizing the British empire so as to defeat the tyranny which Americans thought English statesmen were developing in the extension of taxation. If a British legislature, in which the colonists were not represented, could govern them, then neither British nor colonial freedom could be safe. Americans without a voice in the government could not defend their rights against corrupt rulers. Englishmen, relieved of expenses by American taxation, might rejoice for the moment, but their rulers, no longer dependent on them financially, would be able to govern as they pleased and would eventually escape popular control altogether. The only solution was to give each legislature power only over the people who chose it.

In the 1770's England was unwilling to listen to the colonial arguments, but ultimately adopted the American principle in forming the Commonwealth of Nations. The independent United States applied the principle not only in the confederation of states but in the annexation of other areas. When Virginia in 1781 offered the United States Congress her superior claim to the old Northwest, it was with the stipulation that the region be divided into separate republican states, each of which was to be admitted to the Union on equal terms with the old ones. The stipulation, though not accepted by Congress at the time, was carried out in Jefferson's land ordinance of 1784 and in the Northwest Ordinance of 1787 which superseded it. The United States never wavered from the principle until after the Spanish-American War, when it temporarily accepted government of areas which it had no intention of admitting to the union on equal terms.

The second contribution of the American Revolutionists was an application of the assumption, implicit in the whole ideas of a compact between rulers and people, that a people can exist as a people before they have a government and that they can act as a people independently of government. The Puritans had distinguished between the compact of a group of individuals with God, by which they became a people, and the subsequent compact between this people and their rulers, by which government was created. John Locke had similarly distinguished between the dissolution of society and of government, and so, at least tacitly, had the Revolutionists. They would have been more daring, not to say foolhardy, if they had undertaken to destroy the bonds

[14] E. S. Morgan, *Prologue to Revolution: Sources and Documents on the Stamp Act Crisis* (Chapel Hill, 1959), pp. 73, 91.

[15] Verner Crane, *Benjamin Franklin's Letters to the Press, 1758–1775* (Chapel Hill, 1950), p. xlii.

[16] Thomas Jefferson, *A Summary View of the Rights of British America* (Williamsburg, 1774); James Wilson, *Considerations on the Nature and the Extent of the Legislative Authority of the British Parliament* (Philadelphia, 1774); John Adams, *Works*, ed. C. F. Adams (Boston, 1850–56), IV, 3–177.

of society as well as of government. But in their haste to form new governments after the royal government in each colony dissolved, the Revolutionists followed a procedure that did not clearly distinguish the people from the government. Provincial congresses, exercising a *de facto* power, drafted and adopted permanent constitutions, which in most cases then went into effect without submission to a popular vote.

When the Massachusetts provincial congress proposed to follow this procedure in 1776, the citizens of the town of Concord pointed out the dangerous opening which it offered to human depravity. A *de facto* government that legitimized itself could also alter itself. Whatever safeguards it adopted against corruption could easily be discarded by later legislators: "a Constitution alterable by the Supreme Legislative is no Security at all to the Subject against any Encroachment of the Governing part on any or on all of their Rights and privileges." The town therefore suggested that a special popularly elected convention be called for the sole purpose of drafting a constitution, which should then be submitted to the people for approval.[17]

It is impossible to determine who was responsible for Concord's action, but the protest displays a refinement in the application of republican ideas that does not appear to have been expressed before. Concord's suggestion was eventually followed in the drafting and adoption of the Massachusetts constitution of 1780 and of every subsequent constitution established in the United States. By it the subservience of government to the people was secured through a constitution clearly superior to the government is created, a constitution against which the people could measure governmental performance and against which each branch of government could measure the actions of the other branches. The separation of governmental powers into a bicameral legislature, an executive, and a judiciary, which was an older and more familiar way of checking depravity, was rendered far more effective by the existence of a written constitution resting directly on popular approval. The written constitution also proved its effectiveness in later years by perpetuating in America the operation of judicial review, of executive veto, and of a powerful upper house of the legislature, all of which had been or would be lost in England, where the constitution was unwritten and consisted of customary procedures that could be altered at will by Parliament.

Thus by the time the Revolution ended, Americans had devised a way to establish the superiority of the people to their government and so to control man's tyranny over man. For the same purpose Americans had formulated the principle that no people should exercise dominion over another people. But the way in which they first employed the latter principle in running the new nation did not prove satisfactory. As thirteen separate colonies the people of America had joined to combat Parliamentary taxation, and the result had been thirteen independent republics. It had been an exhilarating experience, and it had led them almost from the beginning to think of themselves in some degree as one people. But the thought was not completed: they did not coalesce into one republic with one government. Instead, as thirteen separate and equal peoples, they set up a "perpetual union" in which they were joined only through a Congress in which each state had one vote. They gave the Congress responsibility for their common concerns. But they did not give it the ordinary powers of a government to tax or legislate.

Because of the straightforward equality of the member states and because the Con-

[17] Robert J. Taylor, ed., *Massachusetts, Colony to Commonwealth: Documents on the Formation of its Constitution, 1775–1780* (Chapel Hill, 1961), p. 45.

gress did not possess the means by which governments generally ran to tyranny, the confederation seemed a safe shape in which to cast the new nation. Actually danger lurked in the fact that the Congress had insufficient power to carry out the responsibilities which the states assigned to it. After the British troops were defeated and the need for united action became less obvious, state support of the Congress steadily declined. Without coercive powers, the Congress could not act effectively either at home or abroad, and the nation was increasingly exposed to the danger of foreign depredations. At the same time, the state governments were proving vulnerable to manipulation by corrupt or ambitious politicians and were growing powerful at the expense not only of the Congress but of the people. Some undertook irresponsible inflationary measures that threatened property rights. Unless the state governments were brought under more effective control, local demagogues might destroy the union and replace the tyranny of Parliament with a new domestic brand.

Although a few men foresaw the drawbacks of a weak Congress from the beginning, most people needed time to show them. The Massachusetts legislature, perceiving that the experience of the state could be applied to the whole United States, in 1785 suggested a national constitutional convention to create a central authority capable of acting effectively in the interests of the whole American people. But in 1785, Americans were not yet convinced that what they had was inadequate. The Massachusetts delegates to the Congress replied to their state's suggestion with the same arguments that had in the first place prompted Americans to base their union on a weak coordinative Congress rather than a real national government: it would be impossible, they said, to prevent such a government from escaping popular control. With headquarters remote from most of its constituents, with only a select few from each state engaged in it, a national government would offer too many opportunities for corruption.[18] The fear was supported by the views of respected European political thinkers. Montesquieu, who had been widely read in America, maintained that republican government was suited only to small areas. A confederation of republics might extend far, but a single republican government of large extent would either fall a prey to the ambitions of a few corrupt individuals, or else it would break up into a number of smaller states.[19]

These sentiments were so widely held that they prevented any effort to establish a national government until 1787. And when a convention was finally called in that year it was charged, not to create a new government, but simply to revise the Articles of Confederation. The members of the Convention, without authorization, assumed the larger task and turned themselves into a national Constitutional Convention. They did so because they became convinced that, contrary to popular belief, a large republic would not necessarily succumb to corruption. The man who persuaded the Convention, insofar as any one man did it, was James Madison, one of the delegates from Virginia.

In the month before the Convention assembled, Madison had drawn up some observations on the "Vices of the Political System of the United States." Following a hint thrown out by David Hume, he reached the conclusion that "the inconveniences of popular States contrary to the prevailing Theory, are in proportion not to the extent, but to the narrowness of their limits." In the state governments that had oper-

---

[18] Edmund C. Burnett, ed., *Letters of Members of the Continental Congress* (Washington, 1921–36), VIII, 206–210.

[19] Montesquieu, *Spirit of the Laws* (New York, 1949), p. 120 (Book VIII, c. 16).

ated since 1776, the great defect was a tendency of the majority to tyrannize over the minority. Madison took it as axiomatic that "in republican Government the majority however composed, ultimately gave the law." Unless a way could be found to control them, the majority would inevitably oppress the minority, because the individuals who made up the majority were as susceptible as any king or lord to the operation of human depravity. The most effective curb, Madison suggested, was to make the territory of the republic so large that a majority would have difficulty forming. Men being hopelessly selfish would inevitably seek to capture the government for selfish purposes, and in a small republic they might easily form combinations to secure the necessary majority. But in a large republic, "the Society becomes broken into a greater variety of interests, of pursuits of passions, which check each other, whilst those who may feel a common sentiment have less opportunity of communication and concert." [20]

The insight, later given classic expression in the tenth *Federalist* paper, was the most fruitful intellectual achievement of the Revolutionary period, the third of the three principles mentioned earlier. It gave Madison and his colleagues at Philadelphia the courage to attempt a republican government for the whole nation. The constitution which they drew up would provide the American peoples with a government that would effectively make them one people. The government would incorporate all the protections to liberty that they still cherished from their British heritage; it would preserve both imported and home-grown republican traditions; and it would employ the political principles developed during the Revolution. It would be a government inferior to the people and one in which no people should have dominion over another, a government in which almost every detail was prompted by the framers' determination to control the operation of human depravity. Many Americans, doubting that the safeguards would work, opposed the adoption of the Constitution. But the character of American politics from 1789 to the present day has borne out Madison's observation: majorities in the United States have been composed of such a variety of interests that they have seldom proved oppressive, and the national government has been a stronger bulwark of freedom than the state governments.

The establishment of a national republic renewed the challenge which the contest with Great Britain had presented to the best minds of America. In the Constitutional Convention and in the conduct of the new national government, Americans found scope for talents that the Revolution had uncovered. Jefferson, Hamilton, Madison, and John Adams received from national politics the stimulus that made them great. The writings in which they embodied their best thoughts were state papers.

In the course of the nineteenth century the stimulus was somehow lost, in hard cider, log cabins, and civil war. Intellect moved away from politics; and intellectual leadership, having passed from clergy to statesmen, moved on to philosophers, scientists, and novelists. But during the brief period when America's intellectual leaders were her political leaders, they created for their country the most stable popular government ever invented and presented to the world three political principles which men have since used repeatedly and successfully to advance human freedom and responsible government.

[20] James Madison, *Writings,* ed. Gaillard Hunt (New York, 1900–1910), II, 361–369.

4 / Rhetoric and Reality
in the American Revolution

Gordon S. Wood

Describing the dominant theme of many contemporary historians as "the American Revolution considered as an intellectual movement," Gordon Wood considers the limitations and the relationships of "idealist" and "behaviorist" views of history. Wood contrasts the traditional emphasis of historians of the first part of this century upon social and economic influences and motives with the concern of present-day historians with the ideals and ideas of the revolutionary generation. He argues that this latter interest had tended to give a neo-Whiggish cast to recent interpretations, tended, that is, to make many authors accept the idealistic claims of the revolutionaries at close to full-value. Thus, contemporary writers have returned to the view of the Revolution as primarily a struggle over abstract rights, a struggle in which these authors often favored the American claims to freedom. In this context, Wood describes the work of Bernard Bailyn as going well beyond the simplistic idealist interpretation of the Revolution and as providing an insight into the complexities of the interaction of ideas and events. Ideas changed rapidly with actions and "men were involved in a complicated web of phenomena, ideas and situations, from which in retrospect escape seems impossible." In Wood's view, Bailyn may thus provide "a point of departure for a new look of the social sources of the Revolution." The ferment of ideas may be related to a ferment in American society that may be contrasted with the relatively static approach of Englishmen to political ideas and the relatively static forms of English politics. Wood's argument thus leads to the view that the very frenzy of American arguments suggests deep problems within the social order and that these problems went far beyond simply an increasing alienation from British authority. For example, he suggests, that there were deep conflicts within the society of Virignia that developed separately from controversies over British policy. These conflicts were somehow entwined with issues that led Virginia's statesmen to the belief that the answer to their social problems might be found in independence from the mother country. In effect, Wood raises a series of questions about the rela-

Reprinted by permisson of the author from *The William and Mary Quarterly,* 3rd series, XXIII (1966), 3–32.

tionships between what Americans said and what they believed, between their ideals and the social pressures upon them—questions that should be kept in mind by readers of the remaining material in this volume.

For further reading: for a view criticized by Wood, see Edmund Morgan, *The Birth of the Republic* (1956) or the essay by Morgan later in this volume, "Colonial Ideas of Parliamentary Power, 1764–1766"; Bernard Bailyn, *Pamphlets of the American Revolution,* I (1965), particularly "The Introduction"; and for studies of recent historical writings, Jack P. Greene, "Changing Interpretations of Early American Politics," in *The Reinterpretation of Early American History: Essays in Honor of John Edwin Pomfret* (1966), or W. F. Craven, "The Revolutionary Era," in John Higham (ed.), *The Reinterpretation of American History* (1962).

If any catch phrase is to characterize the work being done on the American Revolution by this generation of historians, it will probably be "the American Revolution considered as an intellectual movement." [1] For we now seem to be fully involved in a phase of writing about the Revolution in which the thought of the Revolutionaries, rather than their social and economic interests, has become the major focus of research and analysis. This recent emphasis on ideas is not of course new, and indeed right from the beginning it has characterized almost all our attempts to understand the Revolution. The ideas of a period which Samuel Eliot Morison and Harold Laski once described as, next to the English revolutionary decades of the seventeenth century, the most fruitful era in the history of Western political thought could never be completely ignored in any phase of our history writing. [2]

It has not been simply the inherent importance of the Revolutionary ideas, those "great principles of freedom," [3] that has continually attracted the attention of historians. It has been rather the unusual nature of the Revolution and the constant need to explain what on the face of it seems inexplicable that has compelled almost all interpreters of the Revolution, including the participants themselves, to stress its predominantly intellectual character and hence its uniqueness among Western revolutions. Within the context of Revolutionary historiography the one great effort to disparage the significance of ideas in the Revolution—an effort which dominated our history writing in the first half of the twentieth century—becomes something of an anomaly, a temporary aberration into a deterministic social and economic explanation from which we have been retreating for the past two decades. Since roughly the end of World War II we have witnessed a resumed and increasingly heightened insistence on the primary significance of conscious beliefs, and particularly of constitutional principles, in explaining what once again has become the unique character of the American Revolution. In the hands of idealist-minded historians the thought and

[1] This is the title of a recent essay by Edmund S. Morgan in Arthur M. Schlesinger, Jr., and Morton White, eds., *Paths of American Thought* (Boston, 1963), 11–33.

[2] Samuel E. Morison, ed., "William Manning's *The Key of Libberty,*" *William and Mary Quarterly,* 3rd Ser., XIII (1956), 208.

[3] Edmund S. Morgan, "The American Revolution: Revisions in Need of Revising," *Wm. and Mary Qtly.,* 3d Ser., XIV (1957), 14.

principles of the Americans have consequently come to repossess that explanative force which the previous generation of materialist-minded historians had tried to locate in the social structure.

Indeed, our renewed insistence on the importance of ideas in explaining the Revolution has now attained a level of fullness and sophistication never before achieved, with the consequence that the economic and social approach of the previous generation of behaviorist historians has never seemed more anomalous and irrelevant than it does at present. Yet paradoxically it may be that this preoccupation with the explanatory power of the Revolutionary ideas has become so intensive and so refined, assumed such a character, that the apparently discredited social and economic approach of an earlier generation has at the same time never seemed more attractive and relevant. In other words, we may be approaching a crucial juncture in our writing about the Revolution where idealism and behaviorism meet.

I

It was the Revolutionaries themselves who first described the peculiar character of what they had been involved in. The Revolution, as those who took stock at the end of three decades of revolutionary activity noted, was not "one of those events which strikes the public eye in the subversions of laws which have usually attended the revolutions of governments." Because it did not seem to have been a typical revolution, the sources of its force and its momentum appeared strangely unaccountable. "In other revolutions, the sword has been drawn by the arm of offended freedom, under an oppression that threatened the vital powers of society." [4] But this seemed hardly true of the American Revolution. There was none of the legendary tyranny that had so often driven desperate peoples into revolution. The Americans were not an oppressed people; they had no crushing imperial shackles to throw off. In fact, the Americans knew they were probably freer and less burdened with cumbersome feudal and monarchical restraints than any part of mankind in the eighteenth century. To its victims, the Tories, the Revolution was truly incomprehensible. Never in history, said Daniel Leonard, had there been so much rebellion with so "little real cause." It was, wrote Peter Oliver, "the most wanton and unnatural rebellion that ever existed." [5] The Americans' response was out of all proportion to the stimuli. The objective social reality scarcely seemed capable of explaining a revolution.

Yet no American doubted that there had been a revolution. How then was it to be justified and explained? If the American Revolution, lacking "those mad, tumultuous actions which disgraced many of the great revolutions of antiquity," was not a typical revolution, what kind of revolution was it? If the origin of the American Revolution lay not in the usual passions and interests of men, wherein did it lay? Those Americans who looked back at what they had been through could only marvel at the rationality and moderation, "supported by the energies of well weighed choice,"

---

[4] [William Vans Murray], *Political Sketches, Inscribed to His Excellency John Adams* (London, 1787), 21, 48.

[5] [Daniel Leonard], *The Origin of the American Contest with Great-Britain . . . [by] Massachusettensis . . .* (New York, 1775), 40; Douglass Adair and John A. Schutz, eds., *Peter Oliver's Origin and Progress of the American Rebellion: A Tory View* (San Marino, 1963), 159.

involved in their separation from Britain, a revolution remarkably "without violence or convulsion." [6] It seemed to be peculiarly an affair of the mind. Even two such dissimilar sorts of Whigs as Thomas Paine and John Adams both came to see the Revolution they had done so much to bring about as especially involved with ideas, resulting from "a mental examination," a change in "the minds and hearts of the people." [7] The Americans were fortunate in being born at a time when the principles of government and freedom were better known than at any time in history. The Americans had learned "how to define the rights of nature,—how to search into, to distinguish, and to comprehend, the principles of physical, moral, religious, and civil liberty," how, in short, to discover and resist the forces of tyranny before they could be applied. Never before in history had a people achieved "a revolution by reasoning" alone.[8]

The Americans, "born the heirs of freedom," [9] revolted not to create but to maintain their freedom. American society had developed differently from that of the Old World. From the time of the first settlements in the seventeenth century, wrote Samuel Williams in 1794, "every thing tended to produce, and to establish the spirit of freedom." While the speculative philosophers of Europe were laboriously searching their minds in an effort to decide the first principles of liberty, the Americans had come to experience vividly that liberty in their everyday lives. The American Revolution, said Williams, joined together these enlightened ideas with America's experience. The Revolution was thus essentially intellectual and declaratory: it "explained the business to the world, and served to confirm what nature and society had before produced." "All was the result of reason. . . ." [10] The Revolution had taken place not in a succession of eruptions that had crumbled the existing social structure, but in a succession of new thoughts and new ideas that had vindicated that social structure.

The same logic that drove the participants to view the Revolution as peculiarly intellectual also compelled Moses Coit Tyler, writing at the end of the nineteenth century, to describe the American Revolution as "preeminently a revolution caused by ideas, and pivoted on ideas." That ideas played a part in all revolutions Tyler readily admitted. But in most revolutions, like that of the French, ideas had been perceived and acted upon only when the social reality had caught up with them, only when the ideas had been given meaning and force by long-experienced "real evils." The American Revolution, said Tyler, had been different: it was directed "not against tyranny inflicted, but only against tyranny anticipated." The Americans revolted not

[6] Simeon Baldwin, *An Oration Pronounced Before the Citizens of New-Haven, July 4th, 1788* . . . (New Haven, 1788), 10; [Murray], *Political Sketches,* 48; David Ramsay, *The History of the American Revolution* (Philadelphia, 1789), I, 350.

[7] Thomas Paine, *Letter to the Abbé Raynal* . . . (1782) in Philip S. Foner, ed., *The Complete Writings of Thomas Paine* (New York, 1945), II, 243; John Adams to H. Niles, Feb. 13, 1818, in Charles Francis Adams, ed., *The Works of John Adams* (Boston, 1850–56), X, 282.

[8] William Pierce, *An Oration, Delivered at Christ Church, Savannah, on the 4th of July, 1788* . . . (Providence, [1788]), 6; Enos Hitchcock, *An Oration; Delivered July 4th, 1788* . . . (Providence, [1788]), 11.

[9] Petition to the King, Oct. 1774, in Worthington C. Ford, ed., *Journals of the Continental Congress, 1774–1789* (Washington, 1904–37), I, 118.

[10] Samuel Williams, *The Natural and Civil History of Vermont* . . . (Walpole, New Hamp., 1794), vii, 372–373; Pierce, *Oration* . . . *4th July, 1788,* p. 8.

out of actual suffering but out of reasoned principle. "Hence, more than with most other epochs of revolutionary strife, our epoch of revolutionary strife was a strife of ideas: a long warfare of political logic; a succession of annual campaigns in which the marshalling of arguments not only preceded the marshalling of armies, but often exceeded them in impression upon the final result." [11]

II

It is in this historiographical context developed by the end of the nineteenth century, this constant and at times extravagant emphasis on the idealism of the Revolution, that the true radical quality of the Progressive generation's interpretation of the Revolution becomes so vividly apparent. For the work of these Progressive historians was grounded in a social and economic explanation of the Revolutionary era that explicitly rejected the causal importance of ideas. These historians could scarcely have avoided the general intellectual climate of the first part of the twentieth century which regarded ideas as suspect. By absorbing the diffused thinking of Marx and Freud and the assumptions of behaviorist psychology, men had come to conceive of ideas as ideologies or rationalizations, as masks obscuring the underlying interests and drives that actually determined social behavior. For too long, it seemed, philosophers had reified thought, detaching ideas from the material conditions that produced them and investing them with an independent will that was somehow alone responsible for the determination of events.[12] As Charles Beard pointed out in his introduction to the 1935 edition of *An Economic Interpretation of the Constitution*, previous historians of the Constitution had assumed that ideas were "entities, particularities, or forces, apparently independent of all earthly considerations coming under the head of 'economic.'" It was Beard's aim, as it was the aim of many of his contemporaries, to bring into historical consideration "those realistic features of economic conflict, stress, and strain" which previous interpreters of the Revolution had largely ignored.[13] The product of this aim was a generation or more of historical writing about the Revolutionary period (of which Beard's was but the most famous expression) that sought to explain the Revolution and the formation of the Constitution in terms of socio-economic relationships and interests rather than in terms of ideas.[14] Curiously, the consequence of this reversal of historical approaches was not the

[11] Moses Coit Tyler, *The Literary History of the American Revolution, 1763–1783* (New York, 1897), I, 8–9.

[12] For a bald description of the assumptions with which this generation of historians worked see Graham Wallas, *Human Nature in Politics,* 3d ed. (New York, 1921), 5, 45, 48–49, 83, 94, 96, 118, 122, 156.

[13] Charles A. Beard, *An Economic Interpretation of the Constitution* (New York, 1935), x, viii.

[14] While the Progressive historians were attempting to absorb and use the latest scientific techniques of the day nonbehaviorists in government departments and others with a traditional approach to political theory—men like Andrew C. McLaughlin, Edwin S. Corwin, William S. Carpenter, Charles M. McIlwain, and Benjamin F. Wright—were writing during this same period some of the best work that has ever been done on Revolutionary constitutional and political thought. However, because most of them were not, strictly speaking, historians, they never sought to explain the causes of the Revolution in terms of ideas.

destruction of the old-fashioned conception of the nature of ideas. As Marx had said, he intended only to put Hegel's head in its rightful place; he had no desire to cut it off. Ideas as rationalization, as ideology, remained—still distinct entities set in opposition to interests, now however lacking any deep causal significance, becoming merely a covering superstructure for the underlying and determinative social reality. Ideas therefore could still be the subject of historical investigation, as long as one kept them in their proper place, interesting no doubt in their own right but not tually counting for much in the movement of events.

Even someone as interested in ideas as Carl Becker never seriously considered them to be in any way determinants of what happened. Ideas fascinated Becker, but it was as superstructure that he enjoyed examining them, their consistency, their logic, their clarity, the way men formed and played with them. In his *Declaration of Independence: A Study in the History of Political Ideas* the political theory of the Americans takes on an unreal and even fatuous quality. It was as if ideas were merely refined tools to be used by the colonists in the most adroit manner possible. The entire Declaration of Independence, said Becker, was calculated for effect, designed primarily "to convince a candid world that the colonies had a moral and legal right to separate from Great Britain." The severe indictment of the King did not spring from unfathomable passions but was contrived, conjured up, to justify a rebellion whose sources lay elsewhere. Men to Becker were never the victims of their thought, always the masters of it. Ideas were a kind of legal brief. "Thus step by step, from 1764 to 1776, the colonists modified their theory to suit their needs." [15] The assumptions behind Becker's 1909 behaviorist work on New York politics in the Revolution and his 1922 study of the political ideas in the Declaration of Independence were more alike than they at first might appear.

Bringing to their studies of the Revolution similar assumptions about the nature of ideas, some of Becker's contemporaries went on to expose starkly the implications of those assumptions. When the entire body of Revolutionary thinking was examined, these historians could not avoid being struck by its generally bombastic and overwrought quality. The ideas expressed seemed so inflated, such obvious exaggerations of reality, that they could scarcely be taken seriously. The Tories were all "wretched hirelings, and execrable parricides"; George III, the "tyrant of the earth," a "monster in human form"; the British soldiers, "a mercenary licentious rabble of banditti," intending to "tear the bowels and vitals of their brave but peaceable fellow subjects, and *to wash the ground with a profusion of innocent blood.*" [16] Such extravagant language, it seemed could be nothing but calculated deception, at best an obvious distortion of fact, designed to incite and mold a revolutionary fervor. "The stigmatizing of British policy as 'tyranny,' 'oppression' and 'slavery,' " [17] wrote Arthur M. Schlesinger, the dean of the Progressive historians, "had little or no objective reality,

---

[15] Carl L. Becker, *The Declaration of Independence: A Study in the History of Political Ideas* (New York, 1922), 203, 207, 133.

[16] Quoted in Philip Davidson, *Propaganda and the American Revolution, 1763–1783* (Chapel Hill, 1941), 141, 373, 150.

[17] Arthur M. Schlesinger, *Prelude to Independence: The Newspaper War on Britain, 1764–1776* (New York, 1958), 34. For examples of the scientific work on which the propagandist studies drew, see note one in Sidney I. Pomerantz, "The Patriot Newspaper and the American Revolution," in Richard B. Morris, ed., *The Era of the American Revolution* (New York, 1939), 305.

at least prior to the Intolerable Acts, but ceaseless repetition of the charge kept emotions at fever pitch."

Indeed, so grandiose, so overdrawn, it seemed, were the ideas that the historians were necessarily led to ask not whether such ideas were valid but why men should have expressed them. It was not the content of such ideas but the function that was really interesting. The Revolutionary rhetoric, the profusion of sermons, pamphlets, and articles in the patriotic cause, could best be examined as propaganda, that is, as a concerted and self-conscious effort by agitators to manipulate and shape public opinion. Because of the Progressive historians' view of the Revolution as the movement of class minorities bent on promoting particular social and economic interests, the conception of propaganda was crucial to their explanation of what seemed to be a revolutionary consensus. Through the use of ideas in provoking hatred and influencing opinion and creating at least "an appearance of unity," the influence of a minority of agitators was out of all proportion to their number. The Revolution thus became a display of extraordinary skillfulness in the manipulation of public opinion. In fact, wrote Schlesinger, "no disaffected element in history has ever risen more splendidly to the occasion." [18]

Ideas thus became, as it were, parcels of thought to be distributed and used where they would do the most good. This propaganda was not of course necessarily false, but it was always capable of manipulation. "Whether the suggestions are to be true or false, whether the activities are to be open or concealed," wrote Philip Davidson, "are matters for the propagandist to decide." Apparently ideas could be turned on or off at will, and men controlled their rhetoric in a way they could not control their interests. Whatever the importance of propaganda, its connection with social reality was tenuous. Since ideas were so self-consciously manageable, the Whigs were not actually expressing anything meaningful about themselves but were rather feigning and exaggerating for effect. What the Americans said could not be taken at face value but must be considered as a rhetorical disguise for some hidden interest. The expression of even the classic and well-defined natural rights philosophy became, in Davidson's view, but "the propagandist's rationalization of his desire to protect his vested interests." [19]

With this conception of ideas as weapons shrewdly used by designing propagandists, it was inevitable that the thought of the Revolutionaries should have been denigrated. The Revolutionaries became by implication hypocritical demagogues, "adroitly tailoring their arguments to changing conditions." Their political thinking appeared to possess neither consistency nor significance. "At best," said Schlesinger in an early summary of his interpretation, "an exposition of the political theories of the antiparliamentary party is an account of their retreat from one strategic position to another." So the Whigs moved, it was strongly suggested, easily if not frivolously from a defense of charter rights, to the rights of Englishmen, and finally to the rights of man, as each position was exposed and became untenable. In short, concluded Schlesinger, the Revolution could never be understood if it were regarded "as a great forensic controversy over abstract governmental rights." [20]

[18] Davidson, *Propaganda,* 59; Schlesinger, *Prelude to Independence,* 20.
[19] Davidson, *Propaganda,* xiv, 46.
[20] Schlesinger, *Prelude to Independence,* 44; Arthur M. Schlesinger, *New Viewpoints in American History* (New York, 1923), 179.

III

It is essentially on this point of intellectual consistency that Edmund S. Morgan has fastened for the past decade and a half in an attempt to bring down the entire interpretive framework of the socio-economic argument. If it could be shown that the thinking of the Revolutionaries was not inconsistent after all, that the Whigs did not actually skip from one constitutional notion to the next, then the imputation of Whig frivolity and hypocrisy would lose its force. This was a central intention of Morgan's study of the political thought surrounding the Stamp Act. As Morgan himself has noted and others have repeated, "In the last analysis the significance of the Stamp Act crisis lies in the emergence, not of leaders and methods and organizations, but of well-defined constitutional principles." As early as 1765 the Whigs "laid down the line on which Americans stood until they cut their connections with England. Consistently from 1765 to 1776 they denied the authority of Parliament to tax them externally or internally; consistently they affirmed their willingness to submit to whatever legislation Parliament should enact for the supervision of the empire as a whole." [21] This consistency thus becomes, as one scholar's survey of the current interpretation puts it, "an indication of American devotion to principle." [22]

It seemed clear once again after Morgan's study that the Americans were more sincerely attached to constitutional principles than the behaviorist historians had supposed, and that their ideas could not be viewed as simply manipulated propaganda. Consequently the cogency of the Progressive historians' interpretation was weakened if not unhinged. And as the evidence against viewing the Revolution as rooted in internal class-conflict continued to mount from various directions, it appeared more and more comprehensible to accept the old-fashioned notion that the Revolution was after all the consequence of "a great forensic controversy over abstract governmental rights." There were, it seemed, no deprived and depressed populace yearning for a participation in politics that had long been denied; no coherent merchant class victimizing a mass of insolvent debtors; no seething discontent with the British mercantile system; no privileged aristocracy, protected by law, anxiously and insecurely holding power against a clamoring democracy. There was, in short, no internal class upheaval in the Revolution.[23]

If the Revolution was not to become virtually incomprehensible, it must have been the result of what the American Whigs always contended it was—a dispute between Mother Country and colonies over constitutional liberties. By concentrating on the

[21] Edmund S. Morgan, "Colonial Ideas of Parliamentary Power, 1764–1766," *Wm. and Mary Qtly.*, 3d Ser., V (1948), 311, 341; Edmund S. and Helen M. Morgan, *The Stamp Act Crisis: Prologue to Revolution*, rev. ed. (New York, 1963), 369–370; Page Smith, "David Ramsay and the Causes of the American Revolution," *Wm. and Mary Qtly.*, 3d Ser., XVII (1960), 70–71.

[22] Jack P. Greene, "The Flight From Determinism: A Review of Recent Literature on the Coming of the American Revolution," *South Atlantic Quarterly*, LXI (1962), 257.

[23] This revisionist literature of the 1950's is well known. See the listings in Bernard Bailyn, "Political Experience and Enlightenment Ideas in Eighteenth-Century America," *American Historical Review*, LXVII (1961–62), 341n; and in Greene, "Flight From Determinism," 235–259.

immediate events of the decade leading up to independence, the historians of the 1950's have necessarily fled from the economic and social determinism of the Progressive historians. And by emphasizing the consistency and devotion with which Americans held their constitutional beliefs they have once again focused on what seems to be the extraordinary intellectuality of the American Revolution and hence its uniqueness among Western revolutions. This interpretation, which, as Jack P. Greene notes, "may appropriately be styled neo-whig," has turned the Revolution into a rationally conservative movement, involving mainly a constitutional defense of existing political liberties against the abrupt and unexpected provocations of the British government after 1760. "The issue then, according to the neo-whigs, was no more and no less than separation from Britain and the preservation of American liberty." The Revolution has therefore become "more political, legalistic, and constitutional than social or economic." Indeed, some of the neo-Whig historians have implied not just that social and economic conditions were less important in bringing on the Revolution as we once thought, but rather that the social situation in the colonies had little or nothing to do with causing the Revolution. The Whig statements of principle iterated in numerous declarations appear to be the only causal residue after all the supposedly deeper social and economic causes have been washed away. As one scholar who has recently investigated and carefully dismissed the potential social and economic issues in pre-Revolutionary Virginia has concluded, "What remains as the fundamental issue in the coming of the Revolution, then, is nothing more than the contest over constitutional rights." [24]

In a different way Bernard Bailyn in a recent article has clarified and reinforced this revived idealistic interpretation of the Revolution. The accumulative influence of much of the latest historical writing on the character of eighteenth-century American society has led Bailyn to the same insight expressed by Samuel Williams in 1794. What made the Revolution truly revolutionary was not the wholesale disruption of social groups and political institutions, for compared to other revolutions such disruption was slight; rather it was the fundamental alteration in the Americans' structure of values, the way they looked at themselves and their institutions. Bailyn has seized on this basic intellectual shift as a means of explaining the apparent contradiction between the seriousness with which the Americans took their Revolutionary ideas and the absence of radical social and institutional change. The Revolution, argues Bailyn, was not so much the transformation as the realization of American society.

The Americans had been gradually and unwittingly preparing themselves for such a mental revolution since they first came to the New World in the seventeenth century. The substantive changes in American society had taken place in the course of the previous century, slowly, often imperceptibly, as a series of small piecemeal deviations from what was regarded by most Englishmen as the accepted orthodoxy in society, state, and religion. What the Revolution marked, so to speak, was the point when the Americans suddenly blinked and saw their society, its changes, its differences, in a new perspective. Their deviation from European standards, their lack of an established church and a titled aristocracy, their apparent rusticity and general

[24] Greene, "Flight From Determinism," 237, 257; Thad W. Tate, "The Coming of the Revolution in Virginia: Britain's Challenge to Virginia's Ruling Class, 1763–1776," *Wm. and Mary Qtly.*, 3d Ser., XIX (1962), 323–343, esp. 340.

equality, now became desirable, even necessary, elements in the maintenance of their society and politics. The comprehending and justifying, the endowing with high moral purpose, of these confusing and disturbing social and political divergences, Bailyn concludes, was the American Revolution.[25]

Bailyn's more recent investigation of the rich pamphlet literature of the decades before Independence has filled out and refined his idealist interpretation, confirming him in his "rather old-fashioned view that the American Revolution was above all else an ideological-constitutional struggle and not primarily a controversy between social groups undertaken to force changes in the organization of society." While Bailyn's book-length introduction to the first of a multivolumed edition of Revolutionary pamphlets makes no effort to stress the conservative character of the Revolution and indeed emphasizes (in contrast to the earlier article) its radicalism and the dynamic and transforming rather than the rationalizing and declarative quality of Whig thought, it nevertheless represents the culmination of the idealist approach to the history of the Revolution. For "above all else," argues Bailyn, it was the Americans' world-view, the peculiar bundle of notions and beliefs they put together during the imperial debate, "that in the end propelled them into Revolution." Through his study of the Whig pamphlets Bailyn became convinced "that the fear of a comprehensive conspiracy against liberty throughout the English-speaking world—a conspiracy believed to have been nourished in corruption, and of which, it was felt, oppression in America was only the most immediately visible part—lay at the heart of the Revolutionary movement." No one of the various acts and measures of the British government after 1763 could by itself have provoked the extreme and violent response of the American Whigs. But when linked together they formed in the minds of the Americans, imbued with a particular historical understanding of what constituted tyranny, an extensive and frightening program designed to enslave the New World. The Revolution becomes comprehensible only when the mental framework, the Whig world-view into which the Americans fitted the events of the 1760's and 1770's, is known. "It is the development of this view to the point of overwhelming persuasiveness to the majority of American leaders and the meaning this view gave to the events of the time, and not simply an accumulation of grievances," writes Bailyn, "that explains the origins of the American Revolution." [26]

It now seems evident from Bailyn's analysis that it was the Americans' peculiar conception of reality more than anything else that convinced them that tyranny was afoot and that they must fight if their liberty was to survive. By an empathic understanding of a wide range of American thinking Bailyn has been able to offer us a most persuasive argument for the importance of ideas in bringing on the Revolution. Not since Tyler has the intellectual character of the Revolution received such emphasis and never before has it been set out so cogently and completely. It would seem that the idealist explanation of the Revolution has nowhere else to go.[27]

[25] Bailyn, "Political Experience and Enlightenment Ideas," 339–351.
[26] Bernard Bailyn, ed., assisted by Jane N. Garrett, *Pamphlets of the American Revolution, 1750–1776* (Cambridge, Mass., 1965–), I, viii, 60, x, 20. The 200-page general introduction is entitled, "The Transforming Radicalism of the American Revolution."
[27] This is not to say, however, that work on the Revolutionary ideas is in any way finished. For examples of the re-examination of traditional problems in Revolutionary political theory see Richard Buel, Jr., "Democracy and the American Revolution: A Frame of Reference," *Wm. and Mary Qtly.*, 3d Ser., XXI (1964), 165–190; and Bailyn's resolution of James Otis's apparent inconsistency in *Revolutionary Pamphlets*, I, 100–103, 106–107, 121–123, 409–417, 546–552.

IV

Labeling the recent historical interpretations of the Revolution as "neo-whig" is indeed appropriate, for, as Page Smith has pointed out, "After a century and a half of progress in historical scholarship, in research techniques, in tools and methods, we have found our way to the interpretation held, substantially, by those historians who themselves participated in or lived through the era of, the Revolution." By describing the Revolution as a conservative, principled defense of American freedom against the provocations of the English government, the neo-Whig historians have come full circle to the position of the Revolutionaries themselves and to the interpretation of the first generation of historians.[28] Indeed, as a consequence of this historical atavism, praise for the contemporary or early historians has become increasingly common.

But to say "that the Whig interpretation of the American Revolution may not be as dead as some historians would have us believe" is perhaps less to commend the work of David Ramsay and George Bancroft than to indict the approach of recent historians.[29] However necessary and rewarding the neo-Whig histories have been, they present us with only a partial perspective on the Revolution. The neo-Whig interpretation is intrinsically polemical; however subtly presented, it aims to justify the Revolution. It therefore cannot accommodate a totally different, an opposing, perspective, a Tory view of the Revolution. It is for this reason that the recent publication of Peter Oliver's "Origin and Progress of the American Rebellion" is of major significance, for it offers us—"by attacking the hallowed traditions of the revolution, challenging the motives of the founding fathers, and depicting revolution as passion, plotting, and violence"—an explanation of what happened quite different from what we have been recently accustomed to.[30] Oliver's vivid portrait of the Revolutionaries with his accent on their vicious emotions and interests seriously disturbs the present Whiggish interpretation of the Revolution. It is not that Oliver's description of, say, John Adams as madly ambitious and consumingly resentful is any more correct than Adams's own description of himself as a virtuous and patriotic defender of liberty against tyranny. Both interpretations of Adams are in a sense right, but neither can comprehend the other because each is preoccupied with seemingly contradictory sets of motives. Indeed, it is really these two interpretations that have divided historians of the Revolution ever since.

Any intellectually satisfying explanation of the Revolution must encompass the Tory perspective as well as the Whig, for if we are compelled to take sides and choose between opposing motives—unconscious or avowed, passion or principle, greed or liberty—we will be endlessly caught up in the polemics of the participants themselves. We must, in other words, eventually dissolve the distinction between conscious and unconscious motives, between the Revolutionaries' stated intentions and their

---

[28] Smith, "Ramsay and the American Revolution," 72.

[29] Morgan, "Revisions in Need of Revising," 13.

[30] Adair and Schutz, eds., *Peter Oliver's Origin,* ix. In the present neo-Whig context, Sidney S. Fisher, "The Legendary and Myth-Making Process in Histories of the American Revolution," in American Philosophical Society, *Proceedings* LI (Philadelphia, 1912), 53–75, takes on a renewed relevance.

supposedly hidden needs and desires, a dissolution that involves somehow relating beliefs and ideas to the social world in which they operate. If we are to understand the causes of the Revolution we must therefore ultimately transcend this problem of motivation. But this we can never do as long as we attempt to explain the Revolution mainly in terms of the intentions of the participants. It is not that men's motives are unimportant; they indeed make events, including revolutions. But the purposes of men, especially in a revolution, are so numerous, so varied, and so contradictory that their complex interaction produces results that no one intended or could even foresee. It is this interaction and these results that recent historians are referring to when they speak so disparagingly of those "underlying determinants" and "impersonal and inexorable forces" bringing on the Revolution. Historical explanation which does not account for these "forces," which, in other words, relies simply on understanding the conscious intentions of the actors, will thus be limited. This preoccupation with men's purposes was what restricted the perspectives of the contemporaneous Whig and Tory interpretations; and it is still the weakness of the neo-Whig histories, and indeed of any interpretation which attempts to explain the events of the Revolution by discovering the calculations from which individuals supposed themselves to have acted.

No explanation of the American Revolution in terms of the intentions and designs of particular individuals could have been more crudely put than that offered by the Revolutionaries themselves. American Whigs, like men of the eighteenth century generally, were fascinated with what seemed to the age to be the newly appreciated problem of human motivation and causation in the affairs of the world. In the decade before independence the Americans sought endlessly to discover the supposed calculations and purposes of individuals or groups that lay behind the otherwise incomprehensible rush of events. More than anything else perhaps, it was this obsession with motives that led to the prevalence in the eighteenth century of beliefs in conspiracies to account for the confusing happenings in which men found themselves caught up. Bailyn has suggested that this common fear of conspiracy was "deeply rooted in the political awareness of eighteenth-century Britons, involved in the very structure of their political life"; it "reflected so clearly the realities of life in an age in which monarchical autocracy flourished, [and] in which the stability and freedom of England's 'mixed' constitution was a recent and remarkable achievement." [31] Yet it might also be argued that the tendency to see conspiracy behind what happened reflected as well the very enlightenment of the age. To attribute events to the designs and purposes of human agents seemed after all to be an enlightened advance over older beliefs in blind chance, providence, or God's interventions. It was rational and scientific, a product of both the popularization of politics and the secularization of knowledge. It was obvious to Americans that the series of events in the years after 1763, those "unheard of intolerable calamities, spring not of the dust, come not causeless." "Ought not the PEOPLE therefore," asked John Dickinson, "to watch? to observe facts? to search into causes? to investigate designs?" [32] And these causes and

---

[31] Bailyn, *Revolutionary Pamphlets*, I, 87, ix.

[32] [Moses Mather], *America's Appeal to the Impartial World* . . . (Hartford, 1775), 59; [John Dickinson], *Letters from a Farmer in Pennsylvania to the Inhabitants of the British Colonies* (1768), in Paul L. Ford, ed., *The Life and Writings of John Dickinson* (Historical Society of Pennsylvania, *Memoirs*, XIV [Philadelphia, 1895]), II, 348. Dickinson hinged his entire argument on the ability of the Americans to decipher the "intention" of parliamentary legislation, whether for revenue or for commercial regulation. *Ibid.,* 348, 364.

designs could be traced to individuals in high places, to ministers, to royal governors, and their lackeys. The belief in conspiracy grew naturally out of the enlightened need to find the human purposes behind the multitude of phenomena, to find the causes for what happened in the social world just as the natural scientist was discovering the causes for what happened in the physical world.[33] It was a necessary consequence of the search for connections and patterns in events. The various acts of the British government, the Americans knew, should not be "regarded according to the simple force of each, but as parts of a system of oppression." [34] The Whigs' intense search for the human purposes behind events was in fact an example of the beginnings of modern history.

In attempting to rebut those interpretations disparaging the colonists' cause, the present neo-Whig historians have been drawn into writing as partisans of the Revolutionaries. And they have thus found themselves entangled in the same kind of explanation used by the original antagonists, an explanation, despite obvious refinements, still involved with the discovery of motives and its corollary, the assessing of a personal sort of responsibility for what happened. While most of the neo-Whig historians have not gone so far as to see conspiracy in British actions (although some have come close),[35] they have tended to point up the blundering and stupidity of British officials in contrast to "the breadth of vision" that moved the Americans. If George III was in a position of central responsibility in the British government, as English historians have recently said, then, according to Edmund S. Morgan, "he must bear most of the praise or blame for the series of measures that alienated and lost the colonies, and it is hard to see how there can be much praise." By seeking "to define issues, fix responsibilities," and thereby to shift the "burden of proof" onto those who say the Americans were narrow and selfish and the empire was basically just and beneficent, the neo-Whigs have attempted to redress what they felt was an unfair neo-Tory bias of previous explanations of the Revolution;[36] they have not, however, challenged the terms of the argument. They are still obsessed with why men said they acted and with who was right and who was wrong. Viewing the history of the Revolution in this judicatory manner has therefore restricted the issues over which

[33] See Herbert Davis, "The Augustan Conception of History," in J. A. Mazzeo, ed., *Reason and the Imagination: Studies in the History of Ideas, 1600–1800* (New York, 1962), 226–228; W. H. Greenleaf, *Order, Empiricism and Politics: Two Traditions of English Political Thought, 1500–1700* (New York, 1964), 166; R. N. Stromberg, "History in the Eighteenth Century," *Journal of the History of Ideas,* XII (1951), 300. It was against this "dominant characteristic of the historical thought of the age," this "tendency to explain events in terms of conscious action by individuals," that the brilliant group of Scottish social scientists writing at the end of the 18th century directed much of their work. Duncan Forbes, " 'Scientific' Whiggism: Adam Smith and John Millar," *Cambridge Journal,* VII (1954), 651, 653–654. While we have had recently several good studies of historical thinking in 17th-century England, virtually nothing has been done on the 18th century. See, however, J. G. A. Pocock, "Burke and the Ancient Constitution—A Problem in the History of Ideas," *The Historical Journal,* III (1960), 125–143; and Stow Persons, "The Cyclical Theory of History in Eighteenth Century America," *American Quarterly,* VI (1954), 147–163.

[34] [Dickinson], *Letters from a Farmer,* in Ford, ed., *Writings of Dickinson,* 388.

[35] Bailyn has noted that Oliver M. Dickerson, in chap. 7 of his *The Navigation Acts and the American Revolution* (Philadelphia, 1951), "adopts wholesale the contemporary Whig interpretation of the Revolution as the result of a conspiracy of 'King's Friends.' " Bailyn, *Revolutionary Pamphlets,* I, 724.

[36] Morgan, "Revisions in Need of Revising," 7, 13, 8; Greene, "Flight From Determinism," 237.

historians have disagreed to those of motivation and responsibility, the very issues with which the participants themselves were concerned.

The neo-Whig "conviction that the colonists' attachment to principle was genuine" [37] has undoubtedly been refreshing, and indeed necessary, given the Tory slant of earlier twentieth-century interpretations. It now seems clearer that the Progressive historians, with their naive and crude reflex conception of human behavior, had too long treated the ideas of the Revolution superficially if not superciliously. Psychologists and sociologists are now willing to grant a more determining role to beliefs, particularly in revolutionary situations. It is now accepted that men act not simply in response to some kind of objective reality but to the meaning they give to that reality. Since men's beliefs are as much a part of the given stimuli as the objective environment, the beliefs must be understood and taken seriously if men's behavior is to be fully explained. The American Revolutionary ideas were more than cooked up pieces of thought served by an aggressive and interested minority to a gullible and unsuspecting populace. The concept of propaganda permitted the Progressive historians to account for the presence of ideas but it prevented them from recognizing ideas as an impotrant determinant of the Americans' behavior. The weight attributed to ideas and constitutional principles by the neo-Whig historians was thus an essential corrective to the propagandist studies.

Yet in its laudable effort to resurrect the importance of ideas in historical explanation much of the writing of the neo-Whigs has tended to return to the simple nineteenth-century intellectualist assumption that history is the consequence of a rational calculation of ends and means, that what happened was what was consciously desired and planned. By supposing "that individual actions and immediate issues are more important than underlying determinants in explaining particular events," by emphasizing conscious and articulated motives, the neo-Whig historians have selected and presented that evidence which is most directly and clearly expressive of the intentions of the Whigs, that is, the most well-defined, the most constitutional, the most reasonable of the Whig beliefs, those found in their public documents, their several declarations of grievances and causes. It is not surprising that for the neo-Whigs the history of the American Revolution should be more than anything else "the history of the Americans' search for principles." [38] Not only, then, did nothing in the Americans' economic and social structure really determine their behavior, but the colonists in fact acted from the most rational and calculated of motives: they fought, as they said they would, simply to defend their ancient liberties against British provocation.

By implying that certain declared rational purposes are by themselves an adequate explanation for the Americans' revolt, in other words that the Revolution was really nothing more than a contest over constitutional principles, the neo-Whig historians have not only threatened to deny what we have learned of human psychology in the twentieth century, but they have also in fact failed to exploit fully the terms of their own idealist approach by not taking into account all of what the Americans believed and said. Whatever the deficiencies and misunderstandings of the role of ideas in human behavior present in the propagandist studies of the 1930's, these studies did for the first time attempt to deal with the entirety and complexity of American Revolutionary thought—to explain not only all the well-reasoned notions of law and lib-

[37] Edmund S. Morgan, *The Birth of the Republic, 1763–89* (Chicago, 1956), 51.
[38] Greene, "Flight From Determinism," 258; Morgan, *Birth of the Republic,* 3.

erty that were so familiar but, more important, all the irrational and hysterical beliefs that had been so long neglected. Indeed, it was the patent absurdity and im-
plausibility of much of what the Americans said that lent credence and persuasiveness
to their mistrustful approach to the ideas. Once this exaggerated and fanatical rhetoric
was uncovered by the Progressive historians, it should not have subsequently been
ignored—no matter how much it may have impugned the reasonableness of the
American response. No widely expressed ideas can be dismissed out of hand by the
historian.

In his recent analysis of Revolutionary thinking Bernard Bailyn has avoided the
neo-Whig tendency to distort the historical reconstruction of the American mind. By
comprehending "the assumptions, beliefs, and ideas that lay behind the manifest
events of the time," Bailyn has attempted to get inside the Whigs' mind, and to experience vicariously all of what they thought and felt, both their rational constitutional beliefs and their hysterical and emotional ideas as well. The inflammatory
phrases, "slavery," "corruption," "conspiracy," that most historians had either ignored
or readily dismissed as propaganda, took on a new significance for Bailyn. He came
"to suspect that they meant something very real to both the writers and their readers:
that there were real fears, real anxieties, a sense of real danger behind these phrases,
and not merely the desire to influence by rhetoric and propaganda the inert minds of an
otherwise passive populace." [39] No part of American thinking, Bailyn suggests—not
the widespread belief in a ministerial conspiracy, not the hostile and vicious indictments of individuals, not the fear of corruption and the hope for regeneration, not
any of the violent seemingly absurd distortions and falsifications of what we now
believe to be true, in short, none of the frenzied rhetoric—can be safely ignored by
the historian seeking to understand the causes of the Revolution.

Bailyn's study, however, represents something other than a more complete and uncorrupted version of the common idealist interpretations of the Revolution. By viewing from the "interior" the Revolutionary pamphlets, which were "to an unusual degree, *explanatory*," revealing "not merely positions taken but the reasons why positions were taken," Bailyn like any idealist historian has sought to discover the motives the participants themselves gave for their actions, to re-enact their thinking at
crucial moments, and thereby to recapture some of the "unpredictable reality" of the
Revolution.[40] But for Bailyn the very unpredictability of the reality he has disclosed
has undermined the idealist obsession with explaining why, in the participants' own
estimation, they acted as they did. Ideas emerge as more than explanatory devices,
as more than indicators of motives. They become as well objects for analysis in and
for themselves, historical events in their own right to be treated as other historical
events are treated. Although Bailyn has examined the Revolutionary ideas subjec-
tively from the inside, he has also analyzed them objectively from the outside. Thus,
in addition to a contemporary Whig perspective, he presents us with a retrospective
view of the ideas—their complexity, their development, and their consequences—that
the actual participants did not have. In effect his essay represents what has been
called "a Namierism of the history of ideas," [41] a structural analysis of thought that
suggests a conclusion about the movement of history not very different from Sir Lewis

[39] Bailyn, *Revolutionary Pamphlets*, I, vii, ix.
[40] *Ibid.*, vii, viii, 17.
[41] J. G. A. Pocock, "Machiavelli, Harrington, and English Political Ideologies in the Eighteenth
Century," *Wm. and Mary Qtly.*, 3d Ser., XXII (1965), 550.

Namier's, where history becomes something "started in ridiculous beginnings, while small men did things both infinitely smaller and infinitely greater than they knew." [42]

In his *England in the Age of the American Revolution* Namier attacked the Whig tendency to overrate "the importance of the conscious will and purpose in individuals." Above all he urged us "to ascertain and recognize the deeper irrelevancies and incoherence of human actions, which are not so much directed by reason, as invested by it *ex post facto* with the appearances of logic and rationality," to discover the unpredictable reality, where men's motives and intentions were lost in the accumulation and momentum of interacting events. The whole force of Namier's approach tended to squeeze the intellectual content out of what men did. Ideas setting forth principles and purposes for action, said Namier, did not count for much in the movement of history. [43]

In his study of the Revolutionary ideas Bailyn has come to an opposite conclusion: ideas counted for a great deal, not only being responsible for the Revolution but also for transforming the character of American society. Yet in his hands ideas lose that static quality they have commonly had for the Whig historians, the simple statements of intention that so exasperated Namier. For Bailyn the ideas of the Revolutionaries take on an elusive and unmanageable quality, a dynamic self-intensifying character that transcended the intentions and desires of any of the historical participants. By emphasizing how the thought of the colonists was "strangely reshaped, turned in unfamiliar directions," by describing how the Americans "indeliberately, half-knowingly" groped toward "conclusions they could not themselves clearly perceive," by demonstrating how new beliefs and hence new actions were the responses not to desire but to the logic of developing situations, Bailyn has wrested the explanation of the Revolution out of the realm of motivation in which the neo-Whig historians had confined it.

With this kind of approach to ideas, the degree of consistency and devotion to principles become less important, and indeed the major issues of motivation and responsibility over which historians have disagreed become largely irrelevant. Action becomes not the product of rational and conscious calculation but of dimly perceived and rapidly changing thoughts and situations, "where the familiar meaning of ideas and words faded away into confusion, and leaders felt themselves peering into a haze, seeking to bring shifting conceptions somehow into focus." Men become more the victims than the manipulators of their ideas, as their thought unfolds in ways few anticipated, "rapid, irreversible, and irresistible," creating new problems, new considerations, new ideas, which have their own unforeseen implications. In this kind of atmosphere the Revolution, not at first desired by the Americans, takes on something of an inevitable character, moving through a process of escalation into levels few had intended or perceived. It no longer makes sense to assign motives or responsibility to particular individuals for the totality of what happened. Men were involved in a complicated web of phenomena, ideas, and situations, from which in retrospect escape seems impossible. [44]

[42] Sir Lewis Namier, *England in the Age of the American Revolution,* 2d ed. (London, 1961), 131.

[43] *Ibid.,* 129.

[44] Bailyn, *Revolutionary Pamphlets,* I, 90, x, 169, 140. See Hannah Arendt, *On Revolution* (New York, 1963), 173: "American experience had taught the men of the Revolution that action, though it may be started in isolation and decided upon by single individuals for very different

By seeking to uncover the motives of the Americans expressed in the Revolutionary pamphlets, Bailyn has ended by demonstrating the autonomy of ideas as phenomena, where the ideas operate, as it were, over the heads of the participants, taking them in directions no one could have foreseen. His discussion of Revolutionary thought thus represents a move back to a deterministic approach to the Revolution, a determinism, however, which is different from that which the neo-Whig historians have so recently and self-consciously abandoned. Yet while the suggested determinism is thoroughly idealist—indeed never before has the force of ideas in bringing on the Revolution been so emphatically put—its implications are not. By helping to purge our writing about the Revolution of its concentration on constitutional principles and its stifling judicial-like preoccupation with motivation and responsibility, the study serves to open the way for new questions and new appraisals. In fact, it is out of the very completeness of his idealist interpretation, out of his exposition of the extraordinary nature—the very dynamism and emotionalism—of the Americans' thought that we have the evidence for an entirely different, a behaviorist, perspective on the causes of the American Revolution. Bailyn's book-length introduction to his edition of Revolutionary pamphlets is therefore not only a point of fulfillment for the idealist approach to the Revolution, it is also a point of departure for a new look at the social sources of the Revolution.

V

It seems clear that historians of eighteenth-century America and the Revolution cannot ignore the force of ideas in history to the extent that Namier and his students have done in their investigations of eighteenth-century English politics. This is not to say, however, that the Namier approach to English politics has been crucially limiting and distorting. Rather it may suggest that the Namier denigration of ideas and principles is inapplicable for American politics because the American social situation in which ideas operated was very different from that of eighteenth-century England. It may be that ideas are less meaningful to a people in a socially stable situation. Only when ideas have become stereotyped reflexes do evasion and hypocrisy and the Namier mistrust of what men believe become significant. Only in a relatively settled society does ideology become a kind of habit, a bundle of widely shared and instinctive conventions, offering ready-made explanations for men who are not being compelled to ask any serious questions. Conversely, it is perhaps only in a relatively unsettled, disordered society, where the questions come faster than men's answers, that ideas become truly vital and creative.[45]

Paradoxically it may be the very vitality of the Americans' ideas, then, that suggests the need to examine the circumstances in which they flourished. Since ideas and beliefs are ways of perceiving and explaining the world, the nature of the ideas expressed is determined as much by the character of the world being confronted as

motives, can be accomplished only by some joint effort in which the motivation of single individuals . . . no longer counts. . . ."

[45] See Sir Lewis Namier, *The Structure of Politics at the Accession of George III*, 2d ed. (London, 1961), 16; Sir Lewis Namier, "Human Nature in Politics," in *Personalities and Power: Selected Essays* (New York, 1965), 5–6.

by the internal development of inherited and borrowed conceptions. Out of the multitude of inherited and transmitted ideas available in the eighteenth century, Americans selected and emphasized those which seemed to make meaningful what was happening to them. In the colonists' use of classical literature, for example, "their detailed knowledge and engaged interest covered only one era and one small group of writers," Plutarch, Livy, Cicero, Sallust, and Tacitus—those who "had hated and feared the trends of their own time, and in their writing had contrasted the present with a better past, which they endowed with qualities absent from their own, corrupt era." [46] There was always, in Max Weber's term, some sort of elective affinity between the Americans' interests and their beliefs, and without that affinity their ideas would not have possessed the peculiar character and persuasiveness they did. Only the most revolutionary social needs and circumstances could have sustained such revolutionary ideas.[47]

When the ideas of the Americans are examined comprehensively, when all of the Whig rhetoric, irrational as well as rational, is taken into account, one cannot but be struck by the predominant characteristics of fear and frenzy, the exaggerations and the enthusiasm, the general sense of social corruption and disorder out of which would be born a new world of benevolence and harmony where Americans would become the "eminent examples of every divine and social virtue." [48] As Bailyn and the propaganda studies have amply shown, there is simply too much fanatical and millennial thinking even by the best minds that must be explained before we can characterize the Americans' ideas as peculiarly rational and legalistic and thus view the Revolution as merely a conservative defense of constitutional liberties. To isolate refined and nicely-reasoned arguments from the writings of John Adams and Jefferson is not only to disregard the more inflamed expressions of the rest of the Whigs but also to overlook the enthusiastic extravagance—the paranoiac obsession with a diabolical Crown conspiracy and the dream of a restored Saxon era—in the thinking of Adams and Jefferson themselves.

The ideas of the Americans seem, in fact, to form what can only be called a revolutionary syndrome. If we were to confine ourselves to examining the Revolutionary rhetoric alone, apart from what happened politically or socially, it would be virtually impossible to distinguish the American Revolution from any other revolution in modern Western history. In the kinds of ideas expressed the American Revolution is remarkably similar to the seventeenth-century Puritan Revolution and to the eighteenth-century French Revolution: the same general disgust with a chaotic and corrupt world, the same anxious and angry bombast, the same excited fears of conspiracies by depraved men, the same utopian hopes for the construction of a new and virtuous order.[49] It was not that this syndrome of ideas was simply transmitted from

[46] Bailyn, *Revolutionary Pamphlets*, I, 22. The French Revolutionaries were using the same group of classical writings to express their estrangement from the *ancien régime* and their hope for the new order. Harold T. Parker, *The Cult of Antiquity and the French Revolutionaries: A Study in the Development of the Revolutionary Spirit* (Chicago, 1937), 22–23.

[47] The relation of ideas to social structure is one of the most perplexing and intriguing in the social sciences. For an extensive bibliography on the subject see Norman Birnbaum, "The Sociological Study of Ideology" (1940–60), *Current Sociology*, IX (1960).

[48] Jacob Duché, *The American Vine, A Sermon, Preached . . . Before the Honourable Continental Congress, July 20th, 1775 . . .* (Philadelphia, 1775), 29.

[49] For recent discussions of French and Puritan revolutionary rhetoric see Peter Gay, "Rhetoric and Politics in the French Revolution," *Amer. Hist. Rev.*, LXVI (1960–61), 664–676; Michael

one generation or from one people to another. It was rather perhaps that similar, though hardly identical, social situations called forth within the limitations of inherited and available conceptions similar modes of expression. Although we need to know much more about the sociology of revolutions and collective movements, it does seem possible that particular patterns of thought, particular forms of expression, correspond to certain basic social experiences. There may be, in other words, typical modes of expression, typical kinds of beliefs and values, characterizing a revolutionary situation, at least within roughly similar Western societies. Indeed, the types of ideas manifested may be the best way of identifying a collective movement as a revolution. As one student of revolutions writes, "It is on the basis of a knowledge of men's beliefs that we can distinguish their behaviour from riot, rebellion or insanity." [50]

It is thus the very nature of the Americans' rhetoric—its obsession with corruption and disorder, its hostile and conspiratorial outlook, and its millennial vision of a regenerated society—that reveals as nothing else apparently can the American Revolution as a true revolution with its sources lying deep in the social structure. For this kind of frenzied rhetoric could spring only from the most severe sorts of social strain. The grandiose and feverish language of the Americans was indeed the natural, even the inevitable, expression of a people caught up in a revolutionary situation, deeply alienated from the existing sources of authority and vehemently involved in a basic reconstruction of their political and social order. The hysteria of the Americans' thinking was but a measure of the intensity of their revolutionary passions. Undoubtedly the growing American alienation from British authority contributed greatly to this revolutionary situation. Yet the very weakness of the British imperial system and the accumulating ferocity of American antagonism to it suggests that other sources of social strain were being fed into the revolutionary movement. It may be that the Progressive historians in their preoccupation with internal social problems were more right than we have recently been willing to grant. It would be repeating their mistake, however, to expect this internal social strain necessarily to take the form of coherent class conflict or overt social disruption. The sources of revolutionary social stress may have been much more subtle but no less severe.

Of all of the colonies in the mid-eighteenth century, Virginia seems the most settled, the most lacking in obvious social tensions. Therefore, as it has been recently argued, since conspicuous social issues were nonexistent, the only plausible remaining explanation for the Virginians' energetic and almost unanimous commitment to the Revolution must have been their devotion to constitutional principles.[51] Yet it may be that we have been looking for the wrong kind of social issues, for organized conflicts, for conscious divisions, within the society. It seems clear that Virginia's difficulties were not the consequence of any obvious sectional or class antagonism, Tidewater versus Piedmont, aristocratic planters versus yeomen farmers. There was ap-

---

Walzer, "Puritanism as a Revolutionary Ideology," *History and Theory,* III (1963), 59–90. This entire issue of *History and Theory* is devoted to a symposium on the uses of theory in the study of history. In addition to the Walzer article, I have found the papers by Samuel H. Beer, "Causal Explanation and Imaginative Re-enactment," and Charles Tilly, "The Analysis of a Counter-Revolution," very stimulating and helpful.

[50] Bryan A. Wilson, "Millennialism in Comparative Perspective," *Comparative Studies in Society and History,* VI (1963–64), 108. See also Neil J. Smelser, *Theory of Collective Behaviour* (London, 1962), 83, 120, 383.

[51] Tate, "Coming of the Revolution in Virginia," 324–343.

parently no discontent with the political system that went deep into the social structure. But there does seem to have been something of a social crisis within the ruling group itself, which intensely aggravated the Virginians' antagonism to the imperial system. Contrary to the impression of confidence and stability that the Virginia planters have historically acquired, they seemed to have been in very uneasy circumstances in the years before the Revolution. The signs of the eventual nineteenth-century decline of the Virginia gentry were, in other words, already felt if not readily apparent.

The planters' ability to command the acquiescence of the people seems extraordinary compared to the unstable politics of the other colonies. But in the years before independence there were signs of increasing anxiety among the gentry over their representative role. The ambiguities in the relationship between the Burgesses and their constituents erupted into open debate in the 1750's. And men began voicing more and more concern over the mounting costs of elections and growing corruption in the soliciting of votes, especially by "those who have neither natural nor acquired parts to recommend them." [52] By the late sixties and early seventies the newspapers were filled with warnings against electoral influence, bribery, and vote seeking. The freeholders were stridently urged to "strike at the Root of this growing Evil; be influenced by Merit alone," and avoid electing "obscure and inferior persons." [53] It was as if ignoble ambition and demagoguery, one bitter pamphlet remarked, were a "Daemon lately come among us to disturb the peace and harmony, which had so long subsisted in this place." [54] In this context Robert Munford's famous play, *The Candidates*, written in 1770, does not so much confirm the planters' confidence as it betrays their uneasiness with electoral developments in the colony, "when coxcombs and jockies can impose themselves upon it for men of learning." Although disinterested virtue eventually wins out, Munford's satire reveals the kinds of threats the established planters faced from ambitious knaves and blockheads who were turning representatives into slaves of the people.[55]

By the eve of the Revolution the planters were voicing a growing sense of impending ruin, whose sources seemed in the minds of many to be linked more and

[52] Robert E. and B. Katherine Brown, *Virginia, 1705–1786: Democracy or Aristocracy?* (East Lansing, Mich., 1964), 236; Alexander White to Richard Henry Lee, 1758, quoted in J. R. Pole, "Representation and Authority in Virginia from the Revolution to Reform," *The Journal of Southern History*, XXIV (1958), 23.

[53] Purdie and Dixon's *Virginia Gazette* (Williamsburg), Apr. 11, 1771; Rind's *Virginia Gazette*, Oct. 31, 1771. See Lester J. Cappon and Stella F. Duff, eds., *Virginia Gazette Index, 1736–1780* (Williamsburg, 1950), I, 351, for entries on the astounding increase in essays on corruption and cost of elections in the late 1760's and early 1770's.

[54] *The Defence of Injur'd Merit Unmasked; or, the Scurrilous Piece of Philander Dissected and Exposed to Public View. By a Friend to Merit, wherever found* (n.p. 1771), 10. Robert Carter chose to retire to private life in the early 1770's rather than adjust to the "new system of politicks" that had begun "to prevail generally." Quoted in Louis Morton, *Robert Carter of Nomini Hall: A Virginia Tobacco Planter of the Eighteenth Century* (Williamsburg, 1941), 52.

[55] Jay B. Hubbell and Douglass Adair, "Robert Munford's *The Candidates*," *Wm. and Mary Qtly.*, 3d Ser., V (1948), 246, 238. The ambivalence in Munford's attitude toward the representative process is reflected in the different way historians have interpreted his play. Cf. *ibid.*, 223–225, with Brown, *Virginia*, 236–237. Munford's fear of "men who aim at power without merit" was more fully expressed in his later play, *The Patriots*, written in 1775 or 1776. Courtlandt Canby, "Robert Munford's *The Patriots*," *Wm. and Mary Qtly.*, 3d Ser., VI (1949), 437–503, quotation from 450.

more with the corrupting British connection and the Scottish factors, but for others frighteningly rooted in "our Pride, our Luxury, and Idleness." [56] The public and private writings of Virginians became obsessed with "corruption," "virtue," and "luxury." The increasing defections from the Church of England, even among ministers and vestrymen, and the remarkable growth of dissent in the years before the Revolution, "so much complained of in many parts of the colony," further suggests some sort of social stress. The strange religious conversions of Robert Carter may represent only the most dramatic example of what was taking place less frenziedly elsewhere among the gentry.[57] By the middle of the eighteenth century it was evident that many of the planters were living on the edge of bankruptcy, seriously overextended and spending beyond their means in an almost frantic effort to fulfill the aristocratic image they had created of themselves.[58] Perhaps the importance of the Robinson affair in the 1760's lies not in any constitutional changes that resulted but in the shattering effect the disclosures had on that virtuous image.[59] Some of the planters expressed openly their fears for the future, seeing the products of their lives being destroyed in the reckless gambling and drinking of their heirs, who, as Landon Carter put it, "play away and play it all away." [60]

The Revolution in Virginia, "produced by the wantonness of the Gentleman," as one planter suggested,[61] undoubtedly gained much of its force from this social crisis within the gentry. Certainly more was expected from the Revolution than simply a break from British imperialism, and it was not any crude avoidance of British debts.[62] The Revolutionary reforms, like the abolition of entail and primogeniture, may have signified something other than mere symbolic legal adjustments to an existing reality. In addition to being an attempt to make the older Tidewater plantations more economically competitive with lands farther west, the reforms may have represented a real effort to redirect what was believed to be a dangerous tendency in social and family development within the ruling gentry. The Virginians were not after all aristocrats who could afford having their entailed families' estates in the hands of weak or ineffectual eldest sons. Entail, as the preamble to the 1776 act abolishing it stated, had often done "injury to the morals of youth by rendering them independent of, and disobedient to, their parents." [63] There was too much likelihood, as the Nelson

---

[56] [John Randolph], *Considerations on the Present State of Virginia* ([Willamsburg], 1774), in Earl G. Swem, ed., *Virginia and the Revolution: Two Pamphlets, 1774* (New York, 1919), 16; Purdie and Dixon's *Virginia Gazette,* Nov. 25, 1773.

[57] Rind's *Virginia Gazette,* Sept. 8, 1774; Brown, *Virginia,* 252–254; Morton, *Robert Carter,* 231–250.

[58] See George Washington to George Mason, Apr. 5, 1769, in John C. Fitzpatrick, ed., *The Writings of George Washington* (Washington, 1931–44), II, 502; Carl Bridenbaugh, *Myths and Realities: Societies of the Colonial South* (New York, 1963), 5, 10, 14, 16; Emory G. Evans, "Planter Indebtedness and the Coming of the Revolution in Virginia," *Wm. and Mary Qtly.,* 3d Ser., XIX (1962), 518–519.

[59] Rind's *Virginia Gazette,* Aug. 15, 1766. See Carl Bridenbaugh, "Violence and Virtue in Virginia, 1766: or The Importance of the Trivial," Massachusetts Historical Society, *Proceedings,* LXXVI (1964), 3–29.

[60] Quoted in Bridenbaugh, *Myths and Realities,* 27. See also Morton, *Robert Carter,* 223–225.

[61] John A. Washington to R. H. Lee, June 20, 1778, quoted in Pole, "Representation and Authority in Virginia," 28.

[62] Evans, "Planter Indebtedness," 526–527.

[63] Julian P. Boyd and others, eds., *The Papers of Thomas Jefferson* (Princeton, 1950–), I, 560. Most of our knowledge of entail and primogeniture in Virginia stems from an unpublished

family sadly demonstrated, that a single wayward generation would virtually wipe out what had been so painstakingly built.[64] George Mason bespoke the anxieties of many Virginians when he warned the Philadelphia Convention in 1787 that "our own Children will in a short time be among the general mass." [65]

Precisely how the strains within Virginia society contributed to the creation of a revolutionary situation and in what way the planters expected independence and republicanism to alleviate their problems, of course, need to be fully explored. It seems clear, however, from the very nature of the ideas expressed that the sources of the Revolution in Virginia were much more subtle and complicated than a simple antagonism to the British government. Constitutional principles alone do not explain the Virginians' almost unanimous determination to revolt. And if the Revolution in the seemingly stable colony of Virginia possessed internal social roots, it is to be expected that the other colonies were experiencing their own forms of social strain that in a like manner sought mitigation through revolution and republicanism.

It is through the Whigs' ideas, then, that we may be led back to take up where the Progressive historians left off in their investigation of the internal social sources of the Revolution. By working through the ideas—by reading them imaginatively and relating them to the objective social world they both reflected and confronted—we may be able to eliminate the unrewarding distinction between conscious and unconscious motives, and eventually thereby to combine a Whig with a Tory, an idealist with a behaviorist, interpretation. For the ideas, the rhetoric, of the Americans was never obscuring but remarkably revealing of their deepest interests and passions. What they expressed may not have been for the most part factually true, but it was always psychologically true. In this sense their rhetoric was never detached from the social and political reality; and indeed it becomes the best entry into an understanding of that reality. Their repeated overstatements of reality, their incessant talk of "tyranny" when there seems to have been no real oppression, their obsession with "virtue," "luxury," and "corruption," their devotion to "liberty" and "equality"—all these notions were neither manipulated propaganda nor borrowed empty abstractions, but ideas with real personal and social significance for those who used them. Propaganda could never move men to revolution. No popular leader, as John Adams put it, has ever been able "to persuade a large people, for any length of time together, to think themselves wronged, injured, and oppressed, unless they really were, and saw and felt it to be so." [66] The ideas had relevance; the sense of oppression and injury, although often displaced onto the imperial system, was nonetheless real. It was indeed the meaningfulness of the connection between what the Americans said and what they felt that gave the ideas their propulsive force and their overwhelming persuasiveness.

---

doctoral dissertation, Clarence R. Keim, Influence of Primogeniture and Entail in the Development of Virginia (University of Chicago, 1926). Keim's is a very careful and qualified study and conclusions from his evidence—other than the obvious fact that much land was held in fee simple—are by no means easy to make. See particularly pp. 56, 60–62, 110–114, 122, 195–196.

[64] Emory S. Evans, "The Rise and Decline of the Virginia Aristocracy in the Eighteenth Century: The Nelsons," in Darrett B. Rutman, ed., The Old Dominion: Essays for Thomas Perkins Abernethy (Charlottesville, 1964), 73–74.

[65] Max Farrand, ed., The Records of the Federal Convention of 1787 (New Haven, 1911), I, 56; Bridenbaugh, Myths and Realities, 14, 16.

[66] John Adams, "Novanglus," in Charles F. Adams, ed., The Works of John Adams (Boston, 1851), IV, 14.

It is precisely the remarkable revolutionary character of the Americans' ideas now being revealed by historians that best indicates that something profoundly unsettling was going on in the society, that raises the question, as it did for the Progressive historians, why the Americans should have expressed such thoughts. With their crude conception of propaganda the Progressive historians at least attempted to grapple with the problem. Since we cannot regard the ideas of the Revolutionaries as simply propaganda, the question still remains to be answered. "When 'ideas' in full cry drive past," wrote Arthur F. Bentley in his classic behavioral study, *The Process of Government,* "the thing to do with them is to accept them as an indication that something is happening; and then search carefully to find out what it really is they stand for, what the factors of the social life are that are expressing themselves through the ideas." [67] Precisely because they sought to understand both the Revolutionary ideas and American society, the behaviorist historians of the Progressive generation, for all of their crude conceptualizations, their obsession with "class" and hidden economic interests, and their treatment of ideas as propaganda, have still offered us an explanation of the Revolutionary era so powerful and so comprehensive that no purely intellectual interpretation will ever replace it.

[67] Arthur F. Bentley, *The Process of Government: A Study of Social Pressures* (Chicago, 1908), 152.

Part II

FROM RESISTANCE TO REVOLUTION

5 / The American Revolution as an Aftermath of the Great War for the Empire, 1754–1763

Lawrence Henry Gipson

The end of The Great War for the Empire, more commonly known to Americans as the French and Indian War, did—in so far as most public statements and manifestations were concerned—mark a high point of colonial allegiance to the mother country and to "good" King George III. Yet Professor Gipson argues that, somewhat ironically, this war, fought in his opinion largely to preserve and enhance the value and safety of Britain's New World Empire, helped pave the way for American Independence. It did so first by leading the British government to enforce more vigorously its control over colonial trade, then to adopt new measures designed to bring order to the colonial frontiers and in the newly acquired territories in North America, and to try to obtain some contributions from the colonists to offset the costs of these new measures. The decision to acquire Canada was based, in British eyes, not upon economic considerations but primarily upon a desire to secure for the colonies a safe frontier and for the Empire a new degree of security. Therefore, British politicians naturally looked to the colonists to pay a share of the costs of supporting the newly expanded military establishment in America. The repeated efforts to raise a revenue in America contributed obviously and directly to the growing spirit of resistance in America. Moreover, the eviction of the French from the New World gave the colonists a new freedom of action: where before prudence might have led them to accept some British policies out of a realization of the necessity of maintaining British protection, now there was no enemy on their frontiers, no clear compulsion to moderate protests that might lead to an eventual end of that British presence.

For further reading: Lawrence Henry Gipson, *The Coming of the Revolution* (1954) and *The British Empire before the American Revolution;* (1936–   ); E. I. McCormac, *Colonial Opposition to Imperial Authority*

Reprinted with permission from the *Political Science Quarterly,* LXV (March 1950), 86–104, with minor revisions by the author. This paper was read before the colonial history section of the American Historical Association in December 1948 at the annual meeting held in Washington.

during the French and Indian War (1914); Bernhard Knollenberg, *Origin of the American Revolution* (1960).

Great wars in modern times have too frequently been the breeders of revolution. The exhausting armed struggles in which France became engaged in the latter half of the eighteenth century led as directly to the French Revolution as did the First World War to the Russian Revolution; it may be said as truly that the American Revolution was an aftermath of the Anglo-French conflict in the New World carried on between 1754 and 1763. This is by no means to deny that other factors were involved in the launching of these revolutionary movements. Before proceeding with an analysis of the theme of this paper, however, it would be well to consider the wording of the title given to it.

Words may be used to disguise or to distort facts as well as to clarify them, but the chief task of the historian is to illuminate the past. He is faced, therefore, with the responsibility of using only such words as will achieve this broad objective of his calling and to reject those that obscure or defeat it. For this reason "the French and Indian War," as a term descriptive of the conflict to which we have just referred, has been avoided in this essay as well as in the writer's series on the *British Empire before the American Revolution*. This has been done in spite of the fact that the term has been employed by most Americans ever since the early days of our Republic and that it therefore has the sanctions of long usage—not to mention the sanction of American national tradition which assigns to the revolt of the northern colonies a position of such commanding importance that all other events in American history, both preceding and following it, have been quite subordinated to the War for Independence. In contrast to this traditional interpretation of our history one may affirm that the Anglo-French conflict settled nothing less than the incomparably vital question as to what civilization—what complex cultural patterns, what political institutions—would arise in the great Mississippi basin and the valleys of the rivers draining it, a civilization, whatever it might be, surely destined to expand to the Pacific seaboard and finally to dominate the North American continent. The determination of this crucial issue is perhaps the most momentous event in the life of the English-speaking people in the New World and quite overshadows in importance both the Revolutionary War and the later Civil War, events which, it is quite clear, were each contingent upon the outcome of the earlier crisis.

A struggle of such proportions, involving tremendous stakes, deserves a name accurately descriptive of its place in the history of the English-speaking people, and the title "the French and Indian War," as suggested, in no way fulfills this need. For the war was not, as the name would seem to imply, a conflict largely between English and French New World colonials and their respective Indian allies, nor was it localized in North America to the extent that the name would appear to indicate. In contrast, it was waged with all their resources both before and after an open declaration of war by the British and French nations, for nine years on three oceans, and much of the land washed by the waters of them; it ultimately brought in both Spain, allied to France, and Portugal, allied to Great Britain. While it involved, it is true, wilderness fighting, yet of equal, if not of greater, importance in assessing the final outcome was the pouring forth of Britain's financial resources in a vast program of shipbuilding, in the equipping and support of the British and colonial armies and the royal navy, and in the subsidization both of allies on the European continent and of the colonies in America. If it also involved the reduction of the fortress of Louisbourg, Fort Niagara, Fort Duquesne, Quebec and Montreal in North America—each in turn to fall to British regulars aided by American provincial troops—these highly significant successes, were, in fact, contingent upon the resounding British naval victories. For it was the success of the British Navy off the Straits of Gilbralter, in the Bay of Biscay, and elsewhere, that brought about the virtual extinction of the French navy and merchant marine and thereby presented to France—seeking to supply her forces in Canada and elsewhere with adequate reinforcements and matériel—a logistical problem so insoluble as to spell the doom of her North American empire and of her possessions in India and elsewhere.

If the term "the French and Indian War" meets none of the requirements of accurate historical nomenclature, neither does the term "the Seven Years' War"—a name appropriately enough employed by historians to designate the mightly conflict that raged for seven years in Germany before its conclusion in the Treaty of Hubertusburg in 1763. The principals in this war were Prussia, allied with Great Britain, Hanover, Brunswick and Hesse, facing Austria, most of the Holy Roman Empire, Russia and Sweden, all allied with France and receiving subsidies from her. Although George II, as King of Great Britain and Elector of Hanover, in the Treaty of 1758 with Frederick of Prussia, promised not to conclude peace without mutual agreement with the latter, and although large subsidies were annually paid to Prussia as well as to the other continental allies out of the British treasury and troops were also sent to Germany, it must be emphasized that these aids were designed primarily for the protection of the King's German Electorate. In other words, the British alliance in no way supported the objectives of the Prussian King, when he suddenly began the German war in 1756 by invading Saxony—two years after the beginning of the Anglo-French war. In this connection it should be borne in mind that throughout the Seven Years' War in Germany Great Britain remained at peace with both Russia and Sweden and refused therefore to send a fleet into the Baltic in spite of the demands of Frederick that this be done; nor were British land troops permitted to assist him against Austria, but only to help form a protective shield for Hanover against the thrusts of the French armies. For the latter were determined not only to overrun the Electorate—something that they succeeded in doing—but to hold it as a bargaining point to be used at the conclusion of hostilities with Great Britain, a feat, however, beyond their power of accomplishment. Closely related and intertwined as were the two wars, they were, nevertheless, distinct in their beginning and distinct in their termination.

Indeed, while British historians at length were led to adopt the nomenclature applied by German and other continental historians to all hostilities that took place between 1754 and 1763 in both the Old and New Worlds, American historians, by and large in the past, have rejected, and rightly so, it seems, the name "the Seven Years' War" to designate specifically the struggle during these years in North America with the fate of that continent at stake; so likewise many of them have rejected, as equally inadmissible, the name "the French and Indian War." Instead, the late Professor Osgood employed the title "the Fourth Intercolonial War," surely not a good one; George Bancroft called the war "the American Revolution: First Phase," still more inaccurate in some respects than the names he sought to avoid; Francis Parkman, with the flare of a romanticist, was at first inclined to call it "the Old French War" but finally, under the influence of the great-man-in-history thesis, gave to his two remarkable volumes concerned with it the totally misleading name, *Montcalm and Wolfe;* finally, John Fiske, the philosopher-historian, as luminous in his views as he was apt to be careless in the details of historical scholarship, happily fastened upon the name "the Great War." In the series on the *British Empire before the American Revolution* the writer has built upon Fiske's title and has called it "the Great War for the Empire" in order to emphasize not only the fact that the war was a very great conflict both in its scope and its lasting effects, as Fiske saw with clearness, but also that, as a war entered into specifically for the defense of the British Empire, it was by far the most important ever waged by Great Britain to this end.

It may be pointed out that later charges, especially by American writers, that the war was begun by Great Britain with less worthy motives in mind, are not supported by the great mass of state papers and the private correspondence of British statesmen responsible for making the weighty decisions at the time. The writer has attempted to analyze in detail these materials, now available to the student, in the two volumes of his series that appeared under the title of *Zones of International Friction, 1748–1754.* In other words, the idea that the war was started as the result of European balance-of-power politics or by British mercantilists for the purpose of destroying a commercial rival and for conquering Canada and the French West Indies, and for expelling the French from India, rather than for the much more limited and legitimate objective of affording the colonies—and particularly the new province of Nova Scotia and the Old Dominion of Virginia—protection against the aggressive aims of France, must be dismissed by students brought face to face with impressive evidence to the contrary.

The development of the war into one for the military mastery of the North American continent came with the growing conviction on the part of the British ministers that nothing short of this drastic step would realize the primary aims of the government, once it had reached the determination to respond to the appeals from the colonies for assistance and to challenge the right of French troops to be planted well within the borders of the Nova Scotia peninsula and at the forks of the Ohio. One may go as far as to state that the acquisition of Canada—as an objective sought by mercantilists to contribute to the wealth of Great Britain—would have seemed fantastic to any contemporary who had the slightest knowledge of the tremendous financial drain that that great possession had been on the treasury of the French King for over a century before 1754. Moreover, the motives that ultimately led, after much searching of heart, to its retention after its conquest by Great Britain were not commercial but strategic and had primarily in view the general security and welfare of the older American colonies.

In view of these facts, not to be confused with surmises, the name "the Great War for the Empire" seems to the writer not only appropriate but, among all the names heretofore applied to the war in question by far the most suitable that can be used by anyone concerned with the history of the old British Empire, who seeks earnestly to maintain that standard of exactness in terminology, as well as in other respects, which the public has a right to demand of him.

The description just given of the motives that led to the Great War for the Empire, nevertheless, runs counter, as suggested, to American national tradition and most history that has been written in harmony with it by American historians. This tradition had a curious beginning. It arose partly out of Pitt's zealous efforts to energize the colonies to prosecute the war most actively; but there also was another potent factor involved in its creation. Before the conclusion of hostilities in 1763 certain powerful commercial interests—centered particularly at Newport, Rhode Island, Boston, New York City, and to a less extent in Philadelphia—in a desire to continue an enormously lucrative trade with the French West Indies, and therefore with the enemy, all in the face of Pitt's determination to keep supplies from the French armed forces operating in the New World, began to express themselves in terms that implied that the war was peculiarly Great Britain's war and only incidentally one that concerned her colonies and that the French, really friendly to the aspirations of British colonials, were opposed only to the mercantilistic ambitions of the mother country. By 1766—just twelve years after the beginning of the war and three years after its termination—this extraordinary tradition had become so well established that Benjamin Franklin, astonishingly enough, could actually assert in his examination before a committee of the House of Commons:

> I know the last war is commonly spoke of here as entered into for the defence, or for the sake of the people of America; I think it is quite misunderstood. It began about the limits between Canada and Nova Scotia, about territories to which the crown indeed laid claim, but were not claimed by any British colony. . . . We had therefore no particular concern or interest in that dispute. As to the Ohio, the contest there began about your right of trading in the Indian country, a right you had by the Treaty of Utrecht, which the French infringed . . . they took a fort which a company of your merchants, and their factors and correspondents, had erected there to secure that trade. Braddock was sent with an army to retake that fort . . . and to protect your trade. It was not until after his defeat that the colonies were attacked. They were before in perfect peace with both French and Indians. . . .

By the beginning of 1768 the tradition had been so extended that John Dickinson—voicing the popular American view in his highly important *Letters from a Farmer in Pennsylvania,* No. VIII—felt that he not only could affirm, as did Franklin, that the war was strictly Britain's war and fought for selfish purposes, but could even insist that the acquisition of territory in North America as the result of it "is greatly injurious to these colonies" and that they therefore were not under the slightest obligation to the mother country.

But to return to the last phases of the Great War for the Empire. The British customs officials—spurred into unusual activity in the face of Pitt's demand for the strict enforcement of the Trade and Navigation Acts in order to break up the pernicious practice of bringing aid and comfort to the enemy—were led to employ writs of assistance for the purpose of laying their hands upon goods landed in American ports and secured in exchange for American provisions sent for the most part either directly or indirectly to the French West Indies. Although in the midst of hostilities, most of the merchants in Boston showed bitter opposition to the writs and gave ardent support to James Otis' declaration made in open court in 1761 that Parliament was powerless to extend the use of these writs to America, whatever its constitutional authority might be in Great Britain. The importance of this declaration lies not so much in its immediate effect but rather in the fact that it was indicative of the line of attack that would be followed during the developing crisis not only by Otis but also by the Adamses, Warren, Hawley, Hancock, and other popular leaders in the Bay colony as they laid down constitutional restrictions upon the power of Parliament to legislate for America. Further, it is clear that, even before the Great War for the Empire had been terminated, there were those in the province who had begun to view Great Britain as the real enemy rather than France.

Just as clearly related to the war under consideration as the issue over writs of assistance was that growing out of the twopenny acts of the Virginia Assembly. In search of funds for maintaining the frontier defensive forces under the command of Colonel George Washington, the Assembly was led to pass in 1755 and 1758 those highly questionable laws, which were as favorable to the tobacco planters as they were indefensively unjust to the clergy. Even assuming the fact that these laws were war measures, and therefore in a sense emergency measures, it was inconceivable that the Privy Council would permit so palpable a violation of contractual relations as they involved. The royal disallowance of the laws in question opened the way for Patrick Henry, the year that hostilities were terminated by the Peace of Paris, to challenge in the Louisa County courthouse the right of the King in Council to refuse approval to a law passed by a colonial assembly—a good law in the judgment of the colony— and to affirm that such refusal was nothing less than an act of tyranny on the part of the King. It was thus resentment at the overturning of Virginia war legislation that led to this attack upon the judicial authority of review by the Crown—an authority exercised previously without serious protest for over a century. It should also be noted that the Henry thesis helped to lay the foundation for the theory of the equality of colonial laws with those passed by Parliament, a theory of the constitution of the empire that most American leaders in 1774 had come to accept in arguing that if the King could no longer exercise a veto over the acts of the legislature of Great Britain, it was unjust that he should do so over those of the colonial assemblies.

But the most fateful aftermath of the Great War for the Empire, with respect to the maintenance of the historic connection between the mother country and the colonies, grew out of the problem of the control and support of the vast trans-Appalachian interior, the right to which was now confirmed by treaty to Great Britain, as well as of the new acquisitions in North America secured from France and Spain. Under the terms of the royal Proclamation of 1763, French Canada to the east of the Great Lakes was organized as the Province of Quebec; most of old Spanish Florida became the Province of East Florida; and those areas, previously held by Spain as well as by France to the west of the Apalachicola and to the east of New Orleans and its immediate environs, became the Province of West Florida. The Proclamation indicated that proper inducements would be offered British and other Protestants to establish themselves in these new provinces. With respect to the trans-Appalachian region, however, it created there a temporary but vast Indian reserve by laying down as a barrier the crest of the mountains beyond which there should be no white settlement except by specific permission of the Crown.

The Proclamation has been represented not only as a blunder, the result largely of carelessness and ignorance on the part of those responsible for it, but also as a cynical attempt by the British ministry to embody mercantilistic principles in an American land policy that in itself ran counter to the charter limits of many of the colonies and the interests in general of the colonials. Nevertheless, this view of the Proclamation fails to take into account the fact that it was the offspring of the war and that the trans-Appalachian aspects of it were an almost inevitable result of promises made during the progress of hostilities. For both in the Treaty of Easton in 1758 with the Ohio Valley Indians, a treaty ratified by the Crown, and in the asseverations of such military leaders as Colonel Bouquet, these Indians were assured that they would be secure in their trans-Appalachian lands as a reward for deserting their allies, the French. As a sign of good faith, the lands lying within the bounds of Pennsylvania to the west of the mountains, purchased by the Proprietors from the Six Nations in 1754, were solemnly released. Thus committed in honor in the course of the war, at its termination what other step could the Cabinet Council have taken? But the Proclamation of 1763 was in opposition to the interests of such groups of land speculators as, for example, the Patrick Henry group in Virginia and the Richard Henderson group in North Carolina, both of whom boldly ignored the Proclamation in negotiating with the Cherokee Indians for land grants. It also led to open defiance by frontiersmen who, moving beyond the mountains by the thousands, proceeded to settle within the Indian reserve—some on lands previously occupied before the beginning of the late war or before the great Indian revolt in 1763, and others on new lands.

The Proclamation line of 1763 might have become an issue, indeed a most formidable one, between the government of Great Britain and the colonials, had not the former acquiesced in the inevitable and confirmed certain Indian treaties that provided for the transfer of much of the land which had been the particular object of quest on the part of speculators and of those moving westward from the settled areas to establish new homes. Such were the treaties of Hard Labor, Fort Stanwix, Lochaber, and the modification of the last-named by the Donelson agreement with the Cherokees in 1771. Nor did the regulation of the trans-Appalachian Indian trade create serious colonial irritation, especially in view of the failure of the government to implement the elaborate Board of Trade plan drawn up in 1764. The same, however, cannot be said of the program put forward by the ministry and accepted by Parliament for securing the means to maintain order and provide protection for this vast area and the new acquisitions to the north and south of it.

Theoretically, it would have been possible for the government of Great Britain to have dropped onto the lap of the old continental colonies the entire responsibility for maintaining garrisons at various strategic points in North America—in Canada, about the Great Lakes, in the Ohio and Mississippi valleys, and in East and West Florida. In spite, however, of assertions made in 1765 and 1766, by some prominent colonials, such as Franklin, that the colonies would be able and were willing to take up the burden of providing for the defense of America, this, under the circumstances, was utterly chimerical. For it would have involved not only a vast expenditure of funds but highly complicated inter-colonial arrangements, in the face of especially serious inter-colonial rivalries such as that between Pennsylvania and Virginia respecting the control of the upper Ohio Valley. The very proportions of the task were an insuperable obstacle to leaving it to the colonies; and the colonies, moreover, would have been faced by another impediment almost as difficult to surmount—the utter aversion of eighteenth-century Americans, by and large, to the dull routine of garrison duty. This was emphasized by the Massachusetts Bay Assembly in 1755 in its appeal to the government of Great Britain after Braddock's defeat, to send regulars to man the frontier forts of that province; the dispatches of Colonel George Washington in 1756 and in 1757 respecting the shameful desertion of militiamen, ordered to hold the chain of posts on the western frontier of Virginia in order to check the frightful French and Indian raids, support this position, as does the testimony in 1757 of Governor Lyttelton of South Carolina, who made clear that the inhabitants of that colony were not all adapted to this type of work. The post-war task of garrison duty was clearly one to be assumed by regulars held to their duty under firm discipline and capable of being shifted from one strategic point to another as circumstances might require. Further, to be effective, any plan for the defense of the new possessions and the trans-Appalachian region demanded unity of command, something the colonies could not provide. Manifestly this could be done only through the instrumentalities of the mother country.

Confronted with the problem of guaranteeing the necessary security for the extended empire in North America, which it was estimated would involve an annual expenditure of from three to four hundred thousand pounds for the maintenance of ten thousand troops—according to various estimates made by General Amherst and others in 1764 (to be found among the Shelburne Papers)—the British ministry, was impelled to raise the question: Should not the colonials be expected to assume some definite part of the cost? Since the government felt that the colonies were in a position to do so and that the stability of these outlying possessions was a matter of greater concern and importance generally to them, by reason of their proximity, than to the people of the mother country three thousand miles away, the answer was in the affirmative. The reason for this is not hard to fathom. The nine years of war had involved Britons in tremendous expenditures. In spite of very heavy taxation during these years, the people were left saddled at the termination of hostilities with a national debt of unprecedented proportions for that day and age of over one hundred and forty million pounds. It was necessary not only to service and to retire this debt, in so far as was possible, but also to meet the ordinary demands of the civil government and to maintain the navy at a point of strength that would offer some assurance that France and Spain would have no desire in the future to plan a war to recover their territorial losses. In addition to all this, there was now the problem of meeting the charges necessary for keeping the new possessions in North America under firm military control for their internal good order and for protection from outside interference.

It may be noted that before the war the British budget had called for average annual expenditures of six and a half million pounds; between the years 1756 and 1766 these expenditures mounted to fourteen and a half million pounds a year on the average and from the latter date to 1775 ranged close to ten million pounds. As a result, the annual per capita tax in Great Britain from 1763 to 1775, without considering local rates, was many times the average annual per capita tax in even those American colonies that made the greatest contribution to the Great War for the Empire, such as Massachusetts Bay and Connecticut—without reference to those colonies that had done little or nothing in this conflict, and therefore had accumulated little in the way of a war debt, such as Maryland and Georgia. The student of the history of the old British Empire, in fact, should accept with great reserve statements to the contrary—some of them quite irresponsible in nature—made by Americans during the heat of the controversy, with respect to the nature of the public burdens they were obliged to carry in the years preceding the outbreak of the Revolutionary War. In this connection a study of parliamentary reimbursement of colonial war expenses from 1756 to 1763 in its relation to public debts in America between the years 1763 and 1775 is most revealing. As to American public finance, all that space will here permit is to state that there is abundant evidence to indicate that, during the five-year period preceding the outbreak of the Revolutionary War, had the inhabitants of any of the thirteen colonies been taxed in one of these years at the average high per capita rate that the British people were taxed from 1760 to 1775, the proceeds of that one year's tax not only would have taken care of the ordinary expenditures of the colony in question for that year but also would have quite liquidated its war debt, so little of which remained in any of the colonies by 1770. Well may John Adams have admitted in 1780 what was equally true in 1770: "America is not used to great taxes, and the people there are not yet disciplined to such enormous taxation as in England."

Assuming, as did the Grenville ministry in 1764, the justice of expecting the Americans to share in the cost of policing the new possessions in North America, the simplest and most obvious way, it might appear, to secure this contribution to a common end so important to Americans and Britons was to request the colonial governments to make definite grants of funds. This was the requisition or quota system that had been employed in the course of the recent war. But the most obvious objections to it were voiced that same year by Benjamin Franklin, who, incidentally, was to reverse himself the following year in conferring with Grenville as the Pennsylvania London agent. In expressing confidentally his personal, rather than any official, views to his friend Richard Jackson on June 25, 1764 he declared: "Quota's would be difficult to settle at first with Equality, and would, if they could be made equal at first, soon become unequal, and never would be satisfactory." Indeed, experience with this system in practice, as a settled method of guaranteeing even the minimum essential resources for the purpose in view, had shown its weakness and utter unfairness. If it could not work equitably even in war time, could it be expected to work in time of peace? It is, therefore, not surprising that this method of securing even a portion of the funds required for North American security should have been rejected in favor of some plan that presented better prospects of a definite American revenue.

The plan of last resort to the ministry was therefore to ask Parliament to act. That Grenville, however, was aware that serious objections might be raised against any direct taxation of the colonials by the government of Great Britain is indicated by the caution with which he approached the solution of the problem of securing from America about a third of the total cost of its defense. The so-called Sugar Act first of all was passed at his request. This provided for import duties on certain West Indian and other products. Colonial import duties imposed by Parliament, at least since 1733, were no innovation. But the anticipated yield of these new duties would fall far short of the desired one hundred thousand pounds. He therefore, in introducing the bill for the Sugar Act, raised the question of a stamp duty but requested postponement of parliamentary action until the colonial governments had been consulted. The latter were thereupon requested to make any suggestions for ways of raising an American fund that might seem more proper to the people than such a tax. Further, it would appear—at least, according to various London advices published in Franklin and Hall's *Pennsylvania Gazette*—that proposals were seriously considered by the Cabinet Council during the fall of 1764 for extending to the colonies representation in Parliament through the election of members to the House of Commons by various colonial assemblies. However, it is quite clear that by the beginning of 1765 any such proposals as may have been under deliberation by the ministry, had been put aside when Grenville at length had become convinced that representation in Parliament was neither actively sought nor even desired by Americans. For the South Carolina Commons House of Assembly went strongly on record against this idea in September 1764 as did the Virginia House of Burgesses in December. In fact, when in the presence of the London colonial agents the minister had outlined the objections raised by Americans to the idea of such representation, no one of them, including Franklin, was prepared to deny the validity of these objections. That he was not mistaken in the opposition of Americans at large to sending members to Parliament, in spite of the advocacy of this by James Otis, is clear in the resolutions passed both by Colonial assemblies other than the ones to which reference has been made and by the Stamp Act Congress in 1765. Indeed, in 1768 the House of Representatives of Massachusetts Bay went so far in its famous Circular Letter framed in opposition to the Townshend duties as to make clear that the people of that colony actually preferred taxation by Parliament without representation to such taxation with representation.

When—in view of the failure of the colonial governments to suggest any practicable, alternate plan for making some contribution to the post-war defensive program in North America—Grenville finally urged in Parliament the passage of an American stamp bill, he acted on an unwarranted assumption. This assumption was—to paraphrase the minister's remarks to the colonials agents in 1765—that opposition to stamp taxes, for the specific purpose in mind, would disappear in America both in light of the benefits such provision would bring to colonials in general and by reason of the plain justice of the measure itself; and that, in place of opposition, an atmosphere of mutual goodwill would be generated by a growing recognition on the part of Americans that they could trust the benevolence of the mother country to act with fairness to all within the empire. Instead, with the news of the passage of the stamp act, cries of British tyranny and impending slavery soon resounded throughout the entire eastern Atlantic American seaboard. What would have been the fate of the empire had Grenville remained in office to attempt to enforce the act, no one can say. But as members of the opposition to the Rockingham ministry, he and his brother, Earl Temple, raised their voices—one as a commoner, the other as a peer—in warning that the American colonies would inevitably be lost to the empire should Parliament be led to repeal the act in the face of colonial resistance and the pressure of British merchants. Had Parliament determined, in spite of violence and threats of violence, to enforce the act, it might have meant open rebellion and civil war, ten years before it actually occurred. Instead, this body decided to yield and, in spite of the passing of the so-called Declaratory Act setting forth its fundamental powers to legislate on all matters relating to the empire, suffered a loss of prestige in the New World that was never to be regained.

But the Stamp Act was not the sole object of attack by colonials. To many of them not only the Sugar Act of 1764 but the whole English pre-war trade and navigation system was equally, if not actually more, obnoxious. Indeed, the unusual energy displayed by the navy and the customs officials, spurred into action by Pitt during the latter years of the war—bringing with it the condemnation in courts of vice-admiralty of many American vessels whose owners were guilty of serious trade violations, or even greater crimes—generated a degree of antagonism against the whole body of late seventeenth- and early eighteenth-century restrictions on commercial intercourse such as never had previously existed. It is not without significance that the greatest acts of terrorism and destruction during the great riot of August 1765 in Boston were directed not against the Massachusetts Bay Stamp distributor but against those officials responsible for encouraging and supporting the enforcement, during the late war, of the various trade acts passed long before 1754. The hatred

also of the Rhode Island merchants, as a group, against the restrictions of the navigation system as well as against the Sugar Act of 1764, remained constant. Moreover, in
December 1766 most of the New York merchants, over two-hundred in number,
showed their repugnance to the way this system was functioning by a strongly
worded petition to the House of Commons in which they enumerated an impressive
list of grievances that they asked to be redressed. Even Chatham, the great friend of
America, regarded their petition "highly improper: in point of time most absurd, in
the extent of their pretensions, most excessive; and in the reasoning, most grossly
fallacious and offensive." In fact, all the leading men in Great Britain supported the
system of trade restrictions.

Nevertheless, the government was now determined—in view especially of the great
financial burdens that the late war had placed upon the mother country—to enforce
the trade laws much more effectively than had been done before 1754. To that end
in 1767 it passed appropriate legislation in order to secure funds from the colonies by
way of import duties so that public officials in America might be held to greater
accountability when paid their salaries by the Crown. This attempt to enforce the
trade and navigation acts and the Townshend Revenue Acts could have only one
result: the combined resistance of those, on the one hand, opposed to any type of
taxation that Parliament might apply to America and of those, on the other, desiring
to free the colonies of hampering trade restrictions.

The suggestion on the part of the Continental Congress in 1774 that Americans
would uphold the British navigation system, if exempted from parliamentary taxation,
while a shrewd gesture to win support in England, had really, it would seem, no
other significance. For it is utterly inconceivable that the Congress itself, or the individual colonial governments, could have set up machinery capable of preventing violations of the system by those whose financial interests were adversely affected by its
operation. Moreover, it is obvious that, by the time the news had reached America that
Lord North's ministry had secured the passage of the coercive acts—for the most
part directed against Massachusetts Bay for the defiant destruction of the East India
Company's tea—leading colonials, among them Franklin, had arrived at the conclusion that Parliament possessed powers so very limited with respect to the empire that
without the consent of the local assemblies it could pass neither constitutional nor
fiscal legislation affecting Americans and the framework of their governments. It is
equally obvious that this represented a most revolutionary position when contrasted
with that held by Franklin and the other delegates to the Albany Congress twenty
years earlier. For it was in 1754 that the famous Plan of Union was drawn up and
approved by the Congress—a plan based upon the view that Parliament, and not the
Crown, had supreme authority within the empire, an authority that alone was adequate in view of framers of the Plan to bring about fundamental changes in the constitutions of the colonies in order legally to clothe the proposed union government
with adequate fiscal as well as other powers.

In accounting for the radical change in attitude of many leading colonials between
the years 1754 and 1774 respecting the nature of the constitution of the empire, surely
among the factors that must be weighed was the truly overwhelming victory achieved
in the Great War for the Empire. This victory not only freed colonials for the first
time in the history of the English-speaking people in the New World from dread of
the French, their Indian allies, and the Spaniards, but, what is of equal significance,
opened up to them the prospect, if given freedom of action, of a vast growth of

power and wealth with an amazing westward expansion. Indeed, it is abundantly clear that a continued subordination of the colonies to the government of Great Britain was no longer considered the asset in the eyes of many Americans by 1774, it had been judged by them to be in 1754, but was rather an onerous liability. What had the debt-ridden mother country to offer in 1774 to the now geographically secure, politically mature, prosperous, dynamic, and self-reliant offspring along the Atlantic seaboard except the dubious opportunity of accepting new burdens in addition to retaining the old ones? And these burdens would have to be borne in order to lighten somewhat the great financial load that the taxpayers of Great Britain were forced to carry because of obligations the nation had assumed both in the course of the late war and at its termination. If many Americans thought they had a perfect right to profit personally by trading with the enemy in time of war, how much more deeply must they have resented in time of peace the serious efforts made by the home government to enforce the elaborate restrictions on commercial intercourse? Again, if, even after the defeat of Colonel Washington at Great Meadows in 1754, colonials such as Franklin were opposed to paying any tax levied by Parliament for establishing a fund for the defense of North America, how much more must they have been inclined to oppose such taxation with the passing in 1763 of the great international crisis?

At this point the question must be frankly faced: If France had won the war decisively and thereby consolidated her position and perfected her claims in Nova Scotia, as well as to the southward of the St. Lawrence, in the Great Lakes region, and in the Ohio and Mississippi valleys, is it at all likely that colonials would have made so fundamental a constitutional issue of the extension to them of the principle of the British stamp tax? Would they have resisted such a tax had Parliament imposed it in order to provide on an equitable basis the maximum resources for guaranteeing their safety, at a time when they were faced on their highly restricted borders by a militant, victorious enemy having at its command thousands of ferocious redskins? Again, accepting the fact of Britain's victory, is it not reasonable to believe that, had Great Britain at the close of the triumphant war left Canada to France and carefully limited her territorial demands in North America to those comparatively modest objectives that she had in mind at its beginning, there would have been no very powerful movement within the foreseeable future toward complete colonial autonomy—not to mention American independence? Would not Americans have continued to feel the need as in the past to rely for their safety and welfare upon British sea power and British land power, as well as upon British resources generally? In other words, was Governor Thomas Hutchinson of Massachusetts Bay far mistaken in his analysis of the American situation late in 1773, when he wrote to the Earl of Dartmouth:

> Before the peace [of 1763] I thought nothing so much to be desired as the cession of Canada. I am now convinced that if it had remained to the French none of the spirit of opposition to the Mother Country would have yet appeared & I think the effects of it [that is, the cession of Canada] worse than all we had to fear from the French or Indians.

In conclusion, it may be said that it would be idle to deny that most colonials in the eighteenth century at one time or another felt strongly the desire for freedom of action in a wider variety of ways than was legally permitted before 1754. Indeed, one can readily uncover these strong impulses even in the early part of the seventeenth century. Yet Americans were, by and large, realists, as were the British, and under the functioning of the imperial system from, let us say, 1650 to 1750 great mutual advantages were enjoyed, with a fair division, taking everything into consideration, of the financial burdens necessary to support the system. However, the mounting Anglo-French rivalry in North America from 1750 onward, the outbreak of hostilities in 1754, and the subsequent nine years of fighting destroyed the old equilibrium, leaving the colonials after 1760 in a highly favored position in comparison with the taxpayers of Great Britain. Attempts on the part of the Crown and Parliament to restore by statute the old balance led directly to the constitutional crisis, out of which came the War for American Independence. Such, ironically, was the aftermath of the Great War for the Empire, a war that Britons believed, as the Earl of Shelburne affirmed in 1762 in Parliament, was begun for the "security of the British colonies in N. America. . . ."

6 / Colonial Ideas
of Parliamentary Power, 1764–1766

Edmund S. Morgan

The central British constitutional issue of the 1760's and early 1770's was the problem of Parliament's authority over the American colonies. Until 1775 at the earliest, the colonists generally proclaimed their loyalty to King George III and usually did so in unequivocal terms. But their reactions to Parliament's claim to legislative authority over America varied considerably from person to person and from time to time. The Americans often objected vociferously to any actual exercise of Parliament's authority; they were not always so loud or so united in their denunciation of any general but unused claim to legislative power. Thus, as the crisis increased, the colonists seemed to be expanding the scope of their objections and the extent of their claims to legislative autonomy. First, the issue was the "internal" tax embodied in the Stamp Act, then it was the "external" taxes of the "Townshend Acts," and finally it became the complete range of Parliament's "pretended" powers over the New World. Yet the issues of the dispute between Great Britain and its colonies were continually changing and the particular arguments and ideas of debate might have been expected to change with the changing nature of those issues. In the following essay, Edmund S. Morgan argues that Americans were far more consistent than they have often been depicted in their objections to Parliamentary taxation. While their ideas concerning Parliament's general legislative authority between 1764 and 1766 were sometimes ambiguous, their objections to any form of taxation by a British legislature were relatively consistent. Unfortunately in the heat of the debate of these years, the issues were sometimes obscured: the British friends of America, for example, in their attempt to bring about the repeal of the Stamp Act, introduced some distinctions—between external and internal taxation and between taxation and legislation—that were to bring much misunderstanding and subsequently to give the Americans a reputation for bad faith among British politicians.

Reprinted by permission of the author from *The William and Mary Quarterly*, 3rd series, V (1948), 311–341.

For further reading: Edmund S. and Helen M. Morgan, *The Stamp Act Crisis: Prologue to Revolution* (1953); Benjamin H. Newcomb, "Effects of the Stamp Act on Colonial Pennsylvania Politics," *The William and Mary Quarterly*, XXIII (1966), 257–272; Randolph G. Adams, *The Political Ideas of the American Revolution* (1922); and Carl Becker, *The Declaration of Independence* (1922).

I [1]

The distinction between internal and external taxes, said Charles Townshend, was "ridiculous in everybody's opinion except the Americans'." [2] The House of Commons was disposed to agree. Members had declared at the time of the Stamp Act that the distinction was meaningless. Some thought that the Americans were fools for espousing such sophistry; others thought that they were knaves, who would seize any pretext to avoid paying for their own protection. And knaves the Americans certainly appeared to be when they objected to the Townshend Duties almost as vehemently as they had to the Stamp Act. The colonists in fact seemed to be a ridiculous group of hypocrites, who capered from one pious notion of their rights to another. Their conduct was shameful and their efforts to justify it even more so. First they quibbled about external taxes and internal taxes. When this distinction failed them, they talked about taxes for regulating trade as against taxes for revenue. Before long they were denying that Parliament had any authority to tax them, and finally they concluded that they were simply not subject to Parliament at all. The frivolous way in which they skipped from one of these views to the next was sufficient evidence that they had no real devotion to any principle except that of keeping their pockets full. [3]

The modern historian, who has thrown off the mantle of patriotism and Whigism for the more sober garments of impartiality, has tended to accept the Tory analysis of American resistance to taxation. He does not always cast doubt on the sincerity of the successive theories of American constitutional rights, but he agrees with Charles Townshend that it was the Americans who distinguished between internal and external taxes, that they abandoned this distinction for another, which likewise proved

---

[1] This paper, in a shortened version, was read at a meeting of the American Historical Association at Cleveland on December 28, 1947. I wish to express my thanks to the members of the Association who offered comments at that time and to the members of my graduate seminar at Brown University, who criticized the paper at an earlier reading. I also wish to thank Mr. Bernhard Knollenberg, who read the manuscript and made several valuable suggestions.

[2] Quoted in J. C. Miller, *Sam Adams: Pioneer in Propaganda* (Boston, 1936), 115.

[3] See William Knox, *The Controversy between Great-Britain and her Colonies Reviewed* (London, 1769), 34–35: "When the repeal of the stamp-act was their object, a distinction was set up between internal and external taxes; they pretended not to dispute the right of parliament to impose external taxes, or port duties, upon the Colonies, whatever were the purposes of parliament in laying them on, or however productive of revenue they might be. . . . but when parliament seemed to adopt the distinction, and waiving for the present the exercise of its right to impose internal taxes, imposed certain duties on merchandizes imported into the Colonies, . . . the distinction between internal and external taxes is rejected by the colony advocates, and a new one devised between taxes for *the regulation of trade,* and taxes for the *purpose of revenue.*"

untenable, and so on until they reached the Declaration of Independence. Thus in the book which examines the American theories most closely, Doctor Randolph G. Adams' *Political Ideas of the American Revolution*,[4] the American advance toward independence is broken down into three stages:

> In the first, the colonies admitted the right of Parliament to levy customs duties (external taxes), but denied the right of Parliament to levy excise taxes (internal taxes) upon them. In the second, the colonies conceded the right of Parliament to regulate the trade of the Empire, and hence exercise a legislative authority over the unrepresented colonies, but denied the right of Parliament to levy taxes of any kind whatever, internal or external. In the third stage of the controversy, the colonies admitted the right of Parliament to act as a quasi-imperial superintending power over them and over all the dominions, but denied that Parliament had any legislative authority over the colonies as a general proposition, on the ground that the colonies were not represented in Parliament.[5]

The first two stages of American Revolutionary thinking, as defined by Doctor Adams, have received less attention and are consequently less well understood than the last stage. My purpose is to examine the colonial ideas of Parliamentary power in the period covered by Doctor Adams' first stage, the period of the Stamp Act crisis.

It will be remembered that the Stamp Act was under discussion in the colonies from the spring of 1764 to the spring of 1766. Although it was in force for less than four months before its repeal in February, 1766, the colonists had begun to consider it as soon as they received news of the resolution passed by Parliament on March 10, 1764, the resolution which declared, "That, towards further defraying the said Expences, it may be proper to charge certain Stamp Duties in the said Colonies and Plantations." [6] The resolution was one of a series which George Grenville had introduced as the basis of his budget for the ensuing year. The others furnished the substance of the Revenue Act of 1764, the so-called Sugar Act, which became a law two months later. But the resolution for a stamp tax was phrased so as to indicate that no action would be taken on it until the next session, though its ultimate passage was almost a certainty.[7] The colonists were thus presented with two measures which threatened their prosperity and which consequently obliged them to think about the relation which they bore to the body which threatened them. They had to consider the Sugar Act, in which Parliament made use of trade regulations to raise money and which in itself would have been sufficient to set discerning minds at work on the question of Parliamentary taxation. At the same time they had to consider the Stamp Act, an act which would directly affect almost every person in the colonies. Of the

[4] New York, 1939 (second edition).

[5] P. 69. For similar views by other historians, see C. P. Nettels, *The Roots of American Civilization* (New York, 1940), 634–635; C. L. Becker, *The Declaration of Independence* (New York, 1942, 1945), 80–134; H. J. Eckenrode, *The Revolution in Virginia* (Boston and New York, 1916), 28.

[6] *Journals of the House of Commons*, XXIX, 935.

[7] Grenville warned the colonial agents that he would bring in a bill for a stamp tax at the next session of Parliament. See the letter from Jasper Mauduit to Massachusetts, May 26, 1764 (Massachusetts Archives, XXII, 375); the letter from Charles Garth to South Carolina, June 5, 1764 (*English Historical Review*, LIV, 646–648); and the account by William Knox, agent for Georgia, in *The Claim of the Colonies to an Exemption from Internal Taxes Imposed by Authority of Parliament Examined* (London, 1765), 31–35.

two, the Stamp Act appeared to most colonists to be the more dangerous, but in formulating their ideas of Parliamentary power they could not afford to neglect either measure; they had to decide in what way their rights were affected both by the internal taxes of the Stamp Act and by the external taxes of the Sugar Act.

Under the pressure of these two acts colonial ideas reached a remarkable maturity during the period under discussion. In some regions and among some persons the theory of complete colonial autonomy was enunciated. For example a meeting of citizens at New London, Connecticut, on December 10, 1765, adopted resolutions which rehearsed the principles of government by consent, specified that the Stamp Act was a violation of those principles, and finally declared, "That it is the Duty of every Person in the Colonies to oppose by every lawful Means, the Execution of those Acts imposed on them,—and if they can in no other way be relieved to reassume their natural Rights, and the Authority the Laws of Nature and of God have vested them with." [8] If there was any confusion in the minds of the colonists as to how to go about reassuming natural rights, newspaper writers were ready with detailed discussions of the technique of revolution.[9] Short of this, other writers expounded the theory which later found more classic expression in the writings of John Adams and James Wilson, the theory that is assumed in the Declaration of Independence, that the colonies owe allegiance only to the king and are not bound in any way by acts of Parliament.[10]

But in the effort to arrive at what may be called the official colonial position during this period, one cannot rely on newspapers and pamphlets nor on the resolutions adopted by informal gatherings of small groups, for these may represent the views of factions or the idiosyncracies of a single man. Fortunately it is not necessary to depend upon such partial statements, for in every colony except Georgia and North Carolina the formally elected representatives of the people produced some official statement of belief. Five of the colonies which later revolted drew up statements in 1764 while the Stamp Act was pending; nine colonies, including all of the first five, did the same in 1765 after the Act was passed; and in the same year at the Stamp Act Congress, nine colonies combined in a declaration which was formally approved by a tenth. These statements, in the form of resolutions, petitions, memorials, and remonstrances, are the safest index of colonial opinion about Parliamentary power. They were carefully phrased by the regularly elected representatives of the voting population and adopted, in many cases unanimously, after deliberation and debate.

In these formal statements it is scarcely possible to discern a trace of the ideas which the Americans are supposed to have adopted during the period under discussion. Almost universally the documents deny the authority of Parliament to tax the colonies at all. Nowhere is there a clear admission of the right of Parliament to levy external taxes rather than internal, and only in three cases does such a right seem to be implied. In at least one of these three, the implication which may be suggested by

[8] *Boston Post-Boy and Advertiser,* December 16, 1765.
[9] See, for example, *Boston Gazette,* December 2, 1765.
[10] *Maryland Gazette,* May 30, 1765; *Providence Gazette,* May 11, 1765; *Boston Gazette,* February 24, March 3, March 17, 1766. Governor Bernard reported to the Lords of Trade, November 30, 1765, that the Massachusetts politicians were claiming that the colonies "have no Superiors upon Earth but the King, and him only in the Person of the Governor, or according to the terms of the Charter." Bernard Papers, IV, 203, Harvard College Library.

a partial reading is denied by a full consideration of the document and the circumstances under which it was produced.

II

As might be expected, the statements drawn up in 1764 while the Stamp Act was pending were generally not as explicit as those prepared a year later, when the Act had been passed and the colonists had had more time to think over its implications. The clearest of the early statements was that made by the New York Assembly in three petitions, to the King, the Lords, and the Commons, on October 18, 1764. These petitions, in objecting to both the Sugar Act and the proposed Stamp Act, claimed that the colonists should be exempt "from the Burthen of all Taxes not granted by themselves." Far from singling out internal taxes, the New York Assembly stated pointedly:

> . . . since all Impositions, whether they be internal Taxes, or Duties paid, for what we consume, equally diminish the Estates upon which they are charged; what avails it to any People, by which of them they are impoverished? . . . the whole wealth of a country may be as effectually drawn off, by the Exaction of Duties, as by any other Tax upon their Estates.

In accordance with this principle New York admitted the authority of Parliament to regulate the trade of the empire for the good of the mother country, but insisted that

> . . . a Freedom to drive all Kinds of Traffick in a Subordination to, and not inconsistent with, the *British* Trade; and an Exemption from all Duties in such a Course of Commerce, is humbly claimed by the Colonies, as the most essential of all the Rights to which they are intitled, as Colonists from, and connected, in the common Bond of Liberty, with the uninslaved Sons of *Great Britain*.[11]

The statement made by Virginia in 1764 was almost as plain as that of New York. The Virginia Council and House of Burgesses in a petition to the King, a memorial to the House of Lords, and a remonstrance to the Commons, claimed an exemption from all Parliamentary taxation. To the King they asserted their "Right of being governed by such laws, respecting their internal Polity and Taxation,[12] as are derived from their own Consent"; to the Lords they stated their right as British subjects to be exempt from all taxes, "but such as are laid on them by their own Consent, or by those who are legally appointed to represent them"; to the Commons they remonstrated "that laws imposing taxes on the people ought not to be made without the consent of representatives chosen by themselves," and added that they could not discern "by what Distinction they can be deprived of that sacred birthright and most valuable inheritance, by their Fellow Subjects, nor with what Propriety they can be

[11] *Journal of the Votes and Proceedings of the General Assembly of the Colony of New York. Began the 8th Day of November, 1743; and Ended the 23d of December, 1765* (New York, 1766), II, 769–779.

[12] For the question whether or not the adjective "internal" modifies "taxation" as well as "polity" see the discussion below of the same phrase in the Virginia Resolves of 1765.

taxed or affected in their estates by the Parliament, wherein they are not, and indeed cannot, constitutionally be represented." [13]

Rhode Island, Connecticut, and Massachusetts took a less precise view of their rights in 1764 than did New York and Virginia, although Massachusetts and Connecticut, at least, cleared up the uncertainty of their position in the following year. In Rhode Island the General Assembly deputed Governor Stephen Hopkins to write a statement of the colony's rights and in addition sent a petition to the King, dated November 29, 1764. Both Governor Hopkins' pamphlet and the petition ignored the constitutional question raised by the Sugar Act, the question of external taxes; they argued against the act simply as a trade regulation which would have ruinous economic consequences. Since none of the colonies at this time denied Parliament's right to regulate colonial trade, Rhode Island, in considering the Sugar Act simply as such a regulation, made no attempt to deny Parliament's right to enact it. Against the proposed Stamp Act Hopkins and the Assembly did raise the question of right. This proposal, if carried into execution, would be "a manifest violation of their just and long enjoyed rights. For it must be confessed by all men, that they who are taxed at pleasure by others, cannot possibly have any property, can have nothing to be called their own; they who have no property can have no freedom, but are indeed reduced to the most abject slavery." The petition to the King recited the same objections and concluded with a request

> that our trade may be restored to its former condition, and no further limited, restrained and burdened, than becomes necessary for the general good of all your Majesty's subjects; that the courts of vice admiralty may not be vested with more extensive powers in the colonies than are given them by law in Great Britain; that the colonists may not be taxed but by the consent of their own representatives, as Your Majesty's other free subjects are.[14]

Thus Rhode Island sidestepped the question of external taxes by ignoring the declared intent of the Sugar Act to raise a revenue. She took a stand upon constitutional grounds only against the proposed Stamp Act, only, in other words, against internal taxes. Yet she did not quite admit Parliament's right to levy external taxes, because she considered the Sugar Act, erroneously to be sure, as a regulation of trade and not as a tax. Her position on external taxes was ambiguous: she didn't say yes and she didn't say no.

Connecticut in 1764 was guilty of the same ambiguity. Connecticut's statement took the form of a pamphlet drawn up by a committee, consisting of Governor Fitch, Ebenezer Silliman, George Wyllys and Jared Ingersoll, deputed by the General Assembly, "to collect and set in the most advantageous light all such arguments and objections as may justly and reasonably [be] advanced against creating and collecting a revenue in America, more particularly in this Colony, and especially against effecting the same by Stamp Duties &c." [15] This committee, of which Governor Fitch was the working member, produced a pamphlet entitled *Reasons why the British Colonies in America should not be charged with Internal Taxes, by Authority of Parliament*.[16]

---

[13] *Journals of the House of Burgesses of Virginia 1761–1765* (Richmond, 1907), liv–lvii.

[14] James R. Bartlett, ed., *Records of the Colony of Rhode Island and Providence Plantations* (Providence, 1861), VI, 414–427.

[15] C. J. Hoadly, ed., *Public Records of the Colony of Connecticut* (Hartford, 1881), XII, 256.

[16] New Haven, 1764. Reprinted in Hoadly, XII, 651–671.

The pamphlet came as close as any American statement to admitting the right of Parliament to levy external taxes. Like the Rhode Island statement, it confined its constitutional objections to internal taxes and failed to consider the problem, raised by the Sugar Act, of whether Parliament could make use of trade regulations as a source of revenue. Instead, it assumed that Parliament would act for the good of the whole in its regulation of trade. "If Restrictions on Navigation, Commerce, or other external Regulations only are established," it said, "the internal Government, Powers of taxing for its Support, an Exemption from being taxed without Consent, and other Immunities, which legally belong to the Subjects of each Colony . . . will be and continue in the Substance of them whole and entire." [17] This was a rather naive view of the situation, but it did not necessarily commit the colony to a constitutional acceptance of external taxes.

The address of Massachusetts to the House of Commons, dated November 3, 1764, like the pamphlets issued by Rhode Island and Connecticut in this year, was not entirely clear on the question of external taxes. Massachusetts affirmed that the American colonists "have always judged by their representatives both of the way and manner, in which internal taxes should be raised within their respective governments, and of the ability of the inhabitants to pay them." The address concluded with the request that "the privileges of the colonies, relative to their internal taxes, which they have so long enjoyed, may still be continued to them." [18] By specifying internal taxes, the address seemed to imply that the inhabitants of Massachusetts did not object to the idea of an external tax imposed by Parliament. This implication was fortified by the rest of the document, which objected to the Sugar Act on economic rather than constitutional grounds as a measure which would ruin the trade of the colony.

Before this address is interpeted as an implied assent to external taxes the circumstances of its origin must be considered. The General Court adopted the address only because the Council refused to concur in a much more inclusive assertion of rights, originally passed by the lower house. In this version the House affirmed that "we look *upon those Duties as a Tax* [i.e. the duties imposed by the Sugar Act], and which we humbly apprehend ought not to be laid without the Representatives of the People affected by them." [19] The abandonment of this earlier version was regarded in Massachusetts as a victory for the Council under the leadership of Lieutenant-Governor Hutchinson, and the House, even though it acquiesced in the new address, did not consider it a proper statement of colonial rights.[20] Accordingly, when they sent it to their agent in London for presentation, they warned him that it did not represent the views of the House. "The House of Representatives," they said

> were clearly for making an ample and full declaration of the exclusive Right of the People of the Colonies to tax themselves and that they ought not to be deprived of a right they had so long enjoyed and which they held by Birth and by Charter; but they could not prevail with the Councill, tho they made several

[17] *Ibid.,* 661.

[18] Alden Bradford, ed., *Massachusetts State Papers. Speeches of the Governors of Massachusetts from 1765 to 1775 etc.* (Boston, 1818), 21–23.

[19] Massachusetts Archives, XXII, 414.

[20] See the letters by Governor Bernard, November 17 and 18, 1764, to the Earl of Halifax, to John Pownall, and to Richard Jackson, relating the success of the Council in toning down the petition. Bernard Papers, II, 181–187, 189, 260–264.

Tryalls, to be more explicit than they have been in the Petition sent you . . . You will therefore collect the sentiments of the Representative Body of People rather from what they have heretofore sent you than from the present Address.[21]

What the House of Representatives had heretofore sent the agent included a long letter instructing him in the doctrine of natural rights and an explicit statement that any attempt by Parliament to tax colonial trade would be "contrary to a fundamentall Principall of our constitution vizt. That all Taxes ought to originate with the people." [22] The House had also approved and sent to the agent a pamphlet written by one of their members, James Otis, entitled *The Rights of the British Colonies asserted and proved*.[23] In this pamphlet Otis had argued against Parliament's right to tax the colonies and had stated in the most unequivocal manner that "there is no foundation for the distinction some make in England, between an internal and an external tax on the colonies." [24] It would hardly seem proper, then, to draw from the Massachusetts Address the inference that the people of the colonies accepted the right of Parliament to levy external as opposed to internal taxes.

III

At the end of the year 1764, when the five initial colonial statements were all on the books, the colonial position was still a little obscure. New York and Virginia had been plain enough, but Rhode Island, Connecticut, and Massachusetts, while denying Parliament's right to levy a stamp tax, had evaded the question of external taxes. By the close of the following year all signs of hesitation had disappeared. The Stamp Act produced an all-but-unanimous reaction: Parliament had no right to tax the colonies.

The first declaration of rights to be made after passage of the Act was the famous

[21] *Collections of the Massachusetts Historical Society,* LXXIV, 170–171.

[22] *Ibid.,* 39–54, 145–146.

[23] Boston, 1764. See *Journal of the Honourable House of Representatives of His Majesty's Province of the Massachusetts-Bay in New-England, Begun and held at Concord, in the county of Middlesex, on Wednesday the Thirtieth Day of May, Annoque Domini, 1764* (Boston, 1764), 66, 77.

[24] P. 42. Strangely enough these were also the private views of Lieutenant-Governor Hutchinson, who was principally responsible for suppressing the original address of the House. In a piece which he wrote in June or July, 1764, but never published, he argued against the Stamp Act on precisely the same line which was later followed by the House. He pointed out that the Sugar Act had been passed, not for the regulation of trade, but "for the sake of the money arising from the Duties," and that the privileges of the people were no less affected by it than they were by an internal tax. (Massachusetts Archives, XXVI, 90–96.) Moreover, on Nov. 9, 1764, just after he had succeeded in getting the Massachusetts Address toned down, Hutchinson wrote to Ebenezer Silliman in Connecticut, criticizing the Connecticut pamphlet for neglecting to object against external taxes. He told Silliman, who was a member of the Connecticut Committee which drew up the pamphlet, that "the fallacy of the argument lies here it is your supposing duties upon trade to be imposed for the sake of regulating trade, whereas the Professed design of the duties by the late Act is to raise a revenue." (Massachusetts Archives, XXVI, 117–118.) Why Hutchinson should have objected to these views when they came from the Massachusetts House of Representatives is not apparent.

set of resolves which Patrick Henry introduced into the Virginia House of Burgesses on May 30, 1765. As recorded on the Journals of the House of Burgesses there were four of these resolves which passed the House. The first two asserted the right of the inhabitants of Virginia to all the privileges of Englishmen. The third declared "that the Taxation of the People by themselves, or by Persons chosen to represent them" was a "distinguishing Characteristick of *British* Freedom, without which the ancient Constitution cannot exist." The fourth stated that the inhabitants of Virginia had always enjoyed and had never forfeited or yielded up "the inestimable Right of being governed by such Laws, respecting their internal Polity and Taxation, as are derived from their own Consent." [25]

Henry had proposed three more resolutions which either failed of passage or later were expunged from the records. The first of these merely repeated what the others had already implied, namely that the General Assembly of Virginia, in its representative capacity, had "the only exclusive right and power to lay taxes and imposts upon the inhabitants of this colony." The second, more radical, stated "That his Majesty's liege people, the inhabitants of this colony, are not bound to yield obedience to any law or ordinance whatever, designed to impose any taxation whatsoever upon them, other than the laws or ordinances of the General Assembly aforesaid." The last provided that anyone who denied the Assembly's exclusive power of taxation should be considered an enemy of the colony.[26]

The Virginia Resolves even without the inclusion of Henry's three additional clauses, constituted a clear denial of Parliament's right to tax. The only phrase which could be interpreted as distinguishing between internal and external taxes was the phrase in the third resolution "internal polity and taxation." Here it was possible to read the adjective "internal" to modify "taxation" as well as "polity." That such a reading would have been incorrect is suggested by the fact that in the version of the Resolves which was printed in the newspapers this phrase was changed to read "taxation and internal police." [27] Furthermore this was also the wording in a copy of the Resolves endorsed on the back in Patrick Henry's handwriting.[28]

The Virginia Resolves served as a model for similar declarations in most of the other colonies. Rhode Island, where the Virginia Resolves were first published, was the first to copy them. In September, 1765, the Rhode Island General Assembly passed six resolutions, three of which were adapted from those passed by the Virginia House of Burgesses, two from Henry's unsuccessful resolutions (which had been printed in

[25] *Journals of the House of Burgesses of Virginia 1761–1765*, 360.

[26] *Ibid.*, lxvii. When the Resolves were printed in the newspapers, the three unsuccessful resolves were included along with the others as though they had been passed. The Resolves, so far as the incomplete newspaper records enable us to tell, were first printed in the *Newport Mercury* on June 24, 1765, and copied in the Boston papers from the version given there. The text printed in the papers, besides including the three unsuccessful resolves, omitted one of those actually passed (the third) and considerably abridged the others. The abridgment did not seriously alter the meaning of the resolves, but the wording was sufficiently changed to suggest that the newspaper text was obtained from an unofficial source, probably from some member of the assembly who had been present when the Resolves were passed. Possibly the source was Henry himself, for the newspaper version, except in its omission of resolution number 3, closely approximates a copy of the resolves which is endorsed on the back in Henry's handwriting. See *Journals of the House of Burgesses*, frontispiece and lxv.

[27] *Newport Mercury*, June 24, 1765; *Boston Post-Boy and Advertiser*, July 1, 1765; *Boston Gazette*, July 1, 1765; *Georgia Gazette*, September 5, 1765.

[28] *Journals of the House of Burgesses of Virginia, 1761–1795*, frontispiece and lxv.

the newspapers without any indication that they had failed to pass), and one original resolution which, in effect, called upon officers of government to pay no attention to the Stamp Act.[29] On the question of Parliamentary authority the Rhode Island statements, being copied from those of Virginia, were no less definite: the General Assembly of the colony had always enjoyed control over "taxation and internal police" and possessed "the only exclusive right to lay taxes and imposts upon the inhabitants of this colony." [30] Rhode Island in fact went farther than the Virginia Burgesses had been willing to go and farther than any other colony went in the next eight or nine years, by calling for direct disobedience to Parliament. She passed the measure which Virginia had rejected and declared that her inhabitants need not submit to a Parliamentary tax. Yet in so doing Rhode Island added a qualification which makes her position on the question of external taxes open to suspicion. In the fifth Rhode Island resolution it was stated that the inhabitants of the colony were "not bound to yield obedience to any law or ordinance designed to impose any internal taxation whatsoever upon them, other than the laws or ordinances of the General Assembly, aforesaid." [31] In Henry's version the word "internal" had not occurred. Rhode Island by inserting it implied that her citizens could disobey an act of Parliament imposing internal taxes but not one imposing external taxes. It should be noted that this distinction did not appear in the assertions of right contained in the preceding resolutions, where the authority of Parliament to tax the colony was denied without qualification. It was only in the summons to rebellion that the Rhode Island Assembly felt obliged to draw back a little. Though their caution on this score was boldness when compared to the stand of the other colonies, which confined themselves to declarations of right, nevertheless the appearance of the word "internal" makes one wonder whether there may not have been a moderate faction in the assembly which would have allowed Parliament a right over external taxes. If there was such a faction, it was not able to insert its views into the resolutions which defined the rights of the colony but only into the one which proposed open rebellion. Moreover, a few weeks later, on November 6, 1765, Rhode Island's popularly-elected governor, Samuel Ward, wrote to General Conway that the colonists were oppressed, because "duties and taxes" were laid upon them without their knowledge or consent.[32]

If the Rhode Island Resolves of 1765 still left some room for doubt on the question of external taxes, the same was not true of the other colonial statements of that year. The Maryland Assembly, on September 28, passed unanimously resolutions denying Parliament's right to tax, in which the only use of the word "internal" was in the familiar phrase "Taxes, and internal Polity." [33] Meanwhile Pennsylvania, on September 21, had drawn up its own set of Resolves, to much the same effect. The first draught of these resolves, written by John Dickinson, included one clause objecting specifically to internal taxes,[34] but in the version finally adopted by the assembly there was no mention of the word "internal." The crucial item read: "Resolved therefore, N.C.D. That the taxation of the people of this province, by any other persons what-

[29] Bartlett, *Records of the Colony of Rhode Island,* VI, 451–452.
[30] *Ibid.,* 452.
[31] *Ibid.*
[32] *Ibid.,* 473.
[33] *Maryland Gazette,* October 3, 1765.
[34] Charles J. Stillé, *The Life and Times of John Dickinson, 1732–1808* (Philadelphia, 1891), 339–340.

soever than such their representatives in assembly, is UNCONSTITUTIONAL, and subversive of their most valuable rights." [35]

Massachusetts, because of the recess of her assembly, did not take action until October, though the newspapers began to agitate for a more spirited statement of rights as soon as they received news of the Virginia Resolves.[36] Accordingly when the assembly was called together in October, it produced a set of resolutions which defined the rights of British subjects and concluded, "that all acts, made by any power whatever, other than the General Assembly of this province, imposing taxes on the inhabitants, are infringements of our inherent and unalienable rights, as men and British subjects; and render void the most valuable declarations of our charter." [37] The Connecticut Assembly likewise cleared up the ambiguity of its earlier statement by a set of resolves modeled partly on those of Virginia and affirming that an act for raising money in the colonies "by duties or taxes" was beyond the authority of Parliament. Connecticut, like Maryland and Rhode Island, included an item copied after the fourth of the Virginia Resolves, in which once again the questionable phrase was rendered as "taxing and internal police." [38]

South Carolina, on November 29, 1765, denied Parliament's right to tax, in a set of eighteen resolves copied from the declarations of the Stamp Act Congress[39] (see below). New York could scarcely state the colonial position more explicitly than she had done the year before, but nevertheless on December 11, 1765, she adopted three more petitions to King, Lords, and Commons, restating the case with the same clarity.[40] New Jersey in the meantime had adopted eleven resolutions copied principally from those of the Stamp Act Congress, with nothing said about internal taxes;[41] and New Hampshire, which did not participate in the Congress, had given formal approval to all the resolutions and petitions of that body.[42]

The Stamp Act Congress had met in New York during October, attended by delegates from Massachusetts, Rhode Island, Connecticut, New York, New Jersey, Pennsylvania, Delaware, Maryland, and South Carolina. These delegates had produced a set of resolutions and three petitions, to the King, the Lords, and the Commons, all denying the authority of Parliament to tax the colonies.[43] Here as in the other formal colonial statements of this year there is no distinction made between internal and external taxes. The Stamp Act Congress has frequently been treated by historians as a rather conservative body of men, possibly because it acknowledged "all

---

[35] J. Almon, ed., *A Collection of interesting, authentic papers, relative to the dispute between Great Britain and America* (London, 1777), 20–21.

[36] See, for example, the *Boston Gazette* of July 8, 1765: "The People of Virginia have spoke very sensibly, and the frozen Politicians of a more northern Government say they have spoke Treason: Their spirited Resolves do indeed serve as a perfect Contrast for a certain, tame, pusillanimous, daub'd, insipid Thing, delicately touch'd up and call'd an Address; which was lately sent from this Side the Water, to please the Taste of the Tools of Corruption on the other." The reference, of course, was to the Massachusetts Address of 1764.

[37] Bradford, *Massachusetts State Papers*, 50–51.

[38] Hoadly, *Public Records of the Colony of Connecticut*, 421–425.

[39] John Drayton, *Memoirs of the American Revolution* (Charleston, S. C., 1821), I, 39–41.

[40] *Journals of the Votes and Proceedings of the General Assembly of the Colony of New York 1743–1765*, II, 795–802.

[41] *New Jersey Archives*, First Series (Paterson, 1902), XXIV, 683–684.

[42] Nathaniel Bouton, ed., *Documents and Records Relating to the Province of New Hampshire* (Nashua, 1873), VII, 92.

[43] Hezekiah Niles, *Principles and Acts of the Revolution* (Baltimore, 1822), 457–460.

due subordination" to Parliament. But as conservatives at the time recognized, this phrase was an empty one unless you stated what subordination was due. It is true that the conservatives, in Massachusetts at least, had hoped to gain control of the Stamp Act Congress.[44] They actually succeeded in securing Timothy Ruggles as one of the Massachusetts delegates, and Governor Bernard wrote at least one letter to Ruggles before the convention urging him to secure submission to the Stamp Act pending its probable repeal.[45] Ruggles remained faithfully conservative, but the true character of the Congress is sufficiently indicated by the fact that, as a conservative, he refused to sign the Resolutions it adopted and was later reprimanded for his refusal by the not-so-conservative Massachusetts House of Representatives.[46] The Stamp Act Congress, in other words, was no less "radical" than the colonial assemblies which sent delegates to it. Though it acknowledged due subordination to Parliament, it denied without qualification the right of Parliament to tax the colonies.

In sum, during the period of the Stamp Act crisis, fifteen formal statements of colonial rights had been issued. Of these only the three early statements by Rhode Island, Connecticut, and Massachusetts could be interpreted as implying an assent to the constitutionality of external taxes. The statement by Massachusetts was clearly not representative of official opinion, and both the Massachusetts and the Connecticut statements were clarified the following year by resolutions which unequivocally rejected the authority of Parliament to tax the colonies at all.

IV

The question suggested by all these declarations of right is: what did the Americans mean when they admitted due subordination to Parliament and at the same time denied Parliament's right to tax them? What subordination was due? If they did not distinguish between internal and external taxes, but denied all authority to tax, what authority did they leave to Parliament?

The answer is given clearly enough in the documents: the colonists allowed the right of Parliament to legislate for the whole empire in any way that concerned the common interests of all the members of the empire (as yet they made no claim that the colonial assemblies were entirely coordinate with Parliament in legislative authority), but they denied that Parliament's legislative authority extended either to the internal polity of the colonies or to taxation. Not all the colonies insisted on exclusive control of internal polity, for Parliament at this time was not attempting to interfere

[44] Governor Bernard wrote to the Lords of Trade on July 8, 1765, that in Massachusetts, where the proposal for the congress initiated, "It was impossible to oppose this measure to any good purpose and therefore the friends of government took the lead in it and have kept it in their hands in pursuance of which of the Committee appointed by this House to meet the other Committees at New York on 1st of October next. Two of the three are fast friends to government prudent and discreet men such as I am assured will never consent to any undutiful or improper application to the Government of Great Britain." (Sparks Manuscripts 43: British Manuscripts, IV, Harvard College Library).

[45] Bernard Papers, IV, 72. The letter is dated September 28, 1765.

[46] *Boston Gazette*, Feb. 17, 1766. The membership of the Stamp Act Congress has been analysed in an unpublished paper by Mr. David S. Lovejoy, in which it is indicated that of the twenty-seven members only two are known to have become Tories at the time of the Revolution.

in this department. The issue of the day was taxation, and what the colonies insisted on most vigorously was that Parliament's supreme legislative authority did not include the right to tax. Taxation and legislation, they said, were separate functions and historically had always been treated as such. Legislation was a function of sovereignty; and as the sovereign body of the empire, Parliament had absolute legislative authority. Under this authority Parliament was entirely justified in regulating the trade and commerce of the empire. There was, in other words, nothing unconstitutional about the Acts of Trade and Navigation. But taxes were something else. Taxes were the "free gift" of the people who paid them, and as such could be levied only by a body which represented the people. As far as Great Britain was concerned the House of Commons was a representative body and could therefore tax the people of Great Britain; but since the colonists were not, and from their local circumstances could not be, represented in Parliament, they could not be taxed by Parliament. The only body with a constitutional right to tax them was a colonial assembly, in which the people upon whom the tax would fall would be represented. Thus the Connecticut Assembly in October, 1765, resolved,

> That, in the opinion of this House, an act for raising money by duties or taxes differs from other acts of legislation, in that it is always considered as a free gift of the people made by their legal and elected representatives; and that we cannot conceive that the people of Great Britain, or their representatives, have right to dispose of our property.[47]

According to this distinction the power to levy taxes even in Great Britain was limited to the House of Commons, the representative part of Parliament. The petition from the General Assembly of New York to the House of Commons, December 11, 1765, while expressing "all due submission to the supreme Authority of the *British* Legislature," affirmed

> That all parliamentary Aids in *Great-Britain,* are the free Gifts of the People by their Representatives, consented to by the Lords, and accepted by the Crown, and therefore every Act imposing them, essentially differs from every other Statute, having the Force of a Law in no other Respect than the Manner thereby prescribed for levying the Gift.
>
> That agreeable to this Distinction, the House of Commons has always contended for and enjoyed the constitutional Right of originating all Money Bills, as well in Aid of the Crown, as for other Purposes.
>
> That all Supplies to the Crown being in their Nature free Gifts, it would, as we humbly conceive, be unconstitutional for the People of *Great-Britain,* by their Representatives in Parliament, to dispose of the Property of Millions of his Majesty's Subjects, who are not, and cannot be there represented.[48]

It was this distinction which the members of the Stamp Act Congress had in mind when they acknowledged "due subordination" to Parliament, for they asked in their petition to the House of Commons,

> Whether there be not a material Distinction in Reason and sound Policy, at least, between the necessary Exercise of Parliamentary Jurisdiction in general Acts, for

[47] *Public Records of the Colony of Connecticut,* XII, 423.

[48] *Journal of the Votes and Proceedings of the General Assembly of the Colony of New York 1743–1765,* II, 800.

the Amendment of the Common Law, and the Regulation of Trade and Commerce through the whole Empire, and the Exercise of that Jurisdiction by imposing Taxes on the Colonies.[49]

V

Most members of Parliament would have answered this query with a flat denial that the power of taxation could be distinguished from that of legislation. Taxation, they would have said, was inseparable from sovereignty. But there were some members willing to speak in favor of the colonial view. In the debate on the Declaratory Act in the House of Commons the question arose over a motion made by Colonel Barré to omit from the act the phrase "in all cases whatsoever." This motion was intended to exclude Parliament's authority to tax the colonies, and in the debate which followed, Barré and William Pitt the elder argued for the motion in much the same terms as were used in the colonial statements. Visitors were not admitted to Parliament during this session, so that few accounts of the debate have been preserved, but according to Charles Garth, member for Devizes borough, Wiltshire, and agent for several of the southern colonies, the speakers for Barré's motion contended: "That the Principles of Taxation as distinguished from Legislation were as distinct Principles and Powers as any two Propositions under the Sun." The speakers cited the precedents of the counties palatine of Chester and Durham which had been subject to Parliament's legislative authority but had not been taxed until they were represented. The clergy, it was pointed out, taxed themselves separately but did not have separate legislative power. Another indication that the two functions were separate was that taxes were the free gift of the Commons, and tax bills could not be considered by the Lords or the King until the Commons had made a grant. Other bills remained in the Upper House for the King's signature, but tax bills were sent back to the Commons, whose speaker presented them to the King as the free gift of the Commons. All this, it was said, showed that Parliament might legislate as the supreme authority of the realm but that it taxed only in its representative capacity. Since the colonies were not represented in Parliament, they could not constitutionally be taxed by Parliament.[50] In the House of Lords, Lord Camden argued the case to the same effect.[51]

In spite of these arguments Parliament decided by an overwhelming majority[52] to include the words "in all cases whatsoever," and thereby, as far as Parliament was concerned, it was concluded that taxation and legislation were not separate functions and that Parliament's authority over the colonies included the right to tax. But strangely enough the Declaratory Act did not include any explicit statement of the right to tax, so that the colonists could not have recognized that Parliament was deny-

---

[49] *Proceedings of the Congress at New York* (Annapolis, 1766), 23. The reprint of the proceedings in Niles, *Principles and Acts of the Revolution* is inaccurate at this point.

[50] Garth's account is in *Maryland Historical Magazine,* VI, 287–305. Another account is in *American Historical Review,* XVII, 565–574.

[51] *Archives of Maryland* (Baltimore, 1895), XIV, 267–268.

[52] *Maryland Historical Magazine,* VI, 300; *Archives of Maryland,* XIV, 280; Sir John Fortescue, ed., *The Correspondence of King George the Third* (London, 1927), I, 254.

ing their position. What the act said was that the King in Parliament had "full power and authority to make laws and statutes of sufficient force and validity to bind the colonies and people of *America,* subjects of the crown of *Great Britain,* in all cases whatsoever." [53] Though the members of Parliament knew that the words "in all cases whatsoever" meant in cases of taxation, there is nothing in the act itself to give the words that meaning. Nor was the ambiguity entirely accidental. When the act was being drawn up, Charles Yorke, the attorney general, suggested that the crucial phrase should read "as well in cases of Taxation, as in all other cases whatsoever." But when he submitted this suggestion to Rockingham, who was then prime minister, Rockingham thought it impolitic to make any mention of the word "taxation." "I think I may say," he wrote to Yorke, "that it is our firm Resolution in the House of Lords—I mean among ourselves—that that word must be resisted." [54] Thus the omission of any mention of taxation was deliberate. By supporting the act as it stood, with the resounding but ambiguous phrase "in all cases whatsoever," the Rockingham government could gain support in Parliament by encouraging the members to beat the drum of Parliamentary power—behind closed doors—without giving offense to the colonies.

The colonies can hardly be blamed then for not getting the point of the Declaratory Act. They had not generally been informed of the debate which had taken place over the words "in all cases whatsoever," [55] and since the act was accompanied by the repeal of Parliament's most conspicuous attempt to tax them, they might very well interpret it as a simple assertion of legislative authority with no necessary implication of a right to tax. They knew that the Declaratory Act was a copy of the earlier statute of 6 George I regarding Ireland. And they knew also that in spite of this statute Ireland had not been taxed by Parliament. The Massachusetts Assembly even before passage of the Stamp Act had argued from the example of Ireland that the colonies might be dependent on England without allowing England a right to tax them.[56] After passage of the Declaratory Act the Massachusetts agent in London, Richard Jackson, encouraged Massachusetts to believe that the same reasoning was still valid, for he wrote to Governor Bernard that the act would probably affect the colonies as little "as the Power we claim in Ireland, the manner of exercising which you are acquainted with." [57] The same view was expressed by Daniel Dulany of Maryland in a letter to General Conway. According to Dulany the Declaratory Act could not imply a power to tax, because if it did, then the act of 6 George I must give authority to tax Ireland, and such authority had never been claimed or exercised.[58] Thus the fact, so often remarked by historians, that the colonists took little notice of the Declaratory Act does not mean that the colonists were indifferent to the question of principle. They simply did not recognize the Act as a challenge to their views. They could acquiesce

[53] Danby Pickering, ed., *The Statutes at Large* (Cambridge, England, 1767), XXVII, 20.

[54] British Museum Additional Manuscripts 35430, ff. 37–38 (Rockingham's letter). The exchange of correspondence between Yorke and Rockingham is printed, in part in George Thomas, Earl of Albemarle, *Memoirs of the Marquis of Rockingham* (London, 1852), I, 285–288. The date of Yorke's letter is not given. Rockingham's letter is dated January 25, 1766.

[55] So far as I have been able to discover Garth's account was the only one sent to the colonies, and it was not published at the time.

[56] Massachusetts Archives, XXII, 415. The argument is made in the petition to the King passed by the House of Representatives on October 22, 1764, and non-concurred by the Council.

[57] *Ibid.,* f. 458. The letter is dated March 3, 1766.

[58] Sparks Manuscripts 44, bundle 7, ff. 10–11. The letter is not dated.

in it with a clear conscience and without inconsistency, unaware that their interpretation differed radically from that held in Parliament.[59]

VI

Unfortunately this misunderstanding on the part of the Americans was matched by a similar misunderstanding on the part of many people in England with regard to the colonial position. We have seen that the American protests against the Stamp Act did not distinguish between internal and external taxes but denied that Parliament had any right to tax the colonies. Yet some Englishmen, at least, thought that the American protests were directed only against internal taxes. The American misunderstanding of the Declaratory Act is explicable by the vagueness of the act itself, the absence of any official interpretation of it, and the fact that the Parliamentary debate on it had been closed to the public. But the colonial statements had all been communicated to the British government by the beginning of the year 1766, before Parliament began to consider repeal of the Stamp Act. Why then did Englishmen suppose that the Americans distinguished between internal and external taxes?

Of course not all Englishmen did suppose so; those who took the trouble to read the colonial statements knew better. But apparently many Englishmen, including members of Parliament, did not take that trouble. It should be remembered that the colonial petitions were never formally considered by Parliament. Those sent before passage of the Stamp Act were thrown out because of the procedural rule against receiving petitions on money bills. Those sent for repeal of the Act were excluded for other procedural reasons and because they called the authority of Parliament into question. Thus although the contents of the statements could doubtless have been learned by anyone who wished to discover them, they were never given a regular hearing in Parliament.[60]

In the absence of any direct acquaintance with the colonial statements the average member of Parliament must have gained his impressions from one of two sources: either from the multitude of pamphlets dealing with the Stamp Act or from speeches in Parliament. It is possible but not probable that the authors of pamphlets against the Stamp Act were responsible for creating the impression that the Americans did not object to external taxes. We have already observed an ambiguity in the two pamphlets by Stephen Hopkins and John Fitch which received the approval of Rhode Island and Connecticut respectively in 1764. Both these pamphlets used the phrase "internal taxes" in such a way as to suggest that external taxes might be constitutionally acceptable, though neither Hopkins nor Fitch explicitly said as much. Two other pamphlets, which enjoyed a wide circulation though not a formal legislative approval, also used the words "internal taxes" in a way which may have helped

[59] George Grenville wrote that the Americans were justified in rejoicing at the repeal of the Stamp Act "especially if they understand by it, as they justly may, notwithstanding the Declaratory Bill passed at the same time, that they are hereby exempted for ever from being taxed by Great Britain for the public support even of themselves." William J. Smith, ed., *The Grenville Papers* (London, 1853), III, 250.

[60] *Collections of the Connecticut Historical Society*, XVIII, 332–335; *Maryland Historical Magazine*, VI, 282–288.

to bring about a misunderstanding of the American position. Richard Bland in *An Inquiry into the Rights of the British Colonies*[61] demonstrated that the colonists could not constitutionally be subjected to an internal tax by act of Parliament. Anyone reading Bland's conclusions without reading the argument leading to them might get the impression that Bland would have agreed to Parliament's collection of a revenue from customs duties levied in the colonies; but Bland's demonstration of his conclusion showed that Parliament could not constitutionally charge duties in the colony upon either imports or exports. In fact, he even argued that the Navigation Acts were unconstitutional. Bland evidently included in the phrase "internal taxes" the very duties which other people called "external taxes."

Another pamphlet which objected specifically to internal taxes was Daniel Dulany's *Considerations on the Propriety of imposing Taxes in the British Colonies.*[62] This probably had a wider circulation than any other pamphlet against the Stamp Act, and it has frequently been cited as the source of the distinction between internal and external taxes. Although the greater part of Dulany's pamphlet was devoted to general arguments against the constitutionality of Parliamentary taxation, there were a few paragraphs in which he implied that internal taxes alone were unconstitutional. Thus he argued, on page 33, that before the Stamp Act, Parliament had never "imposed an internal Tax upon the Colonies *for the single Purpose of Revenue.*" He went on to deny the contention, which he attributed to the proponents of the Stamp Act, "That no Distinction can be supported between one Kind of Tax and another, an Authority to impose the one extending to the other." Contrary to this erroneous view, he said, "It appears to me, that there is a clear and necessary Distinction between an Act imposing a Tax *for the single Purpose of Revenue,* and those Acts which have been made for the Regulation of Trade, and have produced some Revenue in *Consequence of their Effect* and Operation as *Regulations of Trade.*" According to this distinction Parliament had the right to regulate trade by the imposition of duties, even though those duties should incidentally produce some revenue. Dulany closed the discussion of this point by affirming: "a Right to impose an internal Tax on the Colonies without their consent, *for the single Purpose of Revenue,* is denied; a Right to regulate their Trade without their Consent is admitted."

It will be observed that in the course of this discussion, which occupied two pages of the pamphlet, Dulany had not made entirely clear what he regarded as constitutional and what he considered unconstitutional. He said that internal taxes for the purpose of revenue were unconstitutional, and he said that duties on trade for the purpose of regulation were constitutional, even though an incidental revenue might attend them, but he failed to say explicitly how he regarded duties on trade for the single purpose of revenue. He failed, in other words, to say how he stood on external taxes; in fact he did not even use the words "external tax" at any point in the pamphlet. His readers would perhaps have been justified in thinking that Dulany admitted external taxes as constitutional, since he explicitly objected only to internal taxes. Yet, unless Dulany was simply confused about the matter, it would appear that in his use of the phrase "internal tax" he included all duties levied in the colonies for the single purpose of revenue. In no other way does Dulany's argument make sense, for he contrasted what he called an internal tax for the single purpose of

[61] Williamsburg, 1766.
[62] Annapolis, 1765 (second edition). The succeeding quotations are taken from pp. 30–35.

revenue with duties for the purpose of regulation from which an incidental revenue might arise. The context indicates clearly that the point of the contrast was not the difference between internal taxes as opposed to duties on trade but the difference between an imposition for the purpose of regulation and one for the purpose of revenue. Dulany emphasized the contrast by italicising the phrases: *single purpose of revenue, incidental Revenue,* and *Regulations of Trade.* The whole force of the contrast is lost unless the phrase "internal tax" is taken to include duties on trade collected in the colonies for the purpose of revenue. That this was Dulany's understanding of the term is further indicated in the two paragraphs which follow those summarized above. Here Dulany demonstrated that the duties on trade which had hitherto been collected in the colony had been levied not for the purpose of revenue but for the purpose of regulating trade. The argument which he used to carry this point was drawn from the fact that the customs duties collected in North America brought only £1,900 a year into the treasury while they cost £7,600 a year to collect. Dulany had taken these figures from a pamphlet by Grenville himself. He concluded with some justice that

> It would be ridiculous indeed to suppose, that the Parliament would raise a Revenue by Taxes in the Colonies to defray Part of the national Expence, the Collection of which Taxes would increase that Expence to a Sum more than three Times the Amount of the Revenue; but, the Impositions being considered in their true Light, as Regulations of Trade, the Expence arising from an Establishment necessary to carry them into Execution, is so far from being ridiculous, that it may be wisely incurred.

Thus Dulany demonstrated that Parliament could not levy what he called an internal tax for the purpose of revenue by showing that Parliament had never levied an external tax for the purpose of revenue. The conclusion seems inescapable that he used the phrase "internal tax" in a loose sense, to cover all taxes collected in the colonies, whether excise taxes or customs duties levied for the single purpose of revenue. That this was his meaning is also suggested by the remainder of the pamphlet, in which he argued against Parliamentary taxation in general terms, as when he stated that "the Inhabitants of the Colonies claim an Exemption from *all* Taxes not imposed by their own Consent." (The italics are Dulany's.)

Dulany's pamphlet, though it was widely acclaimed as a defense of colonial rights, certainly employed a confusing terminology, and it would not be surprising if Englishmen at the time had gained the impression that there was some sort of distinction in it between the constitutionality of internal taxes as opposed to that of customs duties. Though Dulany never used the phrase "external tax" and though most of the pamphlet will make sense only if his use of the phrase "internal tax" is taken to include all taxes collected in the colonies, yet if American historians have derived the impression that he distinguished between internal and external taxes, it is not unreasonable to suppose that contemporary Englishmen received the same impression.

What does seem unlikely, however, is that British statesmen would have assumed, as American historians frequently seem to do, that Daniel Dulany was the proper spokesman for all the colonies. His pamphlet was only one of many, and the others ranged in attitude from complete submission to the authority of Parliament (as in Martin Howard's *Letter from a Gentleman at Halifax, to His Friend in Rhode Island* [63])

[63] Newport, 1765.

to complete defiance of Parliament (as in the *Considerations upon the Rights of the Colonists to the Privileges of British Subjects*[64]). Most of the pamphlets against the Stamp Act refrained from discussing the question of constitutional right and argued on the grounds of inexpediency or equity.[65] Those which concerned themselves with the constitutional aspects of the question devoted a major part of their attention to the doctrine of virtual representation.[66] This was an easy target, and in centering the constitutional controversy upon it the American protagonists gained a tactical victory; for when their opponents argued that the Americans might be taxed because they were virtually represented, this was tantamount to admitting that the power to tax depended upon representation. Daniel Dulany put his finger on the weakness of the ministerial position when he wrote to General Conway,

> If the right to tax and the right to regulate had been imagined by Mr. Grenville to be inseparable why did he tax his ingenuity to find out a virtual Representation, why did not some able friend intimate to him his Hazard on the slippery ground, he chose, when the all powerful Sovereignty of Parliament might have afforded so safe a footing? [67]

In other words Grenville himself, by arguing for virtual representation (as he did in *The Regulations Lately Made concerning the Colonies, and the Taxes Imposed upon Them, considered* [68]), had admitted that taxation was not a function of sovereignty but rather, as the colonies were contending, the prerogative of a representative body.

There was no reason why the pamphleteers on the American side should have made a distinction between internal and external taxes when arguing the case against virtual representation; and it is not surprising that with the possible exception of those discussed above, none of them seems to have employed the distinction for purposes of argument. The distinction did appear in some of the literature in support of the Stamp Act, where it served as a whipping boy. It was attributed to the Americans and then demolished under the heavy gunfire of constitutional history.[69] It hardly

[64] New York, 1766.

[65] See for example: John Dickinson's *The Late Regulations Respecting the British Colonies on the Continent of America Considered* (London, 1765); *A Letter to a Member of Parliament, Wherein the Power of the British Legislature, and the Case of the Colonists, Are briefly and impartially considered* (London, 1765); *The true Interest of Great Britain, with respect to her American Colonies, Stated and Impartially Considered* (London, 1766); *The Importance of the Colonies of North America, and the Interest of Great Britain with regard to them, Considered* (London, 1766); *The Necessity of Repealing the American Stamp Act Demonstrated* (London, 1766); *The Late Occurrences in North America, and Policy of Great Britain, Considered* (London, 1766); and Benjamin Franklin's *The General Opposition of the Colonies to the Payment of the Stamp Duty; and the Consequence of Enforcing Obedience by Military Measures; Impartially Considered* (London, 1766).

[66] See for example: Samuel Cooper, *The Crisis. Or, a Full Defense of the Colonies* (London, 1766), 3–30; Maurice Moore, *The Justice and Policy of Taxing the American Colonies, in Great Britain, Considered* (Wilmington, N. C., 1765), 7–14; Richard Bland, *An Inquiry into the Rights of the British Colonies* (Williamsburg, 1766), 5–12. Daniel Dulany, *Considerations on the Propriety of imposing Taxes in the British Colonies* (Annapolis, 1765), 5–14.

[67] Sparks Manuscripts 44, bundle 7, f. 10.

[68] London, 1765.

[69] See *The Rights of Parliament Vindicated, On Occasion of the late Stamp-Act. In which is exposed the conduct of the American Colonists* (London, 1766): *An Examination of the Rights of the Colonies upon Principles of Law* (London, 1766).

seems likely that the defenders of the Stamp Act would have attributed the distinction to the Americans simply in order to discredit the colonial position. It is much more likely that they and the members of Parliament really believed that the colonists did distinguish between internal and external taxes. The question remains as to how they gained this impression.

The source from which, in all probability, it was derived was the speeches made in Parliament by friends of the colonies during the debates on repeal of the Stamp Act and afterwards, not excepting the brilliant interview given at the bar of the House of Commons by Benjamin Franklin. The member of Parliament who heard that carefully rehearsed performance (or who read it afterwards in print) might very justly have concluded that the Americans had no objection to external taxes, for Franklin, the arch-American, at several points had stated that the Americans objected only to internal taxes.[70] When a member had pointed out that the objection to internal taxes could with equal justice be applied to external taxes, Franklin had replied that the Americans did not reason in that way at present but that they might learn to do so from the English. The wit of Franklin's tongue obscured the fact that he was wrong, but the average member could scarcely have known that. Laughing at Franklin's clever answers, he would probably have forgotten the rather pertinent question put by a member of the opposition: "Do not the resolutions of the Pennsylvania Assembly say, all taxes?" This question was evidently asked by a member who knew something about Pennsylvania's attitude. Franklin's answer to it was not as sprightly as his replies to some of the other questions. The best he could say was that if the Pennsylvania resolutions said all taxes, they meant only internal taxes. Actually it would have been impossible to tell from Franklin's testimony exactly what he thought the constitutional position of the Americans to be. At times he seemed to be saying that the Americans assented to external taxes; at other times he implied that they consented only to the regulation of trade. The performance was a good piece of lobbying for repeal of the Stamp Act, but it gave no clear indication of the American position and certainly could have contributed to the idea that the Americans were willing to accept external taxes.

The speeches of Franklin's friend Richard Jackson, member of Parliament for Weymouth, and agent at various times for Pennsylvania, Connecticut, and Massachusetts, may also have contributed to a false impression of the colonial position. Jackson believed that Parliament had a clear right to tax the colonies by duties on trade. Since Parliament by its admitted right to regulate trade could prohibit any branch of colonial trade, he reasoned, Parliament could also tax any branch of colonial trade.[71] Jackson, moreover, had searched the precedents thoroughly and found that Parliament in the past had imposed external taxes on the trade of Chester and Durham and Wales before those areas were represented in Parliament. At the same time Parliament had refrained from taxing them internally until they were granted representation. When Jackson rehearsed these views before Parliament,[72] he must

[70] William Cobbett, ed., *Parliamentary History of England, from the Earliest Period to the Year 1803* (London, 1813), XVI, 137–160.

[71] Carl Van Doren, ed., *Letters and Papers of Benjamin Franklin and Richard Jackson 1753–1785* (Philadelphia, 1947), 123–124, 138–139.

[72] *Ibid.*, 194–196; *Collections of the Connecticut Historical Society*, XVIII, 316; Bradford, *Massachusetts State Papers*, 72–73.

have been listened to as a man of some authority; for he had the reputation of being extraordinarily learned,[73] and he was, besides, the official agent for several colonies. The average member of Parliament could not have known that he had been elected agent for Massachusetts by the political maneuvers of the royal governor,[74] nor that the Connecticut Assembly had written him a letter deploring his insufficient insistence upon colonial rights,[75] nor that he owed his appointment in Pennsylvania to his friend Benjamin Franklin, who had also misrepresented the colonial position.[76]

What must also have impressed the uninformed member was the famous speech by William Pitt, when the Great Commoner had come out of his retirement to urge the repeal of the Stamp act. On this occasion, Pitt had risen to a statement by George Grenville in which the latter had complained that he could not understand the distinction between internal and external taxes. "If the gentleman does not understand the difference between internal and external taxes," said Pitt, "I cannot help it." [77] Pitt's reply, if left there, might have been somewhat misleading. Anyone who listened to the whole of what he had to say would have known that Pitt, like the colonists, was distinguishing, not between internal and external taxes but between taxation and legislation. In an earlier speech he had stated that "Taxation is no part of the governing or legislative power," [78] and now he went on to argue that "there is a plain distinction between taxes levied for the purposes of raising a revenue, and duties imposed for the regulation of trade, for the accommodation of the subject; although, in the consequences, some revenue might incidentally arise from the latter." [79] Pitt was following the argument of Dulany, whom he had read and admired;[80] and if historians have misunderstood Dulany's argument, it is not unlikely that the members of Parliament may have misunderstood Pitt's. Though there was a manifest difference between Pitt's and Dulany's acceptance of trade regulations which might incidentally produce a revenue and Jackson's and Franklin's acceptance of external taxes as such, nevertheless all four men were arguing in behalf of the colonies. The average member may have lumped them all together and come out with the simple conclusion that Americans accepted external taxes.

This conclusion would have been strengthened a little later by a speech of Thomas Pownall. Pownall, speaking with some authority as the former governor of Massachusetts, said explicitly that the colonists *"never objected to external taxes*—to imposts, subsidies and duties. They know that the express conditions of their settlements and establishments were, that they should pay these—and therefore they never have had any disputes with government on this head—but have always found reason to be satisfied *in the moderation with which government hath exercised this power."* [81]

[73] Van Doren, *Letters and Papers of Benjamin Franklin and Richard Jackson,* 1–2.

[74] Bernard Papers, III, 277–283.

[75] *Collections of the Connecticut Historical Society,* XVIII, 366–367.

[76] Van Doren, *Letters and Papers of Benjamin Franklin and Richard Jackson,* 87, 100.

[77] *Parliamentary History,* XVI, 105.

[78] *Ibid.,* 99.

[79] *Ibid.,* 105.

[80] W. S. Taylor and J. H. Pringle, eds., *The Chatham Correspondence* (London, 1838–40), III, 192; Moses C. Tyler, *The Literary History of the American Revolution 1763–1783* (New York, 1941), 111 and n.

[81] *The Speech of Th-m-s P-n-ll, Esq* . . . *in the H—se of C—m-ns, in favor of America* (Boston, 1769), 12.

Pownall had apparently never read any of the colonial statements. Perhaps he derived some of his ideas from his friend Benjamin Franklin.[82] Certainly his authority to represent the views of the colonists was long since out of date. But how was the average member to know that? All the friends of America in Parliament seemed to be of opinion that the Americans were resigned to external taxes.

Why the colonial advocates in Parliament should have joined in conveying so false an impression of the colonial position is not entirely clear. A number of reasons might be offered why Pownall or Jackson or Pitt argued as they did: Pownall may have been misinformed;[83] Jackson may have been speaking for himself rather than for the colonies; and Pitt was misunderstood. But Franklin's testimony is more difficult to explain, for Franklin must have been better acquainted with the colonial declarations than he appeared to be. Why should he have contributed to the general misunderstanding? Furthermore why should all the proponents of colonial rights have misrepresented the colonies in the same way?

In the absence of direct information one can only suggest that political circumstances in 1766 required that every friend of the colonies in England refrain from urging the extreme claims put forward by the colonial assemblies and join in representing the colonies as more moderate than they actually were. The immediate object in 1766 was the repeal of the Stamp Act, and repeal was not to be attained by blunt denials of Parliament's authority. Though the colonists seemed to be unaware of this fact and continued on their intransigent course, their friends in England had to seek support where they could find it. They found it in the Rockingham administration, and consequently when they argued for repeal of the Stamp Act, they argued in Rockingham's terms. Now Rockingham's terms, to judge from at least one account, were a recognition of the distinction between internal and external taxes. According to Charles Garth the administration refused to hear the petition of the Stamp Act Congress, because "it tended to question not only the Right of Parliament to impose internal Taxes, but external Duties." [84] Rockingham, it would appear, was prepared to settle the colonial issue by leaving internal taxes to the colonial assemblies. Though this was not as much as the colonies demanded, it was more than the rest of Parliament was willing to give, for most members were as ready to assert Parliament's right to levy all taxes as the colonists were to deny it.[85] Rockingham in fact was unable to repeal the Stamp Act on the basis of the distinction between internal and external taxes. Instead he was obliged to agree to the Declaratory Act, though worded in the

[82] Pownall cooperated with Franklin on a scheme for raising money in the colonies by interest-bearing paper currency. This scheme was proposed by Franklin as a substitute for the Stamp Tax. For details see V. W. Crane, "Benjamin Franklin and the Stamp Act" *Publications of the Colonial Society of Massachusetts,* XXXII, 56–78. On Pownall's participation, see Pownall's letter to Hutchinson, Dec. 3, 1765, in Massachusetts Archives, XXV, 113.

[83] That Pownall was an unreliable source of information is suggested by the fact that he himself had suggested a stamp tax in his book *The Administration of the Colonies.* Dennys De Berdt later wrote that he was "as irresolute as the Wind, in one days debate a friend to America the next quite with the Ministry." (*Publications of the Colonial Society of Massachusetts,* XIII, 377–378.)

[84] *Maryland Historical Magazine,* VI, 285.

[85] This fact was reported to the colonists in several letters. See, for example, that of Jared Ingersoll in *Collections of the Connecticut Historical Society,* XVIII, 317–326, and that of Richard Jackson in *ibid.,* 349–351.

ambiguous terms already noticed.[86] Rockingham, it is plain, needed all the support he could get, for he could not carry the rest of Parliament even as far as he and his own group were willing to go. In these circumstances it would have been undiplomatic, not to say reckless, for the friends of the colonies to embarrass him by insisting on the politically impossible claims of the colonial declarations. It seems unlikely that there was any formal agreement between the Rockingham group and the other colonial protagonists, whereby the latter agreed to soft-pedal the colonial claims to exclusive powers of taxation, but the pressure of politics undoubtedly dissuaded the friends of the colonies from giving publicity to the colonial declarations, and probably led them to cooperate with Rockingham in adopting a distinction which the colonists would never have allowed.

One conclusion in any case is clear: it was not the Americans who drew the line between internal and external taxes. It was recognized in America at the time by such diverse political personalities as James Otis and Thomas Hutchinson that the distinction was an English one. Otis, as already noticed, in the pamphlet approved by the Massachusetts assembly in 1764, scouted the distinction as one that "some make in England." [87] Hutchinson, in the third volume of his history of Massachusetts, gave credit for it to Pitt. Though it is clear that Pitt did not originate it, Hutchinson evidently thought that he did and was equally certain that the Americans did not accept it; for he averred that in levying the Townshend duties, "government in England too easily presumed, that Mr. Pit's distinction between internal and external taxes would be favourably received in America." [88] There were members of Parliament in England, too, who realized that the distinction was not an American one, for in the debates on the Declaratory Act, Hans Stanley, the member for Southampton, embarrassed the Rockingham administration by pointing out that "The Americans have not made the futile Distinction between internal and external taxes," [89] and Lord Lyttelton did the same thing in the House of Lords in the debate on the repeal of the Stamp Act, when he stated that "The Americans themselves make no distinction between external and internal taxes." [90] The colonial agents also realized that the colonists were talking bigger at home than their friends in England would admit, and the agents repeatedly requested their constituents to be less noisy about their rights. The colonists in return instructed the agents to be more noisy about them.[91]

The colonists were bumptious, blunt, and lacking in diplomacy, but they were not guilty of the constitutional frivolity with which they have been charged. When they objected to the Townshend Duties in 1767, they had in no way changed the concep-

[86] Dennys De Berdt wrote to Samuel White at the time of repeal that there were three parties in Parliament so far as the Stamp Act was concerned, one for enforcing, one for repeal with a declaration of right, and one for repeal without a declaration. According to De Berdt the administration favored the last view but was obliged to take the middle position in order to gain a majority. (*Publications of the Colonial Society of Massachusetts*, XIII, 311–312.)

[87] *The Rights of the British Colonies asserted and proved* (Boston, 1764), 42.

[88] L. S. Mayo, ed., *History of the Province of Massachusetts Bay* (Cambridge, Mass., 1936), III, 130.

[89] *American Historical Review*, XVII, 566.

[90] *Parliamentary History*, XVI, 167.

[91] *Collections of the Connecticut Historical Society*, XVIII, 349–351, 366–367; *Collections of the Massachusetts Historical Society*, LXXIV, 39–54, 145–146; Massachusetts Archives, XXII, 361–363; *Publications of the Colonial Society of Massachusetts*, XIII, 332–333, 335, 337, 354.

tion of Parliamentary power which they avowed at the time of the Stamp Act: they still admitted the authority of Parliament to regulate trade and to legislate in other ways for the whole empire; they still denied that Parliament had a right to tax them. These views they continued to affirm until the 1770's when they advanced to the more radical position of denying the authority of Parliament to legislate as well as to tax. Though this denial was generally accompanied by an allowance of Parliamentary legislation as a matter of convenience, there can be no question that the later position was constitutionally different from the earlier one. But that the colonists were guilty of skipping from one constitutional theory to another, like so many grasshoppers, is a Tory libel that has too readily been accepted by modern historians. American Revolutionary thought went through two stages, not three; the supposed first stage never existed. If anyone took a more advanced position because of the passage of the Townshend Duties, it was not the colonists. They were already there.

7 / John Adams: The American Revolution as a Change of Heart?

John W. Ellsworth

Many years after the accomplishment of American Independence, John Adams wrote of that earlier period of his life:

> . . . what do we mean by the American Revolution? Do we mean the American War? The Revolution was affected before the war commenced. The Revolution was in the minds and hearts of the people. . . . This radical change in the principles, opinions, sentiments, and affectations of the people, was the real American Revolution.

Adams here suggested that the necessary preliminary change in the allegiance of the colonists away from their loyalty to George III and to Great Britain took place in the decade or more before 1776 and that the events of 1774 to 1776 simply provided the occasion for the Americans to proclaim that they were no longer bound by their old allegiances. The process by which Americans moved from their professions of devotion to the King in 1763 to their denunciation of him 13 years later and to their total abandonment of monarchial principles was not a process of simple, progressive alienation from the home country and its institutions. Rather it was a process with many ups and downs, of faith alternating with disillusionment with the government of Great Britain. In the following pages, John Ellsworth examines this growing dissatisfaction as it was expressed in John Adams' contemporary writings (and not as he recorded it, sometimes inaccurately, in his later accounts). Ellsworth notes that, while other events influenced Adams' thought, the two crucial controversies affecting his loyalties were those over the Stamp Act and the Coercive Acts. Even in the mind of this foremost leader of the new nation, there was a long struggle between his traditional loyalties and his new fears and anger over British actions.

For further reading: Richard L. Merritt, *Symbols of American Community, 1733–1775* (1966); Verner W. Crane, *Benjamin Franklin, English-*

Reprinted by permission from *The Huntington Library Quarterly*, XXVIII (1965), 293–300.

man or American (1936); Carl Van Doren, *Benjamin Franklin* (1938); Paul Varg, "The Advent of Nationalism," *American Quarterly*, XVI (1964), 169–181.

John Adams has lent much support to those historians who interpret the American Revolution as caused by slow changes in the sentiments of the American colonists. The main source of this interpretation, in Adams' writings, is a letter addressed to Dr. J. Morse in 1815.[1] Here Adams remarked that the Revolutionary War was only an effect of a previous revolution that had taken place in the "minds and hearts of the people, and in the union of the colonies; both of which were substantially effected before hostilities commenced."[2] In other papers written after his retirement from the presidency in 1801, Adams further developed this view.

If his writings are pieced together, a gradualist, psychological interpretation of the events leading to the war can be constructed, which emphasizes two general propositions regarding the American Revolution. First, it was a revolution in sentiment, a change of heart. Secondly, it was a revolution produced by words, presumably words which were written largely by the hard core of Massachusettsmen who had steadily resisted English policies prior to 1776. The revolution did not proceed steadily, building to a climax in 1775–1776, according to Adams. Revolutionary sentiment rather came to a peak in 1766 and afterward declined. He calls 1760–1766 the "purest period of patriotism," in contrast to 1766–1776, which he labels the "period of corruption" (X, 197–198). During this period, colonial Tories were successful in winning support through "address, intrigue, artifice, and stratagem." "Nearly one-third" of the colonists were "deluded" (X, 193).

After his retirement from the presidency, then, Adams emphasized what we would today call "public opinion." He held that it was largely the actions of propagandists and legislators which had produced the revolutionary spirit in America. He portrayed revolutionary sentiment as peaking at the time of the Stamp Act and gradually dwindling from 1766 to 1776. Despite this "corruption" of revolutionary strength, sentiment favoring a union of the colonies and eventually a separation from Britain somehow crystallized before the first shots of the war were fired.

This interpretation has the clear defect that it does not explain why, if sentiment was eroded in the ten years preceding the Declaration of Independence, the revolu-

[1] Clinton Rossiter, *Seedtime of the Republic* (New York, 1953), and Max Savelle, *Seeds of Liberty* (New York, 1948), are two recent volumes attempting the type of history of opinion that Adams suggested to Dr. Morse. The "Imperial School" emphasizes the idea of maturing American colonists clashing with the devices of imperial control; e.g., L. H. Gipson employs the Morse letter of Nov. 1815 in *The Coming of the Revolution* (New York, 1954), p. 231, and follows the main Adams hypothesis through much of his work. John C. Miller, while ascribing importance to the writing of that era, points out that only the events of the times made the writings significant; *Origins of the American Revolution* (Boston, 1943). Such analyses as Edmund S. Morgan's *Birth of the Republic* (Chicago, 1956) and Oliver M. Dickerson's *The Navigation Acts and the American Revolution* (Philadelphia, 1951) place even more emphasis upon British policies as causes of the revolutionary temper of the American colonists.

[2] *The Works of John Adams*, ed. Charles Francis Adams (Boston, 1850–56), X, 182, 172–173, 197, 282. Future references to this source are indicated by parenthetical notes in the text, containing the volume and pages cited.

tion took place then, rather in 1766 at the height of pure patriotism. In order to explain the violence of 1775, it is essential to determine the impact of policies and actions, as well as words, upon the sentiments of the people. The older Adams, who sat in relation to the period in much the same manner as any historian, did not do this. Nevertheless, careful searching of his correspondence, diary, and other writings of the pre-Revolutionary War period yields a good deal of insight into what made John Adams—one of the prominent people whose minds and hearts were revolutionized prior to 1776—opt for active resistance to England. These documents demonstrate the impact of specific policies and events, without giving substantial support to his post-1800 interpretation.

If we were to accept Adams' later account of the revolution, we would begin our history with the 1761 speech by James Otis against writs of assistance. In accord with his emphasis upon the role of the written and spoken word in awakening revolutionary sentiments, the older Adams emphasized the role of Bostonian propaganda in bringing about the revolution (X, 189, 263, 295–300, 314–316, 327, 348, 355, 364). In his view, alarms had spread from Massachusetts to the other colonies (X, 184, 174–176, 279). James Otis, in particular, by firmly opposing the use of writs of assistance in 1761, had awakened his colony to the impending danger (X, 183–184).

Adams' first written reference to Otis' speech as marking the start of the revolution is found in a letter to Mrs. Adams, written July 3, 1776, the day before the formal declaration of independence from England. This is an early date, and lends credence to Adams' later interpretation; but the letter contains additional references, not to speeches or propaganda, or even to a gradual awakening of the people, but to "political events" as well as to the "suddenness" of the revolution (IX, 418).

It is in vain, however, that we search for revolutionary sentiments in his writings during 1761, the year of the speech, or indeed in any writings prior to 1765 and the Stamp Act. Otis' speech evoked only a minor comment in his diary in 1761 (II, 124). Even in 1774, two years before the Declaration of Independence and his letter to Abigail Adams pinpointing Otis' speech as the beginning of the revolutionary movement, he was more inclined to use the Treaty of Paris (1763) than the events of 1761 as a starting point for a history of the period (II, 337–338). In his 1774 letters to Mrs. Adams he was more inclined to point to Hutchinson, Oliver, parliamentary taxation, and the conduct of the British army as causes of American discontent than to credit James Otis or propaganda as the prime cause.[3] Only after the break with England did Adams find Otis' speech to be of primary importance. During these years, moreover, Adams' entries in the diary not only make scant mention of the Otis speech, but indicate that he was almost totally absorbed in his own private affairs and at times had a negative attitude toward "patriots" (II, 142–143), which seems to belie his later claim to have been steadily aligned with the rebellious elements in Massachusetts.

His first diary entry showing active identification with the rebellious movement concerns the August 1765 riots against Mr. Oliver. Here he gives the first hint that he fears a plot by Hutchinson to tyrannize Massachusetts. But even Adams' suspicions of Hutchinson are tempered by lengthy criticism of the Boston mob (II, 150–151) in connection with its resistance to the Stamp Act. In Adams' contemporaneous

---

[3] *Familiar Letters of John Adams and His Wife Abigail during the Revolution*, ed. Charles Francis Adams (Boston, 1876), pp. 13–15. Subsequent references to the *Familiar Letters* will be denoted by the letter "F" preceding the page citation.

writings this appears to be an event much more likely to trigger massive public resistance to England than was Otis' speech. To illustrate the change the Stamp Act made in Adams' thinking, his essay "On Self-Delusion," printed in 1763, before the Stamp Act, exhorts the rebellious citizens of Massachusetts to use caution. He expresses considerable sympathy for the tasks of the existing authorities and reminds "writers and statesmen" that the colonists "have not yet seen any side as altogether free from atrocious vices" (III, 436). In stark contrast to this 1763 essay, his "Dissertation on the Canon and Feudal Law," published in 1765, asserts that because the colonists "have been *excessively cautious* of giving offense by complaining of grievances," the agents of the crown have deprived them of. their rights (III, 459–460).

The sudden change produced by the Stamp Act is also evident in Adams' diary, where we find no entry from August 15, 1765, until December 18, 1765. On the latter date he expresses regret that his journal has not been kept, and then emphasizes the importance of the year 1765 as the "most remarkable year of my life" because the Stamp Act has raised the "universal" resentment of the people (II, 154). Even in his *Autobiography,* written in 1804 after ample time for reflection, there is nothing definite concerning the revolution in the passages dealing with 1761–1765, except the assertion that he knew a fight was coming.[4] Not even that much appears in his diary or correspondence for the period.

As far as his contemporary utterances can inform us, then, it seems apparent that Adams' basic commitment to resist Parliament was forged in the controversy over the Stamp Act, not in the debates over writs of assistance, however significant the earlier events may have seemed in retrospect. His writings indicate that the Stamp Act, not revolutionary propaganda, aroused Adams and the other colonists. Their resistance— at least as it appears in the form of a popular movement commanding a very high degree of colonial support—appears suddenly, not gradually. It might be called a resistance based upon "pure patriotism" (to use Adams' later term), but if so, it was a one-shot, massive pure patriotism and apparently not characteristic of the entire period 1761–1765, as Adams later maintained.

The crucial role of the Stamp Act in producing rebellious sentiment is also evident in the rapid dissolution of that sentiment after the act was repealed. The Adams diary demonstrates the subsidence of his own rebelliousness after 1765 in striking fashion. From July 24, 1766, until November 8 of the same year, his entries indicate that he was completely absorbed in his private, social, and family affairs (II, 197–202). In November, Adams exhibits a slight ripple of renewed concern over the possibility that the colony will be asked to pay for damages to Governor Hutchinson's house, but his conversations with fellow colonists reflect a general sentiment of gratitude to the king and a desire to please him, even though payment to Hutchinson would work a hardship (II, 202). In fact, until the Boston Tea Party, Adams' contemporaneous writings yield little evidence that he was a pure patriot, or that he felt that his fellow colonists were being "corrupted." His 1804 *Autobiography* tells of the offer of a high colonial post which he declined because of the "unsettled State of the Country." It also provides the only clear account of Adams' shock at finding British troops in Boston and of the Boston Massacre and Adams' subsequent defense of the British soldiers involved (P, III, 288, 290, 292–294). The *Autobiography* account

[4] *The Adams Papers,* ed. L. H. Butterfield (Cambridge, Mass., 1961), III, pp. 277–283. Future references to the Butterfield edition will be denoted by the letter "P" preceding the volume and pages cited.

does not present John Adams as a confirmed and militant revolutionary. He appears to have been one who leaned toward the patriot cause, but he was far from being dislodged from his loyalty to the mother country and her laws.

If Adams was not rabidly partisan, the Boston Tea Party of December 1773 nonetheless provoked great exhilaration in him, and his letters following that event give strong indications that he was firmly and steadily opposed to parliamentary taxation of the colonies. In these letters he acclaims the "sublimity" of the dumping of the tea and crows that the people have "passed the river and cut away the bridge" and that the "spirit of liberty is very high in the country" (IX, 333, 335–337). This would, if an accurate appraisal of public opinion, hardly substantiate the theory that in 1773 the patriotism of the people was in a state of steady decline during a period of corruption wherein Hutchinson was gaining support. Such scanty evidence as three letters may not be conclusive in this regard, but there are no Adams letters that support the "period of corruption" interpretation made latter in his life.

The Coercive Acts were the British response to the Boston Tea Party, and Adams' reaction to these measures is most significant. From May until July of 1774 he expressed apprehension for the fate of Boston and a determination to let the conflict be settled by others without allowing himself to be involved. Particularly interesting is his comment of July 1, 1774, that he may become "foreman upon my own farm and the schoolmaster to my own children," and his comment of the same date which states, "I will laugh and be easy if I can, let the contest of parties terminate as it will" (F, 2, 4, 7, 11).

In spite of this expressed desire to sit on the sidelines while the issues would be resolved by others, Adams, in his letters to his wife, became more and more committed to resistance as the spring and summer passed. Through the summer of 1774 he moves from a statement on July 4 that he has always tried to avoid furthering "tumult or disorder," to an admonition on October 7 that the people should prepare for war, even while trying to avoid it (F, 11, 44). It was, of course, during the summer of 1774 that the organization of the Committees of Correspondence and the Sons of Liberty began to be effective. It is difficult to avoid the conclusion that John Adams, who later counted himself as an early partisan of the patriot cause, tried mightily to remain uninvolved until the concrete evidence of British intent to use force appeared in Massachusetts and triggered general resentment among the people, making the patriot cause both morally attractive and politically expedient.[5] This observation is buttressed by his letters to Abigail, written en route to the first Continental Congress, where he writes of the great support for the Congress expressed by the people of New Jersey and Pennsylvania. His observations of "universal" (F, 26, 27, 32) support for the patriot cause give further indication that the idea of a "period of corruption," a steady decline of support for rebellion, is an inaccurate and oversimplified generalization.

Adams had to wrestle with his convictions before the use of British troops to enforce the Coercive Acts pushed him into a firm commitment to resist this type of military rule. He wrestled even longer over the question of open, violent rebellion and possible independence from England. Though by December of 1774 he was in

[5] The crucial month in transforming John Adams into an active opponent of the crown seems to have been July of 1774. It was during this month that he began to assert the propriety of violence, always being careful to note that it is justified only when basic rights are involved (IX, 333–335).

favor of resisting British rule by force of arms, he was not enthusiastic at the prospect. He feared that if a clash occurred, the breach between England and her colonies could never be healed (IX, 352). Six months later he wrote, "In my opinion, powder and artillery are the most efficacious, sure, and infallible conciliatory measures we can adopt" (IX, 357). The intervening six months had brought armed clashes between colonials and British regulars at Lexington, Concord, and Bunker Hill. These clashes reconciled Adams to the necessity for force and provoked a number of letters which demonstrated a new, exultant patriotism on his part, allying him firmly with those who were working for colonial union (F, 55, 59, 61, 66, 70). By the time of the Second Continental Congress, however much his thoughts may have wavered in earlier times, John Adams was firmly in the rebel camp. The English were in America in force; martial law obtained in Boston; the patriots were armed and ready to resist English troops. Once the armed clash had occurred and the Congress had sanctioned the actions of New England men who had challenged the British soldiers, the move for independence was almost sure to come. Adams wrote home in February of 1776 that "reconciliation if practicable, and peace if attainable, . . . would be as agreeable to my inclinations, and as advantageous to my interest, as to any man's," though he recognized that the chance of healing the break was very small (F, 135). And by July 3, 1776, he came to write, "It is the will of Heaven that the two countries should be sundered forever" (IX, 418). His own personality, his heritage, and his response to the words of those around him cannot be dismissed as irrelevant in the formation of John Adams into a revolutionary, but it seems plain that in this last stage, as in the earlier events and attitudes discussed, it was the course of events and the exercise of odious policies by England which had the largest part in determining his final response.

The gradualist interpretation of the American Revolution which Adams offered in his later writings is not, for all of its oversimplicity, without historical use. The studies that Adams' suggestions have produced are valuable to our understanding of events preceding the Revolutionary War. Nevertheless there is danger in accepting their findings as definitive. For, while a great deal may be learned about current attitudes and clashes of opinion from the writings of the time, these utterances lack significance unless they are related to the very concrete events which were at once their cause and their effect. If John Adams, as a leader of the eventual fight for independence, could waver in the strength of his commitment to the revolutionary cause, it is almost certain that others wavered at least as much. And though his later writings tell us that he was steadily and always on the side of the rebels, his own contemporaneous writings make plain that he was much more concerned with righting wrongs in the existing empire than with inciting rebellion. The Stamp Act and the Coercive Acts produced great bursts of patriotism in him. The Townshend Acts, the Boston Tea Party, and the quartering of troops in Boston produced less intensive patriotic fervor. Adams' prerevolutionary attitudes do not fit so simple a pattern as his later historical generalizations lead us to believe. Grave actions, events of great moment, tangible threats to liberty—these, not merely the words of propagandists, seem most responsible for his change of attitude toward the British Empire.

8 / The Coming of the Revolution in Virginia: Britain's Challenge to Virginia's Ruling Class, 1763–1776

Thad W. Tate

What led individual Americans to join in the revolutionary struggle against Great Britain? The pattern of resistance varied from colony to colony according to local social and political conditions. Virginia had its own particular pattern: While that colony was only incidentally affected by much of the new British legislation of the 1760's and 1770's, it had a political elite almost completely united in its hostility to the actions of the British government. Historians have offered different explanations for this general unity: the impact of the "Parson's Cause," the question of planter debts in a society dominated by planters, Virginians' complaints over limitations on Western expansion, and others. Yet the colonists here as elsewhere emphasized constitutional questions: they protested publicly over what were primarily political issues. In the following essay, Thad W. Tate examines various suggestions as to the reasons for Virginia's opposition to British policies. Some features of the colonists' resistance—the economic measures taken by the planters—are seen not as a way of their avoiding paying money owed to British merchants but rather as a means by which they might bring indirect pressure upon the government in London. He returns to the old view that Virginians rose in protest because of their fears of the constitutional implications of British action, because of their belief that British policy would undermine the political autonomy of Virginia. Tate further argues that the concentration of power in the hands of a relatively small and intertwined group of planters, men who constituted a kind of elite and yet were responsible to a larger electorate, made for nearly unanimous reaction against British policy. In Selection 4 of this volume, Gordon Wood referred to the possibility that social pressures within and upon Virginia's elite helped move it toward revolution. Tate, on the other hand, tends to view the struggle in

Reprinted by permission from *The William and Mary Quarterly,* 3rd series, XIX (1962), 323–343.

Virginia as one between the colony's established native political leadership and the British government.

For further reading: among the better studies of the revolutionary movements in particular colonies are Charles A. Barker, *Background of the Revolution in Maryland* (1940); Carl Becker, *Political Parties in New York 1760–1776* (1909); Robert E. and B. Katherine Brown, *Virginia, 1705–1786: Democracy or Aristocracy?* (1964); David S. Lovejoy, *Rhode Island Politics and the American Revolution, 1760–1776* (1958); Theodore Thayer, *Pennsylvania Politics and the Rise of Democracy, 1740–1776* (1953); and Oscar Zeichner, *Connecticut's Years of Controversy* (1950).

Contemplating the approach of independence in May 1776, Landon Carter, Virginia planter and retired Burgess, recorded in his diary that the Revolution was an unfortunate contest which Great Britain "certainly began with America by attempting to tax her out of the constitutional road." [1] Carter took a view of the predominant issue leading to the American Revolution that every Patriot leader in Virginia shared. All the major public resolutions, addresses, and petitions of the colony spoke against a threat to "ancient, legal, and constitutional Rights." [2]

The final statement, a bill of indictment against George III in the preamble of the 1776 constitution, comprised twenty-two charges, which stand as an official summary of the issues as the colony saw them.[3] Five of the twenty-two related to punitive actions taken after the beginning of hostilities by Dunmore or by British military authorities elsewhere and did not, therefore, concern basic issues from which the conflict had arisen. Two other accusations were too general to relate to specific grievances. Of the remaining fifteen allegations, which were the heart of the case, fourteen attacked British political or military policies. Nine of the fourteen criticized restrictions on colonial legislatures, two objected to abridgment of legal rights of the individual, and three dealt with threats to liberty from the use of armed force. Only a single article from the entire list concerned economic conditions—a complaint against the restriction of colonial trade with non-British ports.[4] Apparently the Virginia protest explained the Revolution as a defense of constitutional rights against their subversion

[1] Entry of May 29, 1776, "Diary of Col. Landon Carter," *William and Mary College Quarterly,* 1st Ser., XVIII (1909–10), 43.

[2] The quotation is from the resolutions of the House of Burgesses creating the Committee of Correspondence, Mar. 12, 1773, in Henry R. McIlwaine and John P. Kennedy, eds., *Journals of the House of Burgesses of Virginia* (Richmond, 1905–15), *1773–1776,* p. 28. Other important statements derived from constitutional arguments are in *ibid., 1761–1765,* pp. 302–304; *1766–1769,* pp. 23–24, 165–171, 214; *1770–1772,* pp. 101–102; *1773–1776,* pp. 28, 124; Purdie and Dixon's *Virginia Gazette* (Williamsburg), July 21, 1768, Aug. 11, 1774.

[3] *Ordinance Passed at a General Convention . . . of Virginia . . . Monday the 6th of May Anno Dom: 1776* (Williamsburg [1776]), 5–7.

[4] Thomas Jefferson, the author of the list of charges in the Virginia Constitution, made a more sweeping condemnation of imperial economic policies in *Summary View of the Rights of British America . . .* (London, 1774). The briefer statement with only a single mention of economic grievances was, however, the version that gained the approval of the Virginia Convention. See Julian P. Boyd, ed., *The Papers of Thomas Jefferson* (Princeton, 1950–), I, 123–124, 329–365, 377–378.

by the British government. Moreover, it made no distinction between measures that affected Virginia directly and those that seemed, by their threat to another colony, to raise the prospect of future tyranny over all. The Virginians seemed content to say they fought over a common issue.

Many historians have been dissatisfied with this answer. In part, they have been influenced by broad currents in historical writing, such as the imperialist view of the colonial period, the economic interpretation of history, and the belief that the American Revolution was primarily an internal conflict, all of which have questioned the traditional constitutional explanation. Doubt has come, too, from certain local characteristics of the Revolution in Virginia. It has not been easy to understand why a colony with Virginia's reputation for conservatism and loyalty reacted with such force and rapidity, when the actual burdens of the British acts fell more lightly upon Virginia than upon many other colonies. The Stamp Act and the Townshend duties, of course, affected all colonies equally; and Virginia was one of the colonies that the framers of the Currency Act of 1764 had particularly in mind. The Sugar Act, however, seemed likely to harm Virginia mostly through higher costs for a gentleman's favorite solace—good Madeira wine.[5] No military commander came to quarter his troops upon unwilling Virginians. The Crown had long enjoyed independent sources of revenue from which to pay royal salaries within the colony.[6] "Customs racketeering" by the American Board of Customs Commissioners and its agents was possibly not so severe as elsewhere—the General Court, for one thing, never issued general writs of assistance.[7] Finally, the Coercive Acts neither affected Virginia directly nor, in the Massachusetts Government Act, imposed any conditions upon the Bay Colony that had not long prevailed in Virginia. Such considerations have caused speculation about the candor of Virginia Patriots and about the accuracy of interpreting the Revolution in that colony solely as a contest for political liberty.

Although no one has made a full-scale attack on the constitutional interpretation as it applied to Virginia, a number of scholars have emphasized other issues. Among the additional sources of conflict to which they have pointed are the existence of

---

[5] "Proceedings of the Virginia Committee of Correspondence, 1759–67," *Virginia Magazine of History and Biography*, XII (1904–5), 6, 9. For a suggestion that the Sugar Act might even benefit Virginia economically, see Charles Steuart to Messrs. [William] Aitchinson and [James] Parker, May 4, 1764, Parker Family Papers, Liverpool Record Office, Liverpool, Eng. (available on microfilm at Colonial Williamsburg, Inc., Research Library).

[6] Note, for example, the reputation for loyalty on the part of Virginia implicit in Halifax's observation that it was "the only province in North America who had granted a permanent revenue to the crown for the support of government." Quoted in Keith B. Berwick, *Loyalties in Crisis: A Study of the Attitudes of Virginians in the Revolution* (unpubl. Ph.D. diss., University of Chicago, 1959), 51.

[7] Treasury, Ser. 1, 501, foll. 181–186, 261–265, 270–275, 308–311, Public Record Office, London (available on microfilm at Colonial Williamsburg, Inc., Research Library); John Randolph to Commissioners of Customs, May 15, 1769, Colonial Office Papers, Ser. 5, 1347, fol. 109, Public Record Office (available on microfilm at Colonial Williamsburg, Inc., Research Library). The fullest discussion of the Virginia General Court's refusal to issue writs of assistance is in Oliver M. Dickerson, "Writs of Assistance as a Cause of the Revolution," in Richard B. Morris, ed., *The Era of the American Revolution* (New York, 1939), 67–73. Dickerson's *The Navigation Acts and the American Revolution* (Philadelphia, 1951), 255, finds little evidence of customs racketeering in Virginia. There is a suggestion of the relative moderation of vice-admiralty court activity in Virginia in Carl Ubbelohde, *The Vice-Admiralty Courts and the American Revolution* (Chapel Hill, 1960), 93–94, 156–167.

earlier disputes, antedating the taxation measures of George Grenville; the massive indebtedness of the planters to British merchants; the clash between imperial policy and speculative interests of Virginians in western lands; and the divisions between radical Patriots of the stripe of Patrick Henry and the entrenched leadership of the House of Burgesses. The over-all effect has been to reduce the importance of the issue of colonial rights, as it developed after 1763, by suggesting either that it was only one among a number of points in dispute or that it was largely an expression of deeper-seated and more material grievances.

Those who believe that there were important beginnings of the Revolution in Virginia before the peace of 1763 have placed their emphasis upon the only serious political controversy at this time—the disputes over the Twopenny Acts, otherwise known as the Parsons' Cause. In the disallowance of these laws they have seen the making of an imperial dispute that commenced as early as 1759 and led directly to Virginia's involvement in the Revolution.[8]

The Twopenny Acts were passed by the Assembly in 1755 and again in 1758 to relieve taxpayers of the necessity of satisfying their public obligations in tobacco during two years of short crops and abnormally high prices. Both laws permitted the commutation of such payments at a rate of two pence per pound of tobacco—well below its market value.[9] The 1755 law was to remain in effect only ten months, and the 1758 law, twelve. Among the obligations affected were the salaries of the clergy of the Established Church, which had been fixed at sixteen thousand pounds of tobacco yearly by a 1748 law that had been confirmed by the Crown. Although the royal instructions stipulated that laws thus confirmed could not be altered without the consent of the Crown and required the insertion of a suspending clause in any amending acts, the Virginia legislature included no such clause in either of the Twopenny Acts.

[8] There are a number of detailed accounts of the Parsons' Cause, many of which vary in their emphasis. Richard L. Morton, Colonial Virginia (Chapel Hill, 1960), II, 751–819, is especially good for its explanation of the background of ill feeling against the Anglican clergy in Virginia; Bernhard Knollenberg, Origin of the American Revolution: 1759–1766, rev. ed. (New York, 1961), 57–66, gives strong emphasis to the Parsons' Cause as a significant source of discontent in Virginia; George Maclaren Brydon, Virginia's Mother Church and the Political Conditions under Which It Grew (Philadelphia and Richmond, 1947–52), II, 288–320, stresses the effect on the clergy; Robert Douthat Meade, Patrick Henry: Patriot in the Making (Philadelphia and New York, 1957), 114–138, has a very full treatment of the suit by the Rev. James Maury in which Henry was involved; Lawrence Henry Gipson, The Coming of the Revolution, 1763–1775 (New York, 1954), 46–54, treats the Parsons' Cause as an aspect of the question of planter debts; the same author's more recent The Triumphant Empire: Thunder-Clouds Gather in the West, 1763–1766 (New York, 1961), Volume X of The British Empire before the American Revolution, 146–157, contains a suggestive treatment of the passage of the Twopenny Acts as part of a broad, determined effort by the Virginia House of Burgesses to modify the constitutional authority of the Crown in the colony; Glenn Curtis Smith, "The Parsons' Cause, 1755–65," Tyler's Quarterly Historical and Genealogical Magazine, XXI (1939–40), 140–171, 291–306, is the fullest discussion of the pamphlet controversy. Two studies of exceptional importance which do not stress the Parsons' Cause as a cause of the Revolution are Arthur P. Scott, "The Constitutional Aspects of the 'Parson's Cause,'" Political Science Quarterly, XXXI (1916), 558–577, which is particularly good in treating the rather questionable legal grounds of the lawsuits of the clergy, and Joseph Henry Smith, Appeals to the Privy Council from the American Plantations (New York, 1950), 607–626, which gives a very thorough analysis of all the legal aspects of the Parsons' Cause.

[9] William Waller Hening, ed., The Statutes at Large: Being a Collection of All the Laws of Virginia . . . (Richmond, 1809–23), VI, 568–569; VII, 240–241.

To have done so, as defenders of the measure later pointed out, would have kept them from going into immediate effect and would have defeated the whole purpose of the legislation. Lieutenant Governor Francis Fauquier realized that he was violating his instructions in assenting to the 1758 measure, but he readily approved it because there had been no repercussions from the approval of the 1755 law by his predecessor Robert Dinwiddie.[10]

Passage of the 1758 act immediately evoked strong opposition from the clergy. Had the law not been enacted, the high-priced tobacco would have meant a substantial addition to their income. To avoid its loss a number of ministers determined to resist the Twopenny legislation. Their opposition took several forms: a convention of some, though not all, of the clergy;[11] a petition to the Privy Council requesting that the 1758 act be declared null and void from its inception;[12] a series of lawsuits for the recovery of the full market value of their assigned quota of tobacco;[13] and a pamphlet and newspaper controvesry.[14] In all of these measures the chief clerical spokesman was the Reverend John Camm, Professor of Divinity at the College of William and Mary and rector of Yorkhampton Parish in nearby York County. It was he who largely instigated the complaints to England, carried the test suit to the Privy Council on appeal, and defended the clerical position in writing against two outspoken burgesses, Landon Carter and Richard Bland.

The resultant controversy continued from 1759 until 1766, and in its course the clerics directly challenged the competence of the Virginia Assembly to pass the Twopenny Acts. Both the timing—its later stages coincided with the taxation dispute with the home government—and the underlying issue—the limits of the legislative power of a colonial assembly—have made it easy to see the Parsons' Cause as one of the first steps of approaching revolution. Patrick Henry's vehement argument in the best-known of the clerical suits that a king who would annul a beneficial law degenerated into a tyrant seems to support this view.[15] The same is true of the more sober arguments advanced by Carter and Bland. They justified the Twopenny Acts on several grounds that touched upon the nature of the imperial constitution: the necessity of the legislation to protect the welfare of the colony, the right of the people to be governed by laws made by their elected representatives, and the claim that a

[10] Morton, *Colonial Virginia,* II, 682, 784–785; Knollenberg, *Origin of the American Revolution,* 57–58; Gipson, *The Triumphant Empire,* 145–147; J. H. Smith, *Appeals to Privy Council,* 608–611.

[11] Richard Bland, *A Letter to the Clergy in Virginia* . . . (Williamsburg, 1760), 3; William Robinson to the Bishop of London, Aug. 12, 1765, in William Stevens Perry, ed., *Historical Collections Relating to the American Colonial Church* ([Hartford], 1870), I, 509–510.

[12] Memorial of the Clergy of Virginia to the Board of Trade, C.O. 5/1329, foll. 119–120.

[13] Morton, *Colonial Virginia,* II, 807–812, and J. H. Smith, *Appeals to Privy Council,* 615–621, are the best accounts of the initiation of all the suits and of their progress through the courts of the colony.

[14] The pamphlets in order of their appearance are: Landon Carter, *A Letter to the Right Reverend Father in God the Lord B——p of L——n* . . . (Williamsburg, 1759); Bland, *Letter to the Clergy in Virginia;* John Camm, *A Single and Distinct View of the Act, Vulgarly Entitled, the Twopenny Act* . . . (Annapolis, 1763); Landon Carter, *The Rector Detected* . . . (Williamsburg, 1764); John Camm, *A Review of the Rector Detected* . . . (Williamsburg, 1764); Richard Bland, *The Colonel Dismounted; or the Rector Vindicated* (Williamsburg, 1764); John Camm, *Critical Remarks on a Letter Ascribed to Common Sense* (Williamsburg, 1765).

[15] James Maury to John Camm, Dec. 12, 1763, in Ann Maury, ed., *Memoirs of a Huguenot Family* (New York, 1853), 421.

governor's instructions from the Crown were not obligatory and did not have the force of law.[16]

Yet it is possible to see the Parsons' Cause in a much different light by considering its full scope, including the progress of the dispute in England as well as in the colony. Patrick Henry's courtroom oration was, after all, only a single episode, occurring in a local case in which the court's initial finding in favor of the clergyman was at variance with the general outcome of the cases.[17] The pamphlet warfare was also a local controversy within the colony and did not directly involve any British officials or political leaders. Far more central to the nature and outcome of the Parsons' Cause were the two appeals to the Privy Council—one legislative and the other judicial— that John Camm instituted. These show the Parsons' Cause as primarily a dispute between the colony and its clergy, not between colony and mother country.[18]

After the failure of every appeal within the colony itself, Camm sailed for England in either late 1758 or early 1759 to represent the clergy in an effort to have the Two- penny Acts declared null and void from the moment of their passage.[19] The memorial of the clergy which Camm presented to the Privy Council did not ask for the cus- tomary disallowance, because the clergy knew that it would not take effect before the expiration of the laws. By customary usage the laws would thereby have the force of law until their expiration or disallowance. A decision that the acts had never pos- sessed the force of law would, on the other hand, open the way for recovery of the full value of the clerical salaries. On August 10, 1759, however, after full hearings before the Board of Trade and before one of its own committees, the Privy Council refused to do more than disallow the laws.[20] Thereupon James Abercromby, who had represented the colony during the hearings, reported with evident satisfaction that "the point was determined in our Favour (to wit) to go no further than the Repeal." [21] Abercromby's attitude reflects something that is often forgotten about the Privy Council decision: that disallowance represented a defeat for the clergy far more than it did for the Virginia Assembly. Certainly Virginians would have preferred not to hear the criticism that the Privy Councilors made of their actions, but it was criticism that had no practical effect.

There were, however, aspects of the decision that created the possibility of more serious objections from Virginia. The action of the Privy Council had, after all, not gone so far as to approve the Twopenny Acts. The Privy Council, moreover, had coupled its disallowance with a tart instruction to Fauquier that he would incur the highest displeasure and face recall if he failed in the future to observe strictly article sixteen of his instructions directing him to assent to no act of less than two years

[16] G. C. Smith, "The Parsons' Cause," 169–171, 291–306, summarizes the constitutional arguments of Bland and Carter.

[17] J. H. Smith, *Appeals to Privy Council*, 617–620.

[18] *Ibid.*, 611–624. In this discussion Smith treats the legal aspects of both cases with far greater precision than earlier accounts and thereby clears the way for a better understanding of whether the home government ruled largely in favor of the clergy or the colony both in disallowing the laws and in upholding the decision of the General Court of Virginia in Camm's lawsuit.

[19] Francis Fauquier to Board of Trade, Jan. 9, 1759, C.O. 5/1329, foll. 119–120.

[20] William L. Grant and James B. Munro, eds., *Acts of the Privy Council of England, Colonial Series* (London, 1908–12), IV, 420–421 (Aug. 29, 1759).

[21] To John Blair, Aug. 3, 1759, James Abercromby Letter book, Virginia State Library, Richmond.

duration and to no act without a suspending clause that repealed any other act, whether confirmed by the King or not.[22] This action by the Privy Council posed a definite future threat for the colony, to which the Assembly responded in the "Humble Representation of the Council and Burgesses of Virginia," prepared in October 1760. The sixteenth article of the governor's instructions had not been observed for a long time, and its enforcement now, the Assembly observed, would "involve the Colony in the most insuperable Difficulties." [23]

Admittedly, the renewed emphasis on a long-dormant royal instruction was a source of concern—and perhaps a harbinger of the over-all shift in imperial policy just getting underway.[24] The tone of the Assembly's representation, however, does not suggest that Virginians yet saw either the disallowance of the Twopenny Acts or the additional instruction as part of a new and general restriction on colonial rights. The language of the document is mild, and its nature is explanatory. "It was not our Intention," the members of the Assembly declared, "by any Act of our's to lessen the Influence and Prerogative of the Crown upon which the Preservation of our privileges and the happy and rightful Administration of the Government depend." [25] The reaction of the colony was not dissimilar to that produced by comparable imperial actions earlier in the century.

The sharpest language of the Humble Representation was reserved for those who were accused of having misrepresented the position of the colony in England, thus constituting a scarcely veiled attack on John Camm and the Virginia clergy. The greater part of the reaction within the colony to the outcome of the Privy Council hearings was, in fact, directed against the ministers. First of all, Camm's return from Britain was the occasion for a well-known and explosive incident in which Fauquier committed the supreme insult of pointing the cleric out to his slaves and ordering them never again to admit him beyond the gates of the Governor's Palace.[26] Another irritant was the circulation within Virginia of the Bishop of London's letter of June 14, 1759, which he had originally written to the Board of Trade in support of the clerical request for nullification of the Twopenny Acts.[27] It was a copy of this letter which stung Carter and Bland into initiating the pamphlet war, although by this time it had failed in the immediate purpose of influencing the Privy Council decision. Still a third cause for anger was the institution of several suits by Virginia clergymen to recover their full salaries.[28] Vexing as all these actions of the clergy were, none of

[22] Leonard W. Labaree, ed., *Royal Instructions to British Colonial Governors, 1670–1776* (New York and London, 1935), I, 128–131.

[23] C.O. 5/1330, foll. 51–53. The Assembly also sent a long letter to its agent with an order to work for countermanding of the additional instruction to Fauquier, but this letter is a paraphrase of the Humble Representation. Committee of Correspondence to Montague, Nov. 5, 1760, "Proceedings of the Virginia Committee of Correspondence, 1759–'67," *Va. Mag. of Hist. and Biog.,* XI (1903–4), 14–16.

[24] The Privy Council, moreover, in 1761 recommended against granting the request of the Humble Representation for modification of the new instruction. C.O. 5/1368, foll. 179–185.

[25] C.O. 5/1330, fol. 53.

[26] Morton, *Colonial Virginia,* II, 802.

[27] The letter is in C.O. 5/1329, foll. 131–133A.

[28] Long before returning from England Camm had written ahead to his attorney to bring suit, and the General Assembly moved before the end of 1759 to support the vestry of Camm's parish in their defense. Morton, *Colonial Virginia,* II, 797–798.

them had anything to do with specific governmental policies adopted by imperial officials.

This fact is even more clear from an examination of the clergy's attempt to recover their money through the courts. Thinking one of the Privy Councilors had suggested he might still recover his money at law, Camm—and ultimately at least four other clergymen—brought suits in various county courts of the colony. In effect, they sought either by deliberate misrepresentation or out of honest misunderstanding to contend that the Order in Council of 1759 had been what it was not: a declaration of nullity rather than a disallowance. Camm's suit, going on appeal from the General Court of Virginia to the Privy Council, became the test case. A committee of the Privy Council decided against him in 1766. The general impression has been that he lost on a question of procedure rather than of right—the implication is that the committee members thought his case valid but found a technical ground for denying his appeal in order to soothe the Virginians without creating a precedent. Nevertheless, the notes of Robert Walpole, clerk for the Privy Council, contain contradictory evidence. As Walpole recorded it, the committee ruled that the 1758 act "passed regularly in the regular course of Legislation" and was "a Law . . . till the disapprobation of the King in Council is signified in the Province." Whatever the basis of the decision, the Virginians had once and for all carried the day against the clergy in the Parsons' Cause.[29]

The view that the dispute over the Twopenny Acts was in its essence a dispute between Virginia and Great Britain depends upon two assumptions: that Patrick Henry's plea was a major event of the controversy in which he and the popular opinion that supported him defied the Privy Council decision of 1759 and that Virginians contended with British officials who generally—at least until a conciliatory gesture in 1766—supported the clerical arguments. Both are in large part erroneous, although it is possible that the clergy themselves helped obscure the issue in Virginia somewhat and although they did enjoy powerful support in England from bishops, merchants, and a few officials of the government.

There is an alternate set of propositions that serves much more accurately to delineate the nature of the Parsons' Cause. First, the dispute originated solely within the colony, between clergy and local political leaders, and was not the result of any deliberate act of imperial policy. The home government, moreover, became involved beyond the routine review of legislation only at the instigation of the Virginia clergy and their friends in England. Whether the action of Crown officials in the Parsons' Cause was, or was understood by Virginians to be, a part of the general tightening of colonial policy that began at much the same time is problematical. In the long run, the Virginians used the machinery of imperial administration, and they lost nothing by it. Two royal governors sided with them, and the Privy Council twice decided more in their favor than against them. If there was a genuine constitutional issue involved, it was that of the additional instruction to Fauquier in 1759, which, as it turned out, was a potential rather than an actual grievance. Unquestionably the pamphlets of Bland and Carter expressed many of the same ideas that soon appeared in more genuine Revolutionary disputes. They were, however, principally answering

[29] Camm's case is treated through its final outcome in great detail by J. H. Smith, *Appeals to Privy Council*, 618–624. The statement of Robert Walpole is quoted by Smith from War Office Papers, Ser. 1, 404, fol. 66, Public Record Office.

the extravagant claims of John Camm and the Bishop of London, whom no one mistook for official interpreters of the British constitution. Furthermore, they wrote in part after the crisis of the Sugar Act and the Stamp Act had begun to affect the controversy. In retrospect the Parsons' Cause may have seemed to some Virginians a grievance against Great Britain. Certainly, had British politicians been observant, it could have warned them of the extent of colonial constitutional claims.[30] This, however, was the extent of its relationship to the Revolution. It was not in the beginning a major issue between Virginia and the home government. At most, it was contributory rather than decisive to the advent of the Revolution in Virginia.

The Parsons' Cause is sometimes also seen as an economic issue, in which Virginians took a first step toward revolution by their reaction to alleged British interference with an effort at debtor relief.[31] But, since disallowance occurred after the expiration of the Twopenny Acts and did not affect their validity during the time they were in force, the British action did not have any practical economic effect. Still the question of whether planter debts influenced the coming of the Revolution, being far broader than a single incident, demands further consideration. Certainly the endless discussions of increasing debts, depressed tobacco prices, and shortages of currency that occupy so large a part of the surviving correspondence of Virginians suggests the possibility of a link between economic conditions in the colony and the Revolutionary movement. Indeed, by 1763 planter debts were already an issue of long standing, as the running controversy in the 1750's over the rate of exchange between Virginia currency and sterling money attested.[32]

In the 1760's and 1770's there are two aspects of the debt question. One centers around the Currency Act of 1764, which extended to the other continental colonies the 1751 restrictions on New England forbidding further emissions of paper money as legal tender.[33] Virginia, where the rate of exchange with sterling money had seldom kept pace with depreciation of the paper bills, had been a principal offender; and the demand for the statute was largely a result of pressure from British merchants who traded there and who were displeased with the persistent refusal of the House of Burgesses to comply with an instruction of 1759 requiring the removal of the legal tender provisions of previous currency issues. Men like Robert Beverley were consequently bitter at the "Machinations of those very Merchants who draw their Subsistence, as it were from our very Vitals." [34] After passage of the Currency Act Virginians were still incensed at the merchants but were surprisingly unconcerned about the act itself. In their communications with Virginia agent Edward Montagu, mem-

[30] In this connection see the conclusion in Scott, "Constitutional Aspects of 'Parson's Cause,' " 577.

[31] Gipson, Coming of the Revolution, 45–54.

[32] It is this earlier period that is emphasized in Lawrence H. Gipson, "Virginia Planter Debts before the American Revolution," Va. Mag. of Hist. and Biog., LXIX (1961), 259–277, and in his The Triumphant Empire, chap. 8. Jack P. Greene and Richard M. Jellison, "The Currency Act of 1764 in Imperial-Colonial Relations, 1764–1776," Wm. and Mary Qtly., 3d Ser., XVIII (1961), 485–488, treat the same period as an immediate background to the Currency Act of 1764. See also Morton, Colonial Virginia, II, 745–749, and William Z. Ripley, The Financial History of Virginia, 1609–1776 (New York, 1893), 153–159.

[33] The fullest treatment of the relationship between the Currency Act and the Revolutionary movement is Greene and Jellison, "Currency Act of 1764 in Imperial-Colonial Relations."

[34] Beverley to John Bland, Apr. 5, 1763, Robert Beverley Letter book, Library of Congress, Washington.

bers of the committee of correspondence expressed no hostility to the act. Rather, they were relieved that, by failing to do more than to demand retirement on schedule of the depreciated money in circulation, it had not gone as far as the merchants demanded.[35] As a result, a sufficient currency for at least a time remained in circulation, a circumstance to which the general lack of immediate protest in Virginia possibly owed a great deal. Beyond a few outbursts against the merchants, the immediate reaction to the Currency Act was mild.

If the prohibition of future paper money issues failed to stir initial hostility against the home government itself, it nevertheless soon created a shortage of circulating currency that brought occasional expressions of dissatisfaction and an unsuccessful attempt by the House of Burgesses in 1768 to obtain permission for a new issue of £200,000.[36] Ultimately, Virginia found ways to mitigate its currency problem through such expedients as non-legal tender issues in 1769 and 1771;[37] and, if there had been sufficient time before Independence for the Parliamentary Act of 1773, which modified the Currency Act of 1764, to run its course, the currency issue might well have disappeared completely. As it is, it is difficult to see the Currency Act as a major grievance in Virginia or as one which the colony believed it could not solve within the normal imperial framework.[38]

The second part of the debt question concerns the debts themselves—the ever increasing sums due British merchants as a consequence of the fortunes of the tobacco trade.[39] If a link does exist between them and the Revolutionary protest, it is not easy to establish, for the Virginians never included complaints about economic conditions in their petitions and resolutions. Between 1764 and 1766 Virginians occasionally grumbled about debts. Governor Fauquier found the people "uneasy, peevish, and ready to murmur at every Occurrence" because of their debts, and he attributed some of the continued unrest after repeal of the Stamp Act to economic hardship.[40] Again, most of the hostility seemed directed against the merchants; the debts were not the occasion for any contests with the government.[41] Probably debtors welcomed the closing of the courts that had occurred while the Stamp Act was in force, because it prevented suits by creditors and put pressure on merchants to work for repeal of the stamp duties.[42] But the benefit to debtors was almost certainly a by-product

[35] "Proceedings of the Virginia Committee of Correspondence, 1759–'67," Va. Mag. of Hist. and Biog., XII (1904–5), 6, 11.

[36] Francis Fauquier to Earl of Halifax, June 14, 1765, C.O. 5/1345, foll. 80–81; C.O. 5/1332, foll. 30–34; Board of Trade to Crown, June 10, 1768, C.O. 5/1346, foll. 9–12; Greene and Jellison, "Currency Act of 1764 in Imperial-Colonial Relations," 503.

[37] Hening, ed., Statutes at Large, VIII, 346–348, 501–503.

[38] Greene and Jellison, "Currency Act of 1764 in Imperial-Colonial Relations," 518.

[39] In addition to the emphasis upon the relevance of planter debts in the works of Professor Lawrence H. Gipson, cited in nn. 31 and 32 above, the study by Isaac S. Harrell of Loyalism in Virginia . . . (Durham, 1926), also stresses the debt question but concentrates upon its outcome in the period after 1776.

[40] Fauquier to Earl of Halifax, June 14, 1765, C.O. 5/1345, foll. 80–81; Fauquier to Commissioners for Trade, C.O. 5/1331, foll. 149–150.

[41] Fauquier to Secretary of State, Nov. 18, 1766, C.O. 5/1345, foll. 157–159; Purdie and Dixon's Virginia Gazette, Oct. 30, 1766.

[42] George Washington to Francis Dandridge, Sept. 20, 1765, in John C. Fitzpatrick, ed., The Writings of George Washington (Washington, 1931–44), II, 425–426; Richard Henry Lee to Landon Carter, Feb. 24, 1766, in James Curtis Ballagh, ed., The Letters of Richard Henry Lee (New York, 1911–14), I, 14–15.

and not a cause of the suspension of the courts, which had occurred very widely to avoid the use of stamped paper. A number of inferior courts, moreover, reopened in Virginia before the repeal of the Stamp Act.[43]

Certainly neither in the period of the Stamp Act nor in the crisis over the Townshend duties did Virginias make a full-scale attack upon the British navigation system and the closed trade by which it presumably held them irretrievably in debt.[44] In the very letter to George Washington in which he outlined his proposals for the nonimportation agreement of 1769, George Mason wrote that "our supplying our Mother Country with gross Materials, and taking her Manufactures in Return is the true Chain of Connection between Us; these are the Bands, which, if not broken by Oppression, must long hold Us together, by maintaining a constant Reciprocation of Interest." [45]

The attitude of Virginians concerning their debts grew harsher in the spring and summer of 1774. These months mark a distinct shift to a new phase of the debt question. The commercial system was still not an object of criticism, but there was frank discussion of withholding the payment of debts.[46] Not all of it came as accusations from diehard Tories like James Parker, whose constant contention was that "the more a man is in debit, the greater patriot he is." [47] Even Parker must be believed, however, when he describes in some detail the advocacy of nonpayment by George Mason, Patrick Henry, Richard Henry Lee, and Robert Carter Nicholas.[48] Feeling reached the point where in November Patriots suspended a bag of feathers over a barrel of tar on the main street of Williamsburg and dragged offending merchants before it to recant their crimes against the people.[49] Moreover, the county courts and the General Court stopped hearing civil cases, giving as their reason the failure of the Assembly during its brief session in May to renew the law fixing court fees.[50] The next year British subjects, permitted to return home by the Virginia Convention, were forbidden to take with them papers or account books belonging to anyone in Great Britain.[51]

The closing of the courts—the most substantial of these actions since it blocked suits for debts—may have served as a weapon in the political struggle, as it had in

[43] See the general discussion on the closing of the courts in twelve of the colonies in Edmund S. Morgan and Helen M. Morgan, *The Stamp Act Crisis: Prologue to Revolution* (Chapel Hill, 1953), 168–179. For the Virginia information see 172–173.

[44] One of the few exceptions is the letter by "A Virginian," Rind's *Virginia Gazette* (Williamsburg), Dec. 11, 1766.

[45] George Mason to George Washington, Apr. 5, 1769, George Washington Papers, Lib. Cong.

[46] Francis Lightfoot Lee to William Lee, July 3, 1774, Lee-Ludwell Papers, Virginia Historical Society, Richmond; James Parker to Charles Steuart, May 17, 1774, Charles Steuart Papers, National Library of Scotland, Edinburgh (available on microfilm at Colonial Williamsburg, Inc., Research Library).

[47] James Parker to Charles Steuart, June 7, 1774, Charles Steuart Papers.

[48] James Parker to Charles Steuart, postcript of June 17, 1774, to letter of June 7, 1774, *ibid.*

[49] James Parker to Charles Steuart, Nov. 14, 1774, Parker Family Papers; Parker to Steuart, Nov. 27, 1774, Steuart Papers.

[50] See, for example, Edmund Randolph, History of Virginia, Va. Hist. Soc.; William Reynolds to George F. Norton, June 3, 1774, William Reynold Letter book, Lib. Cong.; Charles Yates to John Hardy, Dec. 1774, Charles Yates Letter book, Alderman Library, University of Virginia, Charlottesville.

[51] *The Proceedings of the Convention and Delegates for the Counties and Corporations in the Colony of Virginia . . . on the 20th of March, 1775 . . .* (Richmond, 1816), 77.

part in 1765. Some merchants in Virginia conceded that its principal purpose was simply to force the merchants in Great Britain to use their influence against the repressive measures of the ministry instead of supporting them.[52] Any exact apportionment between its political and economic purposes is impossible, but obviously political pressure on the merchants played some part.[53] On the other hand, the atmosphere in 1774 did differ from that of 1765. There was more open complaint about debts, and by 1773 the tobacco trade had entered a new period of depression, bringing a consequent restriction on credit. If there was, however, a genuine economic conflict, it appeared at a late stage in the advance toward revolution, when public sentiment had become sufficiently inflamed to aggravate latent grievances.

In sum, there seems little doubt that there was—and had been for a long time—feeling by the planters on the subject of their financial obligations. That it constituted a basic issue in bringing on the Revolution is questionable. Virginians directed hostility over the debts against the merchants rather than against the economic policies of the government, which in all its measures after 1763 actually exerted less pressure on the matter of debts than it had sometimes done earlier. For most of these years the colonists agitated the debt issue correspondingly less. And in the last five years of the 1760's the Assembly even enacted a few minor safeguards against efforts of debtors to escape their obligations.[54] Only with the interruption of the courts in 1774 did hostility grow notably sharper and did Virginia move to obstruct outright the collection of debts. The debt issue, in short, does not loom particularly large in the years of political conflict with Great Britain. At best, the planter debts were an underlying source of difficulty brought to the surface only late in the Revolutionary crisis under the stimulus of a deepening political crisis.

Virginia had another economic interest—speculation in western lands—which the post-1763 measures of the imperial government affected more directly. The land claims of Virginia were sweeping, and many of the leaders of the colony had acquired a stake in their exploitation. The series of British directives, beginning with the Proclamation Line of 1763, that restricted the confirmation of new grants or the establishment of new settlements in the West ran counter to the plans of Virginians for further acquisitions and profitable sales. Even where lands were to be opened, Virginia investors faced a contest with British rivals. Yet, the West no more figured as an initial issue in the Revolutionary controversy in Virginia than did planter debts. On land questions the colony could usually count upon the royal governor to take its side.[55] Furthermore, the British allowed settlement in some areas west of the

---

[52] Harry Piper to Dixon and Littledale, June 9, 1774, Harry Piper Letter book, Alderman Library. Piper wrote that "it is also proposed to stop all proceedings in the Courts of Justice with regard to the recovery of Debts, so that You see the Merchants are to be distressed at all events in order to make them Active in getting the Acts Repealed." See also Charles Yates to Samuel and William Vernon, Oct. 5, 1774, Charles Yates Letter book.

[53] The point is discussed in some detail in Emory G. Evans, "Planter Indebtedness and the Coming of the Revolution in Virginia," paper delivered at Southern Historical Association Annual Meeting, Chattanooga, Tenn., Nov. 9, 1961, and scheduled for publication. Mr. Evans gives an extended treatment of the debt question from a point of view basically sympathetic with that expressed in this paper.

[54] Hening, ed., *Statutes at Large*, VIII, 118–123, 240–241, 326–332.

[55] Richard Orr Curry, "Lord Dunmore and the West: A Re-evalution," *West Virginia History*, XIX (1958), 231–243, treats Dunmore as a strong champion of colonial "rights" so far as western lands were concerned.

mountains by 1769 and never effectively interfered with it elsewhere. And Virginians, willing to trust their bargaining power with the home government, never questioned the Crown's rights to issue land grants.[56]

Only in the already explosive situation of 1774 did the problem of the West attract complaints.[57] In February of that year Dunmore, along with the other governors, received instructions to sell lands only at public auction, at a quintupled minimum price, and at twice the old rate for quitrents.[58] These requirements, unpopular to a degree that had not been true of earlier British actions on the West, were the first to which Patriot leaders in Virginia seriously protested.[59] As a potential grievance that failed to reach important proportions until the last stages of the controversy, the issue of the West developed in a manner similar to that of the debt question.

Internal divisions appear to have been no more important in bringing on the Revolution. The image of a band of radicals ceaselessly contending against a powerful conservative bloc to move the Revolution at a faster pace and to achieve a stronger voice in the colonial government does not hold for Virginia. At no time during the 1760's and 1770's were there organized or rival groups that might be legitimately classified as factions or parties. In fact, once events moved beyond the apparent challenge by Patrick Henry to the old guard of the House of Burgesses over the Stamp Act Resolves of 1765, it is difficult to find evidence of serious internal disputes among Virginia Patriots.[60] In all the years from 1763 to Independence only one period of obvi-

[56] From the extensive literature on the West and the American Revolution the following are most relevant to the specific question of the degree to which British policy in the West influenced the causes of the Revolutionary controversy in Virginia: Clarence W. Alvord, *The Mississippi Valley in British Politics* (Cleveland, 1917), which emphasizes the general importance of the West; the same author's "Virginia and the West, an Interpretation," *Mississippi Valley Historical Review,* III (1916), 19–38, which applies the same argument more specifically to Virginia; Harrell, *Loyalism in Virginia,* 7–22, which briefly but strongly supports the same view; St. George L. Sioussat, "The Breakdown of the Royal Management of Lands in the Southern Provinces, 1773–1775," *Agricultural History,* III (1929), 67–98, which covers in more detail than anyone else the reaction to British Western policy after 1774; Thomas Perkins Abernethy, *Western Lands and the American Revolution* (New York, 1937), which minimizes the importance of the West as a cause of the Revolution in Virginia; and John R. Alden, *The South in the Revolution, 1763–1789* (Baton Rouge, 1957), 138–139, which is a useful and succinct statement of the Abernethy view.

[57] Through the early 1770's the Vandalia scheme loomed as a potential issue but never materialized as Crown authorities dragged their feet and eventually failed to approve it. Abernethy, *Western Lands and the American Revolution,* 40–58.

[58] Earl of Dartmouth to Governor of Virginia, etc., Feb. 5, 1774, C.O. 5/241, foll. 509–524; Alvord, *Miss. Valley in British Politics,* II, 209–216; Jack M. Sosin, *Whitehall and the Wilderness: The Middle West in British Colonial Policy, 1760–1775* (Lincoln, Nebr., 1961), 226–227.

[59] Jefferson, Draft of Instructions to the Virginia Delegates in the Continental Congress, in Boyd, ed., *Papers of Jefferson,* I, 123.

[60] Writers who have emphasized a conservative-radical split are Charles Henry Ambler, *Sectionalism in Virginia from 1776 to 1861* (Chicago, 1910), 16–23; H. J. Eckenrode, *The Revolution in Virginia* (Boston and New York, 1916), 1–57; and Merrill Jensen, *The Articles of Confederation* (Madison, 1940), 21–25. Carl Bridenbaugh, *Seat of Empire: The Political Role of Eighteenth-Century Williamsburg,* new ed. (Williamsburg, 1958), 54–71, and Meade, *Patrick Henry,* are more moderate and more recent statements of the same view. None of these writers, however, produce detailed evidence to substantiate their case, and the recent tendency has been to minimize the importance of this conflict. See David J. Mays, *Edmund Pendleton, 1721–1803, A Biography* (Cambridge, Mass., 1952), I; Charles S. Sydnor, *Gentlemen Freeholders: Political Practices in Washington's Virginia* (Chapel Hill, 1952), 104–108; and Alden,

ous controversy occurred, and that at a time when the agitation against Great Britain had quieted. A group of conflicts clustered in the months following repeal of the Stamp Act, but none of them were factional in nature. In one of them Richard Henry Lee attacked George Mercer for his acceptance of the Virginia stamp agency. When Mercer answered by disclosing that Lee had himself been an unsuccessful applicant for the post, the debate raged through a series of long newspaper articles.[61] Another dispute occurred when the death of John Robinson, Speaker of the House and Treasurer of the colony, disclosed shortages in his accounts because of secret loans from paper money that had been turned in for destruction. It resulted in the separation of the Treasurer's office and the Speakership.[62] There were additional minor disturbances as well, among them one over the admission to bail of John Chiswell, a member of the gentry accused of murder.[63] As Fauquier observed, the Stamp Act may have left Virginia easily aroused to factional quarrels; but none of them survived for long or created a clear division among Patriots. On only one later occasion, the closing of the courts, in 1774, did Virginians appear close to splitting, and then the minority quickly bowed to the popular decision.[64] Nearly all the various committees and delegations elected in Virginia—the Committee of Correspondence of 1773, the first Committee of Safety, the members of the First Continental Congress—included men labeled both radical and conservative by modern scholars. As the Revolutionary controversy progressed, potential conflicts among the Patriots lessened rather than increased.[65]

What remains as the fundamental issue in the coming of the Revolution, then, is nothing more than the contest over constitutional rights. None of the other potential issues seems to have applied in Virginia at the opening of the struggle. Perhaps after all the Virginians had stated their grievances reasonably accurately. In 1763 there was a tradition of jealously guarded rights and privileges, but no lingering issues capable in themselves of instigating new conflicts. The Revolution did not open in force until the announcement of the Stamp Act. From then until the beginning of armed conflict with Dunmore in the fall of 1775 political or constitutional issues were the occasion for every outbreak of protest within the colony. The Virginians reacted, moreover, to actions affecting other colonies—the suspension of the New York legislature, the threat to Massachusetts after the Circular Letter, the Gaspee incident in Rhode Island—almost as readily as to measures that applied directly to their own colony. They were apparently moved as much by the over-all conflict as by local considerations.

South in the Revolution, 143–145. In this connection, see also the statement by a contemporary observer, St. George Tucker, that he had never witnessed anything in the House of Burgesses "that bore the appearance of *party spirit."* Tucker to William Wirt, Sept. 25, 1815, *Wm. and Mary College Qtly.,* 1st Ser., XXII (1913–14), 252–257.

[61] These appear mostly in Purdie and Dixon's *Virginia Gazette,* July–Oct. 1766.

[62] The best treatment of the Robinson affair is Mays, *Edmund Pendleton,* I, 174–208.

[63] This affair can be traced in Purdie and Dixon's *Virginia Gazette,* July–Oct. 1766. See also Robert Carter to Thomas Bladen, July 26, 1766, Robert Carter Letter book, Colonial Williamsburg, Inc., and William Nelson to John Norton, Sept. 6, 1766, William Nelson Letter book, Va. State Lib.

[64] Edmund Pendleton to Ralph Wormeley, July 28, 1774, Ralph Wormeley Papers, Alderman Library; James Parker to Charles Steuart, postcript of June 17, 1774, to letter of June 7, 1774, Steuart Papers.

[65] Sydnor, *Gentlemen Freeholders,* 106–108.

Insofar as other issues of a more local character concerned Virginia Patriots, they crowded in during the last years of controversy, when, as Edmund Randolph noted, "a deeper tone broke forth." [66] The closing of the courts by the summer of 1774 and complaints against the merchants suggest that the personal debts of the planters might then have become involved in the political conflict. Western lands, on which there was new restrictive action in 1774, aroused the colony as it had not done before. By 1775 Lord Dunmore's personality and conduct became a further irritant. Nevertheless, without the constitutional struggle that had gone before, these issues would not have been productive of revolution.

Earlier local disputes, moreover, were not able of themselves to generate the conflict. The Parsons' Cause, for instance, arose within the colony, not in response to any imperial policy; and, when it did become a matter of concern to the home government, the action taken in the long run failed to constitute a clear invasion of what Virginians held to be colonial rights. The dispute over establishing an Anglican episcopate, which had a brief revival in 1770–71, was not really serious, in part because it, too, was not actually considered and not actively promoted by imperial officials.[67]

In its concentration upon the broader aspects of the constitutional conflict with the mother country, the Revolutionary movement in Virginia appeared lacking in local issues of prime relevance. Yet local conditions and circumstances in Virginia, as well as elsewhere, almost certainly gave distinctive characteristics to the development of this common issue. One such influence was the structure and distribution of political power within the colonies. The Revolution marked not only a clash of constitutional theories but also a contest between rival blocs of power, the British seeing a need to extend their control over the colonies and the Americans determined to preserve the degree of autonomy they had enjoyed. As early as May 1764, Richard Henry Lee referred to the "iron hand of power" raised against the colonies.[68] Although Virginians may have exaggerated in charging that the ministerial policies represented a determined system to reduce them to slavery, they correctly assessed the intent of Great Britain as an over-all decrease in colonial political power. Indeed, American constitutional theories were to some extent a rationalization of the power struggle, not in the sense of attempting to hide narrow self-interest but in the sense of explaining why some degree of political power was essential for the protection of liberty.

The operation of the British challenge upon the structure of power in Virginia did as much as anything to shape the Revolutionary controversy there. The nature of political control within the colony is generally familiar. The catch phrase is planter aristocracy. Historians have described a small, able ruling group, largely members of the planter class and frequently related by family ties. These men governed both through the Council and to an even larger extent through the House of Burgesses, and their dominance of the county courts and the Anglican parish vestries provided

---

[66] Randolph, History of Virginia.

[67] On this point see Arthur Lyon Cross, The Anglican Episcopate and the American Colonies (Cambridge, Mass., 1924), 226–240, and George W. Pilcher, "Virginia Newspapers and the Dispute over the Proposed Colonial Episcopate, 1771–1772," The Historian, XXIII (1960–61), 98–113.

[68] Richard Henry Lee to ———, May 31, 1764, in Ballagh, ed., Letters of Richard Henry Lee, I, 5. See also the first paragraph of the Association of 1774 of the Virginia Convention, in Boyd, ed., Papers of Jefferson, I, 137.

additional bases of local power. A further concentration of influence in the hands of a few leading Burgesses meant that a dozen or so men might dominate the government of the colony. At the same time a relatively wide franchise for the election of Burgesses prevented the ruling elite from completely ignoring the will of the populace and suggested a wide assent to the government of the colony.[69]

In this situation there was little chance for factionalism to arise among the Patriots —the unanimity with which Virginians acted was largely unavoidable. Since there were no separate sources of local power, the Revolutionary movement most likely was directed from the center outward to the counties. The county conventions and other local activities need more study. In all likelihood, those who participated in them may have simply been adopting resolutions and policies that the leaders of the colony wanted rather than instructing the Patriot high command. Moreover, the situation in Virginia left no room for the development of native Loyalist leadership. Loyalist claimants for British compensation after the Revolution numbered only thirteen persons born in Virginia. Even the Council, drawn from the same planter class as the Burgesses, was far from being a center of royalist sympathies. Several councilors were outspoken Patriots, and the others were more properly neutralist than Loyalist. The real explanation for the weakness of Loyalism within the colony may lie deeper than in the common assumption that Dunmore's antics alienated strong potential support for the Crown. It may be attributable instead to the lack of an avenue to political power other than the one already monopolized by the planters.[70]

This combination of unanimity and concentration of political power probably accounts for many characteristic features of the Revolution in Virginia—features that have, at least, given a distinctive coloration to the central issue of political and constitutional rights. For example, the emphasis upon interference with the colonial legislatures in the charges against George III is perhaps a clue to the Virginians' preoccupation with threats to a political power that was centered in the House of Burgesses. Similarly, it suggests less concern about the rights of the individual than we commonly associate with the American Revolution. This may seem a risky supposition to make in the face of George Mason's classic defense of individualism in the Virginia Declaration of Rights, but Virginians may very well have thought they possessed individual liberty in sufficient degree and that their rights were endangered only to the extent that colonial self-government itself was in danger. Certainly, the changes that occurred in Virginia, with the exception of the achievement of religious freedom, had little to do with the extension of individual liberty. The two great consequences of the Revolution within Virginia were the elimination of all British control and the further predominance of the legislative branch of government.

The Virginia leaders, then, did not go far wrong in their attribution of the fateful dispute with Great Britain to an invasion of constitutional rights. The one thing they might perhaps have added, though for them it could hardly have needed to be made explicit, was that the new turn in imperial policy directly challenged an established ruling class who would not lightly give up its power and privileges of self-government. If one is seeking the material and substantial interests that represent the reality behind constitutional principle, this political power is substance enough.

[69] Sydnor, *Gentlemen Freeholders,* 60–119; Jack P. Greene, "Foundations of Political Power in the Virginia House of Burgesses, 1720–1776," *Wm. and Mary Qtly.,* 3d Ser., XVI (1959), 485–506.

[70] On the weakness of Loyalism in Virginia see Berwick, Loyalties in Crisis, 51–58.

9 / The Ward-Hopkins Controversy and the American Revolution in Rhode Island: An Interpretation

Mack E. Thompson

In the quarter-century preceding the American Revolution, Rhode Island had its own peculiar political development. Leadership did change hands—in rough terms, from Southerners to Northerners, from Newport to Providence. But what meaning did this process of change have for the social and political order of the colony? And what significance did it have in the broader context of the developing colonial opposition to the home country? Some historians have been tempted to see Rhode Island as an example of internal social revolution and have identified the losers as "conservative merchants" and the winners as "radical farmers." Moreover, they have attempted to depict these "conservative" and "radical" factions in all colonies as the forerunners of the "Tories" and "Whigs" of the Revolution itself. Mack E. Thompson raises some significant questions with regard to such arguments. He analyzes the nature of the principal factions in Rhode Island politics, the groups headed by Samuel Ward and Stephen Hopkins. He notes the phenomenal rise of Providence and the areas surrounding it to a new and different position of economic importance in the half-century prior to the Declaration of Indepenednce, and he carefully considers the attitudes of leaders of various factions toward the dangers of British interference in the 1760's and 1770's. Perhaps, most importantly, he raises significant doubts as to the meaning and the usefulness of such terms as "radical" and "conservative" in any analysis of the actual situation in Rhode Island in the revolutionary era.

From 1755 to 1770 the colony of Rhode Island was torn by an internal political struggle that historians usually refer to as the Ward-Hopkins controversy, since the two factions contending for political supremacy were led by Samuel Ward from

Reprinted by permission from *The William and Mary Quarterly*, 3rd series, XVI (1959), 363–375.

Westerly and Newport and Stephen Hopkins from Providence. Those who consider the American Revolution as an internal social and political conflict as well as a revolt from political obedience to England seem to see their thesis substantiated by the Ward-Hopkins controversy. Their assumption is that in pre-Revolutionary Rhode Island the people were sharply divided politically along economic class lines. One author states that Rhode Island was "a battleground for conservative merchants and radical farmers," and that "radicalism won victories earlier than in the other colonies." "When the break with England came," this author concludes, "Newport and the Narragansett country remained loyal, whereas the agrarian north, which was in control of the government, declared Rhode Island's independence of Britain two months before the radical party was able to achieve that end in the Continental Congress. Throughout the revolutionary period the Rhode Islanders were staunch defenders of democracy and state sovereignty."[1] In other words, the colony was taken into the Revolution by northern agrarian radicals who had earlier won a victory for democratic rights against southern conservative merchants. The purpose of this paper is to offer an alternative interpretation of the Ward-Hopkins controversy and the Revolution in Rhode Island.

It is true that Rhode Island was split politically along geographic lines. Hopkins's supporters were located in the northern towns and Ward's in the southern. But to view the north's rise to political power as a victory for agrarian radicalism is to miss entirely the significance of Stephen Hopkins's political success. Fundamental to an understanding of domestic politics in Rhode Island is a clear picture of the colony's economic growth during the middle half of the eighteenth century.

To speak of the north as "agrarian" and the south as "mercantile" is a fairly accurate description of Rhode Island in 1720, if we mean that commercial activity was confined largely to Newport and the Narragansett country in the south.[2] Before that date, and for some years after, only in Newport, on Aquidneck Island in Narragansett Bay, did there exist in Rhode Island an urban community with a fairly sizable population employed in commerce and manufacturing. And only in the southern part of the colony, in the Narragansett country, were there substantial numbers of capitalistic farmers. In the rest of the colony an overwhelming majority of the people were en-

---

[1] Merrill Jensen, *The Articles of Confederation: An Interpretation of the Social-Constitutional History of the American Revolution, 1774–1781* (Madison, 1940), p. 40. Marguerite Appleton, in her biographical sketch of Samuel Ward in the *Dictionary of American Biography*, XIX, 437, writes that Rhode Island "was divided into two hostile camps: the conservative group, the merchants, found a champion in Ward, while the radicals looked to Hopkins." Bernhard Knollenberg has a somewhat different view. He writes, "I have found no evidence of such a line of cleavage; personal and sectional rivalry seem to have been the chief factors." *Correspondence of Governor Samuel Ward, May 1775–March 1776, with a Biographical Introduction Based Chiefly on the Ward Papers Covering the Period 1775–1776*, ed. Bernhard Knollenberg (Providence, 1952), p. 6. Carl Becker, in his *History of Political Parties in the Province of New York, 1760–1776* (Madison, 1909), was one of the earliest writers to interpret the American Revolution as the "result of two general movements; the contest for home rule and independence, and the democratization of American politics and society." Recently the Becker-Jensen thesis as applied to Massachusetts has been sharply challenged by Robert E. Brown, *Middle-Class Democracy and the Revolution in Massachusetts, 1691–1780* (Ithaca, 1955).

[2] Carl Bridenbaugh, *Cities in the Wilderness: The First Century of Urban Life in America, 1625–1742* (New York, 1938), pp. 175–205, passim, but see particularly pages 175, 176–177, 182, 184, 190; Richard Pares, *Yankees and Creoles: The Trade between North America and the West Indies before the American Revolution* (London, 1956), p. 33.

gaged in subsistence agriculture, and commercial activity was relatively unimportant.

Until the 1750's the agrarian interests managed to have a decisive voice in the formation of public policy because the architects of the colony's government in the seventeenth century had fashioned a system to serve the needs of an agricultural population, and their charter had placed control of the central government in the hands of men residing in small farming communities.[3] As long as Rhode Island's economic base remained predominantly that of subsistence agriculture the most important unit of government was town, not colony, government. With few exceptions the problems of these people could be solved by the town council. For decades the powers of the General Assembly were neither numerous nor vigorously exercised except in the area of monetary policy. From 1710 to 1751 Rhode Island farmers passed nine paper money bills or "banks" in an attempt to solve their monetary problems.[4] They were forcefully but unsuccessfully opposed by the commercial interests in Newport.[5]

But the Rhode Island economy was not static. During the half century preceding the Revolution, external as well as internal events caused a remarkable economic growth that profoundly altered long existing political conditions. Newport, already one of the five leading ports in America by 1720, continued to grow.[6] As the West India market expanded and the number of trading ships to Newport increased, Narragansett planters geared their production to meet the demands of agricultural exporters. Increasingly these planters turned from subsistence to capitalistic farming, sending their surpluses to Newport for distribution. Opportunities in manufacturing, particularly distilling, shipbuilding, and ropemaking, caused many farmers to diversify their activities and in some cases to leave the land altogether. Long existing cultural, religious, and family affinities between the Newport and Narragansett residents were strengthened by intimate economic association, and the planters of Narragansett drifted slowly into political alliance with merchant, mechanic, and professional classes of Newport. Newporters or men closely identified with the interests of that town began to monopolize the governorship and other important offices in the colonial government. They also tried to run the General Assembly in their own interests but were never quite able to wrest control from the grip of the small farmers.

While Newport was expanding its commercial activities and extending its economic and political influence into the southern agricultural communities, in the north, on the banks of the Seekonk and Providence Rivers, another commercial center was rising. For almost a century Providence, the oldest town in the colony, had remained an agricultural community, but in the second quarter of the eighteenth century it

[3] The unit of representation in the General Assembly was the town: six deputies from Newport, four each from Providence, Portsmouth, and Warwick, and two from each of the remaining towns. As long as the smaller towns remained united they could always defeat the larger towns.

[4] *Records of the Colony of Rhode Island and Providence Plantations in New England,* ed. John Russell Bartlett (Providence, 1856–65), IV, 96, 202, 295, 350, 405, 454, 487, 440, 579, 592, V, 40, 75, 99, 130, 318–319. Hereafter cited as *Rhode Island Records.*

[5] For example, see the protest of Newport deputies against the 1744 "bank," and the "Petition to the King, relative to bills of credit," Newport, Sept. 4, 1750, *ibid.,* V, 75–76, 311–313. Among the 72 signers were Newport's leading merchants. In 1731 Governor Joseph Jenkes vetoed a bill issuing £60,000, but he was overruled by the General Assembly and the home government. *Ibid.,* IV, 456–461.

[6] Bridenbaugh, *Cities in the Wilderness,* pp. 330–363, passim, and particularly pp. 331, 334, 337, 347.

responded to the same influences that were making Newport one of the leading ports in British North America. By the mid 1750's Providence was a thriving port with a young and enterprising group of merchants.[7]

Providence's economic growth is not surprising. In some respects that city was more advantageously located than Newport. Providence not only had a protected outlet to the sea, but her merchants could draw on a larger hinterland for their cargoes than could Newport's. In response to increased demand for exports, several Providence merchants began to manufacture candles, chocolate, barrel hoops, rum, and rope and to serve as middlemen, supplying Newport merchants with cargo they could not find on the island or in the Narragansett country across the bay. By the early 1750's Providence was prepared to challenge Newport for economic leadership of the colony.[8]

It is against this background of economic change that Rhode Island politics must be projected. Newport's continued expansion and Providence's rise as an important commercial center were both cause and effect of the violent political controversy that erupted in 1755 and continued for over a decade. In that year the freemen elected Stephen Hopkins, one of Providence's leading merchants, to the governorship, an office he held for nine of the next thirteen years. His election shows that a realignment of political forces had taken place—the hitherto fairly unified agrarian interest had disintegrated, and two composite factions, one in the north and another in the south, had appeared. The new factions were made up of cross sections of society— large and small farmers, merchants and tradesmen, professional men and other freemen. The previous division of political forces along agrarian-commercial lines was no more. Hopkins's election also shows that political leadership had finally passed from the agrarian-small town interests to commercial and manufacturing groups and that the chief instrument for the promotion of economic growth was likely to be the General Assembly rather than the town council. Although rural towns continued to exert considerable influence in the political life of the colony, thirty years passed before they again consolidated to seize control of the government.[9]

With the disintegration of agrarian solidarity and the growth of two factions composed of men from both the urban and rural areas, political success went to the man who could reconcile conflicting interests within his own section and attract a majority of the few uncommitted freemen. As the contest between the north and south developed, leaders of both sides realized that the voters holding the balance of power were concentrated most heavily in the farming communities in the central part of

[7] William E. Foster, *Stephen Hopkins: A Rhode Island Statesman. A Study in the Political History of the Eighteenth Century* (Providence, 1884), pp. 91–102.

[8] James B. Hedges, *The Browns of Providence Plantations: Colonial Years* (Cambridge, Mass., 1952), pp. 1–69.

[9] There is no recent study of the Ward-Hopkins controversy, but see Hedges, *The Browns of Providence Plantations,* pp. 189–192, and my unpublished Ph.D. dissertation, "Moses Brown, A Man of Public Responsibility," Brown University, 1955, chaps. IV–VI. Carl Bridenbaugh has some interesting remarks concerning the Ward-Hopkins controversy in his *Cities in Revolt: Urban Life in America, 1743–1776* (New York, 1955), pp. 11, 53, 222–223, 264, 378. An older but still valuable treatment is contained in *State of Rhode Island and Providence Plantations at the End of the Century: A History,* ed. Edward Field (Boston, 1902), I, 199–219. A recently published work on the subject by David S. Lovejoy, *Rhode Island Politics and the American Revolution, 1760–1776* (Providence, 1958), arrived too late to be of assistance in the preparation of this paper.

the colony, equidistant from the two commercial centers of Newport and Providence.[10] Stephen Hopkins, one of the most accomplished politicians in colonial America, was more successful in appealing to these freemen and better able to prevent any serious defections in his party than was his opponent, Samuel Ward.

The climax to the prolonged struggle came in the election of 1767, when Hopkins decisively defeated Ward for the governorship and dealt the southern party a shattering blow from which it never recovered. Hopkins's success was the result of a combination of factors. By 1767, after controlling the government for two consecutive years, Ward and his followers in Newport had alienated the Narragansett planters and farmers by refusing to support a measure to regulate interest rates, and some of the latter began to look elsewhere for political leadership. Ward's party was further discredited by the gerrymandering activities of Elisha Brown, the deputy governor.[11]

Hopkins helped his cause by collecting a large election fund and conducting an energetic campaign. Personal influence, money, and liberal amounts of rum were brought to bear, and where possible, the old, the sick, and the infirm were carried to the polls to cast their ballots for Hopkins-party men. Freemen were not only paid to vote for Hopkins and his supporters but "many persons that is stranious for Mr. Ward who may be agreed with for a Small Sum to Lay Still," were also approached.[12] One Hopkins-party campaign worker, "Clostly Engaged in the Grand Cause" in Cumberland, reported that he would "be short with Regard to the Necessary argument (haveing Last Evening fell into Company with Two men who was against us Last year, who was hard to Convince of their Error, but I over come them) shall want five Dollars more which I must have; for I must meat the above two men To morrow morning almost up to Woonsoketfalls where I expect to Settle Some things very favourable To the Campaign. . . ." He ended his urgent letter with the candid remark: "am Engaged Clostly in makeing freemen and hope I shall merrit the Beaver Hat." [13]

Hopkins's success in 1767 was materially aided by the growing identification of outlying towns with Providence as a result of the economic opportunities that flourishing port offered. Providence's economic growth may be compared to an expanding whirlpool; when it began slowly to spin in the second quarter of the century, it drew nearby agricultural communities into its vortex. In the next decades, as its force in-

[10] For a breakdown by towns of votes in the elections of 1761–64, see Ward Manuscripts, Box I, 1725–70, nos. 43, 49, Rhode Island Historical Society, Providence, R. I.; Brown Papers, L63–71M, John Carter Brown Library, Providence, R. I. In the election of 1765, Ward carried every town in King's and Kent counties by substantial majorities. In the election of 1766, while he still won all the towns, his margin of victory had decreased appreciably, and in the next election the drift toward Hopkins had gone so far as to give him the election by 414 votes, the largest majority in years. *The Providence* [Rhode Island] *Gazette and Country Journal*, Apr. 18, 1767, announced that not one vote was cast for Ward in Providence, and that in Cumberland he got only 4 votes. An analysis of the vote by towns above shows that in 1767 Ward lost what little support he had in the north, while Hopkins made large dents in Ward's majorities in South Kingston, North Kingston, Westerly (Ward's home town), Charleston, and East Greenwich. "Public Notice to the Printer," submitted by one of the Browns, Apr. 17, 1767, Brown Papers, P-P6; Field, *State of Rhode Island*, I, 211.

[11] *Acts and Resolves . . . of Rhode Island . . .* (Providence and Newport, 1747–1815), 1765–69, pp. 24, 30–32; *Rhode Island Records*, VI, 436–437; Moses Brown Papers, misc. papers, I, 15, XVIII, 77, R. I. Hist. Soc.

[12] Nicholas Brown and Company, Apr. 9, 1767, Brown Papers, P-P6.

[13] John Dexter to Nicholas Brown and Company, Apr. 14, 1767, *ibid.*, L67M.

creased, it slowly but inexorably sucked more distant towns into its center. Political sympathies apparently were swept along with economic interests, for these towns eventually supported Stephen Hopkins and the northern party. Southern response to this economic and political alignment was what triggered the Ward-Hopkins controversy and kept it alive for over a decade.

Stephen Hopkins's elections to the governorship in 1755 and in subsequent years was not a victory for social and political radicalism. On issues commonly associated with radicalism there was little discussion and almost no discussion at all directly relating to internal political controversies. During Hopkins's numerous administrations no new laws were passed or even introduced in the General Assembly abolishing or lowering the property qualifications for the vote. The people were apparently not concerned with such issues. And ironically, on the most important problem of the period, currency, the men who assumed the leadership in solving it were not the southern "conservative merchants" but the northern "radical farmers." Stephen Hopkins, one of Providence's leading merchants, and the Browns of Providence, Obadiah and his four nephews, Nicholas, Joseph, John, and Moses, who operated one of the largest shipping firms in the colony, led the fight for currency reform.[14] By the early 1760's Stephen Hopkins's northern followers were committed to a program of sound money and in 1763 they were able to push through the assembly the first bill to regulate currency in the history of the colony.[15] While some southerners supported currency reform, the Browns would never have been able to pass the bill without the support of representatives from the nearby agricultural towns, a fact which points up the composite nature of the northern faction. Subsequent legislation provided Rhode Island with a stable currency until the Revolution.

To see in Rhode Island political controversy a class struggle—agrarian radicals fighting conservative merchants—is to see something that did not exist. That came only in the post-Revolutionary years and had its roots in the changes brought about by the war and the success of the Revolution. This is not to say that before 1776 there were no class distinctions or that members of the lower classes did not resent advantages enjoyed by the upper classes; but there is little evidence that such distinctions or sentiments resulted in social tensions serious enough to label revolutionary.

Briefly stated, then, the chief cause for the intense political struggle in Rhode Island before the Revolution was the desire of men in the north and the south to gain control of the government to promote private and public interests. When the

[14] The material on this subject is extensive, but see Governor Stephen Hopkins to the General Assembly, Providence, Oct. 28, 1756, *The Correspondence of the Colonial Governors of Rhode Island, 1723–1775*, ed. Gertrude Selwyn Kimball (Boston, 1902–03), II, 234–236; and Petition to General Assembly, Providence, Feb, 1763, Rhode Island Archives, II, 58, State Archives, State House, Providence, R. I. Over a hundred men signed this petition, including the leading merchants and landowners of Providence, but the names of small businessmen, tradesmen, and farmers also appeared on the list. See also Brown Papers, P-P6, and the *Providence Gazette and Country Journal*, Apr. 2, 1763.

[15] *Rhode Island Records*, VI, 358–362. While Hopkins, the Browns, and other northerners desired currency reform, they did not oppose paper money issues on principle. And in response to the Currency Act of 1764, which prohibited the colonies from making paper money legal tender, proponents of currency reform indicated that paper money was essential to the economic prosperity of the colony. *Rhode Island Records*, VI, 407–410. E. James Ferguson, "Currency Finance: An Interpretation of Colonial Monetary Practices," *William and Mary Quarterly*, 3d Ser., X (1953), 155.

southern and northern economies expanded, and merchants, tradesmen, and capitalistic farmers emerged whose needs could no longer be satisfied by the town meeting, they began to compete with one another for control of the colonial government. The General Assembly could bestow many profitable favors on deserving citizens; it could issue flags of truce to merchants authorizing them to exchange French prisoners and provisions in the West Indies;[16] it could determine which merchants could outfit privateers;[17] it could grant monopolies to enterprising businessmen;[18] it could vote funds to build or repair lighthouses, bridges, schools, and to make other local public improvements,[19] it could alter the apportionment of taxes to the benefit of towns in particular sections.[20] These and other powers only the General Assembly had. The section that controlled the government could use the assembly as an instrument to promote its economic and cultural growth.

A good illustration of this interpretation of domestic politics in Rhode Island occurs in the struggle that took place in 1769 and 1770 over the permanent location of the College of Rhode Island. After considerable discussion, the choice of sites for the college narrowed to Providence and Newport. The contestants considered the controversy one more episode, and perhaps the last, in the long drawn-out competition for economic and political leadership between the north and the south. In a letter to the town councils of Scituate and Gloucester, Stephen Hopkins and Moses Brown of Providence wrote:

> When we consider that the building the College here will be a means of bringing great quantities of money into the place, and thereby of greatly increasing the

[16] Governor Hopkins to William Pitt, Rhode Island, Dec. 20, 1760, *Correspondence of William Pitt when Secretary of State with Colonial Governors and Military and Naval Commissioners in America,* ed. Gertrude Selwyn Kimball (London, 1906), II, 373–378; *Rhode Island Records,* V, 241–242, VI, 173–174, 220, 252.

[17] As governor during the French and Indian War, Stephen Hopkins frequently issued letters of marque to Providence ship captains, among them members of his own family. Rhode Island Historical Society Manuscripts, XII, 17.

[18] In 1765 when the Browns of Providence went into the iron manufacturing business, they had to petition the assembly to get legislation permitting them to build a dam for the furnace on the Pawtuxet River. The petition was considered no less than twelve times by the lower and upper houses within a period of less than two months. Governor Ward and the assistants resorted to numerous devices to block the granting of the petition, and, although they were unsuccessful, they were able to place several restrictions on the construction and use of the dam. The furnace owners had to return to the assembly to get them removed, but they waited until Ward was no longer governor. Journal of the House of Deputies, 1765–66, Sept. sess., 1765, R. I. Archives.

[19] For example, in 1764, Moses Brown, one of the deputies from Providence, tried unsuccessfully to get the assembly to appropriate money to restore the washed out Weybosset Bridge in Providence and to repair the lighthouse on Beavertail Island in Narragansett Bay. Later he was more successful. Brown Papers, P-U5, I. Towns also had to get assembly approval for lotteries, one of the common methods for raising money for local improvements, and their representatives were expected to see that such legislation passed the assembly. *Rhode Island Acts and Resolves,* Sept. sess., 1761, pp. 39–40.

[20] In 1761 Hopkins and his party passed legislation shifting the budren of taxation from commercial interests in the northern towns to agricultural property owners in Narragansett country, a Ward-party stronghold. When Ward gained control of the government in 1765, the assembly lightened the tax burden for some of the southern agricultural towns and increased it for Providence, Scituate, and Cumberland, solid Hopkins-party towns. In 1767, when Hopkins decisively defeated Ward, the assembly not only rescinded the Ward-party legislation but passed a bill acquitting the three northern towns of court judgments for nonpayment of taxes. *Ibid.,* 1765–69, May and June sess., 1767.

markets for all kinds of the countries produce; and, consequently, of increasing the value of all estates to which this town is a market; and also that it will much promote the weight and influence of this northern part of the Colony in the scale of government in all times to come, we think every man that hath an estate in this County who duly weighs these advantages, with many others that will naturally occur to his mind, must, for the bettering of his own private interest, as well as for the public good, become a contributor to the College here, rather than it should be removed from hence. . . .

We are more zealous in this matter as we have certain intelligence that the people in Newport, who are become sinsible of the importance of this matter, are very deligently using every method in their power to carry the prize from us, and as the few remaining days of this month is the whole time in which we can work to any purpose, we hope none will slumber or sleep. We think ourselves in this matter wholly engaged for the public good; and therefore hope to be borne with when we beg of you and all our neighbors, to seriously consult their own interest and pursue it with unremitted zeal.[21]

The governing body of the College of Rhode Island eventually voted to make Providence the permanent home of the institution. In the 1770 election, Samuel Ward, his brother Henry, who was the colony secretary, and a few other southern politicians made a determined effort to capture control of the government in order to get a charter for a college in Newport. They failed and their bill to charter a second college was defeated by deputies committed to northern leadership.[22]

To say that the central theme of the Ward-Hopkins controversy was the political struggle between similar interests in two different sections does not necessarily assume a uniformity of motives on the part of the participants. Undoubtedly some men on both sides were propelled above all else by the financial rewards public office afforded, by personal animosities, and by desire for social prestige, while others devoted their time and money to politics because of a sense of public responsibility or simply because they enjoyed the game of politics. But what bound the men of each party together was their recognition that the promotion of their own section, and thus their own interests, could best be done through control of the government.[23] Social and economic classes could co-operate for this purpose in the two sections. In fact, co-operation, not dissension, between classes is the distinctive characteristic of pre-Revolutionary political life in Rhode Island.

If we turn now to consider the claim that Rhode Island split into radical and conservative camps over British attempts to extend Parliamentary authority to America, we find that the facts do not bear out this claim. Rhode Island was one of the first colonies to react to the Sugar Act of 1764 and to the Stamp Act of the following year.[24] In the General Assembly, members of the two factions united to petition the

---

[21] Stephen Hopkins and Nicholas Brown and Company [Moses Brown] to Town Councils of Scituate and Glocester, Providence, Dec. 8, 1769, Rhode Island College Miscellaneous Papers, 1763–82, I, 71, John Hay Library, Providence, R. I.

[22] *The Literary Diary of Ezra Stiles, D. D., LL.D., President of Yale College,* ed. Franklin Bowditch Dexter (New York, 1901), I, 46, 108, 109.

[23] A detailed discussion of these influences is contained in my unpublished Ph.D. dissertation, "Moses Brown, A Man of Public Responsibility," chap. III.

[24] "Remonstrance of the Colony of Rhode Island to the Lords Commissioners of Trade and Plantations," South Kingston, Jan. 24, 1764, and Resolves against the Stamp Act, Sept. 1765, in *Rhode Island Records,* VI, 378–383, 451–452. Rhode Island's response to the Sugar Act and the Stamp Act is described in detail in Edmund S. and Helen M. Morgan, *The Stamp Act Crisis:*

Lords Commissioners for Trade and Plantations for their repeal. This early response set the tone for resistance to subsequent Parliamentary legislation and ministerial attempts to enforce customs regulations.[25]

The political leaders of both factions opposed British policy with equal vigor. Stephen Hopkins made a strong defense of American rights in *The Rights of the Colonies Examined,* and the General Assembly sent this pamphlet to the colony's agent in England for use in the move for repeal of the Stamp Act.[26] Hopkins's subsequent service for the cause of American independence is too well known to necessitate further comment. His political opponent, Samuel Ward, was no less a patriot. In fact, Ward held the governorship during the Stamp Act crisis when the colony successfully prevented the use of stamps. He made every effort to frustrate attempts of the king's officers to enforce the Acts of Trade and was an outspoken critic of British trade regulations. When the First Continental Congress met in Philadelphia in September 1774, Ward and Hopkins attended as delegates from Rhode Island.[27]

Stout resistance by these key figures to Parliament's attempts to extend its authority to the American colonies was emulated by the second rank of leaders of both factions and strongly supported by the freemen. The only person of importance in the north who attempted to abide by the Stamp Act was John Foster, a justice of the peace and clerk of the Inferior Court of Common Pleas for Providence County, who refused to open his court and transact business without stamps.[28] A crowd of angry people gathered before his house and threatened to ride him out of town on a rail unless he changed his mind. This was enough to convince Foster of his error. In 1769 after the Townshend Acts were passed and again in 1772, royal officials trying to perform their duties were roughly treated by the northerners; and in 1773, when British naval vessels were patrolling Narragansett Bay in an effort to stop contraband trade, John Brown, the leading merchant in Providence, and a number of citizens, burned the revenue vessel, the *Gaspee,* to the water's edge. Royal investigators could get no assistance from Rhode Islanders in their search for the culprits. In the south, in Newport, throughout the period 1765–75, the people frequently demonstrated their hostile attitude toward British policy and supporters of the Crown.[29]

Prologue to Revolution (Chapel Hill, 1953), pp. 27–28, 36, 98–99. In connection with Rhode Island's reaction to the Sugar Act, the Morgans note that "In Rhode Island where the whole government was popularly elected, no conservative politicians hampered the preparation of a spirited protest." This statement (p. 36) describes the nature of Rhode Island resistance for the entire period.

[25] *Rhode Island Records,* V, 559–561, 561–566, 563. Arthur M. Schlesinger, *The Colonial Merchants and the American Revolution, 1763–1776,* Library Edition (New York, 1939), p. 112.

[26] *Rhode Island Records,* VI, 412. For Hopkins's pamphlet, see *ibid.,* 416–427.

[27] *Correspondence of Governor Samuel Ward,* pp. 3–36; *Rhode Island Records,* VI, 472–513, passim. As late as December 12, 1774, Governor Joseph Wanton was firm in his opposition to the British efforts to suppress revolt. *American Archives,* ed. Peter Force, 4th ser. (Washington, 1837–46), I, 1039. Rhode Island resolutions against Parliamentary taxation and the Boston Port Act, Newport, June 15, 1774, *ibid.,* 416–417.

[28] Affidavit, Dec. 12, 1765, Moses Brown Papers, misc. MSS, B-815, Box 1, R. I. Hist. Soc.

[29] Oliver M. Dickerson, *The Navigation Acts and the American Revolution* (Philadelphia, 1951), p. 258; Morgan and Morgan, *The Stamp Act Crisis,* pp. 144–151; Bridenbaugh, *Cities in Revolt,* pp. 309–311. *Rhode Island Records,* VI, 593–596; Schlesinger, *Colonial Merchants,* pp. 485–486; *American Archives,* 4th ser., I, 1098–1099. For response of Newport to Boston Port Act, see Resolves of Newport town meeting, May 20, 1774, *ibid.,* 343–344. That there were a few royalists in Newport and Providence during this period is suggested by an "Extract of a

One of the striking things about anti-British leadership in Rhode Island is its continuity. The same people who successfully organized the opposition to the Stamp Act and the Townshend Acts led the resistance to the Tea Act and the Intolerable Acts and declared Rhode Island's independence. For the most part these leaders were not radical agrarians but members of the commercial and professional classes of both Providence and Newport. This does not mean that the farmers were pro-British. There was stronger loyalist sentiment among the merchants in Newport than among the farmers in the agricultural communities.[30] What it does mean is that the farmers were content to follow the lead of men like Hopkins and Ward. The merchants, shipowners, and lawyers who were the leaders in domestic politics were also the leaders in the Revolutionary movement.

Articulate supporters of Parliamentary supremacy in Rhode Island during the 1760's were almost without exception royal government employees.[31] They constituted an infinitesimal percentage of the population and exerted no influence within the colonial government and very little outside it. And when they did speak out, they made every effort to hide their identity and to cloak their real intentions. If discovered, they were either forced into silence or hounded out of the colony. During the five years before the outbreak of violence, supporters of British policy were even less noticeable than during the earlier period. Even Joseph Wanton, Rhode Island's Episcopalian governor who eventually went over to the British, was a strong defender of American liberties throughout these years. When Rhode Island declared its independence, the few citizens who could not accept the decision either withdrew from active participation in public affairs or left the colony.

The colony's vigorous, continuous opposition to British policy proves that Rhode Islanders were trying to preserve a system with which they were well satisfied, rather than to change it. The struggle for home rule in Rhode Island was not paralleled by any fight between agrarian and commercial classes to determine who should rule at home. The transition from colony to commonwealth was made with practically no changes in the existing institutions, leadership, or social structure. And there were few demands for any changes. The struggle for democratic rights came in the postwar decade and its origins must be sought in the changes produced by the war and independence and not in the Ward-Hopkins controversy.

Letter to a Gentleman in New-York, dated Newport, Rhode Island, Dec. 14, 1774," and in a Resolution of the Providence town meeting, Aug. 31, 1774, *ibid.*, 1041, 747.

[30] Carl Bridenbaugh, *Peter Harrison, First American Architect* (Chapel Hill, 1949), p. 125. Most Quakers, of course, opposed the Revolution or tried to remain neutral, and some of the Episcopalians joined the British.

[31] Governor Joseph Wanton refused to sanction General Assembly military preparations and was removed from office. *Rhode Island Records,* VII, 392–393. Deputy Governor Darius Sessions and Assistants William Potter and Thomas Wicks also expressed doubts about military resistance to royal authority, but they soon recovered and became good patriots. *Ibid.,* 311, 398–399, 347–349. There was no great turnover in the personnel sitting in the assembly during 1775–76. Those who left did so to serve in the army or to assume some other government post; their successors were in some instances former members who had retired because of age or to devote full time to business; in other cases they were local leaders who would probably have moved up to the assembly eventually.

Part III

THE WAR
FOR INDEPENDENCE

10 / The Massachusetts Acts of 1774: Coercive or Preventive?

Jack M. Sosin

The famous Boston Tea Party was followed in 1774 by the enactment of a series of Parliamentary statutes that rapidly became known in the American colonies as the "Intolerable Acts." Of these acts, all but one—the Quebec Act, which was in reality a long needed reform of the government of that province—were attempts to deal with the state of near-rebellion that the British believed existed in the Massachusetts Bay Colony. These Intolerable Acts, or as British authors have often referred to them, "Coercive Acts," became in turn the precipitating factor for further colonial resistance. They served to unite the Whigs of the colonies and led directly to the calling of the First Continental Congress. American propagandists widely pictured these pieces of British legislation as unparalleled examples of oppression: they described them as destroying self-government in Massachusetts, threatening to starve the people of Boston, foreshadowing the quartering of an oppressive standing army, and ending such traditional rights as that to trial by jury of one's peers. By adding the Quebec Act to their list of complaints, these writers also made an appeal to the strong anti-Catholic bias of most Americans of this generation. Yet there is little doubt that the British ministry thought itself confronted with a spirit of resistance in Massachusetts so strong that it had to be dealt with by forceful measures. Lord North and those around him believed that the government had been far too lenient toward the colonists in the past and had to adopt a program that was sufficiently stern to prevent the further growth of rebellious spirit. Ironically, their efforts that were intended as a show of strength to lead the colonists to return to their traditional obedience provided the catalyst for the rise of further and united opposition. In the following essay Jack M. Sosin examines the issues involved insofar as the British were concerned in the adoption of the statutes to deal with the crisis facing royal officials and the entire system of royal authority in the Massachusetts Bay Colony.

Reprinted by permission from the *Huntington Library Quarterly,* XXVI (1962–1963), 235–252.

For further reading: Max Beloff, *The Debate over the American Revolution 1761–1783* (1949); Bernard Donoughue, *British Politics and the American Revolution: The Path to War, 1773–1775* (1965); Charles R. Ritcheson, *British Politics and the American Revolution* (1954); Jack M. Sosin, *Agents and Merchants: British Colonial Policy and the Origins of the American Revolution, 1763–1775* (1965); Alan Valentine, *Lord North* (2 vols., 1967).

"The tea that bainful weed is arrived"; so wrote Abigail Adams. The future first lady referred, of course, to the appearance at Boston of three tea ships of the British East India Company.[1] Resistance to the landing of the tea and to the payment of the threepence duty was widespread in America; but the most sensational incident occurred in Boston, where for weeks the local patriots attempted to force the consignees of the East India Company to ship the tea back to England. Richard Clark, Thomas and Elisha Hutchinson (sons of the governor), Benjamin Faneuil, Jr., and Joshua Winslow petitioned the governor, council, and justices of the peace to take charge of the cargoes assigned to them; but to no avail. The councilors contended that they had no authority to take the tea from the consignees; if they advised landing the cargo, the duty would be paid, and they would be advocating a measure inconsistent with the declared sentiments of the Massachusetts legislature. In despair, Governor Thomas Hutchinson wrote to the British secretary of state enclosing the debates of the council; his lordship could see, he remonstrated, "the situation of a Massachusetts Governor, and that he is without the least support in measures for maintaining the authority of the Crown." [2]

Since the governor on his own authority had not been able to help them, the consignees and four of the five royal customs commissioners (John Temple, a colonist, sided with the patriots) fled to the protection of the royal garrison at Castle William in Boston Harbor. Through the Boston town meeting the patriots now organized in defense of the "liberties" of America.[3]

On the night of December 16, 1773, Samuel Adams' "Mohawks" boarded the ships of the East India Company and dumped three cargoes of Bohea tea into the harbor. This "most magnificent movement of all" stirred John Adams to write in his diary: "There is a dignity, a majesty, a sublimity, in this last effort of the patriots, that I greatly admire. The people should never rise without doing something to be remembered, something notable and striking." [4]

But how had the Boston patriots carried out this memorable blow when royal troops and ships were in the vicinity? The military and naval commanders had suspected

[1] Abigail Adams to Mercy Warren, Dec. 5, 1773, *Warren-Adams Letters*, Massachusetts Historical Society Collections, LXXII (Boston, 1917), 18.

[2] See the letter of the Boston consignees, dated Castle William, Dec. 17, 1773, enclosed in one from the chairman of the East India Company to the earl of Dartmouth, Jan. 29, 1774, *Calendar of Home Office Papers of the Reign of George III,* IV, ed. Richard A. Roberts (London, 1899), 176; also the letter from Hutchinson to the earl of Dartmouth (private), Dec. 2, 1773, Historical Manuscripts Commission, *Eleventh Report,* App., Pt. V (London, 1887), 343.

[3] For the "Minutes of the Tea Meetings," 1773, in the hand of the Boston town clerk, William Cooper, see Massachusetts Historical Society, *Proceedings,* XX (Boston, 1884), 10–17.

[4] Diary entry for Dec. 17, 1773, *The Works of John Adams,* ed. Charles Francis Adams, II (Boston, 1850), 323.

they were planning some move but had not been able to act on their own initiative to prevent it. As Admiral Montague, commander of the royal squadron, pointed out, during the crisis neither governor, council, nor revenue officials had called for his assistance. If they had, he could "easily have prevented the execution of this plan," but, he added, he would have "endangered the lives of many innocent people, by firing upon the town." The army could have taken more limited, but effective action. It did not, for Lieutenant Colonel Leslie, commanding the Sixty-fourth Regiment at Castle William, reported that Governor Thomas Hutchinson, the bête noire of the patriots, had shown no desire to march the troops into the town to maintain order.[5] As had been the case during the Stamp Act riots in 1765, the military had been unable to interfere; by the constitutional practice of the time as set forth in the Mutiny Acts, it could only act legally on the call of the civil authorities. For some time the Massachusetts council—elected by the lower house of the legislature—had sided with the patriots. The upper house of the legislature had not responded to the pleas of the governor and consignees for help against the intimidation of the patriots. This was an important factor in determining the passage by the British government of the Massachusetts Acts of 1774. It had to have legal means of supporting order and the authority of the royal government in the Bay Colony.

For some time the administration of Lord North, first lord of the treasury, had been aware of the situation in America. As early as December 17, 1773, the day following the dramatic incident at Boston, London had received news of colonial opposition to the landing of the tea. At that time the secretary of state for the American department, the earl of Dartmouth, had written to the chairman of the East India Company, and in the weeks that followed he received from company officials various accounts transmitted by their correspondents in America.[6] Of particular significance for future British policy were the accounts of the consignees in Boston, relating the efforts of the patriots to prevent the landing of the tea and the reaction of the government of the Bay Colony. In the name of the Boston town meeting, the consignees were summoned to appear at the local Liberty Tree and publicly resign. When they failed to appear, a committee from the patriots demanded that they sign a pledge to send the cargoes back to England. When they refused, they were further threatened by a mob. Still they refused, and again a committee of the town meeting demanded their resignation. Once more they refused. The consignees then petitioned the governor and council to take charge of the tea, but the councilors procrastinated. Finally, adopting a report by James Bowdoin, Samuel Dexter, and John Winthrop, they referred to the justices of the peace the consignees' petition requesting personal protection.[7] Having obtained no satisfaction from the regularly constituted government in the colony, the consignees and royal customs officials fled to Castle William. The destruction of the tea followed.

This was the information received by the ministers in London, and it was on the basis of this information that they acted. From the minutes of the cabinet among the

[5] See Montague to Philip Stevens (secretary to the admiralty board), Dec. 17, 1773, HMC, *Eleventh Report*, App., Pt. V, 344; Leslie's letters of Dec. 6 and Dec. 17, 1773, sent by Viscount Barrington (secretary at war) to the earl of Dartmouth, Jan. 28, 1774, *Cal. H.O. Papers, George III*, IV, 175–176.

[6] These may be found in Public Records Office, London, Treasury Board Papers, Class I, Bundle 505; and *Cal. H.O. Papers, George III*, IV, 116, 117, 118, 164–166, 167, 176–177, 181.

[7] *Cal. H.O. Papers, George III*, IV, 176–177.

papers of the secretary of state for the American department and from other sources, it is possible to construct a more accurate analysis of the motives behind their actions than has been presented heretofore.

The ministry was unwilling to use extreme measures except in case of emergency. The earl of Dartmouth informed Governor William Tryon of New York that during the crisis the civil magistrates should not requisition the army "upon a Slight Ground but only in Cases of absolute Necessity when every other Effort has failed." George III himself was "much hurt that the instigation of bad men hath again drawn the people of Boston to take such injustifiable steps. . . ." [8] Late in January the cabinet met to consider the situation. Lord Chancellor Apsley, Lord President Gower, Lord North, the earl of Sandwich (first lord of the admiralty), and the three secretaries of state, the earls of Rochford, Suffolk, and Dartmouth, agreed that "in consequence of the present disorders in America, effectual Steps be taken to secure the Dependence of the Colonies on the Mother Country." But what steps? [9] At this point Dartmouth proposed to the king that Boston be punished by removing the customs house from the town and convening the Massachusetts assembly elsewhere. This could be done by the "sole power of the Crown. . . ." [10] At first this appeared to be the only course the ministry would follow. Almost two weeks later Dartmouth wrote to the treasury board that in view of the "outrage" in Boston, the open breach of law, and the defiance of the authority of Great Britain, the king thought fit "for the better protection & Security of the Commerce of his Subjects" to remove all officials concerned in the plantation trade from Boston to some other port in Massachusetts.[11]

In the meantime discussions continued in the cabinet. General Thomas Gage, the commander in chief in America, who had been recalled to London the previous June for consultations, personally advised the king on the need for forceful measures in Boston. The colonists "will be Lyons, whilst we are Lambs," he predicted. But if the ministry took "resolute" action, then the Americans will "undoubtedly prove very meek." Four regiments in town would be "sufficient to prevent any disturbance" in the future. George III was not prone to compromise, for (as he wrote to North on February 4) he felt that "all men seem now to feel that the fatal compliance in 1766," the repeal of the Stamp Act, had encouraged the Americans to "encrease in their pretensions" of independence—a doctrine "quite subversive of the obedience which a Colony owes to its Mother Country." The day after the king penned these words, the secretary of state wrote to the temporary commander in chief in America that on the unanimous advice of "His Confidential Servants," the cabinet, the king was resolved to "pursue such measures as shall be effectual for the securing the De-

[8] Dartmouth to Tryon, Jan. 8, 1774, in *Collections of the New-York Historical Society,* LVI (New York, 1923), 202; George III to Dartmouth, Jan. 19, 1774, HMC, *Thirteenth Report,* App. Pt. IV (London, 1892), 499.

[9] The American department was then considering the situation in Boston. John Pownall proposed closing the port, while William Knox, the other undersecretary of state, advised altering the charter of the colony to allow the Crown to appoint the provincial council. Dartmouth supported this last measure. At this point, the former governor of the Bay Colony, Sir Francis Bernard, argued that the government also regulate the town meetings and juries. See Knox's account in HMC, *Report on Manuscripts in Various Collections,* VI (London, 1909), 257.

[10] Minute of cabinet, Jan. 29, 1774, William Salt Library, Stafford, England, Dartmouth Papers, II, 799; Lord North to George III, Jan. [29], 1774, *The Correspondence of King George the Third,* ed. John Fortescue, III (London, 1928), No. 1377.

[11] Dartmouth to the Treasury Board, Feb. 11, 1774, P.R.O., Colonial Office, 5/160: 91–92.

pendence of the Colonies upon this Kingdom." [12] That same day, February 5, the cabinet again discussed the situation in Boston. On the basis of reports from Governor Hutchinson, the ministers decided to take legal action against the offenders. If, in the opinion of the attorney general and solicitor general (Edward Thurlow and Alexander Wedderburn), there were sufficient grounds to institute criminal proceedings "against any of the Persons said to have been concerned in the outrages" at Boston, the ministry would issue a commission under the Great Seal to investigate and apprehend those individuals for trial in England.[13] The crown law officers were also to report whether or not the king by his own authority could appoint justices of the peace in the Massachusetts Bay Colony.

Dartmouth immediately sent to the law officers a "Narrative Case" of the events in Boston and the other colonial ports.[14] It included a list of those regarded as the principal abettors in the Boston episode. Among those named were Jonathan Williams, Samuel and John Adams, William Phillips, John Rowe, William Molineaux, James Warren, and Doctor Thomas Young. The state of the colonies and the "Insults that have been offered to the Authority of this Kingdom," Dartmouth urged the law officers, "require the most serious deliberation and speedy decision. . . ." Consequently Wedderburn and Thurlow were to report immediately on several questions. Did the acts committed at Boston constitute high treason? If so, who were the persons to be charged with the crime? What would be the most proper legal method of proceeding against them? [15]

Perhaps because they hesitated to assume responsibility for the decision, Wedderburn and Thurlow procrastinated. But since some decision was necessary, Dartmouth urged them on, and finally on February 11 the law officers responded.[16] One thing was clear: the proceedings at Boston as described in the "Narrative Case" constituted high treason, namely, "levying War against His Majesty." To Thurlow and Wedderburn those acts were an attempt, concerted with much deliberation, and made with open force in pursuance of such concert, to obstruct the execution of an act of Parliament imposing a duty on tea imported into America. Moreover they sought to impose a general restraint upon the execution of a lawful trade, as if it were a public grievance. The imperial government could proceed against the individuals responsible for these acts as named in the "Narrative Case" in any of three ways: by trying them in Massachusetts "in the ordinary course of Justice"; by arresting them in the colony by justices of the peace and trying them in some English county; or by sending over a warrant of a secretary of state grounded on sufficient information on oath for their arrest and trial in England. The most proper procedure, if the cabinet thought it sufficient in other respects, would be the more ordinary course—that is, trial in Massachusetts.[17]

[12] *Correspondence of George III,* III, No. 1379; Dartmouth to General Frederick Haldimand (secret and confidential), Feb. 5, 1774, C.O. 5/91:23–24.

[13] Minute of cabinet, Feb. 5, 1774, Dartmouth Papers, II, 819.

[14] "Narrative Case," C.O. 5/7:25. Another version of this narrative in C.O. 5/7:606–625 seems to be based on the information (in C.O. 5/113) sent by the East India Company to the ministry.

[15] Dartmouth to Wedderburn and Thurlow, Feb. 5, 1774, C.O. 5/160:1, 25.

[16] Dartmouth to Wedderburn and Thurlow, Feb. 8, 10, 1774; *Cal. H.O. Papers, George III,* IV, 181. They were specific on one point: the Crown on its own authority could remove the customs house from Boston and locate another in any more convenient port in the colony. Report of Feb. 11, C.O. 5/247:192–193.

[17] Report by Wedderburn and Thurlow, Feb. 11, 1774, C.O. 5/160:79–86.

But would justice be done in the ordinary process of law in a colony whose government seemed to sympathize with the suspected traitors? Evidently the ministers thought not and hoped to follow another procedure. That same day, February 11, Dartmouth drafted a letter to Wedderburn and Thurlow requesting them to report whether the king could appoint a commission under the Great Seal to conduct an "Inquisition of the treason committed." They were also to state whether he could invest such a commission with full powers of magistracy comparable to those exercised by the civil magistrates in Massachusetts by virtue of the commissions granted by the governor with the advice of the council, pursuant to the charter of 1691.

Apparently the ministers were also exploring another possibility: direct action against those thought to be responsible for the incidents at Boston, through a warrant from the secretary of state founded on information given under oath. On February 19 a committee of the privy council received the depositions of ten persons present in Boston at the time of the purported treason.[18] On the basis of this evidence the cabinet that same day decided on three points. If the attorney general and solicitor general approved, the ministers would issue a warrant for the arrest and transportation to England of any person in Boston deemed guilty of treason. Secondly, they would move in Parliament for a bill to close the port of Boston until the town, or those who had destroyed the tea, had indemnified the East India Company. And finally, they would move to bring in a bill to alter the charter of the colony; such a bill would be either presented in the current session or suspended until the next in order to give the general court of Massachusetts an opportunity to show cause by "agents deputed for that purpose or other ways as they shall think necessary . . . why such an alteration should not be made." [19]

The cabinet took no further action until nine days later, when it met with Thurlow and Wedderburn. The law officers proved the stumbling block to the ministerial program then being considered. Apparently they had previously agreed with the decision to send over a warrant, but now they argued that the charge of treason could not be upheld merely on the basis of the depositions taken at the council on February 19.[20] Although the ministers continued to bring pressure to bear on the law officers, Wedderburn maintained that the proposal to send over a warrant for the apprehension of the patriot leaders would present difficulties. In view of the unique aspects of the question, he begged for time to consider it until March 7, the day scheduled to bring the situation in Massachusetts to the attention of Parliament.[21] Apparently Wedderburn and Thurlow had reversed themselves and also objected

[18] Dartmouth to Wedderburn and Thurlow (draft), Feb. 11, 1774, C.O. 5/160–187; *Acts of the Privy Council of England, Colonial Series,* ed. James Munro (Edinburgh, 1908–1912), V, 391; VI, 550–555.

[19] Minute of cabinet, Feb. 19, 1774, Dartmouth Papers, II, 834. Present at the meeting were Apsley, Gower, North, Rochford, Sandwich, and Dartmouth.

[20] Minute of cabinet, Feb. 28, 1774, Dartmouth Papers, II, 839. Thurlow and Wedderburn may have had another motive: they may not have wanted to take sole responsibility for the decision to send the warrants. See the amusing account left by William Knox, undersecretary of state for the American department. HMC, *Report on . . . Various Collections,* VI, 270. See also the entries for July 5 and August 14, 1774, *The Diary and Letters of Thomas Hutchinson,* ed. Peter Orlando Hutchinson, I (London, 1884), 183, 219, for the purported influence of William Murray, Lord Mansfield. The cabinet minutes by Dartmouth do not, however, indicate that Mansfield was present.

[21] Minute of cabinet, March 1, 1774, with attached memorandum, Dartmouth Papers, II, 842; and George III to Dartmouth, March 1, 1774, HMC, *Thirteenth Report,* App., Pt. IV, 500.

to removing the customs house from Boston by executive action, pointing out that ship captains producing their clearance papers were legally entitled to require that a customs official attend them in any particular port. They raised another sore point: making charges of high treason against the patriot leaders for the advice they had allegedly given at the town meeting and for their recommendation that the patriots station guards on the tea ships. Although Wedderburn seemed to think that the leaders could be tried, Thurlow disagreed. According to the depositions given the council, John Hancock purportedly had recommended stationing guards so that others might not destroy the tea and blame the patriots.

Since the proposed executive action was of doubtful legality, the ministers were forced to attempt another course of action. Parliamentary legislation would close the port of Boston and declare it a "crime and misdemeanor" to dispute at any public meeting the sovereign legislative authority of Great Britain. To insure that in the future justices of the peace would not be lax in their duty, they too would be regulated by an alteration of the charter of the colony.[22]

Except for the bill closing the port of Boston, the ministers were still not committed to the specific program to be brought into Parliament. While Lord Chancellor Apsley urged a general bill for the "Security of the Military" in America, he thought it would be "prudent" for the government to comply should "any Person of Consequence" wish the provisions of the bill restricted to Boston. But such an act, he felt, should be in effect only for a short time, perhaps two years. Not only was it desirable to distinguish between Boston and the "rest of the Delinquents" but, if possible, to select a half dozen of the "Ring leaders & separate them from the rest of the town." A bill to alter the "Constitution of the Government of Boston" was necessary, he thought, but at all events the king must be empowered to appoint justices of the peace. Apsley hoped that the apprehensions of his fellow ministers over the opposition they might encounter would not "deter us from acting with Spirit," for it "has been the giving into palliative measures that has brought us to the present Scituation." Evidently the lord chancellor still hoped to prosecute the ringleaders in Boston, but he drew a distinction between outlawing individuals for a capital offense and for a misdemeanor.[23]

But the ministers did not press either charge; apparently Wedderburn and Thurlow would not approve the warrants. Consequently the government had to act through Parliament, not to punish those responsible for past offenses, but to prevent a recurrence in the future.

On March 7 Lord North, through the King's Speech from the Throne, introduced the ministerial program into the House of Commons. He termed the events at Boston "violent and outrageous," carried on with a "View to obstructing the Commerce of this Kingdom, and upon Grounds and Pretences immediately subversive of the Constitution thereof. . . ." The administration now called on the imperial legislature to enact "permanent Provisions" for the "better securing the Execution of the Laws and the just Dependence of the Colonies upon the Crown and Parliament of Great Britain."[24] It viewed the crisis in Boston as a challenge to the authority of

[22] Minute of cabinet, Feb. 28, 1774, Dartmouth Papers, II, 839; minutes of a conversation between the earl of Buckinghamshire and Dartmouth, March 2, 1774, HMC, *Report on the Manuscripts of the Marquess of Lothian* (London, 1905), pp. 290–291; and George III to Dartmouth, March 1, 1774, HMC, *Thirteenth Report*, App., Pt. IV, 500.

[23] Apsley to Dartmouth [March 6, 1774], Dartmouth Papers, II, 849.

[24] *Journals of the House of Commons* (London, 1803–13), XXXIV, 541.

the mother country. Convinced that years of procrastination and conciliation had merely strengthened a movement aimed at independence, the ministers originally considered two measures only: compelling the town to compensate for the destruction of the tea and acting against the ringleaders in the anti-British movement. But the information on which they could legally act through the courts was insufficient. The crown law officers would not sanction such prosecution. Now the ministers would have to operate through Parliament, but for a limited objective: the suppression by legal means of any future challenge. The ineffectiveness of local traditional government in Massachusetts had been decisive. Royal authority would now be enforced by the army if necessary, but it must be used in a legal, constitutional manner. To ensure proper facilities for the troops, a quartering act would be passed. The military had been unable to function in the crisis late in 1773 simply because no civil magistrate had called on these forces. For this reason the elected council of Massachusetts would be replaced by a body appointed by the Crown. To eliminate the center of the radical movement, all town meetings, except those held with the sanction of the governor or those for the purpose of electing representatives, would be prohibited. This alteration of the charter of the Bay Colony was not designed to subvert local democratic government as such, but only the revolutionary movement. Town meetings for the purpose of electing members to the general court and local officials were still allowed, and the Massachusetts House of Representatives was not disturbed. As the method of appointing the council had been altered, the army could now be legally called out to enforce order and support the government. The danger in meeting force with force to execute parliamentary legislation was that royal officials might be indicted and tried before prejudiced or inflamed local juries in the colony. To provide for the more impartial administration of justice in such cases, trials would be held in some other colony or in England. These were the goals behind the four acts relating to Massachusetts passed by Parliament in the spring of 1774 and termed "intolerable" or "coercive" by the Americans. The Quebec Act passed later that session was conceived before December 1773 and was not related to the tea incident.

The economic aspect of the destruction of the tea was not the primary consideration, as Lord North made clear in the House of Commons on March 14. As reported by Edmund Burke, he stressed that the government must meet the political problem. The question was no longer the "degrees of freedom or restraint in which they [the colonies] were to be held, but whether they should be totally separated from their connexion with and dependence on . . . Great Britain." [25] According to another account, North observed that in Boston, England and America are "considered as two independent States"—not an inappropriate conclusion to draw from the position previously adopted by Benjamin Franklin and the Massachusetts legislature.[26] And North continued: "but we are no more to dispute between legislation and taxation" but to consider whether "we have any authority there. . . ." It was very clear "we have none," he maintained, "if we suffer the property of our subjects

[25] Edmund Burke to the New York committee on correspondence, April 6, 1774, *Edmund Burke, New York Agent*, ed. Ross J. S. Hoffman (Philadelphia, 1956), pp. 245–246.

[26] See, for example, Franklin to Samuel Cooper, June 8, 1770, *The Writings of Benjamin Franklin*, ed. Albert H. Smyth, V (New York, 1905), 259–261; and the exchange between Governor Hutchinson and the Massachusetts legislature in *Speeches of the Governors of Massachusetts*, ed. Alden Bradford (Boston, 1918), pp. 340–365.

to be destroyed." The town of Boston, he charged, "had been the ringleader in all riots, and at all times shewn a desire of seeing the laws of Great Britain attempted in vain" in the colony. The destruction of the tea and the other proceedings "belonged to the act of the publick meeting" of Boston. He concluded with the hope that all —peers, members, and merchants—would agree unanimously "to animadvert upon such parts of America as deny the authority of this country." "We must," he concluded, "punish, controul, or yield to them." [27]

But some British merchants, at least those trading to Boston, would not agree. Their trade would suffer if the ministry closed the port, as it proposed to do when North put the finishing touches to the Boston port bill on March 16. As soon as they learned of its contents, the "most considerable among them went in a Body" to call on the first lord of the treasury. They were prepared to go far and offered "to be answerable" to the East India Company for over £16,000—double the value of the tea destroyed—"by way of Compensation. . . ." The lord mayor of London himself "repeatedly & publicly declared that he would be Security to the amount of £20,000 for the People of Boston." They requested six months to come to a "settlement with the Town or the Assembly" of Massachusetts, "confiding in their disposition" to reimburse the sum. But North replied that he would "proceed upon no other Ground" than the merchants being "answerable for the future peaceable conduct & entire acquiescense" of the Bostonians in receiving tea. This the merchants "utterly refused, as absurd, and impossible," as North probably knew they would. Yet he protested that he meant "nothing inimical to the Trade of Boston or the Liberties of America. . . ." Consequently the merchants "ought to return & set quietly at their Compting Houses & leave their Affairs to his Direction for that their Property should henceforth be better secured than heretofore. . . ." [28] North brought in the Boston Port Bill on March 18, and it passed the House of Commons without a division a week later.

The ministry also introduced two other bills in the Commons, one altering the charter of Massachusetts and the other providing for the trial—either in some other colony or in England—of persons accused of crimes in enforcing acts of Parliament. During the debate on the Boston Port Bill the ministry's spokesmen indicated the need for these additional measures. They proposed to alter the charter of the colony to enable the executive branch of the civil government to us troops legally in putting down a revolutionary movement and upholding royal authority. No civil officer or magistrate in Massachusetts had been willing to call them out; consequently some method was necessary whereby "the military force may act with effect, and without bloodshed" in supporting and maintaining "the authority of Great Britain. . . ." Governor Hutchinson had claimed that it had been impossible to proceed against those concerned in the riots, since the patriots had intimidated the judges in the colony by threatening their families, property, and persons. The grand jurors of

[27] [John Debrett], *The History, Debates and Proceedings of Both Houses of Parliament,* VII (London, 1792), 70–72. Benjamin Franklin wrote to a committee of the town of Boston that as the tea had been destroyed by "Persons unknown" who probably would not "be found or brought to answer for it" there seemed "to be some reasonable Claim on the Society at large in which it happened." Franklin to Samuel Adams, John Hancock, William Phillips, and Thomas Cushing, Feb. 2, 1774, Smyth, *Writings of Franklin,* VI, 179.

[28] See the undated, unsigned account of this meeting in the Chatham Papers, Public Record Office, 30/8/97:260–261. The writer was hostile to North, accusing him of "extreme duplicity."

Boston, Hutchinson charged, were the "persons who were among the principal promoters" at the town meetings "which occasioned the destruction of the tea. . . ." No doubt, he conjectured, they were selected to quash indictments. There was no prospect of restoring order without interposing the power of the mother country. "I rather think the anarchy will continually increase until the whole Province is in confusion," he predicted. Whether or not the governor's sentiments were decisive is not certain, but it is clear that by mid-March the ministry was intent on altering the government of Massachusetts in order legally to use the army.[29]

On March 28 when the Boston Port Bill was before the House of Lords, Lord North asked leave to bring in a bill regulating the government of Massachusetts. It was apparent, he observed, that "an executive power was wanting" in the colony and that it was necessary to strengthen the magistracy. The force of the civil power consisted of the *"posse comitatus,"* but since the *posse* evidently "are the very people who have committed all these riots, little obedience to the preservation of the peace is to be expected of them." There appeared to be a "total defect in the constitutional power" of the government. If the "democratic part shews that contempt for obedience to the laws," he asked, "how is the governor to execute any authority vested in him?" If he wanted any magistrate to act, he did not have the power to appoint one; nor could he remove any magistrate who would not act. Only the council had that authority—a council "whose dependence is on the democratic part of the constitution." For years it had appeared that the civil magistrates had been "uniformly inactive" and that the governor on his own authority could do "nothing," for he needed the consent of seven of the council. To remedy the situation, North proposed a bill "to take the executive power from the hands of the democratic part of the Government" and to have the governor as a justice of the peace with the power of appointing civil officials, such as sheriffs, who could be removed only by royal orders. The town meetings were also a problem. Every member of Parliament could see, North argued, the impropriety of "such irregular assemblies" as existed in Boston. He would not have them meet except with the consent of the governor unless for the annual election of "certain officers, which it is their province to chuse." The juries were also improperly selected and must be regulated. North claimed he was open to any suggestion, but he emphasized that "until the executive power is free, it cannot act; our regulations here are of no import, if you have nobody" in Massachusetts to give them force.

There was little question. The House of Commons voted the ministry leave to bring in the bill.[30]

The Massachusetts Government Bill led to the passage of another statute—the act for the impartial administration of justice. General Thomas Gage, commander in chief of the forces in America and soon to be governor of the Bay Colony, had certain reservations about the program for Massachusetts—questions which he broached with Dartmouth. In turn, the secretary of state brought them to the attention of the cabinet on April 7. Could Gage, the new governor, on his own authority and without the advice of the council, call out troops to assist him in quelling riots and disturbances? What could he do if "any Accident should happen that might expose any

---

[29] Debrett, *Debates and Proceedings,* VII, 88; Hutchinson to Dartmouth (private), Feb. 17, 1774; HMC, *Eleventh Report,* App., Pt. V, 348–349; *Correspondence of George III,* III, No. 1416. See also William Knox's account in HMC, *Report on . . . Various Collections,* VI, 257.

[30] Debrett, *Debates and Proceedings,* VII, 104–105; *Commons Journals,* XXXIV, 601.

persons employed in quelling such disturbances to any Prosecution" and trial was instituted in a civil court in the colony? Gage doubted if royal officials would receive a fair hearing in the Massachusetts courts. After consulting the attorney general and solicitor general, Dartmouth, North, Sandwich, Rochford, and Apsley informed Gage that in case of "dangerous Tumult & Insurrection," every man was bound to "interpose for the preservation of the public Peace"; the governor must call on all subjects to assist him in quelling "tumults" and repelling "force & violence" by every means at his disposal. But to protect officials charged with crimes in the enforcement of acts of Parliament from "unjust prosecution," the ministers agreed to advise the king to invest the governor with the power of pardon in cases where he thought it necessary to the "due administration of Justice to interpose that power." [31] This would have granted wide discretion to the executive, a dangerous tactic; and ultimately the ministry decided not to rely on executive pardon, but on legislative authority. On April 15, when North introduced into the House of Commons the bill for regulating the Massachusetts government, he also moved for leave to bring in a bill for the impartial administration of justice in cases of persons questioned for any acts performed in executing laws or suppressing riots. Such individuals would be tried in England or in a neighboring colony. By substantial margins the House of Commons passed the regulation bill on May 2 and the bill for the administration of justice four days later. Both measures easily passed the House of Lords on May 20. The Massachusetts government Act (14 George III, cap. 45) and the Act for the Impartial Administration of Justice (14 George III, cap. 39) then received the royal assent. [32]

One further measure remained to complete the ministerial program for Massachusetts. Some provision must be made for better securing quarters for the army in the colony. In the past there had been some difficulty in quartering troops, since implementation of previous mutiny acts had depended on local officials. To correct this situation, Viscount Barrington, the secretary at war, on May 3 introduced a quartering bill into the House of Commons. There was little difficulty in the lower chamber, but for some reason the ministry expected trouble in the House of Lords on the third reading, scheduled for May 26. Six days before, Rochford, one of the secretaries of state, sent what seems to have been a "whip" in the form of a circular letter to the peers requesting their attendance on the third reading. The ministry had an easy time of it, but significantly those who called themselves friends of the colonists (seven peers belonging to the faction of the marquis of Rockingham) did not vote on the measure but "went away" instead. [33] The act (14 George III, cap. 54) "for the better providing suitable Quarters for Officers and Soldiers . . . in *North America*" provided that in case there were insufficient barracks for the troops, persons authorized by law in any of the colonies, on a requisition from the commander

---

[31] Minute of cabinet, April 7, 1774, Dartmouth Papers, II, 883; and Gage's questions, ibid., II, 884.

[32] *Commons Journals*, XXXIV, 667–689, 696, 702, 712; *Journals of the House of Lords*, (London, 17–?–1833), XXXIV, 182.

[33] *Commons Journals*, XXXIV, 695; *Lords Journals*, XXXIV, 217. Rochford's note, dated May 20, 1774 (Public Record Office, State Papers, 37/10:220R) reads: "Lord Rochford presents his Compliments to ———— and begs leave to remind His ———— that there will be business of very great Importance in the House of Lords on Thursday next the 26th Inst upon the third reading of the Bill for quartering Troops in America." Lists of peers voting for and against the measure (but with the headings reversed) and those who left before the vote are in State Papers 37/10:219–220.

in chief, could billet soldiers in such manner as was already provided by the Mutiny Act. If they failed to comply within twenty-four hours, the governor could order and direct that uninhabited houses, barns, outbuildings, and other structures be used. The new law merely implemented the provisions of the previous mutiny acts.

By passing the Boston Port, Massachusetts Government, Impartial Administration of Justice, and Quartering Acts, the British government had reacted to the crisis in Massachusetts. Its aims were limited: *legally* to put down what appeared a revolutionary movement aimed at overthrowing its authority. The ministers did not act arbitrarily or order the arbitrary use of military force. Nor did they attempt to "render the Military independent of and superior to the Civil Power" as the Americans were to charge in the Declaration of Independence. They merely sought to arrest a revolutionary challenge through legally constituted civil officers. Initially the North administration only sought to hold Boston and the patriot leaders responsible for the destruction of the tea. But since the crown law officers held that the ministers had insufficient evidence to prosecute them for treason, another course of action was necessary—legislation by Parliament to prevent a recurrence of such acts and to strengthen the colonial executive. Events in Massachusetts demonstrated that the executive had insufficient power, or at least that the legislative branch and the extra-legal bodies so favored the patriot cause that they could nullify any act of the governor and intimidate judicial officials. Had the civil magistrates, justices of the peace, or the council (elected by the House of Representatives) called on the military, they might have averted the crisis. By the legislation passed in 1774 the new governor could rely on a royally appointed council and magistrates subject to his removal. Consequently the civil government could requisition the army.

This legislation was not designed to limit the democratic or representative elements of the Massachusetts government as such, but only to restrict the town meetings in so far as they were used by the revolutionary patriots. The Massachusetts Government Act did not restrict the representative assembly or prohibit town meetings called to elect officials. The imperial government did not eliminate the democratic part of the colonial government but sought, as Lord North put it in the House of Commons on March 28, 1774, to remedy a "defect in the constitutional power" of the governor to execute the authority vested in him.[34] It aimed at restoring that balance in government embodied in the Glorious Revolution, a blended government in which the executive checked the excesses of the representative assembly. As one writer has noted, many of the colonists themselves shared this ideal. They did not consider democracy or any other form of government as practical or desirable in its pure form. To them the ideal was a combination, a blended government. "Most colonists regarded the English constitution as the ideal mixed government"; moreover, they "believed that their own colonial governments were copies, or imitations, of the English." [35] After all, the alteration of the Massachusetts government merely imposed on that colony a system which had existed for some time in the other royal provinces. One may be struck by the common appeal to the principles of popular sovereignty and rule of the people in the arguments the colonial patriots used against British measures. But this appeal may have been an aberration. In the newly declared states after 1776, government was based on the consent of property holders, not on the consent of the

[34] Debrett, *Debates and Proceedings*, VII, 104.
[35] Roy N. Lokken, "The Concept of Democracy in Colonial Political Thought," *William and Mary Quarterly*, 3rd Ser., XVI (1959), 570, 573, 574.

governed; and popular sovereignty was not the basis of American government as established by the federal constitution of 1787, when the founding fathers returned to the principle of a mixed government, although in a more attenuated form than existed in the colonial period. Despite the recent attacks on particular economic interpretations of the Constitution, valid as they may be, "it yet remains true," as Bellot has said, "that the Constitution was not, and was not intended to be, a democratic document, in the sense that it was meant to set bounds to legislative authority and to check the power of majorities." [36] Not until the rise of organized political parties in the nineteenth century, both in England and America, could the ideal of representative government be realized.

In 1774 the British government attempted to restore mixed government in Massachusetts in order to support the authority of Parliament. As the earl of Dartmouth put it, a "little time" would convince all who "can think with coolness and temper, that the liberties of America are not so much in danger from any thing that Parliament has done, or is likely to do here, as from the violence and misconduct of America itself." The idea prevalent in the colonies that the imperial government intended to "enslave" the Americans was an "absurdity"; on the contrary, it wished the colonists "to enjoy all the freedom and all the rights which belong to British subjects," without any restraints except those arising from the nature of their connection with the mother country. Dartmouth then posed the crucial issue as he saw it. The supreme legislature of the empire had levied a tax on tea; the colonists, particularly the Bostonians, had resisted its authority and opposed the execution of its laws "in a manner clearly treasonable." Consequently the mother country, although unwilling to proceed to extremes, had, on the "principles of every government upon earth," passed laws—which it had an undisputed right to do—to punish the most flagrant offenders, reform abuses, and prevent "like extremities in the future." The question was now whether the colonists would submit to this legislation. If they did not, in effect they were declaring themselves no longer a part of the British empire. They would alter the basis of the controversy, for no longer would they be contending that Parliament did not have the right to pass particular acts, but that it had no right to legislate at all.[37] In two years this was just the position the patriots proclaimed in the Declaration of Independence: that Parliament did not have, and had never had, any authority over the colonies.

[36] Hugh Hale Bellot, "The Literature of that Last Half-Century on the Constitutional History of the United States," Royal Historical Sociey, *Transactions,* 5th Ser., VII (1957), 167. For an opposing point of view see Eric Robson, *The American Revolution in Its Political and Military Aspects, 1763–1783* (London, 1955), p. 221.

[37] Dartmouth to Joseph Reed, July 27, 1774, Dartmouth Papers, I, ii, 991. This point has been debated at length by many historians, principally by Charles McIlwain and Robert Livingston Schuyler.

11 / King George III:
A Study of Personality

Lewis B. Namier

As the symbol of British authority and as the target of the charges of the Declaration of Independence, King George III has, quite naturally, not enjoyed favorable treatment in American studies of the Revolution. As the symbol of the government that lost America and the target of a long tradition of English Whig polemic and history, he has enjoyed scarcely better handling by many English historians. As Americans denounced George III as the invader of their rights, so have British Whigs condemned him as an ambitious man designing to upset the constitutional order of their own country. Lewis B. Namier in this study of the "personality" of George III considers the broad question of the constitutional role of this monarch. He suggests some features of the political system of the eighteenth century that have been largely ignored by many contemporary and later critics of George III. As the founder of a school of "Namierist" analysis of English politics, Namier has considerable authority as a critic of the traditional Whig approach. His interpretation of the King suggests some of the anomalies in the American criticism of George III: it was precisely the Monarch's determination to defend Parliamentary power that first led him into the bad graces of his colonial subjects. For years Americans regarded him as "good" King George who was misguided by his ministers into supporting the pretended authority of Parliament to tax the Americans. Only in 1775 and 1776 did he and the entire system of monarchy come under the attack of such writers as Thomas Paine and Thomas Jefferson. Beyond his analysis of the system of British politics, Namier describes some of the unfortunate traits of George III's character, traits that helped to contribute to his political decline as they helped to contribute to his eventual insanity. But Namier insists that these undeniable weaknesses of character should not be confused with a kind of grasping ambition that was and has continued to be attributed to him by his detractors. George III's highest goal was to be a good king operating in and through the British constitutional system as it was widely understood at the time of his accession in 1760.

For further reading: Lewis B. Namier, *The Structure of Politics at the Accession of George III* (2 vols., 1929), *England in the Age of the American Revolution* (1930), and with John Brooke, *The House of Commons, 1754–1790* (3 vols., 1964); Richard Pares, *King George III and the Politicians* (1953); Jacob Price, "Party, Purpose and Pattern: Sir Lewis Namier and His Critics," *Journal of British Studies,* I (1961), 71–93; Herbert Butterfield, *George III, Lord North, and the People, 1779–1780* (1949), *George III and the Historians* (1957).

There were three large pictures of George III at the exhibition of Royal Portraits arranged by the Academy of Arts in the spring of 1953. Looking at the first, by Reynolds, painted when the King was 41, I was struck by the immaturity of expression. The second, by Lawrence, painted in 1792 at the age of 54, depicts him in Garter robes; face and posture seem to attempt in a naive, ineffective, and almost engaging manner to live up to a grandeur which the sitter feels incumbent on him. The third, by Stroehling, painted in November 1807 at the age of nearly 70, shows a sad old man, looking dimly at a world in which he has no pleasure, and which he soon will not be able to see or comprehend.

A picture in a different medium of the King and his story presents itself to the student when in the Royal Archives at Windsor he surveys the papers of George III. They stand on the shelves in boxes, each marked on a white label with the year or years which it covers. The eye runs over that array, and crucial dates recall events: 1760, '65 and '67, '74 and '75, '82 and '83, 1789, '93, '96, 1802, 1805—the series breaks off in 1810; and brown-backed volumes follow, unlabelled: they contain the medical reports on a man shut off from time, which means the world and its life.

Fate had made George III ruler when kings were still expected to govern; and his active reign covered half a century during which the American conflict posed the problem of Imperial relations, while at home political practice constantly ran up against the contradiction inherent in the then much belauded 'mixed form of government': personal monarchy served by Ministers whose tenure of office was contested in Parliament. Neither the Imperial nor the constitutional problem could have been solved in the terms in which the overwhelming majority of the politically minded public in this country considered them at the time; but George III has been blamed ever since for not having thought of Dominion status and parliamentary government when constitutional theory and the facts of the situation as yet admitted of neither.

In the catalogue, *Kings and Queens,* on sale at the exhibition, the introduction dealing with the reign of George III gave the traditional view of his reign:

> Conscientious and ambitious, he tried to restore the political influence of the Crown, but his intervention ended with the humiliating American War of Independence.

Conscientious he certainly was, painstakingly, almost painfully, conscientious. But was he ambitious? Did he try to exercise powers which his predecessors had relinquished, or claim an influence which was not universally conceded to him? And was it the assertion of Royal, and not of Parliamentary, authority over America which brought on the conflict and disrupted the First British Empire?

Let us place ourselves in March 1782. Dismal, humiliating failure has turned public opinion, and the House of Commons is resolved to cut losses and abandon the struggle; it is all over; Lord North's government has fallen; and the King is contemplating abdication. He has drafted a message to Parliament (which was never sent); here are its first two paragraphs:

> His Majesty during the twenty-one years he has sate on the throne of Great Britain, has had no object so much at heart as the maintenance of the British Constitution, of which the difficulties he has at times met with from his scrupulous attachment to the rights of Parliament are sufficient proofs.
> His Majesty is convinced that the sudden change of sentiments of one branch of the legislature has totally incapacitated him from either conducting the war with effect, or from obtaining any peace but on conditions which would prove destructive to the commerce as well as essential rights of the British nation.[1]

In the first paragraph the King declares his unswerving devotion to the British Constitution, and shows himself conscious of his difficulties in America having arisen through 'his scrupulous attachment to the rights of Parliament'; the second paragraph pointedly refers to the Commons as 'one branch of the legislature', and gives the King's view of the American war; he is defending there the vital interests and essential rights of the British nation.

A year later, in March 1783, when faced by the necessity of accepting a Government formed by the Fox-North coalition, George III once more contemplated abdication; and in a letter (which again was never sent) he wrote to the Prince of Wales:

> The situation of the times are such that I must, if I attempt to carry on the business of the nation, give up every political principle on which I have acted, which I should think very unjustifiable, as I have always attempted to act agreeable to my duty; and must form a Ministry from among men who know I cannot trust them and therefore who will not accept office without making me a kind of slave; this undoubtedly is a cruel dilemma, and leaves me but one step to take without the destruction of my principles and honour; the resigning my Crown, my dear Son to you, quitting this my native country for ever and returning to the dominions of my forefathers.
> Your difficulties will not be the same. You have never been in a situation to form any political system, therefore, are open to adopt what the times may make necessary; and no set of men can ever have offended you or made it impossible for you to employ them.[2]

Alongside this consider the following passage from a letter which George III wrote on 26 December 1783, after having dismissed the Coalition and while he was trying to rally support for the newly formed Administration of the younger Pitt:

> The times are of the most serious nature, the political struggle is not as formerly between two factions for power; but it is no less than whether a desperate faction shall not reduce the Sovereign to a mere tool in its hands: though I have too much principle ever to infringe the rights of others, yet that must ever equally prevent my submitting to the Executive power being in any other hands, than where the Constitution has placed it. I therefore must call on the assistance of

[1] Fortescue, *op. cit.*, vol. v, No. 3061. [J. W. Fortescue, *Correspondence of King George III from 1760 to December 1783* (London, 1927–1928).]
[2] Windsor MSS.

every honest man . . . to support Government on the present most critical occasion.[3]

Note in these two passages the King's honest conviction that he has always attempted to do his duty; that he has been mindful not to infringe the rights of others; but that it would be equally wrong in him to submit 'to the Executive power being in any other hands, than where the Constitution has placed it'. And while I do not for a moment suggest that these things could not have been done in a happier manner, I contend that the King's statements quoted above are substantially correct.

In the eighteenth century, a proper balance between King, Lords, and Commons, that is, the monarchical, aristocratic, and representative elements of the Constitution acting as checks on each other, was supposed to safeguard the property and privileges, the lives and liberty of the subjects. Single-Chamber government would have been no less abhorrent to the century than Royal autocracy. The Executive was the King's as truly as it is now of the President in the United States; he, too, had to choose his Ministers: but from among Parliamentary leaders. And while aspirants to office swore by the 'independency' of the Crown and disclaimed all wish to force themselves on the King, if left out they did their level best to embarrass and upset their successful rivals. The technique of Parliamentary opposition was fully established long before its most essential aim, which is to force a change of government, was recognized as legitimate; and because that aim could not be avowed in its innocent purity, deadly dangers threatening the Constitution, nay the life of the country, had to be alleged for justification. Robert Walpole as 'sole Minister' was accused of arrogating to himself the powers of both King and Parliament; the very tame Pelhams of keeping George II 'in fetters'; Bute, who bore the name of Stuart, of 'raising the standard of Royal prerogative'; and George III of ruling not through the Ministers of his own choice whom he avowed in public, but through a hidden gang of obscure and sinister 'King's friends'. It is obviously impossible here to trace the origin and growth of that story, or to disprove it by establishing the true facts of the transactions to which it has become attached—it was a figment so beautifully elaborated by Burke's fertile imagination that the Rockinghams themselves finished by believing it, and it grew into an obsession with them. In reality the constitutional practice of George III differed little from that of George I and George II. William Wyndham was proscribed by the first two Georges as a dangerous Jacobite, and C. J. Fox by the third as a dangerous Jacobin; while the elder Pitt was long kept out by both George II and George III on personal grounds. But for some the Royal veto and Royal influence in politics lose their sting if exercised in favour of successful monopolists in Whiggery.

I go one step further: in the eighteenth century the King had to intervene in politics and was bound to exercise his political influence, for the party system, which is the basis of Parliamentary government, did not exist.[4] Of the House of Commons itself probably less than half thought and acted in party terms. About one-third of the House consisted of Members who looked to the King for guidance and for permanency of employment: epigoni of earlier Courts or forerunners of the modern Civil Service; and if they thus pursued their own interest, there is no reason to treat them as more corrupt than if they had done so by attaching themselves to a group of politicians. Another one-fifth of the House consisted of independent country gentlemen, ready

[3] Windsor MS. 5709.

[4] For a fuller discussion of this point see Lewis B. Namier, *Crossroads of Power*, pp. 220–229.

to support the King's Government so long as this was compatible with their conscience, but averse to tying themselves up with political groups: they did not desire office, honours, or profits, but prided themselves on the disinterested and independent line they were pursuing; and they rightly claimed to be the authentic voice of the nation. In the centre of the arena stood the politicians, their orators and leaders fighting for the highest prizes of Parliamentary life. They alone could supply the façade of governments: the front benches in Parliament. But to achieve stability a Government required the active support of the Crown and the good opinion of the country. On matters about which public opinion felt strongly, its will would prevail; but with the House constituted as it was, with the electoral structure of the unreformed Parliament, and an electorate which neither thought nor voted on party lines, it is idle to assume that modern Parliamentary government was possible.

I pass to the next point: was George III correct in saying that it was 'his scrupulous attachment to the rights of Parliament' which caused him the difficulties in America? Undoubtedly yes. It was not Royal claims that the Americans objected to, but the claims of 'subjects in one part of the King's dominions to be sovereigns over their fellow-subjects in another part of his dominions'.[5] 'The sovereignity of the Crown I understand,' wrote Benjamin Franklin; 'the sovereignty of Britain I do not understand. . . . We have the same King, but not the same legislature.' Had George III aspired to independent Royal Power nothing could have suited him better than to be Sovereign in America, the West Indies, and possibly in Ireland, independent of the British Parliament; and the foremost champions of the rights of Parliament, recalling the way in which the Stuarts had played off Ireland and Scotland against England, would have been the first to protest. But in fact it would be difficult to imagine a King simultaneously exercising in several independent countries executive powers in conjunction with Parliamentary leaders. It will suffice to remember the difficulties and jealousies which Hanover caused although itself politically inert. The two problems which George III is unjustly accused of having mismanaged, those of Imperial and constitutional relations, were inter-connected: only after responsible government had arisen did Dominion status within the Commonwealth become possible. Lastly, of the measures which brought on the American conflict none was of the King's making: neither George Grenville's Stamp Act, nor the Declaratory Act of the Rockinghams, nor the Townshend Duties. All that can be said against him is that once the struggle had started, he, completely identifying himself with this country, obstinately persevered in it. He wrote on 14 November 1778:

> If Lord North can see with the same degree of enthusiasm I do the beauty, excellence, and perfection of the British Constitution, as by law established, and consider that if any one branch of the Empire is alowed to cast off its dependency, that the others will infalably follow the example . . . he . . . will resolve with vigour to meet every obstacle . . . or the State will be ruined.[6]

And again on 11 June 1779, expecting that the West Indies and Ireland would follow:

> Then this island would be reduced to itself, and soon would be a poor island indeed.[7]

[5] Benjamin Franklin to the Rev. Samuel Cooper of Boston, 8 June 1770.
[6] Fortescue vol. iv, No. 2451.
[7] *Ibid.*, No. 2649.

On 7 March 1780:

> I can never suppose this country so far lost to all ideas of self importance as to be willing to grant America independence, if that could ever be universally adopted, I shall despair of this country being ever preserved from a state of inferiority and consequently falling into a very low class among the European States. . . .[8]

And on 26 September 1780:

> . . . giving up the game would be total ruin, a small State may certainly subsist, but a great one mouldering cannot get into an inferior situation but must be annihilated.[9]

When all was over, Lord North wrote to the King on 18 March 1782:

> Your Majesty is well apprized that, in this country, the Prince on the Throne, cannot, with prudence, oppose the deliberate resolution of the House of Commons . . . Your Majesty has graciously and steadily supported the servants you approve, as long as they could be supported: Your Majesty has firmly and resolutely maintained what appeared to you essential to the welfare and dignity of this country, as long as this country itself thought proper to maintain it. The Parliament have altered their sentiments, and as their sentiments whether just or erroneous, must ultimately prevail, Your Majesty . . . can lose no honour if you yield at length . . .
>
> Your Majesty's goodness encourages me . . . to submit whether it will not be for Your Majesty's welfare, and even glory, to sacrifice, at this moment, former opinions, displeasures and apprehensions (though never so well-founded) to . . . the public safety.[10]

The King replied:

> I could not but be hurt at your letter of last night. Every man must be the sole judge of his feelings, therefore whatever you or any man can say on that subject has no avail with me.[11]

What George III had never learnt was to give in with grace: but this was at the most a defect of character.

II

Lord Waldegrave, who had been Governor to the Prince of Wales 1752–6, wrote in 1758 a character sketch of him so penetrating and just that it deserves quoting almost in full.[12]

> The Prince of Wales is entering into his 21st year, and it would be unfair to decide upon his character in the early stages of life, when there is so much time for improvement.

[8] Fortescue vol. v, No. 2963.
[9] *Ibid.*, No. 3155.
[10] *Ibid.*, No. 3566.
[11] *Ibid.*, No. 3567.
[12] James, 2nd Earl Waldegrave, *Memoirs* (1821), pp. 8–10.

A wise preamble; yet a long and eventful life was to change him very little. Every feature singled out by Waldegrave finds copious illustration in the fifty years that followed (in one case in a superficially inverted form).

> His parts, though not excellent, will be found very tolerable, if ever they are properly exercised.
> He is strictly honest, but wants that frank and open behaviour which makes honesty appear amiable. . . .
> His religion is free from all hypocrisy, but is not of the most charitable sort; he has rather too much attention to the sins of his neighbour.
> He has spirit, but not of the active kind; and does not want resolution, but it is mixed with too much obstinacy.
> He has great command of his passions, and will seldom do wrong, except when he mistakes wrong for right; but as often as this shall happen, it will be difficult to undeceive him, because he is uncommonly indolent, and has strong prejudices.
> His want of application and aversion to business would be far less dangerous, was he eager in the pursuit of pleasure; for the transition from pleasure to business is both shorter and easier than from a state of total inaction.
> He has a kind of unhappiness in his temper, which, if it be not conquered before it has taken too deep a root, will be a source of frequent anxiety. Whenever he is displeased, his anger does not break out with heat and violence; but he becomes sullen and silent, and retires to his closet; not to compose his mind by study or contemplation, but merely to indulge the melancholy enjoyment of his own ill humour. Even when the fit is ended, unfavourable symptoms very frequently return, which indicate that on certain occasions his Royal Highness has too correct a memory.

Waldegrave's own endeavour was to give the Prince 'true notions of common things'[13]. But these he never acquired: which is perhaps the deepest cause of his tragedy.

The defect Waldegrave dwells upon most is the Prince's 'uncommon indolence', his 'want of application and aversion to business'. This is borne out by other evidence, best of all by the Prince's own letters to Bute:[14]

> *July 1st, 1756:* I will throw off that indolence which if I don't soon get the better of will be my ruin.
> *March 25th, 1757:* I am conscious of my own indolence . . . I do here in the most solemn manner declare, that I will throw aside this my greatest enemy. . . .
> *September 25th, 1758:* . . . . that incomprehensible indolence, inattention and heedlessness that reigns within me . . .

And he says of his good resolutions: 'as many as I have made I have regularly broke'; but adds a new one: 'I mean to attempt to regain the many years I have fruitlessly spent.'

> *December 19th, 1758:* . . . through the negligence, if not the wickedness of those around me in my earlier days, and since perhaps through my own indolence of temper, I have not that degree of knowledge and experience in business, one of my age might reasonably have aqcuir'd . . .

[13] *Ibid.,* p. 64.
[14] See *Letters from George III to Lord Bute* (1939), edited by Romney Sedgwick.

> *March* 1760: . . . my natural indolence . . . has been encreas'd by a kind of
> indifference to the world, owing to the number of bad characters I daily see. . . .

By shifting the blame on to others, he tries to relieve the bitter consciousness of
failure: which is one source of that excessive 'attention to the sins of his neighbour'
mentioned by Waldegrave. Indeed, George III's letters, both before and after his
accession, are full of it: 'the great depravity of the age', 'the wickedest age that ever
was seen', 'a degenerate age', 'probity and every other virtue absorb'd into vice, and
dissipation'; etc. 'An ungrateful, wicked people' and individual statesmen alike receive castigation (*in absentia*) from this very young Old Testament prophet. Pitt 'is
the blackest of hearts', 'the most dishonourable of men', and plays 'an infamous and
ungrateful part'; Lord Temple, an 'ungrateful arrogant and self-sufficient man';
Charles Townshend is 'a man void of every quality', 'the worst man that lives',
'vermin'; Henry Fox, a man of 'bad character', 'void of principles'; Lord Mansfield is
'but half a man'; the Duke of Bedford's character 'contains nothing but passion and
absurdity'; etc. As for George II, the Prince felt ashamed of being his grandson.
And on 23 April 1760, half a year before his accession, aged twenty-two he wrote to
Bute: '. . . as to honesty, I have already lived long enough to know you are the only
man who possesses that quality . . .'

In Bute he thought he had found the tutelary spirit who would enable him to live
up to his future high vocation. Here are further excerpts from the Prince's letters
to him:

> *July* 1*st*, 1756: My friend is . . . attack'd in the most cruel and horrid man-
> ner . . . because he is my friend . . . and because he is a friend to the bless'd
> liberties of his country and not to arbitrary notions . . .
> By . . . your friendship . . . I have reap'd great advantage, but not the
> improvement I should if I had follow'd your advice . . . I will exactly follow
> your advice, without which I shall inevitably sink.
> *March* 25*th*, 1757: I am resolved . . . to act the man in everything, to repeat
> whatever I am to say with spirit and not blushing and afraid as I have hitherto
> . . . my conduct shall convince you that I am mortified at what I have done
> and that I despise myself . . . I hope this will persuade you not to leave me
> when all is at stake, when nobody but you can stear me through this difficult,
> though glorious path.

In June 1757 Leicester House were alarmed by rumours of an alliance between the
Duke of Newcastle and Henry Fox, and were ascribing fantastic schemes to the Duke
of Cumberland. The Prince already saw himself compelled to meet force by force
or to 'yield up the Crown',

> for I would only accept it with the hopes of restoring my much beloved country
> to her antient state of liberty; of seeing her . . . again famous for being the
> residence of true piety and virtue, I say if these hopes were lost, I should with
> an eye of pleasure look on retiring to some uninhabited cavern as this would pre-
> vent me from seeing the sufferings of my countrymen, and the total destruction
> of this Monarchy . . .
> *August* 20*th*, 1758: . . . by . . . attempting with vigour to restore religion
> and virtue when I mount the throne this great country will probably regain her
> antient state of lustre.

Was this a Prince nurtured in 'arbitrary notions', ambitious to make his own will prevail? or a man with a 'mission', striving after naively visionary aims? No doubt, since early childhood it must have been rammed into him, especially when he was being reproved, to what high station he was born; and disparaging comparisons are said to have been drawn between him and his younger brother. He grew up with a painful consciousness of his inadequacy: 'though I act wrong perhaps in most things', he wrote on one occasion. Excessive demands on a child, complete with wholesome exhortations, are fit to reduce it to a state of hebetude from which it is not easy to recover. A great deal of the pattern of George III's behaviour throughout life can be traced back to his upbringing.

He spent his young years cut off from intercourse with boys of his own age, till he himself ceased to desire it. Bubb Dodington notes in his *Diary* on 15 October 1752 that the Princess Dowager of Wales

> did not observe the Prince to take very particularly to anybody about him, but to his brother Edward, and she was glad of it, for the young people of quality were so ill-educated and so vicious, that they frightened her.

And so they did him for the rest of his life. Isolation by itself would be apt to suggest to a child that there was something wrong with those he had to shun; but this he was probably told in so many words. On 18 December 1753, Dodington records another talk with the Princess:

> I said, it was to be wished he could have more company. She seemed averse to the young people, from the excessive bad education they had, and from the bad examples they gave.

So the boy spent joyless years in a well-regulated nursery, the nearest approach to a concentration camp: lonely but never alone, constantly watched and discussed, never safe from the wisdom and goodness of the grown-ups; never with anyone on terms of equality, exalted yet oppressed by deferential adults. The silent, sullen anger noted by Waldegrave was natural to one who could not hit back or speak freely his mind, as a child would among children: he could merely retire, and nurture his griefs and grievances—and this again he continued through life. On 3 May 1766, during a political crisis, he wrote to Bute: 'I can neither eat nor sleep, nothing pleases me but musing on my cruel situation.' Nor could he, always with adults, develop self-reliance: at nineteen he dreamt of reforming the nation, but his idea of acting the man was to repeat without blushing or fear what he had to say.

For the pious works which were 'to make this great nation happy' Bute's 'sagacious councils' were therefore indispensable. When in December 1758 Bute expressed doubts whether he should take office in the future reign, the Prince in a panic searched his own conscience:

> Perhaps it is the fear you have I shall not speak firmly enough to my Ministers, or that I shall be stagger'd if they say anything unexpected; as to the former I can with great certainty assure that they, nor no one else shall see a want of steadiness either in my manner of acting or speaking, and as to the latter, I may give fifty sort of puts off, till I have with you thoroughly consider'd what part will be proper to be taken. . . .

George III adhered to this programme. On his grandfather's death he waited to hear from Bute what 'must be done'. When expecting Pitt at a critical juncture: 'I would wish to know what I had best say. . . .' With regard to measures or appointments: 'I have put that off till I hear my Dear Friend's opinion'; 'If this [is] agreeable to my D. Friend I will order it to day . . .'; 'I desire my D. Friend to consider what I have here wrote, if he is of a contrary opinion, I will with pleasure embrace it.' And when in November 1762 Bute declared he would retire on conclusion of peace:

> I had flattered myself [wrote the King] when peace was once established that my D. Friend would have assisted me in purging out corruption . . .; . . . now . . . the Ministry remains compos'd of the most abandon'd men that ever had those offices; thus instead of reformation the Ministers being vicious this country will grow if possible worse; let me attack the irreligious, the covetous &c. as much as I please, that will be of no effect . . . Ministers being of that stamp . . .

Two years on the throne had worked little if any change in his ideas and language; nor did the next twenty. The same high claims on himself, and the same incapacity to meet real situations he was faced with: hence his continued dependence on others. By 1765 he saw that Bute could not help him, by the summer of 1766 he had written off Bute altogether. In the spring of 1765 he turned to the Duke of Cumberland, the bugbear of his young years: 'Dear Uncle, the very friendly and warm part you have taken has given me real satisfaction. . . .'[15] And to Pitt, 'the blackest of hearts': 'My friend for so the part you have acted deserves of me. . . .'[16] In July 1765 Cumberland formed for him the Rockingham Administration and presided over it a quasi-Viceroy; but a few months later Cumberland was dead. In July 1766 Chatham formed his Administration; but a few months later his health broke down completely. Still George III clung to him like a molusc (a molusc who never found his rock). 'Under a health so broken', wrote Chatham, 'as renders at present application of mind totally impossible . . .'[17] After nearly two years of waiting for his recovery, the King still wrote: 'I think I have a right to insist on your remaining in my service.'[18] Next he clung to the ineffective Grafton who longed to be relieved of office; and when Grafton resigned, the King wrote to him on 27 January 1770:

> My heart is so full at the thought of your retiring from your situation that I think it best not to say more as I know the expressing it would give you pain.[19]

Then came North. Totally unequal to the difficulties of the American crisis, in letter after letter he begged the King to let him resign. Thus in March 1778:

> Lord North cannot conceive what can induce His Majesty, after so many proofs of Lord North's unfitness for his situation to determine at all events to keep him at the head of the Administration, though the almost certain consequences of His Majesty's resolution will be the ruin of his affairs, and though it can not ward off for a month that arrangement which His Majesty seems to apprehend.[20]

But the King would not hear of it. 2 July, 1779: 'no man has a right to talk of

---

[15] Fortescue vol. i, No. 74.
[16] *Ibid.*, No. 94.
[17] *Ibid.*, No. 538.
[18] Fortescue vol. ii, No. 669.
[19] Grafton MSS.
[20] Fortescue vol. iv, No. 2241.

leaving me at this hour. . . .'[21] 25 October, 1780: he expects North 'will show that zeal for which he has been conspicuous from the hour of the Duke of Grafton's desertion.[22]

George III's attitude to North conformed to the regular pattern of his behaviour. So did also the way in which after a while he turned against North in bitter disappointment. By the '70s the King spoke disparagingly of Bute and Chatham; and in time his imagination enabled him to remember how on the day of his accession he had given the slip to them both. A month after Grafton had resigned, George III wrote to him: 'I . . . see anew that the sincere regard and friendship I have for you is properly placed. . . .'[23] Somewhat later his resignation changed into 'desertion.' When North resigned: 'I ever did and ever shall look on you as a friend as well as a faithful servant. . . .'[24] But incensed at the new situation he soon started attacking North, and treated him niggardly and unfairly over his secret-service accounts. George III's attachment was never deep: it was that of a drunken man to railings—mechanical rather than emotional. Egocentric and rigid, stunted in feelings, unable to adjust himself to events, flustered by sudden change, he could meet situations only in a negative manner, clinging to men and measures with disastrous obstinacy. But he himself mistook that defensive apparatus for courage, drive, and vigour, from which it was as far removed as anything could be. Of his own mental processes he sometimes gave discerning though embellished accounts. Thus to Bute in 1762: 'I . . . am apt to despise what I am not accustom'd to. . . .' And on 2 March 1797, to the younger Pitt when criticizing the way measures were weakened in passing through Parliament:

> My nature is quite different I never assent till I am convinced what is proposed is right, and then . . . I never allow that to be destroyed by after-thoughts which on all subjects tend to weaken never to strengthen the original proposal.[25]

In short: no after-thoughts, no reconsideration—only desperate, clinging perseverance.

Still it might be said: at least he broke through his indolence. Yes, indeed: from pathologically indolent he turned pathologically industrious—and never again could let off working; but there was little sense of values, no perspective, no detachment. There is a legend about a homunculus whose maker, not knowing what to do with him, bid him count poppy-seed in a bag. That George III was doing with his own busy self. His innumerable letters which he copied in his own hand, or the long documents transcribed by him (he never employed an amanuensis till his eyesight began to fail) contains some shrewd perceptions or remarks, evidence of 'very tolerable parts if . . . properly exercised.' But most of his letters merely repeat approvingly what some Minister, big or small, has suggested. 'Lord A. is very right . . .'; 'General B. has acted very properly . . .'; 'the minute of Cabinet meets with my fullest concurrence . . .'; 'Nothing can more deserve my approbation than' —whatever it was. But if a basic change is suggested, his obstinacy and prejudices appear. On 15 March 1778, in a letter to Lord North, he makes an unusual and startling admission:

[21] *Ibid.,* No. 2696.
[22] Fortescue vol. v, No. 3165.
[23] 2 March 1770, Grafton MSS.
[24] Fortescue vol. v, No. 3593.
[25] Windsor MSS.

> I will only add to put before your eyes my most inmost thoughts, that no advan-
> tage to this country nor personal danger can ever make me address myself for
> assistance either to Lord Chatham or any other branch of the Opposition. . . .[26]

As a rule he would sincerely assert, perhaps with somewhat excessive ostentation, that first and foremost he considered the good of the country. When told by Bute that it would be improper for him to marry Lady Sarah Lennox, he replied: 'the interest of my country ever shall be my first care, my own inclinations shall ever submit to it' (and he added: 'I should wish we could next summer . . . get some account of the various Princesses in Germany'—and he settled down to 'looking in the New Berlin Almanack for Princesses'). When considering withdrawal from the German war, he wrote (with a sidelong glance at the late King) about the superiority of his love 'to this my native country over any private interest of my own. . . .' He was 'a King of a free people'; 'I rely on the hearts of my subjects, the only true support of the Crown', he wrote in November 1760. They will not desert him—

> if they could be so ungrateful to me who love them beyond anything else in life,
> I should then I realy believe fall into the deepest melancholy which would soon
> deprive me of the vexations of this life.

The same note, of love for this country and trust that his subjects would therefore stand by him, continues for almost twenty years. But gradually other overtones begin to mix with it. He had become the target of virulent attacks and unjust suspicions which he deeply resented. Thus to Lord North on 7 March 1780: '. . . however I am treated I must love this country'.[27] And to the Prince of Wales on 14 August 1780:

> The numberless trials and constant torments I meet with in public life, must
> certainly affect any man, and more poignantly me, as I have no other wish but
> to fulfill my various duties; the experience of now twenty years has convinced
> me that however long it may please the Almighty to extend my days, yet I have
> no reason to expect any diminution of my public anxiety; where am I therefore
> to turn for comfort, but into the bosom of my own family? [28]

And he appealed to his son, the future George IV, to connect himself only with young men of respectable character, and by his example help 'to restore this country to its former lustre'—the old tune once more. And in another letter:

> From your childhood I have ever said that I can only try to save my country,
> but it must be by the co-operation of my children only that I can effect it.[29]

In the 1780s there is a more than usually heavy crop of bitter complaints about the age by one 'righteous overmuch': 'it has been my lot to reign in the most profligate age', 'depravity of such times as we live in', 'knavery and indolence perhaps I might add the timidity of the times. . . .' And then:

> I thank Heaven my morals and course of life have but little resembled those
> too prevalent in the present age, and certainly of all objects in this life the one

---

[26] Fortescue vol. iv, No. 2221.
[27] Fortescue vol. v, No. 2963.
[28] Windsor MSS.
[29] *Ibid.*

> I have most at heart, is to form my children that they may be useful examples
> and worthy of imitation . . .[30]

With the King's disappointments in country and son another note enters his letters.
He warns the Prince—

> in other countries national pride makes the inhabitants wish to paint their Princes
> in the most favourable light, and consequently be silent on any indiscretion; but
> here most persons if not concerned in laying ungrounded blame, are ready to
> trumpet any speck they can find out.[31]

And he writes of the 'unalterable attachment' which his Electoral subjects have shown
to their Princes. When George III went mad in 1788, he wanted to go back to Hanover. Deep down there was a good deal of the Hanoverian in him.

His insanity was a form of manic-depression. The first recorded fit in March 1765
was of short duration, though there may have been a slight relapse in May; and a
year later he wrote to Bute—

> if I am to continue the life of agitation I have these three years, the next year
> there will be a Council [of] Regency to assist in that undertaking.

During the next twenty-three years he preserved his normal personality. The attack
in 1788 lasted about half a year: the King was over fifty, and age rendered complete
recovery more difficult. His self-control weakened and his irritability increased. He
was conscious of a growing weakness. Yet there was something about him which
more and more endeared him to the people. He was never popular with London
society or the London mob; he was much beloved in the provinces—perhaps it was
his deeper kindness, his real piety, and sincere wish to do good which evoked those
feelings. These appear strikingly, for instance, in his own account of his journey to
Portsmouth in 1788,[32] and in Fanny Burney's account of his progress through Wiltshire in 1789.[33] He was not a politician, and certainly not a statesman. But in things
which he could judge without passion or preconceived ideas, there appears basic
honesty and the will to do the right thing. I shall limit myself to two examples.
When in 1781 a new Provost was to be appointed at Eton, George III insisted on
choosing a man 'whose literary tallents might make the appointment respectable
. . . for Eton should not be bestowed by favour, but merit'.[34] And when in 1787 a
new Lord Lieutenant had to be chosen for Ireland, the King wrote to the younger
Pitt about the necessity

> of looking out for the person most likely to conduct himself with temper, judge-
> ment, and an avowed resolution to avoid partiality and employ the favours he
> has to recommend to with the justice due to my service and to the public. . . .
> When I have stated this Mr. Pitt must understand that I do not lean to any
> particular person . . . when I state that a Lord Lieutenant should have no
> predelection but to advance the public good I should be ashamed to act in a
> contrary manner.[35]

[30] *Ibid.*
[31] *Ibid.*
[32] Windsor MSS.
[33] Fanny Burney, *Diary* (1905), vol. iv, pp. 310–11.
[34] Fortescue vol. v, No. 3455.
[35] Windsor MSS.

I have given here a picture of George III as seen in his letters, 'warts and all'. What I have never been able to find is the man arrogating power to himself, the ambitious schemer out to dominate, the intriguer dealing in an underhand fashion with his Ministers; in short, any evidence for the stories circulated about him by very clever and eloquent contemporaries. He had a high, indeed an exaggerated, notion of royalty but in terms of mission and duties rather than of power; and trying to live up to this idealized concept, he made unreasonable demands on himself. Setting himself unattainable standards, he could never truly come to grips with reality: which condemned him to remain immature, permanency of inner conflict precluding growth. Aware of his inadequacy, he turned to others and expected them to enable him to realize his visionary program (this appears clearest in his relations with Bute); and he bitterly reproached them in his own mind, and blamed the age in which he lived, for his own inevitable failure. The tension between his notions and reality, and the resulting frustration, account to a high degree for his irritability, his deep-seated resentments, and his suppressed anger—for situations intolerable and disastrous for himself and others; and it may have been a contributory factor in his mental breakdowns. The desire to escape from that unbearable conflict repeatedly shows itself in thoughts of abdication which must not be deemed insincere because never acted upon (men of his type cannot renounce their treadmill). He himself did not understand the nature and depth of his tragedy; still less could others. There was therefore room for the growth of an injurious legend which made that heavy-burdened man a much maligned ruler; and which has long been accepted as history.

12 / British Strategy in the War of American Independence

Piers Mackesy

While the architects of British military policy in the New World were to see their efforts end in the loss of the Thirteen Colonies, these men—and particularly, Lord George Germain—did have some reasonable notions as to how the struggle with the colonists might be brought to a successful conclusion. They worked strenuously to establish and to supply a military force "unprecedented" in British military experience. In this essay, Piers Mackesy argues that British forces were often successful in winning their goals on the battlefield. He discusses the strategy of the British and attempts to suggest the extent to which their plans and endeavors were based upon a rational conception of their task in America. And, by implication at least, he indicates the importance of the great turning points of the war for America. In 1776 the Howes lost a chance to destroy the Continental Armies. In the following year, the British continued to follow the same general lines of operation and were defeated at Saratoga. The foreign complications for both sides that resulted from Saratoga were reflected in a change in the British approach. Then the efforts of their armies in America were directed at a piecemeal reconquest, one which particularly emphasized the gradual extension of British authority upward through the Southern colonies. Then the surprising success of American and French cooperation at Saratoga came as a final political blow, one that was less important in its strictly military terms than in its impact upon British politicians who were tired of war and taxes. To a certain extent, Mackesy may be trying too hard to separate strategy and politics and rational planning and accidental happenings. But his general argument is worth understanding: the British planned their war for America, made strenuous efforts to prosecute it, and could have made a harsher peace if they had been willing to continue to prosecute the war. Their efforts were undercut by divisions at home, by political squabblings over the conduct of the war, and by the ineptness of some of their military leaders as much or more than they were by the force of American resistance.

Reprinted by permission from *The Yale Review* (Copyright © 1963 Yale University), LII (1963), 539–557.

For further reading: John Alden, *General Gage in America* (1948); Piers Mackesy, *The War for America, 1775–1783* (1964); Eric Robson, *The American Revolution in its Political and Military Aspects, 1763–1783* (1966); John Shy, *Towards Lexington* (1965); and Christopher Ward, *The War of the Revolution* (2 vols., 1952).

In the first century of American history-writing it seems to have been a necessary part of the national creed that the War of Independence was won primarily by the tactical prowess of the rebels on the field of battle; and though interest in the war has widened and deepened, there are places where the old legend still holds on tenaciously. One of those places is the battlefields themselves, and the legend is preserved in cast iron along the roads of the eastern seaboard. There is a particularly striking example in New Jersey on the site of the successful rearguard action which General Clinton fought at Monmouth Court House during his withdrawal from Philadelphia in 1778. There, with twelve miles of baggage to protect, and Washington close on his heels, he turned and launched a local counterstroke which enabled him to disengage in the night and make his way without further danger to Sandy Hook. Yet the historical marker by the roadside characterizes the battle in a succinct and confident phrase as An Important American Victory.

Now the truth of course is that in so far as the war was won on the battlefield it was won by the attrition of British resources and the avoidance of decisive defeat —to which the British commanders greatly contributed. The decisive factors in the American success were strategic. Obviously in a sense this is true of all wars; yet there can have been few in which ultimate victory was gained to the accompaniment of so consistent a record of defeat in the field. As one British staff officer wrote admiringly of General Greene, "the more he is beaten, the farther he advances in the end. He has been indefatigable in collecting troops, and leading them to be defeated." I can think of only one important tactical defeat of British troops in the field, the battle of the Cowpens in January 1781; and had it not been for the misconduct of Colonel Rahl and the miscalculations of Burgoyne, the same would have been true of the Germans. This fact accounts for the bitterness of the British and Hessian troops who surrendered at Yorktown. They had fought the rebels for five years, and their superior training and discipline had told in their favor on countless battlefields; and they felt that if history was on the side of the men who carried the muskets, they would not now be piling their arms and colors. When they heard their bands playing "The World Turned Upside Down," these men did not look into the future or realize the long-term repercussions of the American victory throughout the world. Their own world was their regiments, and they knew the words of the tune the bands were playing:

> If ponies rode men, and if grass ate the cows,
> And cats should be chased into holes by the mouse . . .
> If summer were spring and the other way round,
> Then all the world would be upside down.

All this is now common ground. The causes of the British failure were political and strategic; they were failures of a negative kind through most of the war, since except on rare occasions the British held the strategic initiative, yet failed to win a decision; failures of a positive kind when they suffered their two great strategic disasters at Saratoga and Yorktown. Yet the history of the British conduct of the war still remains unwritten. This is partly because the war was lost, and it is painful to dwell on defeat; partly because George III and his Ministers were vilified by domestic enemies, whose accusations, perpetuated in the *Parliamentary Debates,* form the most accessible source of information. There one may read the half-informed and wholly disingenuous criticisms of the opposition, and the misleading and partial replies of Ministers. These, supplemented by the *Annual Register* and memoirs like Horace Walpole's, dominated the entire history of this period for many generations. They are riddled with lies, special pleading, and gossip. Though the political history of the reign has been rewritten from better sources, the major decisions of the war have still to be reassessed.

From the very beginning of the war a few people maintained that the cause was hopeless: and hindsight has strengthened and extended their argument. The Americans, it now runs, were numerous, skilled in handling weapons, and defending a country of limitless space and limited resources: they had no cities whose loss would be fatal to the political, moral, or industrial foundations of their military effort; they were free to refuse battle except on favorable terms, and to retreat into fastnesses where the British could not follow or attack them. When the maritime powers of Europe intervened in the struggle, the argument continues, its futility became all too evident. The British Army was now drawn into defensive commitments throughout the globe which made it impossible to reinforce or even keep up the strength of the force in America, while the navy faced odds which meant that it could no longer guarantee the Atlantic supply-line or the army's lateral communications on the American coast. Only the blindness and folly of the King and his immediate advisers, particularly Lord George Germain, forced England to continue the struggle.

So runs the indictment, delivered from the godlike pinnacles of after-knowledge. But I have spent some time looking at British documents on the conduct of the war, and have tried to look at it from a point where the view is more constricted— let us say from the middle of St. James's Square in London—and with the help of the eyes of two men whom it has only recently become respectable to consult: King George III and Lord George Germain.

Now it is possible to argue that the political objectives of the war were so ill-conceived that the success or failure of the strategy is a matter of indifference: that if America had been reconquered it would have done England no good in the long run anyway, and that it was more important to withdraw from the struggle by an act of political discretion than to wage it against heavy odds in a spirit of military optimism. To this argument there was one reply which was absolutely conclusive if it was true. It was used with much vividness of expression by the King and many other people, but I will put it in the words which Germain used after Yorktown: "we can never continue to exist as a great and powerful nation, after we have lost or renounced the sovereignty of the American colonies."

Now we, being wise after the event, know that this idea was wrong. But to reject it before 1783 was to reject the whole system of economic beliefs which had shaped the British Empire. Statesmen are not built in that mould; and there are enough examples in our own day of policy firmly based on fossilized assumptions to make an Englishman at least somewhat wary of condemning George III and those who shared his beliefs. And they were not all simple souls like the King. When the cause was lost and it was becoming apparent that trade with America did not depend on political sovereignty, a sophisticated mind like Lord Sheffield's could still fight for the Navigation System as the foundation of power on which wealth must ultimately be rooted. And there was another strategic argument which is worth considering: that in time of future war a hostile America would wreck the British homeward-bound West Indian trade and make the West Indies untenable. It is true that in the War of 1812 British trade was not much inconvenienced, but in fact the danger was never fully tested. If America had intervened when Britain's European enemies had powerful navies intact and British resources were already at full stretch, American warships and American bases might have achieved very different results.

But even supposing that the loss of America would be disastrous, the administrative difficulties of the task facing the Ministry were appalling. Setting aside the naval effort, the British government committed itself in the course of the war to transporting, reinforcing, and supplying between fifty and sixty thousand troops in the Western Atlantic between Newfoundland and Tobago. The initial effort of lifting the army which was to fight the campaign of 1776 in Canada and around New York completely swamped the country's shipping resources. Had it not been for the determination of Germain and the support of the King, the Admiralty and Navy Board would have thrown in their hand and declared it to be impossible. It was certainly, as Lord Sandwich declared, unprecedented. Contemporaries, including Sir William Howe, acknowledged the greatness of the achievement, for which the credit lay principally with Germain; and in our own day Walter Millis has written that it is entitled to the respect of modern staff officers and logisticians.

It had been assumed at the outset that the army would quickly recover a sufficient depth of country in America to supply most of its own needs in the way of provisions, fodder, and fuel. But this hope was constantly disappointed in the coming years, and Germain found himself responsible for seeing that fifty thousand troops were fully supplied across three thousand miles of ocean. This he achieved, with the cordial help of the Treasury and at the cost of a good deal of friction. The maintenance of the armies abroad in the last year of the war was to require 120,000 tons of shipping, composed of ships of between 250 and 400 tons. The whole effort across the ocean was unparalleled in the history of the world, and it was successful. A good deal has sometimes been made of the pressure of these supply problems on the commanders in the field, but any excuse was good enough to shift responsibility for failure onto the home government, and the difficulties of the Atlantic pipeline made relatively little difference to the course of operations on land. The pressure was felt most in a different quarter; for the continuing financial burden of the operation fell heavily on Lord North, as head of the Treasury and Exchequer, and it probably did more to depress his spirits and undermine his resolution than did the operational problems of the war.

The course of operations was nevertheless influenced by a problem which might be described as administrative, and in a disastrous manner. The selection of theatre commanders had always been a difficult task: difficult not only because political and social pressures sometimes pushed bad candidates forward, but also because of the genuine impossibility of foretelling how an officer would measure up to the command of a theatre of war when the only evidence available related to his record in peace-time or as a subordinate on the battlefield. The Elder Pitt had fired two commanders on the main front in America in the course of two years; and the problem in the American Rebellion was yet more difficult. In the first place the commanders' task was infinitely more complicated and diffuse, calling for a rare combination of tactical and strategic ability with statesmanship; and in the second place the intense political warfare at home constantly handicapped the government in its choice of commanders and inhibited them from removing failures.

At the very outset the American theatre was saddled with three fairly junior generals who were sent out to give some much-needed military help to General Gage. For that purpose skill in training troops and handling them in the field was most needed; and Howe, Burgoyne, and Clinton all had good reputations. But much more was needed in a commander-in-chief who had to deal with the intensely complicated strategic and political situation in the rebel colonies; and all these men in turn found themselves handling problems that were too big for them. Howe conveniently resigned when he had failed; but Clinton held the command for four years in which he gave ample reasons for removing him. But the political situation when he took over was becoming so tricky that it was very difficult to do so. Generals and admirals who thought they had a grievance mostly had seats in Parliament, where they found eager support from the political enemies of the Ministry. After the naval storms which centered on the Keppel affair, and the return from America of Howe, Burgoyne, and Carleton, it was very difficult indeed to remove the well-connected Clinton, and the Ministry was saddled with him for the rest of its existence. The only soldier who emerged who might have had the stature for the American command was Carleton, who fell out with Germain in 1777; but though Germain handled him unwisely and probably with a degree of personal rancor, I am inclined to believe that Carleton gave some grounds for criticism by his operations in Canada in 1776, and responded to it with an intemperate violence which was difficult to overlook.

The operation consequences of inadequate commanders are all too obvious. They meant lost tactical opportunities, apathetic direction in the theatre, and the muffling of the strategic designs laid down by the Ministry. Less obvious perhaps was the dearth of advice on which the government could rely, and of constructive plans from the men who were in the best position to put them forward. For the campaign of 1777 Howe sent home no less than three separate plans, but provided no general reasoning about how the war should be won. The Ministry accepted his proposals, and indeed the final one reached them so late that they were presented with a *fait accompli* and had to accept it, relying on Howe's common sense to relate his own movements to the general plan which included Burgoyne's advance from Canada. Clinton was worse than Howe. His psychology has recently been explored in an interesting experiment by Professor Willcox of the University of Michigan and a psychologist colleague, and the facts are certainly curious enough to make him a profitable subject for study: on occasion a bold tactician, a bold memorialist on paper when he was a subordinate, but in supreme command reduced to a kind of paralysis, incapable of decision and execution, withdrawing himself from his army, and throwing his energies into violent quarrels with his naval colleagues and the Ministry. Germain and the Cabinet attempted to supply the general planning of which he was apparently incapable; and in return they received endless complaints of interference and appeals to be left alone, but never any counterproposals of Clinton's own, and seldom any action. It is worth contrasting Clinton with the Duke of Wellington, who laid the foundation of his Peninsular victories with a lucid memorandum to the Cabinet on the strategic situation of Portugal, and from this proceeded by rational and systematic steps to develop his strategy as the war progressed. I think it is true to say that in the whole course of his command Clinton never put forward a clear appreciation of his task or any rational suggestions for advancing it.

It was of course difficult in the extreme to form a reliable intelligence appreciation. There was little understanding of the political situation and attitudes of the rebels, and their fighting qualities were difficult to assess, for those who knew the Americans best in 1775 respected them the least. Nor was the government free to use every means known to warfare. British hands were tied by considerations of policy and sentiment. This truth has not always been recognized, but when one considers the usages of eighteenth-century war and the methods employed by occupying armies throughout history against insurgent populations, one realizes that the army behaved with a moderation which may have been to its detriment. I do not mean to suggest that rebels taken in arms should have been treated as traitors, which, as Carleton once had cause to remind Washington, could only lead to mutual massacre; but the strict usages of war could have been enforced with a rigor which might have considerably reduced the rebels' already somewhat qualified enthusiasm for the military life. It is possible to speculate, as Major Mackenzie did, on the consequences of a tougher policy about giving quarter. At the attack on Fort Washington, for instance, the American commander rejected the preliminary summons, and considerable casualties were inflicted on the Hessians when they stormed the outworks. Howe would have been perfectly entitled to let them storm the inner defenses, and the Germans would have made a considerable butchery in the crowded enclosure. It is at least conceivable that Washington would thereafter have found it even more difficult to gather an army, and that garrisons like those of the Delaware forts in 1778 might have been more hesitant about standing an assault in the future. Again, if warnings had been issued that partisans not in uniform would be executed out of hand, and a few examples had been made, it is possible that the population as a whole would have lost some of its taste for killing couriers and annoying the army's communications. This of course is an uncertain presumption: it did not work for the French in Spain, but the Americans were mostly members of a prosperous farming and mercantile community, and suffered neither from the poverty nor the fanaticism of the Spaniards. And again, if the coastal towns had been systematically ravaged as Marlborough ravaged Bavaria, instead of being spasmodically and half-heartedly raided, the rebels' privateers and merchant shipping would have been hard hit and their importing of supplies and munitions seriously impeded.

But from all this the British recoiled. Nor was it wholly a matter of political calculation, though that played its part. Conscience as well as policy was at work. "Here pity interposes," wrote General Phillips, "and we cannot forget that when we strike we wound a brother." When General Tryon burned the village of New Haven in 1779 he thought it necessary to send a sort of apologia to his commander-in-chief for his action; and when Clinton himself was presented with a loyalist proposal to kidnap Washington he turned it down because the proposers were evidently determined to kill the American commander if they could not bring him off alive. I am not aware that this objection was ever raised when Colonel Keyes went into the western desert to collect the scalp of General Rommel. Even the King, in spite of his constant insistence that the British must strike hard, never forgot the distinction between subjects and enemies: "Notes of triumph would not have been proper," he wrote after Howe's Long Island victory, "when the successes are against subjects not a foreign foe." And when a foreign officer proposed to raise a body of troops on an avowed principle of plunder he dismissed it as "very diverting . . . very curious, when intended to serve against the colonies."

To turn from the difficulties of planning to the plans themselves, I think it is pretty plain that until Saratoga at least, organized resistance in the colonies could have been broken; and though disorganized resistance by guerrilla bands would have been impossible to suppress with regular forces over so vast an area, Germain was one of many who believed that once the Continental Army was destroyed and Congress dispersed, the policing could be done by loyalist militias with no more than a stiffening of regulars. This belief was held by colonial governors and officials as well as by statesmen in London. The assumption behind it was that the rebellion was the work of a highly organized and determined minority. At one time it would have been difficult to find historians on either side of the Atlantic who would have admitted such a possibility for a moment, but today there would be more hesitation in rejecting it. It is now clear at any rate that the loyalists did indeed form a high percentage of the population, though since the local machinery of government and coercion had been seized by the rebels before conservative opinion was formed or countermeasures organized, it was exceedingly difficult for the loyalists to organize an opposition or resistance and in the longer run even to maintain their courage. And here too the twentieth century has something to teach us. It is too easily assumed by exiles and officials that a population which is not constructively in favor of rebels is positively against them. Furthermore, it is very difficult to take miltary action against a rebel nucleus without inconveniencing and antagonizing the population as a whole and giving the movement a general cohesion it may have lacked. Both these things happened in the American Revolution. Armies, for instance, could not operate without requisitioning, a procedure known by that name when Washington did it and by the name of plunder when it was done by Howe.

Thus the difficulties of mobilizing loyalist support was certainly considerable; but Germain's views on strategy at the outset were at least as sound as those of the school which advocated purely external pressure on the colonies by blockade, coastal attacks, and Indian raiding. The reasoning of the maritime school was that England could maintain only small forces beyond the Atlantic in proportion to the size of the country, and could not replace her casualties: therefore British casualties were more telling than rebel ones, and a series of winning battles which did not lead to a decision would destroy the army and mean ultimate defeat, while a single serious reverse might destroy the moral asset of superior discipline and training. Therefore, said this school of thought, the war should be conducted with the minimum of risk to the British troops: their commitments should be limited to the defense of bases for the fleet, and to coastal raiding.

This maritime policy might have made life intolerable for the colonists: it was not likely to make them love the mother country more, or pave the way to an enduring political settlement. Germain's view was different: "one decisive blow on land" was essential, then loyal support could be rallied while the navy commanded the rebel coasts. Before one condemns this policy one must ask oneself the question: "What would have happened if Howe had destroyed the rebel army around New York in 1776 and reached Philadelphia?" I believe the whole course of the rebellion would have been changed. To support the policy there was the memory of American jealousies and failures in the Seven Years' War, which encouraged the hope that the colonies would fall apart if a decisive defeat were inflicted on their troops. And there was the international scene to be considered. France was certain to try to exploit Britain's embarrassments, and the sooner the whole dispute was settled by victory the better. The great effort mounted in 1776 was in a sense a gamble on quick results to forestall and discourage the French.

On how to apply the force which was being collected there was general agreement from the beginning. It was the Hudson Valley plan—the plan which led two years later to Saratoga. New England is the heart of the rebellion, so ran the argument; isolate her, and the rest of the colonies will come to their senses. Isolate her, therefore, by striking north from New York and south from Lake Champlain to seize control of the crossings of the Hudson. Then the army in Canada can be used in an offensive role. Afterwards New England may be invaded on a broad front from the rear, in conjunction with a force from Rhode Island. This plan was put forward in the autumn of 1775 not only by Gage, the returning commander-in-chief, but also by Howe and Burgoyne, who came to grief over it two years later. Its execution got off to a slow start in 1776 because Howe had been unable to evacuate Boston before the winter, while in Canada Carleton had been driven back to Quebec and had to reconquer the country in order to reach his intended starting point on Lake Champlain. The offensive was resumed in 1777.

This is not the place to go into the arguments over the responsibility for Saratoga. I will say no more than this: both Howe and Burgoyne had endorsed the general outlines of the plan; Howe was fully aware of the general plan when to the astonishment of all he sailed away from New York to the Chesapeake; and Burgoyne had served in Canada throughout 1776, so that when he virtually wrote his own instructions over Germain's signature he was in a better position than most people to assess the difficulties of his enterprise. The decisions that led to his misfortune were operational ones taken by himself; and his claim that he was rigidly bound by his instructions to persevere in face of the certain destruction of his army has no more substance than Howe's contrary claim that he was left without orders and in ignorance of the general plan. The only avoidable error on the part of Germain and the Ministry was the choice of Burgoyne to lead the northern force.

The disaster at Saratoga of course was the end of the Hudson plan, and the intervention of France a few months later followed by that of Spain and Holland altered the framework of the American War entirely. But before I go on to consider the implications of the intervention of the European maritime powers, I will carry the story of American strategy through to its conclusion. By "American strategy" I mean the master plan for bringing the colonies back into the Empire. The changing situation modified but did not alter the fundamental assumptions on which Germain's strategy was based. The first year after Saratoga was spent in contracting and re-deploying the army to meet the requirements of the wider war against France: Philadelphia was abandoned in order to reinforce the West Indies and Florida. But the forward policy in America was resumed at the beginning of 1779 with a new directive from Germain. It was framed in consultation with North and Amherst and with the advice, not merely of "sycophantic refugees" as was alleged, but with the help of Lord Carlisle and William Eden, the newly returned Peace Commissioners, which in the circumstances was perhaps the best advice available. The plan had military support; and if Clinton disliked it he let his case go by default.

The new directive recognized the improbability that Washington could now be forced to a decisive battle, though this was still regarded as the most hopeful method of winning the war, and the fact that there were no strategic or political objectives in the colonies whose seizure could of itself lead to the collapse of the rebellion. If Clinton could not bring Washington to action, he was to contain the Continental Army with his main force, and make it possible for detachments to recover and protect individual provinces till a loyalist militia could be organized and an assembly could meet. That is to say, instead of a single decisive campaign, there was to be piecemeal recovery and reintegration of individual provinces behind the umbrella of the main army.

Clinton had difficulties and shortages to contend with, but he did as little as possible to give the scheme a fair trial. He always opposed the restoration of civil government, even in New York. Nothing whatever was accomplished in 1779, and the first offensive was mounted in South Carolina in the spring of 1780. Georgia had been recovered by a small force at the end of 1778; and the American Department had great faith in the policy of attacking from the southern end of the rebellion, where the colonies were believed to be especially vulnerable through their dependence on importing their means of existence and their large slave populations. At first all went well. The rebel southern army surrendered in Charleston, and by the middle of the summer the entire province of South Carolina seemed to have been pacified. But as soon as a guerrilla leader appeared in the field the rebellion flared up again, and a ferocious civil war broke out between loyalist and rebel militias. It was a struggle in which the balance of terror favored the rebels, since Cornwallis's aim was to conciliate and pacify, and that of the rebels was to stoke the flames of hatred. In due course nevertheless Cornwallis's mobile columns should have been able to suppress the trouble; but now a detachment of American regu-lars under Gates approached from the north, gathering the rebel militia around it as it advanced. Cornwallis dealt with that force at Camden, but he came to the conclusion that he could not protect and pacify South Carolina unless he overran the rebel strongholds further north. This conclusion drew him into the great advance across North Carolina which realized the fears of those who had predicted from the beginning that the British Army would be ruined by a series of winning battles, and it eventually led Cornwallis empty-handed and with depleted ranks to the Jamestown Peninsula in the Chesapeake.

Did Cornwallis's misfortune justify the original predictions of disaster? Only in a limited and special sense. It is true that the numberless militia played a decisive part in frustrating the British hopes; but the element which first necessitated Cornwallis's offensive and then enabled the militia to hold together and resist it was the continued existence of a force of American regular troops. The nature of the problem was described a few months afterwards on the other flank of the theatre by General Haldimand, the commander-in-chief in Canada:

> It is not the number of troops Mr. Washington can spare from his army that is to be apprehended, it is the multitude of militia and men in arms ready to turn out at an hour's notice at the shew of a single Regiment of Continental Troops. . . .

As the great nineteenth-century student of war Jomini pointed out in connection with the Spanish guerrilla effort against Napoleon, it was the presence in the theatre of war of an intact force of regulars which made it possible for the irregulars to operate with real effect, by forcing the French occupying troops to concentrate and give up their hold on the countryside. This was the main achievement of the Continental troops in the southern colonies. Their presence in North Carolina encouraged the militia to prevent the loyalists from joining Cornwallis, to sever the communications between Cornwallis's main force of regulars concentrated to the northward and his outlying detachments of militia, and thus to lay the foundations of Ferguson's defeat at King's Mountain in a battle between militias. They enabled them too to play their part in regular battle, to inflict casualties on Cornwallis's irreplaceable regulars, to defeat Tarleton at the Cowpens, and to force on Cornwallis the Pyrrhic victory of Guilford.

In other words, as Germain had appreciated, it was essential to the plan of piece-meal pacification and resettlement that Washington's regular forces should be effectively contained and prevented from intervening. Much more could have been done in this direction by a more active policy on the part of Clinton and the northern wing of the army based on New York. An earlier and stronger diversion in Virginia might have made a great difference. More effective and perhaps decisive in itself would have been the seizure of the forts guarding the Highlands of the Hudson, which Benedict Arnold maintained could be stormed. For one brief moment while Burgoyne was being surrounded at Saratoga, the forts were actually in British hands, and were abandoned only because Howe's removal to the Chesapeake had stripped New York of troops. Later Clinton was undoubtedly handicapped by shortages of men; and though his own character contributed most to the prevailing inertia at New York, a stronger force might have made him happier about the security of his base and encouraged him to be more venturesome. More troops, however, were out of the question, owing to the pressure which the European powers were exerting against the West Indies and British Isles themselves.

So far I have tried to suggest that British military policy in America had at least a rational basis. I now want for a moment to consider the American struggle in the context of the wider war against France, Spain, and Holland. England had allowed herself to slip into the situation which her statesmen had always dreaded, a war against the maritime powers of Europe with no Continental allies to impose a check on France's freedom to devote her resources to naval warfare. Now these maritime powers held colonial bases from which they could and indeed intended to strike the most damaging blows against the British colonies and economy. The American colonies had been permanently settled, creating a new race which was producing its own political and social traditions, which had a somewhat imponderable economic value to the mother country, and whose sentiments were rapidly drifting away from sympathy with the British people. The case of the colonies which the French now threatened was entirely different. In the West Indies and India the settlers did not form complete social and economic units capable of exercising political choice: they were planter or trader societies exploiting alien populations. The loss of British sovereignty here would not mean independence: it would mean the transfer of their wealth to a supplanting power and a European rival; and the wealth at stake was immense. India was so distant that it was only slowly pulled into the war, and began to exert a strategic pull on British resources from about 1780; but the West Indies exerted their full pressure from the moment France's intentions became clear. The reinforcements drawn from America in 1778 to defend the Lesser Antilles was the beginning of a struggle which contracted the scale of effort in America and drew in all the additional resources which became available as the war went on. It was announced at the time that the main effort was now directed against France, and an attempt was made by means of the Carlisle Mission to reach a settlement with the Americans. That of course failed. When Spain entered the war the evacuation of America was ruled out once more. The depressed and indeterminate Lord North murmured something about the objects of the American War not being worth the cost of obtaining them, to which the King replied that this was "only weighing such events in the scale of a tradesman behind his counter." King George and Lord George Germain were agreed that the loss of the American colonies would mean the loss of the sugar islands, and that therefore England must play for the whole stakes.

This may seem unwise, but there were several grounds for hoping that England might eventually prevail. In the first place one or two victories at sea would have altered the balance completely and given England the strategic initiative. France would have been unable to deploy her military power beyond the seas; and England, after sweeping up as many of the French and Spanish islands in the Caribbean as she thought necessary to her security and prosperity, would have been free to concentrate her military resources in America. With another ten thousand men and the assured command of American waters, even Clinton should have been able to destroy or paralyze Washington's army and enable Cornwallis to consolidate his hold in the south.

The naval victories were not achieved, though there was no inherent reason why they should not have been. A stronger hope, however, was that if the country could keep afloat it would win a war of attrition through its longer purse and the disunity of its enemies. Germain and the King intended to hasten the process and at the same time provide the best defense of England's Caribbean colonies by taking the offensive wherever it was possible. One aspect of this was the succession of small but potentially damaging blows which Germain mounted against the Spanish possessions in Central America, attacks which were intended both to protect Jamaica and to push Spain into making a separate peace without the bribe of Gibraltar. Another aspect of Germain's offensive spirit was his constant effort to mount offensives against the French islands in the Lesser Antilles. But success depended on assembling enough troops to take the islands and, more important, on collecting enough ships to win the command of West Indian waters. He was frustrated in this by the departmental opposition of the two armed services: that is to say, by Lord Amherst and Lord Sandwich.

The British Isles were in some danger of invasion, and while the commander-in-chief of the army resisted the dispatch of troops from the home forces, Sandwich at the Admiralty insisted on retaining a fleet in the English Channel strong enough to challenge the enemy if they attempted to seize the command of the water and pass an army across it. The Admiralty has always had a tendency to be riveted by the fear of invasion and consequently to overinsure in home waters. The effect of this is a strategic paralysis: the sacrifice of the initiative to the enemy. To this line of thinking Germain and the King were strongly opposed. A tame defensive war, said Germain, would be fatal. He and King George believed that it would be disastrous for England to insist on an impenetrable shield of warships: the country must be willing to resist a landing on the beaches with her troops, so that enough ships could be spared to gain the initiative in overseas theatres, and especially the vital Caribbean. There was at least some naval support for this view. The officer who later became Lord Barham wrote a powerful memorandum in the autumn of 1779 in favor of taking the offensive in the West Indies as the only way of defending the British sugar islands; and before the end of the war he came to the conclusion that too much had been sacrificed to an overstrong Channel fleet—a fleet which in no circumstances could be made strong enough to give battle to the combined fleets of France and Spain if they made a really determined attempt at invasion, yet was nevertheless stronger than was necessary for the purpose of impeding the movement of invasion craft from the French coast. If bolder use had been made of the fleet to obtain a strategic surprise in the West Indies, the shape of things in the western Atlantic might have been very different.

But though Germain's hope of winning the local initiative in the western Atlantic was disappointed, there still seemed a real likelihood by 1781 that the enemy alliance would crack from within. The Americans were at the end of their tether, the French officers at Rhode Island were appalled by what they saw of the political and military condition of the rebellion, and the French government was making provisions for pulling its forces out of America at the end of the campaign. In the diplomatic sphere a mediation was being floated by Austria and Russia, and France's need of peace to mend her financial troubles was so great that Vergennes was prepared if necessary to lead the Americans up the garden path to a peace conference and desert them. Spain had given him a bad fright in the previous year by engaging in separate peace talks with England, and in order to keep Madrid in the war French naval resources were being drawn increasingly into the pursuit of such purely Spanish objects as Gibraltar, Minorca, and Jamaica. So confident was the British Cabinet in June 1781 that the tide was flowing in its favor that it actually rejected the Austro-Russian mediation on the grounds that it could admit no discussion by other powers of the American colonies' future. In the light of what followed this was a mistake, but it must be remembered that they were playing for high stakes, and I believe their calculations had a fair chance of being justified. As late as October 1781 Germain was looking forward to a campaign in the Chesapeake-Delaware area, and warning Haldimand in Canada to make the most of Ethan Allen's secessionism in Vermont. At the very moment when he wrote, French siege guns were battering the new earthworks in Cornwallis's position at Yorktown.

Yorktown changed everything. It was the result of a strategic surprise at sea which completely upset the calculations of statesmen. The British admirals in the West

Indies had assumed that their opponent de Grasse would send a large part of his fleet home to Europe at the end of the summer to convoy the trade and refit in their home yards, and thought they were safe in frittering away their own strength for convoys and refitting. De Grasse's orders told him to do exactly what the British assumed—to send home ten sail of the line to Europe—but he ignored them. On receiving appeals to save the desperate situation in Virginia he let his merchant shipping wait for their convoy, and took his whole fleet to the Chesapeake: about 27 sail of the line instead of 17. He thus prevented the relief of Cornwallis, and the army besieged in Yorktown was forced to surrender.

The 7000 troops lost at Yorktown seem trifling in numbers. They would have been very difficult to replace in the circumstances of the war and at that distance from home, but even without them a desultory pressure could have been kept up on the coasts and estuaries of the American colonies. This was what Germain would have done till the tide of fortune changed; but Yorktown produced a consequence which ruled it out. The country gentlemen in Parliament despaired of bringing the American struggle to a successful conclusion, and there was a revolt in the House of Commons against the policy of coercing America. Germain was thrown overboard, but the Ministry failed to stay afloat. In March 1782 a new government came into power, dedicated to abandoning America and ending the war. But while the negotiations dragged on the operations of war were taking a turn which raised a question about the future. While the American theatre was reduced to total stalemate, Rodney won a victory at the Saints which turned the tide in the Caribbean, and Lord Howe relieved Gibraltar under the eyes of the main fleets of France and Spain. When the negotiations were concluded at the turn of the year Vergennes was as desperate for peace as Lord Shelburne himself. Half the members of Shelburne's Cabinet were in favor of continuing the struggle; and it may well be that with a little more perseverance the country would have won a very different settlement at the end of another twelve months.

13 / Lord Howe and Lord George Germain: British Politics and the Winning of American Independence

Ira D. Gruber

The interplay of politics and war could not be ignored by the makers of British strategy. Obviously, the American rebellion had to be suppressed by the display and use of force; equally obviously, a people crushed by excessive military oppression would be of little value to the British. Yet the majority of British leaders by late 1775 were bent upon employing military means to bring the American rebellion to an end. The uses made of the army and navy depended upon the strategic conceptions examined in the previous essay and also upon political considerations within the government. A remnant of conciliatory sentiment had to be handled and a number of demanding officers with political connections had to be satisfied. One of these demanding officers, Admiral Richard Lord Howe, in the view of the author of the following selection, almost accidentally became commander in chief of the great British military and naval efforts of 1776. The majority of the ministry, however, was bent upon stern measures; it instructed Lord Howe and his brother, the commander of the British Army in the colonies, to act promptly. Yet the Howes' desire to conciliate, their reliance upon a show of massive force and a series of successes to suggest the invincibility of their arms, and their unwillingness to use more drastic means undermined the ministry's hope for the kind of overwhelming victory that would have destroyed the Continental Army as a fighting force. And while the Howes' slow triumphal procession showed some signs of converting those who were wavering and bringing them back to loyal devotion to the crown, that procession came to an end with the small but highly significant battles of Trenton and Princeton. Thus, whatever the orders of Germain, the men in America enjoyed an independence that prevented the British from enjoying the advantages of a unified and determined direction of their military efforts. The Howes had political importance in their own right, were not easily ordered about, and

Reprinted by permission from *The William and Mary Quarterly,* 3rd series, XXII (1965), 225–243.

enjoyed the advantage of great distance from the direct wishes and orders of the ministers in Whitehall.

For further reading; in addition to items listed for the preceding article, see T. S. Anderson, *The Command of the Howe Brothers* (1936); Gerald Saxon Brown, *The American Secretary: The Colonial Policy of Lord George Germain, 1775–1778* (1963); and Alan Valentine, *Lord George Germain* (1962).

In the past four decades many historians have tried to determine why Britain failed to win the War for American Independence. Most have agreed that the war was decided in the opening campaigns and that the failure of the British commanders could be fully explained only by considering the rebellion as both a military and a political problem. Because most reasoned that unrestricted warfare "would have defeated the real purpose of the British government, which was to make the colonies once more useful parts of the empire," they assumed that the government ruled out "mere force" and that its commanders had to combine "military pressure and persuasion."[1] These assumptions, theoretically sound and entirely plausible, are not historically correct. British politics and political considerations did, in fact, contribute significantly to the winning of American independence, but not in the way that historians have assumed.

By the autumn of 1775 most members of the British government thought of the rebellion in their American colonies as a military problem. Though the origins of the rebellion were political, there seemed little prospect of finding a political settlement. The colonists insisted that Parliament had no right to tax them or to regulate their domestic affairs; moreover they seemed determined to support their arguments with force. As the King and an overwhelming majority of the members of Parliament believed that they could make laws binding the colonies in all cases whatsoever, no British ministry dared accept the American claims.[2] When, therefore, the colonists

---

[1] Quoting Troyer S. Anderson, *The Command of the Howe Brothers During the American Revolution* (New York, 1936), 10–13, 18. For similar interpretations see: W. M. James, *The British Navy in Adversity* . . . (London, 1926), 47, 426; Weldon A. Brown, *Empire or Independence: A Study in the Failure of Reconciliation, 1774–1783* (Baton Rouge, 1941), 6, 243 (though the narrative and his conclusion, p. 297, belie these generalizations); Eric Robson, *The American Revolution in its Political and Military Aspects, 1763–1783* (New York, 1955), 113–122; Alan Valentine, *Lord George Germain* (Oxford, 1962), 145; William B. Willcox, *Portrait of a General, Sir Henry Clinton in the War of Independence* (New York, 1964), 119; and Piers Mackesy, *The War for America, 1775–1783* (Cambridge, Eng., 1964), 33. Other historians have correctly stated the government's intentions for dealing with the rebellion but have not related them specifically to Britain's failure to win the war. See, for examples, George H. Guttridge, "Lord George Germain in Office, 1775–1782," *American Historical Review*, XXXIII (1927–28), 28; Gerald S. Brown, *The American Secretary: The Colonial Policy of Lord George Germain, 1775–1778* (Ann Arbor, 1963), 63–80; and John R. Alden, *The American Revolution, 1775–1783* (New York, 1962), 66.

[2] For examples, the King to Frederick Lord North, Sept. 11, 1774, in John W. Fortescue, ed., *The Correspondence of King George the Third from 1760 to December 1783* (London, 1927–28), III, 130–131; the King to William Legge, Earl of Dartmouth, June 10, 1775, in Great Britain, Historical Manuscripts Commission, *The Manuscripts of Rye and Hereford Corporations* . . .

had rejected Britain's meager offers of compromise and had taken up arms against the King, the North ministry was forced either to resign or to pursue a policy of military coercion. The ministers, with several exceptions, kept their places and prepared for war. Declaring the colonies in rebellion, they recruited their forces and ordered their commanders in chief to wage unlimited war on the rebels.[3]

But even amid the preparations for war, a few members of the British government remembered that the rebellion was in fact a political as well as a military problem, and these few would have an importance well out of proportion to their number. Most influential among the advocates of a political settlement was Frederick Lord North, the head of the ministry. North had no intention of attenuating Parliament's power in the colonies but was far too practical to prefer a punitive war to a negotiated peace. He favored compromises on specific problems, providing these compromises did not involve constitutional changes. He would, for example, have been willing to suspend parliamentary taxation in America if the colonial assemblies had agreed to the support of imperial defense—an arrangement that promised to give Britain a revenue without raising the question of Parliament's right to tax the colonists.[4]

Indeed, while in October of 1775 most British leaders were thinking of ways to crush the rebellion, North was gathering support for a peace commission. Having learned by experience that the ministry and Parliament were violently opposed to any measure that appeared concessive,[5] he described his commission as an instrument for accelerating colonial surrender, a complement to military operations.[6] In this way he soon won the support of the ministry and Parliament for a commission that would grant pardons, receive surrender, and possibly remove restrictions on colonial trade. Subsequently he even managed to have the powers of the commission enlarged, so that it might have unquestioned authority to remove the prohibition on colonial trade and to discuss grievances.[7] What Parliament did not prescribe, however, was the order in which the commission would exercise its powers. Apparently a majority of Parliament assumed that the commission would accept the surrender of a particular colony or town before doing anything else.[8] If this were to be the case, the com-

---

(London, 1892), 501–502; J. Almon, ed., *The Parliamentary Register* . . . (London, 1775–1804), I, 133–170, 468–478; Hutchinson's diary, May 12, 1775, in Peter O. Hutchinson, ed., *The Diary and Letters of . . . Thomas Hutchinson* . . . (London, 1883–86), I, 445.

[3] Dartmouth to General Thomas Gage, Aug. 2, 1775, separate, and Dartmouth to General William Howe, Sept. 5, 1775, secret, Dartmouth to W. Howe, Sept. 22, 1775, Colonial Office Papers, Class 5, Vol. 92, Public Record Office, London; William Eden to Lord George Germain, Sept. 27, [1775], in Hist. MSS. Com., *Report on the Manuscripts of Mrs. Stopford-Sackville* . . . (London, 1904–10), II, 9–10.

[4] Almon, ed., *Parliamentary Register,* I, 196–214; Eden to Germain, Oct. 3, 1775, Germain Papers, William L. Clements Library, Ann Arbor, Mich.

[5] Feb. 27, 1775, in Hutchinson, ed., *Diary and Letters,* I, 399–400; Edward Gibbon to J. B. Holroyd, Feb. 25, 1775, in J. E. Norton, ed., *The Letters of Edward Gibbon* (London, 1956), II, 60–61; North to the King, [Feb. 20, 1775], in Fortescue, ed., *Correspondence of George Third,* III, 178–179.

[6] Eden to Germain, Oct. 3, 1775, Germain Papers.

[7] Almon, ed., *Parliamentary Register,* III, 1–3; 16 George III c.5, in Danby Pickering, ed., *The Statutes at Large* (Cambridge, Eng., 1762–1807), XXXI, 135–154; Germain to W. Howe, Dec. 23, 1775, Headquarters Papers of the British Army, photostats, I, no. 100, Colonial Williamsburg, Inc., Research Library, Williamsburg, Va.

[8] Augustus Henry Duke of Grafton certainly interpreted the powers of the commission in this way and on Mar. 14, 1776, proposed that they be modified to allow negotiations before the

mission would have little chance of negotiating an end to the war, as North hoped it could. But whether or not the commission would be able to fulfill his expectations depended on the commissioner and on the instructions he received.

In appointing Admiral Richard Lord Howe to the new commission, North did his best to produce a negotiated settlement. By temperament, reputation, and inclination Howe was well qualified to conciliate the rebels. A man who was adept in dealing with subordinates, who (in spite of his connections with men in high places) was not closely associated with the government or the policy of coercion, and whose name was well known in America, Howe was an ideal candidate from North's point of view.[9] But even more important, he had a strong personal interest in reconciliation, an interest born of his family's close ties with New England. His older brother had been so popular with the colonial militia while serving in America during the French and Indian War that when he was killed at Fort Ticonderoga the General Court of Massachusetts Bay voted 250 pounds to erect a monument to his memory in Westminster Abbey. Remembering this gesture and the affection it symbolized, Howe was prompt to offer his services as mediator when in late 1774 the Anglo-American quarrel threatened to become a war.[10] In so doing he did not propose alterations in the imperial constitution; he merely suggested that kind words would make British authority more palatable, whereas coercive measures would frustrate a genuine reconciliation.[11] Though the ministry was unwilling in early 1775 to sponsor a peace commission and rejected his offer, he continued to urge his friends in the administration to accept his mediation.[12] When finally, in October, North gained Parliament's approval for a commission, Howe's persistence was rewarded. North not only promised him the commission but also encouraged him to think he would have authority enough to negotiate a settlement.[13] But North's wishes did not necessarily determine what the ministry's policy would be.

A better forecast of that policy was provided by the reorganization of the ministry

---

colonists had surrendered unconditionally. William R. Anson, ed., *Autobiography and Political Correspondence of Augustus Henry Third Duke of Grafton* (London, 1898), 282–283.

[9] Sir John Barrow, *The Life of Richard, Earl Howe . . .* (London, 1838); Sir Lewis Namier and John Brooke, *The History of Parliament: The House of Commons, 1754–1790* (New York, 1964), II, 647–649.

[10] [J. A. Holden], "Description of the Howe Monument, Westminster Abbey," in N. Y. State Historical Association, *Proceedings*, X (Albany, 1911), 323–325; Franklin's "An Account of Negotiations in London . . . ," Mar. 22, 1775, in Albert H. Smyth, ed., *The Writings of Benjamin Franklin* (New York, 1905–7), VI, 345–354. Though there is no great collection of Lord Howe's papers, his motives may be judged from his sister's letters, several thousand of which are in the possession of the Earl of Spencer at Althorp, Northamptonshire, and from the correspondence of his political broker, Thomas Villiers, Baron Hyde, Earl of Clarendon, whose letter books are in the Bodleian Library, Oxford. Among his sister's letters, for example, are repeated expressions of the family's desire to promote a reconciliation: "we have nothing to wish but that he [General Howe] may be the means of a satisfactory peace. . . ." (Mrs. Caroline Howe to Georgiana, Lady Spencer, Aug. 11, [1775]).

[11] Richard Lord Howe to Hyde, [Feb. 9, 1775], Hyde to Howe, Feb. 10, 1775, Dartmouth Papers, William Salt Library, Stafford, England.

[12] Hyde to North, Jan. 10, 1776, Clarendon Deposit, Bodleian Library.

[13] William Knox's account of the first peace commission of 1776, in Knox Papers, Clements Lib.; Hyde to Howe, Nov. 2, 1775, and Howe to [Dartmouth] Nov. 4, 1775, Dartmouth Papers; Howe to Mark Huish, Nov. 2, 1775, Miscellaneous Manuscripts under Howe, New York Public Library, New York.

that took place in November. The most important change came at the colonial office where the Earl of Dartmouth, who had recoiled from his responsibility for managing the war, yielded to Lord George Germain, a man with unusual enthusiasm for crushing the rebellion.[14] Germain had never been considerate of his inferiors or tolerant of insubordination. He had spoken in favor of the Declaratory Act and against the repeal of the Stamp Act in 1766, declared that leniency bred trouble both in Ireland and America, supported the Massachusetts acts in 1774, and during the first half of 1775 advocated that the colonists be forced to acknowledge Parliament's supremacy in all cases whatsoever. But Lord George's interest in the American rebellion was more than the result of his passion for upholding authority; in the American war he saw a chance to redeem a military reputation that had been ruined in 1760 when he was convicted of cowardice and found " 'unfit to serve his Majesty in any military capacity whatsoever.' "[15] Although as colonial secretary he would not serve in a military capacity, he would, as virtual minister of war, have ample opportunity to demonstrate his talent for military planning and administration. It is little wonder that he was enthusiastic over his new job. Scorning Dartmouth's moderation and saying one decisive victory, together with a blockade, would end the rebellion, he was impatient for a quick decision: "I always wished that the whole power of the state should be Exerted, that one Campaign might decide whether the American Provinces were to be subject to G. B. or free States."[16]

Before Germain had grown accustomed to the colonial office, and before the ministry had decided what the peace commission might do, chance, domestic politics, and dubious assumptions conspired to make Admiral Howe commander in chief as well as peace commissioner. In early December of 1775 a senior admiral died, vacating a lucrative sinecure North had promised to Howe. When North, forgetting his promise, awarded the sinecure to another officer, Howe threatened to resign from the navy. The ministry was, of course, anxious to avoid a breach with one of its ablest admirals and tried to find some other reward to satisfy him.[17] After more

[14] Charles Greville to Sir William Hamilton, Oct. 31, 1775, in Hamilton-Greville Correspondence, Henry E. Huntington Library, San Marino, Calif. In addition to the changes affecting Dartmouth and Germain, Augustus Henry Duke of Grafton, who actively opposed a coercive war, and William Henry Zuylestein, Earl of Rochford, who had little liking for it, retired, while Thomas Thynne, Viscount Weymouth, who shared Germain's views, joined the government. After Nov. 10, therefore, only North and Dartmouth among the ministers favored moderation; Parliament was even more anxious than the ministry to wage a punitive war: "We have a warm Parliament but an indolent Cabinet." Gibbon to Holroyd, Oct. 31, 1775, in Norton, ed., *Letters of Gibbon*, II, 91–92. But no one was more determined than the King to drive the colonists to submission. The King to North, Dec. 15, 1774, and Aug. 18, 1775, in Fortescue, ed., *Correspondence of George Third*, III, 156, 247–248.

[15] Namier and Brooke, *House of Commons, 1754–1790*, III, 390–306; Brown, *American Secretary*, 11–26; Valentine, *Germain*, 9–100.

[16] Germain to [General Sir John Irwin], June 13, 1775, and July 20, 1775, quoting Germain to Eden, [Oct. 7, 1775], Germain Papers; Germain to [Henry Howard, Earl of Suffolk], July 26, 1775, Miscellaneous Manuscripts, XIV, 1771–1775, Massachusetts Historical Society, Boston; Germain to Irwin, Sept. 13, 1775, in Hist. MSS. Com. *Report on the Manuscripts of Mrs. Stopford-Sackville*, I, 137.

[17] Hans Stanley to [Andrew S. Hamond], Jan. 27, 1776, Hamond Papers, Alderman Library, University of Virginia, Charlottesville; John Robinson to John Montagu, Earl of Sandwich, [Dec. 8, 1775], in G. R. Barnes and J. H. Owen, eds., *The Private Papers of John, Earl of Sandwich, First Lord of the Admiralty, 1771–1782* (London, 1932–38), II, 201.

than a month of futile negotiations, it accepted his own suggestion that he be made commander in chief in America.[18] As Howe had no desire to fight against the colonists, he apparently applied for the American command to strengthen his hand as a negotiator. A majority of the ministry, for their part, were willing to appoint him commander in chief because they wanted the services of a fine professional officer and because they assumed he would not allow his hopes for peace to interfere with his conduct of the war. Germain and the King, who were the stanchest advocates of coercive measures and who saw little need for a peace commission, were delighted to employ Howe at sea;[19] in fact the King stifled the only opposition to his appointment, which came from the Earl of Sandwich and was based mainly on personal considerations.[20] Though North and Dartmouth did not share the other ministers' aversion to a negotiated settlement, they fully supported Howe's candidacy,[21] thinking him well qualified to use whatever combination of force and persuasion was needed to end the war. If chance had given Howe the opportunity to ask for a dual commission, he obtained it by exploiting the dubious assumption, held by a majority of the ministry, that he would not mix politics and strategy.

The King, Germain, and many of the administration may have misunderstood Howe's intentions, but they made no mistake in drafting his orders. When he refused to share his peace commission with someone of less conciliatory views, Germain insisted that his instructions should preclude concessions. When North, Dartmouth, and Howe argued that the colonies should not be forced to acknowledge, as a prerequisite to negotiations, Parliament's right to make laws binding the colonies in all cases whatsoever, Germain at length gave in.[22] But Howe's instructions ensured that the commission would remain what Lord George and a majority of Parliament had always intended it to be: a means for accepting colonial surrender. Howe would be able to do no more than grant pardons and wait for the colonists to surrender; until they had dissolved unlawful assemblies, restored royal officials, disbanded their armies, and given up all fortifications, he could not suspend hostilities or discuss the terms of reconciliation. Although he had obtained specific terms for establishing a system of colonial contributions for imperial defense in place of taxation for revenue, a system under which the colonies would have contributed from 5 to 10 per cent of the sum voted annually by Parliament for the army, navy, and ordnance, he was unable to mention these terms until the colonies had surrendered.[23] That he was

[18] Hyde to North, Jan. 11, 1776, and Jan. 10, 1776, Clarendon Deposit; North to the King, Jan. 28, 1776 (misdated by Fortescue as Feb. 4, 1776), Fortescue, ed., *Correspondence of George Third*, III, 338.

[19] Irwin to Francis, Earl of Huntingdon, Feb. 6, 1776, in Hist. MSS. Com. *Report on the Manuscripts of the Late Reginald Rawdon Hastings . . .* , III (London, 1934), 169; Knox's account of the first peace commission of 1776, Knox Papers; Thomas Hutchinson to Thomas Oliver, Feb. 17, 1776, in Hutchinson, ed., *Diary and Letters*, II, 63.

[20] The King to North, Feb. 2, 1776, in Fortescue, ed., *Correspondence of George Third*, III, 336; the King to Sandwich, Feb. 3, 1776, in Barnes and Owen, eds., *Papers of Sandwich*, I, 112–113; Leveson Gower to William Cornwallis, Feb. 27, 1776, Cor/57, 48/MS/9575, National Maritime Museum, Greenwich.

[21] Knox's account of the first peace commission of 1776, Knox Papers.

[22] *Ibid.* and Germain to Eden, Feb. 18, 1776, Auckland Papers, Additions to the Manuscripts, 34, 413, British Museum, London.

[23] Orders and Instructions for the Howe commission, May 6, 1776, C.O. 5/177; Separate instruction to the American commissioners, May 7, 1776, in Hist. MSS. Com., *Sixth Report, Part I* (London, 1877), 400–401.

willing to serve with such a limited commission suggests both his failure to comprehend the depth of colonial dissatisfaction and the confidence he had in his own
powers of persuasion.

While Howe was debating the terms of his peace commission, the government
prepared his instructions for carrying on the war at sea. He was not only to impose
a tight blockade on all the rebellious colonies, bringing economic pressure on the
Americans and denying them military supplies from Europe and the West Indies,
but also to co-operate with the British army in smashing the revolt. So that he would
not mistake the meaning of his orders, the lords of the admiralty gave him specific
suggestions for employing the North American squadron. His cruisers were to shelter
loyal colonists and protect their property, retaliate against coastal towns where the
inhabitants were in rebellion, dismantle American merchantmen that they might
not be fitted for war, destroy all armed vessels, clear colonial ports of sunken ob-
structions and floating batteries, impress rebel seamen, and when necessary, com-
mandeer supplies.[24] To carry out such a variety of measures he would have seventy-
three warships manned by 13,000 seamen, nearly 45 per cent of all the ships and
men on active service in the world's most powerful navy.[25] Although his orders authorized any deviation he thought necessary, their general tone was unmistakable. He was
to use his squadron decisively.

The main British effort in 1776 was, however, to be made ashore. The plans for
the summer campaign were not decreed from London but were worked out in a
series of dispatches between Germain and General William Howe, brother of Admiral
Howe and commander in chief of the British troops at Boston. As early as June 1775,
while still second in command, General Howe had sketched his ideas for 1776.
Rather than compaign from Boston, he would strangle the rebellion in New England
by occupying the Hudson River valley and blockading all ports from New York
to Nova Scotia. In October he expanded this plan, proposing that armies advancing
from New York and Canada should meet along the Hudson and take separate routes
into Massachusetts. If the campaign were to be conclusive, he would need at least
20,000 men, in addition to those in the Canadian army.[26] But Howe by no means
placed his whole reliance on isolating New England and recovering territory piecemeal. He repeatedly declared that he wished to bring the Continental army to a
decisive action, for only a resounding British victory would, he thought, end the
rebellion.[27] Germain, who shared Howe's faith in a climactic battle, not only approved
his plans but also promised him the reinforcements he requested; indeed Lord George's
principal fear during the spring of 1776 was that Howe would risk an engagement
before being fully prepared.[28] On the eve of the campaign of 1776, the Colonial
Secretary had every reason to be satisfied with the Commander in Chief of the army

[24] Admiralty's instructions to Howe, May 4, 1776, and Admiralty to Admiral Samuel Graves,
July 6, 1775, Admiralty Papers, Class 2, Vol. 1332, Public Record Office; Admiralty to Graves,
Aug. 31, Sept. 14, Oct. 23, Oct. 15, and Sept. 14, 1775, Adm. 2/100; Admiralty to Howe, May 4
1776, Adm. 2/101.

[25] Abstract of monthly disposition, July 1, 1776, Adm. 8/52.

[26] W. Howe to Howe, June 12, 1775, Dartmouth Papers; W. Howe to Dartmouth, separate,
Oct. 9, and Nov. 26, 1775, C.O. 5/92; W. Howe to Dartmouth, Jan. 16, 1776, C.O. 5/93.

[27] W. Howe to Dartmouth, Jan. 16, 1776, and W. Howe to Germain, Apr. 25, 1776, C.O. 5/93;
W. Howe to Germain, Apr. 26, 1776, private, in Hist. MSS. Com., *Report on the Manuscripts
of Mrs. Stopford-Sackville*, II, 30–31.

[28] Germain to W. Howe, Jan. 5, Mar. 28, and May 3, 1776, C.O. 5/93.

in America. Although General Howe was temporarily delayed in early July while awaiting reinforcements at Staten Island, his plans remained unchanged. He would take New York and Rhode Island before joining the Canadian army on the Hudson. If he thought his brother's commission might induce many to surrender, he was "still of Opinion that Peace will not be restored in America until the Rebel Army is defeated." [29]

But after Lord Howe joined his brother at New York, the Commanders in Chief soon deviated from the government's plans for ending the rebellion. Though his instructions were inadequate for a negotiation, though he arrived on July 12, a week after Congress had declared the colonies independent, and though his brother did not think the rebels would treat,[30] the Admiral had no intention of applying his sword until he had seen what words might do. He began by issuing a proclamation, telling the colonists that he had been appointed peace commissioner with authority to grant pardon and to end hostilities wherever royal government had been restored. Congress, realizing that he had made no substantial concession in his proclamation, ordered it published throughout the colonies "that the good people of these United States may be informed of what nature are the commissioners, and what the terms, with the expectation of which, the insidious court of Britain has endeavoured to amuse and disarm them." [31] While his proclamation was being distributed, Howe tried to open negotiations with the commander in chief of the Continental army and with Congress, but his overtures had no better reception than his proclamation. When he wrote to Washington asking for a meeting to discuss the provisions of the peace commission, Washington rejected his letter because it was improperly addressed; and when he applied to him again, the American commander refused to discuss an accommodation, saying he understood the Howes were "only to grant pardons [and] that those who had committed no fault wanted no pardon." [32] But even this rejoinder did not deter Howe, who soon attempted to suggest through an emissary that he could discuss a plan for replacing parliamentary taxation in the colonies with a system of fixed colonial contributions. Congress, happy with its independence, would not, however, pursue this suggestion.[33] As one of Howe's juniors remarked, "it has long been too late for Negotiation, yet it is easy to be perceived, My Lord Howe came out with a different Idea." [34]

Lord Howe's desire for a peaceful settlement also seemed to affect military operations. As his brother had neither troops nor equipment enough to attack the rebels

---

[29] W. Howe to Germain, July 7, 1776, C.O. 5/93.

[30] Sir Henry Strachey's journal, July 12, 1776, Hist. MSS. Com., *Sixth Report, Part I,* 402.

[31] Howe to Germain, Aug. 11, 1776, enclosing a copy of his Declaration, C.O. 5/177; July 19, 1776, in Worthington C. Ford, ed., *Journals of the Continental Congress, 1774–1789. Volume V. 1776* (Washington, 1906), 592–593.

[32] Howe to George Washington, July 13, 1776, Howe Papers, Clements Lib.; July 14, 1776, in Edward H. Tatum, Jr. ed., *The American Journal of Ambrose Serle, Secretary to Lord Howe, 1776–1778* (San Marino, 1940), 31–33; Washington to the President of Congress, July 14, 22, 1776, in John C. Fitzpatrick, ed., *The Writings of George Washington . . .* (Washington, 1931–44), V, 273–274, 321n–323n.

[33] Lord Drummond to Howe, Aug. 12, 1776, and Drummond to Washington, Aug. 17, 1776, Washington Papers, XXXII, Library of Congress, Washington; Howe to Drummond, Aug. 15, 1776, in Peter Force, ed., *American Archives . . .* 5th Ser., I (Washington, 1848), 1027; Aug. 20 and 22, 1776, in Ford, ed., *Journals of the Continental Congress,* V, 672, 696.

[34] Hamond to [Stanley], Sept. 24, 1776, Hamond Papers.

until August 14 and as the British offensive began on the twenty-second, Lord Howe cannot be blamed for delaying the opening of the campaign. But he probably did contribute to alterations in General Howe's strategy. The General had appeared eager for a decisive action before the Admiral arrived; thereafter he concentrated on occupying territory rather than on destroying the Continental army. It is true that the American fortifications at New York were too strong to invite a frontal assault, yet the Continental army was precariously divided between Long Island and Manhattan. As British ships could move at will in either the Hudson or the East River, General Howe should have made some effort to trap his enemy.[35] His general plan for taking New York and his conduct on Long Island demonstrated, however, that he was primarily interested in occupying territory. By taking possession of Brooklyn Heights, which commanded the town of New York, he planned to make lower Manhattan untenable for the rebels.[36] His strategy was, in short, to push the Continental army out of New York. The execution deviated little from the design. After landing on Long Island and driving the Americans into their lines at Red Hook and Brooklyn, General Howe made no special effort to keep them there. The rebels were caught against the East River with a superior army in their front, and yet Lord Howe never ordered his captains to block Washington's line of retreat. At least one British officer was extremely disappointed: "had our ships attackd the batteries [at Brooklyn], which we have been in constant expectation of being orderd to do, not a man could have escaped from Long Island." [37] When the Americans fled to Manhattan on the night of August 29, General Howe had accomplished part of his plan, but he had lost his finest opportunity for destroying the Continental army and for ending the rebellion.

After the battle of Long Island, the Howes' conduct of the war assumed a pattern that suggested they were trying to use no more force than they thought necessary to promote a reconciliation. Even before the rebels had fled from Brooklyn, and at a time when Lord Howe might have been devising ways to prevent their escape, he was again trying to open negotiations with Congress.[38] He apparently hoped that the British victory on August 27 would make the rebels more tractable, more willing to put down their arms and hear his terms. Congress responded to his overture by sending three delegates to meet with him on Staten Island, but he soon discovered that the Americans sought only to discredit his peace commission.[39] Frustrated once more, he joined his brother in seeing what a further application of force would do.

[35] Howe ignored Sir Henry Clinton's proposal for a landing at Spuyten Duyvil. Willcox, *Henry Clinton*, 103. The American generals certainly feared that they would be enveloped: John Sullivan to John Hancock, Aug. 5, 1776, in Otis G. Hammond, ed., *Letters and Papers of Major-General John Sullivan . . .* , I (Concord, N.H., 1930), 290–291; Washington to Pres. of Cong., Aug. 9, 1776, in Fitzpatrick, ed., *Writings of Washington*, V, 406.

[36] W. Howe to Germain, private, Aug. 10, 1776, Germain Papers.

[37] Quoting Sir George Collier's journal kept at New York, n.d., in Louis L. Tucker, ed., " 'To My Inexpressible Astonishment' . . . ," *New-York Historical Society Quarterly*, XLVIII (1964), 304. W. Howe to Germain, Sept. 3, 1776, C.O. 5/93; Washington to Pres. of Cong., Aug. 31, 1776, in Fitzpatrick, ed., *Writings of Washington*, V, 508–509.

[38] "Journals of Captain Henry Duncan," Aug. 29–30, 1776, in John K. Laughton, ed., *The Naval Miscellany*, I (London, 1902), 125–126; Aug. 29, 30, 1776, in Tatum, ed., *Journal of Serle*, 80–83; Howe to Germain, Sept. 20, 1776, C.O. 5/177.

[39] Sir Henry Strachey's account of the meeting, Miscellaneous MSS., N.Y. Pub. Lib.; Howe to Germain, Sept. 20, 1776, C.O. 5/177.

After they had driven the Americans from New York, by threatening to trap them there, Lord Howe made still another effort at conciliation. Because he had been unsuccessful in dealing with Congress, he now appealed directly to the colonists, issuing a proclamation that invited them to discuss a reconciliation and that declared the King was disposed to allow them considerable control over their domestic affairs. So unsuccessful was this proclamation that the Howes made no new overtures for several months.[40] In the interim they rolled the Americans back from New York by a series of flanking maneuvers that won territory without forcing a full-scale engagement. Only when the American garrison at Fort Washington refused to escape or surrender did the British make a decisive attack.

The whole campaign of 1776 seemed designed to promote both a restoration of British authority in America and a genuine reconciliation. Lord Howe apparently had persuaded his brother, who shared his desire for peace,[41] to mix stategy and politics. Though the Admiral felt that each battle made conciliation more difficult, he realized that some exertion of force was necessary to make the colonists willing to negotiate. He probably reasoned, therefore, that a steady British advance and a display of overwhelming superiority would force the rebels to treat, without creating an irreparable breach. A ruthless campaign might secure a military victory, but it would never make the colonists into loyal subjects.

If ever this policy of blending strategy and politics seemed likely to succeed, it was in December of 1776, the most critical month in the War for American Independence. After Fort Washington surrendered in mid-November, the Continental army retired rapidly across New Jersey before a seemingly invincible British advance. The loss of Fort Washington, endless withdrawals, and expiring enlistments were destroying the American forces; indeed, on December 1 Washington decided to retreat across the Delaware into Pennsylvania.[42] At New York, where the British heard rumors of dissensions both in Congress and in the Continental army,[43] the Howes were preparing to exploit their belated success. The General, who could no longer expect to open the Hudson before winter, planned to capture Rhode Island and secure New Jersey by the end of the campaign. Nor did he and his brother neglect persuasion, offering a free pardon to anyone who would take an oath of allegiance to George III within sixty days of November 30. This offer, although spurned by leading rebels, was accepted by almost 5,000 colonists and was clearly the most successful of all British efforts toward peace.[44] But before its term had expired, Washington contrived to change the course of the war. On December 26 he destroyed a detachment of Hessians quartered at Trenton and, a week later, won a second battle at Princeton. These

---

[40] The Howes to Germain, Sept. 20, 1776, enclosing a copy of the Declaration, C.O. 5/177; Wilmot Vaughan, Earl of Lisburne to George Jackson, Dec. 22, 1776, Add. MSS., 34, 187.

[41] Mrs. Howe "flatters herself his [General Howe's] advice will be a little attended to, and she knows he wishes to have a peace that is creditable to both." Lady Sarah Bunbury to Lady Susan O'Brien, Aug. 21, 1775, in the Countess of Ilchester and Lord Stavordale, eds., *The Life and Letters of Lady Sarah Lennox, 1745–1826* (London, 1901), I, 244.

[42] Washington to Pres. of Cong., Nov. 23, 30, Dec. 1, 1776, in Fitzpatrick, ed., *Writings of Washington,* VI, 303–304, 314–16, 321–322.

[43] Nov. 1, Dec. 8, 1776, in Tatum, ed., *Journal of Serle,* 135, 155–156; Ambrose Serle to Dartmouth, Dec. 3, 1776, in Benjamin F. Stevens, ed. *Facsimiles of Manuscripts in European Archives Relating to America, 1773–1783* . . . , XXIV (London, 1895), no. 2048.

[44] W. Howe to Germain, Nov. 30, 1776, separate, and Nov. 30, 1776, C.O. 5/93; Howes to Germain, Dec. 22, 1776, and Mar. 25, 1777, C.O. 5/177.

two victories blasted the illusion of British invincibility, restored American morale, and ended the Howes' chances for a negotiated peace.[45] For the Howes the campaign of 1776 was a bitter disappointment; for Great Britain it was a disaster. The British government may not have shown great wisdom in trying to unify an empire by force; but by the summer of 1776 force alone could have restored the colonies to British rule. When the Howes failed to trap and destroy the Continental army during the campaign of 1776, they forfeited Britain's best opportunity for ending the American revolt.

Until February of 1777 most members of the British government were well pleased with the progress of the war in the colonies. If the Howes were not acting with the firmness the ministry desired, a succession of victories obscured the opportunities they had lost. London rejoiced on hearing that Long Island and New York had been captured, and General Howe was knighted for his conduct on August 27.[46] The King found the Howes' dispatches of November 30, which reached England after Christmas, "the more agreeable as they exceed the most sanguine expectations." Germain and Sandwich agreed that the capture of Fort Washington, the occupation of eastern New Jersey, and the sending of an expedition to Rhode Island put a most satisfactory end to the campaign.[47] But Germain was not entirely happy with his commanders. He was pleased with the succession of British victories, but because he had hoped "to reconquer Germany in America"—to redeem his reputation by crushing the rebellion—he was disturbed by the Howes' proclamation of November 30, which offered pardon to rebels and loyalists alike. "This sentimental manner of making war will, I fear, not have the desired Effect." [48] Moreover, having intended that the campaign of 1776 would be decisive and not wishing to overburden the British economy, he was dismayed with General Howe's request for an additional 15,000 men for 1777.[49] He reminded the Howes that those colonists who refused pardon were to be punished and suggested that the General might manage with a reinforcement of less than 15,000 men.[50]

In late February and early March, Lord George's worst fears were realized. On February 23 the *Bristol* reached England, bringing news of Trenton and Princeton together with General Howe's first revision of his plans for 1777. Germain could be

[45] Many British officers and officials thought the battles of Trenton and Princeton had saved the rebellion; for example: William Eddis to Eden, July 23, 1777, C.O. 5/722; Hamond's MS account of his role in the American war, Hamond Papers; Colonel William Harcourt to Simon Harcourt, Earl of Harcourt, Jan. 18, 1777, in Edward W. Harcourt, ed., *The Harcourt Papers* (Oxford, 1880–1905), XI, 203; MS journal kept by a soldier in Howe's army, 1777, MS Am 1562, Houghton Library, Harvard University; Sir George Osborn to [Sir George Pocock], May 15, 1777, Pocock Collection, Huntington Library; Dec. 27, 1776, in Tatum, ed., *Journal of Serle,* 163.

[46] George Bussy Villiers, Earl of Jersey, to Lady Spencer, Oct. 10, 1776; Mrs. Howe to Lady Spencer, Oct. 16, 1776, Spencer Papers, Althorp, Northamptonshire.

[47] The King to Sandwich, Dec. 30, 1776, and Sandwich to Howe, Jan. 6, 1777, in Barnes and Owen, eds., *Papers of Sandwich,* I, 169, 170–172; Germain to Knox, Dec. 31, 1776, Knox Papers.

[48] Gibbon to Holroyd, Nov. 4, 1776, in Norton, ed., *Letters of Gibbon,* II, 119–120; Germain to Knox, Dec. 31, 1776, Knox Papers.

[49] Account of a conversation with Germain, Oct. 26, 1776, Lucas Collection, Bedford County Record Office, Bedford; Germain to Eden, Jan. 1, 1777, Auckland Papers, Add. MSS., 34, 413.

[50] Germain to the Howes, Jan. 14, 1777, C.O. 5/177; Germain to W. Howe, Jan. 14, 1777, C.O. 5/94.

glad that the General no longer asked for a reinforcement (he now proposed leaving 9,000 men to hold Rhode Island, New York, and the lower Hudson while he took Philadelphia with an army of 10,000), but there was nothing else in the dispatches to comfort the Colonial Secretary.[51] Approving Howe's revised plan and urging him to undertake raids on the New England coasts, Lord George lectured his commanders on the importance of acting decisively: "I fear that you and Lord Howe will find it necessary to adopt such modes of carrying on the war, that the Rebels may be effectually distressed; so that through a lively Experience of losses and sufferings, they may be brought as soon as possible to a proper sense of their Duty." [52] Scarcely had he finished these dispatches when he received news of a more serious nature. Copies of Lord Howe's instructions for establishing a blockade reached London on March 4. The Admiral had directed his captains to be lenient with the colonists—to allow subsistence fishing, to "encourage and cultivate all amicable correspondence with the said Inhabitants, to gain their good Will and Confidence, whilst they demean themselves in a peaceable and orderly manner. And to grant them every other Indulgence which the limitations upon their Trade specified in the [Prohibitory] Act . . . will consistently admit: In order to conciliate their friendly Dispositions and to detach them from the Prejudices they have imbibed." Lest they should learn defensive warfare, he also forbade his captains to raid along the coasts.[53] If defeats at Trenton and Princeton could be charged to the misconduct of a Hessian officer, there was no way of excusing Howe's instructions to his captains, which seriously violated the spirit of the orders he had received from the ministry. Because this was the first specific example of such a violation and because he had many powerful friends in England, the government did no more than urge him to be less lenient. Both Germain and Sandwich reproved the Admiral for his indulgence to colonial fishermen, and Lord George sent a Major Nisbet Balfour to ask Sir William what he planned to do in 1777 and when he would do it.[54]

Germain clearly did not like the way the war was being managed; he was especially displeased with Lord Howe[55] and would, no doubt, have been glad to replace him with another admiral; but until he saw the results of Balfour's mission, there was little he could do. He was committed temporarily to a policy of reforming his commanders. In May he accepted their justification of a general pardon and approved Sir William's decision to go to Philadelphia by sea.[56] But when he learned in July that Balfour had failed to convert the Howes and that the British had suffered still another reverse, he began a determined campaign to replace, or at least intimidate, his com-

[51] W. Howe to Germain, separate, Dec. 20, 1776, Dec. 29, 1776, and Jan. 5, 1777, C.O. 5/94; Feb. 24, 1777, in Hutchinson, ed., *Diary and Letters*, II, 139.

[52] Quoting Germain to W. Howe, Mar. 3, 1777, no. 4, citing Germain to W. Howe, Mar. 3, 1777, no. 5, C.O. 5/94.

[53] Quoting Howe to Sir Peter Parker, Dec. 22, 1776, enclosed in Howe to Philip Stephens, Jan. 15, 1777, Adm. 1/487; Stephens to Howe, Mar. 4, 1777, Adm. 2/554.

[54] Sandwich to Howe, Mar. 10, 1777, in Barnes and Owen, eds., *Papers of Sandwich*, I, 288–289; Germain to Knox, June 11, 1777, Knox Papers; Howe to Germain, May 31, 1777, Germain Papers.

[55] "Lord Howe is the most disinterested man I know in permitting the Trade of Charlestown to be carryd on without interruption when he might availe himself of so many rich prizes." Germain to Knox, June 15, 1777, Knox Papers.

[56] Germain to the Howes, May 18, 1777, C.O. 5/177; Germain to W. Howe, May 18, 1777, no. 11, C.O. 5/94.

manders. Lord Howe had stubbornly defended his leniency to fishermen, arguing that by allowing them to fish he kept them from serving in the Continental army or navy. Similarly, he and his brother refused to undertake raids on New England ports, asserting that such raids would interfere with their over-all plan for the campaign. These arguments might have been convincing if they had not arrived with news of a rebel sortie from New England in which a squadron of eighteen armed vessels had put to sea, unopposed, in late May.[57] Germain now had proof of the disastrous consequences of leniency, and he intended to make the most of it. Employing irony in his reply to Lord Howe, he said he was happy that the indulgence "shewn to the Inhabitants upon the Coast, in not depriving them of the means of Subsistance has had so good an Effect"; indeed, he continued, Howe's blockade was so effective that the British Isles were teeming with American privateers. Lord George's argument was stated more bluntly by Sandwich and the lords of the admiralty who, feeling no need for indirection, censured Howe for stationing his cruisers improperly and for failing to provide intelligence of American preparations.[58] Though Germain had more confidence in General Howe than in his brother, he also encouraged Sir William to win the approval of his countrymen by retaliating against the bases of the privateers.[59] Lord George was determined to have a different war in America—with or without the help of the Howes.

Across the Atlantic the campaign of 1777 was scarcely begun. Feeling that there was little chance for ending the war, either by negotiations or by force, and that they were unreasonably harassed from Whitehall, the Howes seemed to exemplify the law of inertia. As early as April of 1777, Lord Howe expressed his sense of frustration by saying he knew not "what were best to be done." His brother, lamenting the weakness of his army, saw no prospect of winning the war in 1777.[60] Nor did his subsequent performance endanger the fulfillment of his prediction. Waiting until mid-June to begin the campaign, he spent two weeks trying to lure Washington away from his fortifications in New Jersey and three more in preparing to sail from New York. He did not reach the Delaware until July 30 and then decided to go to Philadelphia by way of the Chesapeake. This circuitous route combined with colonial opposition kept him from reaching Philadelphia for another eight weeks, and before he and his brother had driven the rebels from their fortifications on the Delaware, Burgoyne had surrendered at Saratoga. Indeed the Howes did not secure their hold on Philadelphia, for which they expended the Canadian army and a whole campaign, until November 23, when British shipping was at last able to reach the town. Even then, the capture of Philadelphia proved no more than an additional drain on British strength: expectations of substantial loyalist support in Pennsylvania turned out to be the private chimera of Joseph Galloway and the Allens.[61]

[57] Stephens to Howe, Aug. 20, 1777, Adm. 2/555; Howe to Germain, May 31, 1777, private, Germain Papers; W. Howe to Germain, June 3, 1777, C.O. 5/94; Howe to Stephens, June 8, 1777, Adm. 1/487.

[58] Germain to Howe, Aug. 4, 1777, Germain Papers; Sandwich to Howe, Aug. 3, 1777, in Barnes and Owen, eds., Papers of Sandwich, I, 293–295; Stephens to Howe, Aug. 20, 1777, Adm. 2/555.

[59] Germain to Irwin, Aug. 29, 1777, Germain to W. Howe, Aug. 4, 1777, Germain Papers.

[60] Apr. 17, 1777, in Tatum, ed., Journal of Serle, 212–213; W. Howe to Germain, Apr. 2, 1777, C.O. 5/94.

[61] W. Howe to Germain, Apr. 2, 1777, C.O. 5/94; W. Howe to Germain, Nov. 30, 1777, C.O. 5/95; Dec. 27, 30, and 31, 1776, in Tatum, ed., Journal of Serle, 163–165.

The Howes received Germain's dispatches of early August in October while they were struggling to open the Delaware. Lord Howe refused at first to be baited by the Colonial Secretary. When Lord George congratulated him on the success of his leniency to colonial fishermen, he paid irony with irony by thanking him for his compliment.[62] His brother was not, however, capable of such self-restraint. Though not yet sure that Burgoyne had surrendered, Sir William already knew that the Canadian army was in trouble. Feeling that he was partially responsible for whatever had happened to Burgoyne and knowing that his conquest of Philadelphia would be poor recompense for the loss of an army, he was in no mood to suffer further taunts from Germain. On October 22 he asked to be recalled, saying his recommendations had been ignored and justifying his conduct toward Burgoyne on the ground that he had warned him to expect no direct support from New York.[63] Lord Howe was more subtle. A month later, without referring to the ministers' dispatches, he quietly asked the admiralty to name an officer to succeed him in case poor health should force him to resign, and not until December 10 did he reply to the charge that he had neglected the blockade of New England. He had been unable to maintain an adequate blockade, he said, because most of his ships had been employed in supporting the army—his primary responsibility.[64] The government might, of course, have made effective replies to both of the Howes had any need for debating remained.

Sir William's resignation reached London on December 1, and Lord Howe's, on January 7.[65] Because the government was busy digesting Burgoyne's surrender and enjoying the Christmas holiday, no formal action was taken on their resignations until January 10, when the cabinet voted unanimously to replace General Howe. If the issue had developed slowly, it now burst forth with unusual intensity, demonstrating the dangers involved in removing any commander blessed with strong political connections. Indeed, when Lord Howe's mother poured a verbal broadside into Germain, the admiralty promptly retracted its censure of her older son and declared its complete satisfaction with his disposition of the American squadron.[66] The battle over Sir William's resignation was not, however, so quickly settled. Germain, a tougher opponent than Sandwich, was determined to replace General Howe at any cost. On January 31 the King told Lord North to decide whether he would keep the Colonial Secretary or the General. When North chose Germain,[67] he precipitated a further outburst from the Howes and their friends. Lord George's own secretary resigned in protest, as did Lord Chancellor Bathurst. Lady Howe demanded that her husband be given leave to return home with his brother, and she was supported by the Earl of Clarendon, who suggested alternatively that both of the brothers be

[62] Howe to Germain, Oct. 18, 1777, Germain Papers.

[63] W. Howe to Germain, Oct. 22, 1777, C.O. 5/94. As early as Oct. 16, the British heard rumors that General John Burgoyne had been defeated and lost his baggage. "Journals of Captain Henry Duncan," Oct. 16, 1777, pp. 152–153.

[64] Howe to Stephens, Nov. 23, and Dec. 10, 1777, Adm. 1/488.

[65] W. Howe to Germain, Oct. 22, 1777, C.O. 5/94; Howe to Stephens, Nov. 23, 1777, Adm. 1/488.

[66] Germain to the King, Jan. 10, 1778, and the King to North, Jan. 13, 1778, in Fortescue, ed., *Correspondence of George Third*, IV, 8, 15; John Hobart, Earl of Buckinghamshire to Sir Charles Hotham Thompson, Jan. 16, 1778, Hotham Deposit, DD HO/4/19, East Riding Record Office, Beverley, Yorkshire; Stephens to Howe, Jan. 15, 1778, Adm. 2/556.

[67] The King to North, [Jan. 31], Feb. 2, 1778, in Fortescue, ed., *Correspondence of George Third*, IV, 13, 33.

retained.[68] The King, interceding in behalf of the Howes, who had long been his personal favorites, ordered the ministry to soften the terms of the General's recall and to give the Admiral complete freedom either to resign or to retain his command.[69] General Howe left America in May, but his brother, trapped by the arrival of a French fleet, did not sail from New York until September. Changing commanders in a war across the Atlantic was no simple matter. Even when the political battles were over, the ocean remained a formidable barrier.

At its outset the American rebellion posed what was primarily a political problem. When it became a military problem as well, a majority of the British government chose to forget politics and to seek a solution by force of arms. Ironically, those Englishmen who continued to work for a political settlement—men like North and Howe— succeeded only in hampering the majority's efforts to achieve a military victory. In persuading the ministry to approve a peace commission, North interjected imperial politics into the government's preparations for war. When subsequently Lord Howe secured the American command as well as the peace commission, strategy became hopelessly enmeshed with politics. His instructions being entirely inadequate for a successful negotiation, his attempts to promote a reconciliation did no more than forfeit Britain's best chances for a military decision. Although Germain realized as early as December of 1776 that the Howes were violating the spirit of their instructions, he could neither alter their performance nor secure their resignations before a second campaign had passed. In the interim, the Howes, shielded by the Atlantic Ocean and their friends at home, made their way dejectedly to Philadelphia, their dreams of reuniting the empire blasted by the political and military realities of the American rebellion.

[68] Germain to Eden, Feb. 10, 1778, Add. MSS., 34, 415; Feb. 10, 1778, in Hutchinson, ed., *Diary and Letters,* II, 184; Henry, Earl Bathurst to North, Feb. 15, 1778, Smith Collection, Morristown National Historical Park, Morristown, New Jersey; Mary Countess Howe to North, Feb. 18, 1778, in Barnes and Owen, eds., *Papers of Sandwich,* II, 292; Clarendon to North, Feb. 22, 1778, in Hist. MSS. Com., *The Manuscripts of the Marquis of Abergavenny . . .* (London, 1887), 20; Clarendon to North, Feb. 19, 1778, Clarendon Deposit.

[69] The King to North, Feb. 18, 1778, in Fortescue, ed., *Correspondence of George Third,* IV, 39; North to Sandwich, Feb. 23, 1778, in Barnes and Owen, eds., *Papers of Sandwich,* II, 292n. For examples of the King's attitude toward Lord Howe see A. M. W. Stirling, *The Hothams . . .* (London, 1918), II, 130–131; and Barrow, *Life of Earl Howe,* vii.

14 / George Washington:
George Washington's Generalship

Marcus Cunliffe

Nineteenth-century propagandists may justly be blamed for giving us the "cherry-tree" picture of a George Washington who "never told a lie." Their romances have tended to obscure his real accomplishments, and in reaction many historians have come to question several aspects of the accomplishments of Washington. Marcus Cunliffe is concerned with his military record as Commander in Chief of the Continental Army. Washington took up that position in mid-1775 and resigned it in 1783. In that period of time, he was actually present at a very limited number of American battlefield victories. More often he commanded forces that were compelled to retreat or won, at best, costly stalemates. Yet other aspects of his military achievement should not be overlooked. When he assumed command, the "Continental Army" was primarily a conglomeration of miscellaneous New England militiamen with little organization of any kind. He rapidly became the very symbol of the Continental Army and kept that symbol in existence throughout the long years of the War for Independence. Whether or not British failure was more important than American success in 1776, Washington saw the end of that year with his army still in existence as a fighting force. Throughout the war, that army gave a certain tone to the struggle. While there were fierce "guerrilla" struggles in many parts of the American states, there was also a real army whose soldiers were something more than shaggy and harassed "rebels." The army was the symbol of the reality of the new American nation, and Washington was the man who in so many ways kept that army in existence. On the following pages, Marcus Cunliffe—an Englishman—is concerned with other questions relating to Washington's leadership, and he contrasts the ultimate success of that leadership with the lesser qualities displayed by the Howe brothers, Burgoyne, and Cornwallis.

For further reading: John R. Alden, *General Charles Lee* (1951); George Athan Billias, *George Washington's Generals* (1964); James Thomas Flexner,

George Washington in the American Revolution, 1775–1783 (1968); Curtis Nettles, *George Washington and American Independence* (1951); Howard H. Peckham, *The War for Independence: A Military History* (1958); and Theodore Thayer, *Nathaniel Greene: Strategist of the American Revolution* (1960).

At first sight there is not much to be said about George Washington's generalship. At least, there is little new to be said. With hardly an exception, his contemporaries and biographers alike have agreed that he was an exemplary leader. Not even his few detractors have denied that he possessed certain essential attributes. To begin with, he was personally brave. In the fighting on Manhattan in September 1776, at Princeton in the following January, and at Germantown in September 1777, he displayed conspicuous courage. Tall, handsome, dignified, an expert horseman, he *looked* the part of a commander. He had great physical stamina; unlike some of his generals he was able to survive years of arduous campaigning without a serious illness. While less well educated than a number of his associates, he managed to express himself, in conversation and correspondence, with clarity and vigor. He was a methodical and energetic administrator. However despondent he might appear in private correspondence, he never wavered in his public insistence that the American cause was righteous and would triumph. Nor did he ever waver in his loyalty; the British admiral, Rodney, hopelessly misread his character in assuring Lord George Germain (as late as December 1780) that "Washington is certainly to be bought— honours will do it." [1] Then, early in the struggle he realized that crisis could be defined as peril plus opportunity. The limitations of his command—miscellaneous and inexperienced troops, indequate equipment and supplies, lack of naval vessels—must determine military policy. "[W]e should on all occasions," he told the President of Congress in September 1776, "avoid a general Action, or put anything to the Risque, unless compelled by a necessity, into which we ought never to be drawn." [2] But these words were written at a time of grave danger, when his troops were raw, hard-pressed and considerably outnumbered. He never ceased to seek out the possibility of what he liked to call a "brilliant stroke": a sudden assault, that is, like the one across the Delaware in December 1776. And when he felt more confidence in the quality of his men, he did not shun large-scale encounters. Finally, though he had a high sense of his own reputation, he resisted the temptation to abuse his authority. No scandal, financial or moral, attached to his name. If he kept a punctilious record of the expenses owed him by the United States, he took no pay for his services. If British propaganda alleged that he had a mistress, the *canard* gained no credence. More important, he made it plain beyond doubt that he cherished no overweening dream of military dictatorship. In emergency Congress twice entrusted him with exceptional powers. Some of his officers were prepared to hint in 1783 that he might become king of the new nation. In such situations he responded with the utmost rectitude.

---

[1] Quoted in Henry S. Commager and Richard B. Morris, eds., *The Spirit of 'Seventy-Six: The Story of the American Revolution as told by Participants,* 2 vols. (Indianapolis, 1958), II, 703.

[2] Letter of September 8, 1776, in John C. Fitzpatrick, ed., *The Writings of George Washington,* 39 vols. (Washington, D.C., 1931–44), VI, 28.

No wonder that the contrast was so often drawn between his own career and that of Napoleon Bonaparte.

On all this there is virtually no argument. But to probe deeper, to offer any reassessment of Washington's relative military talent, or of his standing vis-à-vis his brother generals or the Continental Congress, is difficult. Some of the evidence we need—for example, on the true nature of the so-called Conway Cabal—is lacking and probably never will be available. And the story has become too fixed in its main outlines. Between us and what might be a fresher truth lie all the famous tableaux, apocryphal or authentic. Through portraiture we see Washington as elegant, severe, unruffled. We recall a whole sequence of static scenes: Washington being placed in nomination for the chief command by John Adams at Philadelphia in June 1775; Washington reviewing his army on Cambridge Common a couple of weeks later; Washington sharing the miseries of the Valley Forge winter of 1777–78 with his men, yet (in our minds' eye) less affected by the cold than they; Washington rebuking Charles Lee at Monmouth Court House in June 1778, his soldiers broiled and parched, yet himself neither thirsty nor perspiring though angry enough with Lee; Washington superb in triumph at Yorktown, when Cornwallis surrenders to him in October 1781; Washington equally superb in his fatherly wisdom, when he puts on his spectacles to reply to the Newburgh Address of his discontented officers in March 1783; Washington bidding farewell to his officers, who now weep, at Fraunces Tavern in December of the same year. With such scenes are associated smaller vignettes: of nice young Lafayette, gruff old Steuben, jealous Gates and Conway, robust John Stark, comical Artemas Ward, villainous Arnold, loyal Greene, fat Knox; of Major André the British spy, so polite as to be almost masochistic; and of the Continental Congress, peevish, erratic, self-important. The total effect is like that of an old-fashioned engraving in which a central subject or person (Washington) is surrounded by a decorative border of tiny subordinate figures. The achievements of others are dwarfed, and made to seem dependent upon Washington's direction.

An awareness of this disparity accounts for much of the carping or malicious comment about him that circulated among such prominent soldiers and civilians as Joseph Reed, Charles Lee, Benjamin Rush, James Lovell, and John Adams. Admired, deferred to, secure in seniority, Washington (as they saw it) could easily afford the luxury of *noblesse oblige,* just as the wealthy, well-born Lafayette could easily rise to a nobility of conduct that endeared him to Washington but made him an exasperating example for a hard-up comrade like "Baron" de Kalb.

The nature of the war itself creates further difficulties of interpretation. Though we call it the Revolutionary War, or the War of Independence, it was also a civil war —less so than the War Between the States, but enough to blur conventional military evaluations. It was an improvised, ambiguous struggle. We do well to remember, for instance, that John Stark, the hero of Bennington, had a brother William who fought on the opposite side and was killed in the Battle of Long Island in August 1776.[3] The British were not sure how to regard the conflict. The simplest answer was to call it a rebellion. Indeed, the British might have noted that such disturbances were apparently subject to a thirty-year cycle: 1775 was preceded by the Jacobite risings of 1745 and 1715, and by Monmouth's rebellion of 1685. The difference was that the American rebels were more remote, and the extent of their threat to British power less

[3] Maldwyn A. Jones, *American Immigration* (Chicago, 1960), pp. 53–54.

starkly obvious. So George III's advisers and generals fell into confusions over strategy and policy comparable to those that were later to perplex Abraham Lincoln. Both sides complained bitterly, and with reason, that they did not know where they stood, or where they ought to stand in a war that was much easier to lose than to win.

In the circumstances, British generalship was so hesitant and mediocre at major moments that Washington's own prowess is not easy to determine. When he tried to write this portion of his biography of the American commander-in-chief, Washington Irving confessed his bewilderment. The military campaigns, he said, reminded him of two drunk men trying to hit one another yet failing to connect. An English observer (in *The Gentleman's Magazine* of August 1778), while seeking of course to denigrate Washington, admitted to a similar inability to make sense of events:

> Nature has certainly given him some military talents, yet it is more than probable that he will never be a great soldier. . . . He is but of slow parts, and these are totally unassisted by any kind of education. Now, though such a character may acquit itself with some sort of eclat, in the poor, pitiful, unsoldierlike war in which he has hitherto been employed, it is romantic to suppose he must not fail, if ever it should be his lot to be opposed by real military skill.

The anonymous commentator continues:

> He never saw any actual service, but in the unfortunate action of Braddock. He never read a book in the art of war of higher value than Bland's Exercises; and it has already been noted, that he is by no means of bright or shining parts. If, then, military knowledge be not unlike all other; or, if it be not totally useless as to all the purposes of actual war, it is impossible that ever Mr. Washington should be a great soldier. In fact, by the mere dint and bravery of our army alone, he has been beaten whenever he has engaged; and that this is left to befall him again, is a problem which, I believe, most military men are utterly at a loss to solve.

The author is ungenerously inaccurate. Washington had had several years of soldiering in the French and Indian War. He had "heard the bullets whistle" more than once, before and after Braddock's disaster at the Monongahela. And it would strain the imagination to see the actions at Trenton and Princeton as proofs of British military superiority. Still, the commentator's puzzlement is understandable. For whatever reasons, and with the doubtful exception of Monmouth Court House, Washington *did* get the worst of all the major engagements he had a hand in during the first half of the war. The English writer goes on:

> It should not be denied . . . that all things considered, [Washington] really has performed wonders. That he is alive to command an army, or that an army is left him to command, might be sufficient to insure him the reputation of a great General, if British Generals any longer were what British Generals used to be. In short, I am of the opinion . . . that any other General in the world than General Howe would have beaten General Washington; and any other General in the world than General Washington would have beaten General Howe.[4]

[4] "Particulars of the Life and Character of General Washington, Extracted from a Letter in Lloyd's Evening Post of Aug. 17, Signed An Old Soldier," *The Gentleman's Magazine*, Vol. XLVIII (August 1778). This is conveniently reprinted in Martin Kallich and Andrew MacLeish, eds., *The American Revolution Through British Eyes* (Evanston, 1962), pp. 111–13.

Without taking the last observation too seriously, perhaps we can agree that Washington came very near to catastrophe in the latter part of 1776. With a little more persistence and audacity from Howe, the army led by Washington might have been destroyed. If so, and if he himself had fallen into British hands, the struggle might have continued and Washington would have been dismissed by posterity as a well-intentioned but outmatched amateur.

The situation—to return to the perspective of the period—was certainly novel. As this *Gentleman's Magazine* assessment indicates, the war defied measurement according to European standards. It was a civil war, or a rebellion, or a popular patriotic rising, or a mixture of all three. Washington was a novice, with a reputedly limited intelligence; and yet he had "performed wonders."

In the final analysis the two most decisive factors were perhaps not personal but geographical: the huge extent of America and the width of the Atlantic. We have said that Washington's own eminence has made the activities of his officers seem minuscule. Geography, as Washington Irving came to feel, had a similar diminishing effect upon the commanders of both sides. A third factor, the French alliance, could be held almost equally decisive. Its inception might be counted as a diplomatic rather than a military success, while the all-important victory at Yorktown may be seen primarily as a Franco-British affair—a blow struck in a century-long contest.

If we attach some weight to such elements, what are we left with by way of an estimate of George Washington's generalship? It seems that there must be some scaling-down of the wilder claims: claims, it must be said, that he did not advance on his own behalf and that have not been asserted by reputable historians in the past half-century. We must discard the legend, disproved but still lingering on in folklore, that Frederick the Great ever sent Washington a sword with the engraved inscription, "From the oldest soldier in Europe to the greatest soldier in the world."[5] Instead, let us consider dispassionately his stature as a fighting general, or field commander; and secondly, as an organizing general, or commander-in-chief.

Washington's talents as a field commander were in truth not tested often enough, or upon a big enough scale, to rank him automatically with the prodigies of military history. Like the other American generals at the beginning of the war, he was after all deficient in experience. At the outset this recognition weighed upon them to a perhaps undue extent. None of them had had much formal training on the European pattern. They were at best veterans of colonial warfare, unaccustomed to the handling of large bodies of troops or to the employment of special arms such as cavalry. Washington never had the responsibility for campaigns on the Napoleonic scale, not to mention those of the American Civil War. This is not to maintain that he would have failed to rise to the occasion, but simply to note that the giant occasion did not present itself. We can only guess what his "ceiling" of achievement might have been in the tactical disposition of one big army confronting another.[6]

[5] The results of various scrutinies of the legend are summarized in Francis V. Greene, *The Revolutionary War and the Military Policy of the United States* (New York, 1911).

[6] "His courage is calm and brilliant, but to appreciate in a satisfactory manner the real extent of his . . . ability as a great . . . captain, I think one should have seen him at the head of a greater army, with greater means than he has had, and opposed to an enemy less his superior. At least one cannot fail to give him the title of an excellent patriot, of a wise and virtuous man, and one is . . . tempted to ascribe to him all good qualities, even those that circumstances have not yet permitted him to develop." This is the rather feline opinion of Colonel de Broglie, a

On the debit side, military historians tend to agree that Washington made mistakes. Possibly he was too ready to shift the blame for a reverse onto a subordinate. This has been said of his treatment of Nathanael Greene after the loss of Fort Washington, and of his more peremptory reaction to Charles Lee at Monmouth Court House. The evidence against him is by no means conclusive; and indeed few senior soldiers in history could be held entirely innocent of such a charge. Washington's record is, for example, no worse and probably better than that of Stonewall Jackson in this respect. As for actual mistakes, he is most commonly accused of the following:

> *Long Island* (August 1776): Splitting his army between New York and Brooklyn; failure to appreciate the value of cavalry for reconnaissance purposes, and so being taken by surprise through a flank attack; failure to give close supervision to General Israel Putnam's dispositions, which led to raw troops fighting without benefit of entrenchments.[7]
>
> *Fort Washington* (November 1776): The loss of 3,000 men when the Fort was captured through his own indecision.[8]
>
> *Brandywine* (September 1777): Failure to use his Light Horse to gather information of enemy moves, or in other ways to anticipate Howe's flank attack; general lack of firm direction.[9]
>
> *Germantown* (October 1777): Reliance upon too intricate a plan of battle.[10]
>
> *Campaigns of 1777*: A strategic error in deciding to march south against Howe's invasion of Pennsylvania, instead of joining Gates and Schuyler so as to crush Burgoyne in the north and then swing south, with reinforcements from the Northern army, against Howe.[11]

These charges are not without substance. In extenuation, it should be said that most soldiers, even celebrated ones, make mistakes. Stonewall Jackson, brilliant in the Shenandoah Valley in 1862, was abominably sluggish in the Peninsula fighting a few weeks later. Washington's errors, significantly, were concentrated in the first half of the war, when he was a learner in command of learners, face to face with professionals. Probably Howe could have destroyed him at the end of 1776. But Howe hesitated; Washington's response was the splendidly impudent *coup* at Trenton. It was a raid rather than a battle; part of the plan miscarried; but the effect upon

---

young French nobleman who joined his regiment in 1782. W. S. Baker, *Character Portraits of Washington* (Philadelphia, 1887), pp. 18–21. Perhaps its coolness, unusual for this late stage of the war, has something to do with family history. Four years earlier, another de Broglie was being hinted at as a candidate for what would in effect have been the chief command in America. See Douglas S. Freeman, *George Washington*, 6 vols. (New York, 1948–54), IV, 99.

[7] F. V. Greene, *op. cit.*, p. 41; Christopher Ward, *The War of the Revolution*, 2 vols. (New York, 1952), I, 229; George F. Scheer and Hugh F. Rankin, *Rebels and Redcoats* (Cleveland, 1957), p. 174.

[8] This criticism has been most sharply formulated by Bernhard Knollenberg, in *Washington and the Revolution: A Reappraisal* (New York, 1940), pp. 129–39.

[9] For some representative comments, see Willard M. Wallace, *Appeal to Arms: A Military History of the American Revolution* (New York, 1951), p. 139; John R. Alden, *The American Revolution, 1775–1783* (New York, 1954), p. 123; Freeman, *op. cit.*, IV, 488; and Scheer and Rankin, *op. cit.*, pp. 240, 293–94.

[10] Ward, *op. cit.*, I, 364–71; Alden, *op. cit.*, p. 125; Scheer and Rankin, *op. cit.*, p. 244.

[11] One of the first books in Washington historiography to express serious reservations as to the commander-in-chief's military prowess (including his failure to understand the value of cavalry) was Charles Francis Adams, Jr., *Studies Military and Diplomatic, 1775–1865* (New York, 1911). For the campaigns of 1777 see pp. 132–49.

American morale was tremendous. It was as needed a victory, at the time, as was the more ripely comprehensive and more thoroughly professional victory at York-town five years later. The difference in the scope and context of the two engagements defined the distance that Washington and his army had traveled in skill, in offensive capacity, and in assurance. Valley Forge and the French alliance represent the turning point. After the winter of 1777–78, the troops close to Washington began to correspond to the notion he had always stressed: namely, that America must have a disciplined national force, as trained and tried as the best European ranks that could be brought against them.

Here we come to a point that is worth stressing. Ever since the Revolution, Americans have been debating the respective merits of professional and of amateur soldiery. It has been a heated debate, for it embodies quite fundamental divisions of opinion as to the true nature of American nationalism and democracy. The contenders have both managed to find ammunition in their interpretation of the Revolutionary War. The professionals cite Washington's highly critical references to the militia, and to all short-term enlistments; the conflict was won, they believe, by the Continental regiments. The amateurs dwell upon the battles in which the militia fought stoutly, and upon the superior qualities of initiative, patriotism, and ingenuity which derive from an amateur tradition. George Washington, the Virginia planter, could be seen as the highest product of this essentially civilian approach to warfare.[12]

That he retained some "civilian" characteristics is undeniable. His deference to Congress, and to civilian authority generally, may be seen in this light. It is arguable that the tactics to which he sometimes resorted show a refreshing freedom from military orthodoxy, and that the British generals were hopelessly hidebound. No doubt the achievements of Washington's lieutenants—Greene, Knox and Morgan especially —are striking illustrations of amateur proficiency. But the professional-amateur debate is misleading in various ways. On the British side, many of the officers prided themselves on a dilettante approach to warfare. Nor do we give proper credit to the Americans if we caricature the British conduct of operations as a series of brutally stupid frontal attacks on the Bunker Hill pattern. On occasion the British showed considerable enterprise. One example of this would be Grey's night assault on Anthony Wayne at Paoli in September 1777, when the British killed, wounded, or captured nearly 400 Americans for the loss of only 8 of their own men. On the American side, amateurishness may have been evident—perhaps all too evident— in the war's initial stages. But after two or three years of campaigning, Washington, his officers, and his Continental rank-and-file had become professionals in all important respects.[13]

This was what Washington himself ardently desired. He did not visualize himself as a guerrilla leader, a will-of-the-wisp harassing the stolid British like some brigand chief. From the start he strove to build an army able to meet the British in open

[12] One stout upholder of this view is John A. Logan, *The Volunteer Soldier of America* (Chicago, 1887), p. 484: "No amount of preliminary technical education could have made a greater general of the hero of Trenton, Princeton, and Yorktown. His genius was natural, and bloomed into the perfection attained under the developing influence of actual warfare."

[13] There are intelligent comments on these matters in Walter Millis, *Arms and Men* (New York, 1956), pp. 32–33; Daniel Boorstin, *The Americans: The Colonial Experience* (New York, 1958), pp. 364–71; Theodore Ropp, *War in the Modern World* (Durham, 1959), pp. 71–80; and Alfred Vagts, *A History of Militarism,* revised ed. (New York, 1959), pp. 92–101.

battle and beat them at their own game.[14] He knew that this was only a dream in the early stages, and acted accordingly. But it was no idle dream; it was an ambition that he labored to fulfill. As his correspondence shows, he hammered away at the task of creating an army officered (as far as possible) by gentlemen, observing strict discipline, properly armed, accoutered, paid, rewarded, punished. His was no doubt a sensible conservatism: even the most revolutionary armies discover the advantages of well-established procedures and hierarchical distinctions. "Let us have a respectable Army," was his plea from 1776 onward, "and such as will be competent to every exigency." In other words, an army much like that of Howe or Rochambeau.[15]

But George Washington was not merely a field commander, though he maintained his headquarters in the field with whatever troops seemed to be best placed for his manifold purposes. He was commander-in-chief. The limits of his authority could not be exactly defined, in a situation without precedent. Even if a precise definition could have been formulated, much else would have remained hazy. He had a large but vague jurisdiction. His commission came from the Continental Congress, a body speaking for a then nonexistent nation. Congress entrusted him with considerable powers. But Congress itself was only a comity, or perhaps more accurately a committee, of thirteen semi-sovereign states. Washington was clearly senior in rank to all the other generals. But what control was he to exercise, theoretically or actually, over armies that might be several hundred miles away from his own headquarters? To what extent could he give orders to the French military and naval leaders when their expeditions began to arrive in 1778? Who was to formulate strategy? With whom was he to communicate, and on what terms—governors of states, other commanders, the President of Congress, the Board of War? If he lost favor, was he removable?

Like the rest of his countrymen, Washington had to proceed by trial and error. That he did err now and then seems both undeniable and forgivable. His appointment was meant to symbolize the spirit of union. In 1775 such spirit was more an aspiration than a reality. Through indiscreet early letters he let it be known that he, the Virginian, was not much impressed by New England's military prowess. Some harm was done. He had one or two awkward passages with the French, again through indiscreet and possibly disingenuous correspondence which fell into the wrong hands. For a prudent man he sometimes expressed himself with dangerous candor in letters to his family and to friends in and out of Congress. Yet he learned by his

[14] An excellent recent study is Russell F. Weigley, *Towards an American Army: Military Thought from Washington to Marshall* (New York, 1962). See especially pp. 1–7.

[15] By the closing stages of the war he had gone far enough in this direction to astonish discriminating Frenchmen, although previously Mifflin and other generals had enjoyed a reputation for being somewhat more effective disciplinarians. "I had expected to see," wrote the Comte de Ségur, "unkempt soldiers and officers without training. . . . I saw a well-disciplined army presenting in every detail the very image of order, reason, training and experience." Chastellux was equally impressed: "When one sees . . . the General guards encamped within the precincts of his house; nine waggons, destined to carry his baggage, ranged in his court; . . . grooms taking care of very fine horses belonging to the General Officers and their Aides de Camp; when one observes the perfect order . . . within these precincts, . . . one is tempted to apply to the Americans what Pyrrhus said of the Romans: *Truly these people have nothing barbarous in their discipline!*" Gilbert Chinard, ed., *George Washington as the French Knew Him* (Princeton, 1940), pp. 37, 57. If these officers had visited Washington's headquarters in 1776 or 1777, instead of 1781 or 1782, they would of course have found a more rough-and-ready atmosphere.

mistakes. He shed all trace of Virginia localism, until he, more than any other person or any institution or symbol, became synonymous with America's cause. And compared with most of his prominent fellow countrymen—soldiers and civilians—he was a model of discretion. His letters are sometimes angry and self-righteous; they are never whining, silly or malicious.

It was both a strength and a weakness of his position that he seemed, in more than one sense, irreplaceable. In retrospect the critical mutterings of 1776–77, in Congress and among certain army officers, strike us as petty and perhaps even treasonable. We find it absurd that Washington's military policy should be subject to the scrutiny of the five men whom Congress constituted as the Board of War and Ordnance in June 1776. What assistance could be rendered by such a member of the Board as the utterly unmilitary John Adams? It was replaced in 1777 by a new Board not composed of congressmen. But was this not even worse, when intrigue might place disgruntled army officers upon it? Or what of the six special committees sent by the Continental Congress to inquire into the army's affairs? Knowing what befell Gates at Camden—or thinking we know—we wonder how anyone could have entertained the notion of substituting him for Washington in the supreme command.

But this is hindsight, and a hindsight which may be cruelly unfair. On the whole Congress and Washington worked together well—fantastically well if we compare their relations with those between Congress and Lincoln's wretched generals in the Civil War. The boards and special committees of Washington's day had next to nothing in common with the inquisitorial Committee on the Conduct of the War. They were anxious to help, and rendered all the aid within their power. It is doubtful whether there was any serious and concerted scheme to supplant Washington. There was something of a crisis of confidence in 1777–78. His more demonstratively enthusiastic supporters may have persuaded him that an organized plot existed. In the subsequent jockeying for position certain officers—Conway, Gates, Mifflin— may have been identified as a coalition hostile to Washington. Whether they were is dubious. Washington and posterity have treated them with marked disdain.

Whatever the inner history of a situation that may have had *no* inner history, Washington emerged as the undisputed commander, at the head of a group of competent and devoted officers. If there was a plot, it hardly deserves the name. If there was a counterstroke by Washington, it was far from being a Putsch.[16] In the long run, the effects of the entire episode were probably beneficial. The army could rely on Washington to put its case before the country; Congress could feel reasonably sure that with Washington in command there was no risk of subversion by a military junto. It would have been amazing if there had been no friction, no dissension, no backbiting. Once his position was secure, Washington was able to display a remarkable magnanimity. True, he complained unceasingly of the difficulties in his path. The war dragged on and on. The French had their own views of fruitful strategy. There were ominous mutinies in the Continental line. Yet there was a good deal more acrimony in the British camps and council chambers, and far more in that later American conflict of 1861–65.

[16] The undercurrents of hostility and rivalry are closely analyzed in Knollenberg, *op. cit.,* pp. 30–77, and in Kenneth R. Rossman, *Thomas Mifflin and the Politics of the American Revolution* (Chapel Hill, 1952), pp. 91–139, as well as in Freeman, *op. cit.,* IV, 581–611. An older account, which assumes that opposition to Washington was organized, is Louis C. Hatch, *The Administration of the American Revolutionary Army* (New York, 1904), pp. 23–34.

Washington's ultimate success may owe as much to British limpness as to his own firmness. It has been plausibly maintained that the British situation was impossible from the start, and that no amount of brilliance in leadership could have offset the formidable disadvantages of having to fight an unpopular war, with resources strained by other global commitments, in a terrain in which merely to feed or move an army —let alone fight major battles—was an administrative problem of daunting dimensions.[17] The surrender of Cornwallis could not have been encompassed without the French fleet and army. Washington's own growing military capacity would have counted for little if his generals, junior officers, and enlisted men had not grown commensurately in competence and assurance. The heroic efforts of Greene, Knox, Lafayette, and others ought not to be underrated in the apportionment of credit. Greene was accurate as well as warmhearted in writing to Knox after Yorktown:

> Colonel Lee who has lately returned from the Northern Army says you are the genius of it, and that everything is said of you that you can wish. . . . Your success in Virginia is brilliant, glorious, great and important. The commander-in-chief's head is all covered with laurels, and yours so shaded with them that one can hardly get sight of it.[18]

As Washington himself was quick to acknowledge, there was room for more than one set of laurels.

Nevertheless, his devoted subordinates and his admiring French allies gladly yielded to him a major share of the glory. We may discount some of their compliments as flattery or as formal rhetoric. Yet they knew him, closely and testingly, from day to day and month to month. If he had been indecisive, or unduly arrogant, nervous, or reckless, he could not have won and held their respect. The British army no doubt labored under handicaps; yet those of Washington's army were sometimes very similar. Long after the war, John Adams is said to have growled that Washington was "a block of wood!" [19] If he really made the remark, which is likely enough, it can be understood as an oblique commendation, a grudging testimony to the vital elements of straightforwardness, consistency, and reliability in Washington's character. He won, that is, by taking to the field and staying there: by tenacity rather than by Napoleonic *brio*. Though he could be dashing in action, his overriding service to America lay in his steadfastness. He was a fixed point in a shifting universe.

Washington's role in the War of Independence was extraordinary. There are no close historical parallels. Yet two comparisons can be made, each of which helps to remind us that the commander-in-chief was only in part a military leader. The two comparisons are with Charles de Gaulle and Dwight D. Eisenhower. Like de Gaulle, though with less conscious purpose on his part, George Washington symbolized his country and its will to resist. The new nation insisted upon endowing "His Excellency" George Washington with charismatic glamour.[20] He was able to sustain the

[17] See Eric Robson, *The American Revolution in its Political and Military Aspects* (London, 1955), pp. 93–152.

[18] Greene to Knox, December 10, 1781, quoted in North Callahan, *Henry Knox: General Washington's General* (New York, 1958), p. 190.

[19] An anecdote relating to *circa* 1816, recorded by John G. Palfrey; see *William & Mary Quarterly*, 3rd series, XV (January 1958), 93–94.

[20] Seymour Martin Lipset, *The First New Nation: The United States in Historical and Comparative Perspective* (New York, 1963), pp. 16–23.

role with remarkable modesty, all things considered, as well as with remarkable dignity. Like the French leader, he was a figure of exceptional strength of purpose. And like General Eisenhower, he was a coalition general for a large part of the war. A great proportion of his work went on in conference and in correspondence. Some of his activities were political, or diplomatic, rather than military, as when he had to deal with British offers to negotiate, or with French military and naval chiefs. As with General Eisenhower, major strategic plans usually lay outside his scope; but their implementation often depended upon his advice. Despite his charismatic authority, he was more a mediator than a dictator. He communicated with governors of states, with Congress, with the Board of War, with the whole gamut of overlapping jurisdictions. In this respect, indeed, we might say that he was a dictator: a dictator of letters, not of decisions. If his charismatic symbols were those of the flag, the sword, the beautifully caparisoned horse, his day-to-day responsibilities were more appropriately symbolized by the chairman's gavel, the memorandum, the agenda, and the secretary's quill. It was his task, and his talent, to preside, to inform, to adjudicate, to advise, to soothe, to persuade, to anticipate, to collaborate. He had to weld the states together, as far as he could; to co-operate with the French, harmonizing America's aims and theirs; to reconcile the competing claims of different theaters of war; to face the consequences, in terms of mounting pride and estrangement, of having managed to create a professional army; to remember that though a master of men, he was the servant of his country and of Congress.[21] A co-ordinator, he had to learn how to stay near the scene of military action and yet not allow local problems to narrow his vision. A more mercurial figure might well have lost patience. A more genial one might have found his popularity was too cheaply purchased, and so too rapidly dispersed. For most of the war he had to stand on the defensive, reacting to British pressures. But when the chance came, in 1781, he showed that years of parleying had not eroded his spirit. At a vital moment he seized the initiative, like an ideal coalition leader, in ensuring that he and the French for once acted in entire harmony. In earlier episodes he may perhaps now and then have picked the wrong alternative in what he called his "choice of difficulties." Should he, for instance, have marched north instead of south in 1777? Should he, failing that, have retained the 3,000 men he sent to reinforce Schuyler and Gates? He made up his mind and acted, without vain regrets. He sent help to another army at the expense of his own immediate command. Can we imagine such a response from, say, General George B. McClellan?

What irony has accrued to those grudging judgments from *The Gentleman's Magazine!*

> Now, though such a character may acquit itself with some sort of eclat, in the poor, pitiful, unsoldierlike war in which he has hitherto been employed, it is romantic to suppose he must not fail, if ever it should be his lot to be opposed by real military skill. . . .

If and perhaps. History can only answer that it was Washington who stayed the course; it was Howe and Clinton and Cornwallis who headed back home to their firesides and their extenuating speeches and memoirs.

---

[21] Edmund C. Burnett, *The Continental Congress* (New York, 1941), has some fascinating detail on Congress and the army. See for example pp. 442–67 for the period in 1780 when a committee of Congress visited Washington's headquarters.

Part IV

AN INTERNAL REVOLUTION?

15 / Democracy and the American Revolution

Merrill Jensen

What was "revolutionary" about the American Revolution? To be sure, the American people did fight a "War for Independence" and assumed their "separate and equal station" among the peoples of the world. Moreover, they rebelled against King George III so thoroughly that monarchical sentiment virtually disappeared from the new United States. The "revolutionary" quality of this fact should not be overlooked: the rejection of monarchy and its hereditary basis carried with it the most important implication that the ultimate source of political authority was to be found among the people themselves. By driving the Loyalists or "Tories" from their midst, the Americans expelled those most likely to uphold other vestiges of the old order and confiscated and redistributed a large amount of property. Wherever feudal remnants, such as the established churches, were to be found such remnants were greatly weakened or destroyed in the late 1770's. But, beyond this, did the American Revolution have any specifically "democratic" content? Did it carry some new notions of democracy forward? Or did it merely represent, insofar as it was revolutionary at all, the purging of minor unfree elements from what was already a relatively free society, an adjustment of reality and rhetoric to each other? In the following essay, Merrill Jensen depicts the clearly democratic elements in the revolutionary movement. He notes the spread of revolutionary ideology beyond the original confines of the struggle with Great Britain and the manner by which it became an instrument for domestic reform in 1775 and later. Jensen identifies such particular elements as a popular distrust of men in power and an insistence upon frequent elections of all wielders of political authority. He regards the Articles of Confederation as a success for the new democratic spirit in the states. Readers may wish to compare his viewpoints with earlier discussions of revolutionary ideology and with later ones of the history of the confederation and the constitutional convention. Here, however, they should be clearly aware of Mr. Jensen's definition of what was "democratic" and the suppositions and limitations of that definition.

Delivered at the Conference of Early American History at the Henry E. Huntington Library, February 9, 1957. Reprinted by permission from the *Huntington Library Quarterly*, XX (1957), 321–341.

For further reading: Robert E. Brown, *Middle-Class Democracy and the Revolution in Massachusetts, 1691–1780* (1955); J. Franklin Jameson, *The American Revolution Considered as a Social Movement* (1926); Merrill Jensen, *The Articles of Confederation* (1947) and *The New Nation* (1950); Allan Nevins, *The American States during and after the Revolution* (1924); and J. R. Pole, *Political Representation in England and the Origins of the American Republic* (1966).

The historian who ventures to talk about democracy in early America is in danger because there are almost as many opinions as there are writers on the subject. The Puritans have been pictured as the founders of American democracy, and it is vigorously denied that they had anything to do with it. Some have seen in Roger Williams the father of American democracy, and others have denied that he was a democrat, whatever his putative progeny may be. The conflict is equally obvious when it comes to the American Revolution, and the problems of solution are far more complex than they are for the seventeenth century. The difficulty is compounded, for all too often men's emotions seem to become involved.

It is sometimes suggested that we avoid the use of the word "democracy" when discussing the seventeenth and eighteenth centuries. It seems to me that this is a flat evasion of the problem, for the Americans of those centuries used the word and they meant something by it. Our task, then, is not to avoid the issue but to try to understand what they meant, and understand what they meant in the context of the times in which they lived. What we must not do is to measure the seventeenth and eighteenth centuries in terms of our own assumptions about what democracy is or should be. This is all the more important since many of us do not seem to be too clear about our assumptions, even for the century in which we live.

A number of years ago I took the position that "in spite of the paradoxes involved one may still maintain that the Revolution was essentially, though relatively, a democratic movement within the thirteen American colonies, and that its significance for the political and constitutional history of the United States lay in its tendency to elevate the political and economic status of the majority of the people." And then, with a somewhat rhetorical flourish which I have sometimes regretted but have not as yet withdrawn, I went on to say that "the Articles of Confederation were the constitutional expression of this movement and the embodiment in governmental form of the philosophy of the Declaration of Independence." [1] One thing can be said for this statement at least: reviewers read it and quoted it, some with raised eyebrows, and some with approval, whether or not they said anything at all about the rest of the book.

During most of the present century historians have assumed that democracy was involved somehow or other in the American Revolution. They have assumed also that there were conditions within the American colonies that were not satisfactory to at least some of the American people. The causes of internal discontent were various, ranging all the way from religious to economic differences. The discontent was of

---

[1] Merrill Jensen, *The Articles of Confederation: An Interpretation of the Social-Constitutional History of the American Revolution, 1774–1781,* reprint with new foreword (Madison, Wis., 1948), pp. 15, 239.

such intensity that in certain colonies it led to explosive outbreaks in the 1760's such as the Regulator movements in the Carolinas, the Paxton Boys' uprising in Pennsylvania, and the tenant farmer revolt in New York, outbreaks that were suppressed by the armed forces of the colonial governments and with the help of British power.

Most historians have agreed also that the individual colonies were controlled politically by relatively small groups of men in each of them, allied by family, or economic or political interests, or by some combination of these. The colonial aristocracies owed their position to many things: to their wealth and ability, to their family connections and political allies, and to the British government which appointed them to office. As opposed to Britain, they had won virtual self-government for the colonies by 1763. Yet in every colony they were a minority who managed to maintain internal control through property qualifications for the suffrage, especially effective in the growing towns, and through refusal or failure to grant representation in any way proportional to the population of the rapidly growing frontier areas. Probably more important than either of these was the fact that in most colonies the aristocracies manned the upper houses of the legislatures, the supreme courts, and other important posts—all by royal appointment. Beyond this, their control extended down through the county court system, even in Massachusetts. In short, colonial political society was not democratic in operation despite the elective lower houses and the self-government which had been won from Great Britain.[2]

This is a brief but, I think, fair summary of a widely held point of view concerning the political actualities at the beginning of the revolutionary era.

This view has been challenged recently. A writer on Massachusetts declared that "as far as Massachusetts is concerned, colonial society and the American Revolution must be interpreted in terms something very close to a complete democracy with the exception of British restraints." It was not controlled by a wealthy aristocracy. There was little inequality of representation, and property was so widely held that virtually every adult male could vote.[3] The assumption that Massachusetts was an idyllic democracy, united in the fight against British tyranny, will be somewhat surprising to those who have read the letters of Francis Bernard and the diary of John Adams, not to mention the history of Thomas Hutchinson, and, I suspect, would be even more surpising to those gentlemen as well. Elsewhere, this writer has implied that what was true for Massachusetts was probably true for other colonies and for the United States after the Revolution.[4]

On the other hand it is asserted that democracy had nothing to do with the Revolution. Such an assertion made in connection with Pennsylvania is a little startling, for ever since C. H. Lincoln's work of more than a half century ago, down to the present, it has been held that there was a democratic movement in Pennsylvania during the revolutionary era. Not so, says a reviewer of the most recent study. He declares that "the attribution of democratic motivations and ideas to eighteenth century colonists

[2] *Ibid.*, ch. iii, "The Internal Revolution"; Leonard W. Labaree, *Conservatism in Early American History* (New York, 1948); and Robert J. Taylor, *Western Massachusetts in the Revolution* (Providence, 1954), as examples. For methods of local control see Charles S. Sydnor, *Gentlemen Freeholders: Political Practices in Washington's Virginia* (Chapel Hill, 1952).

[3] Robert E. Brown, "Democracy in Colonial Massachusetts," *New England Quarterly*, XXV (1952), 291–313, and at length in *Middle Class Democracy and the Revolution in Massachusetts, 1691–1780* (Ithaca, N. Y., 1955).

[4] Robert E. Brown, "Economic Democracy Before the Constitution," *American Quarterly*, VII (1955), 257–274.

is a common fault among many historians of the colonial period. . . ." He argues that the struggle in Pennsylvania before 1776 was one between "radical and conservative variants of whiggism," which he defines as one between "those who held privilege most dear and those who valued property above all." The Pennsylvania Constitution of 1776 itself was not democratic, but a triumph of "colonial radical whiggism." [5]

It is clear that a considerable diversity of opinion prevails. It is also clear that the time has come to set forth certain propositions or generalizations which seem to me to have a measure of validity.

First of all, a definition of democracy is called for. And just to face the issue squarely, I will offer one stated at Newport, Rhode Island, in 1641 when a meeting declared that "the government which this body politic doth attend unto . . . is a democracy or popular government; . . . that is to say: It is in the power of the body of freemen, orderly assembled, or the major part of them, to make or constitute just laws, by which they will be regulated, and to depute from among themselves such ministers as shall see them faithfully executed between man and man." That such an idea was not confined to Newport was shown six years later when the little towns in Rhode Island formed a confederation, the preamble of which states: "It is agreed, by this present assembly thus incorporate, and by this present act declared, that the form of government established in Providence Plantations is democratical; that is to say, a government held by the free and voluntary consent of all, or the greater part of the free inhabitants."

These are simple but, I think, adequate definitions. I will go even further and offer as a theoretical and philosophical foundation for democracy the statement by Roger Williams in the *Bloudy Tenent* of 1644. After describing civil government as an ordinance of God to conserve the civil peace of the people so far as concerns their bodies and goods, he goes on to say: "The sovereign, original, and foundation of civil power lies in the people (whom they must needs mean by the civil power distinct from the government set up). And if so, that a people may erect and establish what form of government seems to them most meet for their civil condition. It is evident that such governments as are by them erected and established have no more power, nor for no longer time, than the civil power or people consenting and agreeing shall betrust them with. This is clear not only in reason, but in the experience of all commonweals where the people are not deprived of their natural freedom by the power of tyrants." [6]

The central issue in seventeenth-century New England was not social equality, manhood suffrage, women's rights, or sympathy for the Levellers, or other tests which have been applied. The central issue was the source of authority for the establishment of a government. The English view was that no government could exist in a colony without a grant of power from the crown. The opposite view, held by certain English dissenters in New England, was that a group of people could create a valid government for themselves by means of a covenant, compact, or constitution. The authors of the Mayflower Compact and the Fundamental Orders of Connecticut operated on this assumption, although they did not carry it to the logical con-

[5] Roy N. Lokken, review of Theodore Thayer, *Pennsylvania Politics and the Growth of Democracy, 1740–1776* (Harrisburg, 1953), in *William and Mary Quarterly*, XII (1955), 671.

[6] *English Historical Documents,* IX, *American Colonial Documents to 1775,* ed. Merrill Jensen (London and New York, 1955), pp. 168, 226, 174.

clusion and call it democracy as did the people in Rhode Island. It is the basic assumption of the Declaration of Independence, a portion of which reads much like the words of Roger Williams written 132 years earlier.

The second proposition is that colonial governments on the eve of the Revolution did not function democratically, nor did the men who controlled them believe in democracy. Even if we agree that there was virtually manhood suffrage in Massachusetts, it is difficult, for me at least, to see it as a democracy. In 1760 the government was controlled by a superb political machine headed by Thomas Hutchinson, who with his relatives and political allies occupied nearly every important political office in the colony except the governorship. The Hutchinson oligarchy controlled the superior court, the council, the county courts, and the justices of the peace; with this structure of appointive office spread throughout the colony, it was able to control the house of representatives elected by the towns. For six years after 1760 the popular party in Boston, lead by Oxenbridge Thacher and James Otis, suffered one defeat after another at the hands of the Hutchinson machine. The popular leaders in the town of Boston tried everything from slander to mob violence to get control of the government of the colony but it was not until after the Stamp Act crisis that they were able to win a majority of the house of representatives to their side. Even then, men like James Otis did not at first realize that the Stamp Act could be turned to advantage in the fight against the Hutchinson oligarchy.[7] In terms of political support between 1760 and 1765, if Massachusetts had a democratic leader, that man was Thomas Hutchinson, a charge to which he would have been the first to issue a horrified denial.

The third proposition is that before 1774 or 1775 the revolutionary movement was not a democratic movement, except by inadvertence. The pamphleteers who wrote on political and constitutional questions, and the town and county meetings and legislatures that resolved endlessly between 1763 and 1774, were concerned with the formulation of constitutional arguments to defend the colonies and their legislatures from interference by parliament.

The colonial theorists wrote much about the British constitution, the rights of Englishmen, and even of the laws of nature, but they accepted the British assumption that colonial governments derived from British charters and commissions. Their essential concern was with the relationship that existed, or ought to exist, between the British government and the colonial governments, and not with the relationship between man as man, and government itself. Such writers showed no interest in domestic problems, and when it was suggested that the arguments against taxation by parliament were equally applicable to the taxation of under-represented areas in the colonies, or to dissenting religious groups, such suggestions were looked upon as being quite out of order.

The same indifference was displayed in the realm of political realities. The ardent leaders of the fight against British policies showed no interest in, or sympathy for, the discontent of back-country farmers or religious groups such as the Baptists. Instead, they temporarily joined with their political enemies to suppress or ignore it. Such sympathy as the discontented got, they got from the British government, or from colonial leaders charged with being tools of the British power.

----

[7] See Ellen E. Brennan, *Plural Office Holding in Massachusetts 1760–1780* (Chapel Hill, 1945), and "James Otis: Recreant and Patriot," *New England Quarterly,* XII (1939), 691–725.

The fact is that the popular leaders of the revolutionary movement had no program of domestic reform.[8] Instead, their program was a combination of a continuous assault on the local officeholding aristocracies and an ardent attack on British policies; and in the course of time they identified one with the other. It is sometimes difficult to tell with which side of the program the popular leaders were more concerned. In Massachusetts, for instance, before 1765 they were so violent in their attack on Hutchinson that they prevented Massachusetts from joining the other colonies in making formal protests against British legislation.

The fourth proposition is related to the third. It is that although the popular leaders in the colonies showed no interest in internal political and social change, they were still able to build up a political following, particularly in the seacoast towns. They were superb organizers, propagandists with a touch of genius, and possessed of an almost demonic energy in their dual fight against the local political aristocracies and British policies. After a few false starts such as that of James Otis, who at first called the Virginia Stamp Act Resolves treason,[9] the popular leaders took an extreme stand on the subject of colonial rights. The political aristocracies might object to British policies, as most of them did, but considering what they owed to British backing, they displayed an understandable caution, a caution that made it impossible for them to pose as patriotic leaders.

The popular leaders were also willing to take extreme measures in practical opposition to British policies, ranging all the way from mob violence to non-importation agreements forced upon unwilling merchants. And with ever more force and violence they accused Americans who did not agree with them or their methods of knuckling under to British tyranny and of readiness to sell the liberties of their country for a little pelf. In the course of this campaign they appealed to the people at large. Men who normally could not or did not take part in political life, particularly in the cities, were invited to mass meetings where the rules of suffrage were ignored and where they could shout approval of resolutions carefully prepared in advance by their leaders. In addition, the mob was a constant factor in political life, particularly in Boston where it was efficiently organized. Mobs were used to nullify the Stamp Act, to harass British soldiers, to hamper the operations of the customs service, and to intimidate office holders.

All these activities on the part of the disfranchised, or the hitherto politically inactive, accustomed men to taking part in public affairs as never before; and it gave them an appetite for more. From the beginning of the crisis in 1774 onward, more and more "new men," which was the politest name their opponents called them, played an ever more active role, both on the level of practical politics and on the level of political theory. They began writing about and talking about what they called "democracy." And this was a frightening experience, not only to the conservative-minded leaders of the colonies, but to many of the popular leaders as well.

For instance, when a New York mass meeting gathered in May 1774 to answer the letter of the Boston Town Meeting asking for a complete stoppage of trade with Britain as an answer to the Boston Port Act, the people talked about far more than letter writing. One alarmed observer wrote: "I beheld my fellow-citizens very accu-

[8] For example, see Irving Mark, *Agrarian Conflicts in Colonial New York, 1711–1775* (New York, 1940); *The Carolina Background on the Eve of the Revolution,* ed. Richard J. Hooker (Chapel Hill, 1953); and Elisha Douglass, *Rebels and Democrats* (Chapel Hill, 1955).

[9] Brennan, "James Otis: Recreant and Patriot," p. 715.

rately counting all their chickens, not only before any of them were hatched, but before above one half of the eggs were laid. In short, they fairly contended about the future forms of our government, whether it should be founded upon aristocratic or democratic principles." The leaders had "gulled" the mob for years, and now, said Gouverneur Morris, the mob was waking up and could no longer be fooled. The only salvation for the aristocracy of New York was peace with Britain at almost any price.[10]

Another witness to the stirrings among the people was John Adams. Unlike Gouverneur Morris, he never wavered in his belief in independence, but at the same time he was constantly concerned with the danger of an internal upheaval. Years later in his "Autobiography," he recalled as vividly as if it had happened the day before an event that took place while he was home in Massachusetts in the fall of 1775. While there he met a man who had sometimes been his client. "He, though a common horse jockey, was sometimes in the right, and I had commonly been successful in his favor in our courts of law. He was always in the law, and had been sued in many actions at almost every court. As soon as he saw me, he came up to me, and his first salutation to me was, 'Oh! Mr. Adams, what great things have you and your colleagues done for us! We can never be grateful enough to you. There are no courts of justice now in this province, and I hope there never will be another.' " Then Adams goes on: "Is this the object for which I have been contending? said I to myself, for I rode along without any answer to this wretch. Are these the sentiments of such people, and how many of them are there in the country? Half the nation for what I know; for half the nation are debtors, if not more, and these have been, in all countries, the sentiments of debtors. If the power of the country should get into such hands, and there is great danger that it will, to what purpose have we sacrificed our time, health, and everything else? Surely we must guard against this spirit and these principles, or we shall repent of all our conduct." [11]

In May of 1776, with the talk of independence filling the air and the Virginia convention planning to draft a constitution, old Landon Carter of Virginia wrote to Washington bewailing the "ambition" that had "seized on so much ignorance all over the colony as it seems to have done; for this present convention abounds with too many of the inexperienced creatures to navigate our bark on this dangerous coast. . . ." As for independence, he said, "I need only tell you of one definition that I heard of Independency: It was expected to be a form of government that, by being independent of the rich men, every man would then be able to do as he pleased. And it was with this expectation they sent the men they did, in hopes they would plan such a form. One of the delegates I heard exclaim against the Patrolling Law, because a poor man was made to pay for keeping a rich man's slaves in order. I shamed the fool so much for it that he slunk away; but he got elected by it." [12]

One could go on endlessly giving examples like these from the hectic days between 1774 and 1776, examples of the fear among leaders of all shades of opinion that the people would get or were getting out of hand. Meanwhile there was an increasing amount of political writing in the newspapers, writing which was pointing in the

[10] Gouverneur Morris to [John] Penn, May 20, 1774, in *English Historical Documents,* IX, 861–863.

[11] John Adams, "Autobiography," *The Works of John Adams,* ed. Charles F. Adams (Boston, 1856), II, 420–421.

[12] *American Archives,* ed. Peter Force, 4th ser. (Washington, 1837–1846), VI, 390–391. May 9, 1776.

direction of independence and the creation of new governments in America. More than a year before *Common Sense,* a piece which appeared first in the *Pennsylvania Packet* declared that "the history of kings is nothing but the history of the folly and depravity of human nature." "We read now and then, it is true, of a good king; so we read likewise of a prophet escaping unhurt from a lion's den, and of three men walking in a fiery furnace without having even their garments singed. The order of nature is as much inverted in the first as it was in the last two cases. A good king is a miracle." [13]

By early 1776 the debate over future governments to be·adopted was in full swing. Disliking intensely the ideas of government set forth in *Common Sense,* John Adams drafted his *Thoughts on Government.* His plan was modeled on the old government of Massachusetts, with an elective rather than a royal governor, of course, but it certainly contemplated no radical change in the political structure.[14] John Adams was no innovator. He deplored what he called "the rage for innovation" which had appeared in Massachusetts by June of 1776. The projects, said he, are not for repairing the building but for tearing it down. "The projects of county assemblies, town registers, and town probates of wills are founded in narrow notions, sordid stinginess, and profound ignorance, and tend directly to barbarism." [15]

There was equal alarm in the south at demands for change and new governments. Among those who sought to defend the old order was Carter Braxton. In a long address to the Virginia convention he praised the British constitution and declared that it would be "perverting all order to oblige us, by a novel government, to give up our laws, our customs, and our manners." The spirit or principles of limited monarchy should be preserved. Yet, he said, we daily see it condemned by the advocates of "popular governments. . . . The systems recommended to the colonies seem to accord with the temper of the times, and are fraught with all the tumult and riot incident to simple democracy. . . ." Braxton declared that democracies would not tolerate wealth, and that they could exist only in countries where all the people are poor from necessity. Nowhere in history could he find an example of a successful democracy. What he proposed for Virginia was a three-part government with a house of representatives elected by the voters for three years. The house, in turn, would choose a governor to serve during good behavior and a council of twenty-four to hold their places for life and to act as an upper house of the legislature.[16] Braxton in Virginia, like John Adams in Massachusetts, hoped to make the transition from dependence to independence without any fundamental political change.

But change was in the air, and writer after writer sought to formulate new ideas about government and to offer concrete suggestions for the theoretical foundations and political structures of the new states to be. In 1775, on hearing that congress had given advice to New Hampshire on the establishment of a government, General John Sullivan offered his thoughts to the revolutionary congress of his colony. All

---

[13] *English Historical Documents,* IX, 816–817.

[14] *Works of John Adams,* IV, 189–200.

[15] To John Winthrop, Philadelphia, June 23, 1776, in Mass. Hist. Soc. *Collections,* 5th ser. (Boston, 1878), IV, 310. This was in reply to a letter of John Winthrop, written on June 1, in which he reported to Adams on the various schemes afoot in Massachusetts. *Ibid.,* 305–308.

[16] *The Virginia Gazette* (Dixon and Hunter), June 8, 1776. This had been printed earlier in pamphlet form. For similar ideas see the letter of William Hooper, North Carolina delegate to the Continental Congress, to the North Carolina Provincial Congress, October 26, 1776, in *The Colonial Records of North Carolina,* ed. W. L. Saunders, X (1890), 866–869.

government, he wrote, ought to be instituted for the good of the people. There should be no conflicting branches in imitation of the British constitution "so much celebrated by those who understand nothing of it. . . ." The two houses of the legislature and a governor should all be elected by the people. No danger can arise to a state "from giving the people a free and full voice in their own government." The so-called checks upon the licentiousness of the people "are only the children of designing or ambitious men, no such thing being necessary. . . ." [17]

In the middle colonies appeared an address "To the People of North America on the Different Kinds of Government." After defining monarchy, aristocracy, oligarchy, and democracy, the anonymous writer said: "Popular government—sometimes termed democracy, republic, or commonwealth—is the plan of civil society wherein the community at large takes the care of its own welfare, and manages its concerns by representatives elected by the people out of their own body."

"Seeing the happiness of the people is the true end of government; and it appearing by the definition, that the popular form is the only one which has this for its object; it may be worth inquiring into the causes which have prevented its success in the world."

This writer then undertakes to explain the failure of former democracies. First of all, he says that past republics tried democracy too late and contained within them remnants of aristocracies and military cliques which disliked it. A second cause was that men did not have adequate knowledge of representation and that their large and tumultuous assemblies made it possible for unscrupulous men to charge all troubles to the constitution. A third cause of failure has been the political writers who from ignorance or ulterior motives have tried to discredit democracy. "This has been carried to such a length with many, that the mentioning a democracy constantly excites in them the idea of anarchy; and few, except such as have emancipated themselves from the shackles of political bigotry and prejudice, can talk of it with patience, and hearken to anything offered in its defence." Such are the causes of the destruction of former republics, but the Americans have the best opportunity ever open to mankind to form a free government, "the last and best plan that can possibly exist." [18]

In "The Interest of America," another writer says that new governments must soon be created in America and that "the good of the people is the ultimate end of civil government." Therefore, "we should assume that mode of government which is most equitable and adapted to the good of mankind . . . and I think there can be no doubt that a well-regulated democracy is most equitable." The annual or frequent choice of magistrates is "most likely to prevent usurpation and tyranny; and most likely to secure the privileges of the people." Legislatures should be unicameral, for a plurality of branches leads to endless contention and a waste of time.[19]

In New England, where the revolutionary congresses of Massachusetts and New Hampshire were controlled by leaders along the seacoast, there was a growing discontent among the people of the back-country counties. Out of it came one of the clearest democratic statements of the times: "The People are the Best Governors." The author starts with the premise that "there are many very noisy about liberty, but are aiming at nothing more than personal power and grandeur." "God," he said,

[17] John Sullivan to Meshech Weare, Winter Hill [Mass.], December 11, 1775, in *American Archives,* IV, 241–242.

[18] *American Archives,* V, 180–183. [March 1776.]

[19] *Ibid.,* VI, 840–843. [June 1776.]

"gave mankind freedom by nature, made every man equal to his neighbor, and has virtually enjoined them to govern themselves by their own laws." Representatives in legislatures should have only the power to make laws. They should not have power to elect officials or to elect councils or senates to veto legislation. Only the people have this power. If there must be senates, they should be elected by the people of the state at large and should have only advisory powers. Representation should not be according to taxable property, for "Nature itself abhors such a system of civil government, for it will make an inequality among the people and set up a number of lords over the rest." Representation according to population also has its difficulties. The solution is for each town to have one representative, with more for larger towns if the legislature thinks fit. So far as property qualifications for representatives are concerned, there should be none. "Social virtue and knowledge . . . is the best and only necessary qualification of the person before us." If we have property qualifications "we root out virtue; and what will then become of the genuine principle of freedom?" "Let it not be said in future generations that money was made by the founders of the American states an essential qualification in the rulers of a free people." The writer proposed annual elections of a one-house legislature, of a governor, and of the judges of the superior court. The people in the counties should elect annually all their own officials—judges, sheriffs, and others—as should the inhabitants of the towns. And in all elections "any orderly free male of ordinary capacity" should have the right to vote if he has lived in a town for a year.[20]

From such discussions one may sum up certain of the essential ideas. (1) They agree that the "good" or the "happiness" of the people is the only end of government. (2) They agree that "democracy" is the best form of government to achieve that end. (3) They show a distrust of men when in power—a distrust shared with far more conservative-minded writers of the times.

As to details of government there are variations, but they do agree on fundamentals. (1) The legislatures, whether one or two houses, are to be elected by the people. (2) Public officials, state and local, are to be elected by the people or by their representatives in the legislatures. (3) There should be annual elections. (4) Some argue for manhood suffrage, and one writer even advocated that tax-paying widows should vote. (5) There should be freedom of religion, at least for Protestants; in any case, freedom from taxation to support established churches.

One may well ask: did such theoretical discussions have any meaning in terms of practical politics, or were they idle speculations by anonymous writers without influence? The answer is that they did have meaning. I have already cited the discussion of the principles of government in New York in the spring of 1774, and the litigious jockey in Massachusetts in 1775 who hoped that the courts would remain closed forever. These are not isolated examples. By the end of 1775 all sorts of organized activity was under way, ranging in place from North Carolina to New Hampshire, and from militia groups to churches.

In North Carolina the defeat of the Regulators in 1771 had not ended discontent but merely suppressed it. By September 1775 Mecklenburg County was instructing its delegates in the provincial congress to work for a plan of government providing for equal representation and the right to vote for every freeman who supported the

---

[20] Reprinted in Frederick Chase, *A History of Dartmouth College and the Town of Hanover, New Hampshire* (Cambridge, 1891), I, Appendix D, 654–663.

government, either in person or property. Legislation should not be a "divided right"; no man or body of men should be "invested with a negative on the voice of the people duly collected. . . ." [21] By November 1776, when North Carolina elected a congress to write its first state constitution, Mecklenburg County was even more specific in its instructions. It told its delgates that they were to endeavor to establish a free government under the authority of the people of North Carolina, and that the government was to be a "simple democracy, or as near it as possible." In fixing fundamental principles, the delegates were to "oppose everything that leans to aristocracy or power in the hands of the rich and chief men exercised to the oppression of the poor." [22]

In the middle colonies militia organizations made demands and suggestions. Pennsylvania was in turmoil, with the assembly controlled by the opponents of independence and the revolutionary party working in large measure through a voluntary militia organization called the Associators. In February 1776 a committee of privates from the Philadelphia Associators told the assembly "that it has been the practice of all countries, and is highly reasonable, that all persons . . . who expose their lives in the defense of a country, should be admitted to the enjoyment of all the rights and privileges of a citizen of that country. . . ." All Associators should be given the right to vote.[23]

In June the committee of privates again protested to the legislature. This time they denied the right of the assembly to appoint two brigadier generals for the Associators as recommended by the Continental Congress. The privates declared that since many of them could not vote, they were not represented in the assembly. Furthermore, many counties where the Associators were most numerous did not have proportional representation. And for that matter, since many members of the assembly were members of a religious profession "totally averse to military defense," they could not possibly be called representatives of the Associators.[24]

While such ideas were being expounded in Pennsylvania, some militia in Maryland were proposing a new constitution. There was a growing discontent in Maryland with the revolutionary convention which was opposed to independence, and whose members were appointing one another to military posts. Government by convention should stop, said one writer, and regular government be instituted.[25]

Later in June 1776 deputies from the militia battalions in Anne Arundel County met and proposed a constitution to be submitted to the people of the county. They started out with the declaration that the right to legislate is in "every member of the community," but that for convenience the right must be delegated to representatives chosen by the people. The legislature must never form a sepaiate interest from the community at large, and its branches must "be independent of and balance each other, and all dependent on the people." There should be a two-house legislature chosen annually "as annual elections are most friendly to liberty, and the oftener power reverts to the people, the greater will be the security for a faithful discharge of it." All provincial officials, including judges, should be elected annually by joint

---

[21] Colonial Records of North Carolina, X, 239–242. [Sept. 1775.]

[22] Ibid., 870, a–f. [Nov. 1776.]

[23] Votes and Proceedings of the Assembly, Feb. 23, 1776, in Pennsylvania Archives, 8th ser. [Harrisburg, 1935], VIII, 7406.

[24] Ibid., 7546–47. June 14, 1776.

[25] "An American" in "To the People of Maryland," American Archives, VI, 1094–96.

ballot of the two houses. All county officials should be chosen annually by the people of each county. Nothing is said of property qualifications for either voting or office-holding. So far as taxes are concerned, "the unjust mode of taxation by poll" should be abolished, and all monies raised should be according to a fair and equal assessment of people's estates.[26]

In New Jersey the revolutionary congress, like that in other colonies, was trying to prevent change and was maintaining the land qualification for voting for its members. But the complaints grew so loud that it was forced to yield. One petition in 1776, for instance, declared that "we cannot conceive the wise author of our existence ever designed that a certain quantity of earth on which we tread should be annexed to a man to complete his dignity and fit him for society. Was the sole design of government either the security of land or money, the possession of either or both of these would be the only necessary qualifications for its members. But we apprehend the benign intentions of a well regulated government to extend to the security of much more valuable possessions—the rights and privileges of freemen, for the defense of which every kind of property and even life itself have been liberally expended." [27]

In Massachusetts the Baptists were quick to draw a parallel between the fight for civil liberty against England and their own fight for religious liberty. Baptists were being jailed for refusal to pay taxes to support churches. Their leader, the Reverend Isaac Backus, put Sam Adams squarely on the spot in January 1774. "I fully concur with your grand maxim," wrote Backus, "that it is essential to liberty that representation and taxation go together." Hence, since the representatives in the Massachusetts legislature have only civil qualifications, how can they levy ecclesiastical taxes? "And I am bold in it," Backus goes on, "that taxes laid by the British Parliament upon America are not more contrary to civil freedom, than these taxes are to the very nature of liberty of conscience. . . ." He hopes, he says, that Adams will do something about it so that a large number of peaceable people "may not be forced to carry their complaints before those who would be glad to hear that the legislature of Massachusetts deny to their fellow servants that liberty which they so earnestly insist upon for themselves. A word to the wise is sufficient." [28]

Samuel Adams was not interested in liberty of conscience, particularly for Baptists, and he did not reply. But Backus pursued him to the first Continental Congress in Philadelphia where a four-hour meeting was held in Carpenter's Hall one night. The Massachusetts delegation met with the Baptists, but with a large audience present, among whom were the Quaker leaders James and Israel Pemberton, and members of congress like Joseph Galloway. The Backus diary gives a picture of Sam and John Adams quite literally squirming as the Baptists cited the facts of religious life in Massachusetts.[29] One can well imagine with what delight Galloway and the Pembertons looked on as the Massachusetts delegation vainly tried to wriggle out of a dilemma produced by the contradiction between their theory and their practice.

The Declaration of Independence was taken seriously by many Americans, or at least they found its basic philosophy useful in battling for change in the new states.

[26] *Ibid.*, 1092–94. June 26–27, 1776.

[27] Richard P. McCormick, *The History of Voting in New Jersey . . . 1664–1911* (New Brunswick, 1953), pp. 66–68.

[28] To Samuel Adams, Jan. 19, 1774, in Alvah Hovey, *A Memoir of the Life and Times of the Rev. Isaac Backus* (Boston, 1859), pp. 195–197.

[29] *Ibid.*, ch. xv.

Nowhere was this done more neatly than in Grafton County, New Hampshire. The Provincial Congress was in the control of eastern leaders and they refused to grant representation that the western towns thought adequate. In calling elections in the fall of 1776, the Congress grouped various towns together for electing representatives and told them that the men they elected must own real estate worth £200 lawful money. Led by professors at an obscure little college at Hanover, the people of Grafton County went on strike. They refused to hold elections, and town after town met and passed resolutions. The whole procedure of the Congress was unconstitutional. No plan of representation had been adopted since the Declaration of Independence. By the Declaration, said Hanover and two other towns in a joint statement, "we conceive that the powers of government reverted to the people at large, and of course annihilated the political existence of the Assembly which then was. . . ." Six other towns joined together and declared it to be "our humble opinion, that when the declaration of independency took place, the Colonies were absolutely in a state of nature, and the powers of government reverted to the people at large. . . ." Such being the case, the Provincial Congress has no authority to combine towns, each of which is entitled to representation as a corporate entity. And it has no right to limit the choice of representatives to the owners of £200, said the people of Lyme, because "every elector in free states is capable of being elected." [30]

It seems clear, to me at least, that by 1776 there were people in America demanding the establishment of democratic state governments, by which they meant legislatures controlled by a majority of the voters, and with none of the checks upon their actions such as had existed in the colonies. At the same time there were many Americans who were determined that there should be no changes except those made inevitable by separation from Great Britain.

The history of the writing of the first state constitutions is to a large extent the history of the conflict between these two ideals of government. The conflict can be exaggerated, of course, for there was considerable agreement on structural details. Most of the state constitutions worked out in written form the structure of government that had existed in the colonies, all the way from governors, two-house legislatures, and judicial systems, to the forms of local government. In terms of structure, little that is revolutionary is to be found. Even the much maligned unicameral legislature of Pennsylvania was only a continuation of what Pennsylvania had had since the beginning of the century.

The significant thing is not the continuity of governmental structure, but the alteration of the balance of power within the structure, and in the political situation resulting from the break away from the supervising power of a central government— that of Great Britain.

The first and most revolutionary change was in the field of basic theory. In May 1776, to help bring about the overthrow of the Pennsylvania assembly, the chief stumbling block in the way of independence, Congress resolved that all governments exercising authority under the crown of Great Britain should be suppressed, and that "all the powers of government [be] exerted under the authority of the people of the colonies. . . ." John Adams described it as "the most important resolution that ever was taken in America." [31] The Declaration of Independence spelled it out in terms

[30] *American Archives*, 5th ser. (Washington, 1848–1853), III, 1223–24, and Chase, *History of Dartmouth*, I, 426–433.

[31] *Warren-Adams Letters*, I (Boston, 1917), 245; in Mass. Hist. Soc. *Collections*, Vols. 72, 73.

of the equality of men, the sovereignty of the people, and the right of a people to change their governments as they pleased.

Second: the Revolution ended the power of a sovereign central government over the colonies. Britain had had the power to appoint and remove governors, members of upper houses of legislatures, judges, and other officials. It had the power to veto colonial legislation, to review cases appealed from colonial supreme courts, and to use armed force. All of this superintending power was wiped out by independence.

Third: the new central government created in America by the Articles of Confederation was, in a negative sense at least, a democratic government. The Congress of the United States had no power over either the states or their citizens. Hence, each state could govern itself as it pleased, and as a result of some of the new state constitutions, this often meant by a majority of the voters within a state.

Fourth: in writing the state constitutions, change was inevitable. The hierarchy of appointed legislative, executive, and judicial officials which had served as a check upon the elective legislatures was gone. The elective legislature became the supreme power in every state, and the lower houses, representing people however inadequately, became the dominant branch. The appointive houses of colonial times were replaced by elective senates, which in theory were supposed to represent property. They were expected to, and sometimes did, act as a check upon the lower houses, but their power was far less than that of pre-war councils.

Fifth: the office of governor underwent a real revolution. The governors of the royal colonies had, in theory at least, vast powers, including an absolute veto. In the new constitutions, most Americans united in shearing the office of governor of virtually all power.

Sixth: state supreme courts underwent a similar revolution. Under the state constitutions they were elected by the legislatures or appointed by governors who were elected officials. And woe betide a supreme court that tried to interfere with the actions of a legislature.

What such changes meant in terms of political realities was that a majority of voters within a state, if agreed upon a program and persistent enough, could do what it wanted, unchecked by governors or courts or appeals to a higher power outside the state.

There were other areas in which changes took place, although they were only beginnings. A start was made in the direction of ending the property qualification for voting and office-holding. A few states established what amounted to manhood suffrage, and a few years later even women voted in New Jersey although that was stopped when it appeared that woman suffrage meant only a means of stuffing ballot boxes. A few states took steps in the direction of representation according to population, a process as yet unsolved in the United States. A large step was taken in the direction of disestablishing state churches, but on the whole one still had to be a Protestant, and a Trinitarian at that, to hold office.

In connection with office-holding, there is one eighteenth-century American idea that is worthy of a whole study by itself, and that is the concept of rotation in office. Many Americans were convinced that office-holding bred a lust for power in the holder. Therefore there must be frequent, if not annual, elections; and there must be a limitation on the time one might spend in certain offices. There is probably no more remarkable self-denying ordinance in the history of politics than the provision in the Articles of Confederation that no man could be a member of Congress more than three years out of any six. I have often been accused of wanting to go back to the Articles of Confederation, which is nonsense, but there are times when I do wish that this one provision might be revived in the twentieth century.

What I have done in this paper is to set before you some of the reasons for believing that the American Revolution was a democratic movement, not in origin, but in result. Certainly the political leaders of the eighteenth century thought the results were democratic. Whether they thought the results were good or bad is another story.

16 / Historians and the Problem of Early American Democracy

J. R. Pole

In the preceding essay, Merrill Jensen presented his views on the democratic impetus behind part of the revolutionary movement in America. On the following pages, an English scholar, J. R. Pole, carefully considers the relevance of modern "democratic" values in assessing some aspects of eighteenth-century politics. At the present it is perhaps understandable—if theoretically regrettable—that so many writers and readers adopt an almost apologetic tone in explaining that colonial America had not yet achieved all of the wonders of modern democratic life, that its laws still restricted the franchise to property-holders, and that its practices still restricted office-holding to the richer property-holders. Pole raises some serious objections to such anachronistic approaches to the political life of the American colonies as they became the American states and suggests that such approaches obscure some of the important features of the way in which politics actually functioned during the eighteenth century. Two matters mentioned in his essay should perhaps be emphasized. While the author notes the persistence of a habit of deference in selecting political leaders, he also mentions what modern scholarship has generally borne out: even though there was a universal property qualification for voting in the years before 1776, the franchise was widespread among adult males in colonial America. Secondly, the Americans, as they established their new governments, did engage in a series of notable experiments in the exercise of the constituent power. In Massachusetts, for example, all adult males—property-owners or not—were eligible to vote on the ratification of the new state Constitution of 1780. In ratifying that Constitution, however, the voters of Massachusetts restricted the future exercise of the franchise— as it had been restricted under the colonial Charter of 1691—to certain classes of property-holders. The inhabitants of Massachusetts thus exercised their constituent power so as to limit some kinds of popular participation in politics. Europeans noted the experiment of Americans in employing the

Reprinted by permission of the author from the *American Historical Review,* LXVII (1962), 626–646.

"people" as the constituent power; present-day Americans should perhaps note that this activity did not necessarily lead in a direction that later generations would regard as "democratic."

The earliest national period of United States history combines two themes. It is a period of revolution and also of constitution making. Charter governments, whether royal or proprietary, give way to new governments which claim to derive the whole of their authority from the American electorate. The Americans, though working from experience, build for the future. This fact is of cardinal importance for any attempt to understand their work or the state of mind in which it was undertaken.

The claim of the new government raises a problem that was not solved by the mere exercise of effective, but revolutionary powers. Was their authority strictly compatible with the doctrine that governments derive their just powers from the consent of the governed? What was meant by "consent"? How was such consent obtained or certified?

The attempt to answer these questions leads the historian into a reconstruction of the character of these early institutions and an inquiry into the ideas by which they were governed. In the light of subsequent American development, it has led historians to address themselves to the problem of deciding whether or not these institutions were democratic. Whether or not we choose to adopt this particular definition, whether or not we regard it as a useful tool of analysis, the underlying problem is one that the historian cannot easily avoid. No history of the American Revolution and of constitution making could be written without discussion of the doctrines on which the Americans based their resistance, the question of what meaning these doctrines bore for the different American participants, and of the degree of participation, the attitude and purposes of different elements in American society.

There is a problem of the relationship of ideas to institutions; there is a previous problem of the ideas themselves. I do not think that the broad and undifferentiated use of the term "democracy" helps either to describe the institutions or to explain the ideas. I do not even think that our analysis of these matters will be much affected by the use of this concept. But the thesis has been advanced [1] that the American colonies were already full-fledged democracies before the American Revolution began, from which it follows that the cardinal principle of the Revolution was a defense of democratic institutions against royal or parliamentary tyranny. It is a thesis that has the advantage of an attractive simplicity, and it is one that can be supported by a good deal of evidence, especially if that evidence is read without much relation to the context of eighteenth-century political ideas. It also has the merit of providing the occasion, and in order that the argument should not go by default, the necessity of a more searching inquiry into the realities.

To use the word "democracy" is to raise, but not I think to solve, a problem of definition. And it is not an easy one. There is so little agreement about what is meant by "democracy," and the discussion has such a strong tendency to slide noiselessly from what we *do* mean to what we *ought* to mean, that for purposes of definition it seems to be applicable only in the broadest sense. And this sense has the effect of limiting, rather than of advancing, our understanding of the past.

[1] Robert E. Brown, *Middle-Class Democracy and the Revolution in Massachusetts, 1691–1780* (Ithaca, N. Y., 1955), esp. 401–408.

But I must certainly admit that if I did think the word "democracy" in fact did justice to the problem, then I would have to accept it despite the risks involved. More than this: we ought to have some agreement as to what meaning it can be made to bear. It makes good sense in a purely comparative view to call the American colonies and early states democratic when contrasting them with the Prussia of Frederick II or the Habsburg Empire; they were in the same sense democratic compared with France or with England, with which they had so much in common. There might be less unintended irony in calling them part of the "free world" than in doing the same today with Spain, Formosa, or the Union of South Africa. In the broad strokes we use to differentiate between tyrannies and free states the term will serve as a starting point, but not as a conclusion. It is interesting, when one begins to look more closely at the structure of the complex societies of the eighteenth century, how rapidly these broad distinctions lose their value and cease to serve any analytical purpose. As R. R. Palmer has recently remarked, surveying the Western world before the French Revolution, "No one except a few disgruntled literary men supposed that he lived under a despotism." [2] When one considers how complex the machinery of administration, of justice, for the redress of grievances and, if any, of political representation must become in any ancient and intricately diversified society, it is easy to feel that the more democratic virtues of the American societies were related, more than anything else, to their relative simplicity and lack of economic and functional diversity. But a closer inspection, not only of the structure, but of the development, of colonial institutions reveals a tendency that puts the matter in another light; for these institutions were unmistakably molded in the shape of English institutions and were conforming themselves, both socially and politically, to the conventions of the period.

The alternative view, which I want to suggest, does not confine itself merely to rejecting the "democratic" interpretation by putting in its place a flat, antidemocratic account of the same set of institutions. What it does, I think, is to see the democratic elements in their proper perspective by adding a further dimension without which the rest is flat, incomplete, and, for all its turbulence, essentially lifeless. This is the dimension of what Cecelia Kenyon has called "institutional thought." [3]

To take this view, one has to free oneself from a tendency that has become very difficult to resist. I mean the strong, though wholly anachronistic tendency to suppose that when people who were accustomed to ways and ideas which have largely disappeared into the past felt grievances against their government, they must necessarily have wanted to express their dissatisfaction by applying the remedies of modern democracy; and, again, that when their demands were satisfied, the aspirations thus fulfilled must have been modern, democratic aspirations.

The idea that the great mass of the common people might actually have given their consent to concepts of government that limited their own participation in ways completely at variance with the principles of modern democracy is one that lies completely outside the compass or comprehension of the "democratic" interpretation. That interpretation insists on the all-importance of certain democratic features of political life, backed by certain egalitarian features of social life having a strong influence on political institutions. What it misses is that these features belonged within a frame-

[2] R. R. Palmer, *The Age of the Democratic Revolution* (Princeton, N. J., 1959), 51.
[3] Cecelia M. Kenyon, "Men of Little Faith: The Anti-Federalists on the Nature of Representative Government," *William and Mary Quarterly*, XII (Jan. 1955), 4.

work which—to polarize the issue at the risk of using another broad term—was known to the world as Whiggism. The institutions of representative government derived from the time when the Whig concept of representative government was being worked out in England and, both by extension and by original experience, in the American colonies (and when the foundations were laid for the Whig interpretation of history). Even where democratic elements were strong and dominant, the animating ideas belonged to a whole Whig world of both politics and society. More than this, the colonial and early national period in which they played so important a part was pervaded by a belief in and a sense of the propriety of social order guided and strengthened by principles of dignity on the one hand and deference on the other. It was, to use the term coined by Walter Bagehot in his account of Victorian England, a deferential society.[4]

There is, of course, nothing very new about the theory that early American society was relatively egalitarian and that this situation was reflected in political institutions and conduct. It was a view that became fashionable in the days of George Bancroft. But it has been reformulated, with formidable documentation, in Robert E. Brown's work on Massachusetts and in his attack on Charles Beard.[5] To regain our perspective it seems necessary for a moment to go back to Beard.

Beard, as we know, distinguished in his study of the Constitution between two leading types of propertied interest, basically those of land and commerce. Commercial property was supposed to have been strongly represented in the Constitutional Convention, landed property outside. The opposition in some of the state ratifying conventions was supposed to have arisen from the outraged interests of the landed classes.

Despite intense opposition in certain states, the Constitution was eventually ratified. But here Beard went further. He asserted that ratification was not a true expression of the will of the people. He based this argument on the prevalence of property qualifications for the suffrage, which meant that only a minority of freeholders and other owners of property could participate in the elections to the ratifying conventions, which in consequence were not truly representative. There are two elements in Beard's hypothesis, as Brown has pointed out.[6] On the one hand, Beard advances the alleged clash between the mercantile and landed interests, with the mercantile coming out on top because of the power conferred by its economic advantages; on the other, he implies the existence of a connection between the landed opposition to ratification and the supposedly disfranchised masses, whose silence so damagingly detracts from the authority of the Constitution. It is not my purpose to discuss the question as to whether Beard's argument has stood the test of recent scrutiny. Another aspect, which may be called that of the moral consequences of Beard's work, deserves more consideration than it has received.

The Philadelphia Convention was described by Thomas Jefferson as "an assembly of demi-gods," a judgment to which posterity murmured "Amen." There are, however,

---

[4] See also E. S. Griffith, *History of American City Government: Colonial Period* (New York, 1938), 191; Clifford K. Shipton, review of Brown, *Middle-Class Democracy, Political Science Quarterly,* LXXI (No. 2, 1956), 306–308.

[5] Robert E. Brown, *Charles Beard and the Constitution: A Critical Analysis of "An Economic Interpretation of the Constitution"* (Princeton, N. J., 1956).

[6] *Ibid.,* 50–51, 53–55, 180–81, 194.

marked disadvantages about being descended from demi-gods; they not only lack a sense of humor, but they set an appallingly high standard. What a relief it must have been, after the first shock of Beard's iconoclasm had died down, to find that they were only human after all! Beard had questioned the Constitution at two points. In the first place, by implying that it was the work of men motivated by private economic interests he made it possible to reconsider its wisdom and justice; but in the second place, when he denied that it had received the sanction of a genuine, popular ratification he made it possible—perhaps obligatory—to question the authority of the Constitution precisely because it did not owe its origin to the only recognized source of such authority in the whole science of government as understood in America: the consent of the governed.

To this problem, Brown's critique of Beard is directly relevant. He not only pursues Beard with a determination that recalls John Horace Round's pursuit of Edward Freeman, but in his work on Massachusetts, he makes a thorough and painstaking investigation of the institutions of that province, in which he reaches the conclusion that colonial Massachusetts was already so fully democratic that no case can be made for an interpretation of the American Revolution there in terms of an internal "class war." It is in this connection that Brown broadens his front to develop an attack on Carl Becker.[7] The Revolution was a war of secession, fought for the preservation of American democracy against the antidemocratic policy of the crown. Nothing more, and nothing less. The joint foundations of all this are the wide extent of the suffrage franchise and the wide distribution of middling quantities of property.

The consequences are obvious. If the states, and not only the states but the colonies, were ruled by the consent of the governed, then Beard's unenfranchised masses disappear, and the Constitution is restored to its high place not only in the affection of the American people, but in their scale of approbation.

American history has been written not merely as the story of the people who went to, and lived in, America. It has been developed as the history of liberty. Innumerable books carry in their titles the message that colonial development was a progress toward liberty; since the Revolution, it has sometimes been possible to discern in accounts of American history a certain messianic quality, which some have felt to have been reflected periodically in American diplomacy. History written in this way frequently finds itself obliged to ask how a man, or a movement, stands in relation to the particular values for which American history is responsible. A recent study of Alexander Hamilton's place in the origins of political parties, for example, speaks of the need to determine Hamilton's "rightful place in our history." [8] It becomes important, not just to write a man's biography or to assess his contribution, but to place him correctly on the eternal curve upon which American political performances seem to be graded.

The writing of history thus becomes a matter, not only of finding out what actually happened, but of judging the past. It is a process that cuts both ways. For earlier generations of Americans were keenly—almost disconcertingly—aware of the example they were setting for their descendants. (There is a town meeting entry in Massachu-

[7] Brown, *Middle-Class Democracy*, Chap. IV.

[8] Joseph E. Charles, "Hamilton and Washington," *William and Mary Quarterly*, XII (Apr. 1955), 226. A further example in connection with Hamilton, whose career provokes this kind of judgment, is found in the title of Louis M. Hacker's *Alexander Hamilton in the American Tradition* (New York, 1957).

setts, in 1766, which calls the attention of future generations to the sacrifices the townsmen were making for their liberties.[9]) They knew that they would be judged. They were not only building institutions, they were setting standards, for the future. This can become a nerve-racking business. As has been remarked in a different connection (by a writer in the *Times Literary Supplement*) the past and the present seem to watch each other warily as from opposite boxes at the opera, each suspecting the other of being about to commit a *faux pas*.[10]

The two great instruments of American nationhood were the Revolution, with its banner, the Declaration of Independence, and the Constitution. Baptism and confirmation. It would be hard to imagine a more important commitment, not only for the interpretation of the American experience, but one might almost say for the emotional stability of the interpreter, than to place his own values in their proper relation to these events, or if that cannot be done, then to place these events in their proper relation to his values.

Accordingly, historians have brought the problem of values firmly into their assessment of history. They ask, "How democratic was early American society?" And they do not hesitate to reply, if their findings tell them so, that it was not democratic enough. Or, which is still more confusing, that it was struggling forward toward a fuller ideal of democracy. Accounts of this period repeatedly explain that such features of government as property qualifications for the suffrage and political office were still regarded as necessary at that time. "Still." These people had the right instincts; they were coming on nicely; but, unlike ourselves, they had not yet arrived.

There thus develops a tendency to adopt a completely anachronistic note of apology for the insufficiency of democratic principles in early American institutions.[11]

I would like here to anticipate the objection that I am advocating that moral judgments should be taken out of historical writing. Neither do I deny that major developments can and ought to be traced to their minor origins. Moral judgments about the past are not necessarily anachronistic. It is not, I think, unhistorical to believe that some of the acts of treachery and cruelty or of violent aggression which comprise so great a proportion of recorded human activity were morally wrong, or even to maintain that they influenced the course of events for the worse. But when judgments of moral value are applied to complex social systems, they expose the judge to a peculiar danger of self-deception, perhaps even of self-incrimination. The historian must not only be careful, he must also be highly self-critical, when he embarks on assessments of the moral shortcomings of the past.

The reading of values into historical analysis is particularly liable to deception when the values of the present are themselves made the basis for the selection of materials, which are then judged in the light of the values in question. This may happen when the importance of different institutions or opinions is estimated on the basis of our own opinion of the role they ought to have played in their own time.

[9] Lucius R. Paige, *A History of Cambridge, Massachusetts, 1630–1877* (New York, 1883), 137.

[10] "Imaginative Historians: Telling the News about the Past," *Times Literary Supplement, Special Supplement on The American Imagination*, Nov. 6, 1959.

[11] Even Brown does so. In pointing out how few men were disfranchised in Massachusetts, he significantly remarks, "We cannot condone the practice of excluding those few," though he rightly adds that it makes a tremendous difference whether they were 95 per cent or 5 per cent. Brown, *Middle-Class Democracy*, 402.

Without doubt there is a place for such judgments. There is a place for criticism of the Hanoverian House of Commons—rather a large place. But when we discuss that body our task is not that of apologizing for the fact that the bright light of nineteenth-century democracy had not yet broken on such persons as Pitt or Burke or Shelburne or Fox. Our problem, as I understand it, is that of reconstructing the inner nature of political society in their age and of asking how far Parliament answered the needs of that society, and how far it did not. And that is a matter of what history was actually about, not what it ought to have been about. The historian has a responsibility to the past, but it is not that of deciding within what limits he can recommend it to the approbation of his readers.

The American Revolution was certainly a war for self-determination. But self-determination and democracy are not interchangeable terms, though they can be confused with a facility that has not been without its significance in American diplomacy. A society need not be democratic in order to achieve a high degree of internal unity when fighting for self-determination. Again, a measure of democracy, or a wider diffusion of political power, may well be brought about as an outcome of such a struggle. Such a development was in fact one of the most important consequences of the American Revolution.

It must be acknowledged that the sources of colonial history supply an impressive quantity of material that can be marshaled against my own views of this subject, though not enough as yet to weaken my conviction of the validity of historical evidence.

Much evidence of this sort comes from New England, and Massachusetts is rich in examples. In 1768 General Thomas Gage wrote to Viscount Hillsborough, "from what has been said, your lordship will conclude, that there is no government in Boston, there is in truth, very little at present, and the constitution of the province leans so much to democracy, that the governor has not the power to remedy the disorders which happen in it." [12] The next year Sir Francis Bernard wrote to Viscount Barrington,

> . . . for these 4 years past so uniform a system for bringing all power into the hands of the people has been prosecuted without interruption and with such success that all fear, reverence, respect and awe which before formed a tolerable balance against the power of the people, are annihilated, and the artificial weights being removed, the royal scale mounts up and kicks the beam. . . . It would be better that Mass. Bay should be a complete republic like Connecticut than to remain with so few ingredients of royalty as shall be insufficient to maintain the real royal character. [13]

In 1766 Thomas Hutchinson reported: "In the town of Boston a plebeian party always has and I fear always will command and for some months past they have governed the province." [14] Describing elections in 1772, Hutchinson told Hillsborough, "By the constitution forty pounds sterl.—which they say may be in clothes household furniture or any sort of property is a qualification and even into that there is scarce

[12] *Correspondence of General Thomas Gage* . . . , ed. Clarence E. Carter (2 vols., New Haven, Conn., 1931, 1933), I, 205.

[13] Quoted by R. V. Harlow, *History of Legislative Methods before 1825* (New Haven, Conn., 1917), 39–40.

[14] Brown, *Middle-Class Democracy*, 57.

ever any inquiry and anything with the appearance of a man is admitted without scrutiny." [15]

The franchise was certainly broad. Brown has shown that in many towns as many as 80 per cent of the adult male population, in some more than 90 per cent, were qualified by their property to vote in provincial elections.[16] Three towns appear in the nineties, three in the fifties, the rest in between. These findings tend to confirm and strengthen the impression that prevailed among contemporaries, that Massachusetts was a hotbed of "democratical" or "levelling" principles: the more so after the Boston junta got control of the General Court.

These expressions raise two issues, one of definition, the other of interpretation.

The point of definition first: when the indignant officers of government described these provinces as "democratical," they were of course not talking about representative government with universal suffrage. They shared not only with their correspondents, but in the last analysis even with their political opponents, the assumption that the constitutions of the colonies, like that of Britain, were made up of mixed elements; they were mixed constitutions, in which the commons were represented in the assembly or commons house. In each constitution there were different orders, and the justification, the *raison d'être,* of such a constitution was that it gave security to each. When they said that the government was becoming "too democratical" or "leaned towards democracy" they meant that the popular element was too weighty for the proper balance of a mixed constitution. They used these expressions as terms of abuse. Not that that matters: we may be impressed by their indignation, but we are not obliged to share it. What is more important to the historian is that the leaders of these movements which took control of the assemblies were in general prepared to accept the same set of definitions.

This they demonstrated when they came to establish new constitutions. The theory of mixed government was maintained with as little adulteration as possible. The difference they had to face was that all the "orders" now drew their position in the government from some form of popular representation. Most of the new constitutions represented the adaptation of institutions which undeniably received their authority from the people, an authority conceived, if not in liberty, then certainly in a revolutionary situation, to the traditional and equally important theory of balanced government.

This does not dispose of the second point, that of interpretation. Suppose that, in this form of mixed government, the "democratical" arm actually gathers up a preponderance of political power. This, after all, was what happened in the Revolution and had been happening long before. Does this give us a democracy? It is a question of crucial importance and one to which one school of thought returns an uncritically affirmative answer. Much of the power and internal influence within each colony was indeed concentrated in its assembly. This concentration reflected, or rather represented, the distribution of power and influence in the colony in general. If the domestic distribution of power tends toward oligarchy rather than democracy—to use the language of the time—then the power of that oligarchy will be exercised in, and through, the assembly itself: just as in the House of Commons. A difference of degree,

[15] *Ibid.*, 291.
[16] *Ibid.*, 50.

not of kind. And in fact this most significant aspect of the domestic situation in the colonies applied with hardly less force in leveling Boston than in high-toned Virginia.

In Virginia one feels that an immigrant from England would at once have been at home.[17] There were many instances of hotly contested elections, of treating and corruption, of sharp practice by sheriffs. It would not be difficult, however, to adduce evidence of democratic tendencies in Virginia elections. Especially in the spring elections of 1776 there were many signs that the freeholders were taking their choice seriously, and several distinguished gentlemen were either turned out of their seats or given a nasty fright. But it is an unmistakable feature of Virginia elections that although the freeholders participated often quite fully, the contests were almost invariably between members of the gentry. To seek election to the House of Burgesses was to stake a distinct claim to social rank. Virginia elections were of course conducted viva voce under the friendly supervision of the local magnates. The comparatively broad base of politics in Virginia makes it all the more instructive to look into the real concentration of political power. There were two main areas: the House of Burgesses and the county courts (not taking account of the council and governor).

Effective power in the House of Burgesses was concentrated in a few hands. The house began to use the committee system in the late seventeenth century and had brought it to a high efficiency well before the middle of the eighteenth.[18] The famous Virginia ruling families of this era always occupied a large share of the key positions, enough to ensure their own domination. Before the Revolution, of some hundred members who regularly attended the house, only about twenty took an active part in proceedings. Three families, the Robinsons, the Randolphs, and the Lees, provided most of the leaders. A very recent study shows that of 630 members between 1720 and 1776, only 110 belonged throughout the period to the "select few who dominated the proceedings of the house." [19]

These men, many of whom were linked by ties of family, had the characteristics of a strong social and political elite. They were large landowners and generally were substantial slaveowners. Some were merchants. A few, such as Edmund Pendleton, had arrived by intellectual ability and hard work combined with legal training. But Pendleton had the patronage of a great family. All those with ambition were land speculators. This gave them an interest in western development, an interest which no doubt extended to the policy of making western areas attractive to the prospective settler. Probably for this reason they wanted to extend the suffrage, which they twice tried to do in the 1760's by reducing the amount of uncleared land required as a qualification. The crown disallowed these acts, though on other grounds. This reform was completed in the first election law after the Revolution. Despite the famous reforms pressed through by Jefferson, no concessions were made on matters of fundamental importance. It is a striking tribute to the tremendous security of their hold on the country that in the new state constitution there was no provision for special quali-

[17] Charles S. Sydnor, *Gentlemen Freeholders* (Chapel Hill, N. C., 1952); David J. Mays, *Edmund Pendleton, 1721–1803* (2 vols., Cambridge, Mass., 1952); J. R. Pole, "Representation and Authority in Virginia from the Revolution to Reform," *Journal of Southern History,* XXIV (Feb. 1958), 16–50.

[18] Harlow, *Legislative Methods,* 10–11.

[19] Jack P. Greene, "Foundations of Political Power in the Virginia House of Burgesses, 1720–1766," *William and Mary Quarterly,* XVI (Oct. 1959), 485–506; quotation from p. 485.

fications for membership in the legislature. The qualifications of voters and of representatives for the time being remained as before. It is a silent piece of evidence, possibly, but one that speaks loudly of their eminent self-confidence.

Life in the counties was dominated by the county courts, which touched the interests of the common people far more closely than did the remote and occasional meetings of the legislature. The courts, which knew little of any doctrine of separation of powers, exercised all the main functions of both legislative and judicial administration. These included tax assessment, granting licenses, supervising highways, and authorizing constructions. They had nothing elective in their nature. Membership was by co-option. The courts made the important county nominations for confirmation by the governor. And the county courts were made up of the leading men of the county, representing at the local level the material of which the House of Burgesses was composed at the central. They seem on the whole to have worked well enough. And it is likely that if they had in fact been elected by the freeholders, their membership would have been about the same. Assuredly they were not tyrannical; equally certainly they were not democratic. They were a good example of what is usually meant by oligarchy.

What happened in the American Revolution in Virginia was that the policies of the British government clashed with the interests of this ambitious, proud, self-assured, and highly competent provincial government. In arguing its case, both to the British authorities and to its own people, this government appealed to the principles on which it claimed to be founded, which were philosophically the same and historically comparable to those of Parliament itself. For historical reasons, the Virginia Whigs were somewhat closer to the radical, or popular side, of the Whig spectrum. But in Virginia as in other provinces, it was the principles generally understood as Whig principles that were at stake, and it was these principles which were affirmed and re-established in the new set of domestic state constitutions.

From time to time, as the war went on, the upper classes felt tremors of alarm in which they revealed something of their relationship to the common people.

Thus John Augustine Washington, writing to Richard Henry Lee of the difficulties of getting the militia to obey a marching order, and the secret proceedings by which they bound themselves to stand by each other in refusing to leave the state, remarked: "I fear we have among us some designing dangerous characters who misrepresent to ignorant, uninformed people, the situation of our affairs and the nature of the contest, making them believe it is a war produced by the wantonness of the gentlemen, and that the poor are very little, if any interested." [20] Another of Lee's correspondents, on the need to arouse popular support, wrote: "The spark of liberty is not yet extinct among our people, and if properly fanned by the Gentlemen of Influence will, I make no doubt, burst out again into a flame." [21]

These hints, these references which illuminate the assumptions of political life, often reveal more than formal expositions of doctrine, or even the official records.

These "Gentlemen of Influence," the ruling class, were prepared to extend the suffrage when it suited their interest to do so in the 1760's, but refused to take the same step when it would have opened the question of political power, a generation later. The first demands for reform, in both suffrage and distribution of representa-

---

[20] Quoted in Pole, "Representation and Authority in Virginia," 28.
[21] Ibid., 28–29.

tion, began to appear about the turn of the century. And these demands were met with a prolonged and bitter resistance, leading only to reluctant and unsatisfactory concessions even in the famous constitutional convention of 1829–1830. The struggle was carried on until a more substantial extension of political rights was at last achieved in 1850. The forces that Virginia's political leadership so long and so determinedly held at bay can, I think, without exaggeration, be called the forces of democracy.

It is a very familiar fact about the early state constitutions that they were generally conservative in character, in that they retained much of the principles and structure of the governments of the colonies. The colonies were already self-governing in the main, and this self-government was administered by representative institutions. When one's attention is confined to these institutions, it can soon become rather difficult to see in what respect they were not, in a common-sense use of the word, democratic. After all, they were accessible to the people, they received petitions and redressed grievances, they possessed the inestimable right of free speech, and in the battles they fought, they were often engaged, in the interest of the colonies, against royal governors.

All these features were not merely consistent with, they were the formative elements of, the great Whig tradition of Parliament since the Glorious Revolution and before. They were, like so many other things, derivable from Locke. With certain exceptions, such as the difficulty of the Regulator rising in North Carolina, it would be true that colonial assemblies lay closer to the people than did the British House of Commons. For one thing, there were far more representatives per head of population in the colonies than in Britain. Parliament had 1 member to every 14,300 persons, the colonies approximately 1 to every 1,200.[22] And this meant that legislative methods and principles were more likely to be familiar to the ordinary colonist. To put it in contemporary terms, the colonies, on the whole, had a great many more constituencies like Middlesex or Westminster, except that they were mostly country and not town constituencies. It might be very close to the mark to press the analogy further and say that they had a great many constituencies that very much resembled Yorkshire—the Yorkshire of Sir George Savile, the Yorkshire of Christopher Wyvill.

What does seem striking about these in many ways highly representative colonial assemblies is, as I suggested earlier, the determination and sureness of touch with which they assumed the characteristics of Parliament. These were characteristics originally designed to secure the liberty of the people's representatives: free speech in debate, freedom of members from arrest or molestation, and freedom of the assembly from abuse by breach of privilege. But there were all too many occasions on which it must have seemed that these safeguards were designed to secure the assemblies against abuse, in the form of free speech and fair comment, by their own constituents.[23]

The colonial assemblies became extraordinarily sensitive to the question of privilege. Strictly from an institutional viewpoint, they were deliberately building on the tradition of Parliament. But institutional studies always seem to tempt the historian to arrive at his answer the short way, by examining structure, without asking questions about development.

[22] Mary P. Clarke, *Parliamentary Privilege in the American Colonies* (New Haven, Conn., 1943), 268.
[23] *Ibid.*, 127.

Much research has recently been done on what Palmer calls the "constituted bodies" [24] which held a strong and growing position in the Western world in the eighteenth century. They were numerous and differed greatly, one from another, and from one century to another—first of all the variety of political or judicial bodies: diets, estates, assemblies, parlements; then the professional associations or guilds; as well as religious orders, and those of the nobilities of Europe.

There seems strong reason for holding that the colonial assemblies were behaving in close conformity with the other bodies of this general type. At their best they were closer to local interests, but no less characteristically, they displayed a remarkable diligence in the adoption of parliamentary abuses. They would send their messengers far into the outlying country to bring to the bar of the house some individual who was to be humbled for having committed a breach of privilege, which very often meant some private action affecting the dignity or even the property of the sitting member. Criticism of the assemblies, either verbal or written, was a risky business. The freedom of the colonial press was very largely at the mercy of the assembly's sense of its own dignity, so much so that a recent investigator doubts whether the famous Zenger case,[25] which is supposed to have done so much toward the establishment of freedom of the press in the colonies, really had any general significance or immediate consequences. The fact is that restrictions on free press comment on assembly actions were not the policy of the crown but the policy of the assemblies.

Expulsions from colonial assemblies were frequent. And in case a parallel with the action of the Commons in the Wilkes case were needed to round off the picture, we may remark that colonial assemblies repeatedly excluded members who had been lawfully elected by their constituents.[26]

There was another feature in which these assemblies showed their affinity with the outlook of their times. In spite of the amount of choice open to the electors, there was a growing tendency for public office, both the elective and the appointive kinds, to become hereditary. It was of course very pronounced in Europe; it is surely no less significant when we see it at work in America. The same family names occur, from generation to generation, in similar positions. And this was no less true in New England than in Virginia or South Carolina or Maryland.

If this was democracy, it was a democracy that wore its cockade firmly pinned into its periwig.

One of the most interesting consequences of the revolutionary situation was that it demanded of political leaders a declaration of their principles. Thus we get the famous Virginia Bill of Rights, the work of George Mason; the Declaration of Rights attached to the 1780 constitution of Massachusetts; and the constitutions themselves, with all that they reveal or imply of political ideas; and in the case of Massachusetts we can go even further, for there survive also, in the archives of that state in Boston, the returns of the town meetings which debated that constitution and in many cases recorded their vote, clause by clause.

This constitution, in fact, was submitted to the ratification of what counted then as the whole people—all the adult males in the state. The constitutional convention had been elected on the same basis. The constitution which was framed on this im-

[24] Palmer, *Democratic Revolution*, 27–44.

[25] Leonard W. Levy, "Did the Zenger Case Really Matter? Freedom of the Press in Colonial New York," *William and Mary Quarterly*, XVII (Jan. 1960), 35–50.

[26] Clarke, *Parliamentary Privilege*, 194–96.

pressive foundation of popular sovereignty was certainly not a democratic instrument. It was an articulate, indeed a refined expression, of the Whig view of government— of government-in-society—as applied to the existing conditions in Massachusetts, and as interpreted by John Adams.

The property qualifications for the suffrage were, in round figures, about what they had been under the charter. In practice they proved to have very little effect by way of restricting participation in elections. The introduction of decidedly steeper qualifications for membership in the assembly meant that that body would be composed of the owners of the common, upward of one-hundred-acre family farm, and their mercantile equivalent. The pyramid narrowed again to the senate, and came to a point in the position of governor. These restrictions were new, but gave little offense to the general sense of political propriety; the suffrage qualifications were objected to in about one-fifth of the recorded town meeting debates.[27]

The house and senate represented different types of constituency, and the difference is one of the clues to institutional thought. The house represented the persons of the electorate living in corporate towns, which were entitled to representation according to a numerical scale of population; very small communities were excluded. The town remained the basic unit of representation. The senate, on the other hand, represented the property of the state arranged in districts corresponding to the counties; the number of members to which each county was entitled depended, not on population, but on the taxes it had paid into the state treasury. The result in distribution of representatives in the senate was not actually much different from the apportionment that would have been obtained by population,[28] but the intention was there, and the plan conformed to the principles of political order by which the delegates were guided.[29]

New York, which established popular election of its governor, and North Carolina took the matter further by differentiating between the qualifications of voters for the senate and the house of representatives.

How then are we to explain the paradox of popular consent to a scheme of government which systematically excluded the common people from the more responsible positions of political power? The historian who wishes to adopt the word "democracy" as a definition must first satisfy himself that it can be applied to a carefully ordered hierarchy, under the aegis of which power and authority are related to a conscientiously designed scale of social and economic rank, both actual and prospective; if this test fails him, then he must ask himself whether he can call the system a democracy, on the ground that it was a form of government established with the consent of the governed. Those who wish to argue this line have the advantage of finding

[27] The constitution of 1780 is discussed in: S. E. Morison, "The Struggle over the Adoption of the Constitution of Massachusetts, 1780," Massachusetts Historical Society *Proceedings*, L (Boston, 1916–17), 353–412; Robert J. Taylor, *Western Massachusetts in the Revolution* (Providence, R. I., 1954); J. R. Pole, "Suffrage and Representation in Massachusetts: A Statistical Note," *William and Mary Quarterly*, XIV (Oct. 1957), 560–92. The town meeting records are in Volumes CCLXXVI and CCLXXVII in the Massachusetts Department of Archives, the State House, Boston.

[28] As noted by Palmer, *Democratic Revolution*, 226.

[29] It may be permissible to mention that Brown, in his study of this constitution, omits to note this provision for tax payment as the basis of county representation. In itself, this may seem a small clue, but the thread leads into another world of political ideas than that of modern democracy. Brown, *Middle-Class Democracy*, 393.

much serviceable material that can be adopted without the rigors, or the risks, of a historically-minded analysis. It is possible to concentrate all attention on those aspects of the system which we would now call democratic, to assert that these elements exerted a controlling influence and that all the rest was a sort of obsolescent window dressing. Such a view may not be particularly subtle, but on the other hand it is not absolute nonsense. It is, perhaps, the easiest view to arrive at through an extensive reading of local economic records in the light of a clear, but vastly simplified inter-pretation of the political process; but it leaves unfulfilled the rather more complex task of perceiving the democratic elements in their proper place within a system con-ceived in another age, under a different inspiration.

In the Whig philosophy of government the basic principle, preceding representa-tive institutions, is the compact. The people already owned their property by natural right, and they are supposed to have come into the compact quite voluntarily to se-cure protection both to their property and to their persons. For these purposes gov-ernment was formed. What was done in Massachusetts seems to have been a solemn attempt to re-enact the original compact in the new making of the state. It was even possible to deploy the theory of compact as an excuse for seizing other people's prop-erty: in 1782 the legislature of Virginia resolved that the estates of British subjects might be confiscated because they had not been parties to the original contract of the people of that state.[30] And the Virginia constitution had not even been submitted for popular ratification!

Massachusetts and New Hampshire, in fact, were the only states in which popu-lar ratification was sought for the revolutionary constitution. In a society whose moral cohesion was supplied by the sense of deference and dignity, it was possible for the broad mass of the people to consent to a scheme of government in which their own share would be limited. Some of them of course expected to graduate to the higher levels; government was not controlled by inherited rank.

This factor—the expectation of advancement—is an important feature of the Ameri-can experience; it is one which is often used to excuse the injustice of exclusion from government by economic status. The *Address* that the Massachusetts convention dele-gates drew up in 1780 to expound the principles on which they had acted makes the point that most of those excluded by the suffrage qualification could expect to rise sufficiently in their own property to reach the level of voters. The exclusion of the artisan and laborer from the assembly was, however, more likely to prove permanent.

It would be a mistake to suppose that the body of citizens included in the electoral system at one level or another, or expecting to gain their inclusion, was really the whole body. There are always farm laborers, journeymen, migrant workers, and one may suspect that the numbers excluded by law were larger than the terms of the *Address* suggest. But even if we are disposed to accept the high level of popular participation in elections as being weighty enough to determine our definitions, it is surely wise to pause even over the legal disfranchisement of one man in every four or five, and in some towns one man in three.

This constitutional scheme was derived from a mixture of experience, theory, and intention. It is the intention for the future which seems to call for scrutiny when we attempt a satisfactory definition of these institutions.

In the first place there is the deliberate disfranchisement of the small, perhaps the

---

[30] Edmund Randolph to James Madison, Richmond, Dec. 27, 1782, Madison Papers, Manu-script Division, Library of Congress.

unfortunate, minority; the fact that the number is small is not more significant than that the exclusion is deliberate. In the second place, there is the installation of orders of government corresponding to orders of society; the fact that the lines are imprecise and that the results are uncertain is again not more significant than that the scale is deliberate.

It was a rule of Whig ideology that participation in matters of government was the legitimate concern only of those who possessed what was commonly called "a stake in society." In concrete terms this stake in society was one's property, for the protection of which, government had been originally formed. As a means to that protection, he was entitled, under a government so formed, to a voice: to some form of representation.

But there is a further problem. To put it briefly, what is to happen if the expected general economic advancement does not take place? Accumulations of wealth were far from being unknown; what if the further accumulation of wealth and the advance of the economy were to leave an ever-increasing residue of the population outside the political limits set by these constitutions? It is unlikely that their framers were ignorant of such possibilities. The growth of Sheffield, Manchester, and Leeds was not unknown; London was not easy to overlook; the Americans had close ties with Liverpool and Bristol. The fact is that a future town proletariat would be specifically excluded by the arrangements that were being made.

The historian who insists that this system was a model of democracy may find that the advance of the economy, a tendency already affecting America in many ways, leaves him holding a very undemocratic-looking baby. In the Philadelphia Convention, James Madison bluntly predicted that in future times "the great majority" would be "not only without landed, but any other sort of, property"—a state in which they would either combine, to the peril of property and liberty, or become the tools of opulence and ambition, leading to "equal danger on the other side." [31] The objection became common when state constitutions were under reform. Opponents of suffrage extension in the constitutions of the 1820's, who included many of the recognized leaders of political life, had a better right than their opponents to claim to be the legitimate heirs of the Whig constitution makers of the revolutionary era.

The constitution of the two legislative houses was based on the view that society was formed for the protection of persons and their property and that these two elements required separate protection and separate representation. This was one of the leading political commonplaces of the day. It is implied by Montesquieu; Jefferson accepts it in his *Notes on Virginia*; Madison held the view throughout his career; Hamilton treated it as a point of common agreement.[32] It is worth adding that it lay behind the original conception of the United States Senate in the form envisaged by the Virginia plan, a form which was subverted when the Senate became the representative chamber of the states. The whole subject was, of course, familiar to John Adams, who went on thinking about it long after he had drawn up a draft for the constitution of his state in 1780.

[31] *Records of the Federal Convention,* ed. Max Farrand (4 vols., New Haven, Conn., 1927), II, 203–204.

[32] Charles de Secondat, Baron de Montesquieu, *Oeuvres complètes* (Paris, 1838), *De l'esprit des lois,* 267; James Madison, *Writings,* ed. Gaillard Hunt (9 vols., New York, 1910), V, 287; Hamilton's speech in *Debates and Proceedings of Convention of New York, at Poughkeepsie 1788* (Poughkeepsie, N. Y., 1905), 26.

John Adams, as he himself anticipated, has been a much-misunderstood man. But it is important that we should get him right. No American was more loyal to Whig principles, and none was more deeply read in political ideas.

Adams is often said to have been an admirer of aristocracy and of monarchy. His admiration for the British constitution was easy to treat as an admission of unrepublican principles. But he really believed in the British constitution as it ought to have been, and he prudently averted his gaze from what it was in his own day. If Adams had lived in England in the 1780's, he would have been an associator in Wyvill's parliamentary reform movement, rather than a Foxite Whig.

Adams was profoundly impressed with the advantages enjoyed by birth, wealth, superior education, and natural merit, and the tendency for these advantages to become an inherited perquisite of the families that enjoyed them. He was equally clear about the corrupting influence of this sort of power. For this reason he wanted to segregate the aristocracy in an upper chamber, a process which he called "a kind of ostracism." The strong executive in which he believed was intended as a check not on the commons so much as on the aristocracy.

He developed this view of the function of the upper chamber in his *Defence of the Constitutions of the United States* (1786–1787). It is not wholly consistent with the view given in the *Address*[33] attached to the draft Massachusetts constitution of 1780, in which the line taken was that persons and property require separate protection in different houses. This view is itself a reflection of more than one tradition. It reflects the traditional structure of the legislature—council and assembly, lords and commons; it reflects also the idea that the state is actually composed of different orders (a word of which John Adams was fond) and that these orders have in their own right specific interests which are entitled to specific recognition. They are entitled to it because it is the purpose of the state to secure and protect them: that in fact was why the state was supposed to have come into existence.

Adams once, in later years, wrote to Jefferson: "Your *aristoi* are the most difficult animals to manage in the whole theory and practice of government. They will not suffer themselves to be governed." [34] Yet in spite of his intense distrust of them, I think his attitude was two sided. I find it difficult to read his account of the role played in society by the aristocracy without feeling that there was to him, as there is to many others, something peculiarly distinguished and attractive about these higher circles, elevated by nature and sustained by society above the ordinary run of men. And had he not, after all, sons for whom he had some hopes? Some hopes, perhaps, for the family of Adams?

Governor Bernard had lamented the disappearance from prerevolutionary Massachusetts of those balancing factors, "Fear, reverence, respect and awe." Disappearance at least toward the royal authority. They did not disappear so easily from domestic life. There is nothing which reveals these deferential attitudes more fully than in respect to birth and family, given on trust. Adams therefore tells us much, not only of himself but of his times, when he draws attention to inequality of birth:

> Let no man be surprised that this species of inequality is introduced here. Let the page in history be quoted, where any nation, ancient or modern, civilized or

---

[33] This, however, was the work of Samuel Adams. (William V. Wells, *The Life and Public Services of Samuel Adams* [3 vols., Boston, 1865], III, 89–97.)

[34] Quoted in Palmer, *Democratic Revolution*, 273, n. 52.

savage, is mentioned, among whom no difference was made, between the citizens, on account of their extraction. The truth is, that more influence is allowed to this advantage in free republics than in despotic governments, or would be allowed to it in simple monarchies, if severe laws had not been made from age to age to secure it. The children of illustrious families have generally greater advantages of education, and earlier opportunities to be acquainted with public characters, and informed of public affairs, than those of meaner ones, or even than those in middle life; and what is more than all, a habitual national veneration for their names, and the characters of their ancestors, described in history, or coming down by tradition, removes them farther from vulgar jealousy and popular envy, and secures them in some degree the favour, the affection, the respect of the public. Will any man pretend that the name of Andros, and that of Winthrop, are heard with the same sensations in any village of New England? Is not gratitude the sentiment that attends the latter? And disgust the feeling excited by the former? In the Massachusetts, then, there are persons descended from some of their ancient governors, counsellors, judges, whose fathers, grandfathers, and great-grandfathers, are mentioned in history with applause as benefactors to the country, while there are others who have no such advantage. May we go a step further,—Know thyself, is as useful a precept to nations as to men. Go into every village in New England, and you will find that the office of justice of the peace, and even the place of representative, which has ever depended only on the freest election of the people, have generally descended from generation to generation, in three or four families at most.[35]

Deference: it does not seem, in retrospect, a very secure cement to the union of social orders. Yet to those who live under its sway it can be almost irresistible.

It was beginning to weaken, no doubt, in Adams' own political lifetime. "The distinction of classes," Washington said to Brissot de Warville in 1788, "begins to disappear." But not easily, not all at once, not without a struggle.

It was this which collapsed in ruins in the upheaval of Jacksonian democracy. And that, perhaps, is why the election of so ambiguous a leader was accompanied by such an amazing uproar.

[35] John Adams, *Defence of the Constitutions of the United States* . . . (3 vols., Philadelphia, 1797), I, 110–11.

17 / The American Revolution Considered as an Economic Movement

Clarence L. Ver Steeg

In the following essay, Clarence Ver Steeg raises a number of questions concerning the impact of the War for Independence upon the American economy. Some of these questions are answered, most are presented as appropriate issues for further study. Of the subjects he treats, a few may need some special introduction. The trading pattern of the American colonies before 1775 was subject to British controls. It was a pattern to which most American merchants had become accustomed and upon which they depended. While the overriding British concern in the design of this trading system was profit to British merchants and the home country, the Americans were given a share in some highly desirable aspects of this trade. Certainly they were treated better as colonial subjects than after the war when they were thought of as ungrateful rebels outside the privileges of the British mercantilist system. Thus, Americans in the 1780's had to engage in a wild pursuit of new trading opportunities to replace the ones they had lost. As colonists they had indulged in a large number of necessary experiments with paper money, and the dearth of specie in colonial America was not a problem cured by independence. As a result, monetary experimentation continued throughout the war and the period of Confederation. The war itself encouraged some growth of production in America—although to an extent that has not been and cannot be precisely measured. The war brought the first foreign investments, in the form of loans and subsidies, which aided capital formation in the new country where non-British investment had been discouraged before 1775. In short, the economic impact of the Revolution needs further examination and Ver Steeg here suggests some of the many areas in which investigation should perhaps be carried out by future scholars.

For further reading: Stuart Bruchey, *The Roots of American Economic Growth, 1607–1861* (1965); J. Franklin Jameson, *The American Revolution Considered as a Social Movement* (1926); Curtis P. Nettels, *The Emergence*

Reprinted by permission from the *Huntington Library Quarterly*, XX (1957), 361–372.

of a National Economy, 1775–1815 (1962); George R. Taylor, "American Economic Growth Before 1840: An Exploratory Essay," *Journal of Economic History*, XXIV (1964), 427–444; Philip L. White, *The Beekmans of New York in Politics and Commerce, 1647–1877* (1956).

Historians for a generation or more have been so sensitive to economic influences during the Revolutionary period that a modern scholar places his reputation in jeopardy if he fails to take account of such forces, regardless of what phase of political, social, or cultural life he is investigating. Although this sensitivity did not have its birth with the notable works of Charles A. Beard, they assuredly stand as an unmistakable landmark. The results, in the main, have been good. Our perspective of the Revolutionary generation has broadened, our understanding deepened; and the main stream of events has often been magnificently illuminated.

In contrast, historians have tended to neglect the other side of the coin, giving relatively little, if any, attention to the influences that political, social, and cultural forces might have had upon economic development. Even studies embracing what are normally considered "economic" subjects—such as the role of merchants, the course of trade, the change in the land systems—have almost invariably been oriented toward a distinct vantage point: What effect did a change in land policy have upon social structure? How did the course of trade affect diplomatic policy? How significant was the position of the merchant in the formulation of political decisions? As illuminating as such studies have been, the results have given us only a partial view, for we have yet to answer the questions which arise when economic developments are approached from the reverse, and what many economists would call the proper perspective. Did the modification of political institutions affect the economy? Did political action influence economic change? Were social theories produced that modified the actions of merchant and planter capitalists? Did American society by its very structure circumscribe or direct the course of economic change? How significant was the American Revolution generally upon the rise of capitalism in America? If historians are to assess the impact of the American Revolution upon the whole of American life, these questions and others of equal importance need more precise answers than we now possess.

To illustrate the lack of balance in current historical writing, one need only compare the emphasis given by scholars to the social rather than the economic consequences of the Revolution. Numerous monographic and more general works covering the period could be cited to support this point, but textbooks in United States history give as reliable a testimony as one would wish. Whereas none would be considered complete without its section neatly entitled "Social Impact of the Revolution," or something similar, followed by appropriate paragraphs of description and analysis, no textbook examined by the writer has a similar section devoted to the economic impact. Indeed, it is rare when the possibility of economic results is so much as mentioned. The textbooks in American economic history offer little more. A chapter on the Revolution is seldom included. When it is, too often its focus is "economic causation"; in fact, most economic histories are organized in such a way that one would scarcely realize that a Revolution had taken place. Let it be quickly said that this comparison casts no reflection whatsoever on the textbook writers; the texts, quite properly, merely show the trend of scholarship. Although individual scholars, treating isolated subjects, have sometimes attempted to evaluate the economic effect of the Revolution, no major attempt has been made to bring together the existing material, much less to strike out into unexplored areas where fresh insights and new material would provide the ingredients for a solid synthesis. The only possible exception in the literature of the Revolution is Evarts B. Greene's helpful chapter on "The War's Economic Effects" in his *The Revolutionary Generation, 1763–1790* (New York, 1943). Greene gives a useful summary of some of the scholarship, but his approach is rather limited. Furthermore, Greene's chapter has never caught the attention of scholars; it has not been a departure point for new investigation.[1]

What becomes increasingly obvious, therefore, is that this significant theme, the impact of the Revolution upon the course of economic development, rates a thorough book-length study. This article can be little more than an introduction to an exciting historical problem. Its primary purpose is to focus attention upon the importance of the theme in terms of an area for research and in terms of a more complete understanding of the Revolutionary epoch. It will also attempt to indicate possible approaches to the problem, to make a preliminary assessment of some of the existing material, and, on occasion, to suggest additional theses that might help to define the problem. Part of the following discussion, therefore, will view familiar material from a somewhat different perspective, while other parts will suggest areas that seem to deserve more elaborate consideration if historians are eventually to make a realistic evaluation, and to see the Revolution in its fullest context.[2]

One of the most obvious, but largely overlooked, changes brought by the Revolution, carrying with it the broadest economic implications, was the new relationship between the rights of private property and mineral rights or, to use a broader term, natural resources. A careful study of this transition has never been made, but it is clear that whereas mineral rights in colonial times resided with the sovereign, to be granted or reserved as circumstances dictated, the Revolution saw such rights brought eventually within the purview of private property. The control of natural resources, therefore, was secured more firmly by private enterprisers.

It will be recalled that the charters of most colonies, though granting the rights to minerals and mines, contained a clause reserving the fifth part for the crown. This figure was more than a token; it represented an acknowledgment that the crown, when it disposed of land, possessed the power to grant or retain natural resources under the soil. That such grants were made at all merely indicates that the crown did not believe such resources existed in quantity and, in consequence, it could be generous with an added "inducement" to colonization. As a result, there was some mining activity in the majority of colonies before the Revolution. It is interesting, however, to speculate how magnanimous the crown would have been in granting any mineral rights if precious metals, the priority minerals of the seventeenth and eight-

---

[1] It will be interesting to see whether or not the volume in Rinehart's series on the *Economic History of the United States,* covering the period 1776–1815, will grapple with this problem or whether it will be a straight narrative. There are three places where a summary of the general economic development for these years can be found: Edward Channing, *History of the United States* (New York, 1912), III, ch. iii; Clarence L. Ver Steeg, *Robert Morris, Revolutionary Financier* (Philadelphia, 1954), ch. iii, stressing the period up to 1781; and Merrill Jensen, *The New Nation* (New York, 1950), pp. 179–244, stressing the Confederation period.

[2] Because of the exploratory nature of this article, only a few citations have been made.

eenth centuries, had suddenly been discovered in the colonies; given the basic mercantile position of the mother country it is safe to say that its terms would have been somewhat less liberal.

From the point of view of this article, it is significant that the sovereign right of the central government over mineral resources, though retained as a matter of form, apparently was not preserved in substance. So far as my investigation goes, there seems to be no discussion of this point in the exhaustive debates that took place on the land question during the Revolution. The Land Ordinance of 1785, it is true, reserved "one-third part of all gold, silver, lead, and copper mines" for the national government, but if a scholar relies on the standard monographs on the national land system, nothing seems to have come of it. Although the problem requires more exhaustive study, it would seem that one of the legacies of the Revolution, established almost by default, made an incalculable impact on American society where the command of critical natural resources—coal, iron ore, oil and gas, precious metals, and many others—has been a key factor.

Two of the basic elements in eighteenth-century economic life, farming and land policy, were also greatly influenced by the Revolution. Quite naturally, the celebrated Land Ordinance of 1785 comes immediately to mind, for it was largely responsible for "institutionalizing" the basic productive unit in Midwestern agriculture, the family farm. What this meant for the course of economic development is significant; interestingly enough, arguments are still raging as to the merits of the established family farm as compared with a much larger unit, seemingly more suitable to the complex economy of modern times. The Land Ordinance is only the most obvious of more subtle changes from the land practices of the colonial period, some of them procedural and others substantive, depending upon the region studied. Moreover, the stimulus given to land speculation by some of the interstate and international business groups—an area in which additional research would clarify many issues— is of great importance in itself.[3]

Farming, at least in two regions, the South and New England, underwent a profound change. That historian of agriculture, Lewis C. Gray, whose discriminating analysis and careful judgment commands respect if not always agreement, goes so far as to assert: "For the South it [the American Revolution] was also a great economic Revolution."[4] He particularly emphasizes that general farming, as distinguished from the production of staples in certain areas, was stimulated; and he stresses the importance of the new internal lines of communication and trade. Gray has received additional ammunition from Professor Lawrence Harper who has traced the relative production of specific staples. Indigo, for example, ceased to be produced soon after the Revolution, not so much because indigo failed to enjoy the British subsidy of colonial times, but rather because the British subsidy after the Revolution, applying as it did only to producers within the empire, resulted in a price advantage that the

[3] Payson J. Treat's standard monograph, *The National Land System, 1785–1820* (New York, 1910), ch. ii, makes some comparison between colonial land systems and that evolved after the Revolution. It is entirely possible, however, that the "New England influence" on the national land system has been overstated. It was a thesis that was given wide currency before new research revised some previously accepted assumptions on eighteenth-century New England land policy.

[4] Lewis C. Gray, *History of Agriculture in the Southern United States to 1860* (New York, 1941), II, 613.

South could not meet.[5] It is also well to remember that the damage caused by the fighting—the crops and livestock destroyed, and the wasted fields—meant that the South needed time to rebuild its plantation economy, especially in South Carolina and Georgia. Indeed, the desperate search for new staples to replace the loss of indigo, together with the limited geographical area where rice could be produced, helps to explain the renewed interest in cotton, which had been experimented with for a century previous to independence but never produced in quantity.

Although the New England farmer generally was not asked to face the ravages caused by military engagements, the Revolution had a profound effect upon New England agriculture. The decisive change that occurred when its customary marketing outlets were eliminated, especially those to the West Indies, was not immediately apparent, for until 1780 war-born markets took up the slack. With the sharp cutback in wartime markets starting late in 1781, and with no comparable peacetime markets to replace them, the New England farmer suffered a blow from which he never fully recovered. It is highly probable that the despair and discontent of agrarian New England in the 1780's is largely explicable in terms of the economic consequences of the Revolution.[6]

Trade, as well as agriculture and land policy, was never the same as a result of the Revolution. In some areas it was greatly broadened; in others it was sharply restricted. Furthermore the lines of trade were modified and mercantile connections were altered to meet the new circumstances. Although this effect of the Revolution has received some attention, more exacting studies are needed before it can be adequately measured.

The opening of the China trade, for example, was a direct consequence of the Revolution. In colonial times, the British imperial system made any notion of such a trade an unattainable dream. With the elimination of the British restrictions, this new vista was opened; and the business enterprisers of the new republic, anticipating its promise of rich rewards, rushed to exploit it. It matters not that their hopes were, in part, built upon illusions, for these illusions were quickly dispelled. What is significant is that the Asiatic trade introduced new products, created new demands, and, in some respects, educated this country's merchants in new trading techniques. William B. Weeden's apt statement deserves to be quoted; he asserts that the Revolution marked a break where one passes "from the Peter Faneuils, the negro and rum dealers of the middle century, to the Derbys, Perkinses, Thorndikes. . . . These men brought the far Eastern world home to its new counterpart in the West." [7] The influence of this trade, of course, was not confined to New England. It was a Pennsylvanian, Robert Morris, who was mainly responsible for outfitting the first Ameri-

[5] Lawrence A. Harper, "The Effect of the Navigation Acts on the Thirteen Colonies," in *The Era of the American Revolution*, ed. R. B. Morris (New York, 1939), pp. 24–25, and n. 61.

[6] There is some difference of opinion among scholars who have recently surveyed this problem. Oscar and Mary Handlin's *Commonwealth; A Study of the Role of Government in the American Economy: Massachusetts, 1774–1861* (New York and London, 1947), pp. 1–52, is a good evaluation for the whole New England economy. Percy Bidwell and John Falconer's *History of Agriculture in the Northern United States to 1860* (Washington, 1925), is of no help.

[7] William B. Weeden, *Economic and Social History of New England, 1620–1789* (Boston and New York, 1890), II, 821–822.

can ship to Asiatic waters, and it was a New Yorker, John Jacob Astor, whose career was built upon the rewards of this trade.

Whereas the Pacific trade was opened, the Caribbean trade was sharply reduced. Many factors were responsible, not the least of course being the British and French imperial systems, which automatically established a barrier against commodities from the new nation. Where the West Indies had served as an important market for fisheries, livestock, lumber, rum, and other goods during the colonial period and had acted as the crucial entrepôt during the War of Independence itself, it was suddenly closed to American products. How significant this result was for the economy of the new country has often been suggested, but it is a theme that still requires more elaborate and precise investigation.[8]

When trade is basically modified, it is axiomatic that mercantile connections are modified as well. As the most casual reading of the recently published volumes on eighteenth-century merchants will testify, the impact of the Revolution was profound. Some trading connections were completely changed; in others the nature of the trade itself was altered; in still other cases, a particular merchant or merchant group either won or lost its relative position in the trading community. The Pepperrells of Piscataqua, remaining loyal to Britain, abandoned American shores; the Browns of Providence, though they maintained their important position in the trading community, modified their business connections and adjusted their manufacturing interest to suit the new era; in New York City, James Beekman, whose business was seriously crippled during the Revolution when he was forced to flee from New York City to escape the British, found after the war that the pattern of trade relationships he used with success before 1776 was no longer applicable; Robert Morris, whose relative position within the mercantile community had improved so significantly that he could properly be called the Prince of Merchants, found it not only necessary after 1783 to establish a new network of business partnerships to adjust to the times, but also advantageous to expand his business operations and diversify his investments.[9]

General business organization, as well as the careers of individual merchants, was influenced by the Revolution. Robert East's indispensable book has demonstrated the intricate connections between business groups during the Revolution; but he was primarily interested in their political and to some extent social impact.[10] Using some of the identical material, it is possible to reverse the coin and see the results upon economic life: the rise of multiple partnerships and the beginnings of the corporate structure; the expansion of business groups to include every major marketing center; and the modification of these connections to meet new trade and business opportunities. When the Revolution so profoundly affected so many of its most representative mercantile leaders and the structure of business generally, how can it ever be

---

[8] Merrill Jensen believes that there was less disruption to the West India trade than most scholars have asserted (op. cit., pp. 198–199).

[9] Byron Fairchild, Messrs. William Pepperrell: Merchants at Piscataqua (Ithaca, N. Y., 1954). James B. Hedges, The Browns of Providence Plantations: Colonial Years (Cambridge, Mass., 1952), pp. 285–286, p. 306. Philip L. White, The Beekmans of New York (New York, 1956), pp. 441–530; Clarence L. Ver Steeg, Robert Morris, Revolutionary Financier (Philadelphia, 1954), ch. x.

[10] Business Enterprise in the American Revolutionary Era (New York, 1938), passim.

said that it had little impact upon the economic development of the United States or the rise of commercial capitalism in the young republic!

A discussion of trade during the Revolution inevitably leads to the subject of interstate commerce, especially of course to the fact that its control was placed within the framework of the national government. This subject has become so commonplace that there is a tendency to dismiss it without relating its significance to the rise of commercial capitalism. During the first six decades of the eighteenth century one of the key signs of economic maturation and of developing commercial capitalism was the increased specialization that occurred within the colonies. Each region—New England, the Middle Colonies, and the South—was producing commodities for market that were best suited to its resources. This specialization, among other things, stimulated intercolonial trade. When the Revolution placed its blessing upon this development by giving control of interstate commerce to the national government (the Articles of Confederation in allocating this power to the individual states were actually running counter to the colonial experience and, it should be added, to reality) the consequences were so significant as to be almost incalculable. An unlimited, unfettered, internal market not only stimulated the fruition of commercial capitalism, but also laid down the basic pattern that was to provide an expanding market for the industrial America that would eventually emerge.

The problem of money and money supply and its relation to economic deevlopment is a theme that runs through American history, but we still need an evaluation of the effect of the financial experience and policies of the Revolution upon the economic development of the nation. For a nation based upon a money economy, the mere act of transfer, shifting the financial problems from Britain to the United States, is obviously important for the direction of economic development, but scholars have yet to study the finances in this context.

There are, however, other promising approaches, one of which could focus around the concept of an expanding economy. It is possible, for example, that the extensive use of paper money—far outreaching any colonial experience—stimulated general economic activity, although this thesis requires a more precise examination before it can be accepted. Moreover, a number of alert minds during these formative years explored the relationship between national credit and an expanded national economy—Peletiah Webster, Robert Morris, Gouverneur Morris, and Alexander Hamilton, to cite the most obvious. Still another part of the story is the creation of commercial banks, made possible only by the act of Independence. Although the Bank of North America, chartered in 1781, was first, it was quickly imitated by banks in Massachusetts and New York and plans were laid to create others. The critical role played by these institutions is a matter of record, particularly in their credit experience and their role in the expansion of the economy. Without question, such ideas, practices, policies, and institutions in financial affairs—the result of the Revolution—played a significant role in the economic development of the period; indeed, it is possible that careful study and analysis will find that not nearly enough stress has been placed on their far reaching effects.

Another area requiring further research is manufactures.[11] At first glance this plea

[11] It is of interest to note that J. Franklin Jameson, *The American Revolution Considered as a Social Movement* (Princeton, 1926), spends an entire chapter on "Industry and Commerce," although it is difficult to see how he relates it directly to social change, except to state that the "Revolution brought ultimate benefit to the agriculture, the manufactures, and the commerce of

may appear unnecessary, for numerous historians assert that manufacturing was greatly extended, often supporting such claims with some specific illustrations. What is overlooked, however, is how often historians are merely quoting each other. The few basic economic studies that have included a section on manufacturing—so far as the writer knows, no single monograph on manufacturing in the Revolution exists —are sadly in need of revision. In addition scholars have failed to distinguish between an increase in production and an increase in total "plant" capacity, a crucial feature of the industrial expansion in the First and Second World Wars. It is logical to assume that the demand for guns, wagons, tents, clothing, and other articles brought an expansion in total productive capacity, but the evidence is not conclusive; nor is there so much as a well-informed estimate as to the degree of expansion.

Another factor that remains virtually unnoticed is the expansion of foreign investments in the United States during and after the Revolution. Before independence, quite naturally, neither French nor Dutch capital was invested in American enterprise; almost immediately upon the outbreak of war, however, key figures in both countries appeared to exploit the opportunities opening up in the new nation. In France such great names as that of Chaumont were prominent; in Holland, the Willinks and the Van Stapenhorsts. Some of the investment was purely speculative —the "investments" in currency, for example. In other cases, it was geared to more lasting enterprises, such as the French financial backing given to several new commercial houses. It can also be assumed that foreign investment in American securities must have played some part in capital formation during this period, but there has not been so much as a scholarly guess as to how significant a part. More important, the question of British investment has been neglected. Leland Jenks's fine study of the migration of British capital to the United States begins too late to throw much light on the Revolutionary epoch, with the result that our information is less than sketchy for the prewar as well as the immediate postwar period. Although historians have not given the entire subject of foreign investment its due, and in consequence we cannot speak of the results with confidence, it most certainly is an area of almost limitless possibilities.

Another promising approach, but one that has attracted little attention, is to use material normally discussed in terms of social history. The abolition of primogeniture and entail is a case in point. In most discussions the social consequences of these acts are emphasized: making the stratification produced by a set land system more flexible and thereby encouraging democratization. Seldom, if ever, is the abolition of primogeniture and entail considered in terms of its economic impact, a perspective of equal, if not greater, importance. To encourage a flexible land system where more efficient producers using up-to-date techniques can thrive, in contrast to a static system that settles for the status quo, is surely a matter of some importance. Indeed, it is instructive that historians have recently discovered that the abolition of primogeniture and entail in Virginia had minor social significance and that support for this act was more universal than had been assumed.[12] It might well be another way of saying that these acts were more important for economic than for social results. More study is

the United States of America" (p. 114). The focus of this article, in contrast, is upon those areas where the Revolution may have altered the direction or emphasis of economic development.

[12] A choice example is to trace the increasing firmness with which this new thesis is accepted in the works of Irving Brant, Dumas Malone, and Nathan Schachner on Madison and Jefferson respectively.

needed before a final conclusion can be drawn, but it is evident that a number of topics customarily considered in a social context will be rewarding avenues of exploration for the historian evaluating the economic consequences of the Revolution.

In fact, the number of essential questions requiring answers that only a thorough investigation can provide is a bit overwhelming. Historians have acknowledged that recent depressions, that of the 1930's in particular, have brought about some profound changes, but they have yet to appraise the lasting effect of the immediate postwar depression upon the course of economic development. Historians have written about the rise of the port of Baltimore, when the British blockade of Philadelphia brought new opportunities to its Maryland neighbor, but they have yet to assess the total effect of the Revolution upon the marketing centers of the new nation, including New York City. Historians have noted the decline of fisheries in New England, the change that took place in whaling, and the move from the outports of Massachusetts to Boston, yet they have been slow to determine whether or not the economy of one region of the nation received a more durable impress from the Revolution than did the others. Historians talk about American society with confidence, but they have never asked whether it contained within itself certain special characteristics that would decisively determine the course of economic life in the New Nation.

These considerations re-emphasize not only the importance of the theme but also the vast number of questions that will need to be asked—and, if possible, answered—if we are to assess the full impact of the Revolution. Although this article is merely an introduction rather than a *summa* and any conclusions are, at best, tentative, the evidence concerning the economic consequences of the Revolution is impressive. It is entirely possible that when scholars have completed their investigations, they will conclude that the American Revolution is of greater importance for its economic consequences, where the surface has scarcely been scratched, than for its social consequences, where the research in the Revolution has been concentrated in recent decades. To use the celebrated phrase of that pioneer in the field, J. Franklin Jameson, as a model, a phrase that has made scholars acutely conscious of the social aspects of the Revolution—the time seems overdue for historians to recognize and develop the idea of "The American Revolution Considered as an Economic Movement."

Part V

CONFEDERATION AND CONSTITUTION

18 / The Founding Fathers: A Reform Caucus in Action

John P. Roche

For most Americans, whatever the myths enshrined in some historical accounts, the years from 1783 to 1787 were a reasonably peaceful period with a gradual adjustment of the economy to changed circumstances and of state governments to their changing functions. Yet the end of the 1780's was marked by the establishment of a new national government, a process supported by most of the famed leaders of the Revolution. Their decision to act was based upon a wide range of motives—from their concern with forming some kind of union capable of defending the new nation among the competing powers of the world to other and perhaps more mundane factors. Whatever the forces that drove them on, their achievement was remarkable. Establishing a new government and gaining general popular consent to its establishment at any time would be a notable act; to do so when there were no emergency conditions compelling a larger public to acquiesce in the formation of the new regime was indeed an extraordinary political accomplishment. The sometimes-heated debate between proponents and opponents of the Constitution should not be allowed to obscure the quality of the work of the members of the Philadelphia Convention. They did convince the people of the American states to adopt a new basic document for their government and to give that government a chance to perform. In the following essay John Roche describes some of the significant features of the Convention. The Convention's debate may perhaps best be understood not in ideological terms but in terms of differences over the practical details of government. The delegates to the Convention sometimes clearly expressed their views on the ideal structure and then often indicated their willingness to accommodate their views of the ideal to their understanding of the possible. William Paterson summed up the attitude of many of these practical politicians and constitutional reformers: "I came here not to speak my own sentiments, but the sentiments of those who sent me. Our object is not such a Governm[en]t as may be best in itself, but such a one as our Constituents have authorized us to prepare, and as they will approve."

Reprinted by permission from the *American Political Science Review*, LV (1961), 799–816.

For further reading: Merrill Jensen, *The New Nation* (1950); Clinton Rossiter, *1787: the Grand Convention* (1966); Carl Van Doren, *The Great Rehearsal* (1948); Richard Hofstadter, "The Founding Fathers: an Age of Realism," in *The American Political Tradition* (1948), 3–17.

Over the last century and a half, the work of the Constitutional Convention and the motives of the Founding Fathers have been analyzed under a number of different ideological auspices. To one generation of historians, the hand of God was moving in the assembly; under a later dispensation, the dialectic (at various levels of philosophical sophistication) replaced the Deity: "relationships of production" moved into the niche previously reserved for Love of Country. Thus in counterpoint to the Zeitgeist, the Framers have undergone miraculous metamorphoses: at one time acclaimed as liberals and bold social engineers, today they appear in the guise of sound Burkean conservatives, men who in our time would subscribe to *Fortune,* look to Walter Lippmann for political theory, and chuckle patronizingly at the antics of Barry Goldwater. The implicit assumption is that if James Madison were among us, he would be President of the Ford Foundation, while Alexander Hamilton would chair the Committee for Economic Development.

The "Fathers" have thus been admitted to our best circles; the revolutionary ferocity which confiscated all Tory property in reach and populated New Brunswick with outlaws has been converted by the "Miltown School" of American historians into a benign dedication to "consensus" and "prescriptive rights." The Daughters of the American Revolution have, through the ministrations of Professors Boorstin, Hartz, and Rossiter, at last found ancestors worthy of their descendants. It is not my purpose here to argue that the "Fathers" were, in fact, radical revolutionaries; that proposition has been brilliantly demonstrated by Robert R. Palmer in his *Age of the Democratic Revolution.* My concern is with the further position that not only were they revolutionaries, but also they were democrats. Indeed, in my view, there is one fundamental truth about the Founding Fathers that *every* generation of Zeitgeisters has done its best to obscure: they were first and foremost superb democratic politicians. I suspect that in a contemporary setting, James Madison would be Speaker of the House of Representatives and Hamilton would be the *eminence grise* dominating (*pace* Theodore Sorenson or Sherman Adams) the Executive Office of the President. They were, with their colleagues, *political men*—not metaphysicians, disembodied conservatives or Agents of History—and as recent research into the nature of American politics in the 1780s confirms,[1] they were committed (perhaps willy-nilly) to working within the democratic framework, within a universe of public approval. Charles Beard *and* the filiopietists to the contrary notwithstanding, the Philadelphia

---

[1] The view that the right to vote in the states was severely circumscribed by property qualifications has been thoroughly discredited in recent years. See Chilton Williamson, *American Suffrage from Property to Democracy, 1760–1860* (Princeton, 1960). The contemporary position is that John Dickinson actually knew what he was talking about when he argued that there would be little opposition to vesting the right of suffrage in freeholders since "The great mass of our Citizens is composed at this time of freeholders, and will be pleased with it." Max Farrand, *Records of the Federal Convention,* Vol. 2, p. 202 (New Haven, 1911). (Henceforth cited as *Farrand.*)

Convention was not a College of Cardinals or a council of Platonic guardians working within a manipulative, pre-democratic framework; it was a *nationalist* reform
caucus which had to operate with great delicacy and skill in a political cosmos full
of enemies to achieve the one definitive goal—popular approbation.

Perhaps the time has come, to borrow Walton Hamilton's fine phrase, to raise the
Framers from immortality to mortality, to give them credit for their magnificent demonstration of the art of democratic politics. The point must be reemphasized; they
made history and did it within the limits of consensus. There was nothing inevitable
about the future in 1787; the *Zeitgeist,* that fine Hegelian technique of begging
causal questions, could only be discerned in retrospect. What they did was to ham-
mer out a pragmatic compromise which would both bolster the "National interest"
and be acceptable to the people. What inspiration they got came from their collective
experience as professional politicians in a democratic society. As John Dickinson put
it to his fellow delegates on August 13, "Experience must be our guide. Reason may
mislead us."

In this context, let us examine the problems they confronted and the solutions they
evolved. The Convention has been described picturesquely as a counter-revolutionary
junta and the Constitution as a *coup d'etat,*[2] but this has been accomplished by withdrawing the whole history of the movement for constitutional reform from its true
context. No doubt the goals of the constitutional elite were "subversive" to the existing political order, but it is overlooked that their subversion could only have succeeded if the people of the United States endorsed it by regularized procedures. In-
dubitably they were "plotting" to establish a much stronger central government than
existed under the Articles, but only in the sense in which one could argue equally
well that John F. Kennedy was, from 1956 to 1960, "plotting" to become President.
In short, on the fundamental *procedural* level, the Constitutionalists had to work
according to the prevailing rules of the game. Whether they liked it or not is a topic
for spiritualists—and is irrelevant: one may be quite certain that had Washington
agreed to play the De Gaulle (as the Cincinnati once urged), Hamilton would willingly have held his horse, but such fertile speculation in no way alters the actual
context in which events took place.

I

When the Constitutionalists went forth to subvert the Confederation, they utilized
the mechanisms of political legitimacy. And the roadblocks which confronted them
were formidable. At the same time, they were endowed with certain potent political
assets. The history of the United States from 1786 to 1790 was largely one of a
masterful employment of political expertise by the Constitutionalists as against bum-
bling, erratic behavior by the opponents of reform. Effectively, the Constitutionalists

[2] The classic statement of the *coup d'etat* theory is, of course, Charles A. Beard, *An Economic
Interpretation of the Constitution of the United States* (New York, 1913), and this theme was
echoed by Vernon L. Parrington, Merrill Jensen and others in "populist" historiographical tradition. For a sharp critique of this thesis see Robert E. Brown, *Charles Beard and the Constitution*
(Princeton, 1956). See also Forrest McDonald, *We the People* (Chicago, 1958); the trail-
blazing work in this genre was Douglas Adair, "The Tenth Federalist Revisited," *William and
Mary Quarterly,* Third Series, Vol. VIII (1951), pp. 48–67.

had to induce the states, by democratic techniques of coercion, to emasculate themselves. To be specific, if New York had refused to join the new Union, the project
was doomed; yet before New York was safely in, the reluctant state legislature had
sua sponte to take the following steps: (1) agree to send delegates to the Philadelphia
Convention; (2) provide maintenance for these delegates (these were distinct stages:
New Hampshire was early in naming delegates, but did not provide for their maintenance until July); (3) set up the special *ad hoc* convention to decide on ratification; and (4) concede to the decision of the *ad hoc* convention that New York
should participate. New York admittedly was a tricky state, with a strong interest in
a *status quo* which permitted her to exploit New Jersey and Connecticut, but the
same legal hurdles existed in every state. And at the risk of becoming boring, it must
be reiterated that the *only* weapon in the Constitutionalist arsenal was an effective
mobilization of public opinion.

The group which undertook this struggle was an interesting amalgam of a few
dedicated nationalists with the self-interested spokesmen of various parochial baili-
wicks. The Georgians, for example, wanted a strong central authority to provide
military protection for their huge, underpopulated state against the Creek Confederacy; Jerseymen and Connecticuters wanted to escape from economic bondage to
New York; the Virginians hoped to establish a system which would give that great
state its rightful place in the councils of the republic. The dominant figures in the
politics of these states therefore cooperated in the call for the Convention.[3] In other
states the thrust towards national reform was taken up by opposition groups who
added the "national interest" to their weapons system; in Pennsylvania, for instance,
the group fighting to revise the Constitution of 1776 came out four-square behind
the Constitutionalists, and in New York, Hamilton and the Schuyler *ambiance* took
the same tack against George Clinton.[4] There was, of course, a large element of personality in the affair: there is reason to suspect that Patrick Henry's opposition to
the Convention and the Constitution was founded on his conviction that Jefferson
was behind both, and a close study of local politics elsewhere would surely reveal
that others supported the Constitution for the simple (and politically quite sufficient)
reason that the "wrong" people were against it.

To say this is not to suggest that the Constitution rested on a foundation of impure
or base motives. It is rather to argue that in politics there are no immaculate conceptions, and that in the drive for a stronger general government, motives of all sorts
played a part. Few men in the history of mankind have espoused a view of the "common good" or "public interest" that militated against their private status; even Plato
with all his reverence for disembodied reason managed to put philosophers on top of
the pile. Thus it is not surprising that a number of diversified private interests joined
to push the nationalist public interest; what would have been surprising was the
absence of such a pragmatic united front. And the fact remains that, however

[3] A basic volume, which, like other works by Warren, provides evidence with which one can
evaluate the author's own opinions, is Charles Warren, *The Making of the Constitution* (Boston,
1928). The best brief summary of the forces behind the movement for centralization is Chapter 1
of *Warren* (as it will be cited hereafter).

[4] On Pennsylvania see Robert L. Brunhouse, *Counter-Revolution in Pennsylvania* (Harrisburg,
1942) and Charles P. Smith, *James Wilson* (Chapel Hill, 1956), ch. 15; for New York, which
needs the same sort of microanalysis Pennsylvania has received, the best study is E. Wilder
Spaulding, *New York in the Critical Period, 1783–1789* (New York, 1932).

motivated, these men did demonstrate a willingness to compromise their parochial interests in behalf of an ideal which took shape before their eyes and under their ministrations.

As Stanley Elkins and Eric McKitrick have suggested in a perceptive essay,[5] what distinguished the leaders of the Constitutionalist caucus from their enemies was a "Continental" approach to political, economic and military issues. To the extent that they shared an institutional base of operations, it was the Continental Congress (thirty-nine of the delegates to the Federal Convention had served in Congress[6]), and this was hardly a locale which inspired respect for the state governments. Robert de Jouvenal observed French politics half a century ago and noted that a revolutionary Deputy had more in common with a non-revolutionary Deputy than he had with a revolutionary non-Deputy;[7] similarly one can surmise that membership in the Congress under the Articles of Confederation worked to establish a continental frame of reference, that a Congressman from Pennsylvania and one from South Carolina would share a universe of discourse which provided them with a conceptual common denominator *vis à vis* their respective state legislatures. This was particularly true with respect to external affairs: the average state legislator was probably about as concerned with foreign policy then as he is today, but Congressmen were constantly forced to take the broad view of American prestige, were compelled to listen to the reports of Secretary John Jay and to the dispatches and pleas from their frustrated envoys in Britain, France and Spain.[8] From considerations such as these, a "Continental" ideology developed which seems to have demanded a revision of our domestic institutions primarily on the ground that only by invigorating our general government could we assume our rightful place in the international arena. Indeed, an argument with great force—particularly since Washington was its incarnation—urged that our very survival in the Hobbesian jungle of world politics depended upon a re-ordering and strengthening of our national sovereignty.[9]

Note that I am not endorsing the "Critical Period" thesis; on the contrary, Merrill Jensen seems to me quite sound in his view that for most Americans, engaged as they were in self-sustaining agriculture, the "Critical Period" was not particularly critical.[10] In fact, the great achievement of the Constitutionalists was their ultimate success in convincing the elected representatives of a majority of the white male population that change was imperative. A small group of political leaders with a Continental vision and essentially a consciousness of the United States' *international* impotence, provided the matrix of the movement. To their standard other leaders rallied with their own parallel ambitions. Their great assets were (1) the presence

[5] Stanley Elkins and Eric McKitrick, "The Founding Fathers: Young Men of the Revolution," *Political Science Quarterly,* Vol. 76, p. 181 (1961).

[6] *Warren,* p. 55.

[7] In *La République des Camarades* (Paris, 1914).

[8] See Frank Monaghan, *John Jay* (New York, 1935), ch. 13.

[9] "[T]he situation of the general government, if it can be called a government, is shaken to its foundation, and liable to be overturned by every blast. In a word, it is at an end; and, unless a remedy is soon applied, anarchy and confusion will inevitably ensue." Washington to Jefferson, May 30, 1787, *Farrand,* III, 31. See also Irving Brant, *James Madison, The Nationalist* (New York, 1948), ch. 25.

[10] Merrill Jensen, *The New Nation* (New York, 1950). Interestingly enough, Prof. Jensen virtually ignores international relations in his laudatory treatment of the government under the Articles of Confederation.

in their caucus of the one authentic American "father figure," George Washington, whose prestige was enormous,[11] (2) the energy and talent of their leadership (in which one must include the towering intellectuals of the time, John Adams and Thomas Jefferson, despite their absence abroad), and their communications "network," which was far superior to anything on the opposition side;[12] (3) the preemptive skill which made "their" issue The Issue and kept the locally oriented opposition permanently on the defensive; and (4) the subjective consideration that these men were spokesmen of a new and compelling credo: *American* nationalism, that ill-defined but nonetheless potent sense of collective purpose that emerged from the American Revolution.

Despite great institutional handicaps, the Constitutionalists managed in the mid-1780s to mount an offensive which gained momentum as years went by. Their greatest problem was lethargy, and paradoxically, the number of barriers in their path may have proved an advantage in the long run. Beginning with the initial battle to get the Constitutional Convention called and delegates appointed, they could never relax, never let up the pressure. In practical terms, this meant that the local "organizations" created by the Constitutionalists were perpetually in movement building up their cadres for the next fight. (The word organization has to be used with great caution: a political organization in the United States—as in contemporary England [13] —generally consisted of a magnate and his following, or a coalition of magnates. This did not necessarily mean that it was "undemocratic" or "aristocratic," in the Aristotelian sense of the word: while a few magnates such as the Livingstons could draft their followings, most exercised their leadership without coercion on the basis of popular endorsement. The absence of organized opposition did not imply the impossibility of competition any more than low public participation in elections necessarily indicated an undemocratic suffrage.)

The Constitutionalists got the jump on the "opposition" (a collective noun: oppositions would be more correct) at the outset with the demand for a Convention. Their opponents were caught in an old political trap: they were not being asked to approve any specific program of reform, but only to endorse a meeting to discuss and recommend needed reforms. If they took a hard line at the first stage, they were put in the position of glorifying the *status quo* and of denying the need for *any* changes. Moreover, the Constitutionalists could go to the people with a persuasive argument for "fair play"—"How can you condemn reform before you know precisely what is involved?" Since the state legislatures obviously would have the final say on any proposals that might emerge from the Convention, the Constitutionalists were merely reasonable men asking for a chance. Besides, since they did not make any concrete proposals at that stage, they were in a position to capitalize on every sort of generalized discontent with the Confederation.

Perhaps because of their poor intelligence system, perhaps because of over-confi-

---

[11] The story of James Madison's cultivation of Washington is told by Brant, *op. cit.,* pp. 394–97.

[12] The "message center" being the Congress; nineteen members of Congress were simultaneously delegates to the Convention. One gets a sense of this coordination of effort from Broadus Mitchell, *Alexander Hamilton, Youth to Maturity* (New York, 1957), ch. 22.

[13] See Sir Lewis Namier, *The Structure of Politics at the Accession of George III,* 2d ed. (New York, 1957); *England in the Age of the American Revolution* (London, 1930).

dence generated by the failure of all previous efforts to alter the Articles,[14] the opposition awoke too late to the dangers that confronted them in 1787. Not only did the Constitutionalists manage to get every state but Rhode Island (where politics was enlivened by a party system reminiscent of the "Blues" and the "Greens" in the Byzantine Empire)[15] to appoint delegates to Philadelphia, but when the results were in, it appeared that they dominated the delegations. Given the apathy of the opposition, this was a natural phenomenon: in an ideologically nonpolarized political atmosphere those who get appointed to a special committee are likely to be the men who supported the movement for its creation. Even George Clinton, who seems to have been the first opposition leader to awake to the possibility of trouble, could not prevent the New York legislature from appointing Alexander Hamilton—though he did have the foresight to send two of his henchmen to dominate the delegation. Incidentally, much has been made of the fact that the delegates to Philadelphia were not elected by the people; some have adduced this fact as evidence of the "undemocratic" character of the gathering. But put in the context of the time, this argument is wholly specious: the central government under the Articles was considered a creature of the component states and in all the states but Rhode Island, Connecticut and New Hampshire, members of the national Congress were chosen by the state legislatures. This was not a consequence of elitism or fear of the mob; it was a logical extension of states-rights doctrine to guarantee that the national institution did not end-run the state legislatures and make direct contact with the people.[16]

II

With delegations safely named, the focus shifted to Philadelphia. While waiting for a quorum to assemble, James Madison got busy and drafted the so-called Randolph or Virginia Plan with the aid of the Virginia delegation. This was a political master-stroke. Its consequence was that once business got underway, the framework

[14] The Annapolis Convention, called for the previous year, turned into a shambles: only five states sent commissioners, only three states were legally represented, and the instructions to delegates named varied quite widely from state to state. Clinton and others of his persuasion may have thought this disaster would put an end to the drive for reform. See Mitchell, *op. cit.*, pp. 362–67; Brant, *op. cit.*, pp. 375–87.

[15] See Hamilton M. Bishop, *Why Rhode Island Opposed the Federal Constitution* (Providence, 1950) for a careful analysis of the labyrinthine political course of Rhode Island. For background see David S. Lovejoy, *Rhode Island Politics and the American Revolution* (Providence, 1958).

[16] The terms "radical" and "conservative" have been bandied about a good deal in connection with the Constitution. This usage is nonsense if it is employed to distinguish between two economic "classes"—*e.g.*, radical debtors versus conservative creditors, radical farmers versus conservative capitalists, etc.—because there was no polarization along this line of division; the same types of people turned up on both sides. And many were hard to place in these terms: does one treat Robert Morris as a debtor or a creditor? or James Wilson? See Brown, *op. cit.*, *passim*. The one line of division that holds up is between those deeply attached to states'-rights and those who felt that the Confederation was bankrupt. Thus, curiously, some of the most narrow-minded, parochial spokesmen of the time have earned the designation "radical" while those most willing to experiment and alter the *status quo* have been dubbed "conservative"! See Cecelia Kenyon, "Men of Little Faith," *William and Mary Quarterly*, Vol. 12 (1955), p. 3.

of discussion was established on Madison's terms. There was no interminable argument over agenda; instead the delegates took the Virginia Resolutions—"just for purposes of discussion"—as their point of departure. And along with Madison's proposals, many of which were buried in the course of the summer, went his major premise: a new start on a Constitution rather than piecemeal amendment. This was not necessarily revolutionary—a little exegesis could demonstrate that a new Constitution might be formulated as "amendments" to the Articles of Confederation—but Madison's proposal that this "lump sum" amendment go into effect after approval by nine states (the Articles required unanimous state approval for any amendment) was thoroughly subversive.[17]

Standard treatments of the Convention divide the delegates into "nationalists" and "states'-righters" with various improvised shadings ("moderate nationalists," etc.), but these are *a posteriori* categories which obfuscate more than they clarify. What is striking to one who analyzes the Convention as a case-study in democratic politics is the lack of clear-cut ideological divisions in the Convention. Indeed, I submit that the evidence—Madison's *Notes,* the correspondence of the delegates, and debates on ratification—indicates that this was a remarkably homogeneous body on the ideological level. Yates and Lansing, Clinton's two chaperones for Hamilton, left in disgust on July 10. (Is there anything more tedious than sitting through endless disputes on matters one deems fundamentally misconceived? It takes an iron will to spend a hot summer as an ideological *agent provocateur*.) Luther Martin, Maryland's bibulous narcissist, left on September 4 in a huff when he discovered that others did not share his self-esteem; others went home for personal reasons. But the hard core of delegates accepted a grinding regimen throughout the attrition of a Philadelphia summer precisely because they shared the Constitutionalist goal.

Basic differences of opinion emerged, of course, but these were not ideological; they were *structural*. If the so-called "states'-rights" group had not accepted the fundamental purposes of the Convention, they could simply have pulled out and by doing so have aborted the whole enterprise. Instead of bolting, they returned day after day to argue and to compromise. An interesting symbol of this basic homogeneity was the initial agreement on secrecy: these professional politicians did not want to become prisoners of publicity; they wanted to retain that freedom of maneuver which is only possible when men are not forced to take public stands in the preliminary stages of negotiation.[18] There was no legal means of binding the tongues of the delegates: at any stage in the game a delegate with basic principled objections to the emerging project could have taken the stump (as Luther Martin did after his exit) and denounced the convention to the skies. Yet Madison did not even inform Thomas Jefferson in Paris of the course of the deliberations[19] and available correspondence indicates that the delegates generally observed the injunction. Secrecy is certainly

[17] Yet, there was little objection to this crucial modification from any quarter—there almost seems to have been a gentlemen's agreement that Rhode Island's *liberum veto* had to be destroyed.

[18] See Mason's letter to his son, May 27, 1787, in which he endorsed secrecy as "a proper precaution to prevent mistakes and misrepresentation until the business shall have been completed, when the whole may have a very different complexion from that in which the several crude and indigested parts might in their first shape appear if submitted to the public eye." *Farrand,* III, 28.

[19] See Madison to Jefferson, June 6, 1787, *Farrand,* III, 35.

uncharacteristic of any assembly marked by strong ideological polarization. This was noted at the time: the *New York Daily Advertiser*, August 14, 1787, commented that the ". . . profound secrecy hitherto observed by the Convention [we consider] a happy omen, as it demonstrates that the spirit of party on any great and essential point cannot have arisen to any height." [20]

Commentators on the Constitution who have read *The Federalist* in lieu of reading the actual debates have credited the Fathers with the invention of a sublime concept called "Federalism." [21] Unfortunately *The Federalist* is probative evidence for only one proposition: that Hamilton and Madison were inspired propagandists with a genius for retrospective symmetry. Federalism, as the theory is generally defined, was an improvisation which was later promoted into a political theory. Experts on "federalism" should take to heart the advice of David Hume, who warned in his *Of the Rise and Progress of the Arts and Sciences* that ". . . there is no subject in which we must proceed with more caution than in [history], lest we assign causes which never existed and reduce what is merely contingent to stable and universal principles." In any event, the final balance in the Constitution between the states and the nation must have come as a great disappointment to Madison, while Hamilton's unitary views are too well known to need elucidation.

It is indeed astonishing how those who have glibly designated James Madison the "father" of Federalism have overlooked the solid body of fact which indicates that he shared Hamilton's quest for a unitary central government. To be specific, they have avoided examining the clear import of the Madison-Virginia Plan,[22] and have disregarded Madison's dogged inch-by-inch retreat from the bastions of centralization. The Virginia Plan envisioned a unitary national government effectively freed from and dominant over the states. The lower house of the national legislature was to be elected directly by the people of the states with membership proportional to population. The upper house was to be selected by the lower and the two chambers would elect the executive and choose the judges. The national government would be thus cut completely loose from the states.[23]

[20] Cited in *Warren*, p. 138.

[21] See, *e.g.*, Gottfried Dietze, *The Federalist, A Classic on Federalism and Free Government* (Baltimore, 1960); Richard Hofstadter, *The American Political Tradition* (New York, 1948); and John P. Roche, "American Liberty," in M. Konvitz and C. Rossiter, eds., *Aspects of Liberty* (Ithaca, 1958).

[22] "I hold it for a fundamental point, that an individual independence of the states is utterly irreconcilable with the idea of an aggregate sovereignty," Madison to Randolph, cited in Brant, *op. cit.*, p. 416.

[23] The Randolph Plan was presented on May 29, see *Farrand*, I, 18–23; the state legislatures retained only the power to *nominate* candidates for the upper chamber. Madison's view of the appropriate position of the states emerged even more strikingly in Yates' record of his speech on June 29: "Some contend that states are sovereign when in fact they are only political societies. There is a gradation of power in all societies, from the lowest corporation to the highest sovereign. The states never possessed the essential rights of sovereignty. . . . The states, at present, are only great corporations, having the power of making by-laws, and these are effectual only if they are not contradictory to the general confederation. The states ought to be placed under the control of the general government—at least as much so as they formerly were under the king and British parliament." *Farrand*, I, 471. Forty-six years later, after Yates' "Notes" had been published, Madison tried to explain this statement away as a misinterpretation: he did not flatly deny the authenticity of Yates' record, but attempted a defense that was half justification and half evasion. Madison to W. C. Rives, Oct. 21, 1833. *Farrand*, III, 521–24.

The structure of the general government was freed from state control in a truly radical fashion, but the scope of the authority of the national sovereign as Madison initially formulated it was breathtaking—it was a formulation worthy of the Sage of Malmesbury himself. The national legislature was to be empowered to disallow the acts of state legislatures,[24] and the central government was vested, in addition to the powers of the nation under the Articles of Confederation, with plenary authority wherever ". . . the separate States are incompetent or in which the harmony of the United States may be interrupted by the exercise of individual legislation."[25] Finally, just to lock the door against state intrusion, the national Congress was to be given the power to use military force on recalcitrant states.[26] This was Madison's "model" of an ideal national government, though it later received little publicity in *The Federalist.*

The interesting thing was the reaction of the Convention to this militant program for a strong autonomous central government. Some delegates were startled, some obviously leery of so comprehensive a project of reform,[27] but nobody set off any fireworks and nobody walked out. Moreover, in the two weeks that followed, the Virginia Plan received substantial endorsement *en principe;* the initial temper of the gathering can be deduced from the approval "without debate or dissent," on May 31, of the Sixth Resolution which granted Congress the authority to disallow state legislation ". . . contravening *in its opinion* the Articles of Union." Indeed, an amendment was included to bar states from contravening national treaties.[28]

The Virginia Plan may therefore be considered, in ideological terms, as the delegates' Utopia, but as the discussions continued and became more specific, many of those present began to have second thoughts. After all, they were not residents of Utopia or guardians in Plato's Republic who could simply impose a philosophical ideal on subordinate strata of the population. They were practical politicians in a democratic society, and no matter what their private dreams might be, they had to take home an acceptable package and defend it—and their own political futures—against predictable attack. On June 14 the breaking point between dream and reality took place. Apparently realizing that under the Virginia Plan, Massachusetts, Virginia and Pennsylvania could virtually dominate the national government—and probably appreciating that to sell this program to "the folks back home" would be impossible—the delegates from the small states dug in their heels and demanded time for a consideration of alternatives. One gets a graphic sense of the inner politics from John Dickinson's reproach to Madison: "You see the consequences of pushing things too far. Some of the members from the small States wish for two branches in the General Legislature and are friends to a good National Government; but we would sooner submit to a foreign power than . . . be deprived of an equality of suffrage

[24] Resolution 6 gave the National Legislature this power subject to review by the Council of Revision proposed in Resolution 8.

[25] Resolution 6.

[26] *Ibid.*

[27] See the discussions on May 30 and 31. "Mr. Charles Pinkney wished to know of Mr. Randolph whether he meant to abolish the State Governts. altogether . . . Mr. Butler said he had not made up his mind on the subject and was open to the light which discussion might throw on it . . . Genl. Pinkney expressed a doubt . . . Mr. Gerry seemed to entertain the same doubt." *Farrand,* I, 33–34. There were no denunciations—though it should perhaps be added that Luther Martin had not yet arrived.

[28] *Farrand,* I, 54. (Italics added.)

in both branches of the Legislature, and thereby be thrown under the domination of the large States." [29]

The bare outline of the *Journal* entry for Tuesday, June 14, is suggestive to anyone with extensive experience in deliberative bodies. "It was moved by Mr. Patterson [*sic,* Paterson's name was one of those consistently misspelled by Madison and everybody else] seconded by Mr. Randolph that the further consideration of the report from the Committee of the whole House [endorsing the Virginia Plan] be postponed til tomorrow, and before the question for postponement was taken. It was moved by Mr. Randolph seconded by Mr. Patterson that the House adjourn." [30] The House adjourned by obvious prearrangement of the two principals: since the preceding Saturday when Brearley and Paterson of New Jersey had announced their fundamental discontent with the representational features of the Virginia Plan, the informal pressure had certainly been building up to slow down the steamroller. Doubtless there were extended arguments at the Indian Queen between Madison and Paterson, the latter insisting that events were moving rapidly towards a probably disastrous conclusion, towards a political suicide pact. Now the process of accommodation was put into action smoothly—and wisely, given the character and strength of the doubters. Madison had the votes, but this was one of those situations where the enforcement of mechanical majoritarianism could easily have destroyed the objectives of the majority: the Constitutionalists were in quest of a qualitative as well as a quantitative consensus. This was hardly from deference to local Quaker custom; it was a political imperative if they were to attain ratification.

III

According to the standard script, at this point the "states'-rights" group intervened in force behind the New Jersey Plan, which has been characteristically portrayed as a reversion to the *status quo* under the Articles of Confederation with but minor modifications. A careful examination of the evidence indicates that only in a marginal sense is this an accurate description. It is true that the New Jersey Plan put the states back into the institutional picture, but one could argue that to do so was a recognition of political reality rather than an affirmation of states'-rights. A serious case can be made that the advocates of the New Jersey Plan, far from being ideological addicts of states'-rights, intended to substitute for the Virginia Plan a system which would both retain strong national power and have a chance of adoption in the states. The leading spokesman for the project asserted quite clearly that his views were based more on counsels of expediency than on principle; said Paterson on June 16: "I came here not to speak my own sentiments, but the sentiments of those who sent me. Our object is not such a Governmt. as may be best in itself, but such a one as our Constituents have authorized us to prepare, and as they will approve." [31] This is Madison's version; in Yates' transcription, there is a crucial sentence following the remarks above: "I believe that a little practical virtue is to be preferred to the

---

[29] *Ibid.,* p. 242. Delaware's delegates had been instructed by their general assembly to maintain in any new system the voting equality of the states. *Farrand,* III, 574.

[30] *Ibid.,* p. 240.

[31] *Ibid.,* p. 250.

finest theoretical principles, which cannot be carried into effect." [32] In his preliminary speech on June 9, Paterson had stated ". . . to the public mind we must accommodate ourselves," [33] and in his notes for this and his later effort as well, the emphasis is the same. The *structure* of government under the Articles should be retained:

> 2. Because it accords with the Sentiments of the People
>
> > [Proof:] 1. Coms. [Commissions from state legislatures defining the jurisdiction of the delegates]
> > 2. News-papers—Political Barometer. Jersey never would have sent Delegates under the first [Virginia] Plan—
>
> Not here to sport Opinions of my own. Wt. [What] can be done. A little practicable Virtue preferrable to Theory. [34]

This was a defense of political acumen, not of states'-rights. In fact, Paterson's notes of his speech can easily be construed as an argument for attaining the substantive objectives of the Virginia Plan by a sound political route, *i.e.,* pouring the new wine in the old bottles. With a shrewd eye, Paterson queried:

> Will the Operation and Force of the [central] Govt. depend upon the mode of Representn.—No—it will depend upon the Quantum of Power lodged in the leg. ex. and judy. Departments—Give [the existing] Congress the same Powers that you intend to give the two Branches, [under the Virginia Plan] and I apprehend they will act with as much Propriety and more Energy . . . [35]

In other words, the advocates of the New Jersey Plan concentrated their fire on what they held to be the *political liabilities* of the Virginia Plan—which were matters of institutional structure—rather than on the proposed scope of national authority. Indeed, the Supremacy Clause of the Constitution first saw the light of day in Paterson's Sixth Resolution; the New Jersey Plan contemplated the use of military force to secure compliance with national law; and finally Paterson made clear his view that under either the Virginia or the New Jersey systems, the general government would ". . . act on individuals and not on states." [36] From the states'-rights viewpoint, this was heresy: the fundament of that doctrine was the proposition that any central government had as its constituents the states, not the people, and could only reach the people through the agency of the state government.

Paterson then reopened the agenda of the Convention, but he did so within a distinctly nationalist framework. Paterson's position was one of favoring a strong central government in principle, but opposing one which in fact *put the big states in the saddle.* (The Virginia Plan, for all its abstract merits, did very well by Virginia.) As evidence for this speculation, there is a curious and intriguing proposal among Paterson's preliminary drafts of the New Jersey Plan:

---

[32] *Ibid.,* p. 258.
[33] *Ibid.,* p. 178.
[34] *Ibid.,* p. 274.
[35] *Ibid.,* pp. 275–76.
[36] "But it is said that this national government is to act on individuals and not on states; and cannot a federal government be so framed as to operate in the same way? It surely may." *Ibid.,* pp. 182–83; also *ibid.* at p. 276.

> Whereas it is necessary in Order to form the People of the U. S. of America in to a Nation, that the States should be consolidated, by which means all the Citizens thereof will become equally intitled to and will equally participate in the same Privileges and Rights . . . it is therefore resolved, that all the Lands contained within the Limits of each state individually, and of the U. S. generally be considered as constituting one Body or Mass, and be divided into thirteen or more integral parts.
>
> Resolved, That such Divisions or integral Parts shall be styled Districts.[37]

This makes it sound as though Paterson was prepared to accept a strong unified central government along the lines of the Virginia Plan if the existing states were eliminated. He may have gotten the idea from his New Jersey colleague Judge David Brearley, who on June 9 had commented that the only remedy to the dilemma over representation was ". . . that a map of the U. S. be spread out, that all the existing boundaries be erased, and that a new partition of the whole be made into 13 equal parts." [38] According to Yates, Brearley added at this point, ". . . then a government on the present [Virginia Plan] system will be just." [39]

This proposition was never pushed—it was patently unrealistic—but one can appreciate its purpose: it would have separated the men from the boys in the large-state delegations. How attached would the Virginians have been to their reform principles if Virginia were to disappear as a component geographical unit (the largest) for representational purposes? Up to this point, the Virginians had been in the happy position of supporting high ideals with that inner confidence born of knowledge that the "public interest" they endorsed would nourish their private interest. Worse, they had shown little willingness to compromise. Now the delegates from the small states announced that they were unprepared to be offered up as sacrificial victims to a "national interest" which reflected Virginia's parochial ambition. Caustic Charles Pinckney was not far off when he remarked sardonically that ". . . the whole [conflict] comes to this": "Give N. Jersey an equal vote, and she will dismiss her scruples, and concur in the Natil. system." [40] What he rather unfairly did not add was that the Jersey delegates were not free agents who could adhere to their private convictions; they had to take back, sponsor and risk their reputations on the reforms approved by the Convention—and in New Jersey, not in Virginia.

Paterson spoke on Saturday, and one can surmise that over the weekend there was a good deal of consultation, argument, and caucusing among the delegates. One member at least prepared a full length address: on Monday Alexander Hamilton, previously mute, rose and delivered a six-hour oration.[41] It was a remarkably apolitical speech; the gist of his position was that *both* the Virginia and New Jersey Plans were inadequately centralist, and he detailed a reform program which was reminiscent of the Protectorate under the Cromwellian *Instrument of Government* of 1653. It has been suggested that Hamilton did this in the best political tradition to emphasize the moderate character of the Virginia Plan,[42] to give the cautious delegates something *really* to worry about; but this interpretation seems somehow too

[37] *Farrand*, III, 613.
[38] *Farrand*, I, 177.
[39] *Ibid.*, p. 182.
[40] *Ibid.*, p. 255.
[41] J. C. Hamilton, cited *ibid.*, p. 293.
[42] See, *e.g.*, Mitchell, *op. cit.*, p. 381.

clever. Particularly since the sentiments Hamilton expressed happened to be completely consistent with those he privately—and sometimes publicly—expressed throughout his life. He wanted, to take a striking phrase from a letter to George Washington, a "strong well mounted government";[43] in essence, the Hamilton Plan contemplated an elected life monarch, virtually free of public control, on the Hobbesian ground that only in this fashion could strength and stability be achieved. The other alternatives, he argued, would put policy-making at the mercy of the passions of the mob; only if the sovereign was beyond the reach of selfish influence would it be possible to have government in the interests of the whole community.[44]

From all accounts, this was a masterful and compelling speech, but (aside from furnishing John Lansing and Luther Martin with ammunition for later use against the Constitution) it made little impact. Hamilton was simply transmitting on a different wave-length from the rest of the delegates; the latter adjourned after his great effort, admired his rhetoric, and then returned to business.[45] It was rather as if they had taken a day off to attend the opera. Hamilton, never a particularly patient man or much of a negotiator, stayed for another ten days and then left, in considerable disgust, for New York.[46] Although he came back to Philadelphia sporadically and attended the last two weeks of the Convention, Hamilton played no part in the laborious task of hammering out the Constitution. His day came later when he led the New York Constitutionalists into the savage imbroglio over ratification—an arena in which his unmatched talent for dirty political infighting may well have won the day. For instance, in the New York Ratifying Convention, Lansing threw back into Hamilton's teeth the sentiments the latter had expressed in his June 18 oration in the Convention. However, having since retreated to the fine defensive positions immortalized in *The Federalist,* the Colonel flatly denied that he had ever been an enemy of the states, or had believed that conflict between states and nation was inexorable! As Madison's authoritative *Notes* did not appear until 1840, and there had been no press coverage, there was no way to verify his assertions, so in the words of the reporter, ". . . a warm personal altercation between [Lansing and Hamilton] engrossed the remainder of the day [June 28, 1788]." [47]

IV

On Tuesday morning, June 19, the vacation was over. James Madison led off with a long, carefully reasoned speech analyzing the New Jersey Plan which, while intellectually vigorous in its criticisms, was quite conciliatory in mood. "The great difficulty," he observed, "lies in the affair of Representation; and if this could be adjusted, all others would be surmountable." [48] (As events were to demonstrate, this diagnosis was correct.) When he finished, a vote was taken on whether to continue with the Virginia Plan as the nucleus for a new constitution: seven states voted "Yes";

[43] Hamilton to Washington, July 3, 1787, *Farrand,* III, 53.
[44] A reconstruction of the Hamilton Plan is found in *Farrand,* III, 617–30.
[45] Said William Samuel Johnson on June 21: "A gentleman from New-York, with boldness and decision, proposed a system totally different from both [Virginia and New Jersey]; and though he has been praised by every body, he has been supported by none." *Farrand,* I, 363.
[46] See his letter to Washington cited *supra* note 43.
[47] *Farrand,* III, 338.
[48] *Farrand,* I, 321.

New York, New Jersey, and Delaware voted "No"; and Maryland, whose position often depended on which delegates happened to be on the floor, divided.[49] Paterson, it seems, lost decisively; yet in a fundamental sense he and his allies had achieved their purpose: from that day onward, it could never be forgotten that the state governments loomed ominously in the background and that no verbal incantations could exorcise their power. Moreover, nobody bolted the convention: Paterson and his colleagues took their defeat in stride and set to work to modify the Virginia Plan, particularly with respect to its provisions on representation in the national legislature. Indeed, they won an immediate rhetorical bonus; when Oliver Ellsworth of Connecticut rose to move that the word "national" be expunged from the Third Virginia Resolution ("Resolved that a *national* Government ought to be established consisting of a *supreme* Legislative, Executive and Judiciary" [50]), Randolph agreed and the motion passed unanimously.[51] The process of compromise had begun.

For the next two weeks, the delegates circled around the problem of legislative representation. The Connecticut delegation appears to have evolved a possible compromise quite early in the debates, but the Virginians and particularly Madison (unaware that he would later be acclaimed as the prophet of "federalism") fought obdurately against providing for equal representation of states in the second chamber. There was a good deal of acrimony and at one point Benjamin Franklin—of all people—proposed the institution of a daily prayer; practical politicians in the gathering, however, were meditating more on the merits of a good committee than on the utility of Divine intervention. On July 2, the ice began to break when through a number of fortuitous events[52]—and one that seems deliberate[53]—the majority against

[49] Maryland's politics in this period were only a bit less intricate than Rhode Island's: the rural gentry, in much the same fashion that Namier described in England, divided up among families—Chases, Carrolls, Pacas, Lloyds, Tilghmans, etc.—and engaged in what seemed, to the outsider, elaborate political Morris dances. See Philip A. Crowl, *Maryland During and After the Revolution* (Baltimore, 1943). The Maryland General Assembly named five delegates to the Convention and provided that "the said Deputies or such of them as shall attend . . . shall have full Power to represent this State," *Farrand*, III, 586. The interesting circumstance was that three of the delegates were Constitutionalists (Carroll, McHenry and Jenifer), while two were opposed (Martin and Mercer); and this led to an *ad hoc* determination of where Maryland would stand when votes were taken. The vote on equality of representation, to be described *infra*, was an important instance of this eccentricity.

[50] This formulation was voted into the Randolph Plan on May 30, 1787, by a vote of six states to none, with one divided. *Farrand*, I, 30.

[51] *Farrand*, I, 335–36. In agreeing, Randolph stipulated his disagreement with Ellsworth's rationale, but said he did not object to merely changing an "expression." Those who subject the Constitution to minute semantic analysis might do well to keep this instance in mind; if Randolph could so concede the deletion of "national," one may wonder if any word changes can be given much weight.

[52] According to Luther Martin, he was alone on the floor and cast Maryland's vote for equality of representation. Shortly thereafter, Jenifer came on the floor and "Mr. King, from Massachusetts, valuing himself on Mr. Jenifer to divide the State of Maryland on this question . . . requested of the President that the question might be put again; however, the motion was too extraordinary in its nature to meet with success." Cited from "The Genuine Information, . . ." *Farrand*, III, 188.

[53] Namely Baldwin's vote *for* equality of representation which divided Georgia—with Few absent and Pierce in New York fighting a duel, Houston voted against equality and Baldwin shifted to tie the state. Baldwin was originally from Connecticut and attended and tutored at Yale, facts which have led to much speculation about the pressures the Connecticut delegation

equality of representation was converted into a dead tie. The Convention had reached the stage where it was "ripe" for a solution (presumably all the therapeutic speeches had been made), and the South Carolinians proposed a committee. Madison and James Wilson wanted none of it, but with only Pennsylvania dissenting, the body voted to establish a working party on the problem of representation.

The members of this committee, one from each state, were elected by the delegates —and a very interesting committee it was. Despite the fact that the Virginia Plan had held majority support up to that date, neither Madison nor Randolph was selected (Mason was the Virginian) and Baldwin of Georgia, whose shift in position had resulted in the tie, was chosen. From the composition, it was clear that this was not to be a "fighting" committee: the emphasis in membership was on what might be described as "second-level political entrepreneurs." On the basis of the discussions up to that time, only Luther Martin of Maryland could be described as a "bitter-ender." Admittedly, some divination enters into this sort of analysis, but one does get a sense of the mood of the delegates from these choices—including the interest-ing selection of Benjamin Franklin, despite his age and intellectual wobbliness, over the brilliant and incisive Wilson or the sharp, polemical Gouverneur Morris, to repre-sent Pennsylvania. His passion for conciliation was more valuable at this juncture than Wilson's logical genius, or Morris' acerbic wit.

There is a common rumor that the Framers divided their time between philosoph-ical discussions of government and reading the classics in political theory. Perhaps this is as good a time as any to note that their concerns were highly practical, that they spent little time canvassing abstractions. A number of them had some acquaint-ance with the history of political theory (probably gained from reading John Adams monumental compilation *A Defense of the Constitutions of Government*,[54] the first volume of which appeared in 1786), and it was a poor rhetorician indeed who could not cite Locke, Montesquieu, or Harrington *in support* of a desired goal. Yet up to this point in the deliberations, no one had expounded a defense of states'-rights or the "separation of powers" on anything resembling a theoretical basis. It should be reiterated that the Madison model had no room either for the states or for the "separa-tion of powers": effectively *all* governmental power was vested in the national legislature. The merits of Montesquieu did not turn up until *The Federalist*; and although a perverse argument could be made that Madison's ideal was truly in the

---

may have brought on him to save the day (Georgia was the last state to vote) and open the way to compromise. To employ a good Russian phrase, it was certainly not an accident that Baldwin voted the way he did. See *Warren,* p. 262.

[54] For various contemporary comments, see *Warren,* pp. 814–818. On Adams' technique, see Zoltan Haraszti, "The Composition of Adams' *Defense,*" in *John Adams and the Prophets of Progress* (Cambridge, 1952), ch. 9. In this connection it is interesting to check the Con-vention discussions for references to the authority of Locke, Montesquieu and Harrington, the theorists who have been assigned various degress of paternal responsibility. There are no explicit references to James Harrington; one to John Locke (Luther Martin cited him on the state of nature, *Farrand,* I, 437); and seven to Montesquieu, only one of which related to the "separation of powers" (Madison in an odd speech, which he explained in a footnote was given to help a friend rather than advance his own views, cited Montesquieu on the separation of the executive and legislative branches, *Farrand,* II, 34). This, of course, does not prove that Locke and Co. were without influence; it shifts the burden of proof, however, to those who assert ideological causality. See Benjamin F. Wright, "The Origins of the Separation of Powers in America," *Economica,* Vol. 13 (1933), p. 184.

tradition of John Locke's *Second Treatise of Government*,[55] the Locke whom the American rebels treated as an honorary president was a pluralistic defender of vested rights,[56] not of parliamentary supremacy.

It would be tedious to continue a blow-by-blow analysis of the work of the delegates; the critical fight was over representation of the states and once the Connecticut Compromise was adopted on July 17, the Convention was over the hump. Madison, James Wilson, and Gouverneur Morris of New York (who was there representing Pennsylvania!) fought the compromise all the way in a last-ditch effort to get a unitary state with parliamentary supremacy. But their allies deserted them and they demonstrated after their defeat the essentially opportunist character of their objections—using "opportunist" here in a non-pejorative sense, to indicate a willingness to swallow their objections and get on with the business. Moreover, once the compromise had carried (by five states to four, with one state divided), its advocates threw themselves vigorously into the job of strengthening the general government's substantive powers—as might have been predicted, indeed, from Paterson's early statements. It nourishes an increased respect for Madison's devotion to the art of politics, to realize that this dogged fighter could sit down six months later and prepare essays for *The Federalist* in contradiction to his basic convictions about the true course the Convention should have taken.

V

Two tricky issues will serve to illustrate the later process of accommodation. The first was the institutional position of the Executive. Madison argued for an executive chosen by the National Legislature and on May 29 this had been adopted with a provision that after his seven-year term was concluded, the chief magistrate should not be eligible for reelection. In late July this was reopened and for a week the matter was argued from several different points of view. A good deal of desultory speech-making ensued, but the gist of the problem was the opposition from two sources to election by the legislature. One group felt that the states should have a hand in the process; another small but influential circle urged direct election by the people. There were a number of proposals: election by the people, election by state governors, by electors chosen by state legislatures, by the National Legislature (James Wilson, perhaps ironically, proposed at one point that an Electroal College be chosen by lot from the National Legislature!), and there was some resemblance to three-dimensional chess in the dispute because of the presence of two other variables, length of tenure and re-eligibility. Finally, after opening, reopening, and re-reopening the debate, the thorny problem was consigned to a committee for resolution.

The Brearley Committee on Postponed Matters was a superb aggregation of talent and its compromise on the Executive was a masterpiece of political improvisation.

[55] I share Willmoore Kendall's interpretation of Locke as a supporter of parliamentary supremacy and majoritarianism; see Kendall, *John Locke and the Doctrine of Majority Rule* (Urbana, 1941). Kendall's general position has recently received strong support in the definitive edition and commentary of Peter Laslett, *Locke's Two Treatises of Government* (Cambridge, 1960).

[56] The American Locke is best delineated in Carl Becker, *The Declaration of Independence* (New York, 1948).

(The Electoral College, its creation, however, had little in its favor as an *institution* —as the delegates well appreciated.) The point of departure for all discussion about the presidency in the Convention was that in immediate terms, the problem was non-existent; in other words, everybody present knew that under any system devised, George Washington would be President. Thus they were dealing in the future tense and to a body of working politicians the merits of the Brearley proposal were obvious: everybody got a piece of cake. (Or to put it more academically, each viewpoint could leave the Convention and argue to its constituents that it had *really* won the day.) First, the state legislatures had the right to determine the mode of selection of the electors; second, the small states received a bonus in the Electoral College in the form of a guaranteed minimum of three votes while the big states got acceptance of the principle of proportional power; third, if the state legislatures agreed (as six did in the first presidential election), the people could be involved directly in the choice of electors; and finally, if no candidate received a majority in the College, the right of decision passed to the National Legislature with each state exercising equal strength. (In the Brearley recommendation, the election went to the Senate, but a motion from the floor substituted the House; this was accepted on the ground that the Senate already had enough authority over the executive in its treaty and appointment powers.)

This compromise was almost too good to be true, and the Framers snapped it up with little debate or controversy. No one seemed to think well of the College as an *institution;* indeed, what evidence there is suggests that there was an assumption that once Washington had finished his tenure as President, the electors would cease to produce majorities and the chief executive would usually be chosen in the House. George Mason observed casually that the selection would be made in the House nineteen times in twenty and no one seriously disputed this point. The vital aspect of the Electoral College was that it got the Convention over the hurdle and protected everybody's interests. The future was left to cope with the problem of what to do with this Rube Goldberg mechanism.

In short, the Framers did not in their wisdom endow the United States with a College of Cardinals—the Electoral College was neither an exercise in applied Platonism nor an experiment in indirect government based on elitist distrust of the masses. It was merely a jerry-rigged improvisation which has subsequently been endowed with a high theoretical content. When an elector from Oklahoma in 1960 refused to cast his vote for Nixon (naming Byrd and Goldwater instead) on the ground that the Founding Fathers intended him to exercise his great independent wisdom, he was indulging in historical fantasy. If one were to indulge in counter-fantasy, he would be tempted to suggest that the Fathers would be startled to find the College still in operation—and perhaps even dismayed at their descendants' lack of judgment or inventiveness.[57]

The second issue on which some substantial practical bargaining took place was slavery. The morality of slavery was, by design, not at issue;[58] but in its other con-

---

[57] See John P. Roche, "The Electoral College: A Note on American Political Mythology," *Dissent* (Spring, 1961), pp. 197–99. The relevant debates took place July 19–26, 1787, *Farrand,* II, 50–128, and September 5–6, 1787, *ibid.,* pp. 505–31.

[58] See the discussion on August 22, 1787, *Farrand,* II, 366–375; King seems to have expressed the sense of the Convention when he said "the subject should be considered in a political light only." *Ibid.* at 373.

crete aspects, slavery colored the arguments over taxation, commerce, and representation. The "Three-Fifths Compromise," that three-fifths of the slaves would be counted
both for representation and for purposes of direct taxation (which was drawn from
the past—it was a formula of Madison's utilized by Congress in 1783 to establish
the basis of state contributions to the Confederation treasury) had allayed some
Northern fears about Southern over-representation (no one then foresaw the trivial
role that direct taxation would play in later federal financial policy), but doubts still
remained. The Southerners, on the other hand, were afraid that Congressional control over commerce would lead to the exclusion of slaves or to their excessive taxation
as imports. Moreover, the Southerners were disturbed over "navigation acts," *i.e.,*
tariffs, or special legislation providing, for example, that exports be carried only in
American ships; as a section depending upon exports, they wanted protection from
the potential voracity of their commercial brethren of the Eastern states. To achieve
this end, Mason and others urged that the Constitution include a proviso that navigation and commercial laws should require a two-thirds vote in Congress.

These problems came to a head in late August and, as usual, were handed to a
committee in the hope that, in Gouverneur Morris' words, ". . . these things may
form a bargain among the Northern and Southern states." [59] The Committee reported its measures of reconciliation on August 25, and on August 29 the package
was wrapped up and delivered. What occurred can best be described in George Mason's dour version (he anticipated Calhoun in his conviction that permitting navigation acts to pass by majority vote would put the South in economic bondage to the
North—it was mainly on this ground that he refused to sign the Constitution):

> The Constitution as agreed to till a fortnight before the Convention rose was
> such a one as he would have set his hand and heart to. . . . [Until that time]
> The 3 New England States were constantly with us in all questions . . . so that
> it was these three States with the 5 Southern ones against Pennsylvania, Jersey
> and Delaware. With respect to the importation of slaves, [decision-making] was
> left to Congress. This disturbed the two Southernmost States who knew that Con-
> gress would immediately suppress the importation of slaves. Those two States
> therefore struck up a bargain with the three New England States. If they would
> join to admit slaves for some years, the two Southern-most States would join in
> changing the clause which required the 2/3 of the Legislature in any vote [on
> navigation acts]. It was done.[60]

On the floor of the Convention there was a virtual love-feast on this happy occasion. Charles Pinckney of South Carolina attempted to overturn the committee's
decision, when the compromise was reported to the Convention, by insisting that the
South needed protection from the imperialism of the Northern states. But his
Southern colleagues were not prepared to rock the boat and General C. C. Pinckney
arose to spread oil on the suddenly ruffled waters; he admitted that:

> It was in the true interest of the S[outhern] States to have no regulation of
> commerce; but considering the loss brought on the commerce of the Eastern States
> by the Revolution, their liberal conduct towards the views of South Carolina [on
> the regulation of the slave trade] and the interests the weak Southn. States had
> in being united with the strong Eastern states, he thought it proper that no fet-

---

[59] *Farrand,* II, 374. Randolph echoed his sentiment in different words.
[60] Mason to Jefferson, cited in *Warren,* p. 584.

ters should be imposed on the power of making commercial regulations; *and that his constituents, though prejudiced against the Eastern States, would be reconciled to this liberality*. He had himself prejudices agst the Eastern States before he came here, but would acknowledge that he had found them as liberal and candid as any men whatever. (Italics added)[61]

Pierce Butler took the same tack, essentially arguing that he was not too happy about the possible consequences, but that a deal was a deal.[62] Many Southern leaders were later—in the wake of the "Tariff of Abominations"—to rue this day of reconciliation; Calhoun's *Disquisition on Government* was little more than an extension of the argument in the Convention against permitting a congressional majority to enact navigation acts.[63]

VI

Drawing on their vast collective political experience, utilizing every weapon in the politician's arsenal, looking constantly over their shoulders at their constituents, the delegates put together a Constitution. It was a makeshift affair; some sticky issues (for example, the qualification of voters) they ducked entirely; others they mastered with that ancient instrument of political sagacity, studied ambiguity (for example, citizenship), and some they just overlooked. In this last category, I suspect, fell the matter of the power of the federal courts to determine the constitutionality of acts of Congress. When the judicial article was formulated (Article III of the Constitution), deliberations were still in the stage where the legislature was endowed with broad power under the Randolph formulation, authority which by its own terms was scarcely amenable to judicial review. In essence, courts hardly determine when ". . . the separate States are incompetent or . . . the harmony of the United States may be interrupted"; the National Legislature, as critics pointed out, was free to define its own jurisdiction. Later the definition of legislative authority was changed into the form we know, a series of stipulated powers, *but the delegates never seriously reexamined the jurisdiction of the judiciary under this new limited formulation*.[64]

[61] August 29, 1787, *Farrand*, II, 449–50.

[62] *Ibid.*, p. 451. The plainest statement of the matter was put by the three North Carolina delegates (Blount, Spaight and Williamson) in their report to Governor Caswell, September 18, 1787. After noting that "no exertions have been wanting on our part to guard and promote the particular interest of North Carolina," they went on to explain the basis of the negotiations in cold-blooded fashion: "While we were taking so much care to guard ourselves against being over reached and to form rules of Taxation that might operate in our favour, it is not to be supposed that our Northern Brethren were Inattentive to their particular Interest. A navigation Act or the power to regulate Commerce in the Hands of the National Government . . . is what the Southern States have given in Exchange for the advantages we Mentioned." They concluded by explaining that while the Constitution did deal with other matters besides taxes—"there are other Considerations of great Magnitude involved in the system"—they would not take up valuable time with boring details! *Farrand*, III, 83–84.

[63] See John C. Calhoun, *A Disquisition on Government* (New York, 1943), pp. 21–25, 38. Calhoun differed from Mason, and others in the Convention who urged the two-thirds requirement, by advocating a functional or interest veto rather than some sort of special majority, *i.e.*, he abandoned the search for quantitative checks in favor of a qualitative solution.

[64] The Committee on Detail altered the general grant of legislative power envisioned by the Virginia Plan into a series of specific grants; these were examined closely between August 16 and

All arguments on the intention of the Framers in this matter are thus deductive and *a posteriori*, though some obviously make more sense than others.[65]

The Framers were busy and distinguished men, anxious to get back to their families, their positions, and their constituents, not members of the French Academy devoting a lifetime to a dictionary. They were trying to do an important job, and do it in such a fashion that their handiwork would be acceptable to very diverse constituencies. No one was rhapsodic about the final document, but it was a beginning, a move in the right direction, and one they had reason to believe the people would endorse. In addition, since they had modified the impossible amendment provisions of the Articles (the requirement of unanimity which could always be frustrated by "Rogues Island") to one demanding approval by only three-quarters of the states, they seemed confident that gaps in the fabric which experience would reveal could be rewoven without undue difficulty.

So with a neat phrase introduced by Benjamin Franklin (but devised by Gouverneur Morris)[66] which made their decision sound unanimous, and an inspired benediction by the Old Doctor urging doubters to doubt their own infallibility, the Constitution was accepted and signed. Curiously, Edmund Randolph, who had played so vital a role throughout, refused to sign, as did his fellow Virginian George Mason and Elbridge Gerry of Masschusetts. Randolph's behavior was eccentric, to say the least—his excuses for refusing his signature have a factitious ring even at this late date; the best explanation seems to be that he was afraid that the Constitution would prove to be a liability in Virginia politics, where Patrick Henry was burning up the countryside with impassioned denunciations. Presumably, Randolph wanted to check the temper of the populace before he risked his reputation, and perhaps his job, in a fight with both Henry and Richard Henry Lee.[67] Events lend some justification to this speculation: after much temporizing and use of conditional subjunctive

---

August 23. One day only was devoted to the Judicial Article, August 27, and since no one raised the question of judicial review of *Federal* statutes, no light was cast on the matter. A number of random comments on the power of the judiciary were scattered throughout the discussions, but there was another variable which deprives them of much probative value: the proposed Council of Revision which would have joined the Executive with the judges in *legislative* review. Madison and Wilson, for example, favored this technique—which had nothing in common with what we think of as judicial review except that judges were involved in the task.

[65] For what it may be worth, I think that judicial review of congressional acts was logically on all fours with review of state enactments and that it was certainly consistent with the view that the Constitution could not be amended by the Congress and President, or by a two-thirds vote of Congress (overriding a veto), without the agreement of three-quarters of the states. *External* evidence from that time supports this view, see Charles Warren, *Congress, the Constitution, and the Supreme Court* (Boston, 1925), pp. 41–128, but the debates *in* the Convention prove nothing.

[66] Or so Madison stated, *Farrand*, II, 643. Wilson too may have contributed; he was close to Franklin and delivered the frail old gentleman's speeches for him.

[67] See a very interesting letter, from an unknown source in Philadelphia, to Jefferson, October 11, 1787: "Randolph wishes it well, & it is thought would have signed it, but he wanted to be on a footing with a popular rival." *Farrand*, III, 104. Madison, writing Jefferson a full account on October 24, 1787, put the matter more delicately—he was working hard on Randolph to win him for ratification: "[Randolph] was not inveterate in his opposition, and grounded his refusal to subscribe pretty much on his unwillingness to commit himself, so as not to be at liberty to be governed by further lights on the subject." *Ibid.*, p. 135.

tense, Randolph endorsed ratifications in Virginia and ended up getting the best of both worlds.

Madison, despite his reservations about the Constitution, was the campaign manager in ratification. His first task was to get the Congress in New York to light its own funeral pyre by approving the "amendments" to the Articles and sending them on to the state legislatures. Above all, momentum had to be maintained. The anti-Constitutionalists, now thoroughly alarmed and no novices in politics, realized that their best tactic was attrition rather than direct opposition. Thus they settled on a position expressing qualified approval but calling for a second Convention to remedy various defects (the one with the most demagogic appeal was the lack of a Bill of Rights). Madison knew that to accede to this demand would be equivalent to losing the battle, nor would he agree to conditional approval (despite wavering even by Hamilton). This was an all-or-nothing proposition: national salvation or national impotence with no intermediate positions possible. Unable to get congressional approval, he settled for second best: a unanimous resolution of Congress transmitting the Constitution to the states for whatever action they saw fit to take. The opponents then moved from New York and the Congress, where they had attempted to attach amendments and conditions, to the states for the final battle.[68]

At first the campaign for ratification went beautifully: within eight months after the delegates set their names to the document, eight states had ratified. Only in Massachusetts had the result been close (187–168). Theoretically, a ratification by one more state convention would set the new government in motion, but in fact until Virginia and New York acceded to the new Union, the latter was a fiction. New Hampshire was the next to ratify; Rhode Island was involved in its characteristic political convulsions (the Legislature there sent the Constitution out to the towns for decision by popular vote and it got lost among a series of local issues);[69] North Carolina's convention did not meet until July and then postponed a final decision. This is hardly the place for an extensive analysis of the conventions of New York and Virginia. Suffice it to say that the Constitutionalists clearly outmaneuvered their opponents, forced them into impossible political positions, and won both states narrowly. The Virginia Convention could serve as a classic study in effective floor management: Patrick Henry had to be contained, and a reading of the debates discloses a standard two-stage technique. Henry would give a four- or five-hour speech denouncing some section of the Constitution on every conceivable ground (the federal district, he averred at one point, would become a haven for convicts escaping from state authority!);[70] When Henry subsided, "Mr. Lee of Westmoreland" would rise and literally poleaxe him with sardonic invective (when Henry complained about the militia power, "Lighthorse Harry" really punched below the belt: observing that while the former Governor had been sitting in Richmond during the Revolution, *he* had been out in the trenches with the troops and thus felt better qualified to discuss military affairs).[71] Then the gentlemanly Constitutionalists (Madison, Pendleton and

---

[68] See Edward P. Smith, "The Movement Towards a Second Constitutional Convention in 1788," in J. F. Jameson, ed., *Essays in the Constitutional History of the United States* (Boston, 1889), pp. 46–115.

[69] See Bishop, *op. cit., passim.*

[70] See *Elliot's Debates on the Federal Constitution* (Washington, 1836), Vol. 3, pp. 436–438.

[71] This should be quoted to give the full flavor: "Without vanity, I may say I have had different experience of [militia] service from that of [Henry]. It was my fortune to be a soldier

Marshall) would pick up the matters at issue and examine them in the light of reason.

Indeed, modern Americans who tend to think of James Madison as a rather dessicated character should spend some time with this transcript. Probably Madison put on his most spectacular demonstration of nimble rhetoric in what might be called "The Battle of the Absent Authorities." Patrick Henry in the course of one of his harangues alleged that Jefferson was known to be opposed to Virginia's approving the Constitution. This was clever: Henry hated Jefferson, but was prepared to use any weapon that came to hand. Madison's riposte was superb: First, he said that with all due respect to the great reputation of Jefferson, he was not in the country and therefore could not formulate an adequate judgment; second, no one should utilize the reputation of an outsider—the Virginia Convention was there to think for itself; third, if there were to be recourse to outsiders, the opinions of George Washington should certainly be taken into consideration; and finally, he knew from privileged personal communications from Jefferson that in fact the latter *strongly favored* the Constitution.[72] To devise an assault route into this rhetorical fortress was literally impossible.

VII

The fight was over; all that remained now was to establish the new frame of government in the spirit of its framers. And who were better qualified for this task than the Framers themselves? Thus victory for the Constitution meant simultaneous victory for the Constitutionalists; the anti-Constitutionalists either capitulated or vanished into limbo—soon Patrick Henry would be offered a seat on the Supreme Court[73] and Luther Martin would be known as the Federalist "bull-dog."[74] And irony of ironies, Alexander Hamilton and James Madison would shortly accumulate a reputation as the formulators of what is often alleged to be our political theory, the concept of "federalism." Also, on the other side of the ledger, the arguments would soon appear over what the Framers "really meant"; while these disputes have assumed the proportions of a big scholarly business in the last century, they began almost before the ink on the Constitution was dry. One of the best early ones featured Hamilton versus Madison on the scope of presidential power, and other Framers characteristically assumed positions in this and other disputes on the basis of their political convictions.

Probably our greatest difficulty is that we know so much more about what the Framers *should have meant* than they themselves did. We are intimately acquainted

of my country. . . . I saw what the honorable gentleman did not see—our men fighting. . . ." *Ibid.,* p. 178.

[72] *Ibid.,* p. 329.

[73] Washington offered him the Chief Justiceship in 1796, but he declined; Charles Warren, *The Supreme Court in United States History* (Boston, 1947), Vol. 1, p. 139.

[74] He was a zealous prosecutor of seditions in the period 1798–1800; with Justice Samuel Chase, like himself an alleged "radical" at the time of the Constitutional Convention, Martir hunted down Jeffersonian heretics. See James M. Smith, *Freedom's Fetters* (Ithaca, 1956) pp. 342–43.

with the problems that their Constitution should have been designed to master; in short, we have read the mystery story backwards. If we are to get the right "feel" for their time and their circumstances, we must in Maitland's phrase, ". . . think ourselves back into a twilight." Obviously, no one can pretend completely to escape from the solipsistic web of his own environment, but if the effort is made, it is possible to appreciate the past roughly on its own terms. The first step in this process is to abandon the academic premise that because we can ask a question, there must be an answer.

Thus we can ask what the Framers meant when they gave Congress the power to regulate interstate and foreign commerce, and we emerge, reluctantly perhaps, with the reply that (Professor Crosskey to the contrary notwithstanding)[75] they may not have known what they meant, that there may not have been any semantic consensus. The Convention was not a seminar in analytic philosophy or linguistic analysis. Commerce was *commerce*—and if different interpretations of the word arose, later generations could worry about the problem of definition. The delegates were in a hurry to get a new government established; when definitional arguments arose, they characteristically took refuge in ambiguity. If different men voted for the same proposition for varying reasons, that was politics (and still is); if later generations were unsettled by this lack of precision, that would be their problem.

There was a good deal of definitional pluralism with respect to the problems the delegates did discuss, but when we move to the question of extrapolated intentions, we enter the realm of spiritualism. When men in our time, for instance, launch into elaborate talmudic exegesis to demonstrate that federal aid to parochial schools is (or is not) in accord with the intentions of the men who established the Republic and endorsed the Bill of Rights, they are engaging in historical Extra-Sensory Perception. (If one were to join this E. S. P. contingent for a minute, he might suggest that the hard-boiled politicians who wrote the Constitution and Bill of Rights would chuckle scornfully at such an invocation of authority: obviously a politician would chart his course on the intentions of the living, not of the dead, and count the number of Catholics in his constituency.)

The Constitution, then, was not an apotheosis of "constitutionalism," a triumph of

---

[75] Crosskey in his sprawling *Politics and the Constitution* (Chicago, 1953), 2 vols., has developed with almost unbelievable zeal and intricacy the thesis that the Constitution *was* designed to establish a centralized unitary state, but that the political leadership of the Republic in its formative years betrayed this ideal and sold the pass to states'-rights. While he has unearthed some interesting newspaper articles and other material, it is impossible for me to accept his central proposition. Madison and the other delegates, with the exceptions discussed in the text *supra,* did *want* to diminish the power of the states and create a vigorous national government. But they were not fools, and were, I submit, under no illusions when they departed from Philadelphia that this end had been accomplished. The crux of my argument is that *political realities* forced them to water down their objectives and they settled, like the good politicians they were, for half a loaf. The basic difficulty with Crosskey's thesis is that he knows *too* much— he assumes that the Framers had a perfectly clear idea of the road they were taking; with a semantic machete he cuts blandly through all the confusion on the floor of the meeting to the *real* meanings. Thus, despite all his ornate research apparatus, there is a fundamentally non-empirical quality about Crosskey's work: at crucial points in the argument he falls back on a type of divination which can only be described as Kabbalistic. He may be right, for example, in stating (without any proof) that Richard Henry Lee did *not* write the "Letters from a Federal Farmer," but in this country spectral evidence has not been admissible since the Seventeenth Century.

architectonic genius; it was a patch-work sewn together under the pressure of both time and events by a group of extremely talented democratic politicians. They refused to attempt the establishment of a strong, centralized sovereignty on the principle of legislative supremacy for the excellent reason that the people would not accept it. They risked their political fortunes by opposing the established doctrines of state sovereignty because they were convinced that the existing system was leading to national impotence and probably foreign domination. For two years, they worked to get a convention established. For over three months, in what must have seemed to the faithful participants an endless process of give-and-take, they reasoned, cajoled, threatened, and bargained amongst themselves. The result was a Constitution which the people, in fact, by democratic processes, did accept, and a new and far better national government was established.

Beginning with the inspired propaganda of Hamilton, Madison and Jay, the ideological build-up got under way. *The Federalist* had little impact on the ratification of the Constitution, except perhaps in New York, but this volume had enormous influence on the image of the Constitution in the minds of future generations, particularly on historians and political scientists who have an innate fondness for theoretical symmetry. Yet, while the shades of Locke and Montesquieu *may* have been hovering in the background, and the delegates *may* have been unconscious instruments of a transcendent *telos*, the careful observer of the day-to-day work of the Convention finds no over-arching principles. The "separation of powers" to him seems to be a by-product of suspicion, and "federalism" he views as a *pis aller*, as the farthest point the delegates felt they could go in the destruction of state power without themselves inviting repudiation.

To conclude, the Constitution was neither a victory for abstract theory nor a great practical success. Well over half a million men had to die on the battlefields of the Civil War before certain constitutional principles could be defined—a baleful consideration which is somehow overlooked in our customary tributes to the far-sighted genius of the Framers and to the supposed American talent for "constitutionalism." The Constitution was, however, a vivid demonstration of effective democratic political action, and of the forging of a national elite which literally persuaded its countrymen to hoist themselves by their own boot straps. American pro-consuls would be wise not to translate the Constitution into Japanese, or Swahili, or treat it as a work of semi-Divine origin; but when students of comparative politics examine the process of nation-building in countries newly freed from colonial rule, they may find the American experience instructive as a classic example of the potentialities of a democratic elite.

19 / The Virginia Convention of 1788:
A Criticism of Beard's
"An Economic Interpretation of the Constitution"

Robert E. Thomas

Of all the historical analyses of the Constitution of 1787 that have been published, the one that has created the most controversy was Charles A. Beard's *An Economic Interpretation of the Constitution*. Beard's iconoclasm led him to question many facets of the constitution-making process of the 1780's. In his view the men at Philadelphia were motivated, at least in part, by economic considerations, particularly by their concern to have a strong government protecting their interests in personalty, such as their holdings of government securities. Moreover, they acted in secrecy, in haste, and in an undemocratic way. The adoption of the Constitution was virtually a *coup d'état* against the old order. Previous essays have examined the place of "democratic" values in eighteenth-century politics. The immediately preceding article at least suggested the involved process by which the Constitution was adopted and the extraordinary share that the people and the states had in that process. In simple progression, the Congress under the Articles had to call a convention, the states' popularly elected legislatures to send delegates, the delegates to act, the Congress to refer their action back to the states, the legislatures to decide to call conventions, the people to elect delegates to the conventions, and the conventions to vote on the new government. More serious attention perhaps should be given to Beard's suggestion of economic motivation. On the following pages, Robert E. Thomas examines the lines dividing proponents and opponents of the Constitution in the key state of Virginia. Without Virginia's acquiescence, there would have been little chance of the new federal government becoming a reality. To readers of earlier selections in this volume, it should come as no surprise that Virginia's politics—however wide the popular basis of participation—were dominated by men loosely categorized as "aristocrats." But how and why did those aristocratic leaders divide over the Constitution?

Reprinted by permission from the *Journal of Southern History*, XIX (1953), 63–72. Copyright 1953 by the Southern Historical Association. Reprinted by permission of the Managing Editor.

For further reading: Douglass Adair, "The Tenth Federalist Revisited," *William and Mary Quarterly,* 3rd series, VIII (1951), 48–67; Richard Hofstadter, "Beard and the Constitution: the History of an Idea," *American Quarterly,* II (1950), 195–213; Charles A. Beard, *An Economic Interpretation of the Constitution* (1913); Lee Benson, *Turner and Beard: American Historical Writing Reconsidered* (1960); Robert E. Brown, *Charles Beard and the Constitution, A Critical Analysis of "An Economic Interpretation of the Constitution* (1956); Forrest McDonald, *We the People; the Economic Origins of the Constitution* (1958).

Perhaps no other book in the past half century has aroused more controversy than Charles A. Beard's *An Economic Interpretation of the Constitution of the United States* (New York, 1913). Yet in spite of the debate which has raged about Beard's thesis and despite its susceptibility to empiric test, few writers have set about to determine inductively whether the poor were generally Anti-Federalists and the rich for the most part Federalists. This essay, a study of the economic and social status of the members of the Virginia state ratifying convention of 1788, is an attempt to answer this question so far as it applies to Virginia.[1]

In his section on Virginia in the chapter entitled "The Economics of the Vote on the Constitution" Beard, drawing heavily on the works of Orin G. Libby[2] and Charles H. Ambler,[3] demonstrates that the vote on the Constitution corresponds rather closely to the four geographical sections within Virginia at that time—the Tidewater, the Piedmont, the Great Valley, and in the far western part of the state, Kentucky. Beard believed that the Tidewater, which was "almost solid in favor of ratifying the Constitution," supported the new government because here were concentrated the greatest number of large slave and landowners, as well as the heaviest concentration of commercial interests; that the Piedmont, which "was largely against ratifying the Constitution," voted as it did because in this region there were fewer personalty interests and a higher percentage of small farming debtors; that the vote of the Great Valley, which was overwhelmingly in favor of the federal government, "has not yet been traced to economic reasons"; and that the Kentucky district, which "was almost solid against ratification of the Constitution," opposed the new government because of the "frontier economic characteristics of the region" (that is, absence of personalty interests) and "the question of the opening of the Mississippi river." Implicit in this picture of the vote on the Constitution is a political contest between the rich and the poor. The rich, because of their excessive numbers in the East,[4]

[1] This essay is based upon economic and social biographies of each of the 167 members of this convention. In the course of compiling these biographies the author unearthed much relevant material which cannot conveniently be summarized, but that which can is contained in these pages.

[2] Orin G. Libby, *The Geographical Distribution of the Vote of the Thirteen States on the Federal Constitution, 1787–8* (Madison, Wis., 1894).

[3] Charles H. Ambler, *Sectionalism in Virginia* (Chicago, 1910).

[4] The "East" is here taken to mean the Tidewater, which voted for the Constitution, while the "West" designates the Piedmont and Kentucky, which opposed the Constitution. In a criticism of Beard's thesis the Great Valley may be forgotten, because Beard himself admitted that the vote of this region could not be traced to economic reasons.

won that region for the Federalists; the poor, because of their preponderance in the West, aligned that region with the Anti-Federalists.

Beard's thesis, however, rests upon no other foundation than Libby's demonstration that the conflict in Virginia was sectional. But to suggest that this was a class conflict because the East—where were concentrated the greatest number of personalty interests—voted for the Constitution, while the West—where was concentrated the highest percentage of small farming debtors—voted against it, overlooks the fact that there were personalty interests in both sections, and that there were small farming debtors in the Tidewater as well as in the West. The question of whether the conflict in Virginia was class as well as sectional depends upon whether the personalty interests in both sections voted as a unit in favor of the Constitution, and whether the debtors in both sections voted against it. Definitive proof of the nature of the contest in Virginia awaits an exhaustive study of "all" the personnel involved. In the meantime the data here presented offer substantial proof that the leaders of both the Federalist and Anti-Federalist parties came from the *same class*—slaveowners, large landowners, land speculators, army officers and professional people, in short, the gentry—and that the conflict, for whatever reasons, was only sectional.

II

Because of the absence of extensive commercial interests in Virginia during this period (in 1790, only 18,539 persons out of a total population of over 700,000 lived in Virginia's nine principal towns) the most extensive personalty was in slaves. Thus any test of the Beardian thesis must concern itself largely with an investigation of the ownership of slaves. Was a substantial majority of Virginia's approximately 290,-000 slaves owned by those who voted to support the new government, were they more or less equally divided between the two parties, or did the weight of Virginia's most extensive personalty lie with the Anti-Federalists? Unfortunately since the returns for Virginia in the first United States census have been almost totally destroyed, no comparison of the holdings of individual members of both parties can be made from this source. However, the white and slave populations by counties have been preserved, and on the basis of a state-wide comparison of all the counties it will be seen, from the chart below, that the greatest number of slaves, both absolutely and relative to the number of whites, was in the *Anti-Federalist* counties:

	Anti-Federalist	Federalist	Divided
Total Number of Whites	176,255	214,986	50,876
Total Number of Slaves	133,155	123,692	35,780
Ratio of Slaves to Whites	0.8	0.6	0.7
Total Number of Counties	35	39	10
Average Slaves per County	3,804	3,171	3,578

It would appear at first glance that the Federalists were by far the poorest in personalty of the three groups above. But this is true only on a state-wide basis. The lower figures (except population) for the Federalists results from the fact that fourteen Federalist counties,[5] lying in or near the Great Valley, with a combined population of 99,890 whites, held only 13,483 slaves: a ratio of .1 slaves to each white. Caroline, a Federalist, Tidewater county, alone held 10,292 slaves, while its white population was only 6,994: a ratio of 1.4 slaves to each white. Thus the Great Valley, whose vote Beard says "has not yet been traced to economic reasons," distorts the Federalist figures for the rest of the state. A better indication of the relative wealth of the Federalists and Anti-Federalists, so far as Beard's thesis is concerned, may be had by a comparison of those Federalist and Anti-Federalist counties which did not lie in either the Federalist Great Valley or the Anti-Federalist southwestern part of the state. The twenty-five remaining Federalist counties, clustered for the most part in the Tidewater, contained 115,096 whites and 110,209 slaves: a ratio of .95 slaves per white. The twenty-five remaining Anti-Federalist counties, which lay generally in the Piedmont, contained 146,196 whites and 129,253 slaves: a ratio of .88 slaves per white.

The conclusion suggested by the above figures is that—whether one views the state as a whole, in which case the Anti-Federalists appears somewhat richer in slaves than the Federalists, or contrasts only the Tidewater and the Piedmont, in which case the Federalists have absolutely fewer, but relatively slightly more slaves than the Anti-Federalists—the slaveholders did not, as a group, support the Federal Constitution. Instead, in the regions where slaves were most widely held, the slaveholders appear to have been more or less equally divided on the issue.

Yet however suggestive the above figures may be, they do not reveal the wealth of individual men who voted to adopt or to reject the Constitution. It is only when county and sectional lines have been breached, and the status of individual men who voted either for or against the Constitution has been determined, that the "economic interpretation" will have been adequately tested. The materials for such a study, unlike those for a county study, are extremely fragmentary; yet the chart which follows offers strong evidence that men owning substantially the same number of slaves were equally divided on the matter of adopting or rejecting the Federal Constitution:

SLAVES HELD BY INDIVIDUAL MEMBERS OF THE VIRGINIA CONVENTION

Anti-Federalists		Federalists	
No. of Owners	No. of Slaves Owned	No. of Owners	No. of Slaves Owned
2	4	1	5
1	6	2	8
1	8	1	9
3	10	1	10
1	13	1	12
1	17	4	15
1	19	2	19
3	21	1	25
1	23	1	26
1	27	1	27
1	30	1	28
1	32	1	31
1	35	1	37
1	38	1	38

[5] Ohio, Harrison, Greenbriar, Randolph, Hardy, Augusta, Rockbridge, Botetourt, Hampshire, Berkeley, Jefferson, Frederick, Shenandoah, and Rockingham counties.

SLAVES HELD BY INDIVIDUAL MEMBERS OF THE VIRGINIA CONVENTION–*Cont.**

Anti-Federalists		*Federalists*	
No. of Owners	*No. of Slaves Owned*	*No. of Owners*	*No. of Slaves Owned*
1	39	1	43
1	124	1	58
1	150	1	62
1	300	1	63
		1	88
		1	143
		1	200

Anti-Federalists		Federalists	
Total number of slaves:	962	Total number of slaves:	1,019
Total number of owners:	23	Total number of owners:	26
Average per owner:	42	Average per owner:	39
Median: 21		Median: 25.5	
(No specific figures for 55 Anti-Federalist delegates)		(No specific figures for 63 Federalist delegates)	

* Figures in this table are taken from biographical sketches of the members of the convention, which were compiled by the author.

In order to heighten the significance of the above figures the following tables are included. They may help to make clearer what constituted a large, medium, and small slaveholder, and to place the above delegates in their proper light:

PRINCESS ANNE COUNTY (Federalist, Tidewater) 1783 48% of the heads of families owned no slaves.		PRINCE EDWARD COUNTY (Anti-Federalist, Piedmont) 1783 37% of the heads of families owned no slaves.		HAMPSHIRE COUNTY (Western County) 1782 88% of the heads of families owned no slaves.	
No. of Owners	*No. of Slaves Owned*	*No. of Owners*	*No. of Slaves Owned*	*No. of Owners*	*No. of Slaves Owned*
98	1	15	1	56	1
60	2	19	2	30	2
53	3	16	3	22	3
34	4	13	4	7	4
29	5	12	5	3	5
26	6	10	6	8	6
25	7	8	7	6	7
9	8	7	8	1	8
9	9	8	9	3	9
10	10	5	10	5	10
13	11	4	11	4	12
7	12	4	12	1	13
6	13	5	13	1	15
7	14	2	15	1	16
7	15	4	16	1	21
5	16	4	17		
6	17	3	18		
4	18	4	19		
3	19	4	20		
4	20	1	22		
3	21	1	25		

PRINCESS ANNE COUNTY*		PRINCE EDWARD COUNTY		HAMPSHIRE COUNTY	
(Federalist, Tidewater) 1783 48% of the heads of families owned no slaves.		(Anti-Federalist, Piedmont) 1783 37% of the heads of families owned no slaves.		(Western County) 1782 88% of the heads of families owned no slaves.	
No. of Owners	No. of Slaves Owned	No. of Owners	No. of Slaves Owned	No. of Owners	No. of Slaves Owned
2	22	1	28		
1	23	1	29		
2	24	1	30		
1	25	1	33		
1	28	1	34		
1	29	1	35		
1	30	1	43		
1	31	1	46		
1	47	1	64		
1	53				
1	72				

Total number of slaves: 2,656	Total number of slaves: 1,468	Total number of slaves: 513
Total number of owners: 431	Total number of owners: 158	Total number of owners: 149
Average per owner: 6.2	Average per owner: 9.2	Average per owner: 3.4

* Although the schedules for the heads of families in Virginia in the first United States census were almost totally destroyed in the War of 1812, the Census Bureau has made an effort to fill this gap by collecting and publishing state census and tax lists for Virginia which cover the period 1782–1785. These lists are published under the title *Heads of Families at the First Census of the United States Taken in the Year 1790; Records of the State Enumerations: 1782 to 1785, Virginia* (Washington, 1908). The tables here are based upon figures taken from that collection.

It will be seen from the tables for Princess Anne, a Tidewater county, Prince Edward, a Piedmont county, and Hampshire, a western county, that anyone owning 15 slaves or more might be considered a large slaveholder for any of these regions. Of the eight Anti-Federalist delegates who owned fewer than 15 slaves two were from western counties, where, in view of the fact that 88 per cent of the heads of families in Hampshire, a western county, held no slaves at all in 1782, it is evident that anyone owning any slaves could be considered one of the wealthier men in that region. Of these western delegates, one, Alexander Robertson, from Mercer County, owned 10 slaves, and may thus be considered a man of extreme wealth for that county; another, Henry Pawling, from Lincoln County, owned 4 slaves, and was consequently a man of some wealth. Two other Anti-Federalists who owned fewer than 15 slaves were Joseph Haden, who owned 8, and Samuel Richardson, who owned 4, both from Fluvanna County. In 1782, 47 per cent of the heads of families in that county held no slaves, while of those who did own slaves 46 per cent owned less than 4, and only 11 per cent owned 8 or more. Thus Haden, with 8 slaves, may be considered one of the larger slaveholders in that county, while Richardson, who owned 4, may be considered one of that county's medium slaveholders. Of the remaining Anti-Federalists who appear above as owning fewer than 15 slaves, one, Joseph Jones, from Dinwiddie, a Piedmont county, owned 10 slaves, and may be considered a medium slaveholder for that region. Another, Jonathan Patteson, from Lunenburg, a Piedmont county, owned 6 slaves in 1769; it may be presumed that his slaveholdings were somewhat larger by the time of the ratifying convention in 1788. Another, David Bell, from Buckingham, a Piedmont county, is listed as owning 13 slaves. This figure represents only those slaves which he inherited from his father-in-law, Henry Cary. It is nearly certain that his total holdings in slaves was considerably higher than this figure indicates. Finally, Theodorick Bland doubtless owned more than the 10 slaves for which he is listed above. This figure represents only those slaves which he owned in Amelia County, and not those which he is certain to have owned in his home county, Prince George, whose records have been destroyed.

Of the six Federalists above who owned fewer than 15 slaves, three were from western counties: Ralph Humphreys, from Hampshire, who owned 10 slaves, Thomas Lewis, from Rockingham, who owned 8, and Alexander White, from Frederick, who owned 9. All of these western delegates were large slaveholders for their region. Of the remaining Federalists who owned fewer than 15 slaves, one, Thomas Matthews was from the borough of Norfolk. Although the schedules for the heads of families in the first census have been destroyed, this census indicates that there were 1,604 whites in Norfolk borough in 1790 and 1,294 slaves: a ratio of .8 slaves per white. Matthews, who owned 12 slaves, was doubtless among the larger slaveholders in that borough. Another of these delegates was Charles Simms, from Fairfax, a Tidewater county, who owned 8 slaves. In 1782, 48 per cent of the heads of families in that county owned no slaves, and of those who did, 77 per cent owned less than 8. Simms may thus be considered of the upper-middle slaveholding class in that county. Finally, James Johnson, from Isle of Wight, a Tidewater county, owned 5 slaves. Forty-four per cent of the heads of families in that county owned no slaves in 1782, and of those who did, 53 per cent held less than 5. Johnson, then, may be considered as belonging to that county's lower-middle slaveholding class.

From the tables and analysis above three conclusions seem warranted: first, a substantial majority of the delegates were among Virginia's largest slaveholders; second, those delegates who appear in the table above as owning fewer than 15 slaves were generally large slaveholders for their particular county; and third, there is no significant difference in the number of slaves held by those who supported and those who opposed the Constitution.

III

Also pertinent to a test of the "economic interpretation" is the position taken on ratification by men who had been officers in the Revolution. Virginia's army officers received for their military service enormous grants of western land. "For instance the basic award for a Major was 5,333 acres; for a Captain, 4,000 acres; for Lieutenants, Ensigns, Cornets, Midshipmen, Surgeon's Mates and Gunners in the Artillery, 2,666 acres. Privates and non-commissioned officers received from 100 to 200 acres. The awards to Generals, Colonels, and Lieutenant Colonels varied, some of them receiving more than 10,000 acres." [6] Army officers, then, constituted a group with

[6] John H. Gwathmey, *Historical Register of Virginians in the Revolution* (Richmond, 1938), iv–v.

extensive holdings in western land. According to Beard, "the weakness of the Confederation, the lack of proper military forces, the uncertainty as to the frontiers kept the values of . . . large sections of the West at an abnormally low price." Consequently, those with large interests in western real estate "foresaw the benefits which might be expected from a new and stable government" and voted in favor of the Constitution. While it may be true that the army officers voted as a bloc in other states, there was no such unanimity among the officers in Virginia.

Army Officers	Anti-Federalists	Federalists
General	1	2
Colonel	23	19
Lt. Colonel	3	5
Major	4	3
Captain	10	13
Lieutenant	5	4
Ensign	2	0
Surgeon's Mate	0	1
Sergeant	0	1
Rank Unknown	2	6
	Total: 50	Total: 54
Members of the Cincinnati	10	8

In comparing these figures, and it must be remembered that there were eleven more Federalists than Anti-Federalists,[7] it is evident that the army officers were not, as a group, "in favor of the new Constitution." Instead, and despite their holdings in western land, it appears that about half of Virginia's officers voted against the Federal Constitution.

IV

Also worth comparing is the number of professional people who appear in each party. There were, of course, more towns in the Tidewater than in the Anti-Federalist regions of the state, and it would be reasonable to expect somewhat more lawyers, doctors, and ministers among the Federalists than among the Anti-Federalists. While this is true, the slight difference in the number of professional people who appear in the two parties suggests that the members of this group voted as Federalists in the Tidewater and as Anti-Federalists in the Piedmont; that they voted, that is, according to region rather than class:

	Anti-Federalist	Federalist*
Lawyers	8	13
Doctors	2	3
Ministers	1	0

* These figures, as well as those for the army officers above, are provisional. There may have been more army officers; there were almost certainly more lawyers.

[7] Jonathan Elliot (ed.), *The Debates in the Several State Conventions on the Adoption of the Federal Constitution* (5 vols., Washington, 1836–1845), III, gives the number of Anti-Federalist delegates to the Virginia convention as 79. The list of these delegates in his volume on Virginia, however, contains only 78 names.

From the tables above it seems clear that "In the ratification . . . the line of cleavage for and against the Constitution was [*not*] between substantial personalty interests on the one hand and the small farming and debtor interests on the other." Instead, the leaders of both parties were recruited from the same class, and the contest over ratification of the Federal Constitution in Virginia was essentially a struggle between competing groups within the aristocracy.

20 / The Anti-Federalists, 1781-1789

Forrest McDonald

The supporters of the Constitution of 1787 included a fair number of men known to present-day Americans; its opponents, by and large, have slipped into historical anonymity. To be sure, there are occasional exceptions—Patrick Henry, for example, although he is remembered primarily for other activities of his long political career. In terms of winning the argument in the eyes of contemporaries and of posterity, the "Federalists" have enjoyed a considerable advantage, an advantage only slightly offset by the implications of the charges of Charles A. Beard and his followers. Yet the questions remain, Who were the "anti-Federalists"? What were their concerns? Some, to be sure, argued on a relatively high level about constitutional principle: they were "ideologues" who doubted the wisdom or possibility of a national republic. Others were simply politicians with particular vested interests in the governments of the states. In an attempt to revise and to make more precise the lines of division among interest groups, Forrest McDonald examines some of the particular economic interests of members of the "anti-Federalist" coalition. As he notes, his argument, unlike the arguments of the two preceding essays, smacks heavily of a "knaves" and "fools" interpretation of the anti-Federalists and he quickly skips over the ideological concerns of the anti-Federalists. In his deepest examination in this essay, that of the interest groups in competition in New York, McDonald perhaps overstates the cynical calculation of the followers of George Clinton. Moreover, he rather readily assumes that a vote for someone associated with Clinton

Reprinted by permission from the *Wisconsin Magazine of History,* XLVI (1963), 206–214. This paper, in slightly different form, was delivered as an address before the annual meeting of the American Historical Association in New York, December 28, 1960. It is published here without any pretensions that it is definitive; rather, it is a condensed forecast of one of the major portions of a forthcoming book on the establishment of the American governmental system, 1781–1792. Nor are the factual data or the documentation represented as adequate to "prove" the thesis; rather, the factual data are only illustrative, and the footnotes only document the illustrative matter. Finally, I am familiar with the several books relating to the subject—including one, Jackson T. Main's *The Anti-federalists* (Chapel Hill, 1961), which has the same main title as this paper—that have been published since the delivery of my address; and am aware that this paper, and the forthcoming book that underlies it, disagree with those works in almost every salient. [AUTHOR'S NOTE]

as a delegate to the New York ratifying convention was a vote against the Constitution. In fact, the New York convention did ratify the Constitution. By doing so, the New Yorkers raised some questions about the validity of this "vested interest" interpretation of anti-Federalism.

For further reading: Linda Grant De Pauw, *The Eleventh Pillar: New York State and the Federal Constitution* (1966); Cecilia Kenyon, "Men of Little Faith: The Anti-Federalist on the Nature of Representative Government," *William and Mary Quarterly,* 3rd series, XII (1955), 3–43, and *The Antifederalists* (1966); Jackson T. Main, *The Antifederalists: Critics of the Constitution, 1781–1788* (1961); Robert Allen Rutland, *The Ordeal of the Constitution: the Anti-Federalists and the Ratification Struggle of 1787–1788* (1965).

The term anti-Federalists[1] means those persons who opposed the establishment of a national government under the Constitution. Anti-Federalists did not use the term to designate themselves; it was coined by Federalists as a term of opprobrium, and was used much as one might today denounce a conservative by calling him a reactionary or a fascist, or denounce a liberal as a radical left-winger or communist. Because the label stuck, however, it can be used here as a convenient term for purposes of communication, without conveying disapproval, at least not in the sense in which it originally conveyed disapproval.

Indeed, the most important point to be made about the anti-Federalists is that they were not, as they were sometimes depicted by the Federalists, uniformly unintelligent, uninformed, and unprincipled; and neither were they the downtrodden masses, the exploited farmers, or the debtor class; nor yet the "agrarian-minded," the old Whigs, or the radicals, as they have been depicted by various twentieth-century historians. Their leadership matched that of the Federalists for intelligence, education, experience, and political savoir faire, and they comprehended a similar assortment of rich men, poor men, virtuous men, and thieves. In short, they cannot be ordered with any rigid or simple system of classification.

Answering the question, Who were the anti-Federalists and how did they come to be that way? involves answering, in large measure, the same question about their opposite number, the Federalists, and neither is an easy undertaking. A suitable point of departure, I think, is a comment made by Edmund Morgan: "The most radical change produced in Americans by the Revolution was in fact not a division at all" —for they began divided—"but the union of three million cantankerous colonists

---

[1] Spellings of the term vary. Mr. Main, cited above, uses a single, unhyphenated word with a capital "A": Antifederalists. This and "Antifœderalists" were as commonly used by Federalist writers as were "Anti-federalists" and "anti-Federalists" and their variants with the "œ" character. Historians have used all these spellings. The single capitalized word, Antifederalists, suggests that the wearers of the term had something positive in common that would justify thinking of them as a group—in general, cohesiveness, organization, self-consciousness, and some existence pre-dating the contest over the Constitution. The term anti-Federalists has a different connotation: it only designates those persons who, on the single issue of the ratification of the Constitution, opposed the persons calling themselves Federalists. It is thus the more neutral term and, in my judgment, the preferable term.

into a new nation." [2] It is explaining why so many people espoused more perfect union through the Constitution, and not why so many people opposed it, that is the difficult task.

This point will be illustrated, and the first basis of division established, by recalling certain facts of life, as life was lived in the eighteenth century, that are so obvious as to be almost invisible. Given the existing technology of communication and transportation—which dictated that these functions be synonymous, and that travel by water was far easier and faster than travel by land—it took about the same amount of time to move men, goods, money, or ideas and information from Portsmouth, New Hampshire, to Liverpool as it did to move them to, say, Augusta, Georgia. Similarly, in point of time Philadelphia—possibly the second largest English-speaking city in the world—was little further from London, the largest, than it was from Pittsburgh, and it was closer to London than was Vienna. Norfolk was closer to the Azores than to the furthermost Virginia town; Charleston was closer to any island in the British West Indies than it was to Raleigh.

It was thus far more natural for most Americans to think in local terms than in national terms, and, when they thought about it at all, to prefer local authority to national authority. If distance made unreasonable the notion that the thirteen colonies could be well governed from London, distance made almost equally far-fetched the notion that the thirteen states could be well governed by a single national government. In short, for most people the natural thing to be was an anti-Federalist, and it took something special to make them think otherwise. Too, simply by virtue of living in one place instead of another, Americans were less or more prone to think nationally: to be aware of the existence of national problems, and to think of themselves as Americans before thinking of themselves as citizens of their states or towns. An inhabitant of, say, Jaffrey, New Hampshire, would normally not have direct contact with the government of the United States from one year to the next, would deal with his state government only through the annual visit of the tax collector, and would come into direct contact with information, ideas, or people from the outside world only two or three times a year. On the other hand, in the normal course of events an inhabitant of Philadelphia would, irrespective of his occupation, wealth, education, or station in life, come into daily contact with persons and news and ideas from the other states and, indeed, from Europe as well.[3]

These were the first and most important factors predisposing Americans towards national or provincial loyalties during the postwar decade, and towards corresponding loyalties during the contest over ratification—and their preponderating weight was on the side of localism. Several other sets of predisposing factors worked the other way: particularly, the wartime experience of some people, the peacetime experience of others, and the economic interests of still others.

Among those who became devoted to the national cause as a result of the war, three groups are most important. First, those who learned at first-hand the idiocy of attempting to wage a war without a government, which would include particularly members of Congress and important administrative officials who served between 1778

---

[2] Edmund S. Morgan, *The Birth of the Republic, 1763–1789* (Chicago, 1956), 100.

[3] Said Alexander Hamilton: "Man is very much a creature of habit. A thing that rarely strikes his senses will generally have but little influence upon his mind. A government continually at a distance and out of sight, can hardly be expected to interest the sensations of the people." *The Federalist* (Modern Library Edition, 1941), 168.

and 1782.[4] Second, those who fought in the war, particularly those in the continental line and most particularly those officers who served close to Washington. Third, those who inhabited areas which suffered great devastation or long occupation at the hands of the British during the war.

The peacetime experience (1783–1787) likewise convinced some that a national government was necessary, but its effect was upon whole populations of whole states —that is, on those states in which the experiments in independence convinced most people that their states could not make a go of it alone. Making a go of it appeared impossible for a variety of reasons: in Connecticut because of a hopelessly ensnarled fiscal system that blocked the successful working of both government and economy; in Maryland because of a political movement that portended great social upheaval; in Georgia because of an Indian uprising that threatened the very survival of the inhabitants; and so on.[5]

As to the role of economic interests, I have previously devoted 435 pages of a book to an effort to delineate how these worked in winning friends for the Constitution, and apart from repeating that they were complex, subtle, and variable, I shall not reiterate the effort here.[6] But I shall return to economic interests that worked for anti-Federalism in a moment.

Now, if one applies to the contest over ratification the several considerations just mentioned, one comes up with a remarkable picture of it. I invite you to try it. Begin with an outline map of the United States, vintage 1787, with counties and towns indicated. Then color in red (for Federalist) all places which had regular intercourse with other states, and color the remainder blue (for anti-Federalist). Then erase and change from blue to red all areas which were occupied by British armies for more than a year, or in which the ascertainable destruction from warfare exceeded, say, 25 per cent of the total value of property other than land. Then repeat the operation for places which furnished members of Congress between 1778 and 1782, and men who served in the continental line with the rank of lieutenant colonel or higher; and do so again for places in which the place itself or three of its half-dozen richest inhabitants stood to profit directly by the adoption of the Constitution. Finally, re-peat the operation for the entirety of the five states which, given the objective condi-

---

[4] This generalization, like all generalizations made here, is only partially valid; an effort will be made later to account for the exceptions. The striking exception to the generalization about Congress is the members of the so-called Lee-Adams Junto—delegates from Virginia and Massachusetts and certain of their allies, especially in New England—who were in Congress for part of the years cited, and some of whom later opposed the Constitution.

[5] These generalizations are drawn largely from manuscript volumes 2, "Industry," and 5, "Finance and Currency," in the Connecticut Archives, Hartford; Hartford *Connecticut Courant,* New London *Connecticut Gazette,* Middletown *Middlesex Gazette,* and New Haven *Connecticut Journal,* 1785–1787, *passim;* Records of the Loan of 1790, especially volumes 174A, 491, 495, and 498, and the New Haven Port Records, all manuscripts in the Fiscal Section of the National Archives; Philip A. Crowl, "Anti-Federalism in Maryland, 1787–1788," in the *William and Mary Quarterly,* 3d Series, 4:446–469 (October, 1947), and the same author's *Maryland during and after the Revolution* (Baltimore, 1943); Baltimore *Maryland Journal,* Annapolis *Maryland Gazette,* 1785–1787, *passim;* Savannah *Gazette of the State of Georgia,* July–December, 1787; Journal of the Assembly of the State of Georgia, September Session, 1787, manuscript in the Georgia Department of Archives and History, Atlanta; and Kenneth Coleman, *The American Revolution in Georgia, 1763–1789* (Athens, 1958).

[6] Forrest McDonald, *We The People: The Economic Origins of the Constitution* (Chicago, 1958).

tions prevailing under the Articles of Confederation, considered themselves the weakest: Connecticut, New Jersey, Maryland, Delaware, and Georgia. The map you end up with will, at a glance, seem scarcely distinguishable from Orin G. Libby's maps showing the geographical distribution of the vote on the ratification of the Constitution.[7]

But only at a glance. Closer inspection will reveal discrepancies, *e.g.*, that thirteen of the fourteen delegates from counties in the Trans-Alleghany region of Virginia, which you have as blue (anti-Federalist) actually voted for ratification; or that the Connecticut Valley and Cape Cod come out as checkerboards, whereas you have them definitely one way or the other. In all, perhaps a fourth or a fifth of the votes are as yet unaccounted for.

And that is as far as a general analysis of the contest can go. For the remainder of the analysis, one must look to individuals and to vested interests in local politics. When the microscope is thus applied, the leaders of anti-Federalism, as well as the most important dynamic elements in their opposition to the Constitution, stand revealed.

Individuals first. For one kind of person, at least, it was possible to be well educated, well informed, disinterested, and genuinely concerned over the national welfare, and yet opposed to ratification. This was the ideologue, the doctrinaire republican in the classical sense, who could oppose the Constitution on the grounds that it contained many imperfections from the point of view of republican principles of political theory. Now, what makes a man a doctrinaire—republican or any other kind—I cannot say, but who these men were and what they believed and how they behaved is easily enough pointed out. In the Constitutional Convention, they were Elbridge Gerry, Edmund Randolph, John Francis Mercer, George Mason, and perhaps others; in the country at large, they were such prominent anti-Federalists as Joshua Atherton of New Hampshire, Rawling Lowndes of South Carolina, George Bryan of Pennsylvania, Timothy Bloodworth of North Carolina, and a host of Virginians. They were men in the rationalist tradition, men who reasoned from principles to particulars, men whose views were the precise opposite of that so well expressed by John Dickinson in the Constitutional Convention: "Experience," said Dickinson, "must be our only guide. Reason may mislead us."[8] Such men viewed Harrington, Locke, and Montesquieu much as a fundamentalist views the Holy Bible; to them, political salvation lay in the difficult but possible task of devising a perfect system. Inasmuch as reason would show that any imperfect form (whether democratic, aristocratic, or monarchistic) would inevitably degenerate into tyranny, it was better to make do without a national government than to create an imperfect one.[9]

[7] Orin Grant Libby, *Geographical Distribution of the Vote of the Thirteen States on the Ratification of the Federal Constitution, 1787–1788* (Madison, 1894).

[8] Madison's Journal, August 13, 1787, in Charles C. Tansill, ed., *Documents Illustrative of the Formation of the Union* (Washington, 1927), 533.

[9] For an elaboration and further development of these comments on the doctrinaire republican mentality, see the introduction to Forrest McDonald, ed., *Empire and Nation: Letters from a Farmer in Pennsylvania by John Dickinson and Letters from the Federal Farmer by Richard Henry Lee* (New York, 1962). For a clear example of how it worked, see Lee's *Letters* in that volume. A lengthy analysis of it, tentatively titled "The Anti-Federalist Papers," is the subject of a forthcoming book by Professor Morton Borden of Montana State University (a preview of which was given in a provocative paper delivered by Professor Borden at the Mississippi Valley Historical Association meeting in Milwaukee, April, 1962).

With the ideologues the Federalists could argue, through the facile pens and dexterous wits of such skilled theoreticians as Hamilton, Madison, Wilson, Coxe, and Webster. Vested interest groups were another matter, and Federalists could cope with them only by hurling derisive epithets—"pretended patriots," "ambitious and interested men," "artful and designing men," "anti-Federalists"—or by attempting to offer contrary interests. A part of the opposition to the Constitution by vested interest groups has long since been recognized: in the very first number of *The Federalist*, Hamilton predicted that "men in every State" would "resist all changes which may hazard a diminution of the power, emolument and consequence of the offices they hold under the State-establishments"; and in 1924 Allan Nevins made it clear that holders of important state offices generally were, in fact, anti-Federalists. But we are dealing here with a much larger field. Lucrative and prestigious state offices were few, and men with vested interests in state primacy were legion.[10]

It is impossible to delineate all such vested-interest groups here, but it is possible to draw lines around enough of them to afford abundant illustration of the point. New York offers a prime example. Governor George Clinton, aspiring to make his the Empire State and to establish a dynasty to rule it, had the good sense to realize that doing so involved the use of political power both to govern well and to buy the loyalties of people through their ambition or avarice.[11]

This was not a simple task, and should not be regarded as such. That is, most modern devices which we associate with the welding of political organizations were not available to Clinton. The functions of government were yet too limited to permit building power through patronage; public works were too few to permit building power through graft in the construction business; and so on. One will search in vain for evidence of modern manifestations of machine politics.

But one can hold to this maxim: wherein lies the profit in dealing with government, there also lies the greatest source of power. In New York, as in most states, profit in dealing with government lay in public lands and the public debt. Salable public lands in New York consisted primarily of confiscated loyalist estates, the total market value of which was some £750,000 New York current, or almost $2,000,000. The unimaginative stirrer of these ingredients might have been disposed simply to sell the estates, pay the debts, and be done with it. Not so with Clinton; no dullard was he. On the theory that one wins friends among the well-to-do by making them better-to-do, he arranged, through a series of acts and administrative decisions, that the confiscated estates be disposed of according to a careful design. So as to insure that the field of buyers would not be cluttered with small purchasers, the lands were sold in large blocs at public auction. So as to insure profits to all speculators, it was provided in 1780 that purchases could be made on the installment plan and in certain kinds of public securities, at par. Since these securities had not yet been provided for, they could be bought on the open market at prices which returned hand-

[10] *The Federalist* (Modern Library Edition, 1941), 4; Allan Nevins, *The American States during and after the Revolution* (New York, 1924).

[11] There is only one full-length biography of Clinton, E. Wilder Spaulding's *His Excellency George Clinton, Critic of the Constitution* (New York, 1938); the same author's *New York in the Critical Period* (New York, 1932) is also useful. See also the *Public Papers of George Clinton* (New York and Albany, 1900), and Hamilton's comments about Clinton and his supporters in Harold C. Syrett and Jacob E. Cooke, eds., *The Papers of Alexander Hamilton*, vols. 2 and 3 (New York, 1962).

some profits to purchasers of confiscated estates. In effect, such operators were enabled to buy on the market at prices ranging from three shillings nine pence to four shillings on the pound, and sell to the state (for confiscated estates) at twenty shillings.[12]

The speculative orgy thus engendered lasted from the latter part of the war to 1786, until a number of rich people had become political friends and a larger number of political friends had become rich people. Then it was time for the next step. It was time to do justice to the suffering public creditors. But not quite all of them. Clinton's chief financial advisor, state treasurer Gerard Bancker, first reckoned how much debt could be supported with the income from the state's lucrative import duties, and then combed the lists of security holders and came up with tables of the various combinations of securities in which a minimum expenditure could result in largesse for a maximum number of voters. In what was offered to the public as a generous, responsible, and patriotic action, the Clintonians decided to fund not only all the state debts but about $1,400,000 of continental debts as well. Two forms of continental debts were assumed: Loan Office Certificates and so-called Barber's Notes, certificates issued by the United States for supplies furnished the continental army. Some 5,000 holders of continental securities—about half the number of voters in a normal election—were provided for under this act. As the system was devised, these securities were neither paid off nor funded: they were simply lent to the state, and the state punctually paid interest on them. Note that the system created, in effect, a list of 5,000 pensioners. Note also that the action could hardly have been inspired by either patriotism or responsibility, for $3,600,000 in other kinds of continental debts held in the state, which were politically less potent because they were concentrated in the hands of only a couple of hundred persons, remained unfunded. This scheme was, as one critic charged, "a studied design to divide the interests of the public creditors." [13]

But it was even more than that. It was also a method for doubly rewarding the faithful and punishing those who had been so wicked as to fail to appreciate past favors. The rise in security prices which quickly followed the funding act caught the speculators in confiscated estates as bears in a bull market. That is, they were in effect short sellers, whose profits depended upon keeping the security market low; they were heavily extended for installment delivery of securities against purchases of confiscated estates. When the securities market rose, they found themselves having to pay roughly 300 per cent as much as they had expected to pay for the securities with which to make their payments. Not surprisingly, many of them were broken.

Those who had appreciated Clinton's generosity, however, those who had given him unreserved political support, were protected. They were informed in advance (1) that the funding would take place, (2) the precise securities which would be

---

[12] For an excellent description of speculation in confiscated estates in New York, see Harry B. Yoshpe, *The Disposition of Loyalist Estates in the Southern District of the State of New York* (New York, 1939), 59–60, 63–78, 114–115, and elsewhere. Prices of public securities have been taken from occasional notices in New York newspapers.

[13] *Laws of the State of New York Passed at the Sessions of the Legislature* (3 vols., Albany, 1886–1888), 2:253ff.; Report of the Committee on the Treasury to the House of Assembly, January 16, 1788, published in the *New York Journal* of January 31, 1788; "Gustavus," in the *New York Packet* of April 13, 1786; and Records of the Loan of 1790, vols. 22, 545, 548, 549, 551, in the National Archives.

funded, and (3) when the operations would occur. Accordingly, they were able to cover their positions and even make a tidy sum by going long in appropriate securities.[14]

These were merely among the more spectacular of Clinton's devices. There were others, and they all worked. Small wonder, then, that when the Constitution came along and threatened to undermine Clinton by transferring control of the more lucrative devices from the state to a general government, as well as similarly transferring that great source of revenue, the tariff, Clinton greeted the document with less than enthusiasm. Small wonder, too, that when he vigorously opposed ratification, the people of the state voted against it, 14,000 to 6,500.[15]

Before proceeding with an effort to outline the development of major vested-interest groups in other states, it is well to pause and observe that by no means all vested interests created during the period were economic interests. Greed may have been the quickest motive to which politicians could appeal, but lust for prestige and power drove most of the managers themselves and, when properly utilized, could provide a continuing basis of strength among the followers. This is clearly seen in a contrasting view of Clinton himself and of the two Clintonian delegates to the Philadelphia Convention, John Lansing and Robert Yates. Clinton was clearly driven by desire for power, and it does not alter the case that he exercised his power judiciously and, for the most part, in the interest of the state. Lansing, on the other hand, liked money. He was a rich man when he began his association with Clinton, and because he capitalized on the opportunities his party afforded, he became a much richer man. He also became a perpetually loyal party adherent. Yates, on the contrary, was incorruptible—at least, he was not corruptible by the love of money. His biographer, writing soon after his death, gives us a moving picture: "He was often urged to unite with some of his friends in speculating in forfeited estates during the war, by which he might easily have enriched himself and his connections without censure or suspicion—and although such speculations were common, yet he would not consent to become wealthy upon the ruin of others." (The biographer adds a touching footnote: "Chief Justice Yates died poor.") [16]

Nor was Yates particularly ambitious for power. But where avarice and ambition were absent, vanity was abundantly and fatally present. Yates was induced to become a loyal Clintonian by the simple expedient of giving him an extremely prestigious position, albeit one which was neither particularly powerful nor remunerative, that of chief justice of the state supreme court. Interestingly, New York Fed-

[14] The statements in the two foregoing paragraphs are inferences drawn from the sources cited in notes 12, 13, and 14, and from the *Votes and Proceedings of the Assembly of the State of New York, 1786–1787,* and New York newspapers for the same period.

[15] A summary of election returns for five counties appears in the *New York Journal* of June 5, 1788; for Orange County, see the *Daily Advertiser,* June 14, 1788; for Queens County (incorrectly called Suffolk therein), *ibid.,* June 7, 1788; for Dutchess County, the Poughkeepsie *Country Journal,* June 3, 1788; and for Westchester County, the *Daily Advertiser,* June 3, 1788. The popular votes in two counties, Washington and Suffolk, are unknown.

[16] On Lansing, see the sketch in the *Dictionary of American Biography;* Spaulding's *New York in the Critical Period,* 237; and scattered references in vol. 3 of Syrett and Cooke, eds., *The Papers of Alexander Hamilton,* especially 3:139–140. On Yates, see the sketch in the *Dictionary of American Biography* and the biography appended to Senate Document 728, 60th Congress, 2d Session, p. 205.

eralists won him away from Clinton in 1789 by offering him their support for governor in a campaign against Clinton himself.[17]

It should be noted that in regard to non-economic vested interests the weight of
advantages favored the anti-Federalists, but in individual instances of particular
strategic importance, the Federalists were invariably in a position to gain. Two well-
known examples illustrate this matter. Massachusetts Federalists won the indispensable support of Governor John Hancock by promising him the vice-presidency, a
promise they subsequently felt no obligation to fulfill; and Virginia Federalists won
the indispensable support of Governor Edmund Randolph by promising him the
attorney-generalship, which he was actually awarded.[18]

Now let us return to a survey of the development of vested interests in the states
of the Confederation. The most fruitful soil for such development existed when a
policy designed for the over-all, best interests of the state as a whole could be combined with policies that worked to the particular advantage of particular individuals.
Such was the case with New York, and in this respect the history of Virginia during
the period strikingly resembles that of New York, though it was different in every
detail. The tangle of interests in Virginia—state, regional, local, and personal—was
so involved that any attempt to discuss them in full here would be folly. Let us, then,
take notice of such matters as confiscated estates, western lands, navigation of the
Mississippi, and the nebulous but vital questions of personal prides and prestiges, but
pass over them and focus on but a single aspect of the problem, Virginia's commercial policy.[19]

Virginia had, at least in considerable measure, been moved to join the revolutionary
movement as a means of dissolving the credit bands which had bound planters to
British and Scotch merchants. The sequestration acts by which prewar private indebtedness, amounting to some £2,000,000, was wiped out are well known. As Isaac
Harrell has so well shown, hordes of planters seized the opportunity to pay nominal
sums into the state treasury and thereby legally expunge their debts to foreign merchants.[20] What is less known is that Virginia's postwar commercial policy, whose
principal architects were Patrick Henry and the Lees, was carefully designed to
preserve the economic independence so unscrupulously won.

To oversimplify considerably, that program was as follows. In the view of the
framers of the program, merchants had been able to enshackle Virginia planters before the war only because they operated in an artificially created oligopolistic (or
semi-monopolistic) marketing system. To prevent the reforging of the chains, all that
was necessary was to create, artificially, a system of excessive competition. The method
chosen was to develop a Virginia mercantile class to conduct about a third of the

[17] *Ibid.*; see also the several New York newspapers, April–June, 1789.

[18] Moncure D. Conway, *Omitted Chapters in History Disclosed in the Life and Papers of
Edmund Randolph* (New York, 1888), 385ff.; Rufus King to Henry Knox, February 1, 1788, in
Charles R. King, *Life and Correspondence of Rufus King* (6 vols., New York, 1894–1900),
1:319; and Samuel B. Harding, *The Contest over the Ratification of the Federal Constitution in
the State of Massachusetts* (New York, 1896), 85–87.

[19] There is no published general history of Virginia during the period; useful secondary
sources include the several biographies of Washington, Henry, Madison, and Jefferson; Freeman
H. Hart, *The Valley of Virginia in the American Revolution, 1763–1789* (Chapel Hill, 1942);
and W. A. Low, "Merchant and Planter Relations in Post-Revolutionary Virginia, 1783–1789,"
in the *Virginia Magazine of History and Biography*, 61: 308–318 (1953).

[20] Isaac S. Harrell, *Loyalism in Virginia* (Philadelphia, 1926).

tobacco business, and to underwrite it with a system of bounties, drawbacks, and so on, that enabled it to operate far more cheaply than foreigners. This and many nicer refinements of the state's commercial policy produced intense competition between British, Scotch, French, and other American carriers and merchants for a share of the business, for there was not enough business to go around. As a result, in the 1780's, *relative to the prewar years*, credit was easy, money was abundant, freight rates were low, and tobacco prices, despite Robert Morris' efforts to drive them down so as to fill his contract with the French Farmers General, were high.[21] In short, because of its political independence, Virginia had been able to liberate a vast number of its inhabitants from the clutches of their foreign creditors, and bring about a prosperity rarely matched in the preceding century.[22]

The ensuing vested interests in Virginia's continued sovereignty are thus obvious. Equally obvious is the fact that the Constitution ran directly counter to these interests in every way. Again, the intense opposition to ratification on the part of state leaders, and the near-success of their efforts, are hardly surprising.[23]

While public policy in these states worked to the advantage of the states as well as to that of rapacious individuals, it was not so in all places. In Massachusetts, for example, public creditors loaded an insupportable burden upon the taxpayers when they succeeded in having all their public paper funded at par in 1784. Private advantage here was contrary to public advantage, and the result was first the weakening of a state whose economy had already been totally disrupted, then in increasing popular discontent, and finally a brief civil war.[24] In Pennsylvania the most important public actions that enriched special groups had a neutral effect upon the welfare of the whole, and consequently won only such friends of state sovereignty as could profit directly from it. In 1785, for example, that state's Constitutionalist Party (those who became anti-Federalists) caused the passage of an act simultaneously funding the state debt and that portion of the national debt owned in the state, and issuing £150,000 ($400,000) in paper money. The Bank of North America opposed this action and offered to lend the state $300,000 if it would not go through with the scheme, but the Constitutionalist majority refused. As one writer said of the entire program, "to unravel the code of policy which it contains, requires no small amount of sagacity and Machiavelian shrewdness." The principal elements in the code of policy it contained, however, are clearly visible: a calculated appeal to an existing interest group and a scheme for enriching the politicians who devised the program. The existing interest group was the public creditors, to whom the program was made

[21] The Farmers General was an organization of French financiers, to whom collection of many indirect taxes had been farmed out, and who had been granted a monopoly on the importation of tobacco.

[22] The development of the program can be traced in the *Journal of the House of Delegates of the State of Virginia* (Richmond, 1828) and in the published statutes. Its operations have been studied in the manuscript Naval Officer Returns in the Virginia State Library, Richmond, and in the quotations of prices and freight rates in the Alexandria *Virginia Journal*, Richmond *Independent Chronicle*, Richmond *Weekly Advistiser*, Richmond *American Advertiser*, Fredericksburg *Advertiser*, Philadelphia *Evening Herald*, and New York *Daily Advertiser*.

[23] The vote of the Virginia convention was 89 to 79 in favor of ratification. The best account of the struggle in the convention is Hugh Blair Grigsby's *The History of the Virginia Federal Convention of 1788*, edited by R. A. Brock (2 vols., Richmond, 1890–1891).

[24] On Massachusetts finance, see Whitney K. Bates, "State Finances of Massachusetts, 1780–1789" (Unpublished master's thesis, University of Wisconsin, 1948).

immediately palatable by the payment of £100,000 of the new money to them for back interest on their holdings of national debt. The remainder of the paper was issued on loan. Constitutionalist insiders borrowed the paper from the state on long-term, easy credit, and invested in the securities being funded. Thus such Constitutionalists as Charles Pettit, William Moore, John Bayard, Frederick Kuhl, William Will, John Steinmetz, and William Irvine, all holders of several thousand pounds of public securities, profited; and such Constitutionalists as Joseph Heister, John Bishop, Nicholas Lotz, John Hanna, William Brown, William Findley, James Martin, and Robert Whitehill, most of them back-country politicians who had not previously owned any securities, suddenly emerged with profits of several thousand dollars apiece from the rise in security prices.[25]

In 1787, Constitutionalist Party leaders formed a strong phalanx against ratification, but, not surprisingly, they were grossly lacking in public support.[26]

If space permitted, similar developments in virtually all other states could be described. In Rhode Island the habit of mixing public policy and private gain was perhaps deepest rooted and highest developed; interestingly, this was also the state that offered the greatest resistance to the Constitution. But the existence of strong vested interest groups in Connecticut, Maryland, and North Carolina—all of whom became anti-Federalists—is abundantly evident, and traces of the phenomenon are visible elsewhere.

I would leave you, not with a summary or a conclusion, but with a question. The foregoing data, all of which are profusely documentable, smack strongly of a knaves-and-fools interpretation of anti-Federalism. Knaves and fools is precisely what Federalists charged their opponents were—the knaves, in their view, being the groups with vested interests in state governments, and the fools being both the ideologues and the uninformed or misinformed. The anti-Federalists, on the other hand, regularly charged that Federalists were knaves, but rarely accused them of being fools. Federalists viewed themselves as friends of the nation; anti-Federalists depicted themselves as friends of the people.

My question is this: if it is true, as I believe it to be, that as a general rule the verdict of history has been the view held by the winner—that of the Patriots over that of the Loyalists, of Jefferson over Hamilton, of Jackson over Biddle, of Franklin Roosevelt over Sam Insull—then how did it happen that historians have, in the main, preferred the anti-Federalists' description of themselves and of their opponents?

---

[25] Merrill Jensen, *The New Nation* (New York, 1950), 316–317; Philadelphia *Evening Herald,* March 8, 1785; Philadelphia *Pennsylvania Packet,* throughout January, 1784, March 31, April 1, 1785; New Loan Certificates, vol. A, accounts 1, 2, 3, 60, 225, 230, 262, 1775–1802, 1954–1958, 2718–2724, 4915, 4919–4925, 5381, vol. B, accounts 10, 391, 6177–6184, 10525–10526, 10528, vol. C, accounts 37, 54, 120, 126, vol. D, 19235–19241, all manuscript volumes in the Public Records Division of the Pennsylvania Historical and Museum Commission; Records of the Loan of 1790, vol. 54–2, folio 330, vol. 610, folios 23, 24, 39, 43, 45, vol. 611, folios 21, 23, 25, 114–115, vol. 612, accounts 8693, 8976–9025, vol. 624, folio 40, vol. 630, folios 48, 49, 122, 309, vol. 631, folios 223, 250, 298.

[26] The Pennsylvania convention ratified the Constitution by a vote of 46 to 23. The standard work on ratification in Pennsylvania is John Bach McMaster and Frederick D. Stone, eds., *Pensylvania and the Federal Constitution, 1787–1788* (Philadelphia, 1888).

Part VI

AMERICA
AND EUROPE

21 / The Dubious Democrat:
Thomas Jefferson in Bourbon France

Robert R. Palmer

Thomas Jefferson has often been depicted as something of a wild visionary, a radical philosopher-revolutionary who believed that the "tree of liberty should be watered with the blood of tyrants." He has been pictured on other occasions as a reflective, impractical gentleman-planter-scholar. Both descriptions share a common view of Jefferson as an ideologue with little concern for or knowledge of the real world of politics and the limitations of humanity. Of course, Jefferson's very success as politician, architect, and master of Monticello belies much in such caricatures of him. For a radical and visionary, Jefferson was strangely uninterested by the more revolutionary possibilities in Europe. On the following pages, Jefferson's relations with Frenchmen in the late 1780's are the primary subject of concern. He was not the emissary of the rebels of the New World to the prospective ones of the Old. As an American, he was quite naturally unable to detect some of the subtle implications of European political arguments. His early comments on the French Revolution reflected his own experiences: he tended to see dangers in the claims of Louis XVI as he had earlier seen them in the policies of George III. His preferences were clearly for some kind of gradual reform and not for sweeping change that would all at once eradicate the evils of the *ancien régime*. Jefferson's attitude was in part an expression of his own kind of moderation. It was also an expression of his understanding of reality: he saw that attempts at massive reform would simply encourage strong resistance and efforts to frustrate any possibility of meaningful change. In short, Jefferson's years in France suggest the limited aims, the sense of realism of this American radical. And, because of his historical role, they reveal something of the nature of the revolutionary movement in which he participated in Virginia as contrasted with that in France. In Virginia the use of violence could be directed primarily against an external foe and not against domestic defenders of the feudal vestiges of the old order.

Reprinted by permission from the *Political Science Quarterly*, LXXII (September 1957), 388–404.

For further reading: Edward Dumbauld, *Thomas Jefferson, American Tourist* (1946); Durand Echeverria, *Mirage in the West; A History of the French Image of American Society to 1815* (1957); Marie Kimball, *Jefferson: The Scene of Europe, 1784–1789* (1950); Dumas Malone, *Jefferson and the Rights of Man* (1952); Robert R. Palmer, "A Neglected Work: Otto Vossler on Jefferson and the Revolutionary Era," *William and Mary Quarterly*, 3rd series, XII (1955), 462–471.

Thomas Jefferson, the second United States minister to France, remained in that country from 1784 until September of 1789, two months after the fall of the Bastille. The author of the Declaration of Independence saw at first hand the collapse of the monarchy by whose aid American independence had been established, and the revolutionary of 1776 was an eyewitness, and even a participant, in the greater revolution of 1789. These activities of Jefferson, inviting as they do a comparison of the American and French revolutions, and raising the whole conundrum of American relationships to Europe, have long offered an intriguing and now ancient subject, on which it yet always seems possible to say more. My own knowledge is more of Europe than of Jefferson. If the following impressions have any value or novelty, it is because the author is no Jefferson expert, but has simply sat down, with a point of view derived from the study of European history, to a fresh reading of Jefferson's letters from France—both his letters to personal friends, and his official communications to John Jay, the American Secretary of State under the Articles of Confederation. The new edition of the *Papers of Thomas Jefferson*, prepared by Julian P. Boyd and his aides with an abundance of useful annotation, is in fact just now approaching the year 1789.[1]

The title that I have ventured upon requires a word of explanation. To call Jefferson a "dubious democrat" is a pretty alliteration, but "democrat" is an anachronism, and "dubious" is ambiguous. Jefferson did not call himself a democrat, and the word itself was then new, first coming into accepted use to describe some of the Dutch Patriots about 1787, a sense in which Jefferson employed it himself. If we nevertheless call Jefferson not only a democrat but a dubious one, at the time of his sojourn in France, we fall into a double meaning. We imply either that he was a questionable democrat or that he was a skeptical one. Either it is we who doubt the extent of his democratic principles, or it is he, a good enough democrat, who took a doubtful view of what he saw happening in France. There is a little of both these meanings in what I have to say.

[1] Julian P. Boyd and others, eds., *The Papers of Thomas Jefferson*, vols. XI–XIII (Princeton, 1955–56). See also Dumas Malone, *Jefferson and the Rights of Man* (Boston, 1951), pp. 180–237; Gilbert Chinard, ed., *The Letters of Lafayette and Jefferson* (Baltimore and Paris, 1929); O. Vossler, *Die amerikanischen Revolutionsideale in ihrem Verhältnis zu den europäischen: Untersuch an Thomas Jefferson* (Munich, 1929), of which there is a digest in the *William and Mary Quarterly*, XII (July 1955), 462–71; Durand Echeverria, *Mirage in the West: A History of the French Image of American Society to 1815* (Princeton, 1957); and my article, "Notes on the Use of the Word 'Democracy,' 1789–1799," *Political Science Quarterly*, LXVIII (June 1953), 203–26. The present article originated as a paper delivered at the Society for French Historical Studies in February 1957.

One day in Paris, in February 1787, Jefferson wrote a letter to his old friend, John Adams, the American minister in London. They had been closely associated in the American Revolution, in which they had both been on the committee to write the Declaration of Independence, and their political ideas were still much alike, as may be seen in their opinions of the constitutions of Virginia and Massachusetts, their respective native states. The political estrangement of a few years later had not yet come. Jefferson had not yet been stigmatized as a Francophile nor Adams as an Anglomaniac; nor was Jefferson yet thought the preëminent father of American democracy, or Adams looked back upon, perhaps mistakenly, as a deep philosopher of conservatism.

Jefferson had two things to say in his letter. He told his colleague of what had happened at Versailles the day before, the meeting of the Assembly of Notables called by the minister Calonne to deal with the crisis of the French finances. He also commented on Adams' new book, *The Defense of the Constitutions of the United States,* of which Adams had sent him a copy, and which he had just finished reading, as he said, "with infinite satisfaction and improvement." He thought it would do "much good in America," and took immediate steps to have it translated into French. A few days later he went off on a three-months' tour of the South of France. His insatiable curiosity turned to the vine, the olive and the fig, to the mysteries of fossil sea shells, Roman ruins and the shifts in the Mediterranean coastline since the building of Aigues-Mortes, to the wages of farm laborers and the hardness or softness of peasants' beds, to the habits of nightingales in Touraine, the introduction of the steam engine at Nîmes, and the precise width of the Languedoc canal at the bottom. Meanwhile he was out of touch with Versailles, where the Assembly of Notables met during his absence.

The point is that when the King of France upon Calonne's advice convened the Assembly of Notables, and when John Adams wrote his *Defense of the Constitutions of the United States,* there was one idea that they had in common, and one that this acute and tireless observer, Thomas Jefferson, seems much less fully to have shared. This was the idea that a strong independent executive might be a good thing for the people.

The drift of Adams' book was to justify, by a survey of Europe, the separation and balance of governmental powers in America, that is of executive, judiciary, and upper and lower houses of legislation; and it was this separation and balance that won Jefferson's approval. For Adams, the main purpose of such separation was to preserve executive independence, and the purpose of executive independence was to prevent public bodies from degenerating into privileged oligarchies. "If there is one certain truth to be collected from the history of all ages," said Adams, "it is this: that the people's rights and liberties . . . can never be preserved without a strong executive." He saw what has become the commonplace of our history textbooks: that an alliance of kings with burghers and peasants, over the centuries, had put down the feudal classes. "What is the whole history of the barons' wars but one demonstration of this truth? What are all the standing armies in Europe, but another? These were all given to the kings by the people, to defend them against aristocracies." And he concluded, in modern vein, indeed disconcertingly like a latter-day Democrat, that the executive (whom he preferred to have popularly elected) was "the natural friend of the people, and the only defense which they or their representatives can have against the avarice and ambition of the rich and distinguished citizens." [2]

It is a curious speculation to wonder what Adams would have thought of Calonne and the Assembly of Notables, if he rather than Jefferson had been the American minister to France. For Calonne called the Assembly because he believed that the rich and distinguished citizens were evading taxes. In his opening speech to the Assembly he denounced the "abuses of pecuniary privileges." [3] He proposed to use the executive authority of the French crown to impose a kind of equality before the law. In his complex program to save the French monarchy by reforming it, in what Miss Wilma Pugh once called Calonne's New Deal, there were two principal proposals: to introduce a new kind of land tax payable in proportion to income by persons of all legal classes alike, cleric, noble and commoner, without privilege or exception; and to introduce certain representative consultative bodies, called provincial assemblies, whose members should qualify as landowners, and be elected by landowners in general, with no regard to the legal system of three estates. Calonne was perfectly aware that he was attacking privilege and aristocracy at their foundation. His plan for provincial assemblies came directly from the thinking of Turgot, Mirabeau and Dupont de Nemours. [4] As for the tax reforms: "Privileges will be sacrificed, yes, as justice demands and as our needs require. Would anyone prefer to put an even heavier load on the unprivileged, the people?" [5] If there was ever a case of the executive defending the people against certain pretensions of aristocracy, in Adams' formula, this last effort of the expiring Bourbon monarchy was such a case.

But Calonne's program met with insuperable resistance in the Assembly of Notables. He and his successor had to abandon the land tax and the principle of equal representation in the new provincial assemblies. There presently followed what we know as the aristocratic resurgence and the Revolt of the Nobles. On this phenomenon historians have come to agree. Albert Mathiez and Georges Lefebvre have described it, and all the great G's of contemporary learning on the French Revolution, Gottschalk and Gershoy in this country, Goodwin in England, Göhring in Germany, Godechot in France, agree in telling the same story, that the privileged classes in the Assembly of Notables blocked the plan for equality of taxation and equality of representation put forward by Calonne.

I do not know what John Adams would have thought of all this. He was in England, and in his letters and diary he made no significant comment on events in France. It seems likely that the crusty New Englander, who inveighed against the maneuvers of "aristocratical gentlemen" even at Geneva, would have had some sardonic reservations on the aristocracy of France. We do know what Jefferson thought. He thought very well of the Assembly of Notables. When the Assembly

---

[2] John Adams, *Defense of the Constitutions of the United States,* in *Works* (Boston, 1851), IV, 290, 355, 585.

[3] *Discours prononcés par S.M. Louis XVI, Msgr. l'archevêque de Narbonne et M. de Calonne à l'Assemblée des Notables le 22 fevrier, 1787* (Versailles, 1787), p. 23.

[4] P. Jolly, *Calonne, 1734–1802* (Paris, 1949), p. 166.

[5] *Collection des mémoires presentées à l'Assemblée des Notables. Première et seconde division* (Paris, 1787). Published by Calonne about March 30, 1787, and widely circulated, to strengthen his case in the Assembly of Notables by an appeal to public opinion. See an unpublished dissertation at Princeton University by Ralph W. Greenlaw, "The French Nobility on the Eve of the Revolution," pp. 22–23.

first met, he blamed the French for their levity toward it;[6] for a great many witticisms were in circulation, chiefly turning on the select composition of its membership, which, beginning with seven princes of the blood and thirty-six dukes and peers, proceeded through the whole array of legalized status to include, in 144 members, only four who were altogether of the Third Estate. Jefferson showed no disposition to be critical on this score. He thought the Notables "the most able and independent characters in the kingdom." [7]

Calonne had explicitly raised the question of privilege. The word "privilege" never occurs in Jefferson's letters until much later in the controversy, until December 1788. And when the provincial assemblies proposed by Calonne did meet, in altered form, a few months later, when, instead of being elected as landowners by land-owners, they represented the three estates of clergy, nobility and commoner, with some of their membership designated by the king, and the rest co-opted, Jefferson made no comment on the change that the plan for provincial assemblies had under-gone. The assemblies "will be of the choice of the people," he wrote to John Jay, long enough after his return to Paris to have learned what had happened. And he told Adams that "the royal authority has lost, and the rights of the nation gained," as much in France in three months, by peaceable change of opinion only, as in England during all the civil wars under the Stuarts. He thought only old people opposed the change. The revolution, so to speak, was over.[8]

It is no news to report that Jefferson, while in France, took a fairly conservative view of the beginnings of the French Revolution. The problem is to examine the quality and content of this so-called conservatism. The problem is to explain why Thomas Jefferson, of all people, was so insensitive to the case for equality of taxation, equality of representation, and equality of citizenship in France.

It is possible that if he saw no issue of privilege, the politically conscious French public still saw no such issue either. It may be that the archbishops and *grands seigneurs* who led the attack on Calonne acted as the accepted leaders of the country, and in the country's interest. Many of the objections of the Notables to Calonne's tax program were perfectly valid. The Notables preferred a continuation of the old *vingtième* to his new land tax, but the *vingtième* was legally payable by both nobles and commoners; and if there were *de facto* inequalities in its incidence, arising from under-assessment, I am not sure that these were much greater than with the land tax in England—at least I would like to see some comparative research on this subject. The tax privileges most hotly defended by the Notables, and those which Calonne most vigorously attacked, were actually, as Ralph Greenlaw has pointed out, the privileges of certain provinces, by which provinces as a whole, and in theory all classes in those provinces, carried a lighter share of the national tax burden. To Jefferson such privileges or liberties, depending on old agreements, might well seem like states' rights within a kind of federal system, and as such perfectly defensible against the crown.

Before judging what he thought, we must ask what it was possible for him to know.

[6] To Abigail Adams, Feb. 22, 1787, *Papers of Thomas Jefferson,* XI, 174. "The people at large view every object only as it may furnish puns and bons mots. . . . When a measure so capable of doing good as the calling of the Notables is treated with so much ridicule, we may conclude the nation desperate. . . ."

[7] To John Jay, June 21, 1787, *ibid.,* p. 489.

[8] To Jay, *ibid.,* p. 490; to Adams, Aug. 30, 1787, *ibid.,* XII, 68.

We must distinguish between what could be seen by contemporaries and what can be seen by historians. The issue was not entirely invisible in 1787. In the past, to be sure, the Bourbon monarchy, in its frequent clashes with the privileged orders, had been highly secretive, and had yielded all the advantages of publicity to spokesmen for the aristocracy and the clergy. But in 1787 Calonne appealed to the public. He himself published, during the sessions of the Assembly, the main substance of his differences with it. Moreover, Dupont de Nemours, with whom Jefferson was in close contact, had been a secretary to the Assembly, and drew up a detailed report of one of its most critical sessions. Dupont was a partisan of Calonne's program, and, though his confidential report was not published, Jefferson could easily have learned from him what went on. Others of Jefferson's circle, Condorcet and Morellet as well as Dupont, friends and supporters of the late Turgot, were outspoken believers in equality of taxation and in provincial assemblies meeting without regard to legal estate. There were men in France in 1787 who distrusted the lead taken by the prelates and the great nobles. Jefferson was not one of them.[9]

The truth seems to be that Jefferson's idea of what was happening was taken almost entirely from his good friend the Marquis de Lafayette, who played an active part in the Assembly of Notables, as in other later events. Professor Gottschalk, in his great work on Lafayette, allows that his hero in the troubled months of 1787 was somewhat naïve, that he only very slowly came to see the character of the aristocratic resistance to proposed reforms, and that in his patriotic and idealistic outbursts he served as a cat's-paw for the privileged interests.[10] At any rate, when Calonne announced that the monarchy was bankrupt, Lafayette and the Assembly refused to believe him. When he revealed the amount of the deficit, which was of old standing and greatly increased by the American war, they attributed it to his own maladministration, insisting that there had been no deficit in Necker's time a few years before. When Calonne desperately asserted that the government's income must be immediately raised, and that certain loopholes and privileges in the tax structure must be stopped, they retorted that economies in expenditure would suffice. They accused Calonne of scandalous waste, graft and corruption, and denounced the monstrous prodigality of the royal court. Lafayette, in high-minded indignation, did as much as any man to draw this red herring of alleged personal dishonesty and courtly extravagance across the trail marked out by Calonne for structural reform. The trouble in this view was not in the legal and social organization of France, but in the misconduct of an overgrown and arrogant government.

This was doctrine that a Virginia gentleman could readily understand. Powerful government was what Jefferson feared; monarchy was his bugaboo; it was resistance to tyrants that expressed the will of God. "You are afraid of the one—I, of the few.

[9] See notes 3 and 5 above. Dupont's report, written in June 1787, was published by P. Renouvin, *L'Assemblée des Notables de 1787: la conférence du mars, texte publié avec introduction et notes* (Paris, 1920). The abbé Morellet, who had translated Jefferson's *Notes on Virginia* the year before, observed in July 1787 to the Earl of Shelburne that the Parlement of Paris demanded "the Estates-General, the most false and vicious representation that any nation ever had, instead of letting us form and develop provincial administrations in which the deputies would become true and perfect representatives, much better than yours." *Lettres de l'abbé Morellet à Lord Shelburne* (Paris, 1898), p. 245. See also Jolly, *Calonne*, pp. 183, 205.

[10] L. R. Gottschalk, *Lafayette between the American and the French Revolution* (1783–1789) (Chicago, 1950), pp. 279, 297 *et seq.*

. . . You are apprehensive of Monarchy; I, of Aristocracy." [11] So John Adams wrote to him, diagnosing the difference between them. It is true that Jefferson shortly revised his opinion of Calonne, finding "him less wicked, and France less badly governed, than I had feared." [12] It was in the nuance, the emphasis, the first impulse, more than in the considered judgment, that he differed from Adams.

It does appear that Jefferson at the moment, in mid-1787, was not very apprehensive of aristocracy in France, or in Europe either. He was aware of the troubles then raging in Holland and Belgium. These, he said in August 1787, were the places where "we have at present two fires kindled in Europe." What we call the reforms of Joseph II in Belgium, which included religious toleration and reduction of the costs of justice, Jefferson described as innovations of a whimsical sovereign.[13] He knew that the incipient Belgian revolution was led by nobles and priests, but was untroubled by this knowledge. In the Dutch provinces the attempted Patriot revolution had reached its climax and was soon to be suppressed by Great Britain and Prussia. Jefferson, who sympathized with the Patriots, described how they were composed of two groups, the Moderate Aristocrats and the Democrats. When the two disagreed, it was the Democrats that he blamed for their unreasonableness.[14] The Dutch Democrats were middle-class burghers who had formed themselves into militia companies, held a National Assembly of such companies, protested at the subservience of the House of Orange to Great Britain, talked of equality of rights for persons of diverse religions, protested at the hereditary monopolizing of office in certain families, repudiated the three-estates system in Utrecht, and believed that they were imitating the American Revolution. Jefferson thought them very immoderate.

At the same time he reported of France that "the constitutional reformations have gone on well," and that the provincial assemblies would probably soon bring "a revolution in the constitution." [15] Lafayette had been designated by the King as one of the noble members in the assembly of Auvergne; and this assembly had hardly met when it began, with Lafayette's enthusiastic agreement, to demand the revival of long obsolete liberties of the province, which is to say more powers for the clergy and nobility of Auvergne. In these demands, echoed by most of the other provincial assemblies, historians nowadays see signs of the aristocratic resurgence, the attempt of some in the privileged orders, as Göhring says, to turn France into a *Ständestaat*, a status state. For Jefferson they seemed to be a liberal movement to check the crown.

In the next year, 1788, we can detect a new dimension in Jefferson's ideas, corresponding to that "widening of political notions" which Gottschalk finds in Lafayette. The summer of 1788 saw the high tide of the aristocratic resurgence, or what we have learned to call the *révolte nobiliaire*. Jefferson's friends Dupont and Condorcet were becoming more radically anti-noble. So was another in Jefferson's circle, Philip Mazzei, an Italian whom Jefferson had known for years in Virginia, and of whom he was now seeing a good deal in Paris. Mazzei now made a living by writing bulletins to the King of Poland. That dignitary was receiving stronger medicine from Mazzei than the American Congress ever got from Jefferson. "Aristocratic tyranny is

[11] Adams to Jefferson, Dec. 6, 1787, *Jefferson Papers*, XII, 396.

[12] E. M. Sowerby, *Catalogue of the Library of Thomas Jefferson*, II (1953), 425, citing a letter of Oct. 18, 1787; *Jefferson Papers*, XII, 247.

[13] *Jefferson Papers*, XI, 672, 679, 685.

[14] *Ibid.*, p. 696.

[15] *Ibid.*, pp. 697–98. To Jay, Aug. 6, 1787.

struggling against despotism and monarchy. The pretext is the good of the people, to which, however, the aristocracy here, as it is everywhere else, and always has been, is far more opposed than the monarchy is." [16] Jefferson never talked this way about aristocracy. At most, he thought the Parlement of Paris rather obstinately selfish.

He did now admit, in the middle of 1788, as Lafayette now did, that the royal reforms were good in substance, but bad in manner. If the king alone has power to reform France, he says, the government is a despotism.[17] He no longer simply sees liberty against tyranny, but a choice of values. Nor, incidentally, do I think that John Adams or any American at the time would have chosen otherwise than as Jefferson did: as between reforms, and even justice, at the hands of an irresponsible and bureaucratic monarchy, however well-intentioned, and a measure of political liberty through elective and representative bodies, even though unequal, Jefferson unhesitatingly chose the latter. We begin to read in his letters of a possible convocation of the Estates-General. Jefferson thinks this a promising step toward a fixed constitution, limitation of the crown and reduction of expense. Equality of representation seems not to enter his mind; he thinks it will be best if the Estates meet in two houses, one representing the people, the other made up of nobles elected by nobles, as, he observes, is done in Scotland.[18] If such a body meets, issues a bill of rights, puts the king on a civil list, and takes care that it shall meet periodically in the future, quite enough will be accomplished. "I think it probable," he wrote to James Monroe in August 1788, "this country will within two or three years be in the enjoyment of a tolerably free constitution, and that without its having cost them a drop of blood." [19]

His ideas continued to develop at deliberate speed, not an inch ahead of average opinion in France, and well behind a good deal of it. Like others, he was dismayed when the Parlement of Paris, in September, ruled that the coming Estates-General must meet as in 1614, in three separate houses—clergy, nobles and commoners. The Parlement, he said, here revealed "the cloven hoof." [20] Now for the first time he began to use the world "privilege," to tell his American correspondents that there were privileged classes in France, and that they paid less than their share of taxes—as Calonne had said publicly almost two years before.[21] But where others, sensing an aristocratic bid for power, moved on the like the Abbé Sieyès to denounce the aristocracy in bitter terms, and to demand equality of representation in the sense of vote by head in a single chamber, Jefferson, still in agreement with Lafayette, hoped for a compromise between nobility and Third Estate. Sieyès, Condorcet and Mirabeau

---

[16] R. Ciampini, ed., *Lettere di Filippo Mazzei alla corte di Polonia* (Bologna, 1937), I, 7. Despatch of July 28, 1788.

[17] Jefferson to Carmichael, June 3, 1788, *Papers,* XIII, 233; to Cutting, July 24, p. 405; to Madison, July 31, p. 441.

[18] To Washington, May 2, 1788, *ibid.,* p. 126. For Jefferson's persistent belief that the French would be wise to model their government on England rather than on America, see Malone, *op. cit.,* pp. 181, 220.

[19] *Ibid.,* p. 489.

[20] *Ibid.,* p. 642.

[21] Jefferson's first use of the term "privilege" seems to be in letters to Paine, Dec. 23, 1788, *Writings,* ed. by Lipscomb and Bergh (Washington, 1903), VII, 246; to Price, Jan. 8, 1789, p. 256; to Jay, Jan. 11, p. 264. The expression "privileged orders" was denounced as a neologism too much favored by the Third Estate in one of Louis XVI's messages of June 1789 to the Estates-General; see Mazzei's report in Ciampini, *op. cit.,* p. 146.

were already chiding Lafayette as an "aristocrat"; I see no reason why they should not have thought the same of Jefferson also.[22] Of the coming Estates-General Jefferson was content to expect very little. If they "do not aim at too much they may begin a good constitution," he told Madison in November. What he meant was that they should obtain, at their first session, only certain rights over taxation and rights to register laws but not take the initiative in legislation, in addition to the assurance of periodic future meeting.[23] The King himself a few weeks later offered more than Jefferson thought the Estate could prudently ask. Nor did his talks with Lafayette about declarations of rights represent any very radical departure. "All the world is occupied at present in framing, every one his own plan, of a bill of rights," he wrote as early as December 1788.[24]

He remained confident for a while that a moderate constitutional "revolution" could be peaceably effected by men of good will, and by men, it must be admitted, occupying a fairly comfortable place in society—"all the honesty of the kingdom," as he put it, "sufficiently at its leisure to think; the men of letters, the easy bourgeois, the young nobility." [25] When a serious working-class riot broke out at a wallpaper factory, just at the moment to jeopardize the harmony of the Estates-General, Jefferson was thrown into an agitation most unusual with him; one is reminded of Luther excoriating the peasants. He called the rioters "wretches" bent only on mischief, "abandoned banditti," whose repression was "unpitied." [26] To the last possible moment he kept his faith in the moderation of the aristocracy, repeatedly declaring, in the first months of 1789, that the clergy would cause the trouble in the coming Estates-General, but that the majority of the nobility might reach an understanding with the Third Estate.[27] He still hoped, at the very opening of the Estates-General, on May 6, 1789, as a means of resolving all difficulties, that the two privileged classes might be persuaded to sit together in one house, the unprivileged in another.[28] This was by no means what was wanted by Frenchmen classified against their will as Third Estate.

His political education, like everyone else's, became dizzily rapid in the next few weeks. He found that the bulk of the Catholic clergy, whom perhaps even ardent admirers of Jefferson would not claim that he well understood, were prepared to take sides with the Third Estate; and that the bulk of the nobles, in whom he had placed his hopes, were less enlightened than he had supposed. He now discovered, seemingly for the first time, that a great many country nobles did not share the affable liberality of the Marquis de Lefayette—that they still entertained, as he put it, "a disposition to keep distinct from the people, and even to tyrannize over them." [29] He readjusted his ideas with alacrity, but no faster than many others. In the very letter

[22] See Gottschalk, *op. cit.*, p. 416; Ciampini, *op. cit.*, pp. 51–56.

[23] *Writings*, VII, 184. Same view expressed to Jay, Nov. 19, 1788, *ibid.*, p. 191; to Washington, Dec. 4, p. 227; to Price, Jan. 8, 1789, p. 258.

[24] To Dr. Currie, Dec. 20, 1788, *ibid.*, p. 239; to Madison, Jan. 12, 1789, p. 268.

[25] To Price, Jan. 8, 1789, *ibid.*, p. 254.

[26] To Carmichael, May 8, 1789, *ibid.*, p. 336; to Jay, May 9, p. 342; to Madison, May 11, p. 354. Contrast the far more understanding account of these Reveillon riots given by Mazzei to the King of Poland, Ciampini, *op. cit.*, pp. 125–27, 136.

[27] To the Count de Moustier, Mar. 13, 1789, *Writings*, VII, 304; to Madison, Mar. 15, p. 313; to Paine, Mar. 17, p. 316; to Humphreys, Mar. 18, p. 321.

[28] To Lafayette, May 6, 1789, *ibid.*, p. 334.

[29] To Madison, May 11, 1789, *ibid.*, p. 355.

of May 6 in which he expressed the hope of compromise to Lafayette, he also urged him, should compromise fail, to repudiate the instructions of his noble constituency and join with the Third Estate before he lost their confidence. By May 20 he was agreeing with the radicals of the Third Estate, or rather with the predominant opinion forming in that body.[30]

On June 17, 1789, the Third Estate took its decisive revolutionary action, passing the point of no return. By a five-to-one majority it declared itself a National Assembly, the only competent representative body, representing not social orders but a nation; it again invited persons from the other two orders to come and merge into this single body; and it arrogated sovereign power to itself, to the extent of gratuitously authorizing all existing taxes, thus implying that it might withdraw authorization and instigate a taxpayers' rebellion. Two days later the clergy joined. The next day came the oath of the Tennis Court. The King mildly resisted, then appeared to accept, then began secretly to prepare the dissolution of the Assembly by armed force. The country trembled with excitement. There was rapturous praise for good King Louis, and an almost religious belief in the dawning of a new era.

Jefferson remained cool and collected. His mind moved with events, but his feelings were scarcely involved in his judgments. "A tremendous cloud hovers over this nation," he reported to Jay on June 17. He gave a sober analysis. If the King, he said, were to

> side openly with the Commons, the revolution would be completed without a convulsion, by the establishment of a constitution, tolerably free, and in which the distinction of Noble and Commoner would be suppressed. But this is scarcely possible. The King is honest and wishes the good of his people; but the expediency of a hereditary aristocracy is too difficult a question for him.[31]

This is substantially the judgment of most historians today. Jefferson had moved a long way since 1787. He no longer saw a Whiggish clash between king and people. He now saw a clash between king and people because the King now supported the aristocracy. Hereditary legal aristocracy was revealed to him as the issue, the stumbling block, the one thing which the commons would not accept, and which the King would not and could not abandon. In short, this was the French Revolution, not the English Revolution of 1689.

Jefferson now felt an optimism qualified by prudent fears. The Assembly, he told Thomas Paine three days before the episode of the Bastille, had by their sagacity and fortitude come into "undisputed possession of sovereignty. The executive and aristocracy are at their feet; the mass of the nation, the mass of the clergy, and the army are with them; they have prostrated the old government, and are now beginning to build one from the foundation." [32] Now that all France seemed to want a radical rebuilding, Jefferson wanted it for them, too. Now that sweeping change seemed to be possible, with nation, clergy and army behind it, he thought it possible also, or at least worthy trying. Materials were at hand for a "superb edifice," he said. But he had his doubts: the Assembly might be too large to do business; it was composed of Frenchmen, that is "more speakers than listeners"; bread shortages, by causing popular violence, might bring division among the leaders; trouble-makers of the Left might

[30] To Crevecoeur, May 20, 1789, *ibid.*, p. 368.
[31] To Jay, June 17, 1789, *Writings,* VII, 379–80.
[32] To Paine, July 11, 1789, *ibid.*, p. 405.

stir up an agitation around the Duke of Orleans; the discomfited aristocrats might organize counter-revolution.[33] All eventually happened much as he feared. Meanwhile, in September 1789 he went home.

What can we conclude? First of all, Jefferson was no visionary. He conducted no apostolate in Europe for the principles set forth in the Declaration of Independence. He engaged in no proselytism; when he gave advice, he was usually more conservative than those who sought his opinions. He had no idea, at this time, that America might be a model for Europe; it was the British government that he thought the French ought to imitate. The existence of the independent United States, simply as a fact, was a subversive influence on the old order in Europe, but Jefferson did nothing to make it more so. He saw Europe and America as quite different societies. Until events taught him otherwise, he accepted the social order in France, the legalized inequalities, as natural and permanent features of the French landscape, like old churches and chateaux. He had no feeling of impending revolution; he was much more concerned in 1787 with the probabilities of European war, and the fires which he saw kindled were in Holland and Belgium.

He was no optimist. Or, rather, he was optimistic because he expected little. He would have been satisfied if the political crises in France had stopped at any point after the middle of 1787. Repeatedly he predicted that all might turn out well, that the French would soon have a "tolerably free constitution" without bloodshed. He wanted for the French "as much liberty as they are capable of managing," but until June of 1789, if then, he did not think they could manage very much. As for equality, that is civil and legal equality, or equality of representation in elected bodies, he believed in it in principle, of course, and had tried to get more of it written into the constitution of Virginia in 1776; but even in Virginia he had failed, and he expected little from Europe. He lacked class-consciousness, being a gentleman rather than an aristocrat, and had little awareness of it in others. There is nothing in his writings of that angry irritability, that sense of downright outrage, or of having been imposed upon flagrantly, that runs through John Adams' account of European patriciates in his *Defense of the Constitutions,* or which animates the Abbé Sieyès' eloquent diatribe, *What Is the Third Estate?* This latter work, which created a stir at the end of 1788, seems to have made no impression on Jefferson. He could with difficulty think of revolution as something demanded from below, by the lower or even the middle classes, or those hitherto excluded from public life. He thought of revolution as something to be arranged by persons already active in political affairs.

Yet he could be realistic in his observations, and was certainly no enthusiast or doctrinaire. His reports are notable for their unimpassioned analysis, the reverse of the ideological, the work of a predominantly intellectual type of man, who sought calmly to weigh the forces at work, and to make reasonable forecasts of the future. It is this practical purpose that we must keep in mind when we speak of his political moderation. If he disapproved of the Dutch Democrats, and thought them dangerously extreme, it was largely because he thought that extremism would provoke reaction, weaken the Patriot coalition, and ruin the Patriot cause. If he thought the French would have a good constitution if they aimed at very little, if as late as the

---

[33] To Shippen, Mar. 11, 1789, *ibid.,* pp. 291–92; to Carmichael, Aug. 9, p. 434; to Jay, Aug. 27, p. 442; to Madison, Aug. 28, p. 447; to Rutledge, Sept. 18, p. 466.

end of 1788 he thought the Estates-General should insist on nothing more than some control of taxation and a right to register proposed laws, it was because he thought that to ask more would consolidate the opposition to any change at all. We can comment on his moderation, if we like, and even on his timidity, at a time when many Frenchmen were getting into a mood to fight, but we cannot easily dismiss his judgment. He was perfectly right in foreseeing that conservative opposition, aroused by revolutionary demands, would make peaceable reformation impossible.

Jefferson's views before he left France must be described as tepid. When he embarked at Le Havre, in September 1789, he was well to the right of the majority in the National Assembly. His hopes for the future were troubled with forebodings. Why then, after his return home, in the great crisis of 1793, did Jefferson emerge as the leading sympathizer with the French Revolution—the great American "Jacobin"? That he was, as his enemies now said, a visionary, a doctrinaire, a facile optimist, a naïve enthusiast for human perfectability, or even much of a democrat, as democracy was already understood in Europe, I do not believe.

There may have been three reasons why our dubious democrat became the great American Jacobin. Indeed, the same three reasons may explain why many Frenchmen became Jacobins, properly so called. First, Jefferson did feel that liberty and equality, if and where possible, were desirable states of being. Second, it was his tendency, as with most people, to accept the accomplished fact, to adjust his ideas in correspondence with the rush of events, to doubt the feasibility of a thing before it occurred, and to accept and defend it after it had happened. Like Frenchmen, he thus accepted the French Republic: perhaps a measure of liberty and equality was possible, after all. Third, he saw the conflict in Europe in 1793 as a conflict of real forces. He did not see the issue, as conservatives then did and still do, as a choice between anarchy and order, or between political metaphysics and political wisdom, or between godless human presumption and Christian civilization. He had learned the hard way himself, and even against his natural inclinations, that hereditary aristocracy was the ultimate issue in the French Revolution. He had found France virtually unanimous—nation, clergy and army—against the claims of the nobility in July of 1789. He thought that in 1793 the Revolution was simply opposed by Counter-Revolution, and that the Counter-Revolution consisted of elements of the old French aristocracy, the Continental monarchies, the European nobilities and patriciates, the wealthy and privileged classes everywhere, the ecclesiastical hierarchies and the Parliamentary oligarchy of Great Britain. No one who has read Jefferson's letters from France could imagine that he thought all the measures taken during the French Revolution to be wise, even those taken at the very beginning. But he compared the wisdom or unwisdom of the French, not with perfect wisdom, but with the wisdom then exhibited by living and actual opponents of developments in France. Given the choice as he saw it, he chose to take sides with the Revolution.

22 / Novus Ordo Seculorum: Enlightenment Ideas on Diplomacy

Felix Gilbert

In declaring their independence from Great Britain, Americans also hoped to establish a political separation from the intrigues, alliances, and wars of the Old World. Thomas Paine, for example, in his *Common Sense* argued that American involvement in colonial wars in the past has been largely the consequence of political ties between the New World and the Old. Once those political ties were severed, Americans might escape this undesirable result of their former subjection to England. Of course, Americans would not be totally isolated from Europe: they would have commercial connections or "alliances." Paine, again as an example, foresaw willingness on the part of France and Spain to enter into trade with America once separation became the avowed aim of the colonists. He also foresaw the future of the new nation in open commerce with all of Europe, without favoritism or particular ties to any part of that continent. Paine was, in part at least, expressing a contempt for the methods and results of traditional diplomacy. Foreign policy of an old kind was simply another instrument of the old politics of European dynasties, an instrument that a new republic would not have to employ. As did Paine, American diplomats of the revolutionary generation had some high and hardly realistic hopes, hopes that gradually became altered in practice to come somewhat closer to reality. In 1776 the Continental Congress really seemed to believe that it could realize the expectations of the Model Treaty described in the following pages. Its fears of old-style entanglements were repeatedly expressed. These fears were given added force by the thought of many of the *philosophes* described by Gilbert. Yet the necessities of the War for Independence forced Americans to accept terms from France that bound the United States to affairs of the Old World for many years. The needs of the moment in 1777 and 1778 were to make Americans somewhat more realistic in their actual negotiations with the European powers; the events of the 1790's and the first decade and a half of

From Felix Gilbert, *To the Farewell Address: Ideas of Early American Diplomacy*, pp. 44–75. Copyright © 1961 by Princeton University Press. Reprinted by permission of Princeton University Press.

the nineteenth century were to reinforce that old hope of escaping from "entangling alliances" with the Old World.

For further reading: Edward Corwin, *French Policy and the American Alliance of 1778* (1916); Richard B. Morris, *The Peacemakers: The Great Powers and American Independence* (1965); Gerald Stourzh, *Benjamin Franklin and American Foreign Policy* (1954); Carl Van Doren, *Benjamin Franklin* (1938).

I

Paine's *Common Sense* was published in January 1776. Throughout the following months, the movement for independence gained increasing momentum. The final stage in the chain of events which led to the foundation of an independent United States was reached on June 7, 1776, when the Congress entered upon the consideration of R. H. Lee's resolution

> that these United Colonies are, and of right ought to be, free and independent States, that they are absolved from all allegiance to the British crown, and that all political connection between them and the State of Great Britain is, and ought to be, totally dissolved; that it is expedient forthwith to take the most effectual measures for forming foreign Alliances; that a plan of confederation be prepared and transmitted to the respective Colonies for their consideration and approbation.[1]

Confederation, foreign alliances, and independence were presented as interconnected measures in this motion; its pivot was the urgent need for foreign assistance. Because of the difficult economic situation which had developed in the colonies, Congress had been forced to admit the failure of a policy, the main weapon of which had been the stoppage of trade between the colonies and the outside world. Thus on April 6, 1776, the Congress ordered the opening of American ports to the ships of all nations except Great Britain. Because of the British supremacy on the seas and the lack of an American navy, the success of this measure depended on the willingness of foreign powers not only to receive American trade, but also to protect it. The American leaders were aware, however, that no foreign power could dare to take the risky step of assisting the American rebels without having a definite guarantee that some stable regime would be created on the North American continent and that return to British rule would be made impossible. "Confederation" and "independence" were the necessary prerequisites for securing "foreign alliances."

But what did the Americans understand by "foreign alliances"? When John Adams, a few years later, reviewed the events of the summer of 1776, he declared that in the debates of 1776, on the application to foreign powers he had laid it down as a first principle that "we should calculate all our measures and foreign negotiations in such a manner, as to avoid a too great dependence upon any one power of Europe—to avoid all obligations and temptations to take any part in future European wars; that

[1] *Journals of the Continental Congress,* ed. Worthington Chauncey Ford, vol. v, Washington 1906, p. 425.

the business of America with Europe was commerce, not politics or war." [2] Yet in 1776, Adams had been a zealous supporter of Lee's resolution which had recommended the conclusion of foreign alliances. At present, the term "alliance" is understood to mean the establishment of cooperation in the political sphere among the contracting parties. If John Adams saw no contradiction between a support of Lee's resolution and an avoidance of political obligations, he must have used the word "alliance" in a sense different from the present-day meaning of a close political bond.

It can probably be said that our identification of "alliance" with political or even political-military commitments derives from the fact that in the modern world, diplomatic instruments which contain political or political-military arrangements are sharply separated from those concerned with regulations of trade, tariffs, and navigation. Yet this separation of political treaties from commercial treaties began only in the eighteenth century. In the Peace of Utrecht of 1713 ending the hostilities of the War of the Spanish Succession between England and France, political and commercial arrangements were dealt with for the first time in separate documents. This new pattern was only slowly adopted; throughout the eighteenth century, one and the same treaty could still contain arrangements about political, commercial, and economic questions. Thus there are many nuances in the seventeenth and eighteenth centuries between the opposite types of the "traité d'alliance offensive et défensive," clearly designating a political-military bond, and the "traité de commerce," exclusively concerned with trade. Such names as "traité d'alliance et de commerce," "traité de paix, de navigation, et de commerce," "traité de navigation et commerce," "traité de marine," suggest the variety of content which could be contained in a single diplomatic document. In the terminology of the eighteenth century, all such treaties established "alliances."

Thus Adams' view that one could have alliances with foreign powers without making political commitments finds its explanation in the usage of the eighteenth century; other Americans used the term "alliance" in the same loose way. In the first six months of the year 1776, before Lee's resolution made the question of foreign alliances an issue of practical politics, the problem had been frequently discussed; and the ambiguity of the term "alliance" had resulted in a great variety of contradictory opinions about the consequences of concluding foreign alliances. They were looked upon with fear, but they were also regarded as the instrument by which America could obtain the necessary assistance without restrictions on her freedom of action. One of the reasons given against the conclusion of alliances with foreign powers was that the bond which had existed between England and the colonies in the past had been an "alliance";[3] Britain had provided military protection for the granting of commercial advantages on the part of the colonies. An alliance with a foreign power might lead to the same consequences which the "alliance" with Britain had had; "an expedient of this kind" would lead the colonists into "having their allies, at last, for their masters." [4] It would produce the exchange of domination by one

[2] John Adams to Secretary Livingston, February 5, 1783, printed in John Adams, *Works,* ed. Charles Francis Adams, vol. VIII, Boston 1853, p. 35.

[3] For instance, Thomas Paine, *Complete Writings,* ed. Philip S. Foner, vol. I, New York 1945, p. 20; John Adams, *Works,* vol. IV, pp. 110, 114; *Letters of Members of the Continental Congress,* ed. Edmund C. Burnett, vol. I, *Washington* 1921, p. 369; *American Archives,* ed. Peter Force, fourth series, vol. V, Washington 1844, p. 1208; and, most of all, Franklin's "Vindication" of 1775, see Benjamin Franklin, *Works,* ed. Jared Sparks, vol. V, Philadelphia 1840, pp. 83–90.

[4] Cato's "Fifth Letter to the People of Pennsylvania," *American Archives,* fourth series, vol. V, pp. 542–543.

power for domination by another. To avoid this danger, it was suggested that the alliance be restricted to "external assistance";[5] a distinction was to be made between cooperation on land and cooperation at sea. While the French navy should be allowed to play a part in the war, no assistance by a French army should be accepted. In general, Americans were very optimistic about the prospects of receiving the protection of the French navy for American trade without having to make political commitments in return; most Americans believed that the separation of the American colonies from Britain's imperial system and the possibility of trade with the colonies would be regarded by the French as a sufficient attraction. Other Americans were less sanguine. When Franklin wrote about the possibility of exchanging "commerce for friendship," [6] he seems to have felt that a somewhat more substantial inducement in the form of some monopoly, at least for a definite period, must be offered to France. Thus when the contingency of entering into alliances with foreign powers was debated in the early part of 1776, such a measure comprised a wide range of possibilities: a purely commercial treaty, or a treaty with commercial obligations from the American side and political-military obligations from the French side, or a treaty with reciprocal political commitments. When Lee proposed his resolution on June 7, 1776, the thinking in the colonies had not yet crystallized into a clear conception of the kind of "alliance" America should conclude. Only when the Congress began to deliberate on the treaty to be proposed to France and on the instruction to be given to the American negotiators did the ideas on this problem take a definite form, a form which was striking and novel.

The external story of the further events is clearly established. On June 11, 1776, in consequence of Lee's resolution, a committee was appointed to prepare the model of a treaty to be proposed to the French court. This committee handed in its report on July 18 and the report was discussed in the Continental Congress on August 22, 27, and 29. Then the Congress referred the report back to the committee for amendment and for preparation of instructions to be given to the American agents. On September 17, this final report of the committee was made to the Congress, and the latter's agreement to the prepared instructions was given on September 24. Two days later, Benjamin Franklin, Silas Deane, and Thomas Jefferson were appointed commissioners to France.

The internal story behind these factual events is much more difficult to disentangle. For its reconstruction we have only a few documents—the Model Treaty and the instructions—and brief remarks in the letters and memoirs of the main actors.

John Adams was a member of the committee entrusted with the preparation of the Model Treaty, and he was assigned to draft this document. Adams must be considered as the chief architect of the Model Treaty and its accompanying instructions. He had given much thought to the subject before he entered upon this task. In March 1776, evidently influenced by Paine's *Common Sense*, he had set down on paper his ideas as to the "connection we may safely form" with France and arrived at the following formula: "1. No political connection. Submit to none of her authority, receive no governors or officers from her. 2. No military connection. Receive no troops from her. 3. Only a commercial connection; that is, make a treaty to receive

[5] Richard Henry Lee to Landon Carter, June 2, 1776, *Letters of Members of the Continental Congress,* vol. I, p. 469.

[6] Franklin to Joseph Priestley, July 7, 1775, *ibid.,* p. 156.

her ships into our ports; let her engage to receive our ships into her ports; furnish us with arms, cannon, saltpetre, powder, duck, steel." [7] How fundamental these ideas were for him can be deduced from the fact that they also appear in letters which he wrote in the spring of 1776. He urged the necessity of sending ambassadors to foreign courts "to form with them, at least with some of them, commercial treaties of friendship and alliance," [8] and when the dangers to American freedom of an alliance with a foreign power were pointed out to him, he stressed that in recommending foreign alliances, he was thinking only of a contractual safeguard of America's trade relations. "I am not for soliciting any political connection, or military assistance, or indeed naval, from France. I wish for nothing but commerce, a mere marine treaty with them." [9]

The Model Treaty was intended to realize the ideas which John Adams had previously developed—namely, that alliance did not imply a political bond and that America's contacts with outside powers should be limited to trade relations. When Adams began to draft the Model Treaty, Franklin put into his hand "a printed volume of treaties" in which he had made some pencil marks beside certain articles. Adams found "some of these judiciously selected, and I took them, with others which I found necessary, into the draught." [10] A comparison of the Model Treaty with earlier documents reveals that Adams relied heavily on two particular treaties: the treaty between James II and Louis XIV of November 16, 1686, concerning the neutrality of the American colonies in case of a conflict between England and France; and the commercial treaty between England and France of 1713. Most of the stipulations of the Model Treaty concerned with the regulation of trade, navigation, and fishing—which is to say, the greater part of the Model Treaty—are taken from these treaties. In other words, agreements which regulated the commercial relations between England and France were used as patterns for the Model Treaty, and, in that, the United States took the place of England. It seems likely that Adams chose the commercial treaty between England and France of 1713 also because its regulations had been of a most liberal character. The liberal spirit which inspired the American draft is reflected particularly in the articles dealing with trade in wartime. The Model Treaty contained a precisely circumscribed and extremely limited list of contraband goods: even foodstuffs and naval stores were excluded from it. Furthermore, neutrals should have the right to trade with belligerents, and the principle was laid down that free ships make free goods. The strongest indication of this tendency towards complete freedom in trade can be found, however, in the first two articles of the Model Treaty, which were concerned with the establishment of basic principles for the future commercial relations between France and America. These articles go beyond anything that Adams could have taken from the treaties between England and France. The Model Treaty suggested that the French should treat the inhabitants of the United States with regard to duties and imports as natives of France and vice versa; moreover, they "shall enjoy all other the Rights, Liberties, Priviledges, Immunities and Exemptions in Trade, Navigation and Commerce, in passing from one port [Part] thereof to another, and in going to and from the same, from and to any

[7] John Adams, *Works*, vol. ii, pp. 488–489.
[8] John Adams to William Cushing, June 9, 1776, *Letters of Members of the Continental Congress*, vol i, p. 478.
[9] John Adams to John Winthrop, June 23, 1776, *ibid.*, p. 502.
[10] John Adams, *Works*, vol. ii, p. 516.

Part of the World, which the said Natives, or Companies enjoy." [11] The "instructions" added that only if "his most Christian Majesty shall not consent" to these articles, the commissioners should try to get the French agreement to a most-favored-nation clause.[12] The latter was proposed only as a less attractive alternative if a reciprocity clause could not be obtained. The fundamental concepts behind these proposals are evident and, as far as the practical policy of the period is concerned, striking: in drafting the Model Treaty, the colonists were thinking not only of France but also of other powers. They were, in effect, creating a general pattern for future commercial treaties. Whereas usually commercial conventions were sources of friction and instruments of power politics reinforcing political alliances by commercial preferences, the Americans wanted to establish a commercial system of freedom and equality which would eliminate all cause for tension and political conflicts.

Although John Adams might have wanted to limit the Model Treaty to questions of trade and navigation, a number of political questions had to be taken up. Thus French protection was to replace the former English protection of American ships against the attacks of the Barbary States. Moreover, a number of articles were concerned with the problems which had arisen from the war against the British and had forced the colonists into "their application to foreign powers." It was stipulated that American ships should be protected and convoyed by their allies and that France should give up any claim to territories of the North American continent, while the Americans would not oppose a French conquest of the West Indies.

Since both countries—France and the United States—were moving in a sharply anti-English direction, would it not be desirable that they agree on common action for war and peace and that the conditions of their political cooperation be clearly defined? A treaty with the colonial rebels would unavoidably involve France in a war with England; and for most of the colonial leaders, this was the purpose of an agreement with France. Hence some statement about the reciprocal obligations of the two powers fighting against the same potential enemy was necessary. The manner in which the Model Treaty dealt with this question was surprising, as it revealed the Americans' disinclination to be forced into a political bond with an outside power even under pressure of war. Article 8 stated that in case the alliance with the United States should involve France in war with England, the United States would not assist England in such a war. The promise offered in this article—namely, that America would not use the opportunity of an Anglo-French war for coming to an understanding with England—was little more than a matter of course. What is astounding is how little the Americans were willing to offer. Political and military cooperation with France was to be avoided even if France should enter the war against England.

In the instructions for the American negotiators, it was said that this "article will probably be attended with some Difficulty," [13] and the article was explained by an unusually long comment. Clearly the article had evoked a heated debate in the committee. A number of members felt that such love of principle defeated its own purpose and that a somewhat more realistic approach was necessary to obtain French participation in the war. Thus they wanted to include in the instructions a para-

[11] *Journals of the Continental Congress,* vol. v, p. 769.
[12] *Ibid.,* p. 813.
[13] *Ibid.,* pp. 814–815.

graph which would have given the American negotiators permission to offer a greater inducement to France: reconquest of the islands in the West Indies which France had ceded to England after the Seven Years' War: "If the Courts of France cannot be prevailed on to engage in the War with Great Britain for any consideration already proposed in this Treaty, you are hereby authorized to agree as a further inducement, that these United States will wage the war in union with France, not make peace with Great Britain until the latter France shall gain the possession of those Islands in the West Indies formerly called Nieutral, and which by the Treaty of Paris were ceded to G. Britain: provided France shall make the conquest of these Islands an early object of the War and prosecute the same with sufficient force." [14] However, the majority of Congress was not willing to make commitments about territorial changes, and this paragraph was omitted from the final instructions. Some concessions were made to those who cared more about getting France into the war than about principles of foreign policy. The commissioners were entitled to make some additional offers: the United States was willing to guarantee that it would grant to no other power trading privileges which it had not granted to the French king; furthermore, in case France should become involved in the present war, neither France nor the United States would conclude peace without notifying the other power six months ahead.

The striking thing about the Model Treaty and the accompanying instructions is that, although the Americans were in a desperate situation in which they looked anxiously for foreign help, their leaders insisted on proposals which were entirely alien to the spirit of the diplomatic practice of the time.

II

It was a long journey from the simple brick building of the State House in Philadelphia, with its unpretentious wood paneling, to the palaces of Paris and Versailles, abounding in marble and rosewood, chinoiseries, mirrors, and silk. How did the American leaders have the courage to proffer to the French government, ensconced in eighteenth-century splendor, a treaty which challenged all the diplomatic traditions of which France was the foremost practitioner?

The Americans were convinced of the immense value of the offer which they made to France: the ending of the English monopoly of trade with North America. The consequence would be not only to increase French economic prosperity, but also to weaken England, France's old rival. The Americans may have somewhat overestimated the extent to which the opening of the American ports to the ships of all nations would revolutionize the European state system. But in the American view, France would gain such far-reaching advantages that America had a right to determine the nature of the relationship which, in the future, should exist between America and the European powers.

The Model Treaty with which the Americans formulated their concept of this relationship shows the impact of the program which Paine had set forth in *Common Sense*. The Model Treaty and the accompanying instructions were designed to keep

[14] *Ibid.*, p. 817.

America out of European struggles and to secure for her peace and freedom by making all European powers interested partners in American trade. But behind these documents there lay an attitude which leads beyond the image which Paine had given of America's role in foreign policy. Paine's ideas are products of the age in which he was born, of the Enlightenment; but in *Common Sense,* he did not share its optimism. To Paine, the world, with the exception of America, was rotten and lost. "Freedom hath been hunted around the globe. Asia and Africa have long expelled her, Europe regards her like a stranger, and England hath given her warning to depart." America was to be preserved as the last bulwark of liberty, "an asylum for mankind." This censure of Europe corresponded to feelings deeply rooted in America's colonial past and facilitated the acceptance of the ideas of *Common Sense* in America. But American intellectual life was also strongly imbued with the spirit of the Enlightenment. Although most Americans may have agreed with Paine's condemnation of Europe's political and social life as it existed at the time, not all of them shared Paine's gloomy prognostications for Europe's future; many were in accord with the Enlightenment belief in progress and were convinced that a new and better age in the history of the human race was approaching. They believed the American Revolution had started a great experiment; they felt they were setting a pattern which the rest of the world would follow. Thus the Model Treaty had a double face. It was intended, on the one hand, as an instrument to achieve an independent existence for America, secure from the corrupting influence of Europe. On the other hand, by eliminating purely political issues like territorial settlements, by focussing on the regulation of commercial relations, and by placing them on such a liberal basis that the arrangements between France and America could easily be extended to the nations of the whole world, the Americans transformed the Model Treaty into a pattern for all future diplomatic treaties. The Americans entered the European scene as the representatives of the diplomacy of a new era. They did not feel confronted by an entirely hostile world. They might find little sympathy for their ideas with the rulers of France, who thought in terms of traditional diplomacy. But they felt they had many friends: their allies were all the progressive minds of Europe, the writers and thinkers whom we now call "the philosophes."

The philosophes' ideas on foreign policy and diplomacy throw light on the broad background from which the American views on this topic developed. The philosophes confirmed the Americans in their outlook on diplomacy and, for a number of years, were an important factor in determining the course of American foreign policy; finally, they infused a lasting idealistic element into the American attitude toward foreign affairs.

The views of the philosophes both on foreign policy and on domestic policy were based on the conviction that history had reached the end of a long and tortuous development; the contrasts and conflicts of the past would now be resolved in a great synthesis, and a permanent order could be accomplished. The confidence of the philosophes in the near approach of a golden age had its foundation in a peculiar constellation of historical factors.

We have spoken of the change in the political system of Europe signified by the Peace of Utrecht. One of the aspects of this change was the growing awareness of the importance of the non-European parts of the globe. The stipulations of the Treaty of Utrecht covered the entire world and thereby demonstrated to what extent the great European powers, though they remained of central importance, drew their strength from the resources of other continents. This is reflected in Turgot's statement that the trend of the time was to make the boundaries of the political world "become identical with those of the physical world." [15]

This feeling that one civilization now encompassed the whole world was reinforced by the astounding growth of economic interdependence. In the centers of European civilization, people could rely on having a regular supply of goods from all over the world: sugar from the West Indies, tea and china from the Far East, coffee and chocolate from the Americas and Africa. The barriers that existed seemed artificial and ephemeral in comparison with the fine net by which the merchants tied the individuals of the different nations together like "threads of silk." [16] As Sédaine says in his famous comedy Le phisosophe sans le savoir, the merchants—whether they are English, Dutch, Russian, or Chinese—do not serve a single nation; they serve everyone and are citizens of the whole world. Commerce was believed to bind the nations together and to create not only a community of interests but also a distribution of labor among them—a new comprehensive principle placing the isolated sovereign nations in a higher political unit. In the eighteenth century, writers were likely to say that the various nations belonged to "one society"; it was stated that all states together formed "a family of nations," and the whole globe a "general and unbreakable confederation." [17]

The social force which carried this development was the bourgeoisie. In the eighteenth century, its members became conscious of being a main prop of social life; they felt entitled to have all obstacles to the development of their interests eliminated. The philosophes gave the claims of this class an ideological form. They did for the bourgeoisie what intellectuals usually do when a new and rising class wants to break the restraints which keep it in a subordinate position. Then intellectuals identify the cause of a class with the cause of the human race in general and explain that the fight is a fight for freedom against tyranny, rather than for special interests against privileges and suppression by a ruling group. The triumph of the new class is to be a victory of humanity, the final solution of all historical conflicts.

Most of the eighteenth-century philosophes were French. France was the most powerful nation of Europe, the theater in which the issues of the century were fought out. In the economically less advanced countries of Central and Eastern Europe, the power of the feudal and agrarian ruling group could not yet be seriously challenged. In England, as a result of the civil wars and revolutions of the previous century, the commercial classes had gained a steadily increasing influence and were becoming gradually amalgamated with the ruling group. In France, monarchy and nobility were still in exclusive political control, but the bourgeoisie had become a powerful economic and social factor; the forces of the old order and of the new faced each other in almost equal poise. Moreover, although the wars of Louis XIV had brought France to the zenith of power in Europe, they had eventually threatened to carry her beyond that point. The French people had entered the century exhausted

---

[15] Turgot, Oeuvres, ed. Gustave Schelle, vol. I, Paris 1913, p. 263.

[16] Michel-Jean Sédaine, Le philosophe sans le savoir, act II, scene 4.

[17] For instance, Mercier de la Rivière, "L'ordre naturel et essentiel des Sociétés Politiques, 1767," in Collection des Économistes et des Reformateurs Sociaux de la France, ed. Edgar Depitre, Paris 1910, pp. 242–252; Le Trosne, De l'Ordre Social, Paris 1777, pp. 355, 392–393; Gaillard, "Les Avantages de La Paix, 1767," in Gabriel-Henri Gaillard, Mélanges Académiques, Poétiques, Littéraires, Philologiques, vol. I, Paris 1806, p. 66.

and dispirited. The traditional policy of territorial expansion on the Continent and the drive for European hegemony had lost much of its glamour. Thus the great concern of the philosophes was domestic policy.

If the ideas of the philosophes on foreign policy have been studied less than those on domestic policy, this one-sidedness of modern interests corresponds to the order of value which the philosophes themselves assigned to these two fields of political activity. Their thesis was that the great role which foreign affairs played in the political life of their time was one of the most fundamental evils of the existing political system. D'Argenson has most succinctly formulated this basic attitude of the philosophes with regard to the relationship between domestic and foreign affairs. "The true purpose of the science called politics is to perfect the interior of a state as much as possible. Flatterers assure the princes that the interior is there only to serve foreign policy. Duty tells them the opposite." [18]

The philosophes directed a systematic attack against the view which regarded foreign policy as the center and culmination of political activities. They assailed the entire concept of man which complements this philosophy of power politics that stresses the qualities of physical prowess, honor, and obedience. The high evaluation of military virtues is a "dangerous prejudice, a carry-over from barbarism, a remnant of the former chaos." [19] True fame consists not in the glory which the stupidity of the people connects with conquests and which the still more stupid historians love to praise to the point of boring the reader;" [20] if the right name were to be given to conquests "which for so long have been praised as heroism," [21] they would be called crimes.

The existing methods of diplomacy were so much geared towards power politics and war that they could never serve the opposite purpose—the preservation of peace. The main target of the philosophes was the assumption that the only possibility and guarantee for peace lay in the maintenance of a balance of power among the states. There is hardly a philosophe and reformer who does not inveigh against the idea of balance of power, "this favorite idea of newspapers and coffee-house politicians." [22] This idea, "reducing the whole science of politics to knowledge of a single word, pleases both the ignorance and the laziness of the ministers, of ambassadors and their clerks." [23] In contrast to the ostensible aim of promoting peace, balance of power had, it was said, always done harm to a system of lasting peace and was opposed to it. The reason was that "the system of balance of power is a system of resistance, consequently of disturbance, of shocks and of explosions." [24] With the overthrow of this central concept of eighteenth-century diplomacy, the other concerns of the traditional diplomacy were also reevaluated and shown up in their futility and dangerousness.

---

[18] D'Argenson, *Considérations sur le Gouvernement Ancient et Présent de la France,* Amsterdam 1764, p. 18.

[19] *Ibid.,* p. 20.

[20] Condillac, "Le Commerce et le Gouvernement, 1776," in Condillac, *Oeuvres Complètes,* vol. IV, Paris 1821, p. 278.

[21] Condorcet, "Discours de Réception à l'Académie Française," in Condorcet, *Oeuvres,* ed. A. C. O'Connor and M. F. Arago, vol. I, Paris 1847–1849, p. 396.

[22] [Mirabeau], *L'Ami des Hommes ou Traité de la Population,* nouvelle édition 1759, 3rd part, p. 368.

[23] Mably, *"Principes des Négociations,"* in Abbé de Mably, *Collection Complète des Oeuvres,* vol. V, Paris 1784, p. 66.

[24] Gaillard, *loc. cit.,* pp. 79–80.

According to the philosophes, the conclusion of treaties and alliances, the most significant activity of eighteenth-century diplomacy, would not serve to establish friendly relations among states; treaties are nothing but "temporary armistices" [25] and alliances "preparations for treason." [26] Even when they are called defensive alliances, they are "in reality always of an offensive nature." [27] Diplomatic activity, thus being identical with double-dealing and pursuing purposes different from those it openly avows, needs to wrap itself in secrecy and has become an "obscure art which hides itself in the folds of deceit, which fears to let itself be seen and believes it can succeed only in the darkness of mystery." [28] Secrecy, therefore, is not—as the diplomats pretend— necessary for the efficient fulfillment of their functions; it only proves that they are conspirators planning crimes. Diderot, in a satirical piece entitled "Political Principles of Rulers," has summarized the views of the philosophes on the diplomacy of their time. "Make alliances only in order to sow hatred. . . . Incite wars among my neighbors and try to keep it going. . . . Have no ambassadors in other countries, but spies. . . . To be neutral means to profit from the difficulties of others in order to improve one's own situation." [29] Though different writers made different aspects of diplomacy—secrecy or formality of etiquette—the chief butts of their criticism, they were all in agreement that diplomacy could not be reformed by redressing any single abuse. The evil inherent in diplomacy could be removed only by a complete change in the attitude of those who ruled. Foreign affairs showed most clearly the ills of a world not yet ruled by reason. "The blind passions of the princes" [30] were the cause of wars, conquests, and all the miseries accompanying them. A favorite story of the eighteenth century illustrating the arbitrariness which dominated foreign policy was the story of the palace window: Louvois, fearing disgrace because Louis XIV had expressed displeasure with Louvois' arrangements concerning the construction of the windows of the Trianon, instigated the King to renew the war against the Hapsburgs in order to divert his attention from architectural matters. As long as foreign policy continued to be determined by passions, by whims and arbitrary proclivities, diplomacy could be nothing else but "the art of intrigue." [31]

If one wants to reduce this whole complex of eighteenth-century ideas on diplomacy to a simple formula, it can be summarized as the establishment of a rule of reason. It is the same solution which the philosophes had for the problems of domestic policy. In view of the pre-eminence which they gave domestic over foreign affairs, they considered the introduction of a new and peaceful era in foreign policy dependent on a reorganization of domestic policy. It would even be enough to put the policy of France on a new basis. Since France was the hub in the wheel of European politics, the other nations would quickly follow the French lead; a new period in world history would begin.

[25] Rousseau, "Extrait du Projet de Paix Perpétuelle de M. L'Abbé de Saint Pierre," in J. J. Rousseau, *Political Writings*, ed. C. E. Vaughan, vol. i, Cambridge 1915, p. 369.

[26] Guillaume-Thomas Raynal, *Histoire Philosophique et Politique des Établissements et du Commerce des Européens dans les deux Indes*, vol. vi, Genève 1781, p. 284.

[27] D'Argenson, *op. cit.*, p. 327.

[28] Le Trosne, *op. cit.*, p. 395.

[29] Diderot, "Principes de Politique des Souverains," in Diderot, *Oeuvres Complètes*, ed. J. Assézat, vol. ii, Paris 1875, pp. 461–502.

[30] Diderot in article "Paix" in *Dictionnaire Encyclopédique*, in Diderot, *Oeuvres Complètes*, vol. xvi, p. 188.

[31] Mably, *Oeuvres*, vol. v, p. 17.

Yet how could this change be effected? As much as the eighteenth-century re-formers agreed on the basic concepts which we have sketched above, they differed on how their ideas could be realized. Some looked for a solution along conservative, others along radical, democratic lines.

Among those who had a more conservative outlook were the physiocrats. A great number of the philosophes—some in a more, others in a less orthodox way—belonged to the physiocratic school. Although today physiocracy is usually regarded as having propounded an original and important economic doctrine, the significance of physio-cratic theories in the eighteenth century seemed to reach far beyond the economic sphere and to range over the entire structure of social and political life. The physio-crats called their political theory "economic policy," not because they were concerned solely with economic questions, but because, to them, economics and politics were identical. They believed that all political problems would be solved if the right eco-nomic principles were followed and the right economic measures adopted. The con-trast to "economic policy" was the "old policy," the "false policy," or "power politics"; all of these terms were alternately used. "The essence of power politics consists of divergence of interests, that of economic policy of unity of interests—the one leads to war, frustrations, destruction, the other to social integration, co-operation, and free and peaceful sharing of the fruits of work." [32] The physiocrats elaborated this con-trast between "the old policy" and "the economic policy," between an "artificial" and a "natural" political situation, with great gusto and especially emphasized that, as a result of the artificiality of the "old policy," dealings had to be shrouded in secrecy and mystery. The diplomats had to be actors—"competitors in grimaces" [33]—and each nation was barricaded behind its own frontiers, intent on making commercial treaties to its own advantage and to the disadvantage of its neighbor. In contrast, the new world in which the "economic policy" was to be realized would have an unrestricted exchange of goods. From mutual interdependence would emerge the realization that increase in one nation's wealth means increased wealth for all other nations, and that the interests of all nations are identical; consequently, there would be no advan-tage in enlarging one's own territory and combatting one's neighbor. A single measure, namely, the establishment of free trade, would bring about this miraculous change; it was up to the rulers of the states to take this one decisive measure. The physiocrats were favorites of many princes, and their faith in the power of reason was so strong that they believed in the probability of persuading the rulers of the states to make this change. They were no opponents of despotism; on the contrary, they were confident that the new order could be introduced quite easily with and by means of the prince's absolute power.

Other philosophes believed that the physiocrats were deceiving themselves by trusting in princely absolutism. These more radical thinkers saw despotism as an integral part of the old order which had to be overcome. The decisive step in estab-lishing the new order was a change in political leadership; the people themselves had to take over control of political life. These writers were concerned with the problem of how to achieve an effective popular control of foreign policy. Condorcet, who was particularly interested in this question, constructed a mechanism which he consid-ered suitable for this purpose. No convention between nations should be valid with-

---

[32] Baudeau, "Première Introduction à la Philosophie Économique, 1767," in *Physiocrates,* ed. Eugène Daire, vol. ii, Paris 1846, p. 742.

[33] [Mirabeau], *op. cit.,* p. 26.

out approval of the legislative body. Moreover, as a further safeguard, he demanded that political treaties should be ratified by the single districts of a state. In case of an enemy attack, war might be declared, but only by the legislative; and a declaration of war would have to be followed immediately by new elections, which would give the people the opportunity to express their views on the war. Evidently Condorcet had no doubt that the people would always be peace-loving; the practical issue was to remove all obstacles to a direct expression of the popular will. Condorcet regarded diplomats as such an obstacle, as unnecessary middlemen. He had no use for them, nor for diplomatic arrangements establishing automatic obligations by which the freedom of action of a nation would be bound. "Alliance treaties seem to me so dangerous and so little useful that I think it is better to abolish them entirely in time of peace. They are only means by which the rulers of states precipitate the people into wars from which they benefit either by covering up their mistakes or by carrying out their plots against freedom, and for which the emergency serves as a pretext." [34] The picture which the philosophes envisaged of the relations among nations after the rule of reason had been established was implied in their criticism of the existing foreign policy: the former would be the reverse of the latter. Foreign policy should follow moral laws. There should be no difference between the "moral principles" which rule the relations among individuals and "moral principles" which rule the relations among states. Diplomacy should be "frank and open." [35] Formal treaties would be unnecessary; political alliances should be avoided particularly. Commercial conventions should refrain from all detailed regulations establishing individual advantages and privileges; they should limit themselves to general arrangements stating the fundamental rules and customs of trade and navigation. In such a world, the connection among the different states would rest in the hands not of governments but of individuals trading with each other.

If this picture of the foreign policy of the future was not very precise, there was a special reason. Foreign policy and diplomacy were regarded as typical phenomena of the *ancien régime;* they owed their importance to the fact that the rulers followed false ideals and egoistic passions instead of reason. The logical consequence was that in a reformed world, based on reason, foreign policy and diplomacy would become unnecessary, that the new world would be a world without diplomats.

III

The visible symbol of the alliance between the new republic and the philosophes was the meeting of Franklin and Voltaire in a Paris theater, embracing and kissing each other while the public applauded. In our context, an equally significant encounter was that of John Adams with the Abbé de Mably, a philosophe especially interested in the problems of foreign affairs; according to Adams, Mably "spoke with great indignation against the practice of lying, chicaning, and finessing, in negotiations; frankness, candor, and probity, were the only means of gaining confidence." [36]

[34] Cordorcet, *Oeuvres,* vol. IX, p. 45; see also pp. 41–46.
[35] Le Trosne, *op. cit.,* p. 421.
[36] John Adams, *Works,* vol. III, p. 350.

The American commissioners were regarded in France as representatives of a new diplomacy, and they behaved as such. Silas Deane, whom the Continental Congress had dispatched to France even before independence had been declared, apologized in his first interview with the French Foreign Minister, Count Vergennes, for any violation of form which, inadvertently, he might have committed. "If my commission or the mode of introducing the subject were out of the usual course, I must rely on his goodness to make allowances for a new-formed people, in circumstances altogether unprecedented, and for their agent wholly unacquainted with Courts." [37] But Deane was not so humble as he pretended to be to Vergennes. The same day, he wrote a letter, full of contempt for ceremony and etiquette: "Parade and Pomp have no charms in the eyes of a patriot, or even of a man of common good sense." [38] When Franklin arrived to negotiate the alliance with France, he emphasized by the simplicity of his dress—his shabby brown coat and unpowdered hair—that he was the representative of a new and uncorrupted world; Franklin was probably too much of a skeptic, even about his own enlightened beliefs, to be unaware of the propagandistic value of such an attention-provoking attire. Such subtle irony was entirely alien to John Adams, who followed the others to Europe. With deadly seriousness, Adams lectured Vergennes, who had advised him to make some adjustment to prevailing diplomatic customs, that "the dignity of North America does not consist in diplomatic ceremonials or any of the subtleties of etiquette; it consists solely in reason, justice, truth, the rights of mankind, and the interests of the nations of Europe." [39]

The diplomatic tasks with which the American agents had to deal could only strengthen their interest in the ideas of the philosophes on foreign policy. The initial concerns of the American diplomats were to conclude an alliance with France and to persuade other Continental powers to an attitude favorable to the American cause. Then they were occupied with the peace negotiations which extended over a long time. When peace with England had finally been concluded, the relations of the newly recognized republic to other powers had to be placed on a permanent footing. As varied as these changing tasks were, one issue was central in all of them: the replacement of the monopolistically arranged bonds between England and America by new regulations of trade and the settlement of the commercial relations which in the future should exist between America and the European powers.

As the Model Treaty, which Congress had adopted in 1776, showed, the problems of trade had two aspects in the American mind: on the one hand, the Americans were anxious to avoid commercial treaties which would make American trade dependent on one power or a bloc of powers and, consequently, draw America into the political rivalries of the European powers. One aim of American policy, therefore, was to make trade as free as possible, because only a complete liberalization of trade could provide full security against the danger that close commercial relations might create a political dependency. On the other hand, the great importance of trade for American economic life made a smooth and uninterrupted flow of commerce urgently desirable; war, in which a strong seapower like England might stop ships and confiscate their goods as contraband or declare wide stretches of a coast as blockaded

[37] Silas Deane to the Secret Committee of Congress, August 18, 1776, in *New York Historical Society Collections,* vol. XIX: The Deane Papers, vol. I, New York 1887, p. 201.
[38] *Ibid.,* p. 219.
[39] John Adams to Vergennes, July 18, 1781, in *The Revolutionary Diplomatic Corespondence of the United States,* ed. Francis Wharton, vol. IV, Washington 1889, p. 590.

area into which no ships should sail, was the great threat, especially since America had no navy sufficient to protect her merchants. Another aim of American foreign policy, therefore, was to persuade other powers to the acceptance of principles of international law which would mitigate the impact of war on civilian life. America was particularly interested in having the neutral trade secured against interference so that "free ships would make free goods," in reducing the number of articles which could be confiscated as contraband, and in permitting application of the concept of blockade only to ports where the access could be effectively controlled.

Peace and commerce were also the focal ideas in the thinking of the philosophes on foreign policy. As we have seen, they were pacifists, deeply convinced of the use-lessness of war and of the necessity to remove war from social life. They saw in commerce a great instrument for bringing about a new age of peace, if nations, in-stead of trying to further their own commerce at the expense of the commerce of another power, would permit a free flow of goods over the entire globe. Relations between nations would become purely commercial contacts, and the need for a po-litical diplomacy with alliances and balance of power would disappear from the international scene. The ideas with which the Americans entered the political theater of Europe were facets of the larger complex of enlightened eighteenth-century thought.

The close connection between the ideas of the philosophes and American foreign policy appeared clearly in the negotiations about commercial treaties which developed after peace with England had been concluded. Even though Americans had tried to hold firm to the principles of the Model Treaty in the preceding years, their foreign policy had naturally been subordinated to the exigencies of the fight for survival and of gaining all possible support against Great Britain. But after the independence of the United States had been internationally recognized, a new and systematic at-tempt at realization of these principles could be made. Several powers had made feelers towards negotiations about commercial treaties with the United States. Con-gress was divided about the handling of this question. Some members felt that the main effort should be directed to the re-establishment of commercial relations with Britain; as one member wrote: "The Treaty with Britain presses upon us with much greater weight than with any other nation." [40] But the majority of Congress was not convinced that the gains which the re-establishment of trade with Britain might bring could compensate for the disadvantages involved in making special concessions to England and in abandoning the attempt to establish trade on an entirely general and liberal basis. The report which Congress finally accepted was drafted by Jeffer-son;[41] it maintained the principles which had first been stated in the Model Treaty of 1776. Great Britain was named as only one among many other states with which the conclusion of treaties of "amity and commerce" would be desirable. The idea of the report was "to form a general system of commerce by treaties with other nations," rejecting special preferences in favor of liberal rules applicable to all nations. Fur-thermore, the report suggested articles which might limit as far as possible disturb-ances of trade in wartime. It recommended the appointment of consuls and general consuls, but it stated that it was "inconvenient at present" "to keep ministers resident

[40] Jefferson, *The Papers of Thomas Jefferson,* ed. Julian P. Boyd, vol. vii, Princeton 1953, p. 467.
[41] *Ibid.,* vol. vi, pp. 393–400.

at the courts of Europe"; this last suggestion, however, was eliminated from the final version of the report. On the basis of this report, Congress issued instructions to its diplomatic agent on May 7, 1784.

The first negotiations to which these new instructions were applied were with Frederick the Great of Prussia. Negotiations with Denmark and Prussia had already been under way when Congress composed its new instructions. Jefferson, who had taken an active part in drafting them, was appointed to serve with Franklin and Adams as American negotiators in Europe. After Jefferson had arrived in Paris and had conferred with Franklin and Adams, he was charged with investigating the changes required to adjust the documents, which had been drafted in the previous negotiations in Europe, to the instructions which Congress had sent. Jefferson decided "to take up the subject as it were anew, to arrange the articles under classes, and while we are reforming the principles to reform also the language of treaties, which history alone and not grammar will justify. The articles may be rendered shorter and more conspicuous, by simplifying their stile and structure." [42] This intention corresponded to a basic feature of Jefferson's mind; to him, style and structure were the external expression of clarity of thought. But one cannot help wondering whether, in simplifying the diplomatic language, Jefferson did not also intend to open the door for a diplomacy which would be divested of its character as a secret science.

Jefferson also drew up the communications which accompanied the revised treaty draft and which explained to the Prussian representative the reasons for the changes in the draft, particularly the insertion of two articles, one providing for the payment of war contraband in case of confiscation, the other protecting civilian life against the ravages of war. The American commissioners wrote that "it is for the interest of humanity in general, that the occasions of war, and the inducements to it should be diminished." [43] Measures to minimize the impact of war were a logical step in the continuing process of improving the law of nations. Since the beginnings of society when "war and extirpation was the punishment of injury," the development of the law of nations had gone forward "humanizing by degrees." Progress had been slow, so that "Ages have intervened between its several steps," but there was no reason why the law of nations should not "go on improving"; it was now a favorable occasion for accelerating this process: "As knowledge of late encreases rapidly, why should not those steps be quickened?" The enlightened belief in progress, coupled with the conviction of being at the threshold of a new age, found expression also in the further correspondence with the Prussian representative. The American commissioners felt that they were leading the way to an "object so valuable to mankind as the total emancipation of commerce and the bringing together all nations for a free intercommunication of happiness." [44] When finally the treaty had been approved by Frederick the Great, John Adams expressed his enthusiasm in words which, although they might indicate some reservation about having these humane measures quickly adopted by the entire world, still suggest that Adams was satisfied with seeing the course of American foreign policy set towards utopia: "I am charmed to find the King do us the Honor to agree to the Platonic Philosophy of some of our Articles, which are at least a good Lesson to Mankind, and will derive more Influence from a Treaty rati-

[42] *Ibid.*, vol. VII, pp. 476–477.
[43] *Ibid.*, pp. 491, 492.
[44] *Ibid.*, vol. VIII, p. 28.

fied by the King of Prussia, than from the writings of Plato, or Sir Thomas More." [45]

The foreign policy of the young republic, with its emphasis on commerce and on avoidance of political connections, has usually been explained as a policy of isolation. Unquestionably, the English background of the ideas which served in the formation of the American outlook on foreign policy contained an isolationist element. However, if we place the ideas which guided early American foreign policy beside those of the European philosophes, it becomes clear that the isolationist interpretation is one-sided and incomplete: American foreign policy was idealistic and internationalist no less than isolationist.

In many minds, these two motives can be found interwoven in such a way that neither of the two elements can be regarded as predominant. This was characteristic of Jefferson. He remained opposed to diplomacy, which he considered as "the pest of the peace of the world, as the workshop in which nearly all the wars of Europe are manufactured." [46] In 1792, when a number of diplomatic nominations had been submitted to the Senate by Washington for approval, Jefferson suggested that diplomatic representatives should be sent by America only to those countries where geographic closeness or interests of commerce demanded a permanent representation; this meant to London, Paris, Madrid, Lisbon, and The Hague. Also, these appointments should be kept "on the lowest grades admissible." [47] Later Jefferson wrote that "Consuls would do all the business we ought to have." [48] Jefferson's inclination towards the adoption of what he called an "a-diplomatic system" sprang from his fear that America might become involved in European politics but, at the same time, he wanted to set an example to the entire world. Jefferson was convinced that the relations between nations in the future would take forms different from those of the diplomacy of the past. His belief in the emergence of a new spirit in international relations is beautifully expressed in a letter to Madison of August 28, 1789. Jefferson pleaded for acknowledging the duties of gratitude in America's relations to France: the often heard view that power and force ruled in the relations between nations "were legitimate principles in the dark ages which intervened between antient and modern civilisation, but exploded and held in just horror in the 18th century. I know but one code of morality for man whether acting singly or collectively." [49]

Thus, although the American outlook on foreign affairs contained two different elements, they could be combined; and then they reinforced each other. But they could also be contradictory. Then those who were concerned with foreign policy suddenly swerved from one extreme to the other. Unexpected resistance or obstacles might turn the utopian hopes for an imminent "reformation, a kind of protestantism, in the commercial system of the world" [50] into its reverse: demand for complete withdrawal from any contact with the outside world. The Americans might have to "recall their Ministers and send no more," [51] as Adams wrote; or they ought "to stand

[45] Ibid., vol. VII, p. 465.

[46] Jefferson to William Short, January 23, 1804, "Documents," American Historical Review, vol. XXXIII (1927/8), p. 833.

[47] Jefferson to a Committee of the Senate, January 4, 1792, in Thomas Jefferson, Writings, ed. Paul Leicester Ford, vol. I, New York 1892, p. 170.

[48] Jefferson to William Short, January 23, 1804, printed loc. cit., p. 833.

[49] Jefferson to James Madison, August 28, 1789, in Jefferson, Papers, vol. XV, p. 367.

[50] John Adams, Works, vol. VIII, p. 298.

[51] John Adams to John Jay, February 26, 1783, The Diplomatic Correspondence of the United States of America from 1783 to 1789, vol. II, Washington 1837, p. 574.

to Europe precisely on the footing of China," [52] as Jefferson formulated it. Yet it was immediately argued that this was not possible, because it would mean that the Americans would have to "give up the most of their commerce, and live by their agriculture." [53] It was "theory only." [54] In such moments, the egoistic insistence on isolation appeared no less unrealistic than the altruistic counsels of internationalism.

This dilemma was reflected in an episode which happened at the time of the end of the War of Independence. Indignation about the brutal way in which England used her seapower had led a number of European states to form a league of "armed neutrality," with the purpose of defending the right of neutrals on the sea. This policy not only corresponded to the general aims of the foreign policy of the United States but also raised the hope of gaining from these powers support in the struggle against Britain. Thus, the United States was anxious to join the league, but, because a belligerent power could hardly become a member of a league of neutrals, the American advances were rebuffed. When, with the signing of the preliminaries of peace, this obstacle was removed and the Netherlands urged America to participate actively in the policy of armed neutrality, Congress took another look at the possible practical consequences of such a policy; it was realized that the league would make the United States a member of a political bloc. Thus Congress, in a resolution[55] which admitted that "the liberal principles on which the said confederacy was established, are conceived to be in general favourable to the interests of nations, and particularly to those of the United States," rejected further negotiations about entry into the league, because "the true interest of these states requires that they should be as little as possible entangled in the politics and controversies of European nations." The principle of avoiding political connections proved to be incompatible with progress toward freeing commerce, which was the great hope for overcoming power politics.

But as contradictory as isolationism and internationalism could sometimes prove themselves to be, these contrasts could be overlooked; and they could be regarded as compatible with each other because there was a common factor between them, though only of a negative character: isolationism existed in a sphere of timelessness; internationalism existed in the future. Neither existed in the world of the present. Thus the attitudes which the young republic had adopted had not yet satisfactorily solved the problem—either practically or theoretically—of how to chart a course in the world as it was.

---

[52] Jefferson, *Papers*, vol. VIII, p. 633.
[53] *The Diplomatic Correspondence of the United States from 1783 to 1789*, vol. II, p. 574.
[54] Jefferson, *Papers*, vol. VIII, p. 633.
[55] *Journals of the Continental Congress*, vol. XXIV, p. 394.

23 / The American Revolution: The People as Constituent Power

Robert R. Palmer

Historians have long debated the ideological significance of the American Revolution. What contribution did it make to the thinking of those who attempted to overthrow so much of the European social order in the 1790's? What principles did it have in common with the great movements that destroyed the *ancien régime* in France in that decade? In a sense, the many sided issue goes back to some of the implications of a question raised earlier, What was revolutionary about what happened in the New World in the years from 1763 to 1787? Robert R. Palmer again argues in the following article from the viewpoint of one whose primary concern is with the events in the Old World. He is concerned not so much with the high-flown language of public statements as with the practical significance of the actions of the colonists as they reorganized their societies and governments. Many of the glorious ideas of the revolutionaries were after all common enough. Certainly some ideas—whatever their precise meaning—such as natural law, were widely discussed in the Old World. The particular contribution in European eyes came in the series of actions by Americans to translate ideas into practical effects. The Americans made a long series of experiments in reconstituting their governments, experiments that became the basis of a set of theories about the nature of the constituent power of the people. As these theories developed, they were expressed in one of their more refined forms by the work of the Philadelphia Convention. The people there exercised their constituent power through a specially chosen convention, a convention that did not govern but did draw up the basic document of government subject to popular approval. It was this refinement of the procedures by which theory became practice and vice-versa that so struck European observers in the 1780's. Beyond this, Palmer returns to examine the nature of the American Revolution from another perspective. His conclusion is simply that its nature was and must continue to be regarded as ambiguous:

From Robert R. Palmer, *The Age of the Democratic Revolution: A Political History of Europe and America, 1760–1800*, Volume I, *The Challenge*, pp. 212–235. Copyright © 1959 by Princeton University Press. Reprinted by permission of Princeton University Press.

it was a revolution fought against some of the pretensions of the Old World by members of the freest society of the Western World; a revolution fought sometimes with ferocity that yet missed the savagery of the French explosion of the last decade of the eighteenth century; a revolution that disturbed relatively few of the structures of society and thus might be regarded in some sense as "conservative" just because it was fought in the most open and thus "radical" society of the time.

For further reading: Elisha P. Douglas, *Rebels and Democrats: the Struggle for Equal Political Rights and Majority Rule During the American Revolution* (1955); John R. Howe, Jr., *The Changing Political Thought of John Adams* (1966); J. R. Pole, *Political Representation in England and the Origins of the American Republic* (1966); J. P. Selsam, *The Pennsylvania Constitution of 1776: A Study in Revolutionary Democracy* (1936); Robert J. Taylor (ed.), *Massachusetts, Colony to Commonwealth: Documents on the Formation of its Constitution, 1775–1780* (1961).

We hold these truths to be self-evident, that all men are created equal, that they are endowed, by their Creator, with certain unalienable rights, that among these are life, liberty, and the pursuit of happiness. That to secure these rights, governments are instituted among men, deriving their just powers from the consent of the governed, that whenever any form of government becomes destructive of these ends, it is the right of the people to alter or to abolish it. . . .—THE DECLARATION OF INDEPENDENCE OF THE UNITED STATES OF AMERICA, 1776

It is a general maxim in every government, there must exist, somewhere, a supreme, sovereign, absolute and uncontrollable power; but this power resides always in the body of the people; and it never was, or can be delegated to one man, or a few.   —THE GENERAL COURT OF MASSACHUSETTS, 1776

. . . those deluded People.   —KING GEORGE III, 1775

If it be asked what the American Revolution distinctively contributed to the world's stock of ideas, the answer might go somewhat along these lines. It did not contribute primarily a social doctrine—for although a certain skepticism toward social rank was an old American attitude, and possibly even a gift to mankind, it long antedated the Revolution, which did not so much cut down, as prevent the growth of, an aristocracy of European type. It did not especially contribute economic ideas —for the Revolution had nothing to teach on the production or distribution of goods, and the most advanced parties objected to private wealth only when it became too closely associated with government. They aimed at a separation of economic and political spheres, by which men of wealth, while free to get rich, should not have a disproportionate influence on government, and, on the other hand, government and public emoluments should not be used as a means of livelihood for an otherwise impecunious and unproductive upper class.

The American Revolution was a political movement, concerned with liberty, and with power. Most of the ideas involved were by no means distinctively American.

There was nothing peculiarly American in the concepts, purely as concepts, of natural liberty and equality. They were admitted by conservatives, and were taught in the theological faculty at the Sorbonne.[1] Nor could Americans claim any exclusive understanding of the ideas of government by contract or consent, or the sovereignty of the people, or political representation, or the desirability of independence from foreign rule, or natural rights, or the difference between natural law and positive law, or between certain fundamental laws and ordinary legislation, or the separation of powers, or the federal union of separate states. All these ideas were perfectly familiar in Europe, and that is why the American Revolution was of such interest to Europeans.

THE DISTINCTIVENESS OF AMERICAN POLITICAL IDEAS

The most distinctive work of the Revolution was in finding a method, and furnishing a model, for putting these ideas into practical effect. It was in the implementation of similar ideas that Americans were more successful than Europeans. "In the last fifty years," wrote General Bonaparte to Citizen Talleyrand in 1797, "there is only one thing that I can see that we have really defined, and that is the sovereignty of the people. But we have had no more success in determining what is constitutional, than in allocating the different powers of government." And he said more peremptorily, on becoming Emperor in 1804, that the time had come "to constitute the Nation." He added: "I am the constituent power." [2]

The problem throughout much of America and Europe, for half a century, was to "constitute" new government, and in a measure new societies. The problem was to find a constituent power. Napoleon offered himself to Europe in this guise. The Americans solved the problem by the device of the constitutional convention, which, revolutionary in origin, soon became institutionalized in the public law of the United States.[3]

The constitutional convention in theory embodied the sovereignty of the people. The people chose it for a specific purpose, not to govern, but to set up institutions of government. The convention, acting as the sovereign people, proceeded to draft a constitution and a declaration of rights. Certain "natural" or "inalienable" rights of

[1] See on Réal de Curban Chapter III above, and my *Catholics and Unbelievers in Eighteenth Century France* (Princeton, 1939), 126, quoting L. J. Hooke, *Religionis naturalis et moralis philosophiae principia, methodo scholastica digesta* (Paris, 1752–1754), I, 623–24: "Status is a permanent condition of man, involving various rights and a long series of obligations. It is either *natural,* constituted by nature itself, or *adventitious,* arising from some human act or institution. . . . By the *status of nature* we understand that in which men would be who were subject to no government but joined only by similarity of nature or by private pacts. . . . In the status of nature all men are equal and enjoy the same rights. For in that state they are distinguished only by the gifts of mind or body by which some excel others." Italics are the Abbé Hooke's.

[2] *Correspondance de Napoleon I,* III (Paris, 1859), 314; R. M. Johnston, *The Corsican* (N.Y., 1910), 182.

[3] See, for example, J. A. Jameson, *The Constitutional Convention: Its History, Powers and Modes of Proceeding* (N.Y., 1867); H. C. Hockett, *The Constitutional History of the United States, 1776–1826* (N.Y., 1939).

the citizen were thus laid down at the same time as the powers of government. It was the constitution that created the powers of government, defined their scope, gave them legality, and balanced them one against another. The constitution was written and comprised in a single document. The constitution and accompanying declaration, drafted by the convention, must, in the developed theory, be ratified by the people. The convention thereupon disbanded and disappeared, lest its members have a vested interest in the offices they created. The constituent power went into abeyance, leaving the work of government to the authorities now constituted. The people, having exercised sovereignty, now came under government. Having made law, they came under law. They put themselves voluntarily under restraint. At the same time, they put restraint upon government. All government was limited government; all public authority must keep within the bounds of the constitution and of the declared rights. There were two levels of law, a higher law or constitution that only the people could make or amend, through constitutional conventions or bodies similarly empowered; and a statutory law, to be made and unmade, within the assigned limits, by legislators to whom the constitution gave this function.

Such was the theory, and it was a distinctively American one. European thinkers, in all their discussion of a political or social contract, of government by consent and of sovereignty of the people, had not clearly imagined the people as actually contriving a constitution and creating the organs of government. They lacked the idea of the people as a constituent power. Even in the French Revolution the idea developed slowly; members of the French National Assembly, long after the Tennis Court oath, continued to feel that the constitution which they were writing, to be valid, had to be accepted by the King as a kind of equal with whom the nation had to negotiate. Nor, indeed, would the King tolerate any other view. On the other hand, we have seen how at Geneva in 1767 the democrats advanced an extreme version of citizen sovereignty, holding that the people created the constitution and the public offices by an act of will; but they failed to get beyond a simple direct democracy; they had no idea of two levels of law, or of limited government, or of a delegated and representative legislative authority, or of a sovereign people which, after acting as a god from the machine in a constituent convention, retired to the more modest status of an electorate, and let its theoretical sovereignty become inactive.

The difficulty with the theory was that the conditions under which it could work were seldom present. No people really starts *de novo;* some political institutions always already exist; there is never a *tabula rasa,* or state of nature, or Chart Blanche as Galloway posited for conservative purposes. Also, it is difficult for a convention engaged in writing a constitution not to be embroiled in daily politics and problems of government. And it is hard to live voluntarily under restraint. In complex societies, or in times of crisis, either government or people or some part of the people may feel obliged to go beyond the limits that a constitution has laid down.

In reality, the idea of the people as a constituent power, with its corollaries, developed unclearly, gradually, and sporadically during the American Revolution. It was adumbrated in the Declaration of Independence: the people may "institute new government." Jefferson, among the leaders, perhaps conceived the idea most clearly. It is of especial interest, however, to see how the "people" themselves, that is, certain lesser and unknown or poorer or unsatisfied persons, contributed to these distinctive American ideas by their opposition to the Revolutionary elite.

There were naturally many Americans who felt that no change was needed except expulsion of the British. With the disappearance of the British governors, and collapse of the old governors' councils, the kind of men who had been active in the colonial assemblies, and who now sat as provincial congresses or other *de facto* revolutionary bodies, were easily inclined to think that they should keep the management of affairs in their own hands. Some parallel can be seen with what happened in Europe. There was a revolution, or protest, of constituted bodies against authorities set above them, and a more popular form of revolution, or protest, which aimed at changing the character or membership of these constituted bodies themselves. As at Geneva the General Council rebelled against the patriciate, without wishing to admit new citizens to the General Council; as in Britain the Whigs asserted the powers of Parliament against the King, without wishing to change the composition of Parliament; as in Belgium, in 1789, the Estates party declared independence from the Emperor, while maintaining the preexisting estates; as in France, also in 1789, the nobility insisted that the King govern through the Estates-General, but objected to the transformation of the three estates into a new kind of national body; as in the Dutch provinces in 1795 the Estates-General, after expelling the Prince of Orange, tried to remain itself unchanged, and resisted the election of a "convention"; so, in America in 1776, the assemblies that drove out the officers of the King, and governed their respective states under revolutionary conditions, sought to keep control of affairs in their own hands, and to avoid reconstitution at the hands of the "people."

Ten states gave themselves new constitutions in 1776 and 1777. In nine of these states, however, it was the ordinary assembly, that is, the revolutionary government of the day, that drafted and proclaimed the constitution. In the tenth, Pennsylvania, a constituent convention met, but it soon had to take on the burden of daily government in addition. In Connecticut and Rhode Island the colonial charters remained in force, and the authorities constituted in colonial times (when governors and councils had already been elected) remained unchanged in principle for half a century. In Massachusetts the colonial charter remained in effect until 1780.

Thus in no state, when independence was declared, did a true constituent convention meet, and, as it were, calmly and rationally devise government out of a state of nature. There was already, however, some recognition of the principle that constitutions cannot be made merely by governments, that a more fundamental power is needed to produce a constitution than to pass ordinary laws or carry on ordinary executive duties. Thus, in New Hampshire, New York, Delaware, Maryland, North Carolina, and Georgia, the assemblies drew up constitutions only after soliciting authority for that purpose from the voters. In Maryland and North Carolina there was a measure of popular ratification.

CONSTITUTION-MAKING IN NORTH CAROLINA, PENNSYLVANIA, AND MASSACHUSETTS

The popular pressures that helped to form American political doctrine are best illustrated from North Carolina, Pennsylvania, and Massachusetts.[4]

[4] Here I am indebted, without sharing all his conclusions, to E. P. Douglass, *Rebels and Democrats: the Struggle for Equal Political Rights and Majority Rule during the American Revolution* (Chapel Hill, 1955).

In North Carolina class lines had been sharply drawn by the Regulator movement and its suppression. The people of the back-country even inclined to be loyalist, not eager for an independence that might only throw them into the hands of the county gentry. In the turbulent election of October 1776 the voters knew that the assembly which they elected would draft a state constitution. There was no demand for a convention to act exclusively and temporarily as a constituent power. But several counties drew up instructions for the deputies, in which the emerging doctrine was set forth clearly.

Orange and Mecklenburg counties used identical language. This is a sign, as in the case of identical phrasing in the French *cahiers* of 1789, where the matter has been carefully studied, that some person of influence and education, and not some poor farmer ruminating in his cabin, had probably written out a draft. Still, the public meetings of both counties found it to their taste. "Political power," they said, "is of two kinds, one principal and superior, the other derived and inferior. . . . The principal supreme power is possessed only by the people at large. . . . The derived and inferior power by the servants which they employ. . . . The rules by which the inferior power is exercised are to be constituted by the principal supreme power. . . ."[5] In other words, government was not a form of guardianship. Office was to be no longer a perquisite of the gentry, or "an aristocracy of power in the hands of the rich," to use their own language, but a form of employment by the people, whom they did not hesitate to call "the poor." Mecklenburg favored a unicameral legislature, Orange a bicameral one, but both called for a separation of powers. It was not that any organ of government should enjoy independence from the electorate (the essence of balance-of-power theory in the European, British, and loyalist view), but rather that the various functions of government should be defined and distributed among different men, to prevent what had happened in colonial times. The fact that before 1776 the council had possessed executive, legislative, and judicial functions, and that members of the assembly had served as justices of the peace, or had their relatives appointed judges and sheriffs, was the basis on which North Carolina had been dominated by small groups of gentry. It was popular objection to this situation, probably more than a reading of European books, that made the separation of powers a principal American doctrine.

The North Carolina constitution, as written and adopted, enlarged the electorate by granting all taxpayers the right to vote for members of the lower house. It equalized the representation by giving more deputies to the western counties. It required a freehold of 100 acres for members of the lower house, and of 300 acres for those of the upper house, who were to be elected only by voters possessing 50 acres. The governor, elected by the two houses, had to have a freehold worth £1,000. The constitution was a compromise between populace and landed gentry. It lasted until the Civil War.[6]

The situation in Pennsylvania was complex. The Quaker colony, idealized by European intellectuals as the haven of innocent equality and idyllic peace, had long been plagued by some of the most acrimonious politics in America. Quaker bigwigs had long clashed with the non-Quaker lesser orders of Philadelphia and the West.

[5] *Ibid.*, 126.

[6] For the text of the constitutions, see F. N. Thorpe, *Federal and State Constitutions, Colonial Charters and Other Organic Laws of the . . . United States of America* (Washington, 7 vols., 1909).

In the spring of 1776 Pennsylvania was the only colony in which the assembly was still legal under the old law. It still showed a desire for reconciliation with England, and, with it, maintenance of the old social and political system. This persistence of conservatism in high places made a great many people all the more radical. A year of open war with Britain had aroused the determination for independence, and in May 1776 a mass meeting of 4,000 people in Philadelphia demanded the calling of a constitutional convention. Various local committees got to work, and a convention was elected by irregular methods. Where the three eastern counties had formerly been heavily over-represented, the situation was now not equalized, but reversed. The West, with the same population as the three eastern counties, had 64 delegates in the convention to only 24 for the East. "The Convention in Pennsylvania was a political expedient, and not, as in Massachusetts, the cornerstone of constitutional government." [7] Its real function was to promote the Revolution, and assure independence from England, by circumventing the assembly and all other opposition. Like the more famous French Convention elected in 1792, it rested on a kind of popular mandate which did not reflect an actual majority of the population; like it, it became the government of the country during war and revolution; like it, it behaved dictatorially. The constitutions drafted in Pennsylvania in 1776, and in France in 1793, were, in their formal provisions, by far the most democratic of any produced in the eighteenth century. The Pennsylvania constitution of 1776, unlike the French constitution of the Year I, was never submitted even to the formalities of popular ratification. But the two constitutions became a symbol of what democrats meant by democracy.

The Pennsylvania constitution vested legislative power in a single house. For the executive it avoided the name and office of governor, entrusting executive power to a council and "president," a word which then meant no more than chairman. All male taxpayers twenty-one years of age had the vote, and were eligible for any office. To sit in the assembly, however, it was necessary publicly to acknowledge the divine inspiration of the Old and New Testaments. Voters elected the legislators, the executive councillors, sheriffs, coroners, tax-assessors, and justices of the peace. Voting was by ballot. The president was chosen by the legislature and the executive council; he had no veto or appointive powers, and what powers he did have he could exercise only in agreement with his council. All officers were elected for one year, except that councillors served for three. Rotation of office was provided for; legislators, councillors, president, and sheriffs could be reelected only a certain number of times, Doors of the legislative assembly must always be open to the public. There was a kind of referendum, in that no bill passed by the assembly, short of emergency, became law until submitted for public consideration and enacted in the assembly of the following year, if there was no public objection. Officeholders received pay, but if revenues of any office became too large the assembly could reduce them. All officers and judges could be impeached by the assembly. Judges of the Supreme Court could be removed by the assembly for "misbehavior." There was an elected council of censors, or board of review, which every seven years ascertained whether the constitution had been preserved inviolate, and called a convention if amendment seemed necessary.

The Pennsylvania constitution represented the doctrine of a single party, namely the democrats, people of the kind who had formerly had little to do with government,

[7] Douglass, *op. cit.*, 260.

and whose main principle was that government should never become a separate or vested interest within the state. This was indeed an understandable principle, at a time when government, in all countries in varying degree, had in fact become the entrenched interest of a largely hereditary governing class. The Pennsylvania constitution substituted almost a direct democracy, in which no one in government could carry any responsibility or pursue any sustained program of his own. Many people in Pennsylvania objected to it from the beginning. It must be remembered that the democratic constitution did not signify that Pennsylvania was really more democratic than some of the other states; it signified, rather, that Pennsylvania was more divided, and that conservatism was stronger, certain upper-class and politically experienced elements, which elsewhere took a leading part in the Revolution, being in Pennsylvania tainted with Anglophilism. Whether the constitution of 1776 was workable or not, these people soon put an end to it. It lasted only until 1790.[8]

The most interesting case is that of Massachusetts. Here the great political thinker was John Adams, who became the main author of the Massachusetts constitution of 1780, which in turn had an influence on the Constitution of the United States. In his own time Adams was denounced as an Anglomaniac and a Monocrat. In our own time some sympathizers with the eighteenth-century democrats have considered him very conservative, while on the other hand theorists of the "new conservatism" would persuade us that John Adams was in truth the American Edmund Burke. I confess that I see very little in any of these allegations.

Adams in January 1776 published some *Thoughts on Government,* for the guidance of those in the various colonies who were soon to declare independence and begin to govern themselves. This was in some ways a conservative tract. Adams thought it best, during the war, for the new states simply to keep the forms of government that they had. He obviously approved the arrangement under the Massachusetts charter of 1691, by which the popular assembly elected an upper house or council. In other ways he was not very conservative. He declared, like Jefferson, that the aim of government is welfare or happiness, that republican institutions must rest on "virtue," and that the people should support a universal system of public schools. He wanted one-year terms for governors and officials (the alternative would be "slavery"), and he favored rotation of office. He quite agreed that someday the state governors and councillors might be popularly elected, as they were in Connecticut already. He gave six reasons for having a bicameral legislature, but in none of these six reasons did he show any fear of the people, or belief that, with a unicameral legislature, the people would plunder property or degenerate into anarchy. He was afraid of the one-house legislature itself. He never committed the folly of identifying the deputies with the deputizers. He was afraid that a single house would be arbitrary or capricious, or make itself perpetual, or "make laws for their own interest, and adjudge all controversies in their own favor." [9] He himself cited the cases of Holland and the Long Parliament. The fear of a self-perpetuating political body, gathering privileges to itself, was certainly better grounded in common observation than vague alarms about anarchy or pillage.

The *Thoughts* of 1776 were conservative in another way, if conservatism be the

[8] *Ibid.,* 214–86; J. P. Selsam, *The Pennsylvania Constitution of 1776: a Study in Revolutionary Democracy* (Philadelphia, 1936).

[9] *Works* (1851), IV, 196.

word. Adams had not yet conceived the idea of a constitutional convention. He lacked the notion of the people as constituent power. He had in mind that existing assemblies would draft the new constitutions, when and if any were drafted. Adams was familiar with all the high-level political theory of England and Europe. But the idea of the people as the constituent power arose locally, from the grass roots.

The revolutionary leadership in Massachusetts, including both Adamses, was quite satisfied to be rid of the British, and otherwise to keep the Bay State as it had always been. They therefore "resumed" the charter of 1691. They simply undid the Massachusetts Government Act of 1774. Some of the commonalty of Boston, and farmers of Concord and the western towns, envisaged further changes. It is hard to say what they wanted, except that they wanted a new constitution. Experts in Massachusetts history contradict each other flatly; some say that debtors, poor men, and Baptists were dissatisfied; others that all kinds of diverse people naturally owed money anyway, that practically no one was too poor to vote, and that Baptists were an infinitesimal splinter group in a solidly Congregationalist population. It may be that the trouble was basically psychological; that many people of fairly low station, even though they had long had the right to vote, had never until the Revolution participated in politics, were aroused by the Revolution, the war, and excitement of soldiering, and, feeling that affairs had always been managed by people socially above them, wanted now to act politically on their own.

Demands were heard for a new constitution. It was said that the charter of 1691 was of no force, since the royal power that had issued it was no longer valid. It was said that no one could be governed without his consent, and that no living person had really consented to this charter. Some Berkshire towns even hinted that they did not belong to Massachusetts at all until they shared in constituting the new commonwealth. They talked of "setting themselves apart," or being welcomed by a neighboring state. Echoes of the social contract floated through the western air. "The law to bind all must be assented to by all," declared the farmers of Sutton. "The Great Secret of Government is governing all by all," said those of Spencer.[10] It began to seem that a constitution was necessary not only to secure liberty but to establish authority, not only to protect the individual but to found the state.

The house of representatives proposed that it and the council, that is, the two houses of legislation sitting together, should be authorized by the people to draw up a constitution. All adult males were to vote on the granting of this authorization, not merely those possessing the customary property qualification. In a sense, this was to recognize Rousseau's principle that there must be "unanimity at least once": that everyone must consent to the law under which he was to live, even if later, when constitutional arrangements were made, a qualification was required for ordinary voting. The council objected to a plan whereby it would lose its identity by merging with the house. A little dispute occurred, not unlike that in France in 1789 between "vote by head" and "vote by order." The plan nevertheless went through. The two houses, sitting as one, and authorized by the people, produced a constitution in 1778. It was submitted for popular ratification. The voters repudiated it. Apparently both democrats and conservatives were dissatisfied. This is precisely what happened in Holland in 1797, when the first constitution of the Dutch revolution was rejected by a coalition of opposite-minded voters.

[10] Douglass, op. cit., 178.

A special election was therefore held, in which all towns chose delegates to a state convention, "for the sole purpose of forming a new Constitution." John Adams, delegate from Braintree, was put on the drafting committee. He wrote a draft, which the convention modified only in detail. The resulting document reflected many influences. It is worth while to suggest a few.

There is a modern fashion for believing that Rousseau had little influence in America, particularly on such sensible characters as John Adams. I do not think that he had very much. Adams, however, had read the *Social Contract* as early as 1765, and ultimately had four copies of it in his library. I suspect that, like others, he found much of it unintelligible or fantastic, and some of it a brilliant expression of his own beliefs. He himself said of the Massachusetts constitution: "It is Locke, Sidney, Rousseau, and de Mably reduced to practice." [11]

Adams wrote in the preamble: "The body politic is formed by a voluntary association of individuals. It is a social compact, by which the whole people covenants with each citizen, and each citizen with the whole people, that all shall be governed by certain laws for the common good." [12] The thought here, and the use of the word "covenant," go back to the Mayflower compact. But whence comes the "social" in *social* compact? And whence comes the word "citizen"? There were no "citizens" under the British constitution, except in the sense of freemen of the few towns known as cities. In the English language the word "citizen" in its modern sense is an Americanism, dating from the American Revolution.[13] It is entirely possible that Jean-Jacques Rousseau had deposited these terms in Adams' mind. The whole passage suggests Chapter vi, Book 1, of the *Social Contract*. The convention adopted this part of Adams' preamble without change.

In the enacting clause of the preamble Adams wrote: "We, therefore, the delegates of the people of Massachusetts . . . agree upon the following . . . Constitution of the Commonwealth of Massachusetts." The convention made a significant emendation: "We, therefore, the people of Massachusetts . . . agree upon, ordain and establish. . . ." The formula, *We the people ordain and establish*, expressing the developed theory of the people as constituent power, was used for the first time in the Massachusetts constitution of 1780, whence it passed into the preamble of the United States constitution of 1787 and the new Pennsylvania constitution of 1790, after which it became common in the constitutions of the new states, and in new constitutions of the old states. Adams did not invent the formula. He was content with the matter-of-fact or purely empirical statement that the "delegates" had "agreed." It was the popularly elected convention that rose to more abstract heights. Providing in advance for popular ratification, it imputed the creation of government to the people.

Adams wrote, as the first article of the Declaration of Rights: "All men are born equally free and independent, and have certain natural, essential and unalienable

[11] *Works* (1851), IV, 216. Adams also, in 1787, cited Rousseau's *Discourse on Inequality* and *Considerations on Poland* with approval, recommending the former for its picture of the evil in civilized men, the latter for its view that Poland was dominated exclusively by nobles. *Works*, IV, 409 and 367.

[12] Ibid., 219; Thorpe, *op. cit.*, III, 1889.

[13] This may be readily confirmed from the Oxford Dictionary, or by comparison of definitions of "citizen" in British and American dictionaries, or by tracing the article "citizen" through successive editions of the Encyclopaedia Britannica, where the modern meaning does not appear until the eleventh edition in 1910.

rights," which included defense of their lives, liberties, and property, and the seek-ing of "safety and happiness." The Virginia Declaration of Rights, drafted by George Mason in June 1776, was almost identical, and Adams certainly had it in mind. The Massachusetts convention made only one change in this sentence. It declared: "All men are born free and equal." The convention, obviously, was thinking of the Dec-laration of Independence, that is, Jefferson's more incisive rewording of Mason's Virginia declaration.

The convention had been elected by a true universal male suffrage, but it adopted, following Adams' draft, a restriction on the franchise. To vote, under the constitu-tion, it was necessary to own real estate worth £3 a year, or real and personal prop-erty of a value of £60. The charter of 1691 had specified only £2 and £40 respec-tively. The state constitution was thus in this respect more conservative than the charter. How much more conservative? Here we run into the difference between experts already mentioned.[14] A whole school of thought, pointing to a 50 per cent increase in the voting qualification, has seen a reaction of property-owners against dangers from below. Closer examination of the values of money reveals that the £3 and £60 of 1780 represent an increase of only one-eighth over the figures of 1691. Even if half the people of Boston were unfranchised, all Boston then had only a twentieth of the population of the state. In the rural areas, where farm ownership was usual, it was mainly grown sons living for a few years with their parents who lacked the vote. There seems to have been only sporadic objection to the suffrage provision.

Adams put into the constitution, and the convention retained it, that ghost of King, Lords, and Commons that now assumed the form of governor, senate, and house of representatives. Partisans of the British system, in England or America, would surely find this ghost highly attenuated. The point about King and Lords, in the British system, was precisely that they were not elected by anyone, that they were immune to popular pressure, or any pressure, through their enjoyment of life tenure and hereditary personal rights to political position. Governor and senators in Massa-chusetts, like representatives, both in Adams' draft and in the final document, were all elected, by the same electorate, and all for one-year terms. To Adams (as, for example, to Delolme), it was of the utmost importance to prevent the executive from becoming the mere creature of the legislature. He even wished the governor to have an absolute veto, which the convention changed to a veto that could be overridden by a two-thirds majority of both houses. Adams continued to prefer a final veto. Jef-fersonians and their numerous progeny found this highly undemocratic. In all states south of New York, at the end of the Revolution, governors were elected by the legislative houses, and none had any veto. Adams justified the veto as a means "to preserve the independence of the executive and judicial departments."[15] And since governors could no longer be appointed by the crown, an obvious way to prevent their dependence on legislatures was to have them issue, like legislators, from the new sovereign, the people. It was legislative oligarchy that Adams thought the most im-

[14] For emphasis on the conservative or reactionary character of the Massachusetts constitution, see Douglass, op. cit., 189–213, and more specialized writers cited there; for the opposite view, which I follow in part, see R. E. Brown, Middle-Class Democracy and the Revolution in Massachusetts, 1691–1780 (Ithaca, 1955), 384–400.

[15] Adams, Works (1851), IV, 231 and 232 note.

minent danger. As he wrote to Jefferson in 1787: "You are afraid of the one—I, of the few." [16]

As for the phantom "lords," or senators, though they were directly elected by the ordinary voters for one-year terms, they were in a way supposed to represent property rather than numbers. They were apportioned among the counties of Massachusetts not according to population but according to taxes paid, that is, according to assessed value of taxable wealth. Suffolk County, which included Boston, thus received 6 senators out of 40, where on a purely numerical basis it would have received only four. The Maine districts, Cape Cod, and the western counties were numerically somewhat underrepresented. The three central and western counties received 11 senators, where a representation in proportion to numbers would have given them 12 or 13. Inequalities in wealth in Massachusetts, as between individuals or as between city and country, were not yet great enough to make a senate apportioned according to "property" (which included the small man's property as well as the rich man's) very different from a senate apportioned according to numbers.[17]

The Massachusetts constitution prescribed certain qualifications for eligibility. The governor was required to have a freehold worth at least £1,000, senators a freehold of £300 or £600 total estate, representatives a freehold of £100 or £200 total estate. (British law at this time required £300 or £600 *annual income* from land to qualify for the House of Commons.) These Massachusetts requirements resembled those in North Carolina, where the governor had to have a £1,000 freehold, and members of the upper and lower houses freeholds of 300 or 100 acres respectively. In the absence of comparative statistics on land values and distribution of land ownership in the two states, it is impossible to compare the real impact of these legal qualifications for office. In Massachusetts, however, whatever may have been true in North Carolina, the average 100-acre one-family farm was worth well over £300, and there were a great many such farms, so that the ordinary successful farmer could qualify for either house of the legislature, and a few well-to-do ones in almost every village might if they chose have aspired to the office of governor.[18] The requirements in Massachusetts, as set forth by John Adams, were, if anything, Jeffersonian or agrarian in their tendency, since they favored the farm population, and made it even harder for middle-class townspeople, who might own no land, to occupy public office. The aim was clearly to limit office to the substantial segment of the population, but the substantial segment was broadly defined. Still, there were people who by this definition were not "substantial," and some of them objected to these provisions, though not many would in any case have ventured to run for office or been elected if they did, in the Massachusetts of 1780.

It was Article III of the Declaration of Rights, both in Adams' draft and in the finished constitution, that caused most debate in the convention and most disagreement among the voters during ratification. This article, declaring religion to be the foundation of morality and of the state, authorized the legislature to "enjoin" people

[16] *Papers of Thomas Jefferson*, xii (Princeton, 1955), 396.

[17] Compare the apportionment of senators in the Massachusetts constitution with the population of counties in the census of 1790. The fact that the senate represented property rather than numbers is stressed by those who see the Massachusetts constitution of 1780 as a very conservative or reactionary document. I confess to sharing the impatience of Professor Brown at academic theories which dissolve under a little grade-school computation.

[18] Brown, *op. cit.*, 18, 394.

to go to church, and required the use of public funds to maintain the churches, while allowing any "subject" to have his own contribution paid to the denomination of his choice. While it received a large majority of the popular vote, 8,885 to 6,225, it was the one article which most clearly failed to obtain a two-thirds majority, and the one which may have never been legally ratified, though declared so by the convention. Those voting against it expressed a desire to separate church and state. These, in turn, included perhaps a few Baptists who favored such separation on religious principle, a great many Protestants who feared that the article might legalize Roman Catholicism, and an unknown number of people, one suspects, who were no longer very regular in attending any church at all.

The Massachusetts constitution of 1780 was adopted by a two-thirds majority in a popular referendum from which no free adult male was excluded. The vote was light, for opinion on the matter seems not to have been excited.[19] It was six years since the rebellion against King George, and four years since the British army had left Massachusetts; doubtless many people wished to be bothered no longer. The action of the people as constituent power is, after all, a legal concept, or even a necessary legal fiction where the sovereignty of any concrete person or government is denied. It does not signify that everyone is actually engrossed in the fabrication of constitutions. On the other hand, it does not seem necessary to believe that the convention, when it declared the constitution ratified, put something over on an innocent or apathetic or reluctant people. The people of Massachusetts had rejected the constitution proposed in 1778. They could have rejected the one proposed in 1780. It was adopted, not because it was thought perfect or final by everyone, but because it offered a frame of government, or basis of agreement, within which people could still lawfully disagree. It has lasted, with many amendments, until the present day.

A WORD ON THE CONSTITUTION OF THE UNITED STATES

The idea that sovereignty lay with the people, and not with states or their governments, made possible in America a new kind of federal structure unknown in Europe. The Dutch and Swiss federations were unions of component parts, close permanent alliances between disparate corporate members. For them no other structure was possible, because there was as yet no Dutch or Swiss people except in a cultural sense. It was in the Dutch revolution of 1795 and the Swiss revolution of 1798 that these two bundles of provinces or cantons were first proclaimed as political nations. In America it was easier to make the transition from a league of states, set

---

[19] About 23 per cent of adult males voted on ratification of the constitution of 1780, a figure which may be compared with 30 per cent of adult males voting on ratification of the French constitution of 1793, with the difference that in the France of 1793 only those voting "yes" took the trouble to vote at all (1,801,918 "ayes" to 11,610 "no's" with some 4,300,000 abstentions). It is a question whether a vote by 23 per cent of the population should be considered "light." This percentage may have been a good measure of the politically interested population; in the annual elections of the governor the ratio of persons actually casting a vote to the total of adult white males ranged between 9 per cent and 28 per cent until it began to rise with the election of 1800. See J. R. Pole, "Suffrage and Representation in Massachusetts: A Statistical Note," in *William and Mary Quarterly*, xiv (October 1957), 590–92, and J. Godechot, *Les institutions de la France sous la Révolution et l'Empire* (Paris, 1951), 252.

up during the Revolution, to a more integral union set up in the United States constitution of 1787. The new idea was that, instead of the central government drawing its powers from the states, both central and state governments should draw their powers from the same source; the question was the limit between these two sets of derived powers. The citizen, contrariwise, was simultaneously a citizen both of the United States and of his own state. He was the sovereign, not they. He chose to live under two constitutions, two sets of laws, two sets of courts and officials; theoretically, he had created them all, reserving to himself, under each set, certain liberties specified in declarations of rights.

It has been widely believed, since the publication in 1913 of Charles A. Beard's *Economic Interpretation of the Constitution,* that the federal constitution of 1787 marked a reaction against democratic impulses of the Revolution, and was a device by which men of property, particularly those holding securities of the state or continental governments, sought to protect themselves and their financial holdings against the dangers of popular rule. The Philadelphia convention has been represented as an almost clandestine body, which exceeded its powers, and which managed (as has also been said of the Massachusetts convention of 1780) to impose a conservative constitution on a confused or apathetic people. Recently the flimsiness of the evidence for this famous thesis has been shown by Professor Robert Brown.[20] The thesis takes its place in the history of historical writing, as a product of that Progressive and post-Progressive era in which the common man could be viewed as the dupe or plaything of private interests.

It seems likely enough that there was a conservative reaction after the American Revolution, and even a movement among the upper class (minus the old loyalists) not wholly unlike the "aristocratic resurgence" which I shall soon describe in the Europe of the 1780's. The difference is that these neo-aristocrats of America were less obstinate and less caste-conscious than in Europe. They did not agree with each other, and they knew they could not rule alone. The men at Philadelphia in 1787 were too accomplished as politicians to be motivated by anything so impractical as ideology or mere self-interest. They hoped, while solving concrete problems, to arouse as little opposition as possible. They lacked also the European sense of the permanency of class status. Thinking of an upper class as something that individuals might move into or out of, they allowed for social mobility both upward and downward. The wealthy Virginian, George Mason, at the Philadelphia convention, on urging that the upper class should take care to give adequate representation to the lower, offered it as one of his reasons that, however affluent they might be now, "the course of a few years not only might, but certainly would, distribute their posterity through the lowest classes of society." [21] No one seems to have disputed this prognostication. Such acceptance of future downward mobility for one's own grandchildren, if by no means universal in America, was far more common than in Europe. Without such downward mobility there could not long remain much room for newcomers at the top, or much assurance of a fluid society. With it, there could not be a permanent aristocracy in the European sense.

[20] R. E. Brown, *Charles Beard and the Constitution: A Critical Analysis of "An Economic Interpretation of the Constitution"* (Princeton, 1956). The critique of Beard is carried even further in a more recent work, Forrest McDonald, *We the People: The Economic Origins of the Constitution* (Chicago, 1958).

[21] *Writings* of James Madison, 9 vols. (N.Y., 1902–1910), III, 47.

It was the state legislatures that chose the delegates to the Philadelphia convention, in answer to a widely expressed demand for strengthening the federal government under the Articles of Confederation. The Philadelphia convention proceeded, not to amend the Articles, but to ignore and discard them. It repudiated the union which the thirteen states had made. Beard in 1913 found it satisfying to call this operation a revolution, a revolution from above to be sure, which he compared to a *coup d'état* of Napoleon. His critic, Professor Brown, in 1956, found it satisfying and important to deny any revolutionary action in what happened.

What did really happen? The men at Philadelphia did circumvent the state governments, and in a sense they betrayed those who sent them. They did so by adopting the revolutionary principle of the American Revolution, which had already become less purely revolutionary and more institutionalized as an accepted routine, as shown in the Massachusetts convention of 1780, which had been followed by a New Hampshire convention, and new constitution for New Hampshire in 1784. The Philadelphia convention went beyond the existing constituted bodies, that is, the state governments and the Congress under the Articles, by appealing for support directly to the people, who in each state elected, for this purpose only, conventions to discuss, ratify, or refuse to ratify the document proposed by the convention at Philadelphia. The authors of the proposed federal constitution needed a principle of authority; they conceived that "the people were the fountain of all power," and that if popularly chosen conventions ratified their work "all disputes and doubts concerning [its] legitimacy" would be removed.[22] In each state, in voting for ratifying conventions, the voters voted according to the franchise as given by their state constitutions. No use was made of the more truly revolutionary idea, still alive in Massachusetts in 1780, that on the acceptance of a government *every* man should have a vote. In some states the authorized voters were a great majority; in none were they a small minority. The actual vote for the ratifying conventions was light, despite protracted public discussion, because most people lost interest, or never had any, in abstract debates concerning governmental structure at the distant federal level. Eleven states ratified within a few months, and the constitution went into effect for the people of those eleven states. The remaining two states came in within three years. The whole procedure was revolutionary in a sense, but revolution had already become domesticated in America. The idea of the people as the constituent power, acting through special conventions, was so generally accepted and understood that a mere mention of the word "convention," in the final article of the proposed constitution, was thought sufficient explanation of the process of popular endorsement.

Nevertheless, men of popular principles, those who would soon be called democrats, and who preferred the arrangements of the Pennsylvania constitution, with its single-house legislature to which the executive was subordinated, found much in the new federal constitution not to their liking, at least at first sight. The new instrument reproduced the main features of the Massachusetts constitution of 1780: the strong president, the senate, the house of representatives, the partial executive veto, the independent judiciary, the separation and balance of powers. In fact, the longer tenure of offices—four years for the president, six for senators, two for representatives, in place of the annual terms for corresponding functionaries in Massachusetts—shows a reaction away from revolutionary democracy and toward the giving

---

[22] Quoted by Brown, *op. cit.,* 140.

of more adequate authority to those entrusted with public power. The president was not popularly elected, like the governor in Massachusetts; but neither was he designated by the legislative assembly, like the president in Pennsylvania and governors in the Southern states. He was elected by an electoral college, with each state free to determine how its own share of these electors should be chosen. Although as early as 1788 almost half the states provided for popular election of presidential electors, it was not until 1828 that this became the general and permanent rule. In the federal constitution the unique feature, and key to the main compromise, was the senate. Not only did large and small states have the same number of senators, but it was the state legislatures that chose them. Since it was the state legislatures that conservative or hard-money men mainly feared in the 1780's, this provision can hardly have been introduced in the hope of assuring economic conservatism. It was introduced to mollify the states as states. In the senate the new union was a league of preexisting corporate entities. In the house of representatives it rested more directly on the people. Anyone who had the right to vote in his state could vote for a member of the lower house of Congress. In one respect the federal constitution, by its silence, was more democratic in a modern sense than any of the state constitutions. No pecuniary or religious qualification was specified for any office.

The new constitution was a compromise, but that it produced a less popular federal government, less close to the people, than that of the Articles of Confederation, seems actually contrary to the facts. It created a national arena for political controversy. There were now, for the first time, national elections in which voters could dispute over national issues. One result was the rise, on a national scale, of the Jeffersonian democratic movement in the 1790's.

AMBIVALENCE OF THE AMERICAN REVOLUTION

In conclusion, the American Revolution was really a revolution, in that certain Americans subverted their legitimate government, ousted the contrary-minded and confiscated their property, and set the example of a revolutionary program, through mechanisms by which the people was deemed to act as the constituent power. This much being said, it must be admitted that the Americans, when they constituted their new states, tended to reconstitute much of what they already had. They were as fortunate and satisfied a people as any the world has known. They thus offered both the best and the worst example, the most successful and the least pertinent precedent, for less fortunate or more dissatisfied peoples who in other parts of the world might hope to realize the same principles.

Pennsylvania and Georgia gave themselves one-chamber legislatures, but both had had one-chamber legislatures before the Revolution. All states set up weak governors; they had been undermining the authority of royal governors for generations. South Carolina remained a planter oligarchy before and after independence, but even in South Carolina fifty-acre freeholders had a vote. New York set up one of the most conservative of the state constitutions, but this was the first constitution under which Jews received equality of civil rights—not a very revolutionary departure, since Jews had been prospering in New York since 1654.[23] The Anglican Church was disestab-

[23] J. R. Marcus, *Early American Jewry* (Philadelphia, 1953), ii, 530.

lished, but it had had few roots in the colonies anyway. In New England the sects obtained a little more recognition, but Congregationalism remained favored by law. The American revolutionaries made no change in the laws of indentured servitude. They deplored, but avoided, the matter of Negro slavery. Quitrents were generally abolished, but they had been nominal anyway, and a kind of manorial system remained long after the Revolution in New York. Laws favoring primogeniture and entail were done away with, but apparently they had been little used by landowners in any case. No general or statistical estimate is yet possible on the disposition of loyalist property. Some of the confiscated estates went to strengthen a new propertied class, some passed through the hands of speculators, and some either immediately or eventually came into the possession of small owners. There was enough change of ownership to create a material interest in the Revolution, but obviously no such upheaval in property relations as in France after 1789.

Even the apparently simple question of how many people received the right to vote because of the Revolution cannot be satisfactorily answered. There was some extension of democracy in this sense, but the more we examine colonial voting practices the smaller the change appears. The Virginia constitution of 1776 simply gave the vote to those "at present" qualified. By one estimate the number of persons voting in Virginia actually declined from 1741 to 1843, and those casting a vote in the 1780's were about a quarter of the free male population over twenty-one years of age.[24] The advance of political democracy, at the time of the Revolution, was most evident in the range of officers for whom voters could vote. In the South the voters generally voted only for members of the state legislatures; in Pennsylvania and New England they voted also for local officials, and in New England for governors as well.

In 1796, at the time of the revolution in Europe, and when the movement of Jeffersonian democracy was gathering strength in America, seven of the sixteen states then in the union had no property qualification for voters in the choice of the lower legislative house, and half of them provided for popular election of governors, only the seaboard South, and New Jersey, persisting in legislative designation of the executive.[25] The best European historians underestimate the extent of political democracy in America at this time. They stress the restrictions on voting rights in America, as in the French constitution of 1791.[26] They do so because they have read the best American historians on the subject and have in particular followed the school of Charles Beard and others. The truth seems to be that America was a good deal more democratic than Europe in the 1790's. It had been so, within limits, long before the revolutionary era began.

Nor in broad political philosophy did the American Revolution require a violent break with customary ideas. For Englishmen it was impossible to maintain, in the eighteenth century or after, that the British constitution placed any limits on the powers of Parliament. Not so for Americans; they constantly appealed, to block

[24] C. S. Sydnor, *Gentlemen Freeholders: Political Practices in Washington's Virginia* (Williamsburg, 1952), 138–39, 143.

[25] W. L. Smith, *A Comparative View of the Several States with Each Other* . . . (Philadelphia, 1796). There are six tables showing comparisons.

[26] See, for example, G. Lefebvre, *La Révolution française* (Paris, 1951), 99, and *Coming of the French Revolution,* Eng. trans. (Princeton, 1947), 180–81; P. Sagnac, *La fin de l'ancien régime et la Révolution américaine 1763–1789* (Paris, 1947), 386–93, where the Beard view of issues involved in the writing and ratification of the federal constitution is clearly expounded.

the authority of Parliament or other agencies of the British government, to their rights as Englishmen under the British constitution. The idea of limited government, the habit of thinking in terms of two levels of law, of an ordinary law checked by a higher constitutional law, thus came out of the realities of colonial experience. The colonial Americans believed also, like Blackstone for that matter, that the rights of Englishmen were somehow the rights of all mankind. When the highest English authorities disagreed on what Americans claimed as English rights, and when the Americans ceased to be English by abjuring their King, they were obliged to find another and less ethnocentric or merely historical principle of justification. They now called their rights the rights of man. Apart from abstract assertions of natural liberty and equality, which were not so much new and alarming as conceptual statements as in the use to which they were applied, the rights claimed by Americans were the old rights of Englishmen—trial by jury, *habeas corpus,* freedom of the press, freedom of religion, freedom of elections, no taxation without representation. The content of rights was broadened, but the content changed less than the form, for the form now became universal.[27] Rights were demanded for human beings as such. It was not necessary to be English, or even American, to have an ethical claim to them. The form also became more concrete, less speculative and metaphysical, more positive and merely legal. Natural rights were numbered, listed, written down, and embodied in or annexed to constitutions, in the foundations of the state itself.

So the American Revolution remains ambivalent. If it was conservative, it was also revolutionary, and vice versa. It was conservative because colonial Americans had long been radical by general standards of Western Civilization. It was, or appeared, conservative because the deepest conservatives, those most attached to King and empire, conveniently left the scene. It was conservative because the colonies had never known oppression, excepting always for slavery—because, as human institutions go, America had always been free. It was revolutionary because the colonists took the risks of rebellion, because they could not avoid a conflict among themselves, and because they checkmated those Americans who, as the country developed, most admired the aristocratic society of England and Europe. Henceforth the United States, in Louis Hartz's phrase, would be the land of the frustrated aristocrat, not of the frustrated democrat; for to be an aristocrat it is not enough to think of oneself as such, it is necessary to be thought so by others; and never again would deference for social rank be a characteristic American attitude. Elites, for better or for worse, would henceforth be on the defensive against popular values. Moreover the Americans in the 1770's, not content merely to throw off an outside authority, insisted on transmuting the theory of their political institutions. Their revolution was revolutionary because it showed how certain abstract doctrines, such as the rights of man and the sovereignty of the people, could be "reduced to practice," as Adams put it, by assemblages of fairly levelheaded gentlemen exercising constituent power in the name of the people. And, quite apart from its more distant repercussions, it was certainly revolutionary in its impact on the contemporary world across the Atlantic.

[27] For a European view, see O. Vossler, "Studien zur Erklärung der Menschenrechte," *Historische Zeitschrift,* vol. 142 (1930), 536–39.